Perl

Annotated Archives

Martin Brown

Osborne/**McGraw-Hill**

Berkeley   New York   St. Louis   San Francisco   Auckland   Bogotá
Hamburg   London   Madrid   Mexico City   Milan   Montreal   New Delhi
Panama City   Paris   São Paulo   Singapore   Sydney   Tokyo   Toronto

Osborne/**McGraw-Hill**
2600 Tenth Street
Berkeley, California 94710
U.S.A.

For information on translations or book distributors outside the U.S.A., or to arrange bulk purchase discounts for sales promotions, premiums, or fund-raisers, please contact Osborne/**McGraw-Hill** at the above address.

Perl Annotated Archives

1234567890 AGM AGM 90198765432109

ISBN 0-07-882557-1

Publisher	**Proofreader**
Brandon A. Nordin	Laurie Stewart
Editor-in-Chief	**Indexer**
Scott Rogers	Valerie Robbins
Acquisitions Editor	**Computer Designers**
Wendy Rinaldi	Michelle Galicia
	Ann Sellers
Project Editor	
Madhu Prasher	**Illustrator**
	Beth Young
Editorial Assistant	
Monika Faltiss	**Series Design**
	Roberta Steele
Technical Editor	Peter Hancik
Mike Stok	
	Cover Design
Copy Editor	Regan Honda
Barbara Brodnitz	

To my wife, who keeps the house running when I'm still sitting at the keyboard.

ABOUT THE AUTHOR

Martin Brown is an IT Manager and freelance consultant with 15 years of multiplatform administration and programming experience in Perl, Shellscript, Basic, Pascal, C/C++, Java, JavaScript, VBScript, and Awk. Martin is also the author of two computer books.

Contents

PART 2

Networking and E-mail

PART 3

World Wide Web

Acknowledgments

It is impossible to list absolutely everybody who gets involved in the process of writing a book. Despite your best efforts, you are bound to forget somebody. Before I mention people specific to this book, I'd like to thank Simon Hayes, who gave me my first opportunity to write books back in '96. To repay him, in some small respect, I've included his e-commerce script, the BookWare online bookstore system, in Chapter 8 of this volume.

I'd like to thank Wendy Rinaldi at Osborne/McGraw-Hill for allowing me to do this book, and for giving me the support and encouragement I needed during the difficult patches. I'd also like to thank the rest of the team at Osborne, including Madhu Prasher, Debbie Escobedo, Monika Faltiss, and Barbara Brodnitz, for keeping me on my toes and the book on the rails and for producing it to a high enough standard for it to be printed. Mike Stok, Piers Cawley, and Jon "Blowfish" Nangle all helped me with the book's technical aspects; for their comments on the scripts and content in the book, I am eternally grateful.

Many of the scripts in this book are contributed by other programmers, or use modules and code from other programmers and authors. These other authors include Larry Wall (who invented Perl in the first place), Alan Citterman, Tim Bunce, Jochen Widdmann, Michael Fuhr, Brian Jepson, Bruce Barnett, Gisle Aas, Joe "Marcus" Clarke, Joe Casadonte, Graham Barr, and Paul Bijnens.

Finally, I'd like to thank the gang on the #beos channel on IRCNet, including Woonjas, RedHeat, drag, Tao, Naguel, and many others who provided me with encouragement, support, and amusement while I was working on the book. Oh, and I mustn't forget to thank Spip, the channel's 'bot, for providing me with endless amusement and filling the role of the ultimate executive toy.

If there's anybody I've forgotten to acknowledge or contact respecting the modules, scripts, and related parties on this book, I apologize unreservedly in advance now. I have done my best to check and verify all sources and contact all parties involved, but it's perfectly possible for me to make a mistake.

Introduction

This book does not aim to teach you every aspect and function that is available within the Perl environment. Nor is it intended to be an example of the perfect path to a particular goal using Perl. There are a number of ways and methods in which different goals can be achieved in any language, and Perl is no exception to this rule. Instead, my aim is to demonstrate the use of Perl in real-world situations, showing examples and detailed reasons as to why the programmer followed a certain path and structure for the script.

Many of the scripts in this book are taken directly from my own toolkit of scripts and utilities that I have been using for many years. Others have been taken from the Internet, with the author's permission, and are included in this book in the same consistent style, with the same level of annotations. In all cases, I'd like to make it clear that the scripts are not taken to be the ultimate or perfect method of achieving a particular goal. What I can say is that all of the scripts work, and they all do what they set out to do.

WHO THIS BOOK IS FOR

I've not targeted the book at any one specific group of Perl users. To put it simply, if you program in Perl, then you will find this book useful. For beginners, the book provides a useful introduction to how programs are structured and how the different functions and constructs in Perl allow you to do both simple and more complex tasks.

For the intermediate programmer, this book should give you ideas and pointers to improving your Perl programming, and what tools and modules to use when approaching different problems with Perl. For the more advanced user, these scripts can help augment and form the basis of other projects you are working on, and they may even open doors to other solutions for particular problems that you had not originally considered.

In all cases, I have designed the scripts to be standalone examples of how to achieve different goals. All of the scripts can be taken directly from the book's CD-ROM and used within your own systems, albeit with minor modifications to take account of your local setup. Any required modules and extensions are supplied—see the section on the CD-ROM at the end of this introduction.

HOW TO USE THIS BOOK

There is no natural progression through the book, so you can pick it up at any point in any chapter, and you should be able to follow the scripts. Keep in mind, though, that a number of the chapters include a module as one of the first annotations. Although reading one of the later scripts without having first studied the module may leave some gaps in your understanding, the script ought to make sense.

When you want to use one of the scripts, copy it off of the CD-ROM (see the section "Using the CD-ROM"), modify it for your own situation (if necessary), and then try using it while studying the annotations to understand how it works. Where applicable, the annotations include possible script modifications and updates so you can customize it for your own environment or expand its capabilities and features.

Alternatively, if the script does exactly what you want, and you are not interested in the annotations, just go ahead and use the script!

CHAPTER BREAKDOWN

Each chapter in the book attempts to cover a different aspect of the solutions that Perl is able to provide.

Chapter 1 covers the use of Perl as a tool for processing and parsing text. It covers the use of Perl as a replacement for tools such as sed and grep, and it also gives an example of a very simple Web log analyzing program.

Chapter 2 shows how to use Perl with the file system to manage, monitor, and report on the files and directory structure. Of particular note in this chapter is a script that expands the specified path, following links and directories to complete the entire path name.

Chapter 3 demonstrates the ways in which you can use Perl as a solution for text-based databases. We look at tools to edit databases using simple delimiters, and we also explore ways of getting around the limitations imposed by using a delimited database.

Chapter 4 expands on the use of text databases by looking at alternatives to implementing direct access to text files for databases. In place of the text interface, we examine DBM databases, interfacing to older database systems, and using the DBD/DBI toolkits for interfacing between SQL databases, such as Oracle, and the structures available within Perl.

Chapter 5 highlights the use of Perl in a networked environment. It covers using Perl to connect to remote TCP/IP sites, as well as the use of Perl as a server platform by creating a very simple HTTP Web server. The use of the correct protocols to communicate between machines is also included in this chapter.

Chapter 6 examines the methods and procedures involved in processing e-mail messages. We learn how to send e-mail without using external applications, how to write a mailbot, and how to dynamically parse and process e-mail through a Perl-based filtering system.

Chapter 7 details the processes involved in checking and working with HTML documents and entire Web sites. The scripts in this chapter include a quick and dirty HTML verification toolkit, a Web site link checker both for remote and local sites, and tools for downloading and uploading Web sites.

Chapter 8 introduces CGI programming and the use of Perl as an interface between the Web and underlying databases. We also take the opportunity to look at the processes involved in using Perl for your e-commerce solution.

Chapter 9 looks at some approaches to security when programming with Perl as a CGI language. It includes the scripts required to register a user with the Apache Web server and how to e-mail users their password when they forget it.

Chapter 10 covers systems administration on all three platforms. In particular we examine ways of extracting data from Unix logs, such as utmp, converting Unix-style crontab entries to NT equivalents, and plugging the gap in the MacOS for df replacement.

Chapter 11 covers the use of Perl within a network administration role. It includes examples of using Perl to manage DNS information and of Perl as an availability and performance monitoring tool for your Unix and NT servers.

The book concludes with three appendixes of reference material. Appendix A covers the differences between the Unix, Windows, and Mac platforms, as they relate to programming in Perl. Appendix B is a list of resources, print and online, that will help you in your quest to master Perl. Appendix C is an introduction to the Perl documentation.

CONVENTIONS USED IN THIS BOOK

Scripts appear twice within the text of the book: first they are shown in their entirety for you to examine, then they are interspersed with the annotations, which are expansions and discussions surrounding the Perl techniques and functions being employed.

In all cases, the lines are numbered, including blank lines. Also, because of the line-length limit within the book's printed page, all scripts are limited to 69 characters on a line. This limit may affect the look of the script on the page, but I can assure you that the script still runs; I have not wrapped or otherwise segmented the lines. Any splitting of the lines follows the Perl convention. Just for completeness, the scripts on the CD-ROM also follow the same line breaks and conventions, so the scripts you see on the printed page should be identical to the scripts you will end up using from the CD-ROM.

All Perl keywords are highlighted in **bold**, and function definitions and descriptions are formatted in different ways to account for abilities and arguments to the individual functions. In all cases the formats and definitions are made clear.

USING THE CD-ROM

In the CD-ROM directory structure, each directory contains all of the scripts and support files relevant to that chapter. If the source is contributed and had to be modified for inclusion in the book, then you will find the original version in the **originals** directory. If the modules require a supported module, then, where permission has been given, the corresponding module is available in the **modules** directory.

All of the scripts assume the following:

- ◆ You are running Unix *or* you have access to an editor that supports reading Unix files. Options for such editors include emacs for the Mac and Windows platforms, or BBEdit on the Mac.

- ◆ Your Perl distribution is located in /usr/local/bin/perl for Perl 4 scripts or in /usr/local/bin/perl5 for Perl 5 or later scripts.

- ◆ Perl 4–compatible scripts require version 4.036.

- ◆ Perl 5–compatible scripts require version 5.004 or later.

The latest version of all scripts, examples, and support files can be found on the Web site http://www.mcwords.com.

CONTACTING THE AUTHOR

I always welcome comments and suggestions on my work. I particularly appreciate guides and recommendations on better ways of achieving different goals, especially with a language as varied and capable as Perl. The best way to contact me is via e-mail; you can use either books@mcwords.com (preferred) or mc@whoever.com. Alternatively, visit my Web site, http://www.mcwords.com, which contains resources and updated information about the scripts and contents of this book.

Text Processing

Analyzing and Modifying Text
File Management
Manipulating Text Data
Using Alternative Database Systems

Analyzing and Modifying Text

ext processing can mean simply replacing a few pieces of text or converting a file from one format to another, and such actions can easily be performed by a good text editor. Perl, short for Programmable Extraction and Report Language, can intelligently handle and process text, making it useful for a number of different tasks; in fact it is often used as a text processor in place of editors like **emacs**. You can use Perl to identify pieces of text, make direct text replacements, and create regular expressions for your searches and replacements. These abilities are similar, and in fact borrowed from, programs like **grep** and **sed**.

Where Perl excels is that it lets you do multiple replacements quickly and easily and, better still, lets you process the text data and then report on it. Analysis of text includes tasks ranging from counting the number of words in a file up to the more complex processes of analyzing log files and providing summaries of the information to the user.

Identifying patterns with Perl is easy when you use the correct regular expression; however, writing the correct regular expression can be somewhat tricky. You can make comparisons within an **if** statement, like this:

```
if ($var =~ /foo/)
```

The special pattern binding operator =~ forces Perl to test the contents on the left-hand side with the regular expression on the right-hand side. In this example, the pattern matches the letter *f* followed by an *o* and then by another *o*. Forward slashes are pattern delimiters, much the same as in the **sed** program. The opposite of the =~ pattern binding operator is !~, which returns true if the regular expression fails to match.

Alternatively, you can place complex match expressions as individual lines in the program, outside of a typical condition statement. These match expressions allow you to identify and split up lines that match a more complicated pattern than you can retrieve using a simple delimiter. For example, we use the following pattern in our second script in this chapter:

```
/^begin\s+(\d+)\s+(.*)/
```

The regular expression is contained within the delimiters //, and notice that we are using a number of special characters within the expression. These characters give regular expressions the flexibility to match more than simple text strings. There are three types of special-character mapping within a Perl regular expression. A *metacharacter*, listed in Table 1-1, is a character that carries special meaning within a regular expression. A *pattern quantifier*, listed in Table 1-2, specifies the number of repetitions to an expression. *Character patterns*, listed in Table 1-3, allow you to specify special characters and character combinations.

Going back to the previous example of **/^begin\s+(\d+)\s+(.*)/**,

◆ The ^ character specifies that the match must start at the beginning of a line.

◆ The next element specifies that a successful match has the sequence of letters **begin**.

Character(s)	Purpose
\	Treats the following character as a real character, ignoring any associations with a Perl regular expression metacharacter
^	Matches from the beginning of a line
$	Matches from the end of a line
.	Matches any character except the new-line character
|	Specifies alternate matches within the same regular expression (an OR operator)
( )	Group expressions together
[ ]	Look for a set of characters

TABLE 1-1.   Regular Expression Metacharacters

◆   **\s+** specifies that the character pattern be followed by one or more spaces.

◆   **(\d+)** specifies that a set of digits follow.

◆   Another **\s+** specifies that one or more spaces follow.

◆   The **(.*)** pattern specifies a character string.

By placing individual elements within parentheses ( ), the results of each match are placed into variables **$1, $2**, and so on, one for each element.

The most common use for regular expressions is to make changes to text or to strip or add characters. The format for a substitution is identical to the **sed** format, so the expression

```
s/foo/bar/
```

Quantifier	Purpose
*	Matches zero or more items
+	Matches one or more items
?	Matches zero or one item(s)
{n}	Matches exactly n times
{n,}	Matches at least n times
{n,m}	Matches at least n times but no more than m times

TABLE 1-2.   Regular Expression Pattern Qualifiers

Sequence	Purpose
\w	Matches an alphanumeric character (including "_")
\W	Matches a nonalphanumeric character
\s	Matches a whitespace character (such as spaces or tabs)
\S	Matches a nonwhitespace character
\d	Matches a digit
\D	Matches a nondigit character
\b	Matches a word boundary
\B	Matches a non–word boundary
\A	Matches only the beginning of a string
\Z	Matches only the end of a string
\G	Matches where previous **m//g (global match)** operation left off (only works with **/g** modifier)
\t	Matches Tab character
\n	Matches new-line character
\r	Matches carriage-return character
\f	Matches form-feed character
\a	Matches alarm (bell) character
\e	Matches Escape character (as used in **troff**, for example)
\033	Matches Octal character (such as a PDP-11)
\x1B	Matches hex character
\c[	Matches Control character
\l	Lowercases next character
\u	Uppercases next character
\L	Lowercases characters until the **\E** character pattern
\U	Uppercases characters until the **\E** character pattern
\E	Ends case modification
\Q	Quotes (disables) regular expression metacharacters till **\E** character pattern

TABLE 1-3.   Regular Expression Character Patterns

replaces the first occurrence of "foo" with "bar." To replace all occurrences of "foo" with "bar," you would add the modifier **g**:

```
s/foo/bar/g
```

Table 1-4 shows a list of the modifiers available for pattern matching, and Table 1-5 shows the additional options available when performing substitutions.

Although they may look like fairly insubstantial elements on their own, regular expressions make processing and using text significantly easier. The ability to use these expressions directly within the code gives Perl an advantage over languages, such as C, which would need a set of library functions to work on text the same way. Even then, a C programmer would struggle to use the expressions as readily and easily as a Perl programmer does.

Throughout this book, we'll be looking at Perl's text processing features and how they can aid all sorts of programs. In this chapter, we look at a range of scripts that perform such simple text replacement tasks as converting documents from UNIX to DOS format and back again. We also examine more complex processing, such as decoding the uuencoded files you might have received by e-mail, and the text analysis associated with processing the log file from a Web server to obtain some very simple statistics.

dos2ux.pl

Converting the Text Format of Multiple Files

Under Unix, there are two commands that allow you to convert text files from DOS to Unix and back again. Rather obviously, the programs are called **ux2dos** and **dos2ux** for converting from Unix to DOS and vice versa. All they actually do is change the end-of-line characters. Under DOS, each line is terminated first by a new-line character (ASCII code 10) and then by a carriage return (ASCII code 13).

Not everybody has Unix, and even if you do, there's no guarantee that the conversion commands will be available for you to use when you need them. You can get around this problem by using a small script that will do the conversion for you. Because Perl is available on most platforms, the script could be employed

Modifier	Description
i	Makes the match case insensitive
m	If the string has new-line or carriage return characters, then the ^ and $ operators (from Table 1-1) will not work correctly. Instead, they will match the start and end of the string, rather than individual lines. This can be useful when matching multi-line strings
s	Allows . to match a new-line character
x	Allows you to use whitespace in the expression for clarity

TABLE 1-4. Perl Regular Expression Modifiers for Matching

Option	Description
g	Matches every occurrence within a string, not just the first
e	Evaluates replacement string as an expression
o	Evaluates the expression only once

TABLE 1-5.   Perl Regular Expression Modifiers for Substitution

anywhere, and with a few modifications could be used to replace any string in any file.

```
1    #!/usr/local/bin/perl -i
2
3    while (<>)
4    {
5        s/\012\015//;
6        print $_ . "\n";
7    }
```

ANNOTATIONS

Line 1 is actually used by Unix to identify which program to run when you execute the file. In this case, I'm using a version from the default installation directory, **/usr/local/bin/perl**. The **-i** option sets up an environment for Perl that will help us convert documents in place, instead of having to create temporary edit files. This is a lot like running the search and replace feature in an editor, where modifications are made to the live version of a file. There are other effects that the **-i** option has, and I'll cover those below.

NT uses the file associations table to match the extension to the program, but the NT version of Perl will look at this first line to identify any additional options that may need to be set. Perl is notoriously difficult to read at the best of times, and line 2 is just a blank line in the script to make it a bit more readable.

```
3    while (<>)
4    {
```

Lines 3 to 7 do the donkey work. Line 3 sets up a **while** loop, which will execute until the expression in the brackets returns false. In this case, we are checking until the end of file is reached on the default input. Because we haven't specified a file, Perl will take its input from this first file on the command line, do the conversion on the entire file, and then move to the next file specified on the command line. In this way, without having to write the extra code, we can make replacements in a number of files quickly and easy. Line 4 opens up the **while** loop; all subsections in Perl, including loops and **if** statements, are contained within the curly brackets. For each loop of the **while** statement, an individual line will be read into the Perl input space.

```
5    s/\012\015//;
6    print $_ . "\n";
7    }
```

The actual substitution takes place on line 5. The format is similar, if not identical in this case, for standard regular expressions. The leading **s** tells us this is a substitution command, and each subsequent element, separated by the forward slash (/), is an argument to the substitution. The first argument is the text to be replaced. We specify the special characters using octal notation, with a preceding backslash and the three-digit octal code for the character we want. The next argument to the substitution is blank, because we're not replacing the text with anything, and no options are specified for the final argument. The last argument specifies additional options, such as global replacement (Perl only replaces the first occurrence in a line or string otherwise). Because we haven't specified a string for this substitution to work on, it will substitute characters in the default-input space.

Line 6 prints out the line, referenced by the special variable **$_**, and then concatenates this with the new-line character, **\n**. String concatenation in Perl is very easy: to merge any data, just place a period between each element. Elements can be strings, numeric variables, or even function calls. The **print** command does not work quite as you might expect. Normally, a print statement would go to the screen, but because we are using the **-i** option, the output is being sent back to the input file, replacing the line that was originally read in. Finally, we close the **while** loop with a curly bracket.

In essence, the script opens the file referenced on the command line, replaces the carriage return and new-line character on each line of the file with a version terminated only with a new-line character. It's quick and easy and very practical. The substitution string could be replaced with anything you like. This same technique, for example, could be used to convert a comma-separated file into a tab-delimited file.

Going back to our example, to convert a Unix file back to DOS, we have to make modifications to lines 5 and 6:

```
5    s/\012//;
6    print $_ . "\n\r";
```

In this case we are replacing only the new-line character on line 5 with a new-line carriage-return sequence in line 6.

Of course, this sequence works only on a Unix machine because the default end-of-line sequence is just a new line. On a DOS or NT machine, the scripts would have to account for the fact that the default end-of-line sequence is a new-line carriage-return.

Faster File Conversions

Using a slightly different format from the previous example, it's possible to make string replacements to all of the files specified on the command line, still without having to worry about processing the command-line argument list.

For simple replacements, we can specify the entire script on the command line. For example, the DOS-to-Unix conversion program can be written like this:

```
perl -p -i.bak -e 's/\012\015//' file.in
```

The **-p** option automatically encloses the command specified in the argument following **-e** into this script:

```
 1    while(<>)
 2    {
 3        rename($ARGV, $ARGV . '.bak');
 4        open(OUT, ">$ARGV");
 5        s/\012\015//;
 6    }
 7    continue
 8    {
 9        print OUT;
10    }
```

The **-i** option creates the backup file that is generated in line 3; line 4 opens the output file; line 5 performs the conversion; and then lines 7 to 10 print out the result. Although this method doesn't require you to write a script in the normal function, it still uses the text processing features of Perl to reach the same goal.

uudecode.pl

Uudecoding Files

The Internet e-mail system was originally supported via a program called **uucp**, short for Unix-to-Unix copy. The system used 7-bit characters, which was fine for e-mail messages and Usenet news but useless for binary files that used the full 8-bit character set. To get around this problem, binary enclosures were encoded from the full 8-bit set to a 7-bit character set so that they could be sent over e-mail. The process of conversion is called Uuencoding, and all modern versions of Unix come with the necessary encoding and decoding programs.

If you don't have Unix decoding, these files can be a problem, although there are plenty of tools available on just about every platform you can find. A quicker way around the problem is to use Perl to convert the document back to its original form. As in our last example, this type of script has the advantage of being able to run on any machine that runs Perl. You could, for example, supply the script within the e-mail message, since the script itself uses only 7-bit characters, and be assured that the process of extraction would work at the other end.

Unlike our last example, we will access the arguments that are passed to the script directly. An error message will be generated if the required argument is not present. The script also opens two files for processing: one for input, using the argument as the source for its name, and one for output, which uses the source file as the source for the file's name.

```perl
1   #!/usr/local/bin/perl
2
3   unless (@ARGV == 1)
4   {
5       die <<EOF
6   Usage: $0 file
7
8   Where file is the name of the file you want to decode
9   EOF
10  ;
11  }
12
13  open(INFILE,"<" . $ARGV [0]) || die "Can't open input file";
14
15  $valid=0;
16
17  while (<INFILE>)
18  {
19      if (/^begin\s+(\d+)\s+(.*)/)
20      {
21          $filemode=$1;
22          $outfile=$2;
23          $valid=1;
24          last;
25      }
26  }
27
28  $valid ? print "Creating $outfile \n" : die "Not a UU file";
29
30  open(OUTFILE, ">$outfile")|| die "Can't open the input\n";
31
32  while(<INFILE>)
```

```
33    {
34          $decodedline = unpack("u",$_);
35          die "Invalid uuencoded line" if (!defined($decodedline));
36          print OUTFILE $decodedline;
37          /^end$/ && last;
38    }
39
40    close (INFILE);
41    close (OUTFILE);
42    chmod oct($filemode), $outfile;
```

ANNOTATIONS

A uuencoded file starts with the first line that has **begin**, followed by the file's mode in Unix octal format and the filename. The script opens the file specified by the first argument on the command line. It processes the first line of the file and identifies it as a uuencoded file. The first line contains the file's name and mode, and we record this information for later use. The script then creates the output file, processes each line of input using the **unpack** command, closes the input and output files, and changes the mode to match the one specified.

The bulk of the script is devoted to identifying the input and setting up the environment so that the actual file processing can take place. We start on line 1, which just sets the Perl command, this time without any arguments to the Perl application itself.

```
1     #!/usr/local/bin/perl
2
3     if (@ARGV < 0)
4     {
5           die <<EOF
6     Usage: $0 file
7
8     Where file is the name of the file you want to decode
9     EOF
10    ;
11    }
12
```

Lines 3 to 11 check for an argument to the script, and then print a usage message if no file was specified. In line 3 we use an **if** statement to check the number of arguments supplied to the script. Arguments are stored in the variable **@ARGV**. The variable is an array, with each element containing the arguments specified on the command line in sequence. The number of elements in an array is returned by @ARGV in a scalar context. Using $#ARGV gives the index of the last element of @ARGV, or –1 if it's empty. Since we require at least one file, we need to check for a minimum of one argument. In this instance, we're not bothered if they supply more than file as an argument, as only the first file will be processed anyway. Line 4 opens up the **if** statement when no files are specified. We use the **die** function that reports an error and then quits Perl.

Normally you would specify the message to be returned within double quotes, but this can be tedious for long statements, such as the usage information we're printing here. Instead, we use the redirect notation on line 5 to accept all the text up to the first line starting with **EOF**. Perl normally refers to this type of text inclusion as a *here* document. Notice that on line 6 I've put **$0** in the error message. Like shellscript, **$0** refers to the name of the script being run. This means that even if the script name changes, the error message will print correctly.

WARNING *The text used to mark the end of the here document must be the only item on the line, and it must match the character sequence after the redirection operators. Inserting a space before the end-of-text mark will cause Perl to fail, so formatting the end-of-text mark is out of the question!*

The end-of-text mark is on line 9, and line 10 contains a single semicolon to act as visual reminder that this section of text within Perl has ended. It is not required, but it helps a reader identify the split.

Assuming we're past the **if** statement, execution continues on line 13:

```
13    open(INFILE,"<" . $ARGV [0]) || die "Can't open input file";
```

Line 13 creates a new file handle to accept input from the file specified on the command line. The first argument to **open** specifies the file handle, which is the name that will be used to identify the file in the rest of the script; the second argument specifies the name of the file to open and how to open it. In Perl, you use the Unix shell redirection operators to specify how to open the file as part of the string that makes up the name. The less-than symbol, <, is the same as opening a file for reading, and the greater-than symbol, >, opens a file for writing. We use the string concatenation system we saw in the last script to specify the full filename, including the style in which we want to open the file.

The **open** function returns true (a positive number) if the command was successful and false if the command was unsuccessful. Combining this with an OR (| |) and the **die** function means we can report on a problem if one occurs. Using the OR test, Perl will execute the first function, running the second function only if the first one does not return true. If the first function does return true, then the second function is not executed. Put simply, it successfully executes the first *or* the second function. Therefore, in line 13, if the log file is not successfully opened, we use **die** to print the reason for the failure and then quit the script.

```
14
15    $valid=0;
```

```
16
17    while (<INFILE>)
18    {
19        if (/^begin\s+(\d+)\s+(.*)/)
20        {
21            $filemode=$1;
22            $outfile=$2;
23            $valid=1;
24            last;
25        }
26    }
27
```

In line 15, I'm setting the **$valid** variable to zero, which Perl will treat as false if it's tested for. We'll use this in line 28 to check if the match statement worked and executed lines 17 to 26 properly.

On line 17, we start a **while** loop where the test will be based on whether we are at EOF (end of file) for the input file. We check each line starting with the first, until we match a **begin** word at the start of a line, followed by the file mode and then filename that is contained at the top of every uuencoded file. The match string in line 19 will return true if a match is found, and then lines 21 and 22 record the information to use later on. We set **$valid** to 1 (true) in line 23, which again we will use later, and then line 24 drops us out of the while loop at the start of the next line.

```
28    $valid ? print "Creating $outfile \n" : die "Not a UU file";
29
```

Line 28 uses a quick check to see if the match worked. If the **begin** word had not been found, we would have dropped out of the **while** loop at the end of file and still reached this line. But because we set **$valid** to false before we started, if we drop out this way, **$valid** will still be false; only if the file was identified as a uuencoded file would **$valid** return true. The quick test puts the condition first, followed by a question mark and then by the argument that will be executed if the expression returns true. The argument after the colon is executed if the condition returns false. Here we give the user some information about the file being created, or we quit with an error message if the file can't be identified.

```
30    open(OUTFILE, ">$outfile") || die "Can't open the output\n";
31
```

We create a new file, using the name we discovered in line 19, with a file handle of **OUTFILE**. We perform the same check as we did when opening the input source to make sure we can recreate the output. You'll also notice that in this example, I've placed the whole file specification, including the redirection operator, directly into the string that forms the second argument. This is called string *interpolation*.

Interpolation can sometimes make the code more readable. Perl evaluates the contents of the string, replacing variable references with their contents. There are times when interpolation doesn't work, and I'll provide examples as we work through the rest of this book.

```
32   while(<INFILE>)
33   {
34       $decodedline = unpack("u",$_);
35       die "Invalid uuencoded line" if (!defined($decodedline));
36       print OUTFILE $decodedline;
37       /^end$/ && last;
38   }
39
```

Lines 32 to 38 process the source file line by line, converting the uuencoded information back into raw data. More specifically, line 34 actually does the work, using the **unpack** command. The **unpack** command converts the data that has been packed out or filled to fit a specific format. Packed data refers to information that has to be recorded in a file in a fixed size or format. We'll look at this in more detail in Chapter 4 when we cover DBM files. The Perl **unpack** command supports uuencoded information, and processes each line (specified by the **$_** special variable), placing the result in **$decodedline**.

Line 35 makes sure the line was understood by **unpack** by checking that **$decodeline** was defined in the previous line. If it wasn't, we use the **die** function to report an error. Line 36 prints the decoded line to **OUTFILE**. Notice that we don't add a new line to the decoded text. This is because a line of uuencoded information will not match a line of textual or binary data. Any new-line characters in the original file will be contained in the variable that is printed, ensuring that the information will be formatted correctly.

We use another logical expression in line 37, this time using logical AND (&&) to match the word **end** on the input file. If found, the **last** function will drop us out of the **while** loop.

```
40   close (INFILE);
41   close (OUTFILE);
42   chmod oct($filemode), $outfile;
```

Lines 40 to 42 complete the script by closing the input and output files and then setting the correct mode, as discovered in the input file, on the output file. This action is performed using the **chmod** function that works identically to the shellscript version. However, the **chmod** function expects a base-ten value, not an octal value, which is what was specified in the uuencoded file. The **oct** functions return a value interpreted from the octal value passed to it in the argument.

That's it. The script is really quite straightforward, but the only reason it can be so short and simple is because the **unpack** function supports uuencoded data as standard. Without this feature, the program would have been a lot more complex, although the basic process of identifying and reading from and writing to a file would have remained the same.

File Encryption

encrypt.pl

Although there are many tools available to securely encrypt a file, many of them rely on a protected, usually precompiled, program. Often there are times when you just want to quickly encrypt a file, not with something bulletproof but with something that will keep a casual user from looking at the file.

The Unix OS includes a program called **crypt** that uses an algorithm similar to that used for password encryption and is based on the Data Encryption Standard (DES) algorithm. The algorithm is one way, the idea being that the time taken to decode the encrypted text would take more processing power than is available in even the fastest computer. The operation for password checking is to store the encrypted password, checking entered passwords by encrypting them, and comparing the two encrypted results.

Although all Unix versions across all countries support **crypt**, in many countries it is not available due to strict U.S. export laws. To make matters worse, the Perl built-in function **crypt** is based on the same C function. This doesn't help us in our goal to be able to encrypt and decrypt files for the purposes of exchanging documents or recording sensitive information. We need a tool that can effectively encrypt and decrypt documents, without making the algorithm so simple that an idiot could break it.

```perl
1   #!/usr/local/bin/perl
2
3   unless (@ARGV == 2)
4   {
5       die <<EOF
6   Usage: $0 password file
7
8   Where
9   password is the password you want to use to encrypt the file
10  file is the name of the file you want to encrypt
11  EOF
12  }
13
14  $passwd=$ARGV [0];
15  $infile=$ARGV [1];
16
17  open(INFILE, "<" . $infile);
```

```
18   open(OUTFILE, ">" . $infile . ".out");
19
20   $j=0;
21
22   while(<INFILE>)
23   {
24       $inline=$_;
25       for($i=0;$i<length($inline);$i++)
26       {
27           $outchar=ord(substr($inline,$i,1))
28               +ord(substr($passwd,$j++,1));
29           $j=0 if $j>length($passwd);
30           print OUTFILE chr($outchar);
31       }
32   }
33
34   close(INFILE) || die "Couldn't close input file $!\n";
35   close(OUTFILE) || die "Couldn't close output file $!\n";
36
```

ANNOTATIONS

In this example, I've used a simple rotating password that adds the ASCII value of the first character of the input file with the ASCII value of the first character in the password. We then move through the password one letter at a time, reading in each character from the input file. When we get to the end of the password, we start at the first character again, and so on, until we reach the end of the file. As an example, the ASCII code for *A* is 65, so if we had a password of "Aardvark," the first character in the output file would have an ASCII value of 130.

```
1    #!/usr/local/bin/perl
2
3    unless (@ARGV ==2)
4    {
5        die <<EOF
6    Usage: crypt.pl password file
7
8    Where
9    password is the password you want to use to encrypt the file
10   file is the name of the file you want to encrypt
11   EOF
12   }
```

```
13
14    $passwd=$ARGV [0];
15    $infile=$ARGV [1];
16
```

   Lines 1 to 16 set us up for the rest of the program. We check the number of
arguments again, this time looking for two arguments, password and filename,
printing a suitable message on failure. Assuming we get this far, lines 14 and 15 set
two global variables for the password and input file.

```
17    open(INFILE, "<" . $infile);
18    open(OUTFILE, ">" . $infile . ".out");
19
20    $j=0;
21
```

   We open the input file in line 17 and the output file in line 18. Rather than making
the changes in the same file, which could obviously cause some corruption, we
create a new output file with an extension of **.out**. Line 20 sets the **$j** variable to zero;
this is the index number we will use to progress through the password. To really
throw people off the scent, we could start at any character within the password,
checking first that the password was long enough before specifying too large a
number. The same number would be required when the file was decrypted. You
might even want to try adding another argument to the script to allow the user to
specify the starting character. That would make the encrypted file even more
difficult to decrypt because the recipient would need to know both the password
and where the password started from to decrypt the file.

```
22    while(<INFILE>)
23    {
24        $inline=$_;
25        for($i=0;$i<length($inline);$i++)
26        {
```

   Opening the file, we look at each individual line that is automatically extracted by
Perl into the special variable **$_**. The **for** statement in line 25 in combination with
line 27 encrypts each individual character in the line.

```
27            $outchar=ord(substr($inline,$i,1))
28                +ord(substr($passwd,$j++,1));
29            $j=0 if $j>length($passwd);
30            print OUTFILE chr($outchar);
```

   Lines 27 and 28 use the **substr** function to extract one character from the line
using the index of **$i** and one character from the password using the index value of
$j. Using the **ord** function, we get the ASCII number of the characters, and then add

them together. We increment the value of **$j** as we step through the password, and then check on line 28 to make sure we don't go over the end, resetting the index to zero so the password character is constantly rotating through the full password.

Finally, we print each character to the output file in line 30, using the **chr** function, which is the exact opposite of the **ord** function, returning the ASCII character associated with a particular number. Since we don't extract or identify a new-line or carriage-return character, this will be encrypted, too, so we output the character on its own. Lines 31 to 36 finish off the loops and then close the two files:

```
31          }
32    }
33
34    close(INFILE) || die "Couldn't close input file $!\n";
35    close(OUTFILE) || die "Couldn't close output file $!\n";
36
```

I haven't taken into consideration at all the performance aspects of this program. Although we read in the file line by line, output is one character at a time, which is inefficient, even allowing for the buffering that exists on all file I/O. To improve the program's performance, you could replace lines 27 to 36 with these lines:

```
25          undef($outline);
26          for($i=0;$i<length($inline);$i++)
27          {
28                  $outline .= chr(ord(substr($inline,$i,1))
29                      +ord(substr($passwd,$j++,1)));
30                  $j=0 if $j>length($passwd);
31          }
32          print OUTFILE $outline;
33    }
34
35    close(INFILE);
36    close(OUTFILE);
37
```

In line 25, we undefine the variable **$outline**, which is the variable we will use to store the encrypted line of the input file. Because it's inside the loop, it will be reset for each line read in by the loop. Lines 28 and 29 (really a single line, but split here for clarity) now concatenate each character previously placed in **$outchar** on to the **$outline** variable. The **chr** function now operates on the result of the calculation that produces the encrypted character. The only other change is that line 32 outputs the entire line to the output file. The line is outside the loop that works through each character of the line, so by the time we get here, the entire line should have been encrypted; then line 33 ends the loop.

These minor changes to the overall layout can increase the speed of encryption quite significantly on large files. Although it's unlikely that we would be encrypting very large files using this script, the point is that doing as much processing as you can within memory will dramatically speed up the execution of your script. On my dual processor BeBox using my own port of Perl, encrypting a 1.1MB tar file took 371 seconds using the first form of the script, but it took only 339 seconds using the second form.

The decryption script, based on the single character output version, follows.

decrypt.pl

```perl
1    #!/usr/local/bin/perl
2
3    if ($#ARGV < 1)
4    {
5        die <<EOF
6    Usage: decrypt.pl password file
7
8    Where
9    password is the password you want to use to decrypt the file
10   file is the name of the file you want to decrypt
11   EOF
12   }
13
14   $passwd=$ARGV [0];
15   $infile=$ARGV [1];
16
17   open(INFILE, "<" . $infile);
18   open(OUTFILE, ">" . $infile . ".out");
19
20   $j=0;
21
22   while(<INFILE>)
23   {
24       $inline=$_;
25       for($i=0;$i<length($inline);$i++)
26       {
27           $outchar=ord(substr($inline,$i,1))
28               -ord(substr($passwd,$j++,1));
29           $j=0 if $j>length($passwd);
30           print OUTFILE chr($outchar);
31       }
```

```
32   }
33
34   close(INFILE) || die "Couldn't close input file $!\n";
35   close(OUTFILE) || die "Couldn't close output file $!\n";
36
```

The only difference between the two scripts is located in lines 27 and 28, where we take the ASCII value of the password away from the encrypted character to give us the original character back.

Because the output of an encrypted file is likely to be binary (that is, having a character value higher than the 127), I can't show you what the output would be like. Run the decryption script with a password of "Come grow old along with me" on the file **source.enc** on the CD-ROM. Make sure you enclose the password in double quotes on the command line using the correct case.

weblog.pl

Processing a Standard Web Log

All the scripts I've shown so far in this chapter concentrate on converting information from one format to another. Although information conversion is a feature of Perl, the last two letters of its name stand for "Report Language." Using some of these same text processing features we already examined, we can analyze and report on the contents of a text file.

Log files are generated by operating systems and application software. Sometimes you can afford to ignore the contents of these files, but most likely you will want to report on the contents and provide a summary of the information contained within. When summarizing, you need to find a common element that you can key on. With most other languages, you need to find a way of recording information about individual keys within a set of variables. When you come across each element, you first have to search for it in the existing list or recognized keys, incrementing the value if it's found or creating a new entry if it isn't found.

With Perl, however, we can use an associative, or hashed, array feature to store the summary information. A *hashed* array is like a traditional array, except that instead of using numbers as indexes to the elements, we can use a text string. To add a new element to a numerically indexed array, you increment the highest index number by one and make the new index within the array equal the data you want to store.

Within a hashed array, you simply reference the array with a new index name. Perl creates the new element within the array, allowing you to get on with extracting and reporting on the information. Perl is therefore easier to program and easier to read—it's obvious what you are doing.

PROGRAMMER'S NOTE   *A hashed array has no logical order or sequence. Although it's possible to sort the information within a hashed array, to access the information you must know the key that was used to identify the data element you want.*

In the following example, I use a combination of regular expressions to extract and identify the information contained within individual lines of a Web server's log file, and I use hashes to tally the information for reporting. The default log style is called common log format and follows this basic structure:

```
Host      Identifier    Username    [Time]      "Request"    Result    Bytes
```

For example:

```
ps2he - - [25/May/1998:02:09:46 +0100] "GET /cyberpat.html HTTP/1.0" 200 2700
ps2he - - [25/May/1998:02:09:47 +0100] "GET /COembossed.gif HTTP/1.0" 200 1821
ps2he - - [25/May/1998:02:09:50 +0100] "GET /persuser48.gif HTTP/1.0" 200 1321
ps2he - - [25/May/1998:02:09:52 +0100] "GET /business48.gif HTTP/1.0" 200 1477
ps1he - - [25/May/1998:02:10:00 +0100] "GET /aboutco.gif HTTP/1.0" 200 6871
ps1he - - [25/May/1998:02:10:00 +0100] "GET /ButtonPanel.gif HTTP/1.0" 200 3811
ps1he - - [25/May/1998:02:10:01 +0100] "GET /pnblank.gif HTTP/1.0" 200 599
ps2he - - [25/May/1998:02:10:03 +0100] "GET /cyberpic.gif HTTP/1.0" 200 48634
ww-t105.proxy.aol.com - - [25/May/1998:04:01:05 +0100] "GET /cyberpat.html HTTP/1.0" 200 1746
ww-t105.proxy.aol.com - - [25/May/1998:04:01:10 +0100] "GET /whatsnew.gif HTTP/1.0" 200 6045
ww-t105.proxy.aol.com - - [25/May/1998:04:01:10 +0100] "GET /pnblank.gif HTTP/1.0" 200 599
ww-t105.proxy.aol.com - - [25/May/1998:04:01:11 +0100] "GET /ButtonPanel.gif HTTP/1.0" 200 3811
ww-t105.proxy.aol.com - - [25/May/1998:04:01:13 +0100] "GET /COembossed.gif HTTP/1.0" 200 1821
ww-t105.proxy.aol.com - - [25/May/1998:04:01:13 +0100] "GET /cyberpat.gif HTTP/1.0" 200 1019
ww-t105.proxy.aol.com - - [25/May/1998:04:01:20 +0100] "GET /download32.gif HTTP/1.0" 200 1107
```

We could use the **split** function to separate the elements, but it would require some careful splitting and examination to extract the information correctly. Using a space as the separation character would also split up the request field incorrectly. Taking into account the square brackets and double quotes makes the extraction even more complex. Using the **match** function, we can split up the logical components, taking into account the physical layout of each line.

```
1   #!/usr/local/bin/perl
2
3   %Months = (
4               "Jan" => "01",
5               "Feb" => "02",
6               "Mar" => "03",
7               "Apr" => "04",
8               "May" => "05",
9               "Jun" => "06",
10              "Jul" => "07",
11              "Aug" => "08",
12              "Sep" => "09",
```

```
13              "Oct" => "10",
14              "Nov" => "11",
15              "Dec" => "12"
16
17
18  open (INLOG, "<" . $ARGV [0] ) || die "Can't open input: $!\n";
19
20  while (<INLOG>)
21  {
22      chomp;
23
24      $matched = /^(\S+)\s+(\S+)\s+(\S+)\s+\[(.*)\]
25                  \s+"(.*)"\s+(\S+)\s+(\S+)$/x;
26      next unless $matched;
27      $host = $1;
28      $ident = $2;
29      $user = $3;
30      $time = $4;
31      $url = $5;
32      $success = $6;
33      $bytes = $7;
34
35      $matched = $time =~ m%(..)/(...)/(....):(..):(..):(..)%;
36
37      $day = $1;
38      $mon = $Months{$2};
39      $year = $3;
40      $hour = $4;
41      $min = $5;
42      $sec = $6;
43
44      $url =~ m%\S+\s+(\S+)%;
45      $url = $1;
46
47      if ($success == 200)
48      {
49       $accesses++;
50       $bytessent += $bytes;
51       $hostaccess{$host}++;
52       $hostbytes{$host} += $bytes;
53       $urlaccess{$url}++;
54       $urlbytes{$url} += $bytes;
55       $urlbyhost{"$host:$url"}++;
```

```perl
56          $urlbyhostbytes{"$host:$url"} += $bytes;
57      }
58 }
59
60 close(INLOG) || die "Couldn't close the input: $!\n";
61
62 print "Web log report\n\n";
63 print "Total number of accesses: $accesses, Bytes: $bytessent\n\n";
64
65 print "Host summary\n\n";
66
67 foreach $host (sort_values_bynum(\%hostaccess))
68 {
69     printf("%-60s\t%10s\t%10s\n","$host",
70         "$hostaccess{$host}","$hostbytes{$host}");
71 }
72
73 print "\n\nURL summary\n\n";
74
75 foreach $url (sort_values_bynum(\%urlaccess))
76 {
77     printf("%-60s\t%10s\t%10s\n","$url",
78         "$urlaccess{$url}","$urlbytes{$url}");
79 }
80
81 print "\n\nURL/Host summary\n\n";
82
83 foreach $urlhost (sort_values_bynum(\%urlbyhost))
84 {
85     printf("%-60s\t%10s\t%10s\n","$urlhost",
86         "$urlbyhost{$urlhost}","$urlbyhostbytes{$urlhost}");
87 }
88
89 sub sort_values_bynum
90 {
91     my $arrayref = shift;
92     my %array = %$arrayref;
93
94     sort { $array{$b} <=> $array{$a}; } keys %array;
95 }
```

ANNOTATIONS

After some initialization, the script reads in each line of the log file and starts recording individual pieces of information into the associative arrays. Once we've finished reading the log, we start reporting the information, sorting it by the number of accesses to give us a chart.

```
1    #!/usr/local/bin/perl5
2
3    %Months = (
4                "Jan" => "01",
5                "Feb" => "02",
6                "Mar" => "03",
7                "Apr" => "04",
8                "May" => "05",
9                "Jun" => "06",
10               "July" => "07",
11               "Aug" => "08",
12               "Sep" => "09",
13               "Oct" => "10",
14               "Nov" => "11",
15               "Dec" => "12"
16               );
17
```

Lines 3 to 16 set up an associative array. The key value of the array is the month in standard three-letter format, with the value being the month number. We'll use this when we match the date information from the log file.

```
18   open (INLOG, "<" . $ARGV [0] ) || die "Can't open input: $!\n";
19
20   while (<INLOG>)
21   {
22       chomp;
23
```

Line 18 opens the log file by using the argument specified on the command line. As usual, we check the result in combination with the **die** function. I've added in this example the error that will be produced if the file can't be opened. Error messages for all functions are placed into the special variable **$!**. We don't need to check whether one is specified on this occasion, since the **die** function will do that for us. (It would be easy to add the facility in to the script if we really needed it, however.) Then we start processing the log file on line 22 by using **chomp** to take the carriage-return character off the end of the line.

```
24        $matched = /^(\S+)\s+(\S+)\s+(\S+)\s+\[(.*)\]
25                   \s+"(.*)"\s+(\S+)\s+(\S+)$/x;
```

Lines 24 and 25 identify the input line; the component parts resulting from the match statement are listed in Table 1-6. Note that we test against the beginning and end of the line to make sure we are extracting the right information. I've also added the **/x** option to the match so that we can split it across two lines for readability.

```
26        next unless $matched;
27        $host = $1;
28        $ident = $2;
29        $user = $3;
30        $time = $4;
31        $url = $5;
32        $success = $6;
33        $bytes = $7;
34
```

Element	Type	Log Element
^	Beginning of line	
(\S+)	Non-whitespace string	Host
\s+	(whitespace separator)	
(\S+)	Non-whitespace string	Identifier
\s+	(whitespace separator)	
(\S+)	Non-whitespace string	Username
\s+	(whitespace separator)	
\[(.*)\]	All characters enclosed in square brackets	Time
\s+	(whitespace separator)	
"(.*)"	All characters enclosed in double quotes	Request
\s+	(whitespace separator)	
(\S+)	Non-whitespace string	Result
\s+	(whitespace separator)	
(\S+)	Non-whitespace string	Bytes sent
$	End of line	

TABLE 1-6.   Log File Match Components

Because we equated the match to the variable **$matched**—which returns true if the match was successful, or false if the input line could not be matched—we can test the validity of the match. Line 26 skips over the line unless the match completed successfully; we don't want to exit at this point, as it could just be a single bad line in the input file. The result of the match is then extracted within lines 27 to 33.

```
35      $matched = $time =~ m%(..)/(...)/(....):(..):(..):(..)%;
36
37      $day = $1;
38      $mon = $Months{$2};
39      $year = $3;
40      $hour = $4;
41      $min = $5;
42      $sec = $6;
43
```

Lines 35 to 43 perform a similar match operation on the time field we extracted earlier. In this case, the match string is identifying a set number of characters within the overall time format. The match string is also referenced differently. This time we have an **m** preceding the match text, and the percent character is used to enclose the entire regular expression. Using the preceding **m** allows us to specify a different character than the default slash for the expression, and in this case it means the match string is more readable because we are not escaping the special forward slash character used to represent a date. Line 38 equates **$mon** to the number stored in the associative array we created in lines 3 to 16.

```
44      $url =~ m%\S+\s+(\S+)%;
45      $url = $1;
46
```

Our final match statement is in line 43, where we extract the URL from the full request that was received by the Web server. For this script, we are not interested in how a user obtained the file, just what file they access. Because I'm only interested in the first element of the request, it's the only one I've extracted on line 44.

```
47      if ($success == 200)
48      {
49       $accesses++;
50       $bytessent += $bytes;
51       $hostaccess{$host}++;
52       $hostbytes{$host} += $bytes;
53       $urlaccess{$url}++;
54       $urlbytes{$url} += $bytes;
55       $urlbyhost{"$host:$url"}++;
56       $urlbyhostbytes{"$host:$url"} += $bytes;
57      }
```

Now we have the information from the line in the log file in a format we can use, we can start to populate the summary tables. We wrap the summary information gathering within an **if** statement that checks if the Web access was successful (a success has a value of 200). By checking the success and only then counting up the summary information, we ensure that the output from the logs contains only valid accesses.

Line 49 counts up the number of accesses to the Web server, and line 50 totals up the number of bytes sent. Line 51 is our first associative or hashed array, and it totals up the number of accesses by a specific host. Line 52 uses the same key value to total the number of bytes sent to the same host. Then we repeat the action for accesses to individual URLs and then finally to a specific URL accessed by a specific host.

In lines 55 and 56, rather than just using the string as a key value, we create a new string made up of the host name and the URL separated by a colon. This creates a new key with the specified key name. Although based on the same basic principles, we have added an extra level of complication not found in most languages by being able to generate new key information within the variable definition.

We close the file on line 60 having read in and summarized all the information into those associative arrays. Just to make sure we've accessed and closed it correctly, we run it past **die** again. All we need to do is extract the information again, using lines 62 to 87.

```perl
60  close(INLOG) || die "Couldn't close the input: $!\n";
61
62  print "Web log report\n\n";
63  print "Total number of accesses: $accesses, Bytes: $bytessent\n\n";
64
65  print "Host summary\n\n";
66
67  foreach $host (sort_values_bynum(\%hostaccess))
68  {
69      printf("%-60s\t%10s\t%10s\n","$host",
70          "$hostaccess{$host}","$hostbytes{$host}");
71  }
72
73  print "\n\nURL summary\n\n";
74
75  foreach $url (sort_values_bynum(\%urlaccess))
76  {
77      printf("%-60s\t%10s\t%10s\n","$url",
78          "$urlaccess{$url}","$urlbytes{$url}");
79  }
80
```

```
81   print "\n\nURL/Host summary\n\n";
82
83   foreach $urlhost (sort_values_bynum(\%urlbyhost))
84   {
85       printf("%-60s\t%10s\t%10s\n","$urlhost",
86           "$urlbyhost{$urlhost}","$urlbyhostbytes{$urlhost}");
87   }
88
89   sub sort_values_bynum
90   {
91       my $arrayref = shift;
92       my %array = %$arrayref;
93
94       sort { $array{$b} <=> $array{$a}; } keys %array;
95   }
```

For each array, we run a **foreach** loop that will work through the keys of each array, reporting on the information. For example, the last item to be reported is the URL/host access information. Line 81 shows the **foreach** statement, which uses the **sort_values_bynum** function to return the keys, in order, and place each key into the **$urlhost** variable on each loop cycle.

Lines 85 and 86 (really a single line, but split here for clarity) print out the information, using **printf**, so that we can format the URL/host string, access count, and byte counts into a text table separated by tabs. We then use the key specified by the **$urlhost** variable to extract the information from the associative array. Because it's already been sorted, the information will be printed out in the correct order.

```
89   sub sort_values_bynum
90     {
91       my $arrayref = shift;
92       my %array = %$arrayref;
93
94       sort { $array{$b} <=> $array{$a}; } keys %array;
95   }
```

The **sort_values_bynum** function, which we use to sort the keys of the array, is in lines 82 to 88. Lines 84 and 85 allow us to use the array passed in the function arguments as an associative array. We then use the **sort** function in line 87 to make comparisons between the values of the array, returning the keys of the array to the calling line in sequential order.

The comparison element of the line

```
{ $array{$b} <=> $array{$a}; }
```

sorts the keys, specified by the element

```
keys %array;
```

into numerical order, highest number first. To sort the keys in reverse numerical order, you can change the variables **$a** and **$b** around, as follows:

```
{ $array{$a} <=> $array{$b}; }
```

If we were sorting string values, then we would use the **cmp** function to make the entire line look like this:

87   `sort { $array{$b} cmp $array{$a}; } keys %array;`

Finally, if we wanted to sort the keys alphabetically, we would replace line 87 with

87   `sort keys %array;`

for a sort in ascending alphabetical order, or

87   `reverse sort keys %array;`

for a reverse alphabetical sort.

This code, however, is quite inefficient because we have to create an explicit copy of the array in order to sort the keys and give this information back to the calling line. A better way of writing this function would be

```
sub sort_values_by_num {
  my $arrayRef = shift;
  sort {$arrayRef->{$b} <=> $arrayRef->{$a}
        ||
        lc ($a) cmp lc ($b)
      } keys %$arrayRef;
}
```

In this function, we use a reference to the original array. References are similar to pointers in C or shortcuts in Windows. A reference is just another name or pointer to the original, and it's used here to save us from creating a copy of the original array. We then sort the array keys as before, but then logically "OR" the result with a lowercase comparison of the two elements. This produces an alphabetical ordering for equal values; even the capitalization it contains is different.

Using a slightly larger version of the sample log file we saw above, running the standard script gives us the following output:

```
Web log report

Total number of accesses: 20, Bytes: 141933

Host summary

ww-t105.proxy.aol.com          7   16148
```

```
ps2he.ss.wave.shaw.ca                      5   55953
151.cambridge-01.ma.dial-access.att.net        5   58551
ps1he.ss.wave.shaw.ca                      3   11281
```

URL summary

```
/col/graphics/pnblank.gif              2    1198
/col/graphics/ButtonPanel.gif          2    7622
/col/graphics/whatsnew.gif             2    12090
/col/graphics/cyberpic.gif             2    97268
/col/graphics/COembossed.gif           2    3642
/col/graphics/download32.gif           2    2214
/col/whatsnew/cyberpat.html            2    3492
/col/graphics/cyberpat.gif             2    2038
/col/graphics/business48.gif           1    1477
/col/graphics/aboutco.gif              1    6871
/col/graphics/persuser48.gif           1    1321
/col/aboutco/cyberpat.html             1    2700
```

URL/Host summary

```
ww-t105.proxy.aol.com:/col/graphics/pnblank.gif              1     599
ps2he.ss.wave.shaw.ca:/col/graphics/COembossed.gif              1    1821
ps1he.ss.wave.shaw.ca:/col/graphics/pnblank.gif              1     599
ps2he.ss.wave.shaw.ca:/col/graphics/persuser48.gif              1    1321
151.cambridge-01.ma.dial-access.att.net:/col/graphics/whatsnew.gif        1    6045
151.cambridge-01.ma.dial-access.att.net:/col/graphics/cyberpic.gif        1    48634
ww-t105.proxy.aol.com:/col/graphics/ButtonPanel.gif              1    3811
ps1he.ss.wave.shaw.ca:/col/graphics/ButtonPanel.gif              1    3811
ps1he.ss.wave.shaw.ca:/col/graphics/aboutco.gif              1    6871
ww-t105.proxy.aol.com:/col/graphics/whatsnew.gif              1    6045
151.cambridge-01.ma.dial-access.att.net:/col/whatsnew/cyberpat.html        1    1746
151.cambridge-01.ma.dial-access.att.net:/col/graphics/cyberpat.gif        1    1019
ps2he.ss.wave.shaw.ca:/col/graphics/cyberpic.gif              1    48634
151.cambridge-01.ma.dial-access.att.net:/col/graphics/download32.gif        1    1107
ps2he.ss.wave.shaw.ca:/col/aboutco/cyberpat.html              1    2700
ww-t105.proxy.aol.com:/col/whatsnew/cyberpat.html              1    1746
ww-t105.proxy.aol.com:/col/graphics/cyberpat.gif              1    1019
ps2he.ss.wave.shaw.ca:/col/graphics/business48.gif              1    1477
ww-t105.proxy.aol.com:/col/graphics/download32.gif              1    1107
ww-t105.proxy.aol.com:/col/graphics/COembossed.gif              1    1821
```

Summary

As we have seen in this chapter, a number of methods exist for manipulating and analyzing textual information. The ability to use regular expressions directly in the

Perl code demonstrates Perl's flexibility, as well as indicating the method employed in developing Perl in the first place. Perl borrows many of the useful abilities and features of a combination of languages, while ignoring features that are infrequently used or badly implemented.

Since text-processing abilities are a core component of the Perl feature set, we'll be revisiting many of the techniques explored here, and examining some new ones, as we progress through the rest of the book.

File Management

A t some point, to make good use of any programming language, you will need to access information about files. Opening them, using them, and reporting about them are relatively easy tasks if you know the exact name of the file; otherwise, you're basically stuck. Perl supports a number of ways of extracting lists of files, either through the familiar wildcard operations that you use within the shell or by reading individual filenames directly from the directory.

It's also often necessary to glean more information about the file that you are using than its name. For instance, you might want to find out the file size or the file permissions to determine if you can access a file. Using symbolic links to help manage and organize the file system on your machine is common practice. But moving symbolic links, or re-attaching symbolic links after a file restoration is a lengthy process, and we will look at ways of accessing and updating the links using regular expressions.

In the last part of the chapter, we will take a look at ways of accessing and modifying symbolic links.

Checking for the Existence of Different Files

filetest.pl

Up to now, we have been checking for successful opening and closing of files. Often, however, all we really want to do is check if a file exists. Using an open command to search for a file is inefficient, and moreover it only checks the current operation. Sometimes it can be useful to check the size of a file or perhaps even the type of a file and who has access to it before we start using the file itself. What would be really useful is if we could do all of this within a standard **if** statement without having to access any functions beforehand. Perl can perform all of these tests natively, in much the same way as the **test** program performs under Unix, or as the built-in test operators perform under many Unix shells. The full list of Perl's available operators is shown in Table 2-1.

WARNING   *Be careful of foreign language files with high-bit or special characters, such as characters with accents. They can sometimes be misinterpreted as a binary file when using -B or -T.*

Inodes

An inode is the name for a directory entry within the file system. The term *inode* comes from Unix, although all operating systems have a similar term for the inode. Both Macs and NT use the term *directory entry*. Under Unix, a change to an inode constitutes a rename, either within the same directory or because the file has been moved to a different directory.

Under NT and MacOS, an inode change can include security, permission, or sharing changes to the underlying file.

Operator	Use to Determine
-A	How many days since the last time the file was accessed
-B	If the file is binary
-C	How many days since the last inode change
-M	How many days since the script was started
-O	If the file is owned by the real user ID
-R	If the file is readable by the real user ID or real group
-S	If the file is a socket
-T	If it is a text file
-W	If the file is writable by the real user or id real group
-X	If the file is executable by the real user ID or real group
-b	If the file is a block special file
-c	If the file is a character special file
-d	If the file is a directory
-e	If the file exists
-f	If it is a plain file
-g	If the file has the **setgid** bit set
-k	If the file has the sticky bit set
-l	If the file is a symbolic link
-o	If the file is owned by the effective user ID
-p	If the file is a named pipe
-r	If the file is readable by the effective user or group ID
-s	The size of the file, with zero referring to an empty file
-t	If the file handle is opened by a TTY (terminal)
-u	If the file has the **setuid** bit set
-w	If the file is writable by the effective user or group id
-x	If the file is executable by the effective user or group id
-z	If the file size is zero

TABLE 2-1. File Test Operators

The **filetest.pl** script uses file tests to identify and report on different information about the file. I've used this program for quite a few years as part of my porting work—it quickly identifies a file that I've extracted from an archive without me having to view the file. Experience has taught me that binary files can cause all sorts of problems, and being able to identify the type of file saves me from freezing the terminal.

```perl
1   #!/usr/local/bin/perl
2
3   ($#ARGV)+1 || die "No file specified";
4
5   $filedesc="";
6   $file=$ARGV[0];
7   if (-e $file)
8   {
9       $filedesc .= " binary," if (-B $file);
10      $filedesc .= " a socket, " if (-S $file);
11      $filedesc .= " a text file, " if (-T $file);
12      $filedesc .= " a block special file," if (-b $file);
13      $filedesc .= " a character special file," if (-c $file);
14      $filedesc .= " a directory," if (-d $file);
15      $filedesc .= " a symbolic link," if (-l $file);
16      $filedesc .= " executable," if (-x $file);
17
18      if ($size = ( -s $file))
19      {
20          $filedesc .= " $size bytes,";
21      }
22      else
23      {
24          $filedesc .= " empty,";
25      }
26
27      chop $filedesc;
28
29      print "$file is" . $filedesc ."\n";
30  }
31  else
32  {
33      die "File does not exist\n";
34  }
```

ANNOTATIONS

```
1    #!/usr/local/bin/perl
2
3    ($#ARGV)+1 || die "No file specified";
4
```

As usual, the first few lines just set us up for the script. In line 3, I've used a different method for checking whether the script has any arguments specified on the command line. Remember that the number of arguments returned by the variable **$#ARGV** is −1 for no arguments, and then 0 and up for each argument. We therefore add 1 to the value before the **die** test to return a true result for one or more files, even though we actually only use one file in the remainder of the script.

```
5    $filedesc="";
6    $file=$ARGV[0];
7    if (-e $file)
8    {
```

The information about the file will be returned in the **$filedesc** variable, which we initialize to an empty string. Unlike C, in Perl these initializations are unnecessary as all variables default to empty, or zero, values, but that doesn't mean we can ignore what is good programming practice. Perl may allow us to get away with it here, but in other scripts not initializing a variable could have unpredictable results. We set **$file** to refer to the file we're checking. Although there are no advantages in this script to using a separate variable for the filename, it just makes the code slightly more readable.

On line 7, we check that the file exists before we test anything else. Assuming the file does exist, then we start checking the different information about the file on lines 9 to 17.

```
9        $filedesc .= " binary," if (-B $file);
10       $filedesc .= " a socket, " if (-S $file);
11       $filedesc .= " a text file, " if (-T $file);
12       $filedesc .= " a block special file," if (-b $file);
13       $filedesc .= " a character special file," if (-c $file);
14       $filedesc .= " a directory," if (-d $file);
15       $filedesc .= " a symbolic link," if (-l $file);
16       $filedesc .= " executable," if (-x $file);
17
```

For each line, we perform a different test, concatenating the description onto the **$filedesc** variable if the test returns true. In this way, we get a summarized listing of the information we want, in a readable way so that other people can spot what we're doing. Each description starts with a space for formatting and ends with a comma to give us a list separated by a comma (from the previous entry) and a space (from the current entry).

A better method would be to "push" the variables onto an array and then take them back off using the **join** function. For example, we might use the following code in place of line 9:

```
push(@filedesc,"binary") if (-B $file);
```

Note that we don't have to include the formatting characters within the string. The formatting will be included when we use **join** to print out the list, separated by the specified characters. The **join** function is the exact opposite of **split**, and it joins together elements of an array separated by the specified string; for example we might use the following line to return the formatted list from the stack of attributes we just created:

```
join(', ',@filedesc);
```

It's worth noting that **join** takes elements from the array in sequence, so the first item put on the stack will be returned first. Using a stack is more efficient and leaves room for further expansion without having to manage the formatting manually. Adding a new attribute to the list of tests is as easy as pushing the necessary text on to the stack.

For each of the tests after the initial one, we could specify the stat buffer that was created by the first test. The stat buffer contains the information about a file and is the structure that supplies the information used to return much of the data used by these tests. This would further shorten line 9 to

```
$filedesc .= " binary," if (-B _);
```

On most systems the stat information will be in the OS's disk cache anyway, but we save time by referring to the information already retrieved by Perl instead of accessing an external data structure to perform the additional tests.

Push and Pop

The functions **push** and **pop** put items onto, and take items off of, an imaginary stack. The stack is treated as FILO (First In Last Out). This allows you to place a list of items in an array without having to use array indexes and then to take the information back off the list in a variety of ways. The **pop** function returns, and removes, the last element of the array. The **shift** function returns the first element of the array and can therefore be used to take information off the stack in the order it was put on (FIFO, First In First Out).

Stacks make it much easier to use lists of sequential, and the data can be extracted easily because the stack is just a normal array.

```
18        if ($size = ( -s $file))
19        {
20               $filedesc .= " $size bytes,";
21        }
22        else
23        {
24               $filedesc .= " empty,";
25        }
26
```

Lines 18 to 26 check the file size and then report the file as either being a specified number of bytes in length or empty. Notice that we use the same formatting for the description.

REMINDER *Perl treats any number other than zero as being true, so returning the file size (which should be a positive number) will result in a true if it is greater than zero or false if the file is empty. This example shows how Perl operates in terms of providing more information than you may want in all situations but still being compatible with all levels. The **-s** test is also a more convenient way of finding out the size of a file without accessing the file information stored in the file's inode.*

```
27        chop $filedesc;
28
29        print "$file is" . $filedesc ."\n";
30  }
```

Line 27 takes the last character off the description. Because we've used the same formatting throughout, the last character will always be a comma. Leaving it on the description doesn't cause a problem, but it looks messy when we print out the information about the file on line 29. For a similar reason, I haven't put a space after **"$file is"** because that space will be provided by the first piece of information returned by the tests. The stack method discussed earlier overcomes these problems.

Note that I've used dot notation to join the strings together. What Perl does behind the scenes with these string sequences is to allocate a new memory block and copy the information into it, which wastes memory (although we're not talking about huge chunks) and time. Using commas allows Perl to print out the items sequentially, as if each item was part of a list of entries to print. No additional memory is required for this action, and it should be faster, although the differences are probably negligible. I tend to use dot notation in scripts where clarity is important, especially when there are commas in the text I'm printing.

```
31  else
32  {
33        die "File does not exist\n";
34  }
```

Finally, lines 31 to 34 print out an error if the file doesn't exist, based on the test we performed on line 7.

Testing the script on itself under Unix returns

```
filetest.pl is a text file, executable, 710 bytes
```

ls.pl

Reading Filenames

There are two basic ways of listing the files within the current directory. The first is to use the directory access function **opendir**, and the second is to use the **glob** function. We will look at the act of "globbing" as part of the next script. The directory access functions open and read directory contents as if the directory were just a plain file. The functions are directly equivalent to the C function set and use a directory handle, rather than a file handle, to refer to the directory contents. You can then step through each file in the directory list until you reach the end, at which point you close the directory handle.

If you need to match a specific set of files, you can use the **grep** function or a pattern match to return a subset of the full list of files. The script **ls.pl** is a very basic version of the ls command, written in Perl.

```
1   #!/usr/local/bin/perl
2
3   opendir(DIR,".") || die "Unable to open directory ($!)\n";
4
5   while(defined($file=readdir(DIR)))
6   {
7       print $file . "\n";
8   }
9
10  closedir(DIR);
```

The opendir Function Set

The full function set consists of the following:

opendir   Returns a directory handle associated with a particular directory
readdir   Returns the file or files sequentially from the directory list
closedir   Closes the directory handle
rewinddir   Moves the handle position within the directory back to the top
telldir   Reports the current location of the handle within the directory
seekdir   Updates the location of the handle to the specified location within the directory

ANNOTATIONS

This example is very concise, but it demonstrates the **opendir** functions clearly. We'll see a more extensive version of the program when we take a look at the programmer's file list later in this chapter.

Line 3 creates a new directory handle, which we will refer to later to extract the file list. The arguments to the **opendir** function are the directory handle and the path you want to view.

```perl
1   #!/usr/local/bin/perl
2
3   opendir(DIR,".") || die "Unable to open directory ($!)\n";
4
```

We OR the contents with the **die** function to make sure we can actually read the current directory. It's important that we make sure that certain commands work before we continue. Although there is often little harm in some of the commands failing, others can cause serious problems, so checking the success of commands is a good habit to get into. Note that we've specified the special variable **$!**, which refers to the last error message generated by Perl.

```perl
5   while(defined($file=readdir(DIR)))
6   {
7       print $file . "\n";
8   }
```

Lines 5 to 8 do the simple part. On each successful loop, the name of the file is printed on line 7, with an appended new-line character. The filename comes from the test in line 5. We put the assignation of the return from the **readdir** function within a **defined** function call to ensure that a successful read is treated as a success. Using the line

```perl
while($file=readdir(DIR))
```

would cause the loop to end if we returned a filename of **0**, because to Perl zero means false.

All we do is assign the result of the **readdir** function to the variable **$file**. Assuming the assignation is successful, the result will be true, and so the **while** loop will continue. When no more files are available, **readdir** will return an undefined value, which Perl treats as false and which will therefore cause the **while** loop to fail.

The final part of the code, on line 10, is to close the directory handle, since we don't need it anymore.

```perl
9
10  closedir(DIR);
```

The . and .. Directory Entries

The . and .. directory entries are used by the system to reference the current directory and the parent of the current directory, respectively. Using these two entries, we can specify a relative reference to a local directory. For example, **./ls.pl** explicitly refers to the file **ls.pl** in the current directory. Parent references are often used with links to refer to a directory or file with reference to the current position.

For example, many Unix systems have a directory called /usr/tmp, which is symbolically linked to /var/tmp. Rather than specify the full directory name, the link simply points to ../var/tmp, which refers to the parent of the /usr directory, which is the root directory, and then to /var/tmp.

renspec.pl

Renaming a Group of Files

The **readdir** group of functions provides an easy way to step through the contents of a directory list, and, used in combination with the **grep** function, you can simulate a lot of the functionality found in the ls and dir commands on Unix and Windows machines, respectively. Using this method, however, is relatively inefficient; there are better ways of getting a list of files based on a file specification.

Globbing File Specifications

The file specifications you use are slightly different than the regular expressions you use in Perl. There are three basic differences:

◆ The asterisk character refers to any character, not multiple repetitions of the previous regular expression segment.

◆ The period is identified as a period, not as any single character.

◆ The question mark is used to represent a single character.

Other than these differences, most of the expressions you are used to, such as character ranges (using []) work as expected.

Globbing means to match a file specification to the list of available files. For example, typing

```
$ ls *.c
```

at a Unix prompt instructs the shell to glob, or match, all the files ending in **.c**. You can use the **glob** function to emulate this functionality within a Perl script. Once you have your file list, you can then perform whatever tasks, replacements, or text processing you want on that selection of files.

In the script below, I've chosen to demonstrate a personal bugbear with Unix, and probably the only thing I don't like about its standard OS. Under DOS, as I'm sure many people are aware, you can rename a group of files based on a new file specification. For example, the DOS command

```
C:\> ren *.c *.o
```

would rename every file with an extension of **.c** and put **.o** as the extension instead. This is a useful feature, and the time you need it most is when you're working on your Unix machine that doesn't support the feature.

Globbing Within the Unix Shell

When you type a file specification into a Unix shell command prompt or shellscript, the globbing, or matching of files to their file specification, is performed by the shell. The expanded file list is passed to the program, each file being a separate argument to the program. The list is passed to the program in deference to most other OSs, where the act of expanding the file specification placed on the command line is executed by the individual program, and not by the command processor (such as command.com under DOS/Windows).

This can cause problems when moving between OSs, especially if you are relying on the expanded file list for an element of your script. You can get around this difference in systems by using Perl's globbing facilities. The only stipulation is that arguments to the original script must be enclosed in double quotes, so that the Unix shell doesn't do the globbing first!

To get around this problem, you can use a quick Perl script to perform the function instead.

```perl
1   #!/usr/local/bin/perl
2
3   die "Usage: renspec.pl from_ext to_ext\n" unless ($#ARGV eq 1);
4
5   $from=shift;
6   $to=shift;
7
8   @files = glob("*.$from");
9
10  foreach $file (@files)
11  {
12      $old=$file;
13      $file =~ s#\.$from#\.$to#g;
14      rename($old,$file);
15  }
```

ANNOTATIONS

Put simply, the program gets a list of all the files matching the extension of the first argument and then, stepping through each one, uses a substitution statement and the **rename** function to replace the old extension with the new one, specified by the second argument.

```perl
1   #!/usr/local/bin/perl
2
3   die "Usage: renspec.pl from_ext to_ext\n" unless ($#ARGV eq 1);
4
```

In line 3 we do the usual checks for command-line arguments. This time I've used the **unless** command to execute **die** only if the test for the number of arguments returns false. We're checking for two arguments this time: the specifications for the extension to look for and what to configure them as.

```perl
5   $from=shift;
6   $to=shift;
7
```

Arguments in the **@ARGV** array can be shifted. The action of shifting is similar to popping elements off of a stack, except that the elements are taken off in the order they were put on. Each time you shift an array, the element is removed from the array. In this example, line 5 shifts the first argument into the variable **$from**. When we get to line 6, the second argument from the command line has become the first element in the **@ARGV** array.

```
8    @files = glob("*.$from");
9
```

Line 8 does the bulk of the work in terms of getting the list of available files. We use the **glob** function, using a file specification made up of the first argument. The list that is returned is put into the **@files** list variable, which is then stepped through, via a **foreach** command on line 10. Each element of the array is put into **$file** for processing in lines 11 to 15.

```
10   foreach $file (@files)
11   {
12       $old=$file;
13       $file =~ s#\.$from$#\.$to#;
14       rename($old,$file);
15   }
```

Line 12 helps us to remember what the old filename was, then we perform a string substitution on the original **file** variable, using hash symbols to separate each regular expression element. Note that because we are looking for an extension I've escaped the period and specified that the extension should only be matched at the end of a string by specifying the dollar sign. Finally, line 14 renames the file.

WARNING   *The **glob** function may return a large number of files causing an error like **Argument List Too Long**. If this happens, you should use the **opendir** functions in combination with the **grep** function to select the list of files.*

rename.pl

Renaming Files with Larry Wall's Rename Script

The previous script may have been a practical solution to the problem of renaming file extensions, but like many quick scripts, it solves only one specific problem when a more flexible solution must be available. For instance, we may want to replace a general piece of text in the filename rather than just the extension.

Since Perl is capable of doing text processing, it's not unreasonable to want to use a regular expression to define how files should be renamed. The **rename.pl** script that follows does exactly this. By specifying a substitution as the first argument to the script, and using the remainder of the arguments as the files to rename, the script gets around the limitations of the previous example.

To emulate the previous script, we could use the following command line:

```
$ rename.pl 's/\.c/\.o/'
```

This script is taken from the Perl 5 distribution, in the eg directory, and is a Larry Wall original. It's provided here verbatim, so what you see here should match the Perl distribution version.

```perl
1   #!/usr/local/bin/perl
2   'di';
3   'ig00';
4   #
5   # $RCSfile: rename,v $$Revision: 4.1 $$Date: 92/08/07 17:20:30 $
6   #
7   # $Log:      rename,v $
8
9   ($op = shift) || die "Usage: rename perlexpr [filenames]\n";
10  if (!@ARGV)
11  {
12      @ARGV = <STDIN>;
13      chop(@ARGV);
14  }
15  for (@ARGV)
16  {
17      $was = $_;
18      eval $op;
19      die $@ if $@;
20      rename($was,$_) unless $was eq $_;
21  }
22  ##################################################
23
24      # These next few lines are legal in both Perl and nroff.
25
26  .00;                # finish .ig
27
28  'di                 \" finish diversion--previous line must be blank
29  .nr nl 0-1          \" fake up transition to first page again
30  .nr % 0             \" start at page 1
31  ';<<'.ex'; #__END__ # From here on it's a standard manual page #
32  .TH RENAME 1 "July 30, 1990"
33  .AT 3
34  .SH NAME
35  rename \- renames multiple files
36  .SH SYNOPSIS
37  .B rename perlexpr [files]
38  .SH DESCRIPTION
```

```
39   .I Rename
40   renames the filenames supplied according to the rule specified
41   as the first argument.
42   The argument is a Perl expression which is expected to modify
43   the $_ string in Perl for at least some of the filenames
44   specified.
45   If a given filename is not modified by the expression, it will
46   not be renamed.
47   If no filenames are given on the command line, filenames will be
48   read via standard input.
49   .PP
50   For example, to rename all files matching *.bak to strip the
51   extension, you might say
52   .nf
53
54        rename 's/\e.bak$//' *.bak
55
56   .fi
57   To translate uppercase names to lower, you'd use
58   .nf
59
60        rename 'y/A-Z/a-z/' *
61
62   .fi
63   .SH ENVIRONMENT
64   No environment variables are used.
65   .SH FILES
66   .SH AUTHOR
67   Larry Wall
68   .SH "SEE ALSO"
69   mv(1)
70   .br
71   perl(1)
72   .SH DIAGNOSTICS
73   If you give an invalid Perl expression you'll get a syntax error.
74   .SH BUGS
75   .I Rename
76   does not check for the existence of target filenames, so use
77   with care.
78   .ex
```

ANNOTATIONS

This script takes the first argument to be a substitution string, and then performs the substitution on each subsequent file specified on the command line.

The wrapper parts that make up a large bulk of the script place an nroff manual page in the same file as the source, which is a good way of supplying a script with its own documentation. The entire "package" is a single file, yet it contains everything you need to know about how to use it. More recently, programmers are using POD (plain old documentation) files to document Perl scripts and packages. The Perl distribution should come with a pod2xxxx script, which converts POD files to a variety of formats, including HTML and plain text.

```
1    #!/usr/local/bin/perl
2    'di';
3    'ig00';
4    #
5    # $RCSfile: rename,v $$Revision: 4.1 $$Date: 92/08/07 17:20:30 $
6    #
7    # $Log:     rename,v $
8
```

Lines 2 and 3 are valid lines in Perl, even though they do nothing. What they do in the nroff page description language is set up a diversion, a section of text that will not be processed as nroff text. Of course, to the reader it's obvious this is a script file. A UNIX shell will ignore everything beyond the first line, as soon as it realizes that the file is intended for a different application. The section is a script, but as far as nroff is concerned, the section will be ignored.

Line 5 is a tag line generated by the RCS (Revision Control System) software. This package allows you to set up and manage revisions to files so that you can record multiple versions of the script. You can see from the tagline that this is version 4.1, last incorporated to the version file on August 7, 1992. For those who didn't realize it, yes, Perl is that old! In fact, Perl stretches back to January 1988, according to the supplied FAQ.

```
9    ($op = shift) || die "Usage: rename perlexpr [filenames]\n";
10   if (!@ARGV)
11   {
12       @ARGV = <STDIN>;
13       chop(@ARGV);
14   }
```

Line 9 performs the usual check for some arguments to the script. Confusingly, what we actually check is if the value of **$op** that is returned by **shift** is logically true, which demonstrates how lax Perl can be in accepting badly written code.

Although the sequence still works, it's not a perfect solution and shows how Perl can be used to quickly write an application to get a job done. This laxity in Perl can cause problems, so you should be aware of the results when the code is not actually doing what you expected, but you are still getting "correct" results. Taking the above example, if the value of the first argument on the command line was logically false, that is, a zero, then the statement would fail, and the whole script would fail, even though the option may well have been legitimate.

We can get away with this test because line 10 checks to see if there are any more arguments. If there aren't any more arguments in the list, then lines 11 to 14 assign individual lines taken from standard input and place them into the argument list. In this way, the script not only supports a command line list of files, but it could also take its input from a file redirection. Line 13 removes the trailing new-line character at the end of each input string. By specifying an array, the **chop** function takes the last character off each element.

This code may look a little strange because you are reassigning values to variables you might normally consider being available only for reading. Although many of the variables within Perl are automatically assigned and populated, there is no reason not to use them. In this example the technique is both practical, because the list is now in one list variable, and has memory and performance advantages, because it lets you avoid making copies of the argument list into a new list.

```
15    for (@ARGV)
16    {
17        $was = $_;
18        eval $op;
19        die $@ if $@;
20        rename($was,$_) unless $was eq $_;
21    }
```

By the time we get to line 15, one way or another we should have a list of filenames to perform the substitution on. Line 17 records the old name. Line 18 does all the work. The **eval** function is, in my opinion, the most powerful single function in the Perl language. The function allows you to evaluate a piece of Perl script that you have placed into a variable. This simple facility means you can create Perl script segments dynamically and have them executed within the execution cycle of the current script. This is semantically the same as being able to write C source code dynamically and have it compiled, and executed, just as if it were another part of your already compiled program.

In this case, we use the **eval** function to run the substitution on the current filename. The $@ variable in line 19 is the syntax error from the previous **eval** statement. Since an error here would signify a major user error, we **die** if a syntax error is returned, displaying the text of the syntax error to the user for information. Finally, line 20 performs the rename as long as the new name is different from the old name.

The script works, but it doesn't check to ensure that the file we are renaming exists or that the new filename does not already exist. It doesn't check whether the rename function succeeds, either. The script is fine for personal use, and it's clear to the reader, but it is not suitable for a serious installation because it's not "industrial strength." Its lack of suitable tests could have serious ramifications, but adding them will confuse the code and make it less obvious what is going on. If you are worried about the reliability of your scripts, then by all means add the necessary tests—just be aware that they are likely to be less portable to casual programmers.

From line 22 onwards, the script becomes the manual page. The end of the diversion in line 2 is shown in line 28. Cleverly, Perl treats lines 26 to 31 as valid, until line 31 where the redirection signifies to Perl the specification of inclusive text. In contrast, nroff sees lines 26 onwards as valid code and displays the formatted manual page, excluding the Perl script part, as it would any other manual page.

With modern POD files, this sequence of events is not necessary, and is not used much anymore. This script was part of the 4.036 distribution of Perl, which is now some years old. We will revisit the use of POD files later in this chapter.

To use the script, just specify the regular expression on the command line. For example:

```
$ rename.pl "s/\.c/\.o/g" *.c
```

would do exactly the same rename operation as the previous script. Because we pass the first argument to the **eval** function, we could do just about anything to the filenames, but there is little point in suggesting something other than a substitution string. The difference is that the substitution could just as easily have replaced any element of the name, not just the extension.

exfi.pl

Getting File Information

Beyond a filename, you may often find yourself requiring more detailed file information about an individual file. More often than not, you will want to know the file size, but you may want to know who can access and modify a file, without actually trying to open the file first. Under Unix, you can see the available extended file information by specifying long format with the ls command; for example:

```
$ ls -l
-r--r--r--    1 300      staff      37921 Sep 19  1997 regcomp.c
-r--r--r--    1 300      staff       9246 Jun  7  1997 regcomp.h
-rw-r--r--    1 root     staff      28116 Jun  3 22:55 regcomp.o
-r--r--r--    1 300      staff      30629 Sep 10  1997 regexec.c
-rw-r--r--    1 root     staff      18912 Jun  3 23:06 regexec.o
-r--r--r--    1 300      staff       1118 Jan 17  1997 regexp.h
```

```
-r--r--r--    1 300       staff        2245 Mar  6  1997 run.c
-rw-r--r--    1 root      staff         976 Jun  3 22:59 run.o
-r--r--r--    1 300       staff       16228 Oct  6  1997 scope.c
-r--r--r--    1 300       staff        4170 Apr  1  1997 scope.h
-rw-r--r--    1 root      staff       18036 Jun  3 23:02 scope.o
-r--r--r--    1 300       staff      101082 Oct  6  1997 sv.c
-r--r--r--    1 300       staff       19815 Apr  1  1997 sv.h
-rw-r--r--    1 root      staff       65604 Jun  3 23:00 sv.o
```

Here you can see, in order from left to right, the file permissions, number of links, owner, group owner, size, last modification time, and then the filename. In addition to this information, you can also find out the last time the file was accessed or, in theory, the time the file status was changed (that is, opened, closed, or renamed). Most OSs don't support the access time because of the obvious overheads of updating this information. It's safe to assume that the access and modification times are identical in most situations.

The permission information, shown in the first column, is based on the Unix permission bits. The first character shows the file type. A single dash signifies a standard file, and a *d* signifies a directory. Other characters identify different types of file, although we're not concerned with this information in this instance. The next nine characters then specify the read, write, and execute status for the file's owner, files group, and everybody else.

Therefore, three sets of three bits specify the read, write, and execute permissions for the user, the group, and everybody else. The best representation for this information is to use an octal number where 4 specifies read permissions, 2 specifies write permissions, and 1 specifies the execute permission. You can combine these numbers to specify the file's permission status; for example, a value of 6 specifies read and write permissions (4 + 2 = 6). By combining the permissions for all three groups, you can set the permissions for a file to 644, which would give read/write permissions to the files owner and read only permissions to the group owner and everybody else. See Figure 2-1 for a clearer picture.

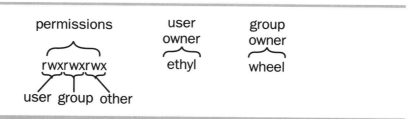

FIGURE 2-1. Permission information under Unix

In addition, there is a further bit set that specifies three special characteristics of a file. The set user ID (**setuid**) bit, which forces the OS to execute the file as the file's owner, has a value of 1. The set group id (**setgid**) bit, which executes the file as the group owner, has a value of 2. The octal value of 4 is the sticky bit, which keeps an executable file resident in memory. The entire permission specification is therefore made up of a four-digit octal number. For example, 0700 specifies read/write/executable for the owner of the file only. The specification shown by the ls command would be **rwx**.

The reason you need to be aware of this information is that the **stat** function returns the value for the permissions. This information can be identified by using logic and bit masks. We'll see how this works as we work through the script.

Windows NT performs slightly differently from Unix. The information displayed by the standard dir command looks like this:

```
19/02/98   03:14                      1,726  VIRUSCAN.MIF
14/10/96   02:38                     24,336  vmmreg32.dll
12/06/98   19:34          <DIR>              Web
20/06/98   12:24                        117  WEBLINK.INI
14/10/96   02:38                     22,288  welcome.exe
22/06/98   16:07                        529  WIN.INI
14/10/96   02:38                          3  WINFILE.INI
14/10/96   02:38                    256,192  WINHELP.EXE
30/04/97   23:00                    311,056  WINHLP32.EXE
14/10/96   02:38                     78,736  winnt.bmp
14/10/96   02:38                    157,044  winnt256.bmp
22/06/98   16:07                      1,749  winzip32.ini
```

Despite the lack of permission information, the same basic information is returned to the user. We get the last modified date, file size (or <DIR> for a directory), and filename. The **stat** function within Perl returns the same basic information to a Perl script. However, because of the differences between the OSs, not all of the information that is returned is usable in the same way. For example, NT is not aware of user or group IDs, so we can't extract information about the owner or group owner of the file. We'll look at specific areas that don't work as we work through the script.

The full list of information returned by the **stat** function is shown in Table 2-2.

PROGRAMMER'S NOTE

The epoch is the reference date used by machines to calculate the time. For most computers, the epoch is Jan 1, 1970, 00:00. Time is calculated as the number of seconds since this date and time. The epoch is calculated from GMT (Greenwich Mean Time) rather than the local time zone.

Element	Description
dev	ID of the device holding the directory entry for the file
inode	File's inode number
mode	Permissions
nlink	Number of links to the file
uid	User ID of the file's owner
gid	Group ID of the file's group
rdev	For character special files, the ID of the device
size	File size, in bytes
atime	Last access time, in seconds since the epoch
mtime	Last modification time, in seconds since the epoch
ctime	Last status change, in seconds since the epoch
blksize	For BSD Unix systems, the preferred I/O block size
blocks	For BSD Unix systems, the number of blocks allocated for storing the file

TABLE 2-2.   Information Returned by the **stat** Command

The **exfi.pl** script that follows uses the **stat** function to extract the extended information about the files specified on the command line.

```perl
#!/usr/local/bin/perl

for $file (@ARGV)
{
    ($ino,$mode,$nlink,$uid,$gid,
        $size,$atime,$mtime,$ctime) = (stat($file))[1..5,7..10];

    $perms = &extperms($mode);
    $user = getpwuid($uid);
    $group = getgrgid($gid);
    print <<EOT;
$file
Size:    \t$size
```

```
14    Inode Number:\t$ino
15    Owner:      \t$user
16    Group Owner:\t$group
17    $perms
18    Links:   \t$nlink
19    EOT
20        print "Last access:\t" . localtime($atime) . "\n";
21        print "Last change:\t" . localtime($mtime) . "\n";
22        print "Status change:\t" . localtime($ctime) . "\n";
23    }
24
25
26    sub extperms ()
27    {
28        ($mode) = @_;
29
30        $user = $group = $other = $special = "";
31
32        $user .= "Read, " if ($mode & 00400);
33        $user .= "Write, " if ($mode & 00200);
34        $user .= "Execute, " if ($mode & 00100);
35        $group .= "Read, " if ($mode & 00040);
36        $group .= "Write, " if ($mode & 00020);
37        $group .= "Execute, " if ($mode & 00010);
38        $other .= "Read, " if ($mode & 00004);
39        $other .= "Write, " if ($mode & 00002);
40        $other .= "Execute, " if ($mode & 00001);
41        $special .= "Setuid, " if ($mode & 04000);
42        $special .= "Setgid, " if ($mode & 02000);
43        $special .= "Sticky Bit " if ($mode & 01000);
44
45        "User:      \t$user\nGroup:      \t$group\nOther:" .
46        "        \t$other\nSpecial:      \t$special";
47    }
```

ANNOTATIONS

The **exfi.pl** script takes the arguments from the command line and then, for each one, runs the **stat** function and post-processes the information to make the output more readable to the user. For simplicity, the permission information is extracted by a single function, which starts on line 26, returning the expanded permissions information as a text string.

```
1    #!/usr/local/bin/perl
2
3    for $file (@ARGV)
4    {
5        ($ino,$mode,$nlink,$uid,$gid,
6            $size,$atime,$mtime,$ctime) = (stat($file))[1..5,7..10];
7
```

Line 3 starts us off by processing each file in the argument list. For a change, this script doesn't contain a check for the number of arguments, although it would be easy to add such a line. Lines 5 and 6 are really the same line, just split for readability. They extract some of the information returned by the **stat** function, placing the results into the variables on the left-hand side of the equal sign.

As further evidence of Perl's flexibility, it is easy to extract multiple pieces of information and assign them to individual variables. In this case, the **stat** function returns a variable list, and we use subscript notation after the function so that only the specified elements of the list are assigned to the variables. The subscript list can specify individual elements, ranges, and combinations and multiples of the two. However, you must enclose the item for which you want to use the subscript notation in parentheses.

```
8        $perms = &extperms($mode);
9        $user = getpwuid($uid);
10       $group = getgrgid($gid);
```

Lines 8 to 10 start to extract the printable information from the **stat** function into variables ready for printing. Line 8 uses the **extperms** function, which we'll look at shortly, to extract a text version of the file permissions. Line 9 gets the user name from the password file, based on the user ID, using the built-in **getpwuid** function. In a similar way, **getgrgid** returns the group name based on the group ID. Neither line 9 nor 10 account for a missing or nonexistent user or group ID. You might want to consider replacing lines 9 and 10 with

```
defined ($user = getpwuid ($uid)) or $user = "($uid)";
```

```
defined ($group = getgruid ($gid)) or $group = "($gid)";
```

These two lines set the user or group string to the corresponding user ID or group ID if the functions don't return a valid user or group name.

Lines 9 and 10 don't work under Windows NT, since the functions are not supported within the OS.

From line 11 onwards, we are printing text directly to the screen until we reach the next **EOT** tag.

```
11       print <<EOT;
12   $file
13   Size:    \t$size
14   Inode Number:\t$ino
```

```
15   Owner:      \t$user
16   Group Owner:\t$group
17   $perms
18   Links:   \t$nlink
19   EOT
```

Lines 12 to 19 print out the information, one line per item. The Tab character is used to separate the title and the data. Make sure you don't indent the **EOT** tag on line 19, which must match the text after the redirection on line 11.

```
20       print "Last access:\t" . localtime($atime) . "\n";
21       print "Last change:\t" . localtime($mtime) . "\n";
22       print "Status change:\t" . localtime($ctime) . "\n";
23   }
24
25
```

Lines 20 to 22 print out the time information, using the **localtime** function to convert the epoch-based reference to a formatted version of the local time. In this scalar context, the Perl **localtime** function emulates the C **ctime** function; the string returned is based on a basic format.

```
26   sub extperms ()
27   {
28       my ($mode) = @_;
29       my ($user, $group, $other, $special);
30       $user = $group = $other = $special = "";
31
32       $user .= "Read, " if ($mode & 00400);
33       $user .= "Write, " if ($mode & 00200);
34       $user .= "Execute, " if ($mode & 00100);
```

Line 26 is the start of the **extperms** function. First, we extract the arguments passed to the function on line 28. Arguments to a function are placed in the special variable @_. We localize the variables to the function in both lines 28 and 29 using the **my** keyword to hide the variables from the rest of the script.

We initialize the descriptive text in line 30 to make sure there is no rollover from a previous call to the function, and then on line 32 we start to identify the elements of the file permissions. Using a logical AND operator, we compare the values of the mode and the known value for user level read access. If the AND is successful, the expression will return true, therefore adding the text "Read," to the description variable.

```
35       $group .= "Read, "      if ($mode & 00040);
36       $group .= "Write, "     if ($mode & 00020);
37       $group .= "Execute, "   if ($mode & 00010);
```

```
38      $other .= "Read, "       if ($mode & 00004);
39      $other .= "Write, "      if ($mode & 00002);
40      $other .= "Execute, "    if ($mode & 00001);
41      $special .= "Setuid, "   if ($mode & 04000);
42      $special .= "Setgid, "   if ($mode & 02000);
43      $special .= "Sticky Bit " if ($mode & 01000);
44
```

Lines 35 to 43 repeat the process for group, other, and then special file permissions, before finally producing the full permission description text on lines 45 and 46.

```
45      "User:      \t$user\nGroup:    \t$group\nOther:" .
46         "    \t$other\nSpecial:    \t$special";
47  }
```

The information returned by a function is either what is specified by a return statement, or it's the value of the last expression in the subroutine. In this case, lines 45 and 46 constitute the last expression, and the string will be returned to the calling line of the script, in this case line 8.

The output, when the script is run on my machine, is as follows:

```
$ exfi.pl exfi.pl
exfi.pl
Size:            1172
Inode Number:    526294
Owner:
Group Owner:     users
User:            Read, Write, Execute,
Group:           Read, Execute,
Other:           Read, Execute,
Special:         Setuid,
Links:           1
Last access:     Wed Jun  3 23:17:30 1998
Last change:     Wed Jun  3 22:47:08 1998
Status change:   Wed Jun  3 22:47:08 1998
```

pl.pl

Generating a Programmer's File List

The ls and dir commands are great general-purpose tools for listing the files on your machine. As we have seen, though, there are often times when some additional information about the files is required or where the layout of the files in the directory could be improved to make using the machine easier or more practical.

A lot of my time is spent porting application software to new platforms, and much of this process involves looking at and working through C source trees. The make program intelligently identifies which files need to be compiled, but it is sometimes necessary to identify which files are up to date and which files need updating as you work through the porting process. The way make works is to check the modification time of the object file and then compare it with the source file. If the object file is newer, then make assumes that the source file does not need to be compiled. If the object file is older, then it's safe to assume to that the source file needs to be recompiled.

We can use the same method to list files intelligently and identify the files that need modification or recompilation. The script below is one I use regularly to give me a quick idea of how far through the compilation process I am. The script looks for all files in a directory, then checks the extensions, creating hash tables based on the filename and extension. Next the information is post-processed and differences in the modification times identified, and then the information is displayed and formatted, including the time difference between the source and object files.

```perl
1   #!/usr/local/bin/perl -w
2
3   my ($maxwidth) = 0;
4   my (%cMTime,%hMTime,%oMTime);
5   my ($file, $base, $fmt);
6
7   opendir(DIR,".") || die "Can't open the directory ($!)\n";
8
9   while (defined($file=readdir(DIR)))
10  {
11      next unless ($base) = $file =~ /(.+)\.c$/;
12
13      $maxwidth = length($file) if (length($file) >= $maxwidth);
14
15      $cMTime{$base} = (stat $file)[9];
16      if (-f "$base.o")
17      {
18          $oMTime{$base} = (stat _)[9];
19      }
20      if (-f "$base.h")
21      {
22          $hMTime{$base} = (stat _)[9];
23      }
24  }
25
26  closedir(DIR);
27
28  $fmt = "%" . ($maxwidth+2) . "s";
29
30  foreach $file (sort keys %cMTime)
```

```
31  {
32      printf($fmt,"$file.c");
33
34      if (defined($oMTime{$file}))
35      {
36          printf($fmt,"$file.o");
37
38          if ($cMTime{$file}>$oMTime{$file})
39          {
40              print &pptime($cMTime{$file}-$oMTime{$file});
41          }
42          else
43          {
44              printf("%12s","");
45          }
46      }
47      else
48      {
49              printf($fmt . "%12s", "NYC","");
50      }
51
52      if (defined($hMTime{$file}))
53      {
54       printf($fmt,"$file.h");
55
56          if ($hMTime{$file}>$cMTime{$file})
57          {
58              print &pptime($hMTime{$file}-$cMTime{$file});
59          }
60      }
61
62      print "\n";
63
64  }
65
66  sub pptime()
67  {
68      my ($time) = @_;
69      my ($min,$hour,$yday) = (gmtime($time))[1,2,7];
70
71      sprintf("(%3sd%2sh%2sm)",$yday,$hour,$min);
72  }
73
```

ANNOTATIONS

We start off by getting a list of all the files in the current directory. Although I could have used **glob** in line 3 to return the information into an array, doing so could cause problems; I've already described how the file list returned by **glob** may be greater than Perl is able to handle. Instead, we'll be using the **opendir** function to create a directory handle, and we'll then process each file individually.

```perl
1    #!/usr/local/bin/perl -w
2
3    my ($maxwidth) = 0;
4    my (%cMTime,%hMTime,%oMTime);
5    my ($file, $base, $fmt);
6
```

In lines 3 to 5 we localize some variables. The **$maxwidth** variable will be used later in the script to help with line formatting. We set the default value to zero; any file will have a filename length greater than zero characters, and this default will make working out the maximum length easier, as we'll see in line 13. The hash arrays will store the modification times of the files. The **$file** and **$base** variables will store the full filename and the base filename without an extension, respectively.

```perl
7    opendir(DIR,".") || die "Can't open the directory ($!)\n";
8
9    while (defined($file=readdir(DIR)))
10   {
11       next unless ($base) = $file =~ /(.+)\.c$/;
12
```

On line 7 we use **opendir** to open the current directory for reading. We check the result of the **opendir** function by combining it in the usual way with **die**. Line 9 sets up a loop that will step through each file in the directory. I've specified the **defined** function around the outside, since **readdir** returns an undefined result when the end of the directory listing is reached.

Line 11 is complex, but it solves two problems in a single line. Working in reverse, the last part is a match string to ensure the **$file** variable is a C source file. The first part of the regular expression is enclosed in brackets, and it sets the **$base** variable. The value of this variable will be set only if the match works, and it will be set to the name of the file without the **.c** extension. Finally, the **next unless** section of the statement skips this cycle of the loop if the file is not a C source file.

In short, this single line sets a new variable to the base name of the file if it is a C source file but skips the file if it isn't C source code. Note that the value of **$file** has not changed, so we can still refer to the original file in the rest of the loop.

```
13      $maxwidth = length($file) if (length($file) >= $maxwidth);
14
15      $cMTime{$base} = (stat $file)[9];
```

Line 13 works out the width of the filename. We'll use this value to help format the output. The quickest way to work out a maximum value is to check if the new value is greater than the existing one recorded. If it is greater, then we set the maximum value to the new value. This line works because we set the starting value of **$maxwidth** to zero in line 3.

Line 15 is the start of the information that we will store for use later. In this line we record the modification time of the C source file, placing the result in a hashed array, using a key of the base name of the file. I've used the subscript notation in the **stat** function to extract only the modification time.

```
16      if (-f "$base.o")
17      {
18          $oMTime{$base} = (stat _)[9];
19      }
20      if (-f "$base.h")
21      {
22          $hMTime{$base} = (stat _)[9];
23      }
24  }
```

Now we have to check for the existence of an object file. We use the base filename, attaching the **.o** extension to the file. If the object file is found in line 16, we set a new hashed array to the modification time of the object file. We use the same key as before, which will make it easier to extract the information again later. In lines 20 to 23 we repeat the exercise with header files. Line 24 is the end of the loop; we've finished extracting all of the information we need to start processing and then outputting the details.

```
26  closedir(DIR);
27
28  $fmt = "%" . ($maxwidth+2) . "s";
29
```

Line 26 closes the directory handle. We don't bother checking that the close completed successfully. By line 28 we will have discovered all of the files we want to report on. We can now use the **$maxwidth** variable to create a new format to be used with **printf** when we come to report the information back to the user. We concatenate here to create the format string because we use a percent sign, which would confuse Perl when combined with the dollar sign to specify the variable. Note that we add two characters to the width to provide a gap between entries. The

format will specify the width of the string to be printed; anything shorter than this
format will be padded with spaces.

```
30  foreach $file (sort keys %cMTime)
31  {
32      printf($fmt,"$file.c");
33
34      if (defined($oMTime{$file}))
35      {
36          printf($fmt,"$file.o");
37
```

Line 30 starts the loop to report the information back. We extract the keys from
the C source file hashed variable we generated earlier. To sort the output, we sort
the keys before passing them to the **$file** variable. The filename reference has no
extension, so we print the C source filename, adding the **.c** extension on line 32. We
check for a corresponding object file in the object hash on line 34. If the object file
exists, we print the filename, adding the **.o** extension.

```
38          if ($cMTime{$file}>$oMTime{$file})
39          {
40              print &pptime($cMTime{$file}-$oMTime{$file});
41          }
42          else
43          {
44              printf("%12s","");
45          }
```

Now we come to the important part. The purpose of the script is to check for
differences in modification times between C source files, object files, and header
files. We verify whether the modification time of the C source is greater than the
object file in line 38. The modification times are contained in the data within the
hash variable, so extracting the information is merely a case of referring to the
corresponding file within the hash.

If the C source file is newer, we print the time difference, formatted by the
pptime function. We pass the result of the subtraction of the modification time of
the source file from the object file to the **pptime** function. The information we
gathered earlier will specify the number of seconds since the epoch that the file was
modified. Therefore, what we send to the **pptime** function is the difference in
seconds between the two files' modification times. If the object file is newer, then we
print a blank space using **printf** and a blank string.

```
46      }
47      else
48      {
49          printf($fmt . "%12s", "NYC","");
```

```
50                 }
51
```

On line 47, we decide what to do if the object file does not exist, or at least if the corresponding object file does not exist in the hash. If it doesn't exist, we print **NYC** for "Not Yet Compiled," with the same format we used for the filename, and the padding we would otherwise use if the time difference had to be printed. We go to all this trouble to ensure the columns are correct in the output.

```
52          if (defined($hMTime{$file}))
53          {
54           printf($fmt,"$file.h");
55
56           if ($hMTime{$file}>$cMTime{$file})
57           {
58               print &pptime($hMTime{$file}-$cMTime{$file});
59           }
60        }
```

Again, we repeat the exercise with the header file in lines 52 to 60. However, we don't print out the padding information if the header file doesn't exist, since it's the last item on the line anyway. We don't bother printing **NYC**; a header file either exists or, if it doesn't, it's not generated by the compilation process.

```
61
62      print "\n";
63
64   }
65
```

By line 61 we have reached the end of the line of information , so we print a new-line character and then cycle around the loop again when we reach line 64.

```
66   sub pptime
67   {
68       my ($time) = @_;
69       my ($min,$hour,$yday) = (gmtime($time))[1,2,7];
70
71       sprintf("(%3sd%2sh%2sm)",$yday,$hour,$min);
72   }
73
```

The **pptime** function starts on line 66. The purpose of the function is to return a "pretty-printed" version of the time passed to it. In this instance, the time will be the number of seconds between the modification time of two files, so we are only printing relatively small amounts of information. Line 68 gets the time from the function arguments, which are stored in the @_variable. We specify the variable as local to this function, just in case. Then on line 69 we use a subscript to extract the number of minutes, hours, and days elapsed from the **$time** variable, assigning the result to some more local variables.

Line 71 then formats the numbers into a string, which is automatically returned to the calling line as the last result of the function. The format used specifies the width of the individual elements, fixing the size of the output string to keep it within our desired formatted layout.

When run, the script reports on all the source files. Object files that are older than the source file have the difference in times between them reported, thereby acting as a quick way of identifying which files have yet to be compiled. We report similar information regarding corresponding header files. Although generally a header file would be used across a range of files, it's safe to assume that matching header and C source files relate to each other. Here is some sample output from part way through a build of Perl 5.004:

```
          av.c            av.o(   0d  0h45m)            av.h
         deb.c           deb.o
        doio.c          doio.o
        doop.c          doop.o
        dump.c          dump.o
     globals.c       globals.o
          gv.c            gv.o(   0d  0h52m)            gv.h
          hv.c            hv.o                          hv.h
      malloc.c        malloc.o
          mg.c            mg.o                          mg.h
 miniperlmain.c  miniperlmain.o
          op.c             NYC                          op.h
        perl.c          perl.o                        perl.h
      perlio.c        perlio.o                      perlio.h
     perlmain.c       perlmain.o
        perly.c         perly.o              perly.h(280d  4h35m)
          pp.c            pp.o                          pp.h
      pp_ctl.c        pp_ctl.o
      pp_hot.c        pp_hot.o
      pp_sys.c        pp_sys.o
      regcomp.c       regcomp.o                    regcomp.h
      regexec.c       regexec.o
         run.c           run.o
       scope.c         scope.o                       scope.h
          sv.c            sv.o                          sv.h
       taint.c         taint.o
        toke.c          toke.o
    universal.c     universal.o
        util.c          util.o               util.h(255d  6h  3m)
```

You can see in this sample that some files are yet to be compiled, such as op.o; others are reporting time differences between the current object file and the current source file. In other cases, including util.h, we can see that the header file is much newer than the source file. These lines prove invaluable when you are programming, by helping you avoid having to run what might be a lengthy "make" process to obtain the information.

mvlink.pl

Moving Links Across File Systems

When you have a symbolic link to a particular directory on another partition, there are times when you want to move the link to another file system. The **rename** function within Perl will fail when you try to move the link from one file system to the other because the OS _rename_ function, on which the Perl _rename_ function is based, updates the directory location contained in the inode within the same file system. Because an inode is attached to an individual drive or file system, it's impossible to copy the inode or update its details so that a different file systems contains the link.

The same problem occurred for older versions of the standard mv command, which was also unable to move files across file systems for exactly the same reason. The trick to moving a file from one file system to another, or from one disk to another, is to create the new file, copy the contents of the old file to the new one, and then remove the old file. The same process can be used to move links across file systems.

Newer versions of the mv command correctly identify that the file is a link. They create a new symbolic link, copy the information for the link to the new link file, and then remove the old link. Unfortunately, the Perl **rename** function is still linked to the OS **rename** function and so is able to update links only on the same file system.

The **mvlink.pl** script that follows uses the **readlink** function to get the details of where the link is currently pointing to, then creates the new link at the new location with the old link information before removing the old link.

```
1   #!/usr/local/bin/perl
2
3   use File::Basename;
4
5   die "Usage: mvlink file [files...] destination\n" if ($#ARGV <1);
6
7   if (!(-d $ARGV [$#ARGV]) && ($#ARGV = 1))
8   {
9       &mvlink($ARGV [0], $ARGV [1]);
10  }
11  elsif ((-d $ARGV [$#ARGV]))
12  {
```

```
13        for($i=0;$i<$#ARGV;$i++)
14        {
15            next unless -l $ARGV [$i];
16            $basefile = basename($ARGV [$i]);
17            &mvlink($ARGV [$i], $ARGV [$#ARGV] . "/" . $basefile);
18        }
19    }
20    else
21    {
22        die "Can't copy multiple links to a single file\n";
23    }
24
25    sub mvlink()
26    {
27        ($old, $new) = @_;
28        local($linkloc);
29
30        die "File $new already exists\n" if (-e $new);
31        $linkloc = readlink($old);
32        unlink($old);
33        symlink($linkloc,$new);
34    }
```

ANNOTATIONS

Put simply, the script checks to see if it's moving a single link to a new directory or a single link to a new name. If the user attempts to copy multiple links into a single file, an error is reported. The function **mvlink** reads the information for the old link, deletes it, and then creates a new link based on the old link information.

```
1    #!/usr/local/bin/perl
2
3    use File::Basename;
4
5    die "Usage: mvlink file [files...] destination\n" if (@ARGV<2);
6
```

In line 3, we incorporate the **Basename** module, which is included under the File hierarchy within the standard Perl module directory. Part of the standard Perl 5 distribution, **Basename** incorporates a number of useful functions, many of which we will look at throughout this book. The **Basename** functions allow you to extract the filename or directory name from an entire path.

Line 5 checks that we have received at least two arguments on the command line. Remember that the script will move a single link or multiple links to a new directory, so we must have at the very least the current link name and the new link location.

```
7    if (!(-d $ARGV [-1]) && (@ARGV == 2))
8    {
9         &mvlink($ARGV [0], $ARGV [1]);
10   }
```

Line 7 identifies the type of move we are conducting. The test checks whether the last command line argument is a directory and how many arguments there were on the command line. You can use negative numbers to refer to entries in an array, starting from the last element. In this example, we've specified a index of **-1**, which Perl interprets as the last element. If the destination is *not* a directory, and there are only two arguments, then it's a case of renaming a link. This is carried out by a single call to the **mvlink** function.

```
11   elsif ((-d $ARGV [-1]))
12   {
13        for($i=0;$i<$#ARGV;$i++)
14        {
15             next unless -l $ARGV [$i];
16             $basefile = basename($ARGV [$i]);
17             &mvlink($ARGV [$i], $ARGV [$#ARGV] . "/" . $basefile);
18        }
19   }
```

If there are two or more arguments and the destination is a directory, we execute lines 11 to 19. Since we know we must have at least two arguments (because otherwise the script will have died on line 5), we just have to check that the last argument refers to a directory.

Line 13 sets up a **for** loop that goes through all of the arguments, up to the second to last one (because we're testing for a value less than the actual number of arguments). In line 15, the argument is tested to make sure it is a link, and not a standard file; if it is a link, we move on to the next argument.

Using the **basename** function we imported on line 3, we extract the filename of the link so that users can specify an absolute path name on the command line, and still be able to handle the move. This filename will be used to specify the full name for the destination. Finally, line 17 calls the same **mvlink** function as before, specifying the original link location, the destination made up of the last argument from the command line, and the base name of the link extracted in line 16.

```
20   else
21   {
22       die "Can't copy multiple links to a single file\n";
23   }
24
```

If we've made it this far, and the arguments have been identified correctly, then the move will have already taken place. So on line 20, we can assume that the arguments are invalid in some way, so we **die** on line 22. The reason for quitting at this point will be that the destination specified was a file, and that there were multiple links to be moved to this new location. This is obviously possible, but not very useful, as every link would be renamed, with subsequent links overwriting previous moves.

```
25   sub mvlink()
26   {
27       my ($old, $new) = @_;
28       my ($linkloc);
29
30       die "File $new already exists\n" if (-e $new);
31       die "$old is not a link\n" if !(-l $old);
32       $linkloc = readlink($old);
33       unlink($old);
34       symlink($linkloc,$new);
35   }
```

The **mvlink** function does the real work. It reads the information from the old link out to the new link, deleting the original link. The arguments to this function are the existing link and the full path name and filename of the destination link.

Line 30 will end the script if the destination already exists, while line 31 ensures that the file we are attempting to move is actually a link. On line 32 we use the **readlink** function to get the detail of where the link currently points. We then remove the old link on line 33 and create the new link on line 34.

Although there is some checking within this function, it is not as bombproof as it could be. We don't check that we read the link information correctly, or whether we managed to remove the old link or create the new one. However, there are tradeoffs in Perl as to where to draw the line when it comes to error checking. Perl will let you get away with a lot before it raises a complaint of any kind. In this case we could easily attempt to move a link, not be able to read it, but successfully delete it and create a new empty link. Adding the error checking I've mentioned would solve this problem, or at least alert the user about it at run time.

Linking

The terms *link* and *unlink* come from the way the original Unix Seventh Edition file system was organized. The basics of the original file system still exist today, even in file systems as advanced as Windows NTFS and Linux ext2.

At the lowest point within a file system, a number is used to refer to each file. The file number is called an *inode*. Each inode specifies the logical location (block number) that the file uses on the disk and the space it uses, and this information is stored in the inode table. This system is essentially the same as the desktop databases used by the Mac or the file allocation tables (FAT) used by DOS and Windows.

At the higher, or user, level, a directory table links the directory names, as we see them, to the inode numbers, as the OS sees them—hence the term *link*. Linking a block of disk space to an inode creates an entry in the directory listing. Adding another link to the same disk block generates an additional filename; both names point to the same file. Unlinking an inode deletes the link, or, if it is the last link, it deletes the file and frees the physical space on the storage device. You can see the inode numbers of files by using the -i option to the ls command, although the information is of little use.

relink.pl

Updating Links

It is common under Unix to use links as a way of moving files and directories about a file system or across disk drives to make better use of the available space. For example, the default location for incoming e-mail under Solaris is **/var/spool/mqueue**, located on the root file system. By default, the space allocated to the root file system is about 40MB, and much of that space is used up by the core OS itself. For a busy mail server, this amount of space is obviously inadequate. The proper solution would be to create and make available another partition on a hard drive somewhere that was a suitable size.

The usual solution, however, is to move the entire directory to an existing file system that has more space, then use a symbolic link to match the old directory location with the new one. The moving about of directories in this manner is common practice; in fact the OS usually uses some symbolic links itself to keep a structured format without duplicating files or folders.

Problems can occur when you have to move a directory around that already has links attached to it. In our previous example, we are moving the link but not changing the information about where that link points to. What we need to do here is leave the link where it is but update the information about where the link points to, to match the location of the moved directory.

We can do this by using a slightly modified version of the previous script. In line 31 of **mvlink.pl** we used the **readlink** function to get the location the link that's pointed to. We can then update this information, delete the old link, and create a new one based on the new destination. I've taken the following example script, **lwrelink.pl**, straight from the Perl 5 distribution, where you can find it in the eg directory. This is another Larry Wall original!

```perl
1    #!/usr/local/bin/perl
2    'di';
3    'ig00';
4    #
5    # $RCSfile: relink,v $$Revision: 4.1 $$Date: 92/08/07 17:20:29 $
6    #
7    # $Log:      relink,v $
8
9    ($op = shift) || die "Usage: relink perlexpr [filenames]\n";
10   if (!@ARGV) {
11       @ARGV = <STDIN>;
12       chop(@ARGV);
13   }
14   for (@ARGV) {
15       next unless -l;              # symbolic link?
16       $name = $_;
17       $_ = readlink($_);
18       $was = $_;
19       eval $op;
20       die $@ if $@;
21       if ($was ne $_) {
22        unlink($name);
23        symlink($_, $name);
24       }
25   }
26   ##############################
```

ANNOTATIONS

This script is a combination of the previous **mvlink.pl** script, and it follows the same basic structure as **rename.pl**, which we covered earlier and is also supplied with the Perl 5 kit. This time, instead of performing a regular expression substitution on the name of the file, the script modifies the location the link points to. The script also uses the same combined file format for keeping the manual page and script in the same file.

```
1    #!/usr/local/bin/perl
2    'di';
3    'ig00';
4    #
5    # $RCSfile: relink,v $$Revision: 4.1 $$Date: 92/08/07 17:20:29 $
6    #
7    # $Log:      relink,v $
8
9    ($op = shift) || die "Usage: relink perlexpr [filenames]\n";
10   if (!@ARGV) {
11       @ARGV = <STDIN>;
12       chop(@ARGV);
13   }
```

We see the same diversion information, used for incorporating the manual page within the script on lines 2 and 3. Line 9 shifts the command line arguments to obtain the regular expression. If there are no arguments specified, then we **die** with a usage message.

Once again, we can get away without specifying any actual files on the command line by importing the information from the keyboard when the script is run. Line 11 attributes everything typed up to the end-of-file character from keyboard into **@ARGV**. Perl will automatically put individual lines into sequential elements of the array. Whether the files were referenced on the command line or standard input, the list of files is now in **@ARGV**.

```
14   for (@ARGV) {
15       next unless -l;            # symbolic link?
16       $name = $_;
17       $_ = readlink($_);
18       $was = $_;
19       eval $op;
20       die $@ if $@;
21       if ($was ne $_) {
22         unlink($name);
23         symlink($_, $name);
24       }
25   }
```

Lines 14 to 25 are responsible for the actual changes. The **for** loop on line 14 sets us up to read through every element of **@ARGV**, with the contents of each element being placed into the default pattern space, $_.

We skip the file if it isn't a link. Note that we don't have to specify the link explicitly. Perl automatically uses the value in the default buffer. The link name is recorded in line 16, because in line 17 we'll put the link location into the pattern searching space. We record the current link location in the **$was** variable on line 18. The regular expression is executed on the pattern search space via the **eval** function. **Eval** executes the specified Perl code; see the earlier section "Renaming Files with Larry Wall's Rename Script" for more details on the **eval** function.

Line 20 drops out of the script if the regular expression failed for any reason. The **$@** variable contains the result from the **eval** statement, but will be empty (or false) if the statement executed without errors. The result from the substitution will be in **$_**, since the expression is executed on that variable.

Lastly, line 21 ensures that the new link location doesn't match the old link location. There is no point updating a link with the same values; it just wastes processor cycles and disk accesses. Line 22 removes the old link, and line 23 creates the new link, using the new link location and the original filename, which we stored back on line 16.

Line 26 and onwards are the built-in manual page, which I've cropped here for brevity. You can view the manual page on a Unix system by using the following command:

```
$ nroff -man relink.pl|more
```

```
RELINK(1)                    User Commands                    RELINK(1)



LINK
     relink - relinks multiple symbolic links

SYNOPSIS
     relink perlexpr [symlinknames]

DESCRIPTION
     Relink relinks the symbolic links  given  according  to  the
     rule  specified  as  the  first  argument.  The argument is a
     Perl expression which is expected to modify the $_  string in
     Perl  for  at  least  some of the names specified.  For each
     symbolic link named on the command line, the Perl expression
     will  be  executed on the contents of the symbolic link with
     that name.  If a given symbolic link's contents is not modi-
     fied  by  the expression, it will not be changed.  If a name
     given on the command line is not a symbolic link, it will be
     ignored.   If  no names are given on the command line, names
     will be read via standard input.
```

For example, to relink all symbolic links in the current directory pointing to somewhere in X11R3 so that they point to X11R4, you might say

```
relink 's/X11R3/X11R4/' *
```

To change all occurences of links in the system from /usr/spool to /var/spool, you'd say

```
find / -type 1 -print | relink 's#/usr/spool#/var/spool#'
```

ENVIRONMENT
No environment variables are used.

FILES
AUTHOR
Larry Wall

SEE ALSO
ln(1)
perl(1)

DIAGNOSTICS
If you give an invalid Perl expression you'll get a syntax error.

BUGS

To the use the script, either type the filenames on the command line, as in:
```
$ relink.pl "s#/var/#/usr/#" /usr/tmp
```
or just specify the substitution, and enter the filenames afterwards:
```
$ relink.pl "s#/var/#/usr/#"
/usr/tmp
EOF
```

Either way, the script will update the links based on the substitution you provide. Remember that this does not physically move or rename any files, just the locations that the symbolic links refer to.

Like the previous script, this one is sadly lacking when it comes to error checking. There is no excuse for not performing at least some checking of the operations concerned, especially when the ramifications of the code could be quite serious. Again, we get to a tradeoff where the quantity of code that actually does the work is smaller than the code that error checks what we do. Using the **die** function in strategic points is often enough to circumnavigate most problems. In this script, it would be safe to assume that if the **unlink** function on line 22 failed, the subsequent line would also fail.

Checking line 22 with a **die** function would prevent any errors, but it could also raise more problems if we get only halfway through a long sequence of files to be modified, leaving the remainder of the files unchanged. One reason for this laxity in error checking is that Perl can perform many things very easily, and the code is often clearer to the programmer and the reader when it's left out. The downside is that the consequences of a badly written script without error checking of any kind can be severe.

explink.pl

Using Link Expander to Locate Files

Links, as we've already seen, can be very useful, but they come with some problems. The previous two scripts help you to move and update links, but what if you just want to identify the real location of a file?

Many links point to a single file, or a single directory, but others may be links to locations that are themselves links to the real directory. You could search through and trawl for this information manually, but it would be a long process and may not be completely successful. The solution is to use a script that is capable of going through the process manually. The **explink.pl** script that follows comes from the CPAN archives. The script is from 1993 and can be found in CPAN/Scripts/File-Handling/EXPAND.SYMLINK.

PROGRAMMER'S NOTE

Most OSs limit the number of links that can be followed to stop you from creating a situation where link A points to link B when link B points to link A. Obviously this pair of links would cause the operating system to permanently follow either of the two links, so the link could never be resolved. To escape from this situation, each time a link is followed by the OS, the link count is increased until the limit is reached. When reached, the OS stops resolving the links and reports an error. For most OSs, that value is between 16 and 32. Under Solaris, for example, it is 20.

```
1    #!/usr/local/bin/perl
2
```

```
3    chop($pwd = `pwd`);
4
5    for $orig (@ARGV)
6    {
7            $expanded = &Expand($orig);
8            print STDERR "$orig -> $expanded\n";
9    }
10
11   sub Expand ()
12   {
13       local($old) = @_;
14       local(*_, *dir);
15       $old =~ s#^#$pwd/# unless $old =~ m#^/#;
16       @dir = split(/\//, $old);
17       shift(@dir);
18       $_ = '';
19       dir: foreach $dir (@dir)
20       {
21           next dir if $dir eq '.';
22           if ($dir eq '..')
23           {
24               s#/[^/]+$##;
25               next dir;
26           }
27           $_ .= '/' . $dir;
28           while ($r = readlink)
29           {
30               if ($r =~ m#^/#)
31               {
32                   $_ = &Expand($r);
33               }
34               else
35               {
36                   s#[^/]+$#$r#;
37                   $_ = &Expand($_);
38               }
39           }
40       }
41       ($_ eq '') ? '/' : $_;
42   }
```

ANNOTATIONS

Basically, the script first identifies the location of the file that it has been requested to expand. The script then goes through the full path of the file, expanding each directory recursively until fully expanded.

```
1    #!/usr/local/bin/perl
2
3    chop($pwd = `pwd`);
4
```

Line 4 stores the output from **pwd**, which returns the current working directory. This information is used to make a full path name out of a locally referenced file. The call to the external program is made via the backquote character (`` ` ``). Perl uses the shellscript notation to identify an external program to be executed, and it works in much the same way as the shell equivalent. Anything returned by the called program is returned by the quoted command, so we can assign the output to a variable.

Because the **pwd** function will add a new-line character, the **chop** function is used to remove the last character from the information returned, and therefore from the **$pwd** variable used to store the output. More recently, with Perl 5 we would use the **chomp** function, which takes the record separator character off the end of the string. By default the record separator is a new-line character.

```
5    for $orig (@ARGV)
6    {
7        $expanded = &Expand($orig);
8        print STDERR "$orig -> $expanded\n";
9    }
10
```

Lines 5 to 10 step through each file specified on the command line. Each file is passed to the **Expand** function, and the output is printed on line 8. In fact, the output is sent to the standard file handle **STDERR**. See the sidebar "Standard File Handles" for more information on file handles.

```
11   sub Expand ()
12   {
13       local($old) = @_;
14       local(*_, *dir);
15       $old =~ s#^#$pwd/# unless $old =~ m#^/#;
```

The **Expand** function starts on line 11. The passed argument is placed into the **$old** variable, which is marked as local to the function only. We also set, in line 14, the **dir** and _ variables as being local. To save time, we use the typeglob character, the asterisk, to refer to all types of the variable of that name within this function. The

Standard File Handles

There are three basic file handles available in every Perl script. These are

STDIN   The default input, usually the keyboard
STDOUT   The default output, usually the screen
STDERR   The default error device, usually the screen

These are equivalent to the **stdin, stdout,** and **stderr** file handles available in C. By default, input is taken from STDIN, print commands output to STDOUT, and errors are sent to STDERR. Because they are separate file handles, we can output and filter the information separately. For example, you may want the output of a script to go to a file, but errors to go to the terminal. By redirecting the standard output to a file, and writing errors to STDERR, you can do exactly that.

specification for these variables to be local will also mean that multiple instances of the function will have their own copy of these variables. We will see later why this is important.

Line 15 puts the current working directory we identified earlier in front of the filename, if the filename doesn't start with a forward slash. This syntax copes with absolute references (that is, those with a leading forward slash) and local references (including those that begin with the current and parent working directory names of . and ..). This works because a path name is just a pointer to a location. Giving directions to a particular location, but then giving directions from that point on, is still valid. For example, take the path name

```
/usr/local/contrib/../../named
```

Although this looks like nonsense, what it actually means is go to **/usr/local/contrib**, then go back up a directory, then back up another, and then go back down into **named**. This specification is equivalent to **/usr/named**, although that is not immediately obvious to the casual observer.

```
16      @dir = split(/\//, $old);
17      shift(@dir);
18      $_ = '';
```

Line 16 splits the full path name into the array **dir**, using the forward slash as the separation character. We now have an array where each element is a single directory within the entire path name. If we expand each of these individual directories, we should end up with the expanded path. On line 17 we ignore the first element of the array because it will be blank—splitting a string where the first character is the same as the split character will produce an empty first element. On line 18, we ensure the pattern matching space is empty before we work through the elements.

```
19        dir: foreach $dir (@dir)
20        {
21            next dir if $dir eq '.';
22            if ($dir eq '..')
23            {
24                s#/[^/]+$##;
25                next dir;
26            }
```

Line 19 sets up a **foreach** loop to go through each directory element. The loop is labeled **dir** so that we can reference this line as the one to continue to from a **next** statement. Line 21 ignores the directory element if it points to the current, ., directory—there is no point expanding a reference to the directory you're currently working on. To give an example, the file foo.bar could just as easily be specified as ./**foo.bar**. The two are identical. In the second example, we could ignore the leading period and still refer to the same file. The **next** statement puts us back up on a new cycle of the **foreach** loop on the next element. In this instance the label is unnecessary since the loop will automatically return to this point anyway.

Lines 22 to 26 account for references to the parent directory. If you consider the path name **/usr/local/..**, you can extract the proper directory by removing the last named directory, which in this example is **/local**. This is exactly what we do on line 24. The regular expression matches a string with a forward slash followed by any character that isn't a forward slash up to the end of the string. Splitting the regular expression up makes it more obvious:

s#	Start of the regular expression
/	A forward slash
[^/]+	One or more characters that aren't a forward slash
$	The end of the string
##	Replacement text (nothing!)

This expression strips the last named directory off the pattern matching space, effectively traversing back up the parent directory. Since we've finished this entry, we can move on to the next element of the array, which is what we do in line 25.

```
27            $_ .= '/' . $dir;
28            while ($r = readlink)
29            {
```

We append the current directory to the pattern space on line 27, and then we expand the link that the directory in the pattern space refers too, placing the result in **$r**. At this point, the loop is flawed. We have already seen that the result of the test in line 28 could equal 0 and yet still refer to an existing file. It would be much better to use the **defined** function to verify that **$r** was set to something sensible.

```
30              if ($r =~ m#^/#)
31              {
32                  $_ = &Expand($r);
33              }
```

If the result of this expansion refers to a directory with an absolute reference (that is, it starts with a forward slash), then we run a new instance of the **Expand** function to work out what its true value should be. This sets up a recursion that will continue to expand links that refer to or contain links to other directories until all the links have been expanded.

```
34              else
35              {
36                  s#[^/]+$#$r#;
37                  $_ = &Expand($_);
38              }
```

If the returned expansion from line 30 doesn't start with a leading forward slash, then we replace the last directory specific in the pattern matching area with the result, setting up a recursion for the full path on line 37.

```
39          }
40      }
41      ($_ eq '') ? '/' : $_;
42  }
```

Once all the recursions have taken place, and all the elements of the recursed directory have been resolved, the result is returned on line 41. However, there is a final test here. If the result from all the recursions is blank, then the result must be the root directory. The only way this would occur is if one of the links had too many references to parent directories, such that it expanded itself to nothing.

You should now be able to see why we used the **local** keyword to specify the variables as being local to the current instance of the function. Without doing so, subsequent recursed calls to the function would overwrite the information stored in the variables with unpredictable results. By using the typeglob option to the variables we ensure that all the different variable types are accounted for.

To understand the script a bit better, a version of the script that supplies a running commentary of what it's doing is supplied as **dexplink.pl** on the CD-ROM.

Here is the output from a Solaris 2.4 box:

```
$ dexplink.pl /usr/tmp
Expanding /usr/tmp
Expanding element usr (result is currently )
Expanding element tmp (result is currently /usr)
Recursively expanding full directory /usr/../var/tmp
Expanding /usr/../var/tmp
```

```
Expanding element usr (result is currently )
Expanding element .. (result is currently /usr)
Expanding element var (result is currently )
Expanding element tmp (result is currently /var)
/usr/tmp -> /var/tmp
```

You see here that the link **/usr/tmp** refers to **../var/tmp**, which is then recursively expanded to replace **/usr** with **/var**.

Summary

As we've seen, there are several ways of accessing and using files within Perl. Once armed with the filenames, it is easy to extract further information about the file. Combining these pieces of information, we can perform some complex reports on the contents of the directory, such as the programmer's file list. We can also use Perl to help with symbolic links, a useful feature of the modern OS, but it's also a source of difficulties when it comes to moving or updating the links.

We haven't covered all of the methods for accessing and using files within this chapter, but we will revisit the topic in later chapters when we look at some more real world examples of scripts.

Manipulating Text Data

I t is impossible in the modern world to escape databases. Most of the time, you are probably unaware of the databases that you are using, and you probably don't even consider some of the files you access to be databases. Think of it this way: a database is defined as a file or system in which data is stored in a structured format. This structure is used to aid the updating and access processes, but it is not designed to constrain the information that you are storing.

For example, the /etc/passwd file is a text database of user properties on a Unix system. The information is stored as plain text, and colons separate the fields in the database. Individual lines make up the records of the database. Here's an extract from one of my machines:

```
root:x:0:1:0000-Admin(0000):/:/sbin/sh
daemon:x:1:1:0000-Admin(0000):/:
bin:x:2:2:0000-Admin(0000):/usr/bin:
sys:x:3:3:0000-Admin(0000):/:
adm:x:4:4:0000-Admin(0000):/var/adm:
lp:x:71:8:0000-lp(0000):/usr/spool/lp:
smtp:x:0:0:mail daemon user:/:
uucp:x:5:5:0000-uucp(0000):/usr/lib/uucp:
nuucp:x:9:9:0000-uucp(0000):/var/spool/uucppublic:/usr/lib/uucp/uucico
listen:x:37:4:Network Admin:/usr/net/nls:
nobody:x:60001:60001:uid no body:/:
noaccess:x:60002:60002:uid no access:/:
martinb:x:1000:1000:Martin C Brown:/users/martinb:/usr/local/bin/bash
```

Extracting the information from this database is relatively easy: all we need to do is read in each line and separate each field. Of course, a read-only database is just a data source. The definition of a database implies that we can use the file, and the format associated with it, to store, update, and report on information.

There is a problem with the preceding type of layout that we'll discover if we start using this technique for standard databases. What happens if the data we are trying to store contains even one colon? As far as the Perl script is concerned, the colon specifies the end of one field and the beginning of the next. An additional colon would upset the information stored in the record. Even worse, what would happen if we wanted to record multiple lines of text in the database? Individual records are stored on individual lines; multiline fields would confuse the script again.

There are ways around these constraints. We could use a different character for the field and record separator, although this fix is still open to the same abuse and possible results. We could just remove the field and record separator characters from the source before we put them in the database, but this fix reduces the utility of being able to store the information in the first place. The simplest solution is to ignore any field or record separators, and instead use fixed-length records to store the information. The use of fixed-length records implies that you know the maximum size of the data that you are storing before you place it into the database.

Using fixed-length records would allow us to store any sort of information in the database, including multiple lines of text, without worrying about how the data may affect the database layout. The only problem with fixed-length databases is that you restrict the amount of information you can store, and you also increase the size of the data file for small records because the individual fields are padded to make up the fixed lengths. To complicate matters further, you may have trouble choosing a padding character that won't affect the contents of the fields you are storing. In these situations, you can usually augment the fixed-length structure by also specifying the field length for each field in each record—which also increases the size of the database.

There is another problem with text databases that is hard to overcome, and that is searching the database for the information you need. Small amounts of information are fine stored in a text database, but if you expect to extract the information from a text database on a individual record basis, then you can run into problems because the only way to access the information is to read the database until you find the information you are looking for. There are some ways to get around this shortcoming, although no perfect solution. For example, we can use index files to store references to particular pieces of information, but we still have to read in the index in order to access the real data.

The most ignored problem with using text databases is concurrent updates. If two processes want to update the same database at the same time, you need to find some way of restricting access so one process does not overwrite the modifications just made by the other process, or make assumptions about the content before it updates. The obvious solution is to use some form of file-locking mechanism. A less obvious solution, but one used by many industrial-strength databases, is to use a "server" process, which performs the updates in sequence, while "clients" talk to the server by some form of interprocess communication (IPC). We'll look at some network-based solutions in Chapter 6.

Throughout this chapter we will look at ways of using text databases, both variable length using field separators and fixed length. We'll also look at some examples of using index files to help with searching text databases. Using the DBI toolkit allows us to make queries on a CSV (comma-separated value) file using SQL statements, and we briefly look at how to use this tool to solve some of our lookup problems. Finally, we will examine ways of sorting the data structures we use in Perl for storing database information. Sorting data is relevant not only to text databases but also to any information we decide to store.

pwls.pl

Reporting from the /etc/passwd File

We have already seen techniques in Chapter 1 for extracting information from text files. Before we leap into using text files for data storage, let's revisit the process of extracting data and introduce the convention of delimited records by reporting on the information contained in the password file on a Unix machine.

The script is simple, but it shows the general method for extracting information from a text database. We open the source, split the "record" up by the field delimiter, and then output the result.

```perl
1    #!/usr/local/bin/perl
2
3    open(D,"</etc/passwd") || die "$0: Can't open passwd file, $!\n";
4
5    while(<D>)
6    {
7        chomp;
8        my ($user,$passwd,$uid,$gid,$info,$home,$shell) = split /:/;
9
10       print <<EOF;
11   User:            $user
12   Password:        <NOT SHOWN>
13   User ID:         $uid
14   Group ID:        $gid
15   User Info:       $info
16   Home Directory:  $home
17   Shell:           $shell
18
19   EOF
20   }
21
22   close(D) || die "$0: Couldn't close the passwd file, $!\n";
```

ANNOTATIONS

In this script, once the /etc/passwd file has been opened, we read in each line, separate the fields, and print out the result.

```perl
1    #!/usr/local/bin/perl
2
```

Line 3 sets up the variables that will be used to hold the information. The format of the /etc/passwd file is

```
login:password:user id:group id:name:home directory:startup shell
```

Each user is listed on a separate line, and colons split up the fields in the line.

```perl
3    open(D,"</etc/passwd") || die "$0: Can't open passwd file, $!\n";
4
```

Line 3 opens the password file, quitting if we can't get access.

```
5    while(<D>)
6    {
7        chomp;
8        my ($user,$passwd,$uid,$gid,$info,$home,$shell) = split /:/;
9
```

Line 7 sets up the loop to work through the file. The **<D>** tests for an end-of-file mark, so the **while** loop will continue as long as the end of the file has not been reached. On line 9 we use the **chomp** function, which strips the default record separator off the current input line. By default, the record separator is an end-of-line character, which is a different character for each platform. This default maintains consistency between Perl programs without you having to make any modifications to account for the OS the script is working on. Line 10 splits the input line by colons into the corresponding variables we defined earlier.

```
10       print <<EOF;
11   User:              $user
12   Password:          <NOT SHOWN>
13   User ID:           $uid
14   Group ID:          $gid
15   User Info:         $info
16   Home Directory:    $home
17   Shell:             $shell
18
19   EOF
20   }
21
```

Lines 12 to 21 set up a here document that presents the results. The loop ends on line 22, and we finish up by closing the file on line 24.

```
22   close(D) || die "$0: Couldn't close the passwd file, $!\n";
```

This script actually emulates part of the functionality of the **getpwent** function, although it demonstrates a basic method we will use throughout the rest of this chapter. The **getpwent** function is part of a family of functions dedicated to extracting and reporting on different elements of the /etc/passwd file.

upddir.pl

Creating and Updating a Simple Text Database

The simplest form of text database is one that relies on a delimiter to separate fields in an individual record, with each record being on an individual line. The password file in our previous script was a good example. The choice of delimiter is important;

for instance, storing URLs in a database where the delimiter is a colon won't work—a URL contains at least one colon.

In our example, we'll create a database containing information about a directory tree. The script is intelligent enough to create a new database if one doesn't exist, and it will update the stored information each time it is run. Because the information we are storing is a combination of filenames and textual information, we can use colons to separate individual fields.

WARNING   *If you are running this script under MacOS, you need to change the delimiter. MacOS uses colons to separate the files and directories in a path name, and using an identical delimiter to separate the fields of information will make the script unable to extract the correct information!*

```
1   #!/usr/local/bin/perl5
2
3   use File::Find;
4
5   die "Usage: $0 dbfile directory\n" if (@ARGV<2);
6
7   $dbfile=shift;
8   $directory=shift;
9
10  if (-f $dbfile)
11  {
12      open(D,"<$dbfile") || die "Can't open the db $dbfile, $!\n";
13
14      while(<D>)
15      {
16          chomp;
17          ($file,@fields) = split /:/;
18          $files{$file} = join ':',@fields;
19      }
20
21      close(D) || "Couldn't close the db, $!\n";
22  }
23
24  find(\&process_file,$directory);
25
26  open(D,">$dbfile") || die "Can't update db $dbfile, $!\n";
27  for $key (keys %files)
28  {
29      print D "$key:$files{$key}\n";
30  }
31  close(D) || "Couldn't close the db, $!\n";
32
33  sub process_file
```

```
34   {
35       if ( -f $_ )
36       {
37           @fields = (stat(_))[2,4,5,7,9];
38           $files{$_} = join(":",@fields);
39       }
40   }
```

ANNOTATIONS

This script examines an entire directory tree, adding or updating information about each file and directory into a file. We record the file's path, and use that path as the key to store the size, user and group IDs, modification time, and permissions. The information is stored in a data file, with individual fields separated by colons.

We also use the **Find** module that is part of the standard Perl 5 distribution. The function will generate a list of files in an entire directory tree, putting each name into the default pattern space and then calling a function to work on each file.

```
1    #!/usr/local/bin/perl5
2
3    use File::Find;
4
5    die a"Usage: $0 dbfile directory\n" if (@ARGV<2);
6
```

We include the **File::Find** module on line 3 and then check for the command-line arguments, reporting a usage message as an error if we can't see enough arguments.

```
7    $dbfile=shift;
8    $directory=shift;
9
```

If we've gotten this far, we can be sure that the command-line arguments exist. Lines 7 and 8 set the **$dbfile** and **$directory** variables to the first and second arguments, respectively.

```
10   if (-f $dbfile)
11   {
12       open(D,"<$dbfile") || die "Can't open the db $dbfile, $!\n";
13
14       while(<D>)
15       {
16           chomp;
17           ($file,@fields) = split /:/;
18           $files{$file} = join ':',@fields;
19       }
20
```

```
21      close(D) || "Couldn't close the db, $!\n";
22  }
23
```

If the database file already exists, we open the file and read in the current version of the database. Line 12 opens the file, and the **while** loop in lines 14 to 20 reads the file in. We put the memory version of the database into a hash, where the key field is the path name of the file, and the value is a colon-separated list of the other fields. Note that on line 17 the first field extracted by **split** is put into **$file**, and the remainder of the fields are put straight into an array. This array is then used by **join** on line 18 to put the extracted fields into the hash. A quicker method than lines 17 and 18 would be to specify the maximum number of times to split on the specified separator. Hence lines 17 and 18 could be written as

```
($file,$rest) = split /:/, $_, 2;
```

This modification saves us a line in the script and a few execution cycles, as we are not relying on another statement to join fields together that were already in one piece to begin with.

```
24  find(\&process_file,$directory);
25
```

Line 24 does most of the work. The call to the **find** function takes two arguments; the first is the function you want to use to process the information, and the second is the directory that you want to generate a listing of. The first argument must be specified as a reference to the function. Placing a preceding slash in front of the object name passes a reference. The directory listing that is produced will contain all of the files in the specified directory, as well as all the subdirectories and files below the specified directory. It's basically equivalent to running the find command under UNIX without any special arguments. For example:

```
$ find . -print
```

However, the **find** function is no more than a directory parser. For each entry in the directory tree, it calls the specified function; any processing of the found file, including selecting particular files from the file list, has to be performed by the function you specify in the first argument.

```
26  open(D,">$dbfile") || die "Can't update db $dbfile, $!\n";
27  for $key (keys %files)
28  {
29      print D "$key:$files{$key}\n";
30  }
31  close(D) || "Couldn't close the db, $!\n";
32
```

Since the file processing is performed by a separate function, lines 26 to 32 are the last lines of the main section of the script. These lines output the details of each file in the internal database (the hashed array) back out to the specified data file. Since we can be sure that the version of the database in memory is the current one for this process, we can overwrite the existing file (line 26). If this script was used to update the database for the same directory tree by a number of users, then the "current" database may be different for each instance of the script. Line 29 shows the benefits of storing the file data in memory as another colon-separated list; outputting the database is simply a case of storing the key and the value separated by a colon into the data file.

```
33   sub process_file
34   {
35       if ( -f $_ )
36       {
37           @fields = (stat(_))[2,4,5,7,9];
38           $files{$_} = join(":",@fields);
39       }
40   }
```

The **process_file** function is called by the **find** function for each directory entry in the tree. The filename is placed in the default IO buffer, **$_**, which we use first on line 35 to check that the result from **find** is actually a file. Provided it is, we use the **stat** function to get the extended information about the file, before placing the information in the hash on line 38. Note that on line 37 the subscript notation is used to extract the fields we want, in this case permissions, user ID, group ID, size, and finally modification time.

The information is joined together, with colons separating each field, and placed into the corresponding hash entry. In fact, line 38 creates new entries and updates existing ones; since we are just updating a variable in memory, it doesn't matter if we overwrite identical information into the variable.

The script gets around the most common problem associated with updating variable-length records by reading in the entire contents of the existing database before updating it in memory, writing out the contents when it's finished. For relatively small databases like this one, it's a good solution to an otherwise complicated problem. For larger databases, the method would be to read in each line, update it, write the line out to a new file, and then move the new file to the old filename.

There are some problems with this script that would require addressing if we used it in a real situation. No attempt is made to check and remove information about files that are in the existing database but not in the new directory tree. An easy way to do this would be to push the file paths into a new array, and then use that array to output the new database. To do this, insert this line before line 37:

```
push(@current,$_);
```

Then change line 27 to read

```
foreach $key (@current)
```

This alteration sets up the array as part of the **find** callback and then uses the list as the keys to the real data. Another, simpler solution would be to recreate the database each time the script was run, instead of reporting it beforehand. There are times when you want a record of the files in a directory, and knowing they no longer exist can be useful.

This method highlights another problem. Files of the same name in different directories are recorded only once within the hash, and therefore only once in the database. The **find** function actually changes the current working directory as it works through the directory tree. Prepending the result of **getcwd** to the filename returned would enable you to record details on a complete directory tree, accounting for duplicate names.

dirdiff.pl

Reporting from a Simple Text Database

In the first script of this chapter, we saw how easy it is to extract the information from a text database to the screen, and in the last script we stored information about a directory tree. With this next script, we will extract the information from the database we created and then perform some further checks on the files. Using this information, we will be able to make comparisons on the state of different files between the point the database was last updated and the state of the same directory tree as it stands now.

```perl
1    #!/usr/local/bin/perl5
2
3    use File::Find;
4
5    die "Usage: $0 dbfile directory\n" if (@ARGV<2);
6
7    $dbfile=shift;
8    $directory=shift;
9
10   open(D,"<$dbfile") || die "Can't open the db, $!\n";
11
12   while(<D>)
13   {
14       chomp;
15       ($file,@fields) = split /:/;
16       $files{$file} = join ':',@fields;
17   }
18
19   close(D) || "Couldn't close the db, $!\n";
20
21   find(\&process_file,$directory);
22
```

```perl
23    sub process_file
24    {
25        ($mode,$uid,$gid,$size,$mtime) = (stat($_))[2,4,5,7,9];
26
27        if (defined($files{$_}))
28        {
29            ($omode,$ouid,$ogid,$osize,$omtime) = split(/:/,$files{$_});
30
31            if ($size != $osize)
32            {
33                print "Size of $_ has changed, was $osize, now $size\n";
34            }
35            if ($mode != $omode)
36            {
37                print "Mode of $_ has changed, was ",extperms($omode),
38                        " now ",extperms($mode),"\n";
39            }
40            if ($uid !=$ouid)
41            {
42                print "User id of $_ has changed, was $ouid, now $uid\n";
43            }
44            if ($gid !=$ogid)
45            {
46                print "Group id of $_ has changed, was $ogid, now $gid\n";
47            }
48            if ($mtime !=$omtime)
49            {
50                $oldtime = localtime($omtime);
51                $newtime = localtime($mtime);
52                print "Modification time of $_ has changed, was ",
53                    $oldtime," now " , $newtime ,"\n";
54            }
55
56        }
57        else
58        {
59            print "File $_ isn't in the database\n";
60        }
61    }
62
63    sub extperms
64    {
65        my ($mode) = @_;
```

```
66      my (@perms) = ("-","-","-","-","-","-","-","-","-");
67
68      $perms[0] = 'r' if ($mode & 00400);
69      $perms[1] = "w" if ($mode & 00200);
70      $perms[2] = "x" if ($mode & 00100);
71      $perms[3] = "r" if ($mode & 00040);
72      $perms[4] = "w" if ($mode & 00020);
73      $perms[5] = "x" if ($mode & 00010);
74      $perms[6] = "r" if ($mode & 00004);
75      $perms[7] = "w" if ($mode & 00002);
76      $perms[8] = "x" if ($mode & 00001);
77      $perms[2] = "s" if ($mode & 04000);
78      $perms[5] = "s" if ($mode & 02000);
79      $perms[8] = "t" if ($mode & 01000);
80
81      join('',@perms);
82  }
```

ANNOTATIONS

The bulk of the script is identical to the update script. However, the **callback**
function used with the **find** function compares the current directory tree with the
database contents.

```
1   #!/usr/local/bin/perl5
2
3   use File::Find;
4
5   die "Usage: $0 dbfile directory\n" if (@ARGV<2);
6
7   $dbfile=shift;
8   $directory=shift;
9
```

Lines 1 to 9 set us up for the rest of the script. We need the same arguments to the
script for it to work correctly: the name of the database file and the directory that we
are comparing.

```
10  open(D,"<$dbfile") || die "Can't open the db, $!\n";
11
12  while(<D>)
13  {
14      chomp;
15      ($file,@fields) = split /:/;
```

```
16        $files{$file} = join ':',@fields;
17    }
18
19    close(D) || "Couldn't close the db, $!\n";
20
```

Lines 10 to 20 read in the existing database into a hashed array for later processing.

```
21    find(\&process_file,$directory);
22
```

Line 21 calls the **find** command with the **process_file** callback function.

```
23    sub process_file
24    {
25        ($mode,$uid,$gid,$size,$mtime) = (stat($_))[2,4,5,7,9];
26
```

The **process_file** function that starts on line 23 will work through each file found in the directory tree, checking the existing file against the existing database. The file status information is extracted on line 25, this time into individual variables for clarity.

```
27        if (defined($files{$_}))
28        {
29            ($omode,$ouid,$ogid,$osize,$omtime) = split(/:/,$files{$_});
30
```

Line 27 checks whether there is information about the current file within the hash and therefore within the internal version of the database imported from the file. The status information of the current file stored within the database is contained within the value of the hashed array pointed to by the file's path name. We extract the fields of information into a parallel set of variables on line 29.

```
31        if ($size != $osize)
32        {
33            print "Size of $_ has changed, was $osize, now $size\n";
34        }
```

Lines 31 to 34 report a difference in the size between the current and old versions of the file, starting with a simple **if** statement on line 31. We use the != numeric inequality test to check whether the old size and the new size do not match. If they don't match, then a suitable message is printed on line 33.

```
35        if ($mode != $omode)
36        {
37            print "Mode of $_ has changed, was ",extperms($omode),
38                    " now ",extperms($mode),"\n";
39        }
```

Lines 35 to 39 repeat the exercise with the file permissions. Note that because the permissions information returned by **stat** is a number, we can make simple comparisons between the two. We can check for the existence of individual settings within the number by interpreting them as a bit field. A number uniquely identifies a particular set of permissions; no two numbers will be identical if the underlying permissions are different. This concept is best understood with the help of the **extperms** function that we use to print out a human-readable form of the permissions on lines 37 and 38.

```
40          if ($uid !=$ouid)
41          {
42              print "User id of $_ has changed, was $ouid, now $uid\n";
43          }
44          if ($gid !=$ogid)
45          {
46              print "Group id of $_ has changed, was $ogid, now $gid\n";
47          }
```

We repeat the exercise again with the user and group IDs on lines 40 to 47.

```
48          if ($mtime !=$omtime)
49          {
50              $oldtime = localtime($omtime);
51              $newtime = localtime($mtime);
52              print "Modification time of $_ has changed, was ",
53                      $oldtime," now " , $newtime ,"\n";
54          }
55
56      }
```

Lines 48 to 54 compare the modification times. The **localtime** function is used to extract an English version of the date and time on lines 50 and 51. The calls to **localtime** could have been made as part of lines 52 and 53, but sometimes it is clearer to use the longer versions so that you know what you are printing.

Note that this time when we call the **localtime** function it is returning a date string, localized for the current time zone, including any daylight saving time. This is because Perl has detected that we expect only one return value, a scalar, from the function. Therefore, the information **localtime** returns is formatted as a text string. If the value on the left-hand side of the statement had been an array, or a string of variables, Perl would have returned the individual date and time elements, placing them in the corresponding variables.

This example demonstrates another of Perl's powerful features. A single function has generated two different responses based on the context in which it is used. Using this feature reduces the number of functions we have to remember when we are programming, but it can also make it less clear to the casual reader what the script is attempting to do.

Line 56 is the end of the **if** statement from line 27, since we have finished processing the differences between the two files.

```
57      else
58      {
59          print "File $_ isn't in the database\n";
60      }
61  }
62
```

If the file currently exists on disk but does not appear in the database, it's safe to assume that the file is new, and we report a suitable message on line 59. Note that at this point we do not check the consistency of the database against the current directory tree. Entries in the database file that are not part of the current directory tree are not reported. We'll look at a solution for this at the end of these annotations.

```
63  sub extperms
64  {
65      my ($mode) = @_;
66      my (@perms) = ("-","-","-","-","-","-","-","-","-");
67
68      $perms[0] = 'r' if ($mode & 00400);
69      $perms[1] = "w" if ($mode & 00200);
70      $perms[2] = "x" if ($mode & 00100);
71      $perms[3] = "r" if ($mode & 00040);
72      $perms[4] = "w" if ($mode & 00020);
73      $perms[5] = "x" if ($mode & 00010);
74      $perms[6] = "r" if ($mode & 00004);
75      $perms[7] = "w" if ($mode & 00002);
76      $perms[8] = "x" if ($mode & 00001);
77      $perms[2] = "s" if ($mode & 04000);
78      $perms[5] = "s" if ($mode & 02000);
79      $perms[8] = "t" if ($mode & 01000);
80
81      join('',@perms);
82  }
```

The **extperms** function is used to print out a standard-style permission list, where each character refers to the permissions of the user, group, and everybody else. The string returned by the function is identical to the last nine characters of the permission string produced by the **ls** command when you do a long directory listing; only the device type, normally at the start, is missing.

First of all, we extract the file permissions from the function arguments on line 65. The value will be a number that we can extract the information from using logic statements. Line 66 sets up the blank array that will contain the final permissions string. We set every element of the array to a single hyphen by specifying the list of values on the right-hand side of the expression, while the left-hand side is just the name of an array. As an alternative you can also do

```
my @perms = '-' x 10;
```

Lines 68 to 79 then do the work, performing a logical test against each portion of the permission variable. If each statement is true, then we put the appropriate letter (**r**, **w**, or **x**) into the corresponding element of the array. Because the set user ID, set group ID, and "sticky-bit" information is ordinarily put into the execute section of the permissions string, we do those last, even though they contain the higher numbers. If any of the permissions are not set, then the element of the array will remain as the default value of a hyphen that we set in line 66.

Once we have extracted all the information, we join all the elements together, without any intervening character, in order to make up the final string. For example, we might get a string returned as

```
rw-r--r--
```

which shows read and write on the user ID, but read-only on the group and everybody else. The octal version of this would be 644.

I stated earlier that no tests were performed to see if the database file referred to files that were not in the current directory tree. In order to check the location of a file, we would have to find some way of detecting which files were in the current tree as part of the **process_files** function.

Because we only test the files in the current directory tree, it would be safe to remove a file from the internal database if it was found successfully. You delete an entry in a hashed array by using the **delete** function. To enable this option, insert the following line before line 54:

```
delete($files{$_});
```

Undefining the entry will not work. The **undef** function will keep the key but delete the value associated with it. To finish it off, we then need to process the list of files still defined in the database back to the user. This is a case of going through an entry that still exists in the hashed array and reporting it back. Before line 23 we would insert a section like this into the code:

```
for each $key (keys %files)
{
    print "File $key was in the database but not the directory tree\n";
}
```

Since we have undefined all of the files we know are in the tree, the resulting list should be the files found only in the database.

phone.pl

Creating a Phone Record Reporter

Many databases you will use are really only there to record information from one source to be reported in another. The file format used by many systems is a simple text file; the Web log reporter we looked at in Chapter 1 is a good example. The format of the common log file is easy to follow and easy to extract information from because all of the records are identical in format.

Not all text databases are as straightforward. The following **phone.pl** script extracts information from a phone log supplied to phone subscribers by British Telecommunications plc. The files are standard comma-delimited text files, but individual records can be of varying formats. The first column contains a code that specifies the type of record. We use that code to identify the format used for the rest of the line, storing and reporting the information differently, based on the corresponding record format.

```perl
1   #!/usr/local/bin/perl5
2
3   open(D,"<" . $ARGV [0]) || die "Couldn't open source file, $!\n";
4
5   while(<D>)
6   {
7       chop;
8       ($codetype, @fields) = split /,/;
9
10      $realcode = substr($codetype,0,3);
11
12      die "Not a valid code $realcode\n"
13       unless ($realcode =~ /[0-9][0-9][0-9]/);
14
15      if ( $realcode eq '100' )
16      {
17          extract_file_header;
18      }
19      elsif ( $realcode eq '200' )
20      {
21          extract_customer_record;
22      }
23      elsif ( $realcode eq '220' )
24      {
25          extract_options_benefits(0);
26      }
27      elsif ( $realcode eq '327' )
28      {
29          extract_buschoice_savings(0);
30      }
31      elsif ( $realcode eq '312' )
32      {
33          item_call_record(0);
```

```
34        }
35     elsif ( $realcode eq '322' )
36     {
37         nonitem_call_summary(0);
38     }
39     elsif ( $realcode eq '380' )
40     {
41         advance_charges(0);
42     }
43 }
44
45 close(D);
46
47 extract_options_benefits(1);
48 extract_buschoice_savings(1);
49 item_call_record(1);
50 nonitem_call_summary(1);
51 advance_charges(1);
52
53 sub extract_file_header
54 {
55     my ($date,$time) = @fields[3,4];
56
57     print <<EOF;
58     <header>
59     <Title>Phone Report for:$ARGV[0]</title>
60     <body bgcolor=#000000 text=#ffffff>
61     <font size=+2><b>Processing Data file $fields[0]
62     (created $date, $time)</font></b><br>\n
63 EOF
64 }
65
66 sub extract_customer_record
67 {
68     my ($accno,$serial,$type,$date,$number)
69         = @fields[1,2,3,4,5];
70
71     print <<EOF
72 <font size=+2><b>Customer no: $accno, Report No: $serial,
73 Report Date: $date, Base Number: $number</font></b><br>
74 EOF
75 }
76
```

```perl
77  sub extract_options_benefits
78  {
79      my ($dosummary) = @_;
80      my ($name,$gdisc,$optch,$ndisc) = @fields[0,1,2,3,4];
81
82      if ($dosummary eq 1)
83      {
84          print <<EOF
85  <p><font size=+2><b>Options Benefits</b></font><br>
86  <table border=1><tr><td>Options Benefits</b><td><b>Gr. Disc.</b>
87  <td><b>Charge</b><td><b>Net Disc.</b>
88  EOF
89      ;
90          foreach $keyname (keys(%obdisc))
91          {
92              printf("<tr><td>%s<td>%10.2f<td>%10.2f<td>%10.2f\n",
93                  $keyname,$obdisc{$keyname},
94                  $oboptch{$keyname},$obndisc{$keyname});
95          }
96          print "</table>";
97      }
98      else
99      {
100         $obdisc{$name}=$gdisc;
101         $oboptch{$name}=$optch;
102         $obndisc{$name}=$ndisc;
103     }
104
105 }
106
107 sub extract_buschoice_savings
108 {
109     my ($dosummary) = @_;
110     my ($cat,$type,$infono,$gross,$disc,$totdisc,$dfee)
111         = @fields[0,1,2,3,4,5,6];
112
113     if ($dosummary eq 1)
114     {
115         print <<EOF
116 <p><font size=+2><b>Business Choice Savings</font></b><br>
117 <table border=1><tr><td><b>Call Type</b>
118 <td><b>Gross</b><td><b>%</b></td><td><b>Disc</b><td><b>Fee
119 EOF
120     ;
```

```
121        foreach $keyname (keys(%bscat))
122        {
123            printf("<tr><td>%s<td>%4.2f<td>%4.2f<td>%4.2f<td>%4.2f\n",
124                $bscat{$keyname},$bsgross{$keyname},$bsdisc{$keyname},
125                $bstotdisc{$keyname},$bsdfee{$keyname});
126        }
127        print "</table>\n";
128    }
129    else
130    {
131        $bscat{$infono}=$cat;
132        $bsgross{$infono}=$gross;
133        $bsdisc{$infono}=$disc;
134        $bstotdisc{$infono}=$totdisc;
135        $bsdfee{$infono}=$dfee;
136    }
137 }
138
139 sub item_call_record
140 {
141    my ($dosummary) = @_;
142    my ($natnum,$line,$infono,$date,$time,$dest,$desc,$cost)
143                    = @fields[0,1,2,3,5,6,7,8];
144    my $previous="";
145
146    if ($dosummary eq 1)
147    {
148        print <<EOF
149 <p><font size=+2><b>Itemised Calls Summary</b></font><br>
150 <Table border=1>\n<tr><td><b>Line</b><td><b>Destination</b>
151 <td><b>Dur</b><td><b>Cost</b>
152 EOF
153        ;
154        foreach $keyname (sort keys(%ldest))
155        {
156            if ($previous eq $lline{$keyname})
157            {
158                printf("<tr><td> <td>$ldest{$keyname}<td>
159                    $ltime{$keyname}<td>%10.2f\n",
160                    $lcost{$keyname});
161            }
162            else
163            {
```

```
164              print "</table>\n";
165              print <<EOF
166     <Table border=1>
167     <tr><td><b>Line</b>
168     <td><b>Destination</b>
169     <td><b>Dur</b>
170     <td><b>Cost</b>
171     EOF
172         ;
173              printf("<tr><td><b>$lline{$keyname}</b><td>$ldest{$keyname}
174                      <td>$ltime{$keyname}<td>%10.2f\n",
175                  $lcost{$keyname});
176           }
177           $previous=$lline{$keyname};
178         }
179
180     print "</table>\n";
181
182     print "<p><font size=+2><b>Itemised Calls Line Summary",
183          "</b></font><br>\n";
184     print "<table border=1\n<tr><td>Line<td>Dur<Td>Cost";
185     foreach $keyname (sort keys(%lltime))
186     {
187          printf("<tr><td>$keyname<td>$lltime{$keyname}
188                  <td>%10.2f\n",$llcost{$keyname});
189     }
190     print "</table>\n";
191     }
192     else
193     {
194     $destnum=substr($dest,11,20);
195     $destnum =~ s/[^0-9]//g;
196     ($refnum,) = split /\//,$line;
197     $refnum =~ s/[^0-9]//g;
198     if (length($refnum) < 6)
199     {
200          $refnum=substr($natnum,5,20);
201     }
202     $ref=$refnum . $destnum;
203     $lline{$ref}=$refnum;
204     $ldest{$ref}=$destnum;
205     $ltime{$ref}=&addtime(2,$ltime{$ref},$time);
206       $lcost{$ref}=$lcost{$ref}+$cost;
```

```perl
207
208            $lltime{$refnum}=&addtime(2,$lltime{$refnum},$time);
209            $llcost{$refnum}=$llcost{$refnum}+$cost;
210        }
211 }
212
213 sub nonitem_call_summary
214 {
215     my ($dosummary) = @_;
216     my ($natnum,$line,$infono,$ncalls,$totcost,$totdur)
217         = @fields[0,1,4,5,6,7];
218
219     if ($dosummary eq 1)
220     {
221         print "<p><font size=+2><b>Non-Itemised Calls Summary",
222             "</b></font>\n";
223         printf("<table border=1><tr><td>%s<td>%s<td>%s<td>%s\n",
224             "Line","Calls","Dur","Cost");
225         foreach $keyname (sort keys(%lnline))
226         {
227             printf("<tr><td>%s<td>%d<td>%s<td>%10.2f\n",
228                 $lnline{$keyname},$lncalls{$keyname},
229                 $lntime{$keyname},$lncost{$keyname});
230         }
231         print "</table>\n";
232     }
233     else
234     {
235         $ref=$natnum;
236         $lnline{$ref}=$natnum;
237         $lncalls{$ref}=$lncalls{$ref}+$ncalls;
238         $lntime{$ref}=&addtime(2,$lntime{$ref},$totdur);
239         $lncost{$ref}=$lncost{$ref}+$totcost;
240     }
241 }
242
243 sub advance_charges
244 {
245     my ($dosummary) = @_;
246     my ($desc,$qty,$qrate,$cost) = @fields[0,1,2,3];
247     my ($i,$localref) = 0,0;
248
249     if ($dosummary eq 1)
```

```
250        {
251            print "<p><font size=+2><b>Advanced Charges</b></font>\n";
252            printf("<table border=1><tr><td>%s<td>%s<td>%s<td>%s\n",
253                    "Description","Qty","Rate","Cost");
254            for($i=1;$i<=$localref;$i++)
255            {
256                printf("<tr><td>%s<td>%d<td>%10.2f<td>%10.2f\n",
257                        $ldesc[$i],$lqty[$i],$lrate[$i],$lacost[$i]);
258            }
259            print "</table>\n";
260        }
261    else
262        {
263            $localref++;
264            $loc=index($desc,"  ");
265            if ( $loc > 0 )
266            {
267                $realdesc=substr($desc,0,$loc);
268            }
269            else
270            {
271                $realdesc=$desc;
272            }
273            $ldesc[$localref]=$realdesc;
274            $lqty[$localref]=$qty;
275            $lrate[$localref]=$qrate;
276            $lacost[$localref]=$cost;
277        }
278 }
279
280 sub addtime
281 {
282    my ($n,$a,$b) = @_;
283    my ($ahour,$amin,$asec);
284    my ($bhour,$bmin,$bsec);
285    my ($chour,$cmin,$csec);
286    my ($retval);
287
288    if ($n eq 3)
289    {
290        if (length($a) eq 0)
291        {
292            $a="00:00";
293        }
```

```
294         ($ahour,$amin,$asec) = split /:/,$a;
295         ($bhour,$bmin,$bsec) = split /:/,$b;
296     }
297     else
298     {
299         if (length($a) eq 0)
300         {
301             $a="00:00";
302         }
303         ($amin,$asec) = split /:/,$a;
304         ($bmin,$bsec) = split /:/,$b;
305     }
306
307     if (($asec+$bsec)>59)
308     {
309         $csec = ($asec + $bsec) % 60;
310         $cmin = int((($asec +$bsec)/60));
311     }
312     else
313     {
314         $csec = $asec + $bsec;
315     }
316     if ($n eq 3)
317     {
318         if (($amin+$bmin+$cmin)>59)
319         {
320             $Dmin = ($amin+$bmin+$cmin) % 60;
321             $chour = int(($amin+$bmin+$cmin)/60);
322             $cmin = $Dmin;
323         }
324         else
325         {
326             $cmin = $amin +$bmin;
327         }
328     }
329     else
330     {
331         $chour=0;
332         $cmin = $amin +$bmin;
333     }
334
335     if ($n eq 3)
336     {
```

```
337        $chour = $chour + $ahour + $bhour;
338        $retval=$chour . ":" . $cmin . ":" . $csec;
339    }
340    else
341    {
342        $retval=$cmin . ":" . $csec;
343    }
344    return $retval;
345
346 }
```

ANNOTATIONS

The script follows the same basic principles of the other scripts in this chapter; we open the source file, read in individual lines, and process them. The difference that we have to handle is that we must first examine the initial field from the source file to discover what type of information is recorded in the remainder of the fields.

In this script, we extract 7 different field types; the full phone log specification contains 24 different types. Each line is read in, the record type extracted, and a corresponding function executed to extract the information from the rest of the fields. Because we need to summarize some of the information, we use an argument as a switch to tell the function whether to calculate the summary information or whether to print out the summary information. Because the different record types could be distributed throughout the file, we need to ensure that the summary information is output only when the entire source file has been processed.

```
1  #!/usr/local/bin/perl5
2
3  open(D,"<" . $ARGV [0]) || die "Couldn't open source file, $!\n";
4
5  while(<D>)
6  {
7      chomp;
8      ($codetype, @fields) = split /,/;
9
```

Lines 1 to 9 open the source file and start the **while** loop that will enable us to step through each line of the source file, stripping off the end-of-line character(s) and then extracting the fields. Note that we don't check for the number of arguments to the script directly because we expect only one argument, and that argument is a file, so we can therefore rely on the open test on line 3. If an argument isn't supplied, or the filename doesn't exist, the user will still get warned.

On line 8, we extract the individual fields of the line. Commas separate the fields, and we use **split** to return a list of the field contents. We place the first field, which is the record type, into the **$codetype** variable, and the rest into the **@fields** array.

```
10      $realcode = substr($codetype,0,3);

11

12      die "Not a valid code $realcode\n"
13        unless ($realcode =~ /[0-9][0-9][0-9]/);

14
```

Just to make sure we have actually extracted a code from the first field, we take the first three characters and place them into a new variable using the **substr** function. Then lines 12 and 13 check that the extracted string is made up of three digits. We don't have to worry about what the digits are at this stage, since we're only attempting to extract information from the codes that we recognize. If we don't recognize a code in the next few lines, then the line will just be ignored.

```
15      if ( $realcode eq '100' )
16      {
17          extract_file_header;
18      }
```

Lines 15 through 18 contain the first of the code extraction functions that we call. Code 100 matches the file header and always comes first and only once in the data file. Once found, we call the corresponding function to report the information that is contained within a single record.

```
19      elsif ( $realcode eq '200' )
20      {
21          extract_customer_record;
22      }
```

Using **elsif** ensures that we only execute one of the matches we are looking for. If a match is found, then all the other **elsif** statements are ignored. Unfortunately, there is no switch or case function in Perl, so in this example we use **elsif** to test for a number of different possibilities on a single variable.

Code 200 is the customer record. The information is contained within a single record, so we can use a straight function call.

```
23      elsif ( $realcode eq '220' )
24      {
25          extract_options_benefits(0);
26      }
```

As part of the phone package, you get a number of optional benefits (cheaper prices for long distance calls and so on), which are stored in records with a code of 220. There may be multiple lines, so we call the **extract_options_benefits** function with an argument of zero that tells the function to process the record but not output the information.

```
27        elsif ( $realcode eq '327' )
28        {
29            extract_buschoice_savings(0);
30        }
31        elsif ( $realcode eq '312' )
32        {
33            item_call_record(0);
34        }
35        elsif ( $realcode eq '322' )
36        {
37            nonitem_call_summary(0);
38        }
39        elsif ( $realcode eq '380' )
40        {
41            advance_charges(0);
42        }
43    }
44
45    close(D);
46
```

Lines 27 to 42 repeat the same process as lines 23 to 26, requesting each function to process a different record type, calculating the summary without printing it out. The **while** loop ends on line 43, and we close the source file on line 45.

```
47    extract_options_benefits(1);
48    extract_buschoice_savings(1);
49    item_call_record(1);
50    nonitem_call_summary(1);
51    advance_charges(1);
52
```

Lines 47 to 51 call the functions we used earlier to process the record information, this time specifying an argument of **1**, which tells the functions to output the information in summary format.

As far as the main execution of the script is concerned, we stop here. The remainder of the script is given over to the individual functions that perform the processing on the source file records.

```
53    sub extract_file_header
54    {
55        my ($date,$time) = @fields[3,4];
56
```

```
57        print <<EOF;
58        <header>
59        <Title>Phone Report for:$ARGV[0]</title>
60        <body bgcolor=#000000 text=#ffffff>
61        <font size=+2><b>Processing Data file $fields[0]
62        (created $date, $time)</font></b><br>\n
63   EOF
64   }
65
```

Lines 53 to 64 are for the **extract_file_header** function. The only useful information contained in this record is the date and time that the data export was conducted. If we look at a sample record from the source file, you can see the individual fields:

`100,DK00625D,07.0,*** CALLBASE EXTRACT FILE ***,19980407,22:59:34,ST`

The fields we are interested in are numbers 4 and 5, and we use subscript notation to extract those fields from the field list array into the **$date** and **$time** variables. Although we don't strictly need to use these variables, since we could just print the field contents directly, it helps to make the function clearer to the casual reader. Lines 57 to 63 are given over to a here document that outputs in HTML format the header information for the entire document.

```
66   sub extract_customer_record
67   {
68        my ($accno,$serial,$type,$date,$number)
69            = @fields[1,2,3,4,5];
70
71        print <<EOF;
72   <font size=+2><b>Customer no: $accno, Report No: $serial,
73   Report Date: $date, Base Number: $number</font></b><br>
74   EOF
75   }
76
```

Lines 66 to 75 extract the customer information, including the account number, the serial number for the data extract, and the date the report was generated. As before, we extract the information into local fields for clarity, then print out the results. This is not a summary function, so we don't have to account for calculating or reporting on summary data.

```
77   sub extract_options_benefits
78   {
79        my ($dosummary) = @_;
80        my ($name,$gdisc,$optch,$ndisc) = @fields[0,1,2,3];
81
```

```
82        if ($dosummary eq 1)
83        {
84            print <<EOF
85  <p><font size=+2><b>Options Benefits</b></font><br>
86  <table border=1><tr><td>Options Benefits</b><td><b>Gr. Disc.</b>
87  <td><b>Charge</b><td><b>Net Disc.</b>
88  EOF
89        ;
90            foreach $keyname (keys(%obdisc))
91            {
92                printf("<tr><td>%s<td>%10.2f<td>%10.2f<td>%10.2f\n",
93                    $keyname,$obdisc{$keyname},
94                    $oboptch{$keyname},$obndisc{$keyname});
95            }
96            print "</table>";
97        }
```

The **extract_options_benefits** function is the first of our summary-based functions. The only argument to these functions is either a zero, which specifies that the function should add the data to the existing summary information, or a 1, which indicates it should report the summary data.

The information in the Option Benefit record is stored in fields 1 to 4 and represents the benefit name, the discount amount, the charge for the option, and the final discount amount. We extract these details from the fields' array into some local variables on line 80.

Line 82 contains the test to find out whether the function should be printing the summary information, with lines 83 to 97 forming the code that does print out the summary details. Note that I've tested for a specific value of the argument passed to us, rather than testing if the function was called with a true or false value. In this example, there is no reason why a simple true/false wouldn't work, but in other scripts we'll look at alternative options within a single function that might require four or five different options.

This function is fairly straightforward: we create a new HTML table and output the summary records we created that were stored in hashes by going through each key of the first hash. The HTML table is closed on line 96.

```
98        else
99        {
100           $obdisc{$name}=$gdisc;
101           $oboptch{$name}=$optch;
102           $obndisc{$name}=$ndisc;
103       }
104
105   }
106
```

Lines 98 to 105 collate the information from the source fields into hashed arrays, using the option name as the key value.

```perl
107  sub extract_buschoice_savings
108  {
109      my ($dosummary) = @_;
110      my ($cat,$type,$infono,$gross,$disc,$totdisc,$dfee)
111          = @fields[0,1,2,3,4,5,6];
112
113      if ($dosummary eq 1)
114      {
115          print <<EOF
116  <p><font size=+2><b>Business Choice Savings</font></b><br>
117  <table border=1><tr><td><b>Call Type</b>
118  <td><b>Gross</b><td><b>%</b><td><b>Disc</b><td><b>Fee
119  EOF
120          ;
121          foreach $keyname (keys(%bscat))
122          {
123              printf("<tr><td>%s<td>%4.2f<td>%4.2f<td>%4.2f<td>%4.2f\n",
124                  $bscat{$keyname},$bsgross{$keyname},$bsdisc{$keyname},
125                  $bstotdisc{$keyname},$bsdfee{$keyname});
126          }
127          print "</table>\n";
128      }
129      else
130      {
131          $bscat{$infono}=$cat;
132          $bsgross{$infono}=$gross;
133          $bsdisc{$infono}=$disc;
134          $bstotdisc{$infono}=$totdisc;
135          $bsdfee{$infono}=$dfee;
136      }
137  }
138
```

Line 107 is the start of **extract_buschoice_savings**. Like the previous function, we first extract the individual fields into local variables. The rest of the function is split into two parts: the summary information is output on lines 113 to 128, and the information is collated on lines 130 to 137.

```perl
139  sub item_call_record
140  {
141      my ($dosummary) = @_;
142      my ($natnum,$line,$infono,$date,$time,$dest,$desc,$cost)
143                      = @fields[0,1,2,3,5,6,7,8];
144      my $previous="";
145
```

The **item_call_record** function starts on line 139. It collates individual phone calls against the phone number they were dialed from and the number that the call was made to. The fields are extracted on line 142. The fields are, in sequence, the phone number the call was made from (**$natnum**); the line of that number (**$line**); a user-set "info" reference (**$infono**); the date of the call (**$date**); the duration of the call (**$time**); the town name and phone number of the destination (**$dest**); a description of the call type, such as local or long distance (**$desc**); and the call's cost (**$cost**). Some of the fields in the full record are ignored; we use the subscript notation to extract the ones we want.

When reporting the phone numbers that calls were made from, we will have a large number of duplications because each source number will be printed for each destination number that was dialed. To get around this, we will use the **$previous** variable to store the last source number printed. By comparing this with the number we are about to print, we will be able to ignore printing the number for each line except the first. We initialize the variable to nothing here to avoid uninitalized variables triggering Perl's warning mechanism.

```
146     if ($dosummary eq 1)
147     {
148         print <<EOF
149 <p><font size=+2><b>Itemised Calls Summary</b></font><br>
150 <Table border=1>\n<tr><td><b>Line</b><td><b>Destination</b>
151 <td><b>Dur</b><td><b>Cost</b>
152 EOF
153     ;
154         foreach $keyname (sort keys(%ldest))
155         {
156             if ($previous eq $lline{$keyname})
157             {
158                 printf("<tr><td> <td>$ldest{$keyname}<td>
159                     $ltime{$keyname}<td>%10.2f\n",
160                     $lcost{$keyname});
161             }
162             else
163             {
164                 print "</table>\n";
165                 print <<EOF
166 <Table border=1>
167 <tr><td><b>Line</b>
168 <td><b>Destination</b>
169 <td><b>Dur</b>
170 <td><b>Cost</b>
171 EOF
172         ;
173                 printf("<tr><td><b>$lline{$keyname}</b><td>$ldest{$keyname}
174                     <td>$ltime{$keyname}<td>%10.2f\n",
```

```
175                           $lcost{$keyname});
176                   }
177               $previous=$lline{$keyname};
178           }
179
180       print "</table>\n";
181
```

Line 146 is the test for printing summary information. Line 148 outputs a suitable HTML header, and then line 154 starts the loop that will work through each entry in the destination number array, printing out the summary results. Line 156 is where we test the current source phone line against the previous source phone line, ending the previous table and starting a new one if the phone lines are different on line 162.

The details are printed out in lines 158 to 160, if the lines are identical. Note that we don't print out the source phone line. Lines 173 to 175 output the summary information for a destination record if this is the first time we have encountered the current source phone line. Line 180 ends this table.

```
182       print "<p><font size=+2><b>Itemised Calls Line Summary",
183               "</b></font><br>\n";
184       print "<table border=1>\n<tr><td>Line<td>Dur<Td>Cost";
185       foreach $keyname (sort keys(%lltime))
186       {
187           printf("<tr><td>$keyname<td>$lltime{$keyname}
188                   <td>%10.2f\n",$llcost{$keyname});
189       }
190       print "</table>\n";
191   }
```

Lines 182 to 191 output the table relating to summary information for all calls from a source line, rather than on a destination-by-destination basis.

```
192   else
193   {
194       $destnum=substr($dest,11,20);
195       $destnum =~ s/[^0-9]//g;
196       ($refnum,) = split /\//,$line;
197       $refnum =~ s/[^0-9]//g;
198       if (length($refnum) < 6)
199       {
200           $refnum=substr($natnum,5,20);
201       }
202       $ref=$refnum . $destnum;
203       $lline{$ref}=$refnum;
204       $ldest{$ref}=$destnum;
205       $ltime{$ref}=&addtime(2,$ltime{$ref},$time);
```

```
206          $lcost{$ref}=$lcost{$ref}+$cost;
207
208          $lltime{$refnum}=&addtime(2,$lltime{$refnum},$time);
209          $llcost{$refnum}=$llcost{$refnum}+$cost;
210      }
211  }
212
```

Line 192 is the start of the summary calculation section of this function. Information about the destination number is stored in a fixed-length field of 20 characters, with the destination phone number being composed of characters 11 to 20. We extract those characters, using **substr** on line 194, into a new variable, and then we ensure that the resulting number is composed only of digits. The regular expression used will delete anything except digits from the variable.

Confusingly, the source line number can be specified in two places. The first place is the first field, which specifies the national phone number, and the other place is the second field (the line number), which contains either the line number or the local number followed by the line number. For example, we may see a record like this:

```
312,01234567890,567890/0001,...
```

Or we may get one like this:

```
312,01234567890,/0001,...
```

Since we want only the local number as a key, the easiest way to extract it is first to use the line field. Line 196 uses **split** to return the first portion of the line reference. Note that although **split** is expected to return more than one element, we take only one. By not specifying any further variables, the rest of the information that may be returned by the **split** function is ignored.

However, if the line field doesn't specify the phone number (which is tested on line 198), then line 200 sets the local number by extracting the last 20 digits from the sixth character of the national phone number.

We create a reference number that will be used as the key on line 202. It is composed of the local phone number we extracted and the destination phone number. Lines 203 to 206 then update the hash arrays with the information. Line 205 is the total duration of all the calls made from the source number to the destination number, and we use a special function (see below) to add the two times together. Line 206 is the sum of the cost of the calls. Here we add the existing value to the new value, placing the result back into the corresponding element of the hash array. A simpler way to write line 206 would be

```
$lcost{$ref} += $cost;
```

Sometimes splitting it out can help clarity. If we had switched warnings on, however, this would have been reported as a problem. The use of **+=** to increment variables lets Perl know that we could be dealing with an uninitialized value.

Lines 208 and 209 store the summary information (duration and cost) for all calls made from a specific source line. The function ends on line 211.

```
213 sub nonitem_call_summary
214 {
215     my ($dosummary) = @_;
216     my ($natnum,$line,$infono,$ncalls,$totcost,$totdur)
217         = @fields[0,1,4,5,6,7];
218
219     if ($dosummary eq 1)
220     {
221         print "<p><font size=+2><b>Non-Itemised Calls Summary",
222                 "</b></font>\n";
223         printf("<table border=1><tr><td>%s<td>%s<td>%s<td>%s\n",
224                 "Line","Calls","Dur","Cost");
225         foreach $keyname (sort keys(%lnline))
226         {
227             printf("<tr><td>%s<td>%d<td>%s<td>%10.2f\n",
228                 $lnline{$keyname},$lncalls{$keyname},
229                 $lntime{$keyname},$lncost{$keyname});
230         }
231         print "</table>\n";
232     }
233     else
234     {
235         $ref=$natnum;
236         $lnline{$ref}=$natnum;
237         $lncalls{$ref}=$lncalls{$ref}+$ncalls;
238         $lntime{$ref}=&addtime(2,$lntime{$ref},$totdur);
239         $lncost{$ref}=$lncost{$ref}+$totcost;
240     }
241 }
242
```

Lines 213 to 241 are the **nonitem_call_summary** function. This function records summary information for the nonitemized calls (those calls that fall below a certain cost limit are not reported individually). Lines 235 to 239 set the summary information into a number of hashed arrays. Note that this time we are interested only in source phone lines, so we use the national phone number as the key.

```
243 sub advance_charges
244 {
245     my ($dosummary) = @_;
246     my ($desc,$qty,$qrate,$cost) = @fields[0,1,2,3];
247     my ($i,$localref) = 0,0;
248
```

```
249      if ($dosummary eq 1)
250      {
251          print "<p><font size=+2><b>Advanced Charges</b></font>\n";
252          printf("<table border=1><tr><td>%s<td>%s<td>%s<td>%s\n",
253                 "Description","Qty","Rate","Cost");
254          for($i=1;$i<=$localref;$i++)
255          {
256              printf("<tr><td>%s<td>%d<td>%10.2f<td>%10.2f\n",
257                     $ldesc[$i],$lqty[$i],$lrate[$i],$lacost[$i]);
258          }
259          print "</table>\n";
260      }
261      else
262      {
263          $localref++;
264          $loc=index($desc,"  ");
265          if ( $loc > 0 )
266          {
267              $realdesc=substr($desc,0,$loc);
268          }
269          else
270          {
271              $realdesc=$desc;
272          }
273          $ldesc[$localref]=$realdesc;
274          $lqty[$localref]=$qty;
275          $lrate[$localref]=$qrate;
276          $lacost[$localref]=$cost;
277      }
278 }
279
```

The **advance_charges** function summarizes the advance charges made on the phone bill. The basic format is familiar: the function is in two sections, with lines 249 to 260 printing the summarized data. However, unlike before, we place the information into a standard array rather than a hash, because there is no unique key we can use to separate the information. Lines 261 to 277 collate the summary information. Line 263 is the counter used to store the array index. The advance charges lines look like this:

```
380,Exchange line + linebox          ,+0000001,000035.840,+0000000035.840
380,Exchange line + linebox          ,+0000001,000035.840,+0000000035.840
380,Exchange line + linebox          ,+0000001,000035.840,+0000000035.840
380,Auxiliary line + master socket   ,+0000001,000035.840,+0000000035.840
```

On line 264 we use the **index** function to discover where the description ends. The **index** function is really the reverse of the **substr** function. Instead of returning the characters at a specific location within a string, the **index** function returns the location within a string where a specified string of characters begins.

Assuming the **index** function found the specified string, which in our case is a double space, then we use **substr** to extract that many characters, starting from the beginning of the description. If **index** fails to find the double space, we just take the entire string.

PROGRAMMER'S NOTE *The reasons for the function failing to find the string may not be immediately clear, but the extra spaces can sometimes confuse an HTML table within some browsers.*

We then add the information to the arrays in lines 273 to 276. We could have used **push** to place these variables on to the array, and it's a case of personal preference in this instance for me to use specific values to the array.

```
280  sub addtime
281  {
282      my ($n,$a,$b) = @_;
283      my ($ahour,$amin,$asec);
284      my ($bhour,$bmin,$bsec);
285      my ($chour,$cmin,$csec);
286      my ($retval);
287
288      if ($n eq 3)
289      {
290          if (length($a) eq 0)
291          {
292              $a="00:00";
293          }
294          ($ahour,$amin,$asec) = split /:/,$a;
295          ($bhour,$bmin,$bsec) = split /:/,$b;
296      }
297      else
298      {
299          if (length($a) eq 0)
300          {
301              $a="00:00";
302          }
303          ($amin,$asec) = split /:/,$a;
304          ($bmin,$bsec) = split /:/,$b;
305      }
306
307      if (($asec+$bsec)>59)
```

```
308        {
309            $csec = ($asec + $bsec) % 60;
310            $cmin = int((($asec +$bsec)/60));
311        }
312        else
313        {
314            $csec = $asec + $bsec;
315        }
```

Lines 280 to 346 are responsible for the **addtime** function. This adds together two times, specified by the first and second arguments. It will add two time specifications, either two elements (minutes and seconds) or three elements (hours, minutes, and seconds), depending on the value of the final argument. The reason for the difference should be clear: if we are adding two element numbers together, then the first element can increase by any size. Additions to the second element must be reflected in the first element if the value is greater than 60. For example:

00:10 + 0:10 = 0:20

but

0:40 + 0:40 = 1:20

For three-element numbers, the first can increase to any value, but the second and third elements have bearings on the value of the first and second elements. For example:

0:00:10 + 0:00:10 = 0:20

0:00:40 + 0:00:40 = 1:20

0:44:44 + 0:44:44 = 1:29:28

Lines 283 to 286 set the local variable we will use. The *a* series are the individual components of the first argument; the *b* series are the individual components of the second argument; and the *c* series are the results.

Lines 288 to 296 extract information from the arguments into the component parts if we are using times with three elements (hours, minutes, seconds). Lines 290 to 293 account for a blank value for the first argument (for example the first time the hash element has been created, if you refer back to the earlier), and lines 294 and 295 use **split** to extract the elements into the component variables.

One line 297 we make the assumption that anything other than three elements is two elements, and extract the corresponding elements in lines 303 and 304.

Lines 307 to 315 add the seconds up. If the value of the **$asec+$bsec** is greater than 59 seconds, then lines 309 and 310 calculate the minutes and seconds equivalent. Line 309 uses the modulus operand, %, to return the remainder from a standard divide calculation. For example, dividing 69 by 60 would give us a floating point value of 1.15. The value of 69 modulus 60 is 9, or the remainder of the calculation after the whole numbers have been removed.

Line 310 calculates the integer value of the same calculation. We use the **int** function to return the integer-only value of the sum of the two seconds divided by 60.

Lines 313 to 315 just add the seconds together if the sum is smaller than 60.

```
316     if ($n eq 3)
317     {
318         if (($amin+$bmin+$cmin)>59)
319         {
320             $Dmin = ($amin+$bmin+$cmin) % 60;
321             $chour = int(($amin+$bmin+$cmin)/60);
322             $cmin = $Dmin;
323         }
324         else
325         {
326             $cmin += $amin +$bmin;
327         }
328     }
329     else
330     {
331         $chour=0;
332         $cmin += $amin +$bmin;
333     }
334
```

Lines 316 to 334 add up the minutes. First we check if we are adding up three element times or only two. If it's three, then lines 318 to 323 add up the minutes in a similar fashion to the seconds. The difference here is that we also have to take into account any existing value of minutes that may have come from the result of the seconds calculation we did earlier. Because we have to use the **$cmin** value a number of times, we put the resulting minutes into **$dmin** and then put this value into **$cmin** once the calculations have been completed.

If we are doing only two-digit calculations, then lines 331 and 332 set the number of minutes to the total of the two values.

```
335     if ($n eq 3)
336     {
337         $chour = $chour + $ahour + $bhour;
338         $retval=$chour . ":" . $cmin . ":" . $csec;
339     }
340     else
341     {
342         $retval=$cmin . ":" . $csec;
343     }
```

Lines 335 to 337 calculate the total number of hours, based on the two arguments and any value calculated by the earlier minute and second calculations. Then line 338, for three elements, and line 342, for two elements, set the time string by concatenating the values into a standard time string separated by colons.

```
344        return $retval;
345
346  }
```

Line 344 then returns the resultant string to the calling function; the function, and the entire script, ends on line 346.

Note that throughout this last function we respecified the calculations each time, instead of putting the result of the basic calculation into a temporary variable. This method is slightly less efficient, but it saves us from creating extra variables and makes it clear to the reader of the script what we are doing.

To be honest, the entire function seems a little cumbersome for what we are trying to achieve. Even accounting for the difference in how the times are displayed, and requested back, the function is overly complicated. A simpler solution may be to calculate the values of the times specified in seconds, add the two numbers together as an integer, and then convert the new time back to a colon-separated format. For example, the following code adds the two numbers together as an integer:

```
for ($a, $b)
{
    next unless defined ($_) && length ($_);
    my $factor = 1;
    for (reverse split /:/)
    {
        $time += $_ * $factor;
        $factor *= 60;
    }
}
```

By extracting the individual elements from the time string, in reverse order, and then multiplying them by the number of seconds in each element (that is, 60 in a minute, 3,600 in an hour), we arrive with a value of **$time** that equals the total number of seconds in both time strings.

```
my @return;
for (my $i = 0; $i < $n - 1; $i++)
{
    unshift @return, $time % 60;
    $time = int ($time / 60);
}
return join ':', $time, map {sprintf '%02d', $_} @return;
```

This script fragment performs the opposite calculation, by taking the full time in seconds, calculating the integer component of the time, and then setting the new time value as the remainder. Results are placed into the **@return** array. The final line joins the values back up with the colon separator. The **map** function performs the specified expression, in this example formatting the elements of the **@return** array using **sprintf**.

The output of the script, using the sample data file phone.txt, looks like the sample in Figure 3-1.

The script demonstrates four main points: the use of a delimited text file as a source for data; the use of fixed-length records within a delimited data file; writing dual-purpose functions that can be used within their own context to calculate and then report on information; and the extraction, conversion, and then recombination of information that forms the **addtime** function.

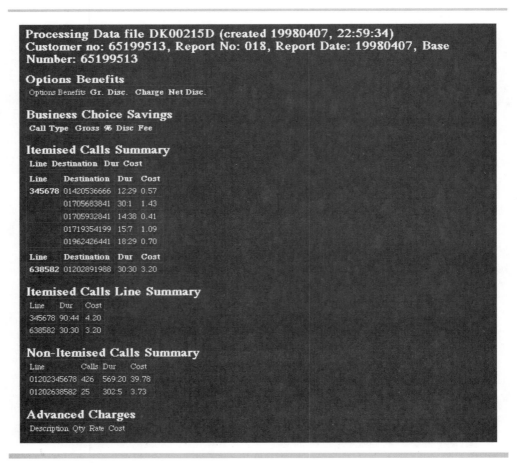

FIGURE 3-1.   Output from phone.pl using sample data

addtask.pl

Using Fixed-length Records to Store Data

There are two problems with the previous examples. First of all, updating the information requires us to create a new version of the database, either within a new file or within the Perl structure. The second problem is less clear, but it creates an equally unpleasant set of problems. Introducing information into the database that contains either the field separator or the record separator would cause significant problems.

To get around these problems, we need to structure the data in some way so that records can easily be updated within the file, so we can forget about field and record separators. The solution is to place the data into a structure whose format is defined outside of the data itself. Using fixed-field lengths, and therefore fixed-record sizes, addresses this problem.

If we have a simple database of words in a file, we could specify that each would be no longer than 20 characters. To store the list, we write out each word, padded to the 20-character length, and write the information, verbatim, out to the file. Each word is added to the file, without line breaks.

Extending this idea, imagine a record from a database where each field is of a fixed length; we know that when the information is written out to a file, the entire record will be the same length. Accessing the information is a case of reading in the number of bytes that make up the record, and then extracting the individual fields from that record. The fields can contain any characters we like, because we know the length of the field.

```perl
1   #!/usr/local/bin/perl5 -w
2
3   use strict;
4
5   my ($taskfile) = "tasks";
6   my ($taskformat) = "A22A40LL";
7   my ($refrnd,$matched);
8   my ($ref,$title,$reqdate,$compdate);
9   my ($sec,$min,$hour,$mday,$mon,$year,$wday,$yday,$isdst)
10      = localtime(time);
11
12  $year += 1900;
13  $mon += 1;
14
15  die "Usage: $0 title required-date\n" if (@ARGV<2);
16
17  srand $sec;
18  $refrnd = rand 32768;
19  $ref=sprintf "%d%02d%02d.%02d%02d%02d.%d",
20              $year,$mon,$mday,$hour,$min,$sec,$refrnd;
```

```
21
22   ($mday,$mon,$year) = split '/',$ARGV[-1];
23   $reqdate = ($year*10000)+($mon*100)+$mday;
24
25   open(D,">>$taskfile") || die "Couldn't open the task file, $!\n";
26   print D pack($taskformat,$ref,$ARGV[0],$reqdate,0);
27   close(D);
```

ANNOTATIONS

Although the entire script is 27 lines long, the bulk of the work is performed by line 26, which takes all the different elements from the command line and creates the corresponding entry into the data file.

```
1    #!/usr/local/bin/perl5 -w
2
3    use strict;
4
5    my ($taskfile) = "tasks";
6    my ($taskformat) = "A22A40LL";
7    my ($refrnd,$matched);
8    my ($ref,$title,$reqdate,$compdate);
9    my ($sec,$min,$hour,$mday,$mon,$year,$wday,$yday,$isdst)
10       = localtime(time);
```

On line 1, I specified Perl's **-w** switch, which will force any warnings about the code that are considered nonfatal to be reported before the script executes. Generally, this is best used when you are developing a script, but it induces an extra overhead once a script is complete. Personally, I leave warnings on permanently, unless the script is going to a production environment where the warnings would otherwise affect the output or response to the script's invocation.

In addition to switching warnings on, we specify on line 3 that Perl should be strict about its error checking. This line is called a *pragma*, short for a pragmatic, and it defines a practical consequence of how the rest of the script is executed. In layman's terms, by defining that strict error checking be enforced, Perl will fail if it spots something that it might otherwise have made a best guess at. This level of error checking forces a programmer to be more precise and exact about the code, so there is no doubt in Perl's "mind" about what the programmer is trying to achieve.

We have already seen on many occasions that Perl is capable of making some educated guesses of what the programmer was trying to achieve, without causing the script to fail, but this sloppy programming can lead to problems if Perl makes the wrong choice. What level you choose depends on what you are producing. If it is a simple, quick script, then it hardly seems necessary to place such restrictions on your code writing. At the other end of the scale, a large, multiple-programmer development effort would benefit from the checks.

One of the consequences of strict error checking is that variables must be defined before they are used, so lines 5 to 10 define all of the variables we will use in this script, setting default values if necessary. You can avoid having to define all the variables by specifying the **use vars** pragma in addition to the **use strict**, which allows you to specify variables without first declaring them.

Line 5 specifies the file where the list of tasks are composing will reside. Line 6 is the format of the packed data string that will be used with the **pack** function to generate a fixed-length record containing the information about the task. It is quite valid to separate the individual elements with spaces, although we've "packed" the string together here. You can see in Table 3-1 the format characters available for the **pack** function. The string passed to **pack** to act as a format is similar in style to that used by **printf**: each element is made up of a character followed by an optional number that specifies the number of repetitions. Line 6 specifies a 22-character space-padded string, followed by a 40-character space-padded string and then two unsigned long integers.

The current time is extracted on lines 9 and 10 by the **localtime** function. Because we have specified individual variables, the returned information is in the form of the individual elements that make up the time information. We'll be using this

Character	Description
@	Null fill to absolute position
a	An ASCII string, which will be null padded
A	An ASCII string, which will be space padded
b	A bit string, in ascending bit order
B	A bit string, in descending bit order
c	A signed character value
C	An unsigned character value
D	A double-precision float in the native format
F	A single-precision float in the native format
h	A hex string, with high nibble first
H	A hex string, with low nibble first
i	A signed integer value
I	An unsigned integer value
l	A signed long value
L	An unsigned long value
n	A long in "network" (big-endian) order
N	A short in "network" (big-endian) order
p	A pointer to a null-terminated string

TABLE 3-1.   Format Characters for the **pack** Function

Character	Description
P	A pointer to a structure (fixed-length string)
s	A signed short value
S	An unsigned short value
U	A uuencoded string
v	A long in "VAX" (little-endian) order
V	A short in "VAX" (little-endian) order
W	A BER-compressed integer
x	A null byte
X	Back up a byte

TABLE 3-1.   Format Characters for the **pack** Function (*continued*)

information to generate a unique code for each task added to the database. Remember that when storing information in a database, the key used to identify an individual record is as important as the data itself when it comes to updating the information.

```
11
12  $year += 1900;
13  $mon += 1;
14
```

One of the problems with the return values from **localtime** is that no account is made for real-world versions of the information. The year returned by **localtime** specifies the numbers of years since 1900, so to get a fully qualified year, we must add 1900 to the value returned.

Finally, the month returned by **localtime** is based on January being month zero, so we add 1 to make January be month 1, and December month 12.

```
15  die "Usage: $0 title required-date\n" if (@ARGV<2);
16
```

Line 15 checks that we have suitable arguments to the script. We expect two arguments, the title of the task and the date it's required. Note that we will have to specify the title within quotes if we want it to have more than one word in it, otherwise the shell (in either Unix or NT) will interpret each word as an argument.

```
17  srand $sec;
18  $refrnd = rand 32768;
19  $ref=sprintf "%d%02d%02d.%02d%02d%02d.%d",
20              $year,$mon,$mday,$hour,$min,$sec,$refrnd;
21
```

Lines 17 to 21 create a unique code to give the task a unique reference in the file. Although these lines seem like overkill for this example (in fact, they are overkill), they do demonstrate a way to produce a near perfect unique code. The code is formed from the current date, the current time, and a random number.

We seed the random number generator (give it a number to calculate from) on line 17, and we obtain a random number with a maximum value of 32,768 on line 18. We generate the reference string on lines 19 and 20 using the **sprintf** function to specify that numbers should be printed with leading zeros and with a width of two characters. For a multiuser system, you may also want to include the process ID, a machine or user name, or some other unique identifier that can be used to reference an instance of the script's invocation.

```
22   ($mday,$mon,$year) = split '/',$ARGV[-1];
23   $reqdate = ($year*10000)+($mon*100)+$mday;
24
```

Lines 22 and 23 first extract the date information from the command line and then format the date as a single number. On line 22 we make the assumption that the date string is in the format of day/month/year, with the separators being slashes. Note that we extract the last argument from the command line using a negative index to **@ARGV**. We also reuse the earlier variable used in the date functions. (Since we no longer need their values, it's safe to reuse them.)

Line 23 generates a number based on the date. The method used here generates a date in ISO format, where the year goes first. This is a sensible approach to the problem of storing dates, especially if you want to sort on a date. An ISO format date is in a perfect sequential format for a simple number sort. The format is

yyyymmdd

where y is the year, m is the month, and d is the day. We could have used **sprintf** to generate the string, but this function wouldn't give us a number but only a string matching the format. A string is more space intensive than an integer to store, so for space sake we use a number instead.

```
25   open(D,">>$taskfile") || die "Couldn't open the task file, $!\n";
26   print D pack($taskformat,$ref,$ARGV[0],$reqdate,0);
27   close(D);
```

Lines 25 to 27 update the data file. Line 25 opens the file for appending using the double redirect. Line 26 prints the results of the **pack** function to the file, and line 27 closes the file.

On line 26, **pack** returns a string packed using the format we specified earlier. The first field, the reference number, is put in the first 22 characters, with spaces used to pad out the string to the full 22 characters. The task title is put into 40 space-padded characters, and the required date and completed date are each put into the two packed long integers. The resulting string is the fixed-length record we will use to store the information.

This code is written using **print**, although we could have used **write** to perform the same operation. The result is a file that contains fixed-length records of information that we can later extract using the **unpack** function.

To use the script, specify the task title and the date the task should be completed by on the command line:

```
$ addtask.pl "Write database" 31/8/1998
```

listtask.pl

Reporting from Fixed-length Records

Before we take a look at how to update the information, we first need to be able to report on the information stored in the file. The **listtask.pl** script is largely the reverse of the previous script; we read in a fixed-length record from the data file, unpack it into its component parts, and then format the parts into a human-readable form.

There are some differences, though, with this script: we can list the tasks in a number of selected orders and ignore tasks that have a completed date. As with most database scripts, the tricks are performed using hashed arrays to store the information temporarily until we are ready to output the final result.

```
1   #!/usr/local/bin/perl5
2
3   use Getopt::Std;
4
5   my ($taskfile) = "tasks";
6   my ($taskformat) = "A22A40LL";
7   my (%lref,%ltitle,%lreqdate,%lcompdate);
8   my ($ref,$title,$reqdate,$compdate);
9   my ($mday,$mon,$year,$key);
10
11  getopts('drc');
12
13  open(D,"<$taskfile") || die "Couldn't open the task file, $!\n";
14
15  while(read(D,$_,70))
16  {
17      ($ref,$title,$reqdate,$compdate) = unpack($taskformat,$_);
18      $lref{$ref} = $title;
19      $lref{$ref} = $reqdate if ($opt_r);
20      $lref{$ref} = $compdate if ($opt_c);
21      $ltitle{$ref} = $title;
```

```
22      $lreqdate{$ref} = $reqdate;
23      $lcompdate{$ref} = $compdate;
24   }
25
26   close(D);
27
28   printf("%-40s  %-10s  %-10s\n","Title","Req. Date","Comp. Date");
29
30   foreach $key (sort_values(\%lref))
31   {
32      $lreqdate{$key} =~ m/(....)(..)(..)/;
33      $reqdate = "$3/$2/$1";
34
35      if ($lcompdate{$key}>0)
36      {
37          next if ($opt_d);
38          $lcompdate{$key} =~ m/(....)(..)(..)/;
39          $compdate = "$3/$2/$1";
40      }
41      else
42      {
43          $compdate="";
44      }
45      printf("%-40s  %10s  %10s\n",$ltitle{$key},$reqdate,$compdate);
46   }
47
48   sub sort_values
49   {
50      my $lref = shift;
51
52      if ($opt_r || $opt_c)
53      {
54          sort {$lref{$a} <=> $lref{$b}} keys %$lref;
55      }
56      else
57      {
58          sort {$lref{$a} cmp $lref{$b}} keys %$lref;
59      }
60   }
```

ANNOTATIONS

As in the **addtask.pl** script, the bulk of the real work is executed in very few lines; the rest of the script is devoted to identifying and using the options we supply on the command line, and sprucing up the raw format of the data into a human-readable format.

```perl
1   #!/usr/local/bin/perl5
2
3   use Getopt::Std;
4
```

I've left warnings and the **strict** pragma out of this script, as they are not really required for such a simple task. We use the standard **Getopt** module to extract command-line arguments. All are optional: **-d** turns off display of completed tasks, **-r** sorts by the required date, and **-c** sorts by the completed date.

```perl
5   my ($taskfile) = "tasks";
6   my ($taskformat) = "A22A40LL";
7   my (%lref,%ltitle,%lreqdate,%lcompdate);
8   my ($ref,$title,$reqdate,$compdate);
9   my ($mday,$mon,$year,$key);
10
```

Local variables are set in lines 5 to 9. Note that the same data file and pack format are set here.

```perl
11  getopts('drc');
12
```

We extract the options in line 11.

```perl
13  open(D,"<$taskfile") || die "Couldn't open the task file, $!\n";
14
```

On line 13, we attempt to open the task file for reading. Up to now, we haven't bothered checking for command-line arguments. There's no point to checking because the script can be run without specifying anything, although it's bad practice not to have some form of description available for the user to find out what the script does and how to use it.

```perl
15  while(read(D,$_,70))
16  {
17      ($ref,$title,$reqdate,$compdate) = unpack($taskformat,$_);
18      $lref{$ref} = $title;
19      $lref{$ref} = $reqdate if ($opt_r);
20      $lref{$ref} = $compdate if ($opt_c);
21      $ltitle{$ref} = $title;
```

```
22        $lreqdate{$ref} = $reqdate;
23        $lcompdate{$ref} = $compdate;
24    }
25
26   close(D);
27
```

Lines 15 to 24 read in the information from the data file. In line 15, we no longer use the default option to the **while** loop of extracting individual lines from the data file. Lines have no meaning here, since the data file contents will be made up of fixed-length records that may or may not contain new-line characters.

Because we are reading in fixed-length records, we use the **read** function to get 70 characters from the data file and place them in the default pattern space, **$_**. The **read** function from the **while** loop returns the number of characters read from the source file. Unless the file is corrupt, **read** will return a value of less than 70 once the end of file has been reached. For a safer loop, we might want to replace line 15 with

```
while (read(D,$_,70) == 70)
```

Or better still, replace line 15 with

```
while ($readbytes=read(D,$_,70))
```

and insert the following line before line 17:

```
unless ($readbytes == 70) die "Invalid record found, bad length";
```

This fact will act as our end-of-file test, which will eventually drop us out after line 24, the end of the loop. We then close the data file on line 26.

How do we know the record length is 70 characters? Well, we know that the format is 22 characters, 40 characters, and then two unsigned long integers. An unsigned long integer is 4 bytes long, so the arithmetic for calculating the size of the record is not that complex. However, an easier way to work out the length, especially for long record formats, is to use a line like this:

```
$reclen = length(pack($taskformat,));
```

This line sets the **$reclen** variable to the size of the pack format string. We could easily have defined this line within the script as a more portable way of specifying the record length.

Line 17 extracts the individual fields from the record using **unpack**. This function returns the list of fields extracted from the byte string (record) based on the pack format string.

Line 18 sets the default sort method to the title of the task. The **%lref** hash will contain a list of all the reference numbers (remember the date/time/random number?) as the key, and the field we want to sort on as the value. This is less messy than other methods, although not quite as efficient since we are creating additional hashes for data we use for nothing more than the sort keys. Lines 19 and 20 set the sort key to the required and the completed dates, based on the options on the command line. Lines 21 to 23 set the remainder of the hashes with the corresponding key value of the reference number to the value of each field.

```
28   printf("%-40s   %-10s   %-10s\n","Title","Req. Date","Comp. Date");
29
```

We print out some header information on line 28 using **printf** so that we can set the string width. We already know what size each element will be, since we are dealing with fixed-length records.

```
30   foreach $key (sort_values(\%lref))
31   {
32       $lreqdate{$key} =~ m/(....)(..)(..)/;
33       $reqdate = "$3/$2/$1";
34
```

We're now ready to print out the data. Line 30 sets up a **foreach** loop to go through each key of the reference hash we created. The **sort_values** function returns a list of keys based on the sorted values contained within the hash. Therefore, the loop will step through a sorted list of keys, where the sort is based on the value we inserted into the reference hash earlier.

Line 32 uses the regular expression **match** to return the individual elements extracted from a string version of the required completion date. Note that the value we extracted with **unpack** was an unsigned long integer. Perl has identified that we want to treat it as a string because of the match format. We could specify a more precise regular expression by specifying that we are looking for numbers, instead of any character, and by anchoring the entire string at either end. However, since we know that the information in the source file will be in the correct format we can get by with being a more simple match. The result is placed into an identifiable format on line 33.

```
35       if ($lcompdate{$key}>0)
36       {
37           next if ($opt_d);
38           $lcompdate{$key} =~ m/(....)(..)(..)/;
39           $compdate = "$3/$2/$1";
40       }
41       else
42       {
43           $compdate="";
44       }
```

We repeat the exercise as part of lines 35 to 44 on the completed date. However, one of the command-line options is to ignore the completed items from the list. On line 35, we check if the completed date is greater than zero, which indicates that the task has been marked as completed. If the user has opted to ignore completed items, then we skip the field on line 37. Skipping this field skips the entire record, and places us at the next key in the list within the loop started on line 30. Lines 38 and 39 repeat the match exercise on the completed date.

If the completed date is not greater than zero, we set the completed date string to be empty on line 43.

```
45      printf("%-40s  %10s  %10s\n",$ltitle{$key},$reqdate,$compdate);
46    }
47
```

Line 45 is where we print out the information for the current record. We use **printf**, as we did for the column headers, with an identical format to ensure consistency. Once the loop ends on line 46, the script is completed.

```
48  sub sort_values
49  {
50      my $lref = shift;
51
52      if ($opt_r || $opt_c)
53      {
54          sort {$lref{$a} <=> $lref{$b}} keys %$lref;
55      }
56      else
57      {
58          sort {$lref{$a} cmp $lref{$b}} keys %$lref;
59      }
60  }
```

The **sort_values** function that starts on line 48 returns a sorted list of keys for the hash specified in the argument list. However, the sort is based on the values within the hash, not the keys.

Line 52 checks if we are sorting by required or completed date. If we are, then the <=> operand in line 54 compares the two scalars as numbers. Remember, the required and completed dates are stored as numbers, not strings. Here, the use of numbers makes sorting dates incredibly easy and straightforward.

Line 58 sorts the values by using the **cmp** function, which is best used on strings because it returns the result of the comparison of the two ASCII strings.

Running the script without any options returns the following:

```
$ listtask.pl
Title                                   Req. Date   Comp. Date
Call Mark                               26/08/1998
E-mail Harry                             14/08/1998
Write accounting software               20/12/1998
```

By specifying the **-r** option, we get the output sorted by the required date:

```
$ listtask.pl -r
Title                                   Req. Date   Comp. Date
E-mail Harry                            14/08/1998
Call Mark                               26/08/1998
Write accounting software               20/12/1998
```

We'll look at the other two options once we've modified the database and marked some of the entries as completed.

This script is a good example of how to sort complex structures and field types easily. First of all, we naturalized the information by converting the machine-unfriendly dates into numbers than could be easily sorted by standard functions. Using this information in combination with a separate field devoted to the sorting process allowed us to sort all the records very quickly and easily using standard Perl functions, without us having to resort to any special code. The same methods can be used elsewhere when working with different types of data that you want to report on.

Preprocessing data into a format that can be easily compared, or sorted on, seems wasteful. However, as this sample shows, it can make certain operations significantly quicker and more straightforward.

modtask.pl

Modifying or Deleting Records from a Packed Database

When using a delimited text database the records are variable lengths. Within the scope of the delimiter, a field could be hundreds or even thousands of bytes long; the length is not fixed in any way. This presents a problem when updating information. We can't simply replace the old record with the new record within the file. If the new record was longer than the old one, we would overwrite the information of the next record, and if it was shorter we could end up with the remnants of the old record tagged on to the end.

The only reliable way of updating a text-delimited database is to read the information in, make a change, and then create a new file with the updated information in it. This is time consuming and wasteful of resources. Even if we read the file into memory before writing it back out, there is still a large overhead for the process, even on small files.

There are even less efficient methods. For example, you could mark the current record as deleted or old with a flag that forms part of the record. Modified versions are then appended to the end.

```perl
1  #!/usr/local/bin/perl5
2
3  use Fcntl;
4
5  my ($taskfile) = "tasks";
6  my ($taskformat) = "A22A40LL";
7  my ($ref,$title,$reqdate,$compdate);
8  my ($mday,$mon,$year,$compdate);
9  my ($lastseek) = 0;
```

```
10
11   die "Usage: modtask.pl title completed-date\n" if (@ARGV<2);
12
13   open(D,"+<$taskfile") || die "Couldn't open the task file, $!\n";
14
15   while(read(D,$_,70))
16   {
17       ($ref,$title,$reqdate,$compdate) = unpack($taskformat,$_);
18       last if (($title eq $ARGV[0]) && ($compdate eq 0));
19       $lastseek=tell(D);
20   }
21
22   if ($lastseek >= (-s $taskfile))
23   {
24       die "Couldn't find the task specified\n";
25   }
26   ($mday,$mon,$year) = split '/',$ARGV[-1];
27   $compdate = ($year*10000)+($mon*100)+$mday;
28
29   seek(D,$lastseek,SEEK_SET);
30
31   print D pack($taskformat,$ref,$title,$reqdate,$compdate);
32
33   close(D) || die "Couldn't close the database\n";
```

ANNOTATIONS

This script is really just a combination of the **addtask.pl** and **listtask.pl** scripts. The difference is that we are no longer outputting the full list of tasks or adding tasks onto the end of the file. Instead, we are searching for a specific entry that we need to update.

```
1    #!/usr/local/bin/perl5
2
3    use Fcntl;
4
5    my ($taskfile) = "tasks";
6    my ($taskformat) = "A22A40LL";
7    my ($ref,$title,$reqdate,$compdate);
8    my ($mday,$mon,$year,$compdate);
9    my ($lastseek) = 0;
10
```

We need the **Fcntl** module to make using the **seek** functions easier. The **seek** function allows us to move to a specific point within a file simply by specifying the byte we want to move to and the reference point used to measure the point from. Its options are to measure the number of bytes from the start of the file (**SEEK_SET**), from the current location (**SEEK_CUR**), and from the end of the file (**SEEK_END**). There is also a corresponding function that reports the current location in bytes within the file, called **tell**.

Lines 5 to 9 set the variables we will use, including the data file and the format string used with **pack** and **unpack**.

```
11  die "Usage: modtask.pl title completed-date\n" if (@ARGV<2);
12
13  open(D,"+<$taskfile") || die "Couldn't open the task file, $!\n";
14
```

Line 11 ensures that the correct number of arguments have been specified on the command line, reporting an error if enough arguments haven't been specified. Line 13 opens the data file. We specify how to open the file with a leading **+**, which allows us to both read and write to the file. However, be careful when you use this option; using **+>** would empty the file before opening it for reading and writing.

```
15  while(read(D,$_,70))
16  {
17      ($ref,$title,$reqdate,$compdate) = unpack($taskformat,$_);
18      last if (($title eq $ARGV[0]) && ($compdate eq 0));
19      $lastseek=tell(D);
20  }
21
```

We now execute a loop to work through the records in the file, extracting the fields and then comparing those details against the title we specified on the command line. Line 15 uses the same **read** function to place 70 bytes from the file into the default pattern space. Line 17 uses **unpack** to extract the info into individual variables. In line 18 we compare the current task title from the data file against the title specified on the command line. To ensure we don't update a file that has already been marked as completed, we combine the check with a verification that the completion date is currently unspecified (zero). If the test returns true, then we drop out of the loop at this point.

In line 19, we use **tell** to report our current location within the file. In line 9, we set this initially to zero, and as we progress through each record, this variable will contain the start location of the next record to be read in from the file.

```
22  if ($lastseek >= (-s $taskfile))
23  {
24      die "Couldn't find the task specified\n";
25  }
26  ($mday,$mon,$year) = split '/',$ARGV[-1];
27  $compdate = ($year*10000)+($mon*100)+$mday;
28
```

In line 22 we check our current location within the file versus the size of the file. If the two match, it means we have reached the end of the file without find a matching task title. We report an error on line 24 if this is the case.

Lines 26 and 27 format the completed date for placement into the data file. The same method is used as before; we convert the completed date into a number so that it can be converted into a packed unsigned long integer for storage.

```
29    seek(D,$lastseek,SEEK_SET);
30
31    print D pack($taskformat,$ref,$title,$reqdate,$compdate);
32
33    close(D) || die "Couldn't close the database\n";
```

In line 29, we **seek** back to the start of the found record using the value set in line 19. This seek will put us back to exactly the start of the found record. Now we output the updated record to the data file in line 31; doing so will overwrite the existing record with the new information. We don't need to worry about overwriting later records: we already know that the record size is consistent. Replacing a 70-byte record with another 70-byte record will not affect the rest of the data file.

Finally, we close the data file on line 33.

To demonstrate the script, let's return to our list of tasks:

```
$ listtask.pl -r
Title                             Req. Date    Comp. Date
E-mail Harry                      14/08/1998
Call Mark                         26/08/1998
Write accounting software         20/12/1998
```

We can mark the first task as completed by specifying the title and the completion date on the command line:

```
$ modtask.pl "Call Mark" 26/8/1998
$ listtask.pl
Title                             Req. Date    Comp. Date
Call Mark                         26/08/1998   26/08/1998
E-mail Harry                      14/08/1998
Write accounting software         20/12/1998
```

Let's repeat the process with the second task:

```
$ modtask.pl "Email Harry" 14/8/1998
Title                             Req. Date    Comp. Date
Call Mark                         26/08/1998   26/08/1998
E-mail Harry                      14/08/1998   14/08/1998
Write accounting software         20/12/1998
```

We can choose to list only the tasks that have not already been completed by specifying the **-d** option to the **listtask.pl** function:

```
$ listtask.pl -d
Title                              Req. Date    Comp. Date
Write accounting software          20/12/1998
```

And with the final task, let's list the tasks this time by their completion date:

```
$ modtask.pl "Write accounting software" 29/8/1998
$ listtask.pl -c
Title                              Req. Date    Comp. Date
E-mail Harry                       14/08/1998   14/08/1998
Call Mark                          26/08/1998   26/08/1998
Write accounting software          20/12/1998   29/08/1998
```

As you can see, the process is fairly straightforward for updating fixed-length records: all you have to do is record the position at which the file you are updating was located, and then overwrite the record with the updated version of the information. The use of a packed record ensures that the record length remains constant—providing you use the same pack format string.

The problem we didn't overcome is that locating the record in the first place required us to move sequentially through each record of the file. There are a number of methods we can get around having to move through the file this way; one method is to use an index to refer to the contents of the actual data. We'll look at an example of this in the next script.

Deleting Fixed-length Records

One other item that we haven't covered yet is deleting records from text databases. The only way to delete a record from a variable-length text database is to copy the contents of the database from one place to another, ignoring the records that you want to delete. You can do this with small files in memory; just read in the existing version of the database into an array, writing the database back out and skipping the records to be deleted. With larger files, copying from one file to another is the best method, as it negates the need for creating larger variables in memory.

With fixed-length records, you have two choices: either set aside a byte in the packed string to mark a record as deleted, or follow the method above. The former is generally quicker since we can use the update method we have already seen to delete a record from the database. However, this method has inherent problems; for example, with large databases where there are a lot of deleted records, the reporting process will be lengthened considerably by having to sift out the deleted records from the report.

Whichever solution you choose, you can use the methods I've described here for the process; the principles are the same.

Creating a Definitions Dictionary

One of the resources I have found on the Internet over the years is a dictionary, not just of words but also their definitions. The dictionary is split into two files. One contains the actual definitions, and the other is an index of the words. This index is simply a list of words with the position of the corresponding definition entry within the full dictionary file.

In theory, this format should make accessing the definitions a quick procedure because we can read in the index, look up the location of the definition for the word we want, and then display the information. To read through the entire definitions file, looking for the specified definition, would take considerably longer then using the index.

Although not strictly a database, the definition directory does demonstrate the use of an index file to speed up access to a database. In practice, the longest part of the process is reading in the index. Incorporating methods used in a larger database context, such as a live query service where the Perl script is resident while the database is in use, would make the access faster.

```perl
1   #!/usr/local/bin/perl
2
3   use POSIX;
4   use Fcntl;
5   use strict;
6
7   my ($dictfile) = "./dict";
8   my ($dictindex) = "./dict.idx";
9   my (%index,@words,$word,$maxword);
10
11  die <<EOF
12  Usage: $0 worddef
13
14  Where worddef can be
15
16  word  - A single word
17  word@ - Any word beginning with these characters
18
19  EOF
20  if (@ARGV<1);
21
22  $maxword = (sort(@ARGV))[-1];
23
24  &read_index($dictindex,$maxword);
```

```
25
26   open(D,"<$dictfile")||die "Couldn't open the dictionary, $!\n";
27
28   for $word (@ARGV)
29   {
30       if ($word =~ /.*\@$/)
31       {
32           $word =~ s/\@$//;
33           push(@words,grep(/^$word.*/,keys %index));
34       }
35       else
36       {
37           push(@words,$word);
38       }
39   }
40
41   for $word (sort @words)
42   {
43       my ($printedDef) = 0;
44       seek(D,$index{$word},SEEK_SET);
45       while(<D>)
46       {
47           last if (($_ =~ /^\@.*/) && ($printedDef));
48           s/^\@//;
49           print $_;
50           $printedDef = 1;
51       }
52       print "\n";
53   }
54
55   close(D)||die "Couldn't close the dictionary, $!\n";
56
57   sub read_index
58   {
59       my ($file,$maxword) = @_;
60       my ($word,$offset);
61
62       open(D,"<$file") || die "$0: Couldn't open index $!\n";
63
64       while(<D>)
65       {
66           chomp;
67           ($word,$offset) = split '\t';
```

```
68        $index{$word} = $offset;
69        last if (($word =~ /^$maxword/) && ($maxword !~ /\@$/));
70    }
71
72    close(D) || die "$0: Couldn't close index $!\n";
73 }
```

ANNOTATIONS

The process of accessing the definition dictionary is two fold. First we must access the index file, and then we need access to the definitions themselves. To make matters more complex, I've included the option to list all the words that match a starting string.

```
1    #!/usr/local/bin/perl
2
3    use POSIX;
4    use Fcntl;
5    use strict;
6
```

We use the **POSIX** and **Fcntl** modules in this script, and I've specified the **strict** pragma for this script. This pragma forces Perl to be a little more fussy about any problems or unclear programming.

```
7    my ($dictfile) = "./dict";
8    my ($dictindex) = "./dict.idx";
9    my (%index,@words,$word,$maxword);
10
```

Lines 7 to 9 specify the local variables we will use, starting with the definition file, and the corresponding index. The locations of the index and dictionary files specified here assume the files are in the local directory, and that we have access to it. If you were installing this as a general tool, then it would make sense to put the dictionary and the script in a publicly accessible location, and change the file locations specified in lines 7 and 8.

```
11   die <<EOF
12   Usage: $0 worddef
13
14   Where worddef can be
15
16   word  - A single word
17   word@ - Any word beginning with these characters
18
```

```
19   EOF
20   if (@ARGV<1);
21
```

Lines 11 to 20 print out the usage instructions if the user fails to supply at least one word on the command line.

```
22   $maxword = lc((sort(@ARGV))[-1]);
23
```

To extract the highest alphabetical word specified on the argument list, we first sort the list and then use subscript notation to identify the last element of the sorted array. The index contains a lowercase version of all the words, so we place the last word extracted into the **lc** function, which returns a lowercase version of the string passed to it.

```
24   &read_index($dictindex,$maxword);
25
```

The **read_index** function will import the dictionary index specified in the first argument into a hashed array. We specify the **$maxword** variable that will be used by the function to identify when it can stop importing the index. See below for more information on how this function operates.

```
26   open(D,"<$dictfile")||die "Couldn't open the dictionary, $!\n";
27
28   for $word (@ARGV)
29   {
30       if ($word =~ /.*\@$/)
31       {
32           $word =~ s/\@$//;
33           push(@words,grep(/^$word.*/i,keys %index));
34       }
35       else
36       {
37           push(@words,lc($word));
38       }
39   }
40
```

On line 26, we open the definition dictionary, checking that we can open it before continuing. Line 28 is the start of a loop that will work through each element of the argument list and extract the list of valid words. The reason for this tiered approach is that by appending an @ sign to the end of a word we can match a list of words contained in the index. For example, specifying **a@** would extract all the words starting with *a*.

Line 30 checks if the current argument ends with an @ sign; if it does, then we strip it from the word, and use **grep** on line 33 to extract the matching words from the index. The **grep** function is almost identical to the **grep** command, except that it operates on arrays and hashes as well as strings. The results of the match are pushed onto the **@words** array. This method works; even if the function returns multiple elements, the **push** function will accept a virtually unlimited number of entries. Lines 30 and 32 could be condensed to

```
if ($word =~ s/\@$//)
```

The regular expression replacement returns true on success, so if it worked, the resultant value would be what we want to use in line 33. In addition, to prevent duplicates ending up in the array, we could assign the results to be the keys of a hash, which would eliminate duplicates, since you can only have one unique key within a hash.

On line 37, if the word does not end in an @ sign, then we just push a lowercase version of the word onto the same **@words** array.

```
41  for $word (sort @words)
42  {
43      my ($printedDef) = 0;
```

The next section works through the **@words** array, in alphabetical order, extracting the full definition from the full definition dictionary file. The format of the definition file is as follows:

```
@word
line2
line3
@word
...
```

Each word that makes up a definition is prepended by an @ sign, and we can use this format to identify where a definition ends.

Line 43 sets the **$first** variable to zero; we'll use this variable to check if the line is the first we have output. We use this value, in combination with the knowledge of the definition layout, to decide when to stop printing the definition.

The format of the index is a list of words and the character position of the definition in the definition file. The index hash created as part of the **read_index** function is made up of the keys, which are the individual words, and the character location, which is stored in the corresponding value.

```
44      seek(D,$index{$word},SEEK_SET);
45      while(<D>)
46      {
47          last if (($_ =~ /^\@.*/) && ($printedDef));
48          s/^@//;
49          print $_;
50          $printedDef = 1;
51      }
52      print "\n";
53  }
54
```

We use this information in line 44 to seek a specific character within the file that is specified by the corresponding hash entry. We then work through the file line by line, using a **while** loop on line 45.

Line 47 skips the loop if the line starts with an @ sign, and if it isn't the first line we have output, because if the definition starts with an @ sign, exiting the loop at this point would skip the printing of the definition entirely. We strip the leading @ sign on line 48, and print out the line on line 49. We don't have to append a new-line character to the print command, because we didn't strip the new-line character from the source file. Remember that Perl includes the new line in the default pattern space when it reads the lines.

Line 50 sets the **$first** variable to 1, which will cause the next call to line 47 to fail if the line starts with an @ sign.

Line 51 is the end of the **while** loop, which has been printing out the definition information. On line 52 we print a blank line to separate each definition, with the loop for the words we are printing ending on line 53.

If the index is accurate (which we can't guarantee in this instance), then we could replace lines 44 to 52 with the following:

```
seek(D,$index{$word},SEEK_SET);
if (defined ($_ = <D>) && s/^\@//)
{
    print $_;
}
else
{
    die "Index doesn't match dictionary\n";
}
while (<D>)
{
    last if /^\@/;
    print $_;
}
```

This sequence reads in the first line of the dictionary and checks that the replacement of a leading @ character completes correctly. Presuming what we've found is a definition, we go on to read the entry until the next definition.

```
55  close(D)||die "Couldn't close the dictionary, $!\n";
56
```

Line 55 closes the database, and we check to make sure that the dictionary file can be closed properly.

```
57  sub read_index
58  {
59      my ($file,$maxword) = @_;
60      my ($word,$offset);
61
```

```
62      open(D,"<$file") || die "$0: Couldn't open index $!\n";
63
64      while(<D>)
65      {
66          chomp;
67          ($word,$offset) = split '\t';
68          $index{$word} = $offset;
69          last if (($word =~ /^$maxword/) && ($maxword !~ /\@$/));
70      }
71
72      close(D) || die "$0: Couldn't close index $!\n";
73  }
```

The **read_index** function imports the dictionary index into a hashed array. We extract the arguments in line 59; the index file is first, and the highest alphabetical word is the second argument.

We open the index on line 62, and then we start working through the file on line 64. The new-line character is stripped off the end on line 66, and we split the line by a tab on line 67 into the word and seek the offset value. This information is used to create the hash entry on line 68.

Line 69 checks the **$maxword** variable against the current word identified on line 67, ensuring the **$maxword** specification is not a word with the completion operator set. Line 69 allows us to exit from the loop, reading in the index if the highest word we are looking for has been found. Exiting the loop saves time: reading in the index is a long process. However, if the highest alphabetical word has been specified as one that needs to be automatically completed, we need to read in the entire index so that the **grep** function on line 33 is allowed to do its work.

This method works even if you specify a completion word within a larger list, since the process will read up to the last full word that was specified, or the entire index.

The index file is closed on line 72, once again checking that the index can be closed properly.

To use the index for a single word, just specify it on the command line:

```
$ lword.pl AND
and \*n(d), (')an(d)\ conj -- used as a function word to indicate
    connection or addition esp. of items within the same class or type
    or to join words or phrases of the same grammatical rank or
    function
```

Alternatively, we can specify the @ sign after a word to list the definitions for words matching the characters up to the @ sign, for example:

```
$ lword.pl AND@
and \*n(d), (')an(d)\ conj -- used as a function word to indicate
    connection or addition esp. of items within the same class or type
    or to join words or phrases of the same grammatical rank or
```

```
function

1 an.dan.te \a_:n-'da_:n-.ta_-, an-'dant-e_-\ adv (or adj) :
  moderately slow -- used as a direction in music

2 andante n : an andante movement

and.iron \'an-.di_-(-*)rn\ n : one of a pair of metal supports for
  firewood in a fireplace

an.dro.gen \'an-dr*-j*n\ n : a male sex hormone
```

Aside from the initial overhead of reading in the index, the process of extracting the definitions from the file is quick, because we have an index that points to the exact character within the file where the information is stored. Without the index, we would have to read in the dictionary until we found the words we were looking for. Reading in the dictionary would be relatively easy, but it would also be significantly slower—the full definitions dictionary is just under six times the size of the index.

Of course, index systems benefit most when the index is permanently in memory and we use the memory-based index to access a static file. The basic method is the same as we used in this script.

Storing Data with the DBI CSV Toolkit

addcsv.pl

The DBI (Data-Base Interface) toolkit is an interface to a range of different databases, including Oracle, Sybase, and other SQL-based RDBMS (relational database management systems). The system is modular, which means you have the base DBI toolkit, which has a submodule used to access the underlying database. Accessing different data sources is as easy as using a different base module, which is specified within the code as an option to the **open** and **close** functions. Each underlying database driver (DBD) may implement a different method for accessing the database, which may lead to some problems when using a mixture of databases, as the error codes returned by each DBD are not consistent across the whole DBI toolkit.

One of the modules allows you to access standard CSV (comma-separated values) files as if they were a SQL-enabled database table. The DBI toolkit supplies all of the functions and constructs required for creating, reporting, and editing information in the database. The CSV functions are written in C for speed, and these functions are interfaced with the Perl CSV module. The DBI module, which supplies the SQL interpretation and the data interface between the database and the Perl script, makes standard calls to the CSV module to read and write the database. The CSV DBD uses the system **flock** function to lock the underlying CSV files, thereby solving one of our earlier concerns. A DBI-managed CSV file will be multiuser compatible without us having to insert any additional code.

The CSV module overcomes many of the problems associated with both text-delimited files and the fixed-length files we have already seen. A CSV file is composed of fields separated by commas; if the field needs to contain commas, then the entire field can be enclosed in double quotes. Updating the file contents is done behind the scenes by the toolkit, so we don't have to worry about duplicating the file or overwriting its contents. Furthermore, the DBI toolkit, via the SQL interface, provides us with a standard way of retrieving the information that doesn't require us to sift through the file looking for the record we want.

In the following example, I've duplicated the functionality of our earlier scripts for recording tasks, using the DBI toolkit in place of our own functions. The scripts are noticeably shorter than the variable- or fixed-record length equivalents, because the DBI module is doing all of the work behind the scenes. All we need to concern ourselves with is writing the correct SQL statement.

For more information on the DBI toolkit, visit the CPAN archives (http://www.cpan.org) or go to the DBI home page (http://www.hermetica.com/technologia/DBI/).

```
1   #!/usr/local/bin/perl5
2
3   use DBI;
4
5   my ($reqdate);
6   die "Usage: $0 title required-date\n" if (@ARGV<2);
7
8   ($mday,$mon,$year) = split '/',$ARGV[-1];
9   $reqdate = ($year*10000)+($mon*100)+$mday;
10
11  my ($table) = "csvtasks";
12
13  my($dbh) = DBI->connect("DBI:CSV:");
14
15  unless (-e $table)
16  {
17      $dbh->do("CREATE TABLE $table (title CHAR(40),
18              reqdate CHAR(8), compdate CHAR(8))")
19          || die "Couldn't create table " . dbh->errstr();
20  }
21
22  $dbh->do("INSERT INTO $table VALUES (" .
23      $dbh->quote($ARGV[0]) . "," .
24      $dbh->quote($reqdate) . "," .
25      $dbh->quote(0) . ")")
26      || die "Couldn't add record, " . $dbh->errstr();
```

ANNOTATIONS

This script is largely identical to the previous, hand-coded example, **addtask.pl**, we saw earlier in this chapter. The difference is that the script can be significantly shorter because we have shifted the database access and update routines over to be the responsibility of the DBI CSV toolkit. All we need to do is collect the information and then compose the SQL statements required to update the CSV file.

```perl
1    #!/usr/local/bin/perl5
2
3    use DBI;
4
5    my ($reqdate);
6    die "Usage: $0 title required-date\n" if (@ARGV<2);
7
```

We incorporate the **DBI** module on line 3. Note that we don't have to specify that we are using the **CSV** module at this point, because the DBI toolkit provides a different interface for specifying the required underlying storage toolkit.

Line 5 sets up the variable we will use to store a formatted version of the date, and a usage error is reported on line 6 if the user fails to supply the task title and the required date.

```perl
8    ($mday,$mon,$year) = split '/',$ARGV[-1];
9    $reqdate = ($year*10000)+($mon*100)+$mday;
10
```

Lines 8 and 9 format the date into a number, first by extracting the individual elements, and then by formatting the date into a numerical value based on the Japanese or Universal date format.

```perl
11   my ($table) = "csvtasks";
12
13   my($dbh) = DBI->connect("DBI:CSV:");
14
```

On line 11 we specify the name of the table we will use to store the information. The DBI CSV toolkit basically emulates a standard SQL database, so individual tables are used to store information. In the case of CSV files, a file will be created with the table name, and each new table created will generate a new file.

Access to a DBI database is via the creation of a database handle. On line 13 we create a new database handle called **$dbh** by making a call to the **connect** function of the DBI toolkit. The options to the **connect** function are specified in a string that is the only argument. The string specifies the toolkit to use, the underlying storage method, and then any additional options to pass to the storage toolkit.

With the CSV toolkit, the main option you will use is **directory** to specify the directory location to use when creating tables. If you fail to specify a directory, the CSV toolkit assumes you want to use the current directory, so the lines

```
      my($dbh) = DBI->connect("DBI:CSV:");
      my($dbh) = DBI->connect("DBI:CSV:directory=.");
```
are identical.

```
15    unless (-e $table)
16    {
17        $dbh->do("CREATE TABLE $table (title CHAR(40),
18                 reqdate CHAR(8), compdate CHAR(8))")
19            || die "Couldn't create table " . dbh->errstr();
20    }
21
```

There is no quick way within the CSV toolkit to check for the existence of a table. Trying a query on a nonexistent table will cause the CSV toolkit to exit without any recourse to the script that made the call. Since we are dealing with simple files, we can use a file test to check if the data file exists, which we do on line 15.

If the table doesn't exist, then we create it on lines 17 to 19. The SQL statement for creating a table follows this format:

CREATE TABLE tablename (field_def, field_def,...)

The latest version of the CSV toolkit discards any definition information about the field type or length.

We execute a SQL statement on the database handle we created earlier by running the function **do**, which is a method within the database handle object we created. By using methods within individual handle objects, we can have many open handles and run different statements on each handle without forgetting where we are. It also ensures that the handle details are attached to the correct storage toolkit, and that using the corresponding functions will use the correct methods when we access the data.

Any statement executed by the DBI toolkit will return a true or false value, depending on its success. If it fails, we use the **die** function to report a suitable error message. The resulting error is accessible by running the **errstr** function as a reference from the database handle.

```
22    $dbh->do("INSERT INTO $table VALUES (" .
23        $dbh->quote($ARGV[0]) . "," .
24        $dbh->quote($reqdate) . "," .
25        $dbh->quote(0) . ")")
26        || die "Couldn't add record, " . $dbh->errstr();
```

Lines 22 to 26 add the task to the database. You add data to a SQL table using the **INSERT** keyword. You must quote a string that is being added to the database. A number will be interpreted correctly, but strings must be escaped to ensure they are stored in a readable format within the CSV file.

The **quote** function takes care of adding quotes to strings; **quote** is again accessed via a reference off the database handle. The alternative method to using **quote** is to use parameters to the **INSERT** command instead of generating a SQL statement for the insert. We could write the preceding line as

```
$dbh->do("INSERT INTO $table VALUES (?,?,?)",ARGV[0],$reqdate,"0")
    || die "Couldn't add record, " . $dbh->errstr();
```

This method saves us from the lengthy process of using the **quote** function around each field.

To use this script, follow the same instructions as for the **addtask.pl** script:

```
$ addcsv.pl "Call Mark" 14/6/1998
$ listcsv.pl
Title                                    Req. Date    Comp. Date
Call Mark                                14/06/1998
```

If you view the CSV file that was created, you can see that it stores the information just as Microsoft Excel or another database that exports CSV files would:

```
$ more csvtasks
"title","reqdate","compdate"
"Call Mark","19980614","0"
```

Notice that the first line contains the list of column names for this table. This information is used by the CSV toolkit to identify which column to use and update. We can refer to these columns by name; we don't have to make mental reminders about what number a particular column is.

listcsv.pl

Reporting from a DBI CSV Database

Reporting from a SQL table is as easy as writing the correct SQL statement. That isn't actually all that easy, but the format is easy to follow. Using the DBI toolkit, the information returned by a query can be placed into familiar hash arrays for processing. More useful, as far as we are concerned, is that sorting is conducted by the toolkit, not by a function we have to write.

```
1   #!/usr/local/bin/perl5
2
3   use DBI;
4   use Getopt::Std;
5
6   my ($reqdate,$compdate);
7   my ($mday,$mon,$year,$key);
8
9   getopts('drc');
10
11  my ($table) = "csvtasks";
12
```

```
13   my($dbh) = DBI->connect("DBI:CSV:");
14
15   my ($query) = "SELECT * FROM $table";
16
17   $query .= " WHERE compdate = 0" if ($opt_d);
18
19   if ($opt_r)
20   {
21       $query .= " ORDER BY reqdate";
22   }
23   elsif ($opt_c && !($opt_d))
24   {
25       $query .= " ORDER BY compdate";
26   }
27   else
28   {
29       $query .= " ORDER BY title";
30   }
31
32   my ($sth) = $dbh->prepare($query)
33              || die "prepare: " . $dbh->errstr();
34
35   $sth->execute() || die "execute: " . $dbh->errstr();
36
37   printf("%-40s  %-10s  %-10s\n","Title","Req. Date","Comp. Date");
38
39   while ($row = $sth->fetchrow_hashref)
40   {
41       $row->{'reqdate'} =~ m/(....)(..)(..)/;
42       $reqdate = "$3/$2/$1";
43
44       if ($row->{'compdate'}>0)
45       {
46           $lcompdate{$key} =~ m/(....)(..)(..)/;
47           $compdate = "$3/$2/$1";
48       }
49       else
50       {
51           $compdate="";
52       }
53       printf("%-40s  %10s  %10s\n",$row->{'title'},
54                                 $reqdate,$compdate);
55   }
```

ANNOTATIONS

In the preceding script, the bulk of the code is given over to creating the initial SQL query string, followed by the code that extracts the date into a human-readable format.

```
1   #!/usr/local/bin/perl5
2
3   use DBI;
4   use Getopt::Std;
5
6   my ($reqdate,$compdate);
7   my ($mday,$mon,$year,$key);
8
```

We'll be using the DBI and standard **Getopt** modules in this script.

```
9   getopts('drc');
10
```

The command-line options are as before: **-d** skips completed tasks, **-r** sorts by required date, and **-c** sorts by completed date. The default sort is by the task title.

```
11  my ($table) = "csvtasks";
12
13  my($dbh) = DBI->connect("DBI:CSV:");
14
```

We specify the table in line 11, and we then attempt to connect to the CSV toolkit in line 13.

```
15  my ($query) = "SELECT * FROM $table";
16
```

The SQL statement that extracts data from a table is **SELECT**. On line 15 we specify that we want to select all the records from the task table. We then proceed in the following lines to specify additional options to the SQL statement to get the list of tasks we want, and we specify the required sort order.

```
17  $query .= " WHERE compdate = 0" if ($opt_d);
18
```

Line 17 appends the SQL options to select only tasks that are not yet completed if we specify the **-d** option on the command line.

```
19  if ($opt_r)
20  {
21      $query .= " ORDER BY reqdate";
22  }
23  elsif ($opt_c && !($opt_d))
24  {
25      $query .= " ORDER BY compdate";
```

```
26   }
27   else
28   {
29       $query .= " ORDER BY title";
30   }
31
```

Lines 19 to 30 set the column we want to sort on. If we want to set the required date as the sort column, we append the necessary options to the SQL statement we will execute on line 21. Alternatively, if we want the completed date to be the sort column, we append the necessary options on line 25. Note that this option is negated if we've chosen not to display tasks that have already been completed. Otherwise, we set the sort column to the title in line 29. In all cases, we have referred to the columns by the names we used to create the original table.

```
32   my ($sth) = $dbh->prepare($query)
33                || die "prepare: " . $dbh->errstr();
34
35   $sth->execute() || die "execute: " . $dbh->errstr();
36
```

We prepare a new select table handle, **$sth**, in line 32, based on the query we have just composed. Any errors raised at this point will relate to the column names or table names we have used, and we check for errors on line 33. The **SELECT** statement is then executed with the **execute** function on line 35.

```
37   printf("%-40s  %-10s  %-10s\n","Title","Req. Date","Comp. Date");
38
```

Line 37 prints out a friendly header row to help us identify the data.

```
39   while ($row = $sth->fetchrow_hashref)
40   {
41       $row->{'reqdate'} =~ m/(....)(..)(..)/;
42       $reqdate = "$3/$2/$1";
43
44       if ($row->{'compdate'}>0)
45       {
46           $lcompdate{$key} =~ m/(....)(..)(..)/;
47           $compdate = "$3/$2/$1";
48       }
49       else
50       {
51           $compdate="";
52       }
53       printf("%-40s  %10s  %10s\n",$row->{'title'},
54                                   $reqdate,$compdate);
55   }
```

Lines 39 to 55 set up the **while** loop that steps through each recovered row from the table. Line 39 is the **while** statement, and the test operation is based around the result of fetching an individual row into the **$row** variables. In fact, each row will be fetched from the table, and the contents of each column will be placed into the hash **%row**, where the key is the column name.

The required date is extracted and then reformatted on line 42. If the contents of the compdate column from the table are greater than zero, we extract a human-readable version of the completed date on lines 46 and 47; otherwise, the completed date is an empty string. Finally, we print out the table row on lines 53 and 54 using **printf** to match the header we output on line 37.

Note that we extracted the field contents by referring to the field by it's name and by using a reference from the **%row** hash array.

This script is used the same way as the fixed-record length version:

```
Title                            Req. Date     Comp. Date
Call Mark                        14/06/1998
Write accounting software        12/12/1998
```

modcsv.pl

Updating a DBI CSV Database

You will remember that when we approached the problem of updating the fixed-length task database earlier, we had to go through a long process to achieve our goal. First we searched through the database until we found the record we were looking for, then we rewound back to the start of that record, and then we output an updated version of the packed data to the data file.

Using the DBI toolkit, which handles most of these options, and a SQL statement that provides an interface to the process, we can shorten the entire script down to just a few lines. The **modcsv.pl** script below provides the same functionality as the **modtask.pl** script we visited earlier, but it is much shorter.

```perl
1   #!/usr/local/bin/perl5
2
3   use DBI;
4
5   die "Usage: $0 title completed-date\n" if (@ARGV<2);
6
7   my ($mday,$mon,$year) = split m:/:,$ARGV[-1];
8   my ($compdate) = ($year*10000)+($mon*100)+$mday;
9
10  my ($table) = "csvtasks";
11
12  my($dbh) = DBI->connect("DBI:CSV:");
13
```

```
14   my($query) = "UPDATE $table SET compdate = " .
15                $dbh->quote($compdate) .
16                " WHERE title = " . $dbh->quote($ARGV[0]);
17
18   $dbh->do($query) || die "Unable to update, " . $dbh->errstr();
```

ANNOTATIONS

Updating the database is also very simple: we just need to write a suitable SQL query to update the database, and the DBI toolkit will handle everything else.

```
1    #!/usr/local/bin/perl5
2
3    use DBI;
4
5    die "Usage: $0 title completed-date\n" if (@ARGV<2);
6
```

We print out the usage message on line 5, since we need at least two arguments—the task title and the date when the task should be marked as completed.

```
7    my ($mday,$mon,$year) = split m:/:,$ARGV[-1];
8    my ($compdate) = ($year*10000)+($mon*100)+$mday;
9
```

We format the date as before, by converting it into a number. In line 7, because we have to specify a regular expression as the first argument to **split** and use a forward slash, we specify it explicitly as a match with a delimiter of a colon. Although the DBI toolkit supports SQL, in its CSV guise it is unable to distinguish between the data types, so we must employ the same method as before to store the date, to make sorting easier.

```
10   my ($table) = "csvtasks";
11
12   my($dbh) = DBI->connect("DBI:CSV:");
13
```

We specify the table name in line 10. We create a new database handle on line 12; remember that the DBI toolkit expects the storage module name to be the second element of the connect string. The third argument we leave blank, in order to set the current directory as the place for storing the tables (CSV files).

```
14   my($query) = "UPDATE $table SET compdate = " .
15                $dbh->quote($compdate) .
16                " WHERE title = " . $dbh->quote($ARGV[0]);
```

```
17
18   $dbh->do($query) || die "Unable to update, " . $dbh->errstr();
```

On lines 14 to 16 we generate a SQL statement to update the table. Within SQL, the command to update a single row is UPDATE. Here's an expanded version of the command:

```
UPDATE csvtasks SET compdate = "19980626" WHERE title = "Call Mark"
```

This line sets the value of the compdate column to **19980626** when the title column has a value of **Call Mark**.

We execute the SQL statement on line 18. Any error generated will be reported as part of the **die** function.

The script works in exactly the same manner as the **modtask.pl** script:

```
$ listcsv.pl
Title                                    Req. Date   Comp. Date
Call Mark                                14/06/1998  14/06/1998
Write accounting software                12/12/1998
$ modcsv.pl "Write accounting software" 20/12/1998
$ listcsv.pl
Title                                    Req. Date   Comp. Date
Call Mark                                14/06/1998  14/06/1998
Write accounting software                12/12/1998  12/12/1998
```

If we view the contents of the CSV file, you can see how the information has been updated:

```
"title","reqdate","compdate"
"Call Mark","19980614","19980618"
"Write accounting software","19981212","19981220"
```

Summary

In general, it's fair to say that for serious applications, especially those requiring a lot of information to be stored, a text-delimited database has too many limitations and problems to make it a practical solution. They make very useful repositories for storing and retrieving static information, but they present too many programming difficulties and performance problems for a database that will be updated.

Fixed-width databases are more practical for most situations. They are easy to create and easy to update and report from. Their only failing is that they can be very wasteful of space. You will always be in a position where there is a tradeoff between the amount of information you want to store and the optimum size of the individual records.

Using the DBI CSV toolkit can help you to get around the difficulties of both systems by completely isolating you from the process of creating, updating, and reporting on the information. The underlying format for the database is a comma-delimited file, no different from our first few examples, but we no longer have to concern ourselves with the problems we encountered earlier. Better still, we can apply the industry-standard SQL interface to a regular text file, and the source for that file could be a spreadsheet or desktop database program.

Even with the DBI toolkit or the indexing model sample we used with the definition dictionary, there is still an overhead associated with accessing the data you are looking for. Searching for a word at the end of the dictionary requires us to read in the index. Even on a fast machine, this can take a second or so, and we're dealing with only about 30,000 words. What would happen if we were attempting to access a 100,000-line text database?

What if we just want one field from one record of that database? First of all, we have to read the file until we find the record we want, and then we need to extract the field in question. That could take seconds, which is not a suitable solution for a time-sensitive application. Even worse, what happens if we want to update the information in that field? If it's a text-delimited file, we'll need to make a copy of it to produce the new version.

Before we disregard text files completely, however, there are times when simply writing out a piece of information to a file for later processing is easier than updating a "real" database. Text files are then the most practical solution: they are easy to write to, and reading the information for processing is as easy as it gets. Let's face it: time-sensitive applications, such as Web servers and phone systems, use a simple, formatted text report to log their execution. Text databases also fill a necessary gap for commonly used files that are updated but so infrequently that the time constraint for the update is negligible. Most of the Unix databases, such as the /etc/password and /etc/hosts files are good examples.

Using Alternative
Database Systems

A lthough text files are practical for many situations, they can be tedious to use and complex to search, especially when a file contains large amounts of information. A better solution is to store the information in a real database, where the information can be recorded and extracted using identified and unique keys. This way you can ignore the searching and storage mechanisms that are required for text databases and instead concentrate on writing the code for using the database, rather than the code for accessing it.

The standard database under Unix is a system called DBM, which is probably short for Data Base Management, although the real description has been lost in the mists of time. DBM is based on a simple key/value pair, which can be thought of as a two-column table. The first column is the key, and the second column is the data. To extract information from the database, you look for the row that contains the key you are looking for, and then extract the value. Perl can extract this information automatically for you if you use a *tied* database that associates a DBM file with a hash.

Although it sounds complicated, it is really no different from the way hash variables are stored within Perl. You access a hashed entry within Perl by specifying a scalar key. With some careful programming and the use of well-worded keys, you can store information in a DBM file in the same way you would store information in any off-the-shelf database. However, be warned that DBM does not use tables like most database applications. The best way to simulate tables within DBM is to format the key according to a predefined layout—we'll see an example of this later in this chapter when we look at "Populating a Semirelational DBM Database."

DBM files are an integral part of many of the standard Unix operating system utilities. Sendmail, for example, uses DBM to store aliases for more efficient accessing. The alias file is converted using the newalias command into a DBM database, and using a DBM file is quicker than manually trawling through the text aliases; this speed is vitally important when processing e-mail messages on large e-mail systems.

Over the years, the original DBM system has been improved and has gone through a number of different incarnations, but the original specification remains the same. Most of the different DBM systems are compatible with each other, but to a greater or lesser extent depending on the platform and implementation involved. They all use the same basic API to access data files, but the underlying storage method varies, so a DBM file won't necessarily be readable by SDBM, for example. It should be noted as well that DBM files are not portable; the storage format used is specific to a particular hardware platform and operating system. In some cases, even different versions of the same OS have incompatible DBM systems.

Because of the way information is stored, it's also difficult to copy the files efficiently using standard tools. A DBM database is composed of two files. One file is a directory containing a bitmap and has .dir as its suffix. The second file contains all the data and has .pag as its suffix. The data file is often full of "holes" where storage space has been allocated, but these holes contain no useful information.

The downside to this method is that some implementations allocate too much storage space, thereby generating a file that is reported to be 10, 100, or even 1,000 times the amount of useful information stored within the file. Although this space use isn't always reflected in the physical disk space used, there are ways around the problems that we will examine in this chapter.

There is a limitation on the storage size of each key/value pair, which is known as the bucket size. Creating entries larger than this limitation will either cause you to exit from Perl with an untrappable error or just truncate the information you attempt to store, depending entirely on how the database has been implemented at C level. Following are the common DBM implementations.

DBM/ODBM   The original implementation of the DBM toolkit. Although included as standard in most Unix variants, it has been replaced almost entirely by NDBM as the DBM implementation of choice. Perl refers to it as ODBM for "Old DBM." The supported bucket size is 1K, although I've noted that on many implementations (notably Hewlett-Packards HP-UX 9.x) this figure includes the storage overhead, so the actual figure is about 980 bytes. If you are expecting to store large amounts of information, either use a different implementation that supports larger bucket sizes or develop a way of splitting the data into multiple buckets.

NDBM   The "new" replacement for the original DBM, with some speed and storage allocation improvements. NDBM has replaced the standard DBM libraries, and in some cases is the only implementation available. Depending on the OS, the bucket size is anything from 1K to 4K.

SDBM   Substitute/Simple DBM, a speed- and stability-enhanced version of DBM. It is included as standard with the Perl distribution, and it supports a bucket size of 1K, which can be modified at compile time.

GDBM   The GNU/FSF implementation of DBM. Faster than all implementations except Berkeley DB, GDBM has been ported to a larger number of platforms than other implementations. GDBM also supports limited file and record locking within the DBM file, which can be useful in a multiuser situation. I've never tested this, however!

Berkeley DB   Berkeley DB is a public domain C library of database access methods, including B+Tree, Extended Linear Hashing, and fixed/variable length records. The **DB_File** Perl module puts a DBM-like wrapper around the B-tree and hash implementations, enabling it to be used like a DBM replacement. The fixed-/variable-length record implementation also has a Perl array wrapper for direct use within Perl scripts.

Berkeley DB libraries also support relational database system facilities, such as multiuser updates and transactions, and the ability to recover corrupt database files.

File and Record Locking with DBM

All of the DBM implementations are quick and easy-to-use database systems, although they lack many of the features that are often required for industrial-strength databases. None of the DBM implementations handle multiuser access very well; it would be quite possible for two invocations of the same script to overwrite information written into a DBM database, or even to corrupt the database entirely.

This limitation means that you will need to use some form of database locking to stop simultaneous updates to the same file. Both the Berkeley DB and GDBM implementations support basic file locking, which can be used to prevent two scripts opening the database at the same time, but this basic file locking is still far from the ideal solution, because it limits access to the database's information. Multiuser access is sacrificed in small, efficient, easy-to-use database systems because for most solutions that use DBM databases, it is a rarely used feature. You should be wary, however, of using such systems in a multiuser setting without accounting for multiuser access in some way.

For the rest of this chapter I will refer to a DBM system simply as DBM, without specifying a precise implementation.

Of course, DBM isn't the only database system, although being part of Unix and standard within Perl does make it the obvious choice for most needs. However, there are some things that DBM doesn't support. It is not a relational database system, although you can make it seem so to a greater or lesser extent, as we'll see later in this chapter. Other databases you may want to use include SQL databases such as Oracle and Sybase, ODBC databases such as Microsoft Access, or the many third-party database extensions to Perl.

There are also other alternatives: the Sprite plain text database can provide an alternative to the DBI toolkits. It stores information in text-delimited files, much like the DBI CSV toolkit mentioned in the last chapter, and uses a reduced version of the SQL language to access information. With Sprite, you can embed Perl-style regular expression into queries.

Later in this chapter ("Reading dBase III Databases") we look at a module and script that enable you to export a text version of an Xbase (dBase, FoxPro, and so on) database. If you want to access these databases directly, you can use the **XBase** module, available along with the rest of the modules I discuss here on the CPAN archives and on the CD. The **XBase** module is available both as a separate module and as an access method for use with the **DBI** module.

In this chapter, we will mostly concentrate on DBM databases, since those are the most readily available. We will also take a brief look at the end of the chapter at some of the database interfaces that are available and how to make the best use of them.

Converting a Text Database to DBM

Text databases have a field layout and a record structure, even if they aren't immediately obvious when you look at the file in question. When converting a text file into a DBM file, you need to be careful about the format and layout of the information you store so that it is easy to recover. We already know that DBM files are composed of key/value pairs, for example:

```
firstname = Martin
lastname = Brown
e-mail = mcslp@hotmail.com
```

How you convert a text file into a DBM file depends on two parameters. How long the information is likely to be, and how you expect to extract the information. Depending on the DBM implementation, you have different maximum record sizes. Storing value information that is larger than 1K in size would be impractical within DBM. You *could* split the data up into lots of key/value pairs at the time the information was stored, and then join it up again at extraction time, but this is messy and time consuming.

DBM implementations are optimized to extract values in a single disk access, although many implementations will tell you that the data is retrieved in "at worst two" access. If you are expecting to extract entire records out of the database, then you should probably put whole records into the values. If you expect to extract individual fields, or a collection of fields, then you need to record field names in the key names and the field values in the value portion. Of course, you should keep both these parameters in mind when designing your DBM database.

To give an example, the Unix alias database stores entire records; the key is the alias name, and the value is the list of e-mail addresses the alias relates to, separated by commas. Sendmail can get away with this method because there is no point extracting the individual "fields," or e-mail addresses, from the alias database, and the size of the alias list is unlikely to be very large. Conversely, a contact database is likely to have long value information (name, address, phone, and so on), which is likely to be looked at one field at a time. You might want a phone number or a list of e-mail addresses from a range of records, but the number of times you need to extract an entire contact record is relatively small.

Let's look at a sample contact database extracted from a desktop application that we want converted into a DBM database as part of a move to an Intranet. The contacts have been extracted into a tab-delimited file, and we need to import this information into a DBM database. The script, **text2dbm.pl**, could be used for converting any tab-delimited file into a DBM file, as the field names are taken from the first line of the source file, and information is put into individual fields within the database.

This script (and the other DBM scripts in this chapter) uses the **tie** function. Normally, accessing different types of variables causes Perl to select the desired option for using that variable type. The **tie** function allows you to bind a particular variable type with a user-defined object so that accessing and using the object causes different functions to be called. In these examples, we tie a hash variable to an external hash file (DBM). You may want to view the **perltie** manual page for more information on the **tie** function.

This process can look alien to most users at first glance; accessing external information using internal variables looks suspicious, but it makes the code easier to write and the programs more readable. For object-oriented programmers, the method is very similar to the constructor and access method classes you design for most objects. For a selected set of known operations, Perl expects to see a function that operates on the corresponding file.

Taking a wider view, the **tie** function can be used with any variable type, allowing you to invoke a user-defined function whenever a particular variable is accessed, without the user being aware of it and without the base code of the script changing. In the case of hash variables and DBM systems, it means we can access and use databases much larger than the size of the available memory while appearing to use an ordinary associative array.

You will see that this script makes the whole conversion process fast and simple. This trend will continue throughout the chapter. You will find that operations that would normally take many more lines of code and, potentially, much more time to implement can be done in a just few lines, or even a single line.

```perl
1    #!/usr/local/bin/perl5 -w
2
3    use NDBM_File;
4    use Fcntl;
5    use POSIX;
6
7    my ($dbfile,%db,$i,@fieldnames,@fields,$key,$n);
8
9    die "Usage:\n$0 source\n" if (@ARGV<1);
10
11   $dbfile = $ARGV [0];
12
13   open(D, "<$dbfile");
14
15   tie (%db, NDBM_File, $dbfile, O_RDWR|O_CREAT|O_EXCL, 0666)
16              || die "$0: Error creating $dbfile database: $!\n";
17
18   while(<D>)
19   {
20       chomp;
21       s/,//g;
```

```
22      @fieldnames = split /\t/;
23      last;
24  }
25
26  $db{fieldlist} = join(",",@fieldnames);
27
28  $i=0;
29  while(<D>)
30  {
31      chomp;
32      @fields = split /\t/;
33
34      for($n=0;$n<=@fields;$n++)
35      {
36          if (length($fields[$n])>0)
37          {
38              $key = $fieldnames[$n] . "-$i";
39              $db{$key} = $fields[$n];
40          }
41      }
42      $i++;
43  }
44
45  $db{seqid} = $i;
46
47  close(D) || die "$0: Couldn't close source, $!\n";
48
49  untie %db;
50
51  print "Read $i records\n";
```

ANNOTATIONS

The script is really quite simple: it opens the source file, reads the first line to get the list of field names, and then reads the rest of the lines, placing field values into corresponding keys composed of the field names and a sequential number.

```
1   #!/usr/local/bin/perl5 -w
2
3   use NDBM_File;
4   use Fcntl;
5   use POSIX;
```

```
6
7    my ($dbfile,%db,$i,@fieldnames,@fields,$key,$n);
8
```

Lines 1 to 8 just set us up for the rest of the script. In line 1 I've specified the warnings argument, **-w**, so that Perl will report anything that it would otherwise make a "best guess" about. We use three external modules with this script: **NDBM_File** supplies us with the facilities for opening NDBM database files as well as the necessary **tie** function definitions. The **Fcntl** and **POSIX** modules are required so that when opening the NDBM file on line 15 we can specify some human-friendly terms about how to open the file. Incorporating the full **POSIX** module, however, can make the initialization of the script much slower and the memory footprint much larger. To get around this problem, we could replace lines 4 and 5 with

```
use POSIX qw/fcntl_h/;
```

This line loads only the Fcntl portions of the entire **POSIX** module, which are all we need within this script. Using this line will therefore speed up initialization and reduce the memory used by the script.

On line 7 I've specified a number of variables that we will use in the rest of the program. Without the **my** keyword, Perl would make the variables global and accessible to every function and module within the script. Since we are using some external modules, it's good practice to use the **my** keyword to protect your own variables from being overwritten by those from imported modules.

PROGRAMMER'S NOTE   *The **my** keyword is part of Perl 5 and can be used in place of and as well as the **local** keyword. Using **local** makes the variable local to the enclosed block and anything called by the block; **my** create a local variable but hides the variable completely from the outside world.*

```
9    die "Usage:\n$0 source\n" if (@ARGV<1);
10
11   $dbfile = $ARGV [0];
12
13   open(D, "<$dbfile");
14
15   tie (%db, NDBM_File, $dbfile, O_RDWR|O_CREAT|O_EXCL, 0666)
16               || die "$0: Error creating $dbfile database: $!\n";
17
```

Line 9 is the usual test function for command-line arguments, and we use the first one to specify the name of the source file on line 11. We also use the name in line 15 as the name of the database file. Line 15 is where we use the **tie** keyword to associate the hash variable, **%db**, with an NDBM_File called **$dbfile**. The next argument specifies the mode to open the file; this mode matches the C specifications. We use **O_RDWR**, which opens a file for reading and writing, and **O_CREAT**, which creates the file if it doesn't already exist. The last flag is **O_EXCL** which will cause the tie to fail if the DBM file already exists. Since we are generating a database from an export file that contains the field headings, adding to an existing file would upset the existing layout and field information. You can see a list of the available file access flags in Table 4-1.

The last argument specifies the file mode, in Unix format, that the file should be created with if it has to be created. As usual, we check that we have been able to open the file correctly by combining the statement with **die.**

PROGRAMMER'S NOTE   *We can use the same name for the source file and DBM file because a DBM database is composed of two files, one ending with .pag and the other ending with .dir. Creating a database with the same name won't overwrite the source file, and it makes it obvious to someone browsing the directory listing what the relationship is. There is one exception to this rule. The Berkeley DB module (DB_File) creates a single file database. Using O_EXCL when opening the database will prevent problems when you move from one implementation to another.*

```
18   while(<D>)
19   {
20       chomp;
21       s/,//g;
22       @fieldnames = split /\t/;
23       last;
24   }
25
```

Flag	Description
O_APPEND	Appends information to the given file
O_CREAT	Creates a new file if it doesn't already exist
O_EXCL	Causes the open to fail if the file already exists, when used with O_CREAT
O_NDELAY	Opens the file without blocking; reads or writes to the file will cause the process to wait
O_NONBLOCK	Behaves the same as O_NDELAY
O_RDONLY	Opens the file as read-only
O_RDWR	Opens the file for reading and writing
O_TRUNC	Opens the file, truncating (emptying) the file if it already exists
O_WRONLY	Opens the file as write-only

TABLE 4-1.   File Access Flags

Lines 18 to 25 get the list of fields contained in the first line of the source file. On line 20 we use **chomp** to strip the end-of-line character(s) off the source line. By default the record separator is a new-line character. You can specify a different character by modifying the variable **$/**, which can be useful if the output of the file has been created by an application that uses a special separator for the records. On line 21 we strip any commas out of the source line because we want to use commas to separate the fields when we write out a field list in line 26.

Then on line 22, we split the line by tabs, assigning the resulting list of fields to the **@fieldnames** array. On line 23 we use the **last** function to get us out of the loop, since we've read in the one line we already need.

We could avoid using a loop in this section by using this line:

```
$_ = <D>;
```

which is effectively what the statement within the **while** loop does anyway. However, there is no checking for the end of the file within this statement, so we would need to expand it to the following to ensure that the source file contained some valid information:

```
defined ($_ = <D>) || die "Unexpected end of $dbfile\n";
```

The same substitutions and the field split could then occur as normal.

```
26    $db{fieldlist} = join(",",@fieldnames);
27
```

On line 26 I've opted to store some sanity information in the database file by recording the list of field names into a key value of **fieldlist** within the database. Since it's safe to assume that we're creating the database to be used by another application, we can use the **fieldlist** key to extract a list of the available fields within the database, thereby giving us access to the information. If we didn't store the information here, we would have to handcode it into the extraction script, which is both messy and cumbersome.

I've used the **join** function to create a new string of the field names, separated by commas. You can see now why I wanted them stripped in line 21. Notice how the information is stored in the database; I've just specified the hash variable we **tied** earlier—the key name that is **fieldlist**—and then assigned the result to it. It really is this easy to put information into the database.

Behind the scenes, Perl has looked up the operation associated with adding information to the tied hash variable and therefore the database, and it has written the information to disk already. Without specifying those options, or even writing a function to do all of that, Perl has shortened the script lines required to just one line!

```
28    $i=0;
29    while(<D>)
30    {
31        chomp;
32        @fields = split /\t/;
33
```

Lines 28 to 43 are also relatively straightforward. They take the individual field data from the source file and place it in the database against a key made up from the field name, which we already know, and a sequential record number. The record number is specified by the variable **$i**, which we initialize to zero in line 28. The **while** loop from line 29 steps through the file, picking out individual lines, which we then take the new-line character off of in line 31.

```
34      for($n=0;$n<=@fields;$n++)
35      {
36          if (length($fields[$n])>0)
37          {
38              $key = $fieldnames[$n] . "-$i";
39              $db{$key} = $fields[$n];
40          }
41      }
42      $i++;
43  }
```

Once again we split the data along tabs into an array called **@fields**. Lines 34 to 41 step through each field from the source line. We use a **for** loop to work through from the first to the last field in the **@fields** array. Since the field sequence matches the field name sequence, we can use the same index within the array to refer to the field name. On line 36 we check that the field actually contains some information, by checking the length of the field data. This check stops the script from putting empty fields into the database.

We create on line 38 a new key based on the matching field name and the sequential record number, separated by a hyphen. Then line 39 puts the field data into the database using this key. Note that the key can contain spaces and other characters; it's not limited to just text. The only caveat is that if you are extracting the information directly, and the key contains spaces and other characters, then it should be enclosed in quotes. If you don't enclose the text in quotes, Perl may attempt to evaluate the contents. In particular, any special operators, such as hyphen (-), period (.), and space, should be quoted. If your key is just an unpunctuated string, you can get away without using quotes.

The process is repeated for each field until we reach the end on line 38. Line 39 increments the record number, and then the whole process starts again for the next record, until we finally finish reading in the information and exit the **while** loop on line 43.

```
44
45  $db{seqid} = $i;
46
47  close(D) || die "$0: Couldn't close source, $!\n";
48
49  untie %db;
```

```
50
51  print "Read $i records\n";
```

As part of the sanity check and future planning for the database, we record the next record number to use in the database against a key of **seqid** in line 45. If we want to add information to this database, we would use this database entry as the starting point for new records so that we didn't overwrite existing information. Since the **$i** variable stores the current record number, it will have been incremented after the last record was added, in line 42. The **while** loop would have ended at the next test, effectively line 29. The **$i** variable will match the next record number that should be used.

On line 47 we close the input source, reporting an error if it doesn't close. We close the database, using the **untie** function on line 49. Finally, we print out the number of records on line 51 to show the user how many records were created in the database.

I used the following database table to populate a short contacts database:

Salutation	First Name	Last Name	Office Tel	E-mail
Mr	Colin	Barker	898 7896	cbarker@nowhere.com
Mr	Simon	Barber	676 9530	
Mr	David	Ewart	846974	
Mr	Tony	Husband	660262	
Mr	Nigel	Taylor	479081	
Mr	Richard	Yonwin		
Ms	Catherine	Watt	231246	cath@dontuse.com
Mr	Michael	Waters	710368	

Using the **dbmdump.pl** script (see "Using the DBM Dumper"), the information was recorded in the DBM database as follows:

```
Salutation-7 = Mr
Salutation-6 = Ms
Salutation-5 = Mr
Salutation-4 = Mr
Salutation-3 = Mr
Salutation-2 = Mr
Salutation-1 = Mr
Salutation-0 = Mr
Office Tel-7 = 710368
Office Tel-6 = 231246
Office Tel-4 = 479081
```

```
Office Tel-3 = 660262
Office Tel-2 = 846974
Office Tel-1 = 676 9530
Office Tel-0 = 898 7896
First Name-7 = Michael
First Name-6 = Catherine
First Name-5 = Richard
First Name-4 = Nigel
First Name-3 = Tony
First Name-2 = David
First Name-1 = Simon
First Name-0 = Colin
Last Name-7 = Waters
Last Name-6 = Watt
Last Name-5 = Yonwin
Last Name-4 = Taylor
Last Name-3 = Husband
Last Name-2 = Ewart
Last Name-1 = Barber
Last Name-0 = Barker
fieldlist = Salutation,First Name,Last Name,Office Tel,E-Mail
E-Mail-6 = cath@dontuse.com
E-Mail-0 = cbarker@nowhere.com
seqid = 8
```

You can see how the information has been split up and that blank fields were not created in the database. The order of the information shown here won't necessarily match what you see when you try the script; the order in which the data is stored is entirely dependent on how the DBM implementation was written. Since the amount of information we are storing is not that large, then it's safe to assume that we could follow the lead of the field list, and put all of the information into one key, separating the fields by commas. This would make the script shorter, but as I've already mentioned, how you store the information depends on both its size and how you expect to extract it again later.

dbmdump.pl

Using the DBM Dumper

Sometimes it's necessary to extract all of the information from a database, not just the records and fields you are looking for, perhaps for reporting purposes or as a debugging tool when you are programming. Dumping information from a DBM database is straightforward: you just need to open the DBM file and then work through the keys of the database displaying the information.

```
1   #!/usr/local/bin/perl5
2
3   die "Usage\n$0 dbmfile.pl\n" if (@ARGV < 1);
4
5   local($df) = $ARGV [0];
6
7   print "Dumping $datafile\n";
8
9   use NDBM_File; use Fcntl;
10
11  tie (%db,NDBM_File,$df,O_RDONLY,0444) || die "$0 ($df) $!\n";
12
13  for $key (keys %db)
14  {
15      print $key, ' = ', $db{$key}, "\n";
16  }
17  untie %db;
```

ANNOTATIONS

Because we used the **tie** function, the script uses the **keys** function to extract all the keys from the hash variable attached to the DBM database, then prints them out.

```
1   #!/usr/local/bin/perl5
2
3   die "Usage\n$0 file\n" if (@ARGV < 1);
4
5   local($df) = $ARGV [0];
6
7   print "Dumping $df\n";
8
```

Lines 1 to 8 perform the usual startup tests and set up the environment. We only report on one file at a time, so we only check for one argument in line 3, and we set the value in the **$df** variable. We let the user know what we're doing in line 7.

```
9   use NDBM_File; use Fcntl;
10
11  tie (%db,NDBM_File,$df,O_RDONLY,0444) || die "$0 ($df) $!\n";
12
```

We need to use the **NDBM_File** and **Fcntl** Perl modules as before, but this time we specify them on a single line within the script. However, because Perl treats the semicolon as a statement separator, we have effectively put three lines into the script. Putting them on one line improves clarity but makes very little difference to Perl. On line 11 we **tie** the database up to the **%db** variable but open the file read only, since we don't need to write to the file. We've specified the file mode here as well, although it's not needed. I personally find that it's good practice to record in what mode the file could be used for our current operation.

```
13   for $key (keys %db)
14   {
15       print $key, ' = ', $db{$key}, "\n";
16   }
```

Lines 13 to 16 do the real work. Line 13 uses a **for** loop to step through all of the keys in the hash variable. Each key will be placed in the **$key** variable, which we can then use to extract the information. Line 15 prints the key and the key's value in the database, separated by an equal sign. Again, you can see how easy it is to extract information from the database: all we have to do is specify the right key to the hash variable, and Perl does the necessary work behind the scenes to find the key in the database and report the information.

```
17   untie %HIST || die "$0: ($df) $!\n";
```

Finally we close the database on line 17 and the script is complete.

Here's the output when dumping the contents of the alias database on my Sun Solaris machine:

```
Dumping /etc/mail/aliases
YP_LAST_MODIFIED = 0898335989
mailer-daemon =  postmaster
YP_MASTER_NAME = twinspark
sharon_brown =  slp
martin_brown =  martinb
postmaster =  root
nobody =  /dev/null
mcslp =  martinb, slp
mc =  martinb
@ = @
```

If you are planning on accessing some of the system-created DBM files, you may want to check the output produced by the **dbmdump.pl** script by piping it through od (which outputs octal or decimal values in place of straight text). I once spent over an hour trying to extract information directly out of the alias database using individual keys. It was only when I studied the output from od that I discovered both the keys and the data within the alias database were terminated with a null (\0) character.

You can use this fact to your advantage. Since a DBM file will store any type of information, we could use it to store data packed by the **pack** function that we saw in the last chapter. This would provide us with all the benefits of a packed data record and the convenience of hashed access to the data.

dbmstore.pl

Adding and Modifying DBM Records

You should have realized by now that using the **tie** function makes creating and accessing records in a DBM database incredibly easy. In fact, because we are using a hash variable, we can do exactly the same things with DBM files as we do with hash variables. We already know how to add information, and modifying information is just as easy.

The following script provides a general-purpose method for adding to and modifying entries within a DBM file. It uses many of the techniques we have already seen, but it also ensures that we don't inadvertently overwrite information we might want to keep.

```perl
1   #!/usr/local/bin/perl5
2
3   use Getopt::Std;
4
5   getopts('u');
6
7   die "Usage:\n$0 [-u] db key value\n" if (@ARGV<3);
8
9   ($dbfile, $key, $value) = @ARGV;
10
11  use POSIX qw/:fcntl_h/; use NDBM_File;
12
13  tie (%db, NDBM_File, $dbfile, O_RDWR|O_CREAT, 0666)
14      || die "$0: Error opening/creating $dbfile: $!\n";
15
16  if (defined($db{$key}))
17  {
18      die "$key already exists\n" unless $opt_u;
19  }
20
21  $db{$key} = $value;
22
23  untie %db;
24
```

ANNOTATIONS

The script opens the DBM file using **tie**, checks to ensure the key doesn't already exist in the database, reporting an error if it does. If the key does not already exist, then we create a new key/value pair using a hash reference which updates the DBM file.

```
1    #!/usr/local/bin/perl5
2
3    use Getopt::Std;
4
5    getopts('u');
6
```

We use the standard **Getopt** module to identify command-line switches. The **getopts** function on line 5 checks all the command-line arguments, looking for strings of the form "-x" where the x is one of the characters specified. In this example we're looking for the **-u** switch, which will be used to update a key if it already exists. If the specified option is found, a new variable, **$opt_u**, will be created with a value of 1.

```
7    die "Usage:\n$0 [-u] db key value\n" if (@ARGV<3);
8
9    ($dbfile, $key, $value) = @ARGV;
10
```

We're looking for three command-line arguments: the database name, the key, and the value. Notice that we check for these arguments after the **getopts** function, because the action of **getopts** will remove the command-line arguments from **@ARGV** if a switch is found. The contents of the resulting list are the remaining arguments. If we had checked the number of arguments before the **getopts** function, then we might have incorrectly identified a command-line switch as a required argument. For example, consider the line

```
$ dbmdump.pl -u dbfile key
```

Checking the number of arguments at the start of the script would return **3**, the minimum we need. But running **getopts** would remove the **-u** argument, effectively making the command line look like this:

```
$ dbmdump.pl dbfile key
```

Now we only have two arguments, but we won't have picked up this user error because we checked the number arguments at the wrong point in the script.

Line 9 associates each of the command-line arguments with the variables shown on the left-hand side of the equal sign in sequence. This grouping is quicker to write than doing each argument individually.

```
11   use POSIX qw/:fcntl_h/; use NDBM_File;
12
13   tie (%db, NDBM_File, $dbfile, O_RDWR|O_CREAT, 0666)
14       || die "$0: Error opening/creating $dbfile: $!\n";
15
```

Lines 11 and 13 include the required Perl modules and then **tie** the **%db** variable to the database specified on the command line. We don't use the **O_EXCL** flag, since we could be adding to an existing database file or creating a new one. Once again, I've used a visual reminder of the required permissions to open the file, even though it's not required for this operation.

```
16   if (defined($db{$key}))
17   {
18       die "$key already exists\n" unless $opt_u;
19   }
```

We use the **defined** function to check whether the specified key value already exists in the database. If it does, then we **die** with a suitable warning, unless we've specified the update option on the command line with the **-u** switch.

```
20
21   $db{$key} = $value;
22
23   untie %db;
24
```

By line 21, we know that we are either adding a new entry or updating an existing one. Either way, the operation is the same: we assign the value to the specified key within the hash variable. Then we close the database on line 23.

To use the script, type a line like this:

```
$ dbmstore.pl new sample value
```

This command line creates a new database (if one called "new" doesn't already exist), storing the value "value" against the key "sample." Trying to store against the same key should produce an error:

```
$ dbmstore.pl new sample neglect
sample already exists
```

If we specify the **-u** option on the command line, we update the value:

```
$ dbmstore.pl -u new sample neglect
```

dbmdel.pl

Deleting DBM Records

DBM files are often used as one-way tickets: information is generally imported from the real source into a DBM file to be used by another program on a read-only basis. This is certainly true for the OS use of DBM files. Although sendmail uses a DBM version of the /etc/aliases file, any updates or edits have to be performed on the original text file with the newalias command, creating a new DBM file to replace the old version. Editing the /etc/aliases file doesn't automatically update the database that sendmail actually uses, and sendmail doesn't write data to the alias file in any form.

PROGRAMMER'S NOTE *One benefit from regenerating the file each time from the source is that the DBM file is as clean and sparse as possible. A DBM file that was modified directly would contain a lot of additional data that was unused, and the size of the file could grow uncontrollably. A sparse file is quicker to access and uses less disk space.*

However, there are many occasions when the DBM file is the working database, the result of some form of conversion. When used as the source, you need routines to create, edit, and delete information from the database. Deletion from a DBM file using tied hash variables is a simple case of deleting the key/value pair in the hash—the tied functions deal with deleting the information from the corresponding datafile.

There is one caveat about deleting data from a DBM file. It doesn't free the space used by the original key/value pair, it simply removes the information from the database file. This can cause storage problems, since a busy DBM file could easily grow to many times the size of useful information stored within it. To get around this problem, I suggest you use the technique in the script **cvdbm.pl**, which we look at in the section "Converting Between DBM Implementations" later in this chapter.

```perl
1   #!/usr/local/bin/perl5 -w
2
3   die "Usage:\n$0 db keys...\n" if (@ARGV<2);
4
5   $dbfile = shift;
6
7   use NDBM_File; use Fcntl; use POSIX;
8
9   tie (%db, NDBM_File, $dbfile, O_RDWR, 0666)
10      || die "$0: Error opening $dbfile: $!\n";
```

```
11
12   foreach $key (@ARGV)
13   {
14       if (defined($db{$key}))
15       {
16           delete $db{$key};
17           print "Deleted key $key\n";
18       }
19       else
20       {
21           print "$key not found\n";
22       }
23   }
24
25   untie %db;
```

ANNOTATIONS

The **dbmdel.pl** script can delete multiple keys from the database. We take the first argument from the command line as the database name, and all subsequent arguments are treated as keys within the database. We step through each key, verify that it exists, and then delete it.

```
1   #!/usr/local/bin/perl5 -w
2
3   die "Usage:\n$0 db keys...\n" if (@ARGV<2);
4
5   $dbfile = shift;
6
```

We're checking for at least two arguments in line 3; a minimum of the database name and one key is required. We use **shift** to return and delete the first element of the @ARGV array and put it in **$dbfile**.

```
7   use NDBM_File; use Fcntl; use POSIX;
8
9   tie (%db, NDBM_File, $dbfile, O_RDWR, 0666)
10      || die "$0: Error opening $dbfile: $!\n";
11
```

On line 9 I've only specified the **O_RDWR** flag. We need to check the existence of the key before we delete it, so we can't get away with just write-only access. Because we should be working on an existing DBM file, we don't specify the **O_CREAT** flag, either. There is no point in creating an empty database to delete a nonexistent key!

Note as well that in all these cases we don't use one of Perl's built-in file test operators to check the existence of the DBM file. We don't check because the name we use and the filename of the real database differ. Although there is no reason why we couldn't check for the database filename, a different implementation could use different file extensions. The other reason is that checking the result of the **tie** function ensures that the file we open or create is a valid DBM file and that the **tie** function to associate the hash to the DBM file succeeds.

```
12   foreach $key (@ARGV)
13   {
14       if (defined($db{$key}))
15       {
16           delete $db{$key};
17           print "Deleted key $key\n";
18       }
```

We set up a loop to step through each element of the **@ARGV** array in line 12, and then we check for the existence of the key on line 14 by using the **defined** function. If the key exists, we delete it on line 16 and report the fact on line 17. I haven't checked if the operation was successful; if you want to do this you can check the result of the **delete** function, which should equal the value of the key/value pair if the deletion was successful. For example, you could replace line 16 and 17 with

```
if (delete $db{$key})
{
print "Deleted key $key\n";
}
else
{
print "Couldn't delete key $key, $!\n";
}
```

However, be warned that the later Perl implementations don't necessarily return anything from the **delete** function. In any case, what is returned is the value element of the key/value pair, which could be a logically false value.

Also note that I've used the **delete** function. It is slower than **undef**, but it will delete both the key and value. Using **undef** only deletes the value, leaving the key intact. This still works if you test for the existence of the key/value pair with **defined**, but it will fail if you use the **exists** function. If you are concerned about performance, use **undef** instead.

PROGRAMMER'S NOTE   *The **defined** function returns true for the specified key within the hash if it contains a value. The **exists** function returns true if the specified key exists, even if there is no value associated with it.*

```
19        else
20        {
21            print "$key not found\n";
22        }
23   }
24
25   untie %db;
```

If the test for the existence of the key on line 14 fails, then we report an error to the user on line 21. We don't **die**, just in case the rest of the keys specified on the command line do exist. Since we're in a loop stepping through each key from the command line, it would be bad practice to drop out on such a simple error—it's not vital to the continuation of the script that all the keys exist. Line 25 closes the database.

Going back to our example from the last script, we could delete the "sample" key using the following command line:

```
$ dbmdel.pl sample
Deleted key sample
```

dbmempty.pl

Emptying a DBM File

Sometimes it is necessary to delete all of the records in a DBM file while leaving the file intact. There are three ways to empty an entire DBM file: delete the file and recreate an empty version; tie the DBM file, step through each element, and then delete each one; or tie a hash to the DBM file and then undefine the hash.

Going in reverse order, the last method is the most efficient and the easiest to implement. The second solution is less elegant, but it is more versatile. With some additional programming, it could be used to delete only certain records or record sets.

The first method is probably the most straightforward, but it does have its disadvantages. If you use a temporary DBM file as part of an update process, but only have access to modify an existing file in the specified directory, then deleting the file may not be possible, or if it is you probably won't be able to recreate it. The advantages of this method, though, are that the space used by the DBM file is completely recovered. It's not difficult with even small amounts of information to create very large DBM files. Using the last two methods deletes only the information in the database files; the space used by the DBM files is still allocated and taking up room on the disk. Deletion and recreation gets around this problem.

In the sample script, I've used the last method as an example of how easy DBM files are to manipulate using Perl.

```
1    #!/usr/local/bin/perl5 -w
2
3    die "Usage:\n$0 db\n" if (@ARGV<1);
```

```
4
5    $dbfile = shift;
6
7    use NDBM_File; use Fcntl;
8
9    tie (%db, NDBM_File, $dbfile, O_RDWR, 0666)
10       || die "$0: $dbfile: $!\n";
11
12   $startrecs = keys (%db);
13   undef %db;
14   $endrecs = keys (%db);
15
16   print "Reduced $dbfile from $startrecs to $endrecs records\n";
17
18   untie %db || die "$0 error closing $dbfile: $!\n";
19
```

ANNOTATIONS

Aside from checking the number of records before and after emptying the file, it's line 13 that does all the work. What happens behind the scenes is that Perl uses the functions **defined** and **associated** with the hash variable via the **tie** function to delete all of the keys from the database.

```
1    #!/usr/local/bin/perl5 -w
2
3    die "Usage:\n$0 db\n" if (@ARGV<1);
4
5    $dbfile = shift;
6
7    use NDBM_File; use Fcntl;
8
9    tie (%db, NDBM_File, $dbfile, O_RDWR, 0666)
10       || die "$0: $dbfile: $!\n";
11
```

Lines 1 to 11 are almost identical to the previous script. We're checking for only one argument, which we get from the argument list by shifting the first value off into the **$dbfile** variable.

```
12   $startrecs = keys (%db);
13   undef %db;
14   $endrecs = keys (%db);
```

Line 12 finds the number of records in the database. The result from the **keys** function, because we are assigning the result to a scalar variable, is the number of keys in the database. We then **undefine** the entire hash array in line 13, and then check the number of records again in line 14.

```
15
16   print "Reduced $dbfile from $startrecs to $endrecs records\n";
17
18   untie %db || die "$0 error closing $dbfile: $!\n";
19
```

We report the number of records before and after the deletion in line 16 as a visual report to the user of how many records were deleted. Although we don't test the result in this script, we could verify that all the records were deleted successfully by checking that **$endrecs** equals zero. We close the database on line 18.

To demonstrate the problems with emptying a DBM file this way, I've shown the directory listing of the database files before and after emptying the contacts database we created in the first script in this chapter.

```
$ ls -l contacts.*
-rw-------   1 martinb  1000              0 Jun 21 11:05 contacts.dir
-rw-------   1 martinb  1000           1024 Jun 21 11:05 contacts.pag
$ dbmempty.pl contacts
Reduced contacts from 35 to 0 records
$ ls -l contacts.*
-rw-------   1 martinb  1000              0 Jun 21 11:05 contacts.dir
-rw-------   1 martinb  1000           1024 Jun 21 13:51 contacts.pag
```

You can see that the database size, although small, has not reduced. The space will be reused when new records are added, although how much is reclaimed is entirely dependent on the DBM implementation in use, the keys being used, and the size of the data being updated. Continually updating the same keys with the same amount of information is unlikely to make a significant difference in the database size.

dbmmerge.pl

Merging DBM Databases

Have you ever had to merge two databases, but you didn't want to go through all the pain of extracting and then recreating the information?

Actually, with DBM files it's not quite that complicated; all you need to do is open the destination file and then read the contents from each file to be merged into the hashed array for the destination file. Before you go ahead and write your own version of the script, however, you need to check some details.

First of all, when copying the information across, you have to make sure that the key name does not already exist in the destination file. In some cases, you may want to merge two DBM files, knowing that the second file could happily overwrite some of the data in the first. The **dbmmerge.pl** script will combine two DBM databases, exiting with an error if duplicate keys are found. With a command-line switch, though, you can tell it to work quietly so it doesn't report the duplicates, or you can tell it to overwrite duplicate keys from later files.

```
1   #!/usr/local/bin/perl5
2
3   use Getopt::Std;
4
5   getopts('oqr');
6
7   die <<EOF
8   Usage:
9   $0 [-qcr] new files...
10
11  Where:
12
13  q Quiet mode (doesn't report duplicate keys)
14  o Overwrite existing keys
15  r Reuse existing DBM file
16  EOF
17  if (@ARGV<2);
18
19  use NDBM_File; use Fcntl;
20
21  $new = shift;
22
23  if ( $opt_r)
24  {
25      tie (%newhash, NDBM_File, $new, O_RDWR, 0666)
26      || die "$0: Error opening $new: $!\n";
27  }
28  else
29  {
30      tie (%newhash, NDBM_File, $new, O_RDWR|O_CREAT|O_EXCL, 0666)
31      || die "$0: Error creating $new: $!\n";
32  }
33
34  foreach $dbmfile (@ARGV)
35  {
36      tie (%inhash, NDBM_File, $dbmfile, O_RDONLY, 0444)
37      || die "$0: Error opening $dbmfile: $!\n";
```

```
38      foreach $key (keys %inhash)
39      {
40          if ((defined($newhash{$key})) && !($opt_o))
41          {
42              print "$key already exists - ignored\n" unless $opt_q;
43          }
44          else
45          {
46              $newhash{$key} = $inhash{$key};
47          }
48      }
49      untie $inhash;
50  }
51
52  untie %newhash;
53
```

ANNOTATIONS

This script is basically identical to the earlier **dbmstore.pl** script, except that the source of the key/value pair is another file rather than an entry from the command line. The script can be used to merge multiple DBM files into one—it joins all the DBM files quoted on the command line sequentially into a new or existing DBM file.

```
1   #!/usr/local/bin/perl5
2
3   use Getopt::Std;
4
5   getopts('oqr');
6
```

We use the **getopts** function from the standard Getopt::Std module on line 5 to identify the three command-line options. You can see from the usage message we print out on lines 8 to 15 what each of the options are used for.

```
7   die <<EOF
8   Usage:
9   $0 [-qcr] new files...
10
11  Where:
12
13  q Quiet mode (doesn't report duplicate keys)
```

```
14   o Overwrite existing keys
15   r Reuse existing DBM file
16   EOF
17   if (@ARGV<2);
18
```

On line 17 we check for a minimum of two arguments. The actual test statement is visibly a long way from the corresponding call to **die**. You can get around this by concatenating lines 7 and 17 into a line like this:

```
die <<EOF if (@ARGV<2);
```

The here document still works because the EOF tag is separated by a space from the rest of the statement. Be careful, though, not to delete this space, because Perl will report an error if it doesn't see the end of the here document.

```
19   use NDBM_File; use Fcntl;
20
21   $new = shift;
22
```

The first argument, which we extract (and delete from the list) by shifting the argument list on line 21, will be used as the destination database, and subsequent files will be merged into the new database. The first file can be an existing file, or a new one will be created. However, the script doesn't merge into an existing database file unless you specify the **-r** option on the command line.

```
23   if ( $opt_r)
24   {
25       tie (%newhash, NDBM_File, $new, O_RDWR, 0666)
26       || die "$0: Error opening $new: $!\n";
27   }
```

We check the command-line switch in line 23. If it is present, then the value of **$opt_r** will be one, or true, and lines 24 to 27 will be executed. The **tie** function on line 25 attempts to open an existing DBM file. By specifying **O_RDWR**, no new file will be created if the specified one doesn't exist, and an error will be returned, causing the **die** function on line 26 to report a suitably worded error.

```
28   else
29   {
30       tie (%newhash, NDBM_File, $new, O_RDWR|O_CREAT|O_EXCL, 0666)
31       || die "$0: Error creating $new: $!\n";
32   }
33
```

If the user hasn't specified that the first argument should be an existing DBM file, we try to open a new one on line 30. This time we specify **O_EXCL** to make sure the user isn't trying to create a new file when one of the same name already exists.

```
34   foreach $dbmfile (@ARGV)
35   {
36       tie (%inhash, NDBM_File, $dbmfile, O_RDONLY, 0444)
37       || die "$0: Error opening $dbmfile: $!\n";
```

By the time we get to line 34, the argument list consists of the files we want to merge. We step through each file using a **foreach** line, and then open it read-only on line 36. Since a missing file that the user wants to merge constitutes a serious error, we **die** on line 37 if the file doesn't exist.

```
38       foreach $key (keys %inhash)
39       {
40           if ((defined($newhash{$key})) && !($opt_o))
41           {
42               print "$key already exists - ignored\n" unless $opt_q;
43           }
```

On line 38 we start a **foreach** loop to work through each key of the database file we just opened. On line 40, we check the existence of the key from the database we're trying to merge in the new database file. We have a command-line argument that allows us to overwrite existing keys. We use a logical AND against the nonexistence of the command-line argument by using the not operator, the exclamation mark. So, line 40 reads as:

If $key is defined in the old file and we haven't specified that they should be overwritten...

On line 42 we print an error message, but we don't use the **die** function to quit the script. This operation could be deliberate, so we just warn the user of the occurrence. If the user had specified the **–q** switch (which specifies "quiet" mode) on the command line, we wouldn't print out the line.

```
44           else
45           {
46               $newhash{$key} = $inhash{$key};
47           }
```

The opposite of line 40 will match any nonexistent key or an existing key when the "overwrite" command-line switch has been set. Lines 44 to 47 then update the key in the new hash file from the merge file.

```
48       }
49       untie $inhash;
50   }
```

```
51
52   untie %newhash;
53
```

Line 48 is the end of the **foreach** loop from line 38. On line 49, we close the database file we were merging; line 50 closes the **foreach** loop from line 34, and we proceed to the next file. When all the files to be merged have been merged, we close the destination database on line 52.

When working with very large databases, the **foreach** statement will consume large amounts of memory as it loads every key from the database into Perl to the form the list that will be stepped through. You can avoid this problem by replacing it with a **while** loop instead:

```
while (($key,$value) = each %inhash)
```

This substitution also has the advantage of accessing the value of the key as part of each loop execution, which may help to reduce some of the overhead.

The script is straightforward; it is only made more complicated by the requirement to step through each key of the files to be merged. The reason for this requirement, however, is to check the existing keys. Even if we knew that existing keys could be overwritten, there is no quicker way to add the contents of one database to another. Using

```
%dba = %dbb;
```

would replace the entire content of **%dba** with **%dbb**, which is not the desired effect!

However, we can use Perl's ability to copy entire hash arrays as shown above to convert from one DBM file to another, which is exactly what we do in the **cvdbm.pl** script in the section "Converting Between DBM Implementations" later in this chapter.

build.pl

Populating a Semirelational DBM Database

As I've already mentioned, DBM was not designed to be a relational database. It should be evident by now that the key/value pairs are flexible enough to simulate many database structures, but they have their limitations. Relational database systems use a key value, a unique identifier of some sort, that can be found in two database structures. Because we can store the same ID in two different tables, the tables can be related to each other. This is the "relational" part of the relational database term.

We already know that with some planning we can simulate a database table in a DBM file, just by some careful naming of the key used to store a particular value. Since the key can actually be made up of anything, what's stopping us from inventing a key that consists of some form of identifier that could be used to match another entry in the DBM file that's logically classed as a separate table?

The answer is, nothing. Let's look at a simple example. If you manage a reasonably sized office network, you are likely to have a patch panel in one corner of the office that relates to a number of floor or wall points (see Figure 4-1). Each of these points can support either a phone or a network connection. The phone side is related to a specific extension, and the network side is connected to a specific piece of network hardware. We can record this information in three "tables." The patch table is a list of patch panel socket numbers; the phone table is the list of phone sockets and their corresponding extension number; and the network table is the list of network hubs.

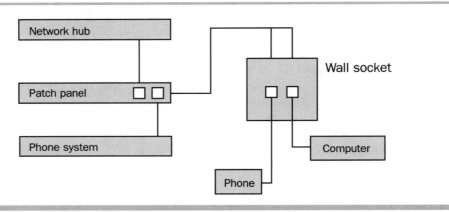

FIGURE 4-1.   The patch panel/wall socket relationship

For our example, the patch table consists of the socket ID number, the type of device (network or phone) plugged into the socket, and the device number of the specified device the socket is connected to. For example:

ID	Device Type	Device Socket
1	Phone	V01
2	Network	43

The phone table contains the voice panel ID and the extension it relates to, such as:

ID	Extension
V01	200

The network table consists of the network socket number, the network device that the socket number corresponds to, and the port on that device the socket is connected to, such as:

ID	Device	Port
43	Bay Switch	1
44	3COM Router	13

To map that information in a DBM file looks impossible, but using a simple key naming system makes it both possible and practical.

First, enter the contents of the patch table, using a key of "patch-*ID*," where *ID* is the ID number. The remainder of the fields should be separated by a comma, colon, or other separator and placed in the corresponding value. A dump of the DBM file would look something like this:

```
patch-1      Phone:V01
patch-2      Network:43
```

Then repeat the exercise with the other two tables. The full DBM dump would then look like this:

```
patch-1      Phone:V01
patch-2      Network:43
phone-V01    200
network-43   Bay Switch:1
network-44   3COM Router:13
```

When it comes to extracting the information, extract the base table, patch. The value for each entry can be transformed into the key of the next table "row" to interrogate. So, to intelligently extract the information for "patch-1" with a value of "Phone:V01," we would look for a key value of "phone-V01," and that entry tells us that patch panel port 1 is connected to extension 200.

It looks complicated at first, but you just have to treat the key of each DBM entry as consisting of the table name and unique identifier within the table. This method emulates the method used by a relational database.

The **build.pl** script uses this technique to build a complete relational database for the patch panel, the network devices those ports might be attached to, and the extensions they might be attached to. To further expand the information, there is also a network device table and an extensions table that maps the extension number to a direct-dial table and the owner of the extension number. The script works by reading in individual files; the name of each file is the table name, and the contents of the file are the fields for each row. The next script, **laypatch.pl**, demonstrates how to extract the information from this relational DBM file.

The example tables build the layout shown in Table 4-2.

PROGRAMMER'S NOTE   *The term DDI is short for Direct Dialing Inwards, and it refers to the phone numbers that go directly to someone's desk, instead of callers having to go through an operator.*

Table	Description
Layout	Consists of power points (static), network ports (from the network table), and voice ports (from the voice table)
Hubs	The list of network devices that network ports are connected to
Network	The available network devices and ports attached to the port ID
Voice	The extension number and DDI number
DDI	The direct dial numbers
Ext	The extensions and their owners

TABLE 4-2.   Semirelational Database Tables

Armed with this information, we can extract all the information about a floorbox, including what hub the network ports are connected to and what extension and DDI number a particular voice port has.

```perl
1    #!/usr/local/bin/perl5
2
3    use NDBM_File;
4    use Fcntl;
5
6    use Getopt::Std;
7
8    tie (%laypatch, NDBM_File, 'patch', O_CREAT|O_RDWR, 0666)
9        || die "$0: Couldn't open the database, $!\n";
10
11   getopts('d');
12
13   die <<EOF
14   Usage:
15   $0 [-d] component
16
17   Where:
18
19   -d Don't generate type contents list
20   EOF
21   if (@ARGV<1);
22
```

```perl
23   for $file (@ARGV)
24   {
25       open (D,"<$file") || die "$0: Can't open $file, $!\n";
26       local($firstrow,$notypelist) = (1,0);
27
28       while(<D>)
29       {
30           chomp;
31           ($id,$type,@data) = split /:/;
32
33           $notypelist=1 if ($opt_d);
34           $firstrow=$notypelist;
35
36           if ($firstrow)
37           {
38               $lastid = $id;
39               $firstrow=0;
40           }
41
42           if ($id ne $lastid)
43           {
44               chop $types;
45               $laypatch{"$file-$lastid"} = $types;
46               $types="";
47               $lastid=$id;
48           }
49
50           $types .= $type . ":";
51
52           $laypatch{"$file-$id-$type"} = join(':',@data);
53
54       }
55       if ($notypelist == 0)
56       {
57           chop $types;
58           $laypatch{"$file-$lastid"} = $types;
59       }
60       $types="";
61   }
62
```

ANNOTATIONS

The script opens and reads files, putting the fields into corresponding key/value pairs in a DBM file. Table names are identified by the filename, and the format of the table data has to match the table names for the script to populate the table correctly.

```
1    #!/usr/local/bin/perl5
2
3    use NDBM_File;
4    use Fcntl;
5
6    use Getopt::Std;
7
8    tie (%laypatch, NDBM_File, 'patch', O_CREAT|O_RDWR, 0666)
9        || die "$0: Couldn't open the database, $!\n";
10
11   getopts('d');
12
```

Lines 1 to 12 do the familiar initialization sequence. Note that on line 8 I'm expecting to either create a new file or update an existing one. I've also hardcoded the filename, since I want to ensure that data goes into the right place for the extraction script.

We use **getopts** to check for a **-d** command-line argument. We'll use this argument to decide whether to generate a type contents list; this is the list of expected types we link to from other "tables" within the DBM database. It's not vital that we switch off the creation, but it might save some space at a future date if we expand this database to include other information.

```
13   die <<EOF
14   Usage:
15   $0 [-d] component
16
17   Where:
18
19   -d Don't generate type contents list
20   EOF
21   if (@ARGV<1);
22
```

The usage message forms lines 13 to 21.

```
23   for $file (@ARGV)
24   {
```

```
25    open (D,"<$file") || die "$0: Can't open $file, $!\n";
26    local($firstrow,$notypelist) = (1,0);
27
```

Line 23 sets up a loop to go through each file specified on the command line. The file is opened on line 25, and we want to quit if there is an error, just in case the user has specified the wrong list of files.

Line 26 initializes two variables. The **$firstrow** variable will be used to determine if we are reading the first line from the script. The **$don't** variable will be used to decide whether we should produce a list of field types; it is calculated in combination with the **$firstrow** and **$opt_d** variables. We set them to 1 and 0, respectively, to signify that to begin with we are on the first line and that we don't want to generate the type list.

```
28    while(<D>)
29    {
30        chomp;
31        ($id,$type,@data) = split /:/;
32
33        $notypelist=1 if ($opt_d);
34        $firstrow=$notypelist;
35
```

Line 28 is the start of the loop that will step through the lines in the source file. We chop off the last character (the new line) on line 30 since we don't want it. Line 31 extracts the data from the source file. The format of an input file is the ID, table name, and data for the record. If the command-line option is set to not create the type list, we set **$don't** in line 33. We make **$firstrow** equal **$don't** in line 34. This information is used in the next few lines to decide whether to generate the type list.

```
36        if ($firstrow)
37        {
38            $lastid = $id;
39            $firstrow=0;
40        }
41
```

If this is the first line, or if we don't want to output the type list, we set a variable called **lastid** to the ID of the current record and then set **$firstrow** to zero again. This is then verified in line 42.

```
42        if ($id ne $lastid)
43        {
44            chop $types;
45            $laypatch{"$file-$lastid"} = $types;
46            $types="";
```

```
47              $lastid=$id;
48          }
49
```

Line 42 decides whether to generate the list of types from the current line. If you've followed the script up to this point, you will know that we identify whether to print the list of types with a combination of the **$don't** variable and the **$firstrow** variable. By the time we get to this line, we will know whether we want the list of device types contained in the *previous* input line placed into the database. The lines from 33 to 42 work out the following:

◆ If **$firstrow** has been set, then we are on the first line in the source, and there is no list to output.

◆ If the **-d** command-line argument has been set, then we don't want to output the list anyway.

If the two statements above are true, then the **$lastid** and **$id** variables will match. In line 42 we are checking for a nonmatch between these two variables and therefore a requirement to add the device-type list to the database. The complexity comes from having to deal with both the first line in the file and the user request to ignore the list anyway.

The recording operation occurs in lines 44 to 47. In line 44 we strip the trailing colon off the string (see line 50), then write out an entry matching the filename and the record ID against which to store the list of device types. We then empty the list, get ready for the next file, and reset the **lastid** so it matches the current ID to prevent us performing this operation again.

This sequence could be neater: we could use an array to store the information and then use **join** to write the information out. However, the intention has always been to update this section to account for duplicate device types (currently it places duplicates in the list) and to intelligently decide which device types aren't already referenced anyway.

```
50          $types .= $type . ":";
51
52          $laypatch{"$file-$id-$type"} = join(':',@data);
53
54      }
```

Line 50 composes the device type list for the current ID. This is an untidy solution to the requirement, but like many programs written in Perl it works, even though it might not be the most effective method.

Line 52 actually writes the data to the file. The format for the table is the filename, the Id, and the device type.

```
55      if ($notypelist == 0)
56      {
57          chop $types;
58          $laypatch{"$file-$lastid"} = $types;
59      }
60      $types="";
61  }
62
```

Lines 55 to 62 polish off the process by adding a type list for the last ID, provided we haven't specified that we don't want the information recorded.

The bulk of the script centers around deciding whether to add a list of the device types against each ID, accounting for multiple files specified on the command line. We could, in theory, strip out half of the script if we made it a requirement that source files were added individually, but such a requirement is cumbersome for a large number of source files.

Incidentally, the reason for recording the information is so that we have a list of device types to look up when it comes time to extract the relational information from the database. Without it, the process of looking up the information would be slower, as we would have to generate a unique list from the database. Using this list, we can attribute the same socket to multiple other tables, purely because we can specify two different devices against the same ID. Better still, we can reference any number of different devices within the source file. We'll see the significance of this ability in the reporting script.

Before we move on to the next script, let's populate the database. Copy the scripts and data files from the CD-ROM and type the following lines:

```
$ build.pl layout hubs network
$ build.pl -d ddi voice ext
```

These commands will create the semirelational database called **patch** in the current directory.

laypatch.pl

Reporting from a Semirelational DBM Database

Keeping the previous script in mind, let's look at how the information we've just incorporated into the database can be extracted. The following script is intended to report the information as part of an Intranet, so the output format is in the form of

HTML tables. I'll assume for the moment that you are comfortable with HTML—it doesn't affect the operation of the script, but it does add extra lines and occasionally extra decisions into the reporting process.

```perl
1    #!/usr/local/bin/perl5
2
3    use NDBM_File;
4    use Fcntl;
5
6
7    print "Content-type: text/html\n\n";
8
9    my $datafile="patch";
10   my (%laypatch,$key,$refno);
11   my ($type,@types,@typedata,%floorpoint,$netsock);
12
13   tie (%laypatch, NDBM_File, $datafile, O_RDONLY, 0444)
14       || die "<h1>Can't open data file, $!</h1>";
15
16   print <<EOF
17   <head>
18   <title>Patches and Floorpoints</title>
19   <h1>Patches and Floorpoints</h1>
20   <table border=1>
21   <tr><td><b>Floorpoint</b>
22   <td><b>Type</b>
23   <td><b>Ref/Qty</b>
24   <td><b>Sub-Type</b>
25   <td><b>Sub-Ref</b>
26   <td><b>Info</b>
27   EOF
28       ;
29
30   for $key (sort keys (%laypatch))
31   {
32       if ($key =~ /layout-[0-9]+$/)
33       {
34           $refno = (split /-/,$key)[1];
35           (@types) = split /:/,$laypatch{$key};
36           for $type (@types)
37           {
38               (@typedata) = split /:/,$laypatch{"$key-$type"};
39
```

```
40              if (!defined($floorpoint{$refno}))
41              {
42                  print "<tr><td>$refno\n";
43                  $floorpoint{$refno}=$refno;
44              }
45              else
46              {
47                  print "<tr><td>\n";
48              }
49
50              if ( $type eq "Power" )
51              {
52                  print "<td>Power Sockets<td>$typedata[0]\n";
53              }
54              elsif ( $type eq "Net" )
55              {
56                  for $netsock (@typedata)
57                  {
58                      &print_netsock_data($netsock,0);
59                  }
60              }
61              elsif ( $type eq "Voice" )
62              {
63                  for $netsock (@typedata)
64                  {
65                      &print_phone_data($netsock,0);
66                  }
67              }
68          }
69      }
70
71  }
72
73  print "</table>";
74
75  sub print_phone_data
76  {
77      my ($voice,$return) = @_;
78          my ($voiceref,@voicedata,$voicedata);
79
80          if ($return)
81          {
82              $voiceref = $laypatch{"voice-$voice-Ext"};
```

```perl
83          (@voicedata) = split /:/,$laypatch{"ext-$voiceref-Ext"};
84     }
85       else
86     {
87         $voiceref = $laypatch{"ext-$voice-Ext"};
88         $voicedata = $laypatch{"ext-$voice-$voiceref"};
89     }
90
91     if ($return)
92     {
93         return("V$voice<td>$voiceref, $voicedata[3]\n");
94     }
95     else
96     {
97         print "<tr><td><td>Voice: Ext: $voice, $voiceref, $voicedata\n";
98     }
99   }
100
101  sub print_netsock_data
102  {
103     my ($netsock,$return) = @_;
104     my ($netsockref,$netsockdata,$fulldata,$subsep,$hub,$hubport);
105
106     $netsockref = $laypatch{"network-$netsock"};
107     $netsockdata = $laypatch{"network-$netsock-$netsockref"};
108
109     if ($return)
110     {
111         $subsep=", ";
112     }
113     else
114     {
115         $subsep="<Td>";
116     }
117
118     if ($netsockref eq "Hub")
119     {
120         ($hub,$hubport) = split /:/, $netsockdata;
121         $fulldata = $laypatch{"hubs-$hub"} . "($hub)<td>$hubport";
122     }
123     elsif ($netsockref eq "Patch")
124     {
125         $fulldata = $netsockref . "<td>to $netsockdata<td>" .
```

```
126                    print_netsock_data($netsockdata,1);
127            }
128        elsif ($netsockref eq "Voice")
129        {
130            $fulldata = $netsockref . "$subsep" .
131                print_phone_data($netsockdata,1);
132        }
133        else
134        {
135            $fulldata = $netsockref . "$subsep" . $netsockdata;
136        }
137
138        if ($return)
139        {
140            return $fulldata;
141        }
142        else
143        {
144        print "<tr><td><Td>Patch<td>$netsock<td>" . $fulldata . "\n";
145    }
146 }
147
```

ANNOTATIONS

The script reads in the database, identifying the key table that is called **layout**. We step through each layout in the table recursively, extracting the information stored against the table key. Because of the nature of the data, and the needs of the relational links, reading information from one table will probably require access to another table to expand all the information.

```
1   #!/usr/local/bin/perl5
2
3   use NDBM_File;
4   use Fcntl;
5
6
7   print "Content-type: text/html\n\n";
8
```

We include the basic database modules we expect to use. Line 7 sends the necessary file type information to the Web browser so it interprets the result as HTML, not plain text.

```
9   my $datafile="patch";
10  my (%laypatch,$key,$refno);
11  my ($type, @types, @typedata,%floorpoint,$netsock);
12
13  tie (%laypatch, NDBM_File, $datafile, O_RDONLY, 0444)
14      || die "<h1>Can't open data file, $!</h1>";
15
```

Lines 9 to 11 localize the variables we will use in the rest of the script. The data file is specified in line 9; because this is a Web-based script, we need to specify the data file filename directly within the script, and we can't use a command-line option the same way as we would a command-line-driven script.

The rest of the variables will store information about the different device types we will look up as part of the relational process. Line 13 opens the data file as read-only, with a suitably formatted HTML message if an error occurs.

```
16  print <<EOF
17  <head>
18  <title>Patches and Floorpoints</title>
19  <h1>Patches and Floorpoints</h1>
20  <table border=1>
21  <tr><td><b>Floorpoint</b>
22  <td><b>Type</b>
23  <td><b>Ref/Qty</b>
24  <td><b>Sub-Type</b>
25  <td><b>Sub-Ref</b>
26  <td><b>Info</b>
27  EOF
28      ;
29
```

Lines 16 to 27 output the table header, which will be populated with information. We report on the base information, the floorpoint reference, the type, the reference number of the device were connecting to, the subtype (network, voice, and so on), the subreference number, and finally any information attached to that subreference. Line 28 is a single semicolon separating the **print** statement from the following **for** statement.

PROGRAMMER'S NOTE   *Using semicolons after here documents also helps emacs to indent the source file correctly.*

```
30  for $key (sort keys (%laypatch))
31  {
32      if ($key =~ /layout-[0-9]+$/)
33      {
```

Line 30 is the start of the real reporting mechanism. We work through each key in the database, sorted alphabetically. We're looking at this stage only for keys starting with "layout" on line 32. In fact, this script is the only key we look for, but it paves the way for expanding the report to include other base keys from the database. For example, we may want to report on extension numbers and how they relate to floorpoints, rather than the other way around. Note that we are looking for a key of "layout-*x*" where *x* is a number.

The value of the"layout-*x*" key is where the device list information is stored. As an example, you could have a floorbox with an ID of 1, which consists of 4 network points and 2 phone points. The device type list would contain "network" and "phone." By identifying the list of devices attached to a single floorbox, we speed up the processing of the related information. Some entries don't need this list, however. For example, an extension entry consists of only the extension number, the direct dial number attached to it, and who owns the extension. There is only one piece of information to look up: the DDI number.

Assuming the key matches the format in line 32, we proceed to extract the information for each device type listed. On line 34 we use the subscript notation to extract the floorpoint ID from the key. Line 35 splits the device list up into an array called **types**.

```
34      $refno = (split /-/,$key)[1];
35      (@types) = split /:/,$laypatch{$key};
36      for $type (@types)
37      {
38          (@typedata) = split /:/,$laypatch{"$key-$type"};
39
```

Line 36 sets up the loop to select each device type and extract the information from the corresponding key. We get the device type–specific information by looking up the existing "layout-*xx*" key combined with the current device type and place it into the **@typedata** array in line 38.

```
40          if (!defined($floorpoint{$refno}))
41          {
42              print "<tr><td>$refno\n";
43              $floorpoint{$refno}=$refno;
44          }
45          else
46          {
47              print "<tr><td>\n";
48          }
49
```

Lines 40 to 44 print out the current floorpoint ID number if it hasn't already been reported on. The list of reported IDs is stored in **%floorpoint**. We update the list of

reported floorpoints on line 43. If the floorpoint has already been reported on, we
start a blank table row.

```
50          if ( $type eq "Power" )
51          {
52               print "<td>Power Sockets<td>$typedata[0]\n";
53          }
```

If the device type is "Power." then we just report the number of power sockets on
line 52. This information is stored in the first field of the value information, which
we have already extracted into the **@typedata** variable.

```
54          elsif ( $type eq "Net" )
55          {
56               for $netsock (@typedata)
57               {
58                &print_netsock_data($netsock,0);
59               }
60          }
```

If the device is not "Power" but rather "Net," then we print out the network socket
information. Each socket in the floorpoint is an individual element of the **@typedata**
array. We work through each floorpoint as part of the for loop on line 56 by calling
the print_netsock_data function, passing the network socket ID and a true/false
variable. We'll see how this is used later in the script.

```
61          elsif ( $type eq "Voice" )
62          {
63               for $netsock (@typedata)
64               {
65                &print_phone_data($netsock,0);
66               }
67          }
```

Lines 61 to 67 perform the same operation if the device type is listed as "Voice."
This time we call the **print_phone_data** function, passing the same ID information
and a similar true/false variable.

```
68     }
69    }
70
71 }
72
73 print "</table>";
74
```

By line 68 we have identified all the types of the devices we want to report on in this script, so we close the loops until we get to the point of closing the final loop on line 71. Line 73 ends the HTML table; without this end tag the table would not be displayed by the browser.

```
75   sub print_phone_data
76   {
77       my ($voice,$return) = @_;
78           my ($voiceref,@voicedata,$voicedata);
79
```

Line 75 is the start of the **print_phone_data** function. The function arguments and local variables are set up in lines 77 and 78.

```
80       if ($return)
81       {
82           $voiceref = $laypatch{"voice-$voice-Ext"};
83           (@voicedata) = split /:/,$laypatch{"ext-$voiceref-Ext"};
84       }
85       else
86       {
87           $voiceref = $laypatch{"ext-$voice-Ext"};
88           $voicedata = $laypatch{"ext-$voice-$voiceref"};
89       }
90
```

The **$return** variable is used to decide whether we are printing the phone information within the function, or whether we are to return the information to the calling function. Which one we want to do affects how we extract the information. The reason for returning the data is that the floorpoint ID is connected to the network patch panel, and therefore we need to extract a different set of information. Lines 82 and 83 extract the voice port and extension number this information relates to and puts it into the **$voiceref** and **@voicedata** variables.

If we are reporting the information locally, it means the floorpoint is a voice port, and therefore we must extract the extension information from the database directly. The information is placed into the same variables on lines 87 and 88.

```
91       if ($return)
92       {
93           return("V$voice<td>$voiceref, $voicedata[3]\n");
94       }
95       else
96       {
97           print "<tr><td><td>Voice: Ext: $voice, $voiceref, $voicedata\n";
98       }
```

```
99  }
100
```

Assuming we are still returning the information, on line 93 we report the voice port number, the floorpoint it relates to, and the extension information as a string. If we are reporting locally, we output the columns of the table on line 97. We could combine these lines with the earlier **if** statement, but I've split them here for a combination of clarity and to offer us the opportunity to further format the information in the intervening lines.

```
101  sub print_netsock_data
102  {
103      my ($netsock,$return) = @_;
104      my ($netsockref,$netsockdata,$fulldata,$subsep,$hub,$hubport);
105
106      $netsockref = $laypatch{"network-$netsock"};
107      $netsockdata = $laypatch{"network-$netsock-$netsockref"};
108
```

Line 101 is the start of the **print_netsock_data** function. The function arguments and local variables are set up in lines 103 and 104. Line 106 composes the key used to extract the network data. Line 107 composes the key relating to the network socket and the hub reference it is connected to.

```
109      if ($return)
110      {
111          $subsep=", ";
112      }
113      else
114      {
115          $subsep="<Td>";
116      }
117
```

Once again, we have the ability to return the information as a string. If we are reporting it as a string, then it is the extended information we're reporting on, and we therefore separate the data with a comma on line 111 or create a column on line 115. We could shorten these lines to just one by using a single test line, like this:

```
$subsep = $return ? ', ' : '<Td>';
```

It achieves the same result, but in fewer lines.

```
118      if ($netsockref eq "Hub")
119      {
120          ($hub,$hubport) = split /:/, $netsockdata;
121          $fulldata = $laypatch{"hubs-$hub"} . "($hub)<td>$hubport";
122      }
```

If the port we are connected to is a hub, we extract the hub information from the database on lines 120 and 121.

```
123     elsif ($netsockref eq "Patch")
124     {
125         $fulldata = $netsockref . "<td>to $netsockdata<td>" .
126          print_netsock_data($netsockdata,1);
127     }
```

If the entry is another patch socket, we fill the **fulldata** variable on lines 125 and 126, adding the information about the port by calling **print_netsock_data** again, specifying the return option to get the extended information returned as a string.

```
128     elsif ($netsockref eq "Voice")
129     {
130         $fulldata = $netsockref . "$subsep" .
131          print_phone_data($netsockdata,1);
132     }
```

If the path port is connected to a voice patch panel, then we fill the **fulldata** variable with the information by calling **print_phone_data** with the return option set to get the data returned by the function as a string. As with line 125, we use concatenation to generate the full string.

```
133     else
134     {
135         $fulldata = $netsockref . "$subsep" . $netsockdata;
136     }
137
```

If the device type that the patch port is connected to has not already been identified, then we must be at the end of the process, and so the patch port is a simple port reference.

```
138     if ($return)
139     {
140         return $fulldata;
141     }
142     else
143     {
144     print "<tr><td><Td>Patch<td>$netsock<td>" . $fulldata . "\n";
145     }
146 }
147
```

On line 138 we decide whether to simply print the information on line 140, or to return the information to the calling function on line 144 as a formatted string.

The script, as I stated earlier, uses a certain level of recursion to extract deeper levels of relational information from the database. Running the script and then viewing it in a browser gives output similar to that below.

Patches and Floorpoints

Floorpoint	Type	Ref/Qty	Subtype	Subref	Info
1	Power Sockets	2			
	Voice: Ext: 2, ,				
	Patch	1	Voice	1	
	Patch	39	CNet 8910 (1)	10	
	Patch	41	Voice	1	
	Patch	53	ISDN	434912	
	Patch	54	CNet 8910 (1)	5	
	Patch	55	AppleTalk	SlowTalk	
	Patch	56			

As I stated at the start of the previous script, writing relational databases in any program requires careful planning. With DBM files, we also need to consider how the information is stored when we have access only to a key/value pair. However, once we get over that hurdle of data modeling, we can very easily and quickly produce an effective relational database.

Under no circumstance, though, should we expect DBM files to replace the traditional relational databases of Microsoft Access, Oracle, and others. But we can make pretty good mock-ups to be used for simple solutions.

cvdbm.pl

Converting Between DBM Implementations

Perl supports a number of different DBM implementations. Because of the differences in DBM implementations, you may find yourself in a position where you need the features of a different implementation, but it seems they can't easily be exported and recreated. Well, of course, we know that's not necessarily true, since extracting the information is easy, and writing that information to a new database is similarly straightforward.

The implementations supported by Perl are dependent on compile time, since it's necessary to include the C code that accesses the DBM files. Perl is capable of supporting of multiple implementations simultaneously, so we can use Perl to convert files between different DBM formats within a single script. Better still, using the **tie** function, converting information from one DBM implementation to the other requires just a single line.

Actually, Perl can dynamically load modules at run time if the Perl port supports dynamic loading, but we won't go into that quite yet.

```
1   #!/usr/local/bin/perl5
2
3   die "Usage:$0 old new\n" if (@ARGV != 2);
4
5   local($old,$new) = @ARGV;
6
7   print "Converting $old -> $new\n";
8
9   use Fcntl; use NDBM_File; use SDBM_File;
10
11  tie (%oldhash, NDBM_File, $old, O_RDONLY, 0444)
12      || die "$0: Error opening source $old: $!\n";
13  tie (%newhash, SDBM_File, $new, O_CREAT|O_RDWR|O_EXCL, 0666)
14      || die "$0: Error opening dest $new: $!\n";
15
16  %newhash = %oldhash;
17
18  untie %oldhash;
19  untie %newhash;
20
```

ANNOTATIONS

The layout of the script is very straightforward, and it follows an identical format to the other scripts in this chapter. Line 16 does all the work, copying the contents of the existing hash file to the new one. Because of the **tie** function matching the DBM files to hashes, all we have to do is copy the old hash to the new hash variable. Perl, and the DBM modules you are using for the DBM files, will do the rest of the work.

There is one major problem with this process that we have touched on before. With very large databases, the script would consume large amounts of memory. We can get around this by using a **while** loop as we have done in other memory intensive examples:

```
$newhash($key) = $value while ($key, $value) = each %oldhash;
```

This still reduces the script to just one line, once we remove the wrapping around the outside.

db3.pl

Reading dBase III Databases

A popular database format in the early days of PC computing was DBF, Data Base Format. Ashton-Tate's dBase I/II/III/III+ and then IV used the same basic format. More recently the DBF file has been the underlying format of Borland's Delphi after their purchase of Ashton-Tate. There are different file format versions, depending on the corresponding version of the dBase application. This script expects to find dBase III files.

The format is very simple and straightforward and has been used for many years both as a database format and as a method for exchanging database-format files between machines, applications, and platforms. Even today, many database and spreadsheet applications still support the DBF format. The database is stored in a single file with a header composed of the field information, name, type, and length and with records that are stored as fixed-length entries. Knowing the format will enable you to pick out the field length, and once you know the field length, you can extract the necessary field data.

The **db3.pl** script that follows is part of the DB3 script from the CPAN archives. This script is a package that defines the basic functions for identifying and reading DBF files. A sample script to extract the information into a text file is shown later in the **db3flat.pl** script. Note that this script was written under Perl 4 and is now six years old. It's not quality assured, although the author confirms that this is still a popular script downloaded from the CPAN archives.

The original script (I've used a slightly modified version here) used a program called repl, written by the same author, to convert accented characters into nonaccent versions. The program is written in C, and I've included the source on the CD-ROM. I've removed the use of this program from the script here, since the need for it related to viewing files on 7-bit terminals.

Also note, as mentioned at the start of this chapter, that a module does exist for use with the DBI toolkit that supports XBase databases. This is a heavyweight solution to the problem we are solving in these scripts, and the example here shows in detail how accessing other databases can be quite straightforward if you know the format of the database you are accessing.

```perl
1   # db3.pl -- routines to read dBaseIII-files
2   # (c) 1992 Paul Bijnens
3
4   package db3;
5
6   # initialise db3-structures from header of the file
7   # usage: db3init(FH);
8   sub main'db3init {
9       local(*Db3) = shift(@_);
```

```
10      local($rec, $pos);
11
12      seek(Db3, 0, 0);
13      read(Db3, $rec, 32);
14      $db3version = &endian(substr($rec,0,1));
15      $db3totrec  = &endian(substr($rec,4,4));
16      $db3lenhead = &endian(substr($rec,8,2)) - 1;
17      $db3lenrec  = &endian(substr($rec,10,2));
18
19      if ($db3version == 0x83) {
20       warn("Cannot handle memo-fields\n");
21      } elsif ($db3version != 0x03) {
22       warn("Not a db3-file\n");
23       return 0;
24      }
25
26      $db3nf = $[;
27      $db3fmt = "a1";
28      for ($pos = 32; $pos < $db3lenhead; $pos += 32) {
29       read(Db3, $rec, 32);
30       $db3fn[$db3nf] = unpack("A11", $rec);
31       $db3fn[$db3nf] =~ s/\000.*//;
32       $db3ft[$db3nf] = substr($rec,11,1);
33       $db3fl[$db3nf] = &endian(substr($rec,16,2));
34       $db3fi{$db3fn[$db3nf]} = $db3nf;
35       $db3fmt .= "A$db3fl[$db3nf]";
36       $db3nf++;
37      }
38
39      if (($c = getc(Db3)) != "\r") {
40       print "Header korrupt...\n";
41      }
42      1;
43  }
44
45
46  # read the next record in the db3-file
47  # usage:  db3read(FH)
48  # return: list of fields, or () on eof or error;
49  sub main'db3read {
50      local(*Db3) = shift(@_);
51      local($rec, $del, @res);
52
```

```
53      do {
54       read(Db3, $rec, $db3lenrec)  ||  return ();
55       ($del, @res) = unpack($db3fmt, $rec);
56      } while ($del ne " ");
57      return @res;
58  }
59
60
61  # print db3-record in flatfile-record format
62  # usage: db3_flat_str
63  sub main'db3_flat_str {
64      local($,) = "\t";
65      local($\) = "\n";
66
67      print @db3fn;
68      print @db3fl;
69      print @db3ft;
70  }
71
72
73  # convert to flatfile-like database
74  # usage: db3_flat(DBHANDLE)
75  sub main'db3_flat {
76      local(*Db3) = shift(@_);
77      local($,) = "\t";
78      local($\) = "\n";
79      local(@flds);
80
81      while (@flds = &main'db3read(*Db3)) {
82       print @flds;
83      }
84  }
85
86
87  # convert little-endian to native machine order
88  # (intel = big-endian  ->  mc68k = big-endian)
89  # usage
90  sub endian
91  {
92      local($n) = 0;
93      foreach (reverse(split('', $_[0]))) {
94       $n = $n * 256 + ord;
95      }
```

```
96      $n;
97   }
98
99   1;
```

ANNOTATIONS

The package is split into five functions: **db3init**, **db3read**, **db3_flat_str**, **db3_flat**, and **endian**. The **db3init** function opens the specified file and determines if it is a DBF file that it can read. Reading records from the file relies on the **db3read** function. To print out the format information in a text format, you use the **db3_flat_str** function, and to print out record contents in text format you would use the **db3_flat** function. Finally, to get around the problems of reading strings from other hardware platforms, we use the **endian** function. See the sidebar for details on the differences between little-endian and big-endian and why they affect storage.

```
1   # db3.pl -- routines to read dBaseIII-files
2   # (c) 1992 Paul Bijnens
3
4   package db3;
5
```

Little-endian or Big-endian

The byte order of an operating system can be described as "big-endian" or "little-endian." Big-endian OSs store the larger portions of the number in the lower bytes, so the number 0x12345678 would have digits 1 and 2 in byte 0, 3 and 4 in byte 1, and so on.

In little-endian OSs the reverse is true: 1 and 2 would be stored in byte 3, 3 and 4 in byte 2, and so on, ending with 78 in byte 0. You can see the difference more clearly if you take a look at the following list:

Byte	Little-endian Value	Big-endian Value
0	78	12
1	56	34
2	34	56
4	12	78

The type of OS affects the storage of numbers and binary strings but not the storage of standard text strings, which are stored sequentially in memory, regardless of the processor.

Because this is a package, we don't need to define the usual first line; it won't be executed as a script from the command line, and the interpreter (Perl) will already be running when the module is incorporated. Instead Paul has given it over to a copyright and information notice. On line 4 we specify the name of the package we are defining as **db3**. By defining a new package, we create a new name space within the script, so all functions and variables we create will be within the db3 name space by default, until a new package is included or defined.

```
6    # initialise db3-structures from header of the file
7    # usage: db3init(FH);
8    sub main'db3init {
9        local(*Db3) = shift(@_);
10       local($rec, $pos);
11
12       seek(Db3, 0, 0);
13       read(Db3, $rec, 32);
```

On line 8 we define the first function, **db3init**. Confusingly, although we specified a new package on line 4, we have explicitly referenced the function to be within the main (default) package name space (usually the calling script). This allows a user calling the function to use **db3init** instead of having to prefix it with the **db3** package name.

Line 9 extracts a file handle reference from the function arguments. This is the file handle that points to an open DBF file. Line 10 defines two local variables: **$rec**, which will hold record information, and **$pos**, which will be used to store the current position within the file. In both lines 9 and 10 we specify the variables as local—Perl 4 didn't have the **my** keyword. The variables will be local to the function and any functions made by **db3init**.

We move to the start of the file in line 12. The **seek** function is identical to the C version and allows us to move to any character within the file, irrespective of the line or other text separation. The first argument specifies the file handle, the second the character number within the file we're seeking, and the third the reference point to make the move from. In this example, we've directly specified a zero, which tells Perl to seek to the specified byte from the beginning of the file. In other words, we are seeking the start of the file (byte 0) from the start of the file (0). This shouldn't be necessary because the file handle that is passed to the function should have only just been opened. But, just in case, we make sure we're starting from the beginning of the file.

Accessing the file byte by byte is vital since we are reading a binary file that doesn't follow the normal format of a text file. As such, we have to access blocks of information directly. On line 13, we read exactly 32 bytes from the DBF file. This is the start of the header information. The **read** function, like the **seek** function, reads 32 bytes straight from the file, ignoring any line or character breaks that may exist in the file and that we would otherwise ignore if we used a **while** loop.

```
14      $db3version = &endian(substr($rec,0,1));
15      $db3totrec  = &endian(substr($rec,4,4));
16      $db3lenhead = &endian(substr($rec,8,2)) - 1;
17      $db3lenrec  = &endian(substr($rec,10,2));
18
```

Lines 14 to 17 extract the header information from the 32 bytes we just read. We use the **substr** function to extract a set number of bytes from a set position within a string. Line 14 extracts the DBF version number, stored in the first byte of the string. Line 15 extracts 4 bytes from the fifth byte of the string, and line 16 extracts 2 bytes from the ninth byte of the string.

In each case, we wrap the **substr** function with the **endian** function, which, as we will see later, converts a multibyte binary number, based on the byte order of the processor we are using. So, in line 16 we extract the number of bytes in the structure definition, and then take 1 off the number returned by the **endian** function. Finally, in line 17, we extract another 2 bytes and convert them to a number.

```
19      if ($db3version == 0x83) {
20       warn("Cannot handle memo-fields\n");
21      } elsif ($db3version != 0x03) {
22       warn("Not a db3-file\n");
23       return 0;
24      }
25
```

Lines 19 to 24 attempt to identify the file type. In line 19 we check for memo fields within the DBF file. A memo field is basically a free text field without a fixed length, used to store more than 255 characters. This package doesn't support this option, so we warn the user with the **warn** function. This function is similar to the **die** function and prints an error, but it doesn't quit the script.

Similarly, on line 21 we double check that the file we have opened is a version 3 DBF or DB3 file, generating a warning if it is not. If the file isn't identified as a valid DB3 file, we also return from the function with a false response. This response can be trapped and handled by the calling script.

Note that in both cases the identity code is specified in hexadecimal by placing **0x** in the front of the number. Perl automatically handles conversions between decimal, octal, and hexadecimal numbers placed in a script as literal text. There are times when a hexadecimal or octal representation of a number is more appropriate than a decimal.

```
26      $db3nf = $[;
27      $db3fmt = "a1";
28      for ($pos = 32; $pos < $db3lenhead; $pos += 32) {
29       read(Db3, $rec, 32);
30       $db3fn[$db3nf] = unpack("A11", $rec);
31       $db3fn[$db3nf] =~ s/\000.*//;
```

```
32      $db3ft[$db3nf] = substr($rec,11,1);
33      $db3fl[$db3nf] = &endian(substr($rec,16,2));
34      $db3fi{$db3fn[$db3nf]} = $db3nf;
35      $db3fmt .= "A$db3fl[$db3nf]";
36      $db3nf++;
37        }
38
```

Lines 26 to 37 extract the field definition information out of the DBF file and create a string that can be used by the **unpack** function to extract the actual records from the rest of the database.

Line 26 sets up a variable that will point to elements in an array. It's initialized at the value of $[, which is the index to the first element of an array; by default this value is zero. The **$db3fmt** variable will be used to hold the format string for the **unpack** function. This is set to **a1**, which is a single byte padded by null characters.

Line 28 sets up a **for** loop to step through each field definition. Individual fields are specified by a 32-byte string, so we start at byte 32 within the file, going up to a maximum of the field definition length we found out earlier, and we increase the position number by 32 bytes for each iteration of the loop. Line 29 reads the next 32 bytes from the file into a variable that will be extracted in the next lines.

Line 30 extracts the 11-character field name from the field definition block, using an 11-byte, space-padded string to the **unpack** function. We strip the null characters from the end of the field name in line 31. Line 32 extracts the single character specifying the field type. Line 33 extracts the field length using the same technique as before, by reading a byte string from the field block and then running the result through the **endian** function. We set up a hash array on line 34 that relates field names to the array index within the field type and field length arrays. Using this array we can refer to field names directly, while getting the index required to extract the information from the field name type and length tables we'll store internally.

Line 35 adds the current field length block information to the **unpack** string. With this string, we will be able to read an entire record from the database, then extract the information from the packed record using the full **unpack** string. The format is simple: for each field of information, we specify a space-padded character block of the correct field length. We'll see how this information is used later. Note that we concatenate the information onto the existing string using the period notation. Line 36 increments the array index.

```
39      if (($c = getc(Db3)) != "\r") {
40        print "Header korrupt...\n";
41      }
42      1;
43    }
44
45
```

Line 39 checks for a trailing carriage-return at the end of the field definition block. The use of **\r** is considered unsafe because the C compiler used to compile Perl may not be aware of the association, or it could have the association wrong. It would have been safer to use **\015**. Assuming we've read the information in correctly in the previous lines, it should be there. If we don't see it, we just warn the user rather than exiting on line 40. Line 42 makes sure that the function returns a true result. If we get to this line, it's safe to assume that the initialization process executed successfully. The function finally ends on line 43.

```
46    # read the next record in the db3-file
47    # usage:   db3read(FH)
48    # return: list of fields, or () on eof or error;
49    sub main'db3read {
50        local(*Db3) = shift(@_);
51        local($rec, $del, @res);
52
53        do {
54          read(Db3, $rec, $db3lenrec)  ||  return ();
55          ($del, @res) = unpack($db3fmt, $rec);
56        } while ($del ne " ");
57        return @res;
58    }
59
60
```

The **db3read** function starts on line 49. Once again, we look for a file handle reference to the function arguments in line 50, and specify some local variables in line 51.

Line 53 sets up a **for** loop to read in the records. We read in an entire record, the length of which was discovered earlier by the **db3init** function and placed into the **$db3lenrec** variable. If the read fails, say because of an end of file character, it will return zero, or false, and we handle this by simply returning to the calling script.

Line 55 extracts the information from the record using the record format string. **Unpack** returns a separate element of an array for each format specification in the format string. The first variable returned will be assigned to the **$del** variable. This will be from the "a1" block we specified in line 27. The block (or single character!) actually records whether the record is marked for deletion. The remainder of the fields, regardless of their length, are placed into the **@res** array. The whole loop from lines 53 to 57 only continues while the record being read is not marked for deletion. In other words, the script will skip over "deleted" records, while returning a valid single record when it reads one. The valid field data (that is, everything except the "deleted" flag) is returned as an array on line 57.

```
61    # print db3-record in flatfile-record format
62    # usage: db3_flat_str
```

```
63  sub main'db3_flat_str {
64      local($,) = "\t";
65      local($\) = "\n";
66
67      print @db3fn;
68      print @db3fl;
69      print @db3ft;
70  }
71
72
```

The **db3_flat_str** function prints out the database field format in human-readable form. Line 64 and 65 set the default field separator and record separator respectively. By setting these values here, lines 67 to 69 will automatically print the elements of the array separated by tabs, with individual arrays being punctuated by a new-line character. By doing it this way, we save having to write the **join** function into the script: Perl can do it all automatically for us. We use the same technique in the **db3_flat** function, next.

WARNING   *Perl's global variables, such as $, and $\ used in lines 64 and 65 of the **db3.pl** script, can only be localized with **local**; you cannot use the **my** keyword.*

```
73  # convert to flatfile-like database
74  # usage: db3_flat(DBHANDLE)
75  sub main'db3_flat {
76      local(*Db3) = shift(@_);
77      local($,) = "\t";
78      local($\) = "\n";
79      local(@flds);
80
81      while (@flds = &main'db3read(*Db3)) {
82       print @flds;
83       }
84  }
85
86
```

Line 76 extracts a file handle reference from the function arguments, which we pass on verbatim to the **db3read** script in line 81. Once again, we set the field and record separators and then create a localized variable to hold the field data in line 79.

Lines 81 to 83 form a loop, which makes continual calls to the **db3read** function to extract valid fields from the database file. If the read has been successful, we print out the fields, separated by tabs and punctuated by a new-line character on line 82.

As soon as we stop reading valid records, the loop ends, and then the function ends on line 84.

```
87  # convert little-endian to native machine order
88  # (intel = big-endian  ->  mc68k = big-endian)
89  # usage
90  sub endian
91  {
92      local($n) = 0;
93      foreach (reverse(split('', $_[0]))) {
94       $n = $n * 256 + ord;
95      }
96      $n;
97  }
98
```

Line 90 is the start of the **endian** function. Note that it is not defined within the main package, but as part of the DB3 package. By doing this, the function is available as a local function within the DB3 package, but it would have to be referenced fully as **db3'endian** if we wanted to use it from another script. We initialize a number variable to zero in line 92. In line 93 we set up a loop that will step through a reversed list of the individual characters of the first argument passed to the function. Taking each element in turn, the section

```
split('', $_[0])
```

returns a list of individual characters that are reversed by the **reverse** function,

```
reverse(split('', $_[0]))
```

The list is then stepped through by the **foreach** loop.

Line 94 sets the real value of the number as we work through each iteration of the loop. The number is calculated as 256 times the current value plus the ASCII value of the current character. Of course, the figure is intended to interpret multibyte numbers in reverse, not normal strings.

```
99  1;
```

Finally, line 99 closes the package. Perl expects a true result from the incorporation of a package, and specifying a 1 on a single line does exactly that. Although we could set the package to return true in some other way, using this method allows us to add more functions without worrying about the format of the package.

The structure of the package is fairly straightforward. Two things are worth a special mention: the package layout and the method used to extract the information. From a package perspective, we have created a set of functions that can be used directly within a calling script. This is possible because the functions (except **endian**) were defined as being part of the main package, even though the variables we used were stored within the DB3 package name space. We can use the **endian** function locally within the functions in the rest of the DB3 package, but to use the function outside of the package would require a direct reference.

The method used is quite complex, but it has been executed in a simple way. Because DBF files store their information in a fixed-width block of data within the file for each record, all we needed to do was find the correct structure and then create a suitable string that could be used to extract the data from the block. By using the **unpack** function, we saved ourselves a lot of time. The **unpack** function handled identification and extraction, simply returning a list of field data that matched the format string it was passed.

Although not always the case, the two methods of extracting information from the DBF file can be transmuted to most file formats. We used both variable-length records (to discover the field format) and fixed-length records (to extract the data) in order to read the information stored in the file. Most database systems will use a similar format, either variable or fixed length, to store information.

Converting dBase III Databases to Text

db3flat.pl

Using the package we just created, we can read in a DB3 file and convert it to text format. The bulk of the **db3flat.pl** script centers on opening the input and output files, with the rest of the work being done by the functions that form the package.

This script is part of the DB3 package available on the CPAN archives and the CD-ROM, and it was written by Paul Bijnens. You can obtain it from the CPAN archives with this URL:

http://www.cpan.org/scripts/dbase/db3.pl

```
1   #!/usr/local/bin/perl5
2
3
4   # convert db3-file to a flatfile (ascii-file with records
5   # consisting of 1 line, and fields separated by a
6   # fieldseparator (tab) character)
7
8   require 'db3.pl';
9
10  foreach $infile (@ARGV) {
11
12      ($basename) = ($infile =~ /(.*)\.dbf$/i);
13      die("$infile: name not like 'name.DBF'\n")  unless $basename;
14
15      open(DB, "< $infile")  ||  die("$infile: cannot open: $!\n");
16      open(OUT, "> $basename")
```

```
17                              ||  die("$basename: cannot open: $!\n");
18      select(OUT);
19
20      &db3init(*DB)  ||  die("$infile: can't init db3-format\n");
21
22      &db3_flat_str;              # print out the structure
23      &db3_flat(*DB);             # followed by the records
24
25      close(DB)   ||  die("$infile: close: $!\n");
26      close(OUT)  ||  die("$basename: close: $!\n");
27   }
```

ANNOTATIONS

This script uses the DB3 package to convert files to text format. The script is very compact, largely because the DB3 package is more or less self-contained. The DB3 package specifies all the functions required for the conversion, this script simply provides a wrapper around the file specification (from the command line) and the initial opening and creation of the dBase file and output file respectively.

```
1    #!/usr/local/bin/perl5
2
3
4    # convert db3-file to a flatfile (ascii-file with records
5    # consisting of 1 line, and fields separated by a
6    # fieldseparator (tab) character)
7
8    require 'db3.pl';
9
```

Lines 4 to 6 are simply comments, but they help to describe to the programmer what the script does. On line 8 we specify that the **db3.pl** package is required to incorporate the scripts and variables in the package into the current script. The difference between **use** and **require** is that the **use** statement is executed as soon as it has been identified. The **use** statement is in fact incorporated at compile time, rather than at run time like the **require** keyword. The **use** statement is better, since it guarantees that all the functions and variables are available to you at run time.

```
10   foreach $infile (@ARGV) {
11
12       ($basename) = ($infile =~ /(.*)\.dbf$/i);
13       die("$infile: name not like 'name.DBF'\n")  unless $basename;
14
```

On line 10 we set up a **foreach** loop to work through each file specified on the command line. Note that we haven't checked for the existence of any arguments. Line 12 is a two-part line. The section

```
($infile =~ /(.*)\.dbf$/i)
```

checks whether the source filename has a trailing ".dbf." If the match succeeds, then the remainder of the line assigns the first part of the regular expression used for the match, "(.*)," to the **$basename** variable. By surrounding both sides of the statement with parentheses, we ensure that the assignation to the **$basename** variable occurs only if the match is successful. This single line is equivalent to

```
if ($infile =~ /.*\.dbf$/I)
{
      $basename = $infile;
      $basename =~ s/\.dbf$//I;
}
```

Obviously the line is much quicker, but also more complex for the casual observer to decode.

```
15      open(DB, "< $infile")  ||  die("$infile: cannot open: $!\n");
16      open(OUT, "> $basename")
17                             ||  die("$basename: cannot open: $!\n");
```

Lines 15 to 17 open the input and output files, quitting if either file can't be opened.

```
18      select(OUT);
19
```

Line 18 looks innocuous enough, but in fact it is quite significant. Since we're using an external package to do the conversion, we could pass the external functions' references to the file handles we have just created. However, as a quick solution, it would be easier to just redirect all the output from **print** functions to a new file. We could close STDOUT and open a new file pointed to by a file handle of the same name. An even better method is to use the **select** function, which sets the default output to the specified file handle. In the case of line 18, it simplifies the process of passing the output file handle to the package functions.

```
20      &db3init(*DB)  ||  die("$infile: can't init db3-format\n");
21
22      &db3_flat_str;            # print out the structure
23      &db3_flat(*DB);           # followed by the records
24
25      close(DB)  ||  die("$infile: close: $!\n");
26      close(OUT)  ||  die("$basename: close: $!\n");
27  }
```

The remainder of the script finishes very quickly. We call the **initialization** function from the DB3 package in line 20. We pass the reference to the input file using typeglob notation. The asterisk at the beginning of the variable can be thought of as a wildcard match for all the different variables in the current name space. To an extent, you can use typeglobs in the same way as you use references; when Perl uses a typeglob variable, it will automatically select the corresponding variable type to use, depending on the context. References, on the other hand, are more specific. A typeglob was the most reliable way of passing a file reference in Perl 4; with Perl 5 the process has become much easier.

Line 22 prints out the structure of input database, which simply outputs the structure information currently held in memory that was imported by the **db3init** function. Line 23 outputs the individual records from the database. Because it requires access to the source file, we have to pass the typeglob again.

Finally, lines 25 and 26 close the input and output files before the loop goes around again as we close the loop on line 27.

Running the script on the dbtest.dbf file supplied yields a file containing the following:

```
MONTH     IN     OUT     BALANCE
10     10       10       10
C       N       N       N
June             1000             500             500
```

The first line contains the field names, the second the field lengths, and the third the field type. Subsequent lines are the individual records. The file was created within Microsoft Excel, which can generate some extraneous information when you export a text- or comma-separated file. Using DBF format files generates more reliable source data. With some work, it would be easy to convert the information from a DBF file into a DBM file; you already have a package that can export the data, and redirecting the output using a technique similar to the **text2dbm.pl** file would yield the required DBM file. Because the DBF file contains information about the length, it would also be possible to check the size of what you were writing into the DBM file to get around any problems with bucket sizes.

Using the DBI Toolkit

We looked in the last chapter at the DBI, Data Base Interface Perl module. This is an extensible kit that we used to provide a SQL interface to CSV files. Further modules exist to access the most popular databases on the market, including Oracle, Sybase, and Informix.

The problem with developing an interface to a commercial database is that although the SQL standard is well adhered to, the different C APIs (Application

Programming Interfaces) that are used to access the information differ enormously. Up until recently, there was no accepted standard. Luckily, Microsoft has bridged the gap on the Wintel machines by creating the ODBC (Open Database Connectivity) initiative, which attempts to standardize the front-end used to access relational databases. The underlying access is still SQL; only the interface to the SQL interpreter on the required database platform has been standardized. We will look at ODBC access via the Windows Win32::ODBC module shortly.

However, back on the Unix platform, there have for a long time been modules from Tim Bunce and others providing connectivity to the different databases via incompatible wrapper modules. The team got together and produced the DBI specification and implementation. The toolkit is flexible, so we can access CSV files (as we've already seen) as easy as we could an Oracle table.

Recently, ODBC has been accepted as the basis for the SQL Call Level Interface ISO standard. Once the database vendors have produced a suitable toolkit, the underlying code for DBI will be changed, and should be smaller and more compact, since the same code should theoretically be compatible with a wide range of database systems.

Although I won't go into detail here, using the DBI toolkit is almost as easy as writing the SQL command you would normally use to extract the information from the database in any package:

```
use DBI;
$db = "fpoints";
$user = "user1";
$password = "nothere";
$dbd = "Oracle";
$dbhandle = DBI->connect($db, $user, $password, $dbd);
die "Error connecting to database, $DBI::errstr\n" if (!$dbhandle);

$dbhandle->do('select id, device from fptable');
...
```

The **connect** function connects you to the database specified, in this case by the **$dbd** variable. Note that we have to specify the user and password in the script. The call returns a database handle, which we can then use to access the database. The **do** function performs the specified SQL command, using the database handle we have already opened.

There are some limits: we can't extract information straight from a SQL table into an array, hashed or otherwise. Also, because of the differences in the way the various implementations handle table creation, there is no reliable cross-portable way of creating tables in a SQL database. This is not a limitation of DBI, but of the database vendors organizing a suitable interface for the process. The recent ODBC initiative should solve this problem.

One other serious problem is error numbers. Because the numbers generated by different database systems are unique, checking for success in a Perl SQL script requires knowledge of the database you are attempting to use. Again, this is not a DBI problem, but it's frustrating nonetheless.

Even with these problems, DBI is a phenomenally useful set of modules, and anybody expecting to use a SQL database could not go far wrong by trying the DBI toolkit.

If you want more information about the DBI modules, visit the Web site at

http://www.hermetica.com/technologia/DBI/

Using ODBC Sources

The ActiveWare port of Perl includes the **Win32::ODBC** module. It follows a similar approach to the DBI system, with a connection being opened, a SQL statement executed, and the information then reported and extracted from the database.

```
use Win32::ODBC;
$dbname = "Floorpoints";
$dbhandle = new Win32::ODBC($dbname);
if dbhandle->Sql("select ID, device from floorpoints")
{
 print 'Error: ", $dbhandle->Error(), "\n";
 $dbhandle->Close();
 exit(1);
}
```

This module has some advantages over the DBI toolkit: we can retrieve multiple rows into arrays and process them without having to keep referring to the ODBC database. Being ODBC, the database could be anything from Oracle to Access to an Excel spreadsheet.

You can find out more information by visiting the ActiveWare Web site, or simply download the ActiveWare port and view the ODBC module that comes with the package.

Comparing Types of Databases

I can't really exit this chapter without taking a look at why you might want to use the different databases in the first place. Essentially, it all comes down to the type of data you are storing. If it can be placed into a single file and is relatively small information, for example, a list of names and e-mail addresses, a flat text file is more than suitable.

You are unlikely to want to pull out individual records from the file, so a DBM file is overkill. You want might want to update a SQL or ODBC table, though, so it's beyond the realm of possibility that you will want to record the information via something like the DBI toolkit.

For more complex information that you want to pull out of a database quickly on a record-by-record or even field-by-field basis, a DBM file is more appropriate. I've used a DBM file for a relatively complex Web site that allows you to configure Hewlett-Packard workstations. It uses a low level of relational ability, but it demonstrates the power of the DBM file. Access is fast, and the databases contain 26 different currencies for each of the product details. The only downside is the time it takes to build the information, and how the information is built in the first place.

It can take 15 to 20 minutes to create the database in the first place, and that information comes from a heavily text-encoded spreadsheet. Since information is only passed one way—from database to Web page—this is not a major headache. But this method would cause difficulties if we decided to make it a two-way process, or to use the DBM file as the working version of the database used for updates to the workstation information. For an effective database, we really need a relational storage mechanism.

For more complex database needs, such as E-Commerce or accounting, it's obvious that a SQL or ODBC source should be the database of choice. With both, we get better reliability and the facility to farm off some of the performance issues to the database engine, instead of relying on Perl scripts to extract and identify the required pieces of information.

Of course, your needs for accessing a database may be one way, as well. Using Perl to extract from a SQL database can give you results that would be difficult to achieve quickly in off the shelf packages. Perl's ability to read different formats makes it an ideal choice for conversions between database formats.

Summary

Whatever your database requirement, you should be able to find a suitable module mentioned in this chapter, or try any of the techniques we have covered here. I hope I've demonstrated the power of the DBM database, and how easy using the **tie** function makes working with DBM files. Moreover, we have looked at the limited or perhaps even advanced relational capabilities built into DBM files, provided you make some intelligent decisions on the use of keys and value information.

I hope I've also shown that, once you know a database file's format, you can use the functions within Perl to extract the information very easily. In our example, a DBF file was converted to text, but it could just as easily have been converted to a DBM file, or even inserted into a SQL table.

As I said at the start of the last chapter, it is difficult to get by in the modern world without using some form of database. You should, by now, see that Perl makes using databases and manipulating the data we extract from databases very easy.

## PART 2

Networking and E-mail

Networking
Working with E-mail

Networking

T he modern world is networked—you can't avoid this technology. And as we march further down the road toward integrating the Internet into our jobs, education, and society, the use of networking technology and the requirement for network-capable scripts will certainly increase.

In this chapter, we will take a close look at TCP/IP (the protocol used on the Internet for communication) by examining the use of sockets. Before we examine the processes behind using network connections in Perl, however, let's look at the general aspects of networks.

Most networking systems are based on the OSI/ISO (Open Systems Interconnection/International Standards Organization) seven-layer model, shown in the following illustration:

Application Layer
Presentation Layer
Session Layer
Transport Layer
Network Layer
Data Link Layer
Physical Layer

Each layer defines an individual component of the networking process, from the physical connection up to the applications that use the network. Each layer is dependent on the layer below to provide the services required. Going from bottom to top, here is what each layer in the illustration represents:

◆ **Physical Layer** Specifies the network's physical operating characteristics, such as voltage and frequency used to transmit data through a piece of cable. This layer is the lowest level and defines the underlying cables and voltages used for communication.

◆ **Data Link Layer**   Defines the method of transferring the digital information to and from the physical medium. This layer is what most people refer to as a network; the terms "Ethernet" and "Token Ring" define systems up to this layer.

◆ **Network Layer**   Defines how information is sent around the network, including the addressing and routing mechanisms, and the low-level flow control of supporting data transfer. One example is the IP (Internet Protocol) component of TCP/IP.

◆ **Transport Layer**   Handles error correction/control and sequence checking to ensure that packets sent over the network are transferred correctly. This layer makes up the TCP (Transmission Control Protocol) element of TCP/IP.

◆ **Session Layer**   Manages the creation of individual sessions, or in other words, the instance of a communication between two machines over the network.

◆ **Presentation Layer**   Presents information to the application in a suitable form. For example, the Perl functions used to access the underlying network provide information to the applications as a data stream.

◆ **Application Layer**   Controls how application programs interface with the network. This control includes everything from the commands used to manage a connection like FTP, to the remainder of the software that supports changing directories and selecting files for transfers.

Beyond the seven-layer model, it is possible to characterize networks by their type of logical connection. A network can either be connection-oriented or connectionless. A connection-oriented network relies on the fact that two computers that want to talk to each other must go through some sort of connection process, usually called a "handshake." This handshake is similar to using the phone: the caller dials a number, and the receiver picks up the phone. In this way, the caller immediately knows if the recipient has received the message because the recipient will have answered the call. This type of connection is supported by TCP/IP and is the main form of communication over the Internet.

In a connectionless network, information is sent to the recipient, without a connection first being set up. This type of network is also a *datagram* or *packet-oriented* network because the data is sent in discrete packets. Each packet consists of the sender's address, recipient's address, and the information, but no response will be provided once the message is received. A connectionless network is therefore more like the postal service: you compose and send a letter, although you have no guarantee that the letter will reach its destination or that the information was received correctly. Connectionless networking is supported by UDP/IP (User Datagram Protocol).

In either case, the "circuit" is not open permanently between the two machines. Data is sent in individual packets that may take different paths and routes to the destination. The routes may involve local area networks, dial-up connections, ISDN routers, and even satellite links. Within the UDP protocol, the packets can arrive in any order, and it is up to the client program to reassemble them into the correct sequence—if there is one. With TCP, the packets are automatically reassembled into the correct sequence before they are presented to the client as a single data stream.

There are advantages and disadvantages to both types of network. A connectionless network is fast because it doesn't have to acknowledge the data or enter into any dialog to set up the connection to receive the data in the first place. However, a connectionless network is also unreliable because there is no way to ensure the information reaches its destination. A connection-oriented network is slow (in comparison to a connectionless network) because of the extra dialog involved, but it guarantees the data sequence, for end-to-end reliability.

Each machine within the networking world has a unique IP address, which is made up of a sequence of 4 bytes that are typically written in *dot notation*, for example, 198.10.29.145. These numbers relate both to individual machines within a network and to entire collections of machines. Because humans are not very good at remembering numbers, there is a system called DNS (Domain Name System) that relates easy-to-remember names to IP addresses. For example, the name "www.mcgraw-hill.com" relates to a single IP address. It is possible to have a single machine that has multiple interfaces, and each interface can have multiple IP addresses assigned to it. However, in all cases, if the interfaces are connected to the Internet in one form or another, then the IP addresses of each interface will be unique.

However, the specification for communication doesn't end there. Many different applications can be executed on the same machine, so a communication must be aimed not only at the machine but also at a *port* on that machine that relates to a particular application. If you think of the IP address as a telephone number, then the port number would be the equivalent of the extension number. The first 1,024 port numbers are assigned to well-known Internet protocols, and different protocols have their own unique port number. For example, HTTP (Hypertext Transfer Protocol), which is used to transfer information between your Web browser and a Web server, has a port number of 80. To connect to a server application, you need both the IP address or machine name and the port number over which the application is "listening."

The BSD socket system was introduced in BSD 4.2 as a way of providing a consistent interface to the different protocols. You must have a socket at each end of the connection in order to communicate between the machines. One end must be set to receive data at the same time as the other end is sending data. As long as each side of the socket connection knows whether it should be sending or receiving information, then the communication can be two-way. Think of a socket like the phone or post office in the examples described above.

There are many different methods for controlling this two-way communication, although none is ultimately reliable. The most obvious is to "best guess" the state that each end of the connection should be in. For example, if one end sends a piece of information, then it might be safe to assume that it should then wait for a response. If the opposite end makes the same assumption, then it can send information after it has just received a data packet. This system is not necessarily reliable; if both ends decide to wait for information at the same time, both ends of the connection are effectively dead. Alternatively, if both ends decide to send information at the same time, the two processes will not lock, but because they use the same send/receive system, once they have both sent information they will both return to the wait state.

A better solution to the problem is to use a protocol that places rules and restrictions on the communication method and order. This is how protocols like SMTP work. The client sends a command to the server, and the immediate response from the server tells the client what to do next. The response may include data and will definitely include an end-of-data string. In effect, it's similar to the technique used when communicating by radio: at the end of each communication, you say, "Over" to indicate to the recipient that you have finished speaking. In essence, it still uses the same best-guess method for communication. Provided the communication starts off correctly, and each end sends the end-of-data signal, then the communication should continue correctly.

Although generally thought of as a technique for communicating between two different machines, we can also use sockets to communicate between two processes on the same machine, which can be useful for two reasons. First of all, communicating between processes on a single machine (IPC, or interprocess communication) allows us to control and cooperatively operate between a number of different processes. Most servers use IPC to manage a number of processes that support a particular service. Perhaps the best example of this is the Apache Web server.

We will begin in this chapter by creating a Perl module that simplifies and unifies the process of creating client and server sockets. We'll then use the Perl module in other scripts to access some standard Internet servers. Using the same module again, we'll look at a simple Web server and then at a combined client/server system that employs a simple protocol system as outlined above. Finally, we'll look at some scripts that use a collection of modules available from the CPAN archives.

If you want more information on networking with sockets and streams under TCP, UDP, and IP, I recommend *The UNIX System V Release 4 Programmers Guide: Networking Interfaces* by AT&T (Prentice Hall, 1990), which covers the principles behind networking, as well as the C source code required to make networking work.

Ssockets.pm

Creating a Simple Socket Module

To use sockets to connect to a server, you must follow a number of steps. First of all, you need to discover the server's IP address, port number, and protocol number. Then you need to create a socket, bind to the socket, and then connect the socket to the remote server. Similarly, creating sockets for use as server processes is also easy: you create the socket, bind to the socket, and then set the socket to a listening state.

These steps are performed by individual functions, and much of the code in the socket module is related to discovering the numbers relating to the individual sockets, ports, and protocols. The rest of the code is dedicated to the error checking surrounding the overall process. However, once completed, these socket functions can be used for a wide range of purposes, as we will see in the following scripts.

```perl
1    package Ssockets;
2
3    require Exporter;
4    @ISA = 'Exporter';
5    @EXPORT = qw (connectsocket listensocket);
6
7    use Socket;
8
9    use vars qw($error);
10
11   sub connectsocket
12   {
13       my ($SOCKETHANDLE, $remotehost_name,
14           $service_name, $protocol_name) = @_;
15       my ($port_num, $sock_type);
16       my ($protocol_num);
17       my ($remote_ip_addr, $remote_socket);
18
19       $protocol_num = getprotobyname($protocol_name);
20       unless ($protocol_num)
21       {
22           $error = "Couldn't find protocol $protocol_name";
23           return;
24       }
25       $sock_type =   $protocol_name eq 'tcp'
26           ? SOCK_STREAM : SOCK_DGRAM;
27
28       unless (socket($SOCKETHANDLE, PF_INET,
29                      $sock_type, $protocol_num))
30       {
31           $error = "Couldn't create a socket, $!";
32           return;
33       }
34
35       if ($service_name =~ /^\d+$/ )
36       {
37           $port_num = $service_name;
38       }
39       else
```

```
40      {
41          $port_num = (getservbyname($service_name,
42                                      $protocol_name))[2];
43          unless($port_num)
44          {
45              $error = "Can't find service $service_name";
46              return;
47          }
48      }
49
50      $remote_ip_addr = gethostbyname($remotehost_name);
51      unless ($remote_ip_addr)
52      {
53          $error
54              = "Can't resolve $remotehost_name to an IP address";
55          return;
56      }
57      $remote_socket = sockaddr_in($port_num, $remote_ip_addr);
58      unless(connect($SOCKETHANDLE, $remote_socket))
59      {
60          $error =
61              "Unable to connect to $remotehost_name: $!";
62          return;
63      }
64      return(1);
65  }
66
67  sub listensocket
68  {
69      my ($SOCKETHANDLE, $service_name,
70          $protocol_name, $queuelength) = @_;
71      my ($port_num, $sock_type, $protocol_num,
72          $local_socket);
73
74      $protocol_num = (getprotobyname($protocol_name))[2];
75      unless ($protocol_num)
76      {
77          $error = "Couldn't find protocol $protocol_name";
78          return;
79      }
80      $sock_type = $protocol_name eq "tcp"
81          ? SOCK_STREAM : SOCK_DGRAM ;
82
```

```
 83    if( $service_name =~ /^\d+$/)
 84    {
 85        $port_num = $service_name;
 86    }
 87    else
 88    {
 89        $port_num = (getservbyname($service_name,
 90                                    $protocol_name))[2];
 91        unless($port_num)
 92        {
 93            $error = "Can't find service $service_name";
 94            return;
 95        }
 96    }
 97
 98    unless(socket($SOCKETHANDLE, PF_INET,
 99                  $sock_type, $protocol_num))
100    {
101        $error = "Couldn't create a socket: $!";
102        return;
103    }
104    unless(setsockopt($SOCKETHANDLE,SOL_SOCKET,
105                      SO_REUSEADDR,pack("l",1)))
106    {
107        $error = "Couldn't set socket options: $!";
108        return;
109    }
110    $local_socket = sockaddr_in($port_num, INADDR_ANY);
111    unless(bind($SOCKETHANDLE, $local_socket))
112    {
113        $error = "Failed to Bind to socket: $!";
114        return;
115    }
116    unless(listen($SOCKETHANDLE, $queuelength))
117    {
118        $error = "Couldn't listen on socket: $!";
119        return;
120    }
121    return(1);
122 }
123
124 1;
```

ANNOTATIONS

As I've already noted, a large proportion of the code relates to the error checking and number discovery. We export two main functions, **connectsocket** and **listensocket**. For error checking, functions return true on success or false on failure. An error message is exported in the variable **$error**, which we can access from a script by specifying the full variable name, including package, such as **$Ssockets::error**.

```
1    package Ssockets;
2
```

We change the default name space to **Ssockets** to create a new package of the same name. The name space we set in this line should match the name of the package, and the name of the file should have an extension of **.pm**, from the term "package module."

```
3    require Exporter;
4    @ISA = 'Exporter';
5    @EXPORT = qw (connectsocket listensocket);
6
```

We use the **Exporter** module, which allows us to specify functions and variables that will be automatically imported into the calling script. This technique is the one employed by the modules that come as part of the standard Perl distribution. The **Exporter** module defines a default import method that can be inherited by other modules. Using the Exporter allows you to select which functions can be automatically imported from the module; only those functions, variables, and other objects specified in the **@EXPORT** array will be imported by the calling script.

Incidentally, the use of **@EXPORT** means that all the specified functions and variables will be imported by the script. So even if we use a line like

```
use Ssockets qw(connectsocket);
```

the **listensocket** function will also be imported. If you want to allow users to selectively import functions, you should use the **@EXPORT_OK** array instead. For more information, view the **pelrmod** and **Exporter** manual pages.

Perl allows us to specify a number of other module names in the special array **@ISA**. When Perl does not find a particular class or instance of an object, it checks the contents of the **@ISA** array to see if any of those modules support the object. It then passes control to that module. This is a function of the object-orientation built into Perl 5. In this instance, we are inheriting the import methods defined in the **Exporter** module. The name comes from the term "is a," specifying the current package is-a member of the specified class.

```
7    use Socket;
8
9    use vars qw($error);
10
```

We also use the **Socket** module, imported here in line 7, which is part of the standard Perl distribution. This module is the set of wrapper functions around the underlying OS functions. The **Perl** function names and arguments match the functions specified by POSIX and, more specifically, Unix for accessing network services.

On line 9 the **use vars** pragma is used to define the **$error** variable. The pragma defines the variable as a package global, so the variable will be available to calling scripts. Had we defined the variable with **my** or **local**, then **$error** would be unavailable to scripts without being specifically imported.

```
11  sub connectsocket
12  {
13      my ($SOCKETHANDLE, $remotehost_name,
14          $service_name, $protocol_name) = @_;
15      my ($port_num, $sock_type);
16      my ($protocol_num);
17      my ($remote_ip_addr, $remote_socket);
18
```

Line 11 is the start of the **connectsocket** function. It takes four arguments, retrieved on lines 13 and 14: the socket handle to use, the remote host name (or IP address), the remote service name (or number), and the remote protocol. We can get away with specifying a simple socket handle, without resorting to references, if we use typeglob notation when the function is called. Lines 15 to 17 declare the local variables that will be used to store the information required to create, bind, and connect the socket. Line 18 defines the variable used to hold the host name.

```
19      $protocol_num = getprotobyname($protocol_name);
20      unless ($protocol_num)
21      {
22          $error = "Couldn't find protocol $protocol_name";
23          return;
24      }
```

Lines 19 to 24 obtain the protocol number associated with the protocol name given in the function's arguments. In general there are two protocols used regularly. The **tcp** protocol is the stream-based protocol used by most communication protocols such as Telnet, FTP, and HTTP. The **udp** protocol is used for the connectionless, datagram communication used in programs like ping.

In practice, the underlying library function under Unix reads the /etc/protocols file or corresponding NIS or similar database to identify the protocol number and proper protocol name. The OS uses this information to decide which driver is required by the remainder of the network calls. Since the Perl function is just a wrapper around the C function, the process is the same. The result of the function call is a protocol number or zero if the protocol cannot be found. We check the result in line 21, and if the protocol could not be found we generate a suitable error in line 23 and return from the function with a zero (false) result.

```
25        $sock_type =    $protocol_name eq 'tcp'
26            ? SOCK_STREAM : SOCK_DGRAM;
27
```

It's safe to assume that if the protocol name is **tcp** we are using a stream-based socket (**SOCK_STREAM**) and that otherwise the socket will be datagram based (**SOCK_DGRAM**). This assumption is not always true, but it is good enough when we expect to work with the basic set of networking protocols.

```
28        unless (socket($SOCKETHANDLE, PF_INET,
29                       $sock_type, $protocol_num))
30        {
31            $error = "Couldn't create a socket, $!";
32            return;
33        }
34
```

The new socket is created on line 28, and the new file handle is attached to the new socket. By attaching the socket to a file handle, we can use the same functions we use with a file. The difference is that the communication is not to a file but to a network connection. You can read and write stream sockets (TCP) in much the same way as you can files. For datagram sockets (UDP), the process is slightly different; we'll see an example when we look at the **pingecho.pl** script.

The arguments to the **socket** function are the file handle that the socket should be attached to, the domain, the socket type, and the protocol number. The domain is either **PF_UNIX** for the Unix domain or **PF_INET** for general Internet sockets. We will be creating and using Internet sockets, as they are the most portable and the most practical for communicating between machines. The socket type is either **SOCK_STREAM** or **SOCK_DGRAM**, depending on the value we selected on lines 25 and 26. The protocol number is the value returned by the earlier function call in line 19.

The result from the **socket** function is true if the socket creation occurred successfully, otherwise undef is returned. If the socket call fails on line 28, then we generate a suitable error string, this time incorporating the OS error string retained by **$!**, returning a false result to the caller in line 32.

```
35        if ($service_name =~ /^\d+$/ )
36        {
37            $port_num = $service_name;
38        }
39        else
40        {
41            $port_num = (getservbyname($service_name,
42                                       $protocol_name))[2];
43            unless($port_num)
44            {
```

```
45              $error = "Can't find service $service_name";
46              return;
47          }
48      }
49
```

On line 35 we identify whether the service name is a string or a number. If it is a number, we can use it directly by setting the **$port_num** variable to the specified number in line 37, without having to call a function to discover the number. Otherwise, we need to call the **getservbyname** function to obtain the service number associated with the service name and protocol. A service can be supported on the same number under both TCP and UDP connections. The result of the **getservbyname** function is an array interpretation of the C **struct servent** structure that is defined as follows:

```
struct  servent {
              char *s_name;            /* official name of service */
              char **s_aliases;        /* alias list */
              int  s_port;             /* port service resides at */
              char *s_proto;           /* protocol to use */
          };
```

The Perl representation sets the first element of the array to the name of the service, the second to a list of aliases, the third to the port number, and the last to the protocol. So in lines 41 and 42 we extract the number by using subscript notation to return the third element. If the number isn't found, then we generate the error string on line 46 and return to the calling script.

```
50      $remote_ip_addr = gethostbyname($remotehost_name);
51      unless ($remote_ip_addr)
52      {
53          $error
54              = "Can't resolve $remotehost_name to an IP address";
55          return;
56      }
```

The **gethostbyname** function in line 50 returns a **hostent** structure, which is defined in C like this:

```
struct hostent {
              char    *h_name;         /* canonical name of host */
              char    **h_aliases;     /* alias list */
              int     h_addrtype;      /* host address type */
              int     h_length;        /* length of address */
              char    **h_addr_list;   /* list of addresses */
          };
```

The discovery of the host information is entirely dependent on the OS configuration. The IP address could come from a local host's file or a DNS server. As before, line 51 checks to ensure a valid response was received, generating the error message on lines 53 and 54 if it wasn't.

```
57      $remote_socket = sockaddr_in($port_num, $remote_ip_addr);
```

The penultimate part to creating the new socket is to create the remote socket structure that we will use, with the **connect** function, to attach the previously created socket handle to the remote connection. We use a function from the **sockaddr_in** utility set to convert Perl variables into the C structures required by the underlying functions. The required information to create the remote socket data is the remote IP address, which we extracted in line 50, and the remote port number, discovered in lines 35 to 49.

```
58      unless(connect($SOCKETHANDLE, $remote_socket))
59      {
60          $error =
61              "Unable to connect to $remotehost_name: $!";
62          return;
63      }
64      return(1);
65  }
66
```

Line 58 is responsible for making the actual connection between the client and the remote socket. If this section fails, the whole connection process fails: there is no way to recover from this option—you can only start again. Provided it doesn't fail, the function returns a true value to the calling script on line 64. If it does fail, then we create an error string and return a false value on line 62.

The **listensocket** function follows a similar sequence to the **connectsocket** function; we have to go through the same motions of discovering the protocol number and service number and creating the socket. However, because we're not connecting to a remote machine, we do not need to work out the remote address or connect to a remote socket. Instead, we set the socket to "listen" for connections.

```
67  sub listensocket
68  {
69      my ($SOCKETHANDLE, $service_name,
70          $protocol_name, $queuelength) = @_;
71      my ($port_num, $sock_type, $protocol_num,
72          $local_socket);
73
74      $protocol_num = (getprotobyname($protocol_name))[2];
75      unless ($protocol_num)
76          {
```

```
77          $error = "Couldn't find protocol $protocol_name";
78          return;
79      }
80      $sock_type = $protocol_name eq "tcp"
81          ? SOCK_STREAM : SOCK_DGRAM ;
82
83      if( $service_name =~ /^\d+$/)
84      {
85          $port_num = $service_name;
86      }
87      else
88      {
89          $port_num = (getservbyname($service_name,
90                                     $protocol_name))[2];
91          unless($port_num)
92          {
93              $error = "Can't find service $service_name";
94              return;
95          }
96      }
97
```

Lines 69 to 72 set up the local variables, and then lines 74 to 97 follow the same basic procedure as for the **connectsocket** function. If the specified ports or protocols do not exist, the error string will be returned.

```
98      unless(socket($SOCKETHANDLE, PF_INET,
99                    $sock_type, $protocol_num))
100     {
101         $error = "Couldn't create a socket: $!";
102         return;
103     }
```

A new local socket is created, using the specified socket handle, Internet domain, socket type, and protocol. As before, we are creating a socket on which to create a connection. The difference with a server socket is that the connection will be, initially, one sided—the remote end of the connection will not become active until a client connects.

```
104     unless(setsockopt($SOCKETHANDLE,SOL_SOCKET,
105                       SO_REUSEADDR,pack("l",1)))
106     {
107         $error = "Couldn't set socket options: $!";
108         return;
109     }
```

Line 104 uses the **setsockopt** function to set the "reuse address" option on the local socket. You can use this function to set all kinds of options on a socket. The format of the function, which is identical to the equivalent C function, is

```
setsockopt(socket,level,option,optvalue)
```

The level will always be **SOL_SOCKET** for sockets; if your OS defines other levels at which you can supply options, you must specify the corresponding level here. The **option** is a value from Table 5-1. The **optvalue** is the value to set for the option. Many options are toggles, where zero means off and 1 means on. Others require a specific value. Table 5-1 shows the options supported by Solaris 2.4. Your operating system may support a different set of options.

```
110     $local_socket = sockaddr_in($port_num, INADDR_ANY);
111     unless(bind($SOCKETHANDLE, $local_socket))
112     {
113         $error = "Failed to bind to socket: $!";
114         return;
115     }
```

The local socket is created based on the requested port name (or number) and a special address of **INADDR_ANY**. This wildcard address allows incoming communication from any other IP address. Table 5-2 shows the list of available values. For most purposes **INADDR_ANY** is the most practical option to choose: it allows you to accept connections from anywhere. You can make decisions about whether to continue the communication based on a specific host name, domain name, or IP address once the connection has been established.

Option	Description
SO_DEBUG	Enable/disable recording of debugging information
SO_REUSEADDR	Enable/disable local address reuse
SO_KEEPALIVE	Enable/disable keep connections alive
SO_DONTROUTE	Enable/disable routing bypass for outgoing messages
SO_LINGER	Linger on close if data is present
SO_BROADCAST	Enable/disable permission to transmit broadcast messages
SO_OOBINLINE	Enable/disable reception of out-of-band data in band
SO_SNDBUF	Set buffer size for output
SO_RCVBUF	Set buffer size for input

TABLE 5-1.   Socket Options Under Solaris 2.4

Address Alias	Description
INADDR_ANY	Returns a packed dotted-quad (that is, IP address) defining the wildcard address to allow any host to connect to the specified socket. Usually equivalent to a packed version of **0.0.0.0**
INADDR_BROADCAST	Returns a packed dotted-quad that specifies the broadcast address to be used on this network. Usually equivalent to a packed version of **255.255.255.255**
INADDR_LOOPBACK	Returns a packed dotted-quad that specifies the local machine address or the special loopback address. Usually equivalent to a packed version of **localhost**
INADDR_NONE	Returns a packed dotted-quad that specifies the wildcard equivalent to no machine on the network. Usually equivalent to a packed version of **255.255.255.255**

TABLE 5-2. Address Type Constants

We bind the socket to the local address on line 111 to create the local end of our server socket.

```
116    unless(listen($SOCKETHANDLE, $queuelength))
117    {
118        $error = "Couldn't listen on socket: $!";
119        return;
120    }
121    return(1);
122 }
123
124 1;
```

On line 116 the socket handle is set to the listen state. Once in this state, we can accept new connections on this socket using the **accept** function. The queue length is the number of requests that will be accepted by the kernel and held in a queue for subsequent **accept** function calls. Once the number of waiting connections reaches the queue length limit, the OS automatically refuses connections.

PROGRAMMER'S NOTE *Not all OSs support varying queue lengths. Some older OSs use a default value for all sockets, irrespective of the value specified in the **listen** function.*

The queue length feature can be used to control server loading and response times. It doesn't affect the maximum number of requests that can be accepted, only the number that are held in the queue before being accepted. For a Web server you could use a high value; the response time on individual requests is quite small, so the time between calls to the **accept** function is likely to be quite low. Setting the queue length too low would mean that connections were refused even if your server weren't very busy.

If the **listen** call fails at this point, the socket is probably already in use. The error generated by the OS will be placed into the error string on line 118.

Using the functions is straightforward. For client processes, you simply call the function, specifying the socket handle, remote host, service, and protocol. The result is a socket handle that can be written and read from much like any file handle. We'll see an example of this in the next script, **remtime.pl**.

For the **listensocket** function, we need a slightly different approach. Once the socket handle has been created, you need to execute the **accept** function to check if an incoming connection is waiting. Once the connection is accepted, you can then read and write to it like any file handle. By building a simple Web server, **httpserv.pl**, we'll see how this works in practice later in this chapter.

Getting the Time Remotely

remtime.pl

There are a number of standard servers available on all Unix systems. They are designed to provide information, usually anonymously, over the network. The one most people are aware of is finger, which provides login information (except the password) about a specified user or a list of connected users if no user is specified. The other regularly used TCP/IP servers return responses to the ping command, which is a built-in function of the inetd daemon under Unix, and the TCP/IP drivers of most other OSs.

PROGRAMMER'S NOTE *By default, many hosts have these services turned off as a security measure. The services supported depend entirely on the server configuration and the network administrator's discretion!*

The service we are going to use is called **daytime**. This is another built-in function of the inetd server. Once the socket has connected, the server immediately responds with the localized time of the machine. Having this time can be handy, both as a test to make sure that the machine is available and as a method of checking the time. There are a number of servers on the Internet that will respond with an exact time based on an external nuclear timepiece.

The best method of accessing these servers is to use the NTP protocol, which can account for network distances and the time zone difference between the client and server machines. For our purposes, we will just use the **daytime** protocol to obtain a **localtime** style formatted time string from a server, using a Perl script and the simple sockets module we created earlier.

```
1   #!/usr/local/bin/perl5
2
3   use Ssockets;
4
5   my $host = shift || 'localhost';
6
7   unless(connectsocket(*TIME, $host, 'daytime', 'tcp'))
8   {
9       die $error;
10  }
11
12  $_ = <TIME>;
13  print "Time on $host is $_";
14  close(TIME);
```

ANNOTATIONS

The script is very simple; much of the complexity of the process has been simplified through the creation and use of the **Ssockets** module. Once the script has connected to the server, we read a single line from the socket handle, and then print it out.

```
1   #!/usr/local/bin/perl5
2
3   use Ssockets;
4
5   my $host = shift || 'localhost';
6
```

We import the **Ssockets** module on line 3. By using a logical OR operator, we take either the first argument off the command-line argument list or we default to a value of **localhost**. This is a good way of setting a default option based on whether the user-selected option exists. **localhost** is the special name for the current machine.

WARNING

It is possible to get invalid results when using this method for defaults if one of the options is naturally false.

```
7   unless(connectsocket(*TIME, $host, 'daytime', 'tcp'))
8   {
9       die $Ssockets::error;
10  }
11
```

The **connectsocket** function returns a positive (true) result if the connection is successful, so we wrap the function call in an **unless** expression so we can check for errors—something that is reported via **die** on line 9. Because we are passing a file handle, we must pass it to the function as a typeglob, then we specify the host, the service name of **daytime**, and a protocol of TCP.

```
12   $_ = <TIME>;
13   print "Time on $host is $_";
14   close(TIME);
```

If the socket connected successfully, we read a single line from the host on line 12. Because we have opened a network socket as if it were a file handle, we can use the normal file handling functions to read and write from the socket handle. In line 13 we print the result, and then close the socket handle on line 14.

To use the script, specify the host you want to obtain the time of, as follows:

```
$ remtime.pl twinspark
Time on twinspark is Sat Jul 25 11:49:05 1998
```

If you are connected to the Internet, you can also ask the time of many available servers. For example, to find out what the time is on the Sunsite UK server,

```
$ remtime.pl src.doc.ic.ac.uk
Time on src.doc.ic.ac.uk is Sat Jul 25 11:49:34 1998
```

Although this script seems trivial, it does demonstrate the ease with which we can use a network socket as a file handle. We'll make more use of this feature in the next few scripts in this chapter.

Pinging a Remote Host

pingecho.pl

We looked briefly at the ping protocol earlier. Using a UDP echo is the simplest method of discovering whether a host is up and responding to TCP/IP packets—although it doesn't guarantee that the machine is also listening on a specific port. The typical way of implementing ping is to use the ICMP protocol instead of the TCP protocol. ICMP is a protocol that sits on top of the underlying IP protocol. It is used for error and control messaging, and it is mostly used for monitoring and diagnostic functions like the ping and traceroute programs. ICMP is also used internally by the TCP and UDP protocols for various purposes, including routing, fault isolation, and congestion control.

However, as has already been mentioned, we can also use the TCP or UDP protocol on the echo service port to emulate the ping function. As the name suggests, the echo command sends back whatever data is sent to it. In the following script, we use UDP on the echo service port to emulate the ping function with Perl.

```perl
1    #!/usr/local/bin/perl5
2
3    use Ssockets;
4    use FileHandle;
5
6    my $host = shift || 'localhost';
7
8    if (ping($host))
9    {
10       print "$host is alive\n";
11   }
12   else
13   {
14       print "$host did not respond\n";
15   }
16
17   sub on_alarm
18   {
19       die "Timed out";
20   };
21
22   sub ping
23   {
24       my ($remhost) = @_;
25       my $outtest = "Echo$/";
26       my $inresponse = ' ' x length $outtest;
27       die $Ssockets::error
28           unless(connectsocket(*PINGHANDLE, $remhost,
29                               'echo', 'udp'));
30       autoflush PINGHANDLE 1;
31       eval
32       {
33           local $SIG{'ALRM'} = \&on_alarm;
34           print PINGHANDLE $outtest;
35           alarm 5;
36           recv(PINGHANDLE, $inresponse, 5, 0);
37           alarm 0;
38       }
39       return($inresponse eq $outtest);
40   }
```

ANNOTATIONS

The **pingecho.pl** script follows a similar sequence to the earlier **remtime.pl** script: we open a socket, send some data, receive it back, and report the success of the process. There are some significant differences, though. A typical ping operation will wait for a few seconds before deciding that the host is not going to respond, which allows for network latency and a busy server responding to the original packet data. We need to account for this waiting within the Perl script.

The easiest way to build in a wait time is to use signals. Most Unix users will have come across signals at some point: a signal is the notification of a particular event to a process. They are used for everything from the job control of subprocesses, as used in the Korn and BASH shells, to allowing a process to accept a quit or kill command from another process. The list of signals varies from machine to machine and OS to OS. Table 5-3 shows a list of the signals that should be supported by any POSIX-compatible system.

Different Perl implementations will support a different range of signals. On most Unix systems, the list will be longer than that shown in Table 5-3 to cater to OS-specific entries. Under Windows NT there is a subset of the full POSIX list, unfortunately not including SIGALRM that we will use in the next script. Under the MacOS implementation there is a similarly short subset, this time including SIGALRM. Refer to Appendix A for more information about the signal differences between operating systems.

There are three types of actions that can be associated with a signal: default, ignore, or function call. The default option is entirely signal independent and may include being ignored, immediately causing the application to quit (as in SIGKILL) or pausing the application. The ignore action allows a signal to be ignored, which means the default option will not take place, and any associated operations are also ignored.

The final action, calling a function, is the useful one. It allows us to execute a function—which can do anything—when the signal is received. Once the function has completed, control returns to the program, at the point it was at when the signal was received. The SIGALRM signal is sent to the process when a timer, set by the **alarm** function, expires. This sequence allows us to set a timeout on an operation. Set the signal to call your desired function when the timeout occurs, set the alarm time (in seconds), and then process as usual.

When the alarm signal is received, regardless of its location in the script, it will automatically jump to the function we set. In our example, the ping test is issued within an **eval** block. By using the test within an **eval**, we can use the **die** function as the timeout handler. Using **die** here causes the script's execution to exit the **eval** block, protecting us from multiple signals and jumping us safely out of the test block.

POSIX Signal Name	Perl Name	Description
SIGABRT	ABRT	Abnormal termination
SIGALRM	ALRM	Timer set by the **alarm** function has expired
SIGFPE	FPE	Arithmetic exceptions, for example divide overflow, or divide by zero
SIGHUP	HUP	Hangup detected on the controlling terminal or death of a controlling process
SIGILL	ILL	Illegal instruction indicating a program error
SIGINT	INT	Interrupt signal (special character from the keyboard or signal from another application)
SIGKILL	KILL	Termination signal—cannot be caught or ignored
SIGPIPE	PIPE	Attempt to write to a pipe with no application reading from it
SIGQUIT	QUIT	Quit signal (special character from the keyboard or signal from another application)
SIGSEGV	SEGV	Attempt to access an invalid memory address
SIGTERM	TERM	Termination signal (from another application or OS)
SIGUSR1	USR1	Application- (user-) defined signal
SIGUSR2	USR2	Application- (user-) defined signal
SIGCHLD	CHLD	A child process terminated or stopped
SIGCONT	CONT	Continue the process if currently stopped
SIGSTOP	STOP	Stop signal—stops the specified process
SIGTSTP	TSTP	Stop signal from special character from keyboard
SIGTTIN	TTIN	A read was attempted from the controlling terminal by a background process
SIGTTOU	TTOU	A write was attempted to the controlling terminal by a background process

TABLE 5-3.   POSIX Signals

For more information on signals, refer to the perlipc manual page.

```
1   #!/usr/local/bin/perl5
2
3   use Ssockets;
4   use FileHandle;
5
```

The simple socket module is incorporated on line 3. We also need the **FileHandle** module that allows us a fine level of control over file handles, or in our case socket handles. We will use it to control the buffering used with the socket handle. Normally, all read and write accesses to a file are buffered. Buffering enhances performance because data is written to or read from a file in chunks. The input or output is flushed only when there's a special request or when the file handle is closed.

When communicating over a network, it is unlikely that you want to buffer the output. The primary reason is that the size of the data you are likely to be transferring is smaller than the size of the buffer used. When writing a small amount of data to a socket handle, you want it transferred immediately to the other end of the network connection.

```
6    my $host = shift || 'localhost';
7
```

On line 6 we use the same trick as before to extract a host from the command line or to choose a default host.

```
8    if (ping($host))
9    {
10       print "$host is alive\n";
11   }
12   else
13   {
14       print "$host did not respond\n";
15   }
16
```

Line 8 calls the local **ping** function that returns true or false upon success or failure. Lines 10 and 14 then print a message based on the function's success or failure.

```
17   sub on_alarm
18   {
19       die "Timed out";
20   };
21
```

Lines 17 to 20 make up the **on_alarm** function that will be called when the SIGALRM signal is received by the script. The **alarm** function, the signal, and this signal handler will form our timeout for the **ping** function.

```
22   sub ping
23   {
24       my ($remhost) = @_;
25       my $outtest = "Echo$/";
```

```
26        my $inresponse = ' ' x length $outtest;
27        die $Ssockets::error
28            unless(connectsocket(*PINGHANDLE, $remhost,
29                                  'echo', 'udp'));
30        autoflush PINGHANDLE 1;
```

Line 22 is the start of the **ping** function. We extract the host on line 24 and set up a variable to hold the test string and response string in lines 26 and 27. By explicitly setting the value of the response to be made up of the same number of spaces as the test string, we can ensure that the returned value is (or is not) identical to the sent string.

Line 27 tests for the successful opening of a new socket using a service of the echo server and the UDP protocol. Using the **connectsocket** function doesn't actually connect to a remote machine; it just sets up a socket handle that will send data to a specified host. No checks are made to ensure that the other end exists or that it opened a receiving socket. The result, therefore, of opening a socket will be true if the process was successful, and false if the name, service, or other lookups associated with creating a local socket failed.

On line 30 we specify that no buffering should take place. Any non-zero value specifies that data should be written immediately to the destination.

```
31        eval
32        {
33            local $SIG{'ALRM'} = \&on_alarm;
34            print PINGHANDLE $outtest;
35            alarm 5;
36            recv(PINGHANDLE, $inresponse, 5, 0);
37            alarm 0;
38        }
39        return($inresponse eq $outtest);
40    }
```

Lines 31 to 38 do the real work, all within the relative safety of the **eval** block. This block protects us from the effects of the signal handling used for the **timeout** function. We set the alarm signal on line 33. To set a signal, you simply set a value of the %**SIG** hash, using the signal name as the key. In this instance, we specify the value of the signal as a function reference. Because the signal handler is simple (one line), we could set the signal with an anonymous handler:

```
local $SIG{'ALRM'} = sub { die 'Timed out' };
```

We send a simple string to the destination on line 34. Remember that we are using UDP, so there is no guarantee that the other end exists or that it will respond. Line 35 sets the alarm timer to 5 seconds: the script will wait 5 seconds before calling **onalarm**, which will then close the socket handle. If we were using a TCP echo, then we would switch lines 34 and 35 around so that we can test that the remote site is accepting the data and responding to it in the allotted time.

Line 36 waits to receive (**recv**) up to 64 bytes of information from the socket handle, placing the result into **$junk**. Because we are using UDP sockets, we must use **recv** to read the data from the socket to ensure we read back up to a set number of bytes.

At this point in the program, one of two things will happen. Either the remote host will respond, in which case **$inresponse** will contain valid information, the alarm will be canceled (before we exit the **eval** block), and the **ping** function will return a positive value to the main sequence. What is printed depends on whether the response from the server was the echoed value of what we sent. Alternatively, the alarm timer will timeout, the alarm signal will be received, and the alarm handler will cause the **eval** block to complete. In this case, **$inresponse** will not equal the string we sent out, so the result of the test in line 39 will be false.

This view of the **ping** function is very simplistic; if you want a more expansive and reliable method of pinging a remote host, you might want to take a look at the **Net::Ping** module, which is part of the standard Perl 5 distribution.

It is also worth noting that this script uses the UDP protocol. The UDP protocol is a datagram service, so it does not guarantee that the remote service is up or responding, or that it received the information correctly or in the right sequence. That said, UDP is a frequently used protocol for sending broadcast information, a situation where the sender is not concerned whether the recipient received the information. If you want a reliable protocol for two-way communication, then you should use TCP.

httpserv.pl

A Simple Web Server

The two previous examples show how to create simple servers using the simple sockets module we created at the start of this chapter. Clients need servers to connect to, and using the socket module simplifies the connection process. However, there are additional issues that need to be addressed when running a server.

Most important of all, we need to get our server to respond to more than one request at a time, otherwise our server will only be able to accept requests sequentially. The other advantage is that individual servers can be serving different clients and be in different states (of sending or receiving). This common technique is used by most Internet servers. The way it works is simple: each time a request is accepted by the server, a new process is created; the sole purpose of the new process is to service the requests of the client.

The **inetd** server is a special case. The **inetd** server listens on multiple ports for a connection, and when one is received, it forks a new process and either services the request itself or executes the program responsible for dealing with that port. Other servers, such as Web servers, pre-fork a number of children to accept requests, which results in higher performance, because the children are not forked at request time, but it induces a higher memory requirement on the server.

This sequence can be done within the Perl script by using the **fork** function: the code following the **fork** statement becomes the code used by the new process. Copies of the data and variables available within the parent process at the time the child was created are also available to each of the subprocesses, or, as they are commonly called, children. This makes multiprocess servers easy to create while still using the same script and other Perl constructs.

There are some problems with the **fork** method. Creating a new process and copying the data demands a lot of the processor and system, and so you sacrifice performance for simplicity and ease of use. The ideal way to proceed, of course, would be to create *threads*, small processes that don't incur the same overheads as creating new processes. They also share data between each other and the parent; with **fork**, data cannot be shared between children without using some form of interprocess communication, or IPC, such as sockets. The data exchange between the parent and children is also one way: the children inherit the data and environment of the parent, but they, too, are unable to communicate any data back to the parent without using some form of IPC. Unfortunately, Perl doesn't yet support threads in a release version. At the time of this writing, beta versions of Perl 5.005, which does support threads, were in the throes of being released.

The **httpserv.pl** script supports a very simple HTTP service and could be used in all sorts of situations where a quick Web server is required, but you don't want to install anything as complex as, say, Apache. Because it's written in Perl, it could be used as a portable way of setting up a Web service on Macs, Unix systems, and PCs. Of course, it has limitations. The script only supports basic GET requests; no CGI or FORM support is included. However, there could be some potential advantages to writing a Perl server program where the Web server itself is written in Perl—it could certainly make Perl-based CGI easier!

```perl
1   #!/usr/local/bin/perl5
2
3   use Ssockets;
4   use FileHandle;
5   use Cwd;
6   use Getopt::Std;
7   use Socket;
8   getopts('d');
9
10  $SIG{'INT'} = $SIG{'QUIT'} = \&exit_request_handler;
11  $SIG{'CHLD'} = \&child_handler;
12
```

```
13
14   my ($SERVERPORT) = 80;
15
16   unless(listensocket(*SERVERSOCKET, $SERVERPORT, 'tcp', 5))
17   {
18       die "$0: ", $Ssockets::error;
19   }
20
21   autoflush SERVERSOCKET 1;
22
23   chroot(getcwd());
24   die "$0: Couldn't change root directory, are you root?"
25       unless (getcwd() eq "/");
26
27   print "Changing root to ", getcwd(), "\n" if $opt_d;
28
29   print "Simple HTTP Server Started\n" if $opt_d;
30
31   while(1)
32   {
33     ACCEPT_CONNECT:
34       {
35           ($remaddr = accept(CHILDSOCKET, SERVERSOCKET))
36               || redo ACCEPT_CONNECT;
37       }
38       autoflush CHILDSOCKET 1;
39       my $pid = fork();
40       die "Cannot fork, $!" unless defined($pid);
41       if ($pid == 0)
42       {
43           my ($remip)
44               = inet_ntoa((unpack_sockaddr_in($remaddr))[1]);
45           print "Connection accepted from $remip\n" if $opt_d;
46           $_ = <CHILDSOCKET>;
47           print "Got Request $_" if $opt_d;
48           chomp;
49
50           unless (m/(\S+) (\S+)/)
51           {
52               print "Malformed request string $_\n" if $opt_d;
53               bad_request(*CHILDSOCKET);
54           }
55           else
```

```perl
56                    {
57                        my ($command) = $1;
58                        my ($arg) = $2;
59                        if (uc($command) eq 'GET')
60                        {
61                            if (open(FILE, "<$arg"))
62                            {
63                                while(<FILE>)
64                                {
65                                    print CHILDSOCKET $_;
66                                }
67                                close(FILE);
68                            }
69                            else
70                            {
71                                bad_request(*CHILDSOCKET);
72                            }
73                        }
74                    }
75                close(CHILDSOCKET);
76                exit(0);
77            }
78        close(CHILDSOCKET);
79    }
80
81    sub bad_request
82    {
83        my ($SOCKET) = shift;
84
85        print $SOCKET <<EOF
86    <html>
87    <head>
88    <title>Bad Request</title>
89    </head>
90    <body>
91    <h1>Bad Request</h1>
92    The file you requested could not be found
93    </body>
94    </html>
95    EOF
96        ;
97    }
98
```

```
99   sub child_handler
100  {
101      wait;
102  }
103
104  sub exit_request_handler
105  {
106      my ($recvsig) = @_;
107      $SIG{'INT'} = $SIG{'QUIT'} = 'IGNORE';
108      close(SERVERSOCKET);
109      close(CHILDSOCKET);
110      die "Quitting on signal $recvsig\n";
111  }
```

ANNOTATIONS

The **httpserv.pl** script is a very simple Web server, supporting a single HTTP command, GET, at a simple level. The GET operation simply sends the requested file back to the client as a data stream, or it returns a formatted (in HTML) error string if the file can't be found. We use the simple sockets module to create a server socket, then spawn new processes as new connections are accepted on the servers port. Each child then reads the request from the client, sending back the requested file. The port number we use in this example is 80, which matches the standard HTTP service number. We could support the Web server on any port.

```
1    #!/usr/local/bin/perl5
2
3    use Ssockets;
4    use FileHandle;
5    use Cwd;
6    use Getopt::Std;
7    use Socket;
```

We import the simple sockets module on line 3. We need the **FileHandle** module to control the socket handle buffering. The **Cwd** module allows us to obtain the current working directory. As part of the simple security for the Web server in this script, we change the root directory to the current directory, which means that when a file is requested, even if an absolute path name is given, all files will be relative to the current directory. We need the **Cwd** function to set the directory value and then report it as part of the debug process. We also need the standard **Getopt** function, which we incorporate on line 6. Line 7 imports the **Socket** module directly, because we use some socket functions within the local code. We could rely on the fact that the **Ssockets** module imports the **Socket** module, but it isn't guaranteed, nor is it good programming practice.

```
8    getopts('d');
9
10   $SIG{'INT'} = $SIG{'QUIT'} = \&exit_request_handler;
11   $SIG{'CHLD'} = \&child_handler;
12
13
```

On line 8 we extract just one argument from the command line: whether we want debugging information switched on or not. Having debugging on will print the progress of the server as it starts up and accepts connections.

Line 10 sets the interrupt (INT) and QUIT signals to call the **exit_request_handler** function. Generally, an interrupt or quit request is received either as part of the shutdown procedures or when the user wants to safely shut down a server. In this case, we call a function that will close the open server port and exit gracefully.

The child (CHLD) signal is received when a child terminates or stops. The **child_handler** function will be called when the script receives this signal.

```
14   my ($SERVERPORT) = 80;
15
16   unless(listensocket(*SERVERSOCKET, $SERVERPORT, 'tcp', 5))
17   {
18       die "$0: ", $Ssockets::error;
19   }
20
21   autoflush SERVERSOCKET 1;
22
23   chroot(getcwd());
24   die "$0: Couldn't change root directory, are you root?"
25       unless (getcwd() eq "/");
26
27   print "Changing root to ", getcwd(), "\n" if $opt_d;
28
29   print "Simple HTTP Server Started\n" if $opt_d;
30
```

We set the default server port in line 14; as explained earlier, we use the standard HTTP port 80. A new server socket is created on line 16. HTTP is a connection-oriented service, so we must use TCP. The last option of the **listensocket** function is to specify the number of waiting socket connections to hold in the queue. This value doesn't restrict the number of servers that are created, but it does specify the number of connections made to the server that will be queued until the server can process them. Once the queue is full, the OS will simply close the client connection. An error is reported on line 18 using **die**. Because failing to create the server socket prevents the rest of the server from running, we quit the script with an error instead of simply giving a warning.

On line 21 we specify the server socket should automatically flush the buffer after each write. Line 23 is the start of our security procedure. The **chroot** function sets the root directory to the specified directory, in this example the current directory, restricting file accesses so a request for "/index.html" will attempt to read index.html from the current directory instead of the real file system root directory.

The **chroot** function can be set only by the super-user on a Unix system, so we check that the directory change worked on lines 24 and 25, again quitting with an error if the process fails. This error is also serious because if we can't change the root directory, the server is not secure even at this basic level. The whole process could be shortened to

```
chroot (getcwd) || die "$0: chroot failed - are you root ($!)\n";
```

We could also check the effective uid (with **geteuid**) of the user to verify if they were root before we called the function.

Lines 27 and 28 print a debug message if we set the debug option on the command line. These serve as simple notifications of the status of the server, rather than provide the sort of logging information available from a standard Web server.

```
31  while(1)
32  {
33    ACCEPT_CONNECT:
34      {
35          ($remaddr = accept(CHILDSOCKET, SERVERSOCKET))
36              || redo ACCEPT_CONNECT;
37      }
38    autoflush CHILDSOCKET 1;
```

Line 31 sets up a perpetual loop. Perl will run the lines of code between 32 and 79 forever because we have set the expression it tests on to be permanently true. This trick is typically used to force a server to work forever. We don't need to worry about quitting out of the application at any point within the main part of the script because we set the INT and QUIT signals to call a suitable function to quit the application upon request.

We label a new block of code on line 33; it stretches from lines 34 to 37. This block will accept new connections on the server port we just created. Line 35 uses the **accept** function to obtain the remote address of a client connection and create a new socket, CHILDSOCKET, which is the socket that connects client to server. The **accept** function will block (stop program execution) until a connection is received. If the connection fails, then we use **redo** to return to the start of the block. If the connection is accepted, execution continues on to line 38, where we set the buffers to flush after each write on the new child network socket.

```
39      my $pid = fork();
40      die "Cannot fork, $!" unless defined($pid);
41      if ($pid == 0)
42      {
43          my ($remip)
44              = inet_ntoa((unpack_sockaddr_in($remaddr))[1]);
45          print "Connection accepted from $remip\n" if $opt_d;
46          $_ = <CHILDSOCKET>;
47          print "Got Request $_" if $opt_d;
48          chomp;
49
```

A new process is created on line 40. The **fork()** function will return **undef** if the forking of a new process fails. We check for possible failure by setting the return value of the function to a new variable and then checking whether the variable was defined on line 40. If a new process could be forked, then a zero will be returned to the child, which we check in line 41.

We will use the forked process to continue the communication with the child socket we obtained on line 35. From line 42 to line 77, the code will be executed by the new child process, not the server process. It's important to remember that even though the code is all contained within the same script, a completely separate process effectively executes these lines. It's also important to remember that the variables you access within the child are copies of the parent versions as they were when the child was created; there is no communication between the two processes. Each new instance of the child will have its own, separate copy of the parent data. The environment is also copied to the child process. Settings like the current directory, including the current root directory as set by **chroot**, will be inherited by the child.

Lines 43 and 44 extract an IP address from the packed remote address returned by the **accept** function in line 35. We first use **unpack_sockaddr_in**, which extracts the packed IP address from the **sockaddr_in** structure that is used by the underlying library function. The second element is the IP address, hence the use of the subscript notation. The result is then converted to a packed IP address by the **inet_ntoa** function. Both functions are defined within the **Socket** module.

Line 45 is a debug line and prints out the connection information. We read the first line of input from the child socket on line 46, printing the request on line 47 if debugging is switched on. Line 48 strips the default record separator off the end of the input line—this separator is usually a new-line character.

```
50              unless (m/(\S+) (\S+)/)
51              {
52                   print "Malformed request string $_\n" if $opt_d;
53                   bad_request(*CHILDSOCKET);
54              }
```

Line 50 is looking for a match of two strings separated by a single space. Line 52 prints out an error when debugging is switched on. We generate a bad request message back to the client by calling the **bad_request** function with a typeglob for the socket's file handle. Remember that file handles can be easily exchanged between functions by using typeglobs.

```
55              else
56              {
57                   my ($command) = $1;
58                   my ($arg) = $2;
59                   if (uc($command) eq 'GET')
60                   {
61                        if (open(FILE, "<$arg"))
62                        {
63                             while(<FILE>)
64                             {
65                                  print CHILDSOCKET $_;
66                             }
67                             close(FILE);
68                        }
```

If the match worked successfully, then we have a correctly formatted request string, and we can extract the command and the argument on lines 57 and 58. Line 59 identifies a GET request. Generally, commands are in capitals, but we effectively ignore any supplied case by comparing an uppercase version (via the **uc** function) against a static string. On line 61 we attempt to open the file specified in the request. We don't perform any regular expression on the argument: if it's a file request, then the file that is opened will be relative to the **chroot** directory we set back in line 23. Using **chroot** allows us to directly support requests for files of the form "/index.html" without having to map the request to the real directory. This method is far less complex and has the added benefit of increasing the security of the server. Provided we don't change the root directory variable to the real root directory, a request for "/etc/passwd" won't respond with the file you might otherwise expect.

If the file exists and is readable, lines 63 to 66 send individual lines of the file back to the client associated with the local CHILDSOCKET. Note that we don't add any extra characters—this method should safely transfer binary files as well as standard HTML text files. We could shorten the lineage in lines 63 to 66 with

```
print CHILDSOCKET while <FILE>;
```

We close the file on line 67.

```
69                    else
70                    {
71                         bad_request(*CHILDSOCKET);
72                    }
73               }
74          }
```

On lines 69 to 72 we report back an error, using the **bad_request** function to send an HTML-formatted text string back to the client socket.

```
75          close(CHILDSOCKET);
76          exit(0);
77     }
78     close(CHILDSOCKET);
79 }
80
```

Up until line 77 we are still executing code within the child process we forked when a new connection was accepted. Line 75 therefore closes the network socket that belongs to the child, which then exits on line 76.

Line 78, on the other hand, closes the network socket that was opened as part of the **accept** function in line 35, and it is part of the parent process. Since each child is given a copy of the child socket handle, closing the parent socket simply frees the child socket for the next incoming connection to be accepted and for the **CHILDSOCKET** handle to be reassigned to the incoming connection.

Line 79 is the end of the perpetual **while** statement, and it returns us to a wait state while the parent process waits for a new client network connection to come in.

```
81 sub bad_request
82 {
83     my ($SOCKET) = shift;
84
85     print $SOCKET <<EOF
86 <html>
87 <head>
88 <title>Bad Request</title>
89 </head>
90 <body>
91 <h1>Bad Request</h1>
92 The file you requested could not be found
```

```
93   </body>
94   </html>
95   EOF
96       ;
97   }
98
```

Lines 81 to 98 form the **bad_request** function, which is really just an entire print statement used to return an error to the client.

```
99   sub child_handler
100  {
101      wait;
102  }
103
```

The **wait** function waits for a child process to exit properly. This function is called when the parent process receives a CHLD signal. Effectively, what happens is that a child exits, the parent is notified, and this function then causes the parent to wait until the child process has completed exiting before continuing.

```
104  sub exit_request_handler
105  {
106      my ($recvsig) = @_;
107      $SIG{'INT'} = $SIG{'QUIT'} = 'IGNORE';
108      close(SERVERSOCKET);
109      close(CHILDSOCKET);
110      die "Quitting on signal $recvsig\n";
111  }
```

The **exit_request_handler** function is called when the parent process receives a QUIT or INT signal. The function's purpose is to close down the parent process gracefully instead of simply quitting and leaving open sockets. The only argument to a signal handling function is the signal that was received, which we extract on line 106. We set the INT and QUIT signals to IGNORE to prevent further interrupts invoking another copy of this function. We then close the open sockets of the parent on lines 108 and 109. Finally, we **die** with an error on line 110.

The **httpserv.pl** script is relatively straightforward. The most complex element to get used to is the **fork** function and how it affects the program execution. In this script, lines 41 to 77 can be thought of as a completely separate script that inherits the variables and open file handles from the parent program.

The execution sequence is therefore different from a standard Perl script. When it first starts, the parent script creates a server socket and listens for new connections. Once a new connection is received, a new Perl script is spawned that handles the communication between the new socket handle on which the client has connected.

Immediately after spawning, the parent closes the child socket, because it is no longer handling the communication, and returns to a wait state for the next incoming connection. This method is fairly typical of server operation and allows the server to support many open client connections very easily.

Obviously, the script is fairly simplistic. Although we have built some security into the script, it's not watertight. The script also supports only one HTTP command. If we wanted to monitor the full list of commands sent to a Web server by a Web browser, we would change line 46 to be a **while** statement like the following:

```
while(<CHILDSOCKET>)
{
...
}
```

By using a dispatch table, we could service any number of commands by assigning functions to the values of hash, the keys of which are the valid commands. We will see an example in the **statserv.pl** script.

We might also want to remove lines 50 to 54 and 69 to 72 to stop the server from returning errors for "incorrect" requests. The result can be quite revealing. Using Netscape to connect to the server with debugging switched on shows us that the typical browser request consists of more than just a simple GET command:

```
$ httpserv.pl -d
Simple HTTP Server Started
Connection accepted from 10.3.3.1
Got Request GET /index.html HTTP/1.0
Got Request Connection: Keep-Alive
Got Request User-Agent: Mozilla/4.05 (Macintosh; I; PPC, Nav)
Got Request Host: 10.3.3.1:4004
Got Request Accept: image/gif, image/x-xbitmap, image/jpeg,
image/pjpeg, image/png, */*
Got Request Accept-Charset: iso-8859-1,*,utf-8
```

Here we can see that Netscape requests that a connection on the server be kept open (if it's available); the name and version number of the client; the host address and port; the list of MIME types supported (Multipurpose Internet Mail Extensions, covered Chapter 7); and the character sets the browser will accept.

statserv.pl

The Machine Status Server

In Chapter 11 we will look at a system that allows us to monitor the status of a number of machines on the network, including their system loading, the available memory and swap space, and the disk space availability. Developing the system to its current late beta state involved a number of different prototypes. The next script is one such prototype.

Building on the HTTP server we developed in the last example, I first built a server capable of accepting different requests or commands from a client. Using this base, I created a number of commands that I could use to remotely interrogate a Solaris machine to obtain the output from the df command, which reports disk storage sizes, and the swap command, which reports the available memory and swap space. Using the same structure, I then decided that using a server to record and track the information, with clients sending in their reports, instead of requesting a report from the server, made more sense from a centralized storage point of view. This decision introduced the need for the server to read and write files over the network to and from the local disk storage.

What I ended up with was the following server, **statserv.pl**. The server works on port 4004 and accepts client requests; the client can request the disk or swap space report from the server. Alternatively, it can supply its own report, which is stored as a file within the local directory; the name is based on the client name and the report type. Finally, the client can request a specific host report from the server.

You can see a typical conversation in Table 5-4. The first command sent by the client is DISK, which requests a disk report from the server. The report is sent back, followed by an EOT (end of transmission string), to show that the report has finished and the server is ready to accept another command. At step 3, we request that a status report for the machine "www" is stored on the server, so we send the command, the report, and then the EOT signal again. The server responds that it has accepted the report and signifies that the transmission has ended before the client quits in step 5.

There are a couple of problems with this system that I'll discuss in more detail in Chapter 11. However, to whet your appetite, the major problem with the script was significant enough to warrant a rewrite. The intention was for regular reports to be submitted to a server machine that would be responsible for holding the data.

Sequence	Server Sends	Client Sends
1		DISK
2	Disk Report EOT	
3		STORE www status Status Report EOT
4	Report Accepted EOT	
5		QUIT

TABLE 5-4. Typical Status Server Conversation

Storing local files on the client which are then sent to the host is not a problem, but if the collection machine is down, it requires a spooling area, and then the files need to be sent individually to the server. Using FTP to perform the uploads was a much simpler and straightforward solution to the upload problem, and it transpired that the performance was improved by uploading files via the standard FTP server to an incoming spool directory, which was then periodically processed. See Chapter 11 for the entire monitoring solution and for the **mstatus.pl** script that has the solution to this specific problem.

Although this script wasn't selected in this instance, it still demonstrates the basic principles behind an application-level protocol and how to implement them over a simple socket link.

```perl
1    #!/usr/local/bin/perl5
2
3    use Ssockets;
4    use FileHandle;
5    use Getopt::Std;
6    use Socket;
7    my %commandlist = (
8                        'DISK'  => 'disk_space_report',
9                        'SWAP'  => 'swap_space_report',
10                       'STORE' => 'store_status_report',
11                       'GET'   => 'get_status_report',
12                       'QUIT'  => 'quit_connection',
13                       );
14   my ($TRANSEND, $SERVERPORT) = ('EOT', 4004);
15
16   getopts('d');
17
18   $SIG{'INT'} = $SIG{'QUIT'} = \&exit_request_handler;
19   $SIG{'CHLD'} = \&child_handler;
20
21   unless(listensocket(*SERVERSOCKET, $SERVERPORT, 'tcp', 5))
22   {
23       die "$0: ", $Ssockets::error;
24   }
25
26   autoflush SERVERSOCKET 1;
27
28   print "Message Server Started, Port $SERVERPORT\n" if $opt_d;
29
30   while(1)
31   {
```

```
32    ACCEPT_CONNECT:
33      {
34          ($remaddr = accept(CHILDSOCKET, SERVERSOCKET))
35              || redo ACCEPT_CONNECT;
36      }
37      autoflush CHILDSOCKET 1;
38      my $pid = fork();
39      die "Cannot fork, $!" unless defined($pid);
40      if ($pid == 0)
41      {
42          my $remip
43              = inet_ntoa((unpack_sockaddr_in($remaddr))[1]);
44          print "Connection accepted from $remip\n" if $opt_d;
45
46          while(<CHILDSOCKET>)
47          {
48              chomp;
49
50              if (m#[/|!]#)
51              {
52                  return_error(*CHILDSOCKET,
53                              "Error: Badly formed command\n");
54                  next;
55              }
56
57              my ($command, $host, $type) = split(' ');
58
59              $command=uc($command);
60              if (defined($commandlist{$command}))
61              {
62                  my ($function) = $commandlist{$command};
63                  die "No $function()" unless defined(&$function);
64                  &$function(*CHILDSOCKET, $host, $type);
65              }
66              else
67              {
68                  return_error(*CHILDSOCKET,
69                              "Error: Not a valid command\n");
70              }
71          }
72          unless (close(CHILDSOCKET))
73          {
74              print "Couldn't close child socket (child), $!\n"
```

```perl
75                        if $opt_d;
76             }
77         exit(0);
78     }
79     unless (close(CHILDSOCKET))
80     {
81         print "Couldn't close the Child socket (parent), $!\n"
82             if $opt_d;
83     }
84 }
85
86 sub return_error
87 {
88     my ($SOCKET, @message) = @_;
89     print $SOCKET @message;
90 }
91
92 sub disk_space_report
93 {
94     my ($SOCKET) = @_;
95
96     if (open(D, "df -k|"))
97     {
98         while(<D>)
99         {
100             print $SOCKET $_;
101         }
102         close(D);
103     }
104     else
105     {
106         print $SOCKET "Error: Could not get disk report\n";
107     }
108     print $SOCKET $TRANSEND, "\n";
109 }
110
111 sub swap_space_report
112 {
113     my ($SOCKET) = @_;
114
115     if (open(D, "swap -s|"))
116     {
117         while(<D>)
```

```
118          {
119              print $SOCKET $_;
120          }
121          close(D);
122      }
123      else
124      {
125          print $SOCKET "Error: Could not get disk report\n";
126      }
127      print $SOCKET $TRANSEND, "\n";
128 }
129
130 sub store_status_report
131 {
132      my ($SOCKET, $host, $type) = @_;
133
134      unless (open(D, ">$host.$type"))
135      {
136          while(<$SOCKET>)
137          {
138              last if ($_ =~ /^\Q$TRANSEND\E$/);
139          }
140          print $SOCKET "Error: couldn't create status file ($!)\n";
141          print SOCKET $TRANSEND, "\n";
142          return;
143      }
144
145      while(<$SOCKET>)
146      {
147          last if ($_ =~ /^\Q$TRANSEND\E$/);
148          print D $_;
149      }
150      close(D);
151      print $SOCKET "Report Accepted\n";
152      print $SOCKET $TRANSEND, "\n";
153 }
154
155 sub get_status_report
156 {
157      my ($SOCKET, $host, $type) = @_;
158      unless(open(D, "<$host.$type"))
159      {
160          print $SOCKET "Error: couldn't open status file ($!)\n";
```

```
161         print SOCKET $TRANSEND, "\n";
162         return;
163     }
164
165     while(<D>)
166     {
167         print $SOCKET $_;
168     }
169     close(D);
170     print $SOCKET $TRANSEND, "\n";
171 }
172
173 sub quit_connection
174 {
175     my ($SOCKET, $host, $type) = @_;
176     close($SOCKET);
177     exit(0);
178 }
179
180 sub child_handler
181 {
182     wait;
183 }
184
185 sub exit_request_handler
186 {
187     my ($recvsig) = @_;
188     $SIG{'INT'} = $SIG{'QUIT'} = 'IGNORE';
189     close(SERVERSOCKET);
190     close(CHILDSOCKET);
191     print "Qutting on signal $recvsig\n" if $opt_d;
192     exit(1);
193 }
```

ANNOTATIONS

The **statserv.pl** script uses the same basic framework as the **httpserv.pl** script. A new server socket is created, then listened to for new connections. As each connection is accepted and opened, we wait for a request from the client. Once the request is received, we process it, sending back data or acknowledgment as required. Then we wait for another request, repeating the process until the client closes the connection.

The big difference is that instead of parsing the requests within the **while** loop that reads the requests, we farm the requests out to specific functions. More significantly, and practically, we use a predefined list of commands matched to function names. Using this "dispatch" list, we can add new commands by updating the list and creating the necessary function. We don't need to add to or modify the main server code. This makes the basic script very extendible and easier to support. Assuming the core code is functionally correct, we can narrow down any other problems to the localized functions supporting individual features.

```perl
1   #!/usr/local/bin/perl5
2
3   use Ssockets;
4   use FileHandle;
5   use Getopt::Std;
6   use Socket;
7   my %commandlist = (
8                       'DISK'   => 'disk_space_report',
9                       'SWAP'   => 'swap_space_report',
10                      'STORE'  => 'store_status_report',
11                      'GET'    => 'get_status_report',
12                      'QUIT'   => 'quit_connection',
13                      );
```

As before, we need the simple sockets module, the **FileHandle** module (for setting the autoflush), and the standard **Getopt** module, which we'll use to select whether we print debug information.

Lines 7 to 13 create a hash that will hold the list of supported commands and the functions that should be called to support them. Each of the lines specifies an individual function. We use the **=>** operator to specify that the key on the left-hand side of the operator relates to the value on the right-hand side. Hence in line 8, the value of **$commandlist{'DISK'}** is **disk_space_report**.

```perl
14  my ($TRANSEND, $SERVERPORT) = ('EOT', 4004);
15
16  getopts('d');
17
18  $SIG{'INT'} = $SIG{'QUIT'} = \&exit_request_handler;
19  $SIG{'CHLD'} = \&child_handler;
20
```

The variable **$TRANSEND** (short for "transmission end") specified in line 14 will be the string used to specify that a file transmission has come to an end. Think of it as the end-of-file marker for the network communication. The server port number is held in the **$SERVERPORT** variable. We can use **-d** on the command line to switch on the printing of debugging information because line 16 extracts the command-line options.

As the final part of our setup procedures, we set the INT and QUIT signals to reference a function that will handle quit requests in line 18, and similarly set the CHLD signal to call the **child_handler** function.

```
21   unless(listensocket(*SERVERSOCKET, $SERVERPORT, 'tcp', 5))
22   {
23       die "$0: ", $Ssockets::error;
24   }
25
26   autoflush SERVERSOCKET 1;
27
28   print "Message Server Started, Port $SERVERPORT\n" if $opt_d;
29
```

The server socket is created on line 21, and we report an error on line 23 if the socket cannot be created using the contents of the **$Ssockets::error** variable, which is exported by the simple sockets module. We set the server socket to autoflush after each write in line 26. Line 28 uses the **$opt_d** variable, created as part of the **getopts** function, to print out a debug message showing the startup status of the server.

```
30   while(1)
31   {
32   ACCEPT_CONNECT:
33       {
34           ($remaddr = accept(CHILDSOCKET, SERVERSOCKET))
35               || redo ACCEPT_CONNECT;
36       }
37       autoflush CHILDSOCKET 1;
```

A perpetual loop is started in line 30, and new child sockets are created when an incoming connection causes **accept** to return the child's socket value. Until then, the **accept** function will block execution. If the child socket creation failed, we skip back to the **ACCEPT_CONNECT** function to repeat the waiting process again. Once accepted, the new child socket is set in line 37 to flush its buffer contents immediately after each write.

```
38       my $pid = fork();
39       die "Cannot fork, $!" unless defined($pid);
40       if ($pid == 0)
41       {
42           my $remip
43               = inet_ntoa((unpack_sockaddr_in($remaddr))[1]);
44           print "Connection accepted from $remip\n" if $opt_d;
45
```

A new process is forked to handle the requests for this client, using the **fork()** function on line 38, which we verify worked correctly in line 39; then we start the child code at line 40. We extract the IP address on line 43, printing it out if debugging is switched on in line 44.

```
46          while(<CHILDSOCKET>)
47          {
48              chomp;
49
50              if (m#[/|!]#)
51              {
52                  return_error(*CHILDSOCKET,
53                              "Error: Badly formed command\n");
54                  next;
55              }
56
57              my ($command, $host, $type) = split(' ');
58
59              $command=uc($command);
60              if (defined($commandlist{$command}))
61              {
62                  my ($function) = $commandlist{$command};
63                  die "No $function()" unless defined(&$function);
64                  &$function(*CHILDSOCKET, $host, $type);
65              }
66              else
67              {
68                  return_error(*CHILDSOCKET,
69                              "Error: Not a valid command\n");
70              }
71          }
```

Lines 46 to 71 process the incoming requests from the client. As long the client does not close the connection, we will sequentially process each line that is sent to us. Any trailing end-of-line characters are stripped on line 48. The regular expression in line 50 checks that the client isn't requesting a file outside of our local directory; anything containing a forward slash, pipe symbol, or exclamation mark is considered to be a badly formed command. We report this information to the client using the **return_error** function on lines 52 and 53. Since the request may be a glitch on the part of a client, or a typo if the server is being accessed manually, we just move on to the next input line, skipping the remainder of the loop.

Line 57 splits the input line by spaces. Commands should be of the form
`command [host] [type]`

The two arguments are optional, and will be ignored by some of the functions. Note that we have specified the variables as local directly within a line of the script in the middle of the program. Unlike in some languages (most notably C), we can create variables, and localize them, at any point within the script. If we wanted to support multiple commands, we could use a line like this one:

```
($command, @args) = split;
```

and then pass the argument list to the function with

```
&$function(@args);
```

Since we are using only two arguments (or no arguments), it seems excessive to pass a list, although it would be more portable and extendible.

Commands, as referenced in the **%commandlist** keys, are uppercase, so we covert to uppercase in line 59. Line 60 verifies that the command just received appears in the known command list. If it does, then we create a new variable in line 62 that points to the correct function. Line 63 ensures that the function defined in the hash is actually defined in the script. We then call the function on line 64, passing the two arguments. We don't need to worry about what the arguments contain, or if the arguments are even valid for the function: it's entirely up to the functions to use or discard these values.

If the function isn't in the known command list, we report an error to the client on lines 68 and 69.

```
72          unless (close(CHILDSOCKET))
73          {
74              print "Couldn't close child socket (child), $!\n"
75                  if $opt_d;
76          }
77          exit(0);
78      }
```

Once the child has closed the socket (or requested that the socket be closed), we will drop out of the loop, reading the lines sent by the client. If the socket can't be closed properly and if debugging is switched on, we print a warning on line 74 before finally exiting the child in line 77.

```
79      unless (close(CHILDSOCKET))
80      {
81          print "Couldn't close the Child socket (parent), $!\n"
82              if $opt_d;
83      }
84  }
85
```

On line 79, we are back within the parent code. We run the same test again; if the **close** function fails and debugging is switched on, then we report an error.

```
86   sub return_error
87   {
88       my ($SOCKET, @message) = @_;
89       print $SOCKET @message;
90   }
91
```

The **return_error** function is used to send an error message back to the client. It's very simple: it takes a typeglob socket handle and a message, printing the message to the socket.

```
92   sub disk_space_report
93   {
94       my ($SOCKET) = @_;
95
96       if (open(D, "df -k|"))
97       {
98           while(<D>)
99           {
100              print $SOCKET $_;
101          }
102          close(D);
103      }
104      else
105      {
106          print $SOCKET "Error: Could not get disk report\n";
107      }
108      print $SOCKET $TRANSEND, "\n";
109  }
110
```

The **disk_space_report** function is called when the client sends the DISK command to the server, requesting a report on disk space, which we do by running the df command and capturing the output. By putting a trailing pipe in the file specification, we cause Perl to run the specified program, and pipe the output back to the specified file handle. The output is read in, line by line, and sent directly to the client; we don't add any trailing new-line character, as it will have been captured from the output of the df command. If the command cannot be executed, we return an error on line 106. The test won't catch everything: if the program is not found, the **open** function returns **undef**, and we don't account for that.

Whether a report is sent back or not, we send the end-of-transmission string back to the client to signify that the transfer has ended. It's up to the client to decide what to do next. Since the client is expecting a multiline response, we have to use the end-of-transmission string to signify the end of transmission. Without it, the client will wait expectantly for the rest of the message, but as far as the server is concerned, the message has been sent. This point is fundamental to application-level protocol: each end must have some indication of the state in which it should be.

Note, by the way, that we extract the host and type values from the arguments sent to us, even though we don't actually use them. They are passed to us by the main child loop, but they are not required for this function.

```perl
111 sub swap_space_report
112 {
113     my ($SOCKET) = @_;
114
115     if (open(D, "swap -s|"))
116     {
117         while(<D>)
118         {
119             print $SOCKET $_;
120         }
121         close(D);
122     }
123     else
124     {
125         print $SOCKET "Error: Could not get disk report\n";
126     }
127     print $SOCKET $TRANSEND, "\n";
128 }
129
```

The swap space report works identically to the disk space report, except this time we run the **swap** function to obtain a report on the used and available swap space. The actual command for reporting the available memory and swap space differs from Unix flavor to flavor. It's swap under Solaris and swapinfo under HP-UX, for example.

```perl
130 sub store_status_report
131 {
132     my ($SOCKET, $host, $type) = @_;
133
134     unless (open(D, ">$host.$type"))
135     {
136         while(<$SOCKET>)
137         {
138             last if ($_ =~ /^\Q$TRANSEND\E$/);
139         }
140         print $SOCKET "Error: couldn't create status file ($!)\n";
141         print SOCKET $TRANSEND, "\n";
```

```
142          return;
143      }
144
145      while(<$SOCKET>)
146      {
147          last if ($_ =~ /^\Q$TRANSEND\E$/);
148          print D $_;
149      }
150      close(D);
151      print $SOCKET "Report Accepted\n";
152      print $SOCKET $TRANSEND, "\n";
153  }
154
```

Storing a status report sent to us from a server is equally straightforward, as long we know the sequence (protocol) required to accept the report. The **store_status_report** function starts on line 130 and takes input from the client, writing the result to a file based on the host and type specified by the client.

If we can't open the output file (line 134), we sink the input from the client in lines 136 to 139. We do this because the client doesn't check to ensure the server is ready to accept the data—it just goes ahead and sends the report. If we were concerned about the size of the data being transferred, this might be a cause for concern, but the short reports we are transferring shouldn't cause a major problem. We must flush the input from the socket before we reply with the error on line 140, so we read the lines from the socket until we receive the end-of-transmission string before replying with an error.

The regular expressions in lines 137 and 148 explicitly look for a single line containing the end-of-transmission string. **\Q** switches off regular expression matching until **\E**.

If we did manage to open the file correctly, then we read each line of input from the network socket and write it straight to the file. We check on line 147 for the end-of-transmission string, breaking out of the loop to close the file on line 150. Finally, we reply to the client with a success message and the **$TRANSEND** string.

```
155  sub get_status_report
156  {
157      my ($SOCKET, $host, $type) = @_;
158      unless(open(D, "<$host.$type"))
159      {
160          print $SOCKET "Error: couldn't open status file ($!)\n";
161          print SOCKET $TRANSEND, "\n";
162          return;
163      }
164
```

```
165     while(<D>)
166     {
167         print $SOCKET $_;
168     }
169     close(D);
170     print $SOCKET $TRANSEND, "\n";
171 }
172
```

The **get_status_report** function is basically the opposite of the **store_status_report** function: we open the local file specified and send it back, over the network socket, to the client. The difference is that we don't have to sink the input; the request calls for a simple reply, and whether the reply contains the actual report or an error message makes no difference to the server. How the client responds is what matters.

So, in this function if **open** fails, we send back the error message and end-of-transmission string. If **open** succeeds, then we send lines from the file to the client, following up with the end-of-transmission string.

```
173 sub quit_connection
174 {
175     my ($SOCKET, $host, $type) = @_;
176     close($SOCKET);
177     exit(0);
178 }
179
```

If the client sends QUIT to the server, then it is a sign for the server to close the connection. We therefore close the socket handle on line 176 before quitting the client on line 177.

```
180 sub child_handler
181 {
182     wait;
183 }
184
185 sub exit_request_handler
186 {
187     my ($recvsig) = @_;
188     $SIG{'INT'} = $SIG{'QUIT'} = 'IGNORE';
189     close(SERVERSOCKET);
190     close(CHILDSOCKET);
191     print "Qutting on signal $recvsig\n" if $opt_d;
192     exit(1);
193 }
```

On line 180 the **child_handler** function uses the **wait** function to wait for the child to quit. It is not a graceful solution, but it does prevent "zombies," processes with no controlling parent or terminal. Lines 185 to 193 handle a quit request to the server. We start on line 188 by setting the INT and QUIT signals to be ignored, then we close the open server and child socket connections. Finally we print a message to the user and exit on lines 191 and 192.

There are two special things to note about this script: the protocol and the function dispatch system. The protocol is very simple. The sequence switches between accepting a line and sending one or more lines in response, separated by an end-of-transmission string. This very simple protocol emulates systems like SMTP, which use the same basic framework for the top-level protocol used to support the transmission of files.

The dispatch service simplifies the process of accepting commands from the client and calling the corresponding function. To add new functionality, we just need to add a new entry to the **%commandlist** hash and create the corresponding function, saving us from having to add extra decision code to the core of the child request loop and allowing us to identify at an early stage if the command sent by the client is not supported.

For an example of how to use the system, refer to the end of the next script, **statclnt.pl**.

The Machine Status Client

statclnt.pl

The **statclnt.pl** script is the client end of the server created in the last example. It allows us to send a status report for the current machine or retrieve a status report for any machine from the server. Obviously, it needs to support the same application-level protocol as the server, but otherwise the client is rather simplistic.

```perl
1   #!/usr/local/bin/perl5
2
3   use Ssockets;
4   use FileHandle;
5   use Getopt::Long;
6
7   my ($DEFAULTPORT) = 4004;
8
9   my ($get, $store, $host, $port, $debug, $type);
10
11  my $goresp = GetOptions("p=i" => \$port,
12                          "h=s" => \$host,
13                          "g" => \$get,
14                          "s" => \$store,
```

```
15                                    "d" => \$debug,
16                                    "t=s" => \$type
17                                    );
18
19   unless ((($get || $store) && ($host && $type)) || !$goresp)
20   {
21       usage_instructions();
22       exit(0);
23   }
24
25   my $remserver = shift || 'localhost';
26   my $SERVERPORT = $port || $DEFAULTPORT;
27   my $TRANSEND = "EOT";
28
29   print "Connecting to $remserver on port $SERVERPORT\n"
30       if $debug;
31
32   unless (connectsocket(*SERVERHANDLE,
33                         $remserver,
34                         $SERVERPORT,
35                         'tcp'))
36   {
37       die "$0: $Ssockets::error";
38   }
39
40   autoflush SERVERHANDLE 1;
41
42   get_status(*SERVERHANDLE, $host, $type) if $get;
43   store_status(*SERVERHANDLE, $host, $type) if $store;
44
45   sub store_status
46   {
47       my ($SOCKET,$host,$type) = @_;
48
49       print $SOCKET "STORE $host $type\n";
50
51       if (open(D, "df -k|"))
52       {
53           while(<D>)
54           {
55               print $SOCKET $_;
56           }
57           close(D);
```

```
58        }
59        else
60        {
61            print "Error: Could not get disk usage\n";
62        }
63        if (open(D, "swap -s|"))
64        {
65            while(<D>)
66            {
67                print $SOCKET $_;
68            }
69            close(D);
70        }
71        else
72        {
73            print "Error: Could not get memory usage\n";
74        }
75        print $SOCKET $TRANSEND,"\n";
76        $_ = <$SOCKET>;
77        unless ($_ =~ /Accepted/)
78        {
79            print "Error: Message not accepted:\n$_";
80        }
81        close($SOCKET);
82    }
83
84    sub get_status
85    {
86        my ($SOCKET, $host, $type) = @_;
87
88        print $SOCKET "GET $host $type\n";
89        while(<$SOCKET>)
90        {
91            last if ($_ =~ $TRANSEND);
92            if ($_ =~ /Error:/)
93            {
94                print "Server Error:\n$_";
95                exit(0);
96            }
97            print $_;
98        }
99        close($SOCKET);
100   }
```

```
101
102 sub usage_instructions
103 {
104     print <<EOF
105 Usage:
106         $0 [-g|-s] [-p port] [-h host] [-d] [-t type]
107
108 Where:
109
110 -g          Get Report
111 -s          Store Report
112 -p port     Use port number instead of default ($DEFAULTPORT)
113 -h host     Use host
114 -d          Turn on debugging
115 -t          Get/Store Report Type
116
117 EOF
118 }
```

ANNOTATIONS

Once the script's environment has been set up, the script connects to the server and then either sends the store command, followed by the report, or the get command, printing the result to the screen.

```
1   #!/usr/local/bin/perl5
2
3   use Ssockets;
4   use FileHandle;
5   use Getopt::Long;
6
7   my ($DEFAULTPORT) = 4004;
8
9   my ($get, $store, $host, $port, $debug, $type);
10
```

We need the client socket function provided by the **Ssockets** module and the **FileHandle** module as before. However, in this script we will use the "Long" version of the **Getopt** system, which allows greater control over the arguments, including allowing us to accept additional information on the command line by specifying the data type expected. We set the default server port to **4004** in line 7. Because we pass a reference to a variable when calling the **GetOptions** function, we first have to declare the variables in line 9.

```
11  my $goresp = GetOptions("p=i" => \$port,
12                          "h=s" => \$host,
13                          "g" => \$get,
14                          "s" => \$store,
15                          "d" => \$debug,
16                          "t=s" => \$type
17                          );
18
```

The command-line options are extracted by the **GetOptions** function. Arguments are sent to the function by creating a hash. The hash key is a letter or word to be identified as an argument, and the value is a reference to the variable in which to store the result. The key value can also have additional options that allow us to specify, for example, that an option can take a string as an argument. Table 5-5 shows the list of available options and their description.

For example, in line 12 the specification **h=s** allows for an argument of **h** with a required string specifying the host; the string will be placed into the **$host** variable. The **GetOptions** function returns false if the argument extraction failed for any reason. We trap for errors as part of the tests on line 19.

```
19  unless (((($get || $store) && ($host && $type)) || !$goresp)
20  {
21      usage_instructions();
22      exit(0);
23  }
24
25  my $remserver = shift || 'localhost';
26  my $SERVERPORT = $port || $DEFAULTPORT;
27  my $TRANSEND = "EOT";
28
```

Option	Description
(none)	Option does not take an argument. The option variable will be set to 1.
!	Option does not take an argument and may be negated, that is, prefixed by "no." For example, "foo!" will allow "—foo" (with value 1) and "-nofoo" (with value 0). The variable will be set to 1, or 0 if negated.
=[sif]	Option takes a mandatory string, integer, or float argument. The corresponding value will be placed into the option variable.
:[sif]	Option takes an optional string, integer, or float argument. The corresponding value will be placed into the option variable.

TABLE 5-5.   Extended Options for Getopt::Long

We expect to obtain either a get option or a store option from the command line, combined with a host and the type of report to retrieve or store. In addition, we check that the result of extracting the options didn't fail. If we don't get the required options, or they are badly supplied, then we print the usage instructions, a process handled by a separate function. The server to connect to is specified by the first of the remaining arguments, and it is extracted on line 25. Line 26 sets the server port to use, either the option specified on the command line or, if it's not specified, the default port. Line 27 specifies the end-of-transmission string, which should match the string we used on the server.

```perl
29    print "Connecting to $remserver on port $SERVERPORT\n"
30        if $debug;
31
32    unless (connectsocket(*SERVERHANDLE,
33                          $remserver,
34                          $SERVERPORT,
35                          'tcp'))
36    {
37        die "$0: $Ssockets::error";
38    }
39
```

If debugging was switched on in the command line, then we print a progress message on line 29 before finally connecting to the server in line 32. (The entire function call is spread over multiple lines in this example for clarity.) If the connection fails, then we report an error on line 37 and exit.

```perl
40    autoflush SERVERHANDLE 1;
41
42    get_status(*SERVERHANDLE, $host, $type) if $get;
43    store_status(*SERVERHANDLE, $host, $type) if $store;
44
```

Line 40 sets the output buffer of the network socket to flush immediately on each write. Lines 42 and 43 execute the corresponding function relating to the service requested on the command line. Both functions take the same basic arguments: the socket handle, the name of the host to store or recover, and the type of report to store or recover.

```perl
45    sub store_status
46    {
47        my ($SOCKET,$host,$type) = @_;
48
49        print $SOCKET "STORE $host $type\n";
50
51        if (open(D, "df -k|"))
```

```
52        {
53             while(<D>)
54             {
55                  print $SOCKET $_;
56             }
57             close(D);
58        }
59        else
60        {
61             print "Error: Could not get disk usage\n";
62        }
```

Line 49 sends the STORE command to the server, adding the host and type specified on the command line. Lines 51 to 62 generate the disk usage element of the report, printing the results to the network socket, and therefore the server, or reporting an error back to the client. We don't need to tell the server that the client is unable to generate a disk report.

```
63        if (open(D, "swap -s|"))
64        {
65             while(<D>)
66             {
67                  print $SOCKET $_;
68             }
69             close(D);
70        }
71        else
72        {
73             print "Error: Could not get memory usage\n";
74        }
```

Lines 63 to 74 repeat the operation with a swap space report.

```
75             print $SOCKET $TRANSEND,"\n";
76        $_ = <$SOCKET>;
77        unless ($_ =~ /Accepted/)
78        {
79             print "Error: Message not accepted:\n$_";
80        }
81        close($SOCKET);
82   }
83
```

Line 75 sends the end-of-transmission string to signify to the server that the report has finished. Line 76 reads a single-line response back from the server. This response should either be "Report Accepted" or "Error...." The result is checked on line 77, with an error reported to the user if the report upload failed. Once the report is sent, we close the network socket on line 81.

```
84   sub get_status
85   {
86       my ($SOCKET, $host, $type) = @_;
87
88       print $SOCKET "GET $host $type\n";
89       while(<$SOCKET>)
90       {
91           last if ($_ =~ /^\Q$TRANSEND\E$/);
92           if ($_ =~ /Error:/)
93           {
94               print "Server Error:\n$_";
95               exit(0);
96           }
97           print $_;
98       }
99       close($SOCKET);
100  }
101
```

The **get_status** function retrieves the report specified by the host and the type from the server, using the open network socket. Line 88 sends the GET command to the server and immediately switches to the listen state on line 89 to read the output received from the server. As each line is received, we check on line 91 whether the end-of-transmission string was sent by the server, skipping the read loop if it was.

If the server reports an error, then line 92 identifies the received error and prints it for the user on line 94. Once the read completes, we close the socket on line 99.

```
102  sub usage_instructions
103  {
104      print <<EOF
105  Usage:
106          $0 [-g|-s] [-p port] [-h host] [-d] [-t type]
107
108  Where:
109
110  -g          Get Report
111  -s          Store Report
112  -p port     Use port number instead of default ($DEFAULTPORT)
113  -h host     Use host
114  -d          Turn on debugging
115  -t          Get/Store Report Type
```

```
116
117 EOF
118 }
```

Lines 107 to 117 print out the usage instructions within the **usage_instructions** function.

Using the client is a simple case of setting the right options on the command line. Assuming the server is already started, the following command will store the current status report on the server:

```
$ statclnt.pl -s -h twinspark -t full -d
Connecting to localhost on port 4004
```

We can then request the status information back from the server:

```
$ statclnt.pl -g -h twinspark -t full -d
Connecting to localhost on port 4004
Filesystem            kbytes    used   avail capacity  Mounted on
/dev/dsk/c0t0d0s0     115504   12951   91003    12%    /
/dev/dsk/c0t0d0s4     240516  169628   46838    78%    /usr
/proc                      0       0       0     0%    /proc
fd                         0       0       0     0%    /dev/fd
/dev/dsk/c0t0d0s3      57487    6748   44999    13%    /opt
/dev/dsk/c0t0d0s6     480509  109053  323406    25%    /users
/dev/dsk/c0t0d0s5    1041732  272289  665273    29%    /usr/local
total: 8564k bytes allocated + 2916k reserved = 11480k used, 25844k available
```

The two scripts, client and server, are prototypes, and have a few minor bugs in them, but they should help to demonstrate the principles behind a two-way communications system based on the TCP/IP network sockets. Most protocols such as HTTP and SMTP work on the same basic principles for communication.

grfile.pl

A Universal File Downloader

When was the last time you were given a URL (uniform resource locator) for a file from a Web site, and it either didn't work or the server was too busy to accept your request? Wouldn't it be great if, rather than using a browser to download the file, you could use a script to do it instead?

I found myself in this situation. I was asked to download a file from an unreliable Web site. The server supported both HTTP and FTP downloads, but it would often drop out during the middle of a transmission. To add insult to injury, I had a whole list of HTTP-sourced files to download from the site, so using FTP to specify a wildcard list to download wasn't an option.

Another common scenario is when you want to look at a page on the Internet. You don't always want to fire up your browser to view it—in some cases you may even be unable to do so. Downloading the page to your local drive would be the ideal solution: you can either view it later in your browser or, if you enjoy manually filtering out the HTML, you can read it directly. (We'll look at ways of stripping the HTML from files in Chapter 7.)

The solution is to write a script that is capable of accepting the URL you have been given and that will then go away and download the file. In this script, I've used two different methods to connect to two different servers. The script decodes a URL from the command line and selects either HTTP or FTP, depending on the URL specification. If an HTTP page is requested, then we use the client socket system we have already used from the simple sockets module we created at the start of the chapter. If FTP is selected, then we use the **Net::FTP** module, which is part of the libnet toolkit written by Graham Barr. You should be able to find the latest modules on CPAN or your local mirror.

```perl
1   #!/usr/local/bin/perl5
2
3   use Ssockets;
4   use FileHandle;
5   use File::Basename;
6   use Net::FTP;
7   use Getopt::Std;
8
9   getopts('d');
10
11  die "Usage: $0 [-d (debug)] URL" unless (@ARGV == 1);
12  my $url = shift;
13
14  my ($protocol, $user, $password, $machine, $port, $path)
15      = decipher_url($url);
16
17  unless ($protocol)
18  {
19      die "Couldn't decipher URL $url";
20  }
21
22  unless($port)
23  {
24      $port = 80 if ($protocol =~ /http/i);
25      $port = 21 if ($protocol =~ /ftp/i);
26  }
27
28  print <<EOF if $opt_d;
29  Retrieving: $path
30  Machine:    $machine
31  Protocol:   $protocol
```

```
32   Port:         $port
33   User:         $user
34   Password:     $password
35   EOF
36
37   if ($protocol =~ /http/i)
38   {
39       get_http_document($machine, $port, $path);
40   }
41   elsif ($protocol =~ /ftp/i)
42   {
43       get_ftp_document($machine, $user, $password, $path);
44   }
45   else
46   {
47       die "Protocol type not recognized/not supported\n";
48   }
49
50   sub decipher_url
51   {
52       my ($url) = @_;
53       my ($matched, $protocol, $host, $path);
54       my ($user, $password, $machine);
55
56       $matched = $url =~ m#(\S+)://([^/ ]+)(.*)#;
57
58       return(undef) unless($matched);
59
60       $protocol = $1;
61       $host = $2;
62       $path = $3;
63
64       $user = 'anonymous';
65       $password = 'me@foo.bar';
66
67       $_ = $host;
68
69       if (m#(\S+):(\d+)#)
70       {
71           $_ = $1;
72           $port = $2;
73       }
74       if (m#(\S+):(\S+)@(\S+)#)
```

```
75          {
76              $user = $1;
77              $password = $2;
78              $machine = $3;
79          }
80          elsif (m#(\S+)@(\S+)#)
81          {
82              $user = $1;
83              $machine = $2;
84          }
85          else
86          {
87              $machine = $host;
88          }
89
90          return($protocol, $user, $password, $machine, $port, $path);
91      }
92
93      sub get_http_document
94      {
95          my ($machine, $port, $path) = @_;
96          my ($localfile);
97          unless (connectsocket(*SERVERHANDLE,
98                                  $machine,
99                                  $protocol,
100                                 'tcp'))
101         {
102             die $Ssockets::error;
103         }
104
105         autoflush SERVERHANDLE 1;
106
107         print SERVERHANDLE "GET $path\n";
108
109         $localfile=basename($path);
110
111         open(D, ">$localfile") || die "Can't write $localfile, $!";
112
113         while(<SERVERHANDLE>)
114         {
115             print D $_;
116         }
117
```

```
118      close(D);
119      close(SERVERHANDLE);
120  }
121
122  sub get_ftp_document
123  {
124      my ($machine, $user, $password, $path, $port) = @_;
125
126      my $file = basename($path);
127      my $dir = dirname($path);
128
129      my $ftp = Net::FTP->new("$machine", "Port" => $port);
130      die "Could not connect to $machine" unless $ftp;
131      $ftp->login($user, $password)
132          || die "Couldn't login to $machine";
133      $ftp->cwd($dir)
134          || die "Invalid directory ($dir) on FTP Server";
135      $ftp->get($file)
136          || die "File ($path) on $machine is not accessible";
137      $ftp->quit();
138  }
```

ANNOTATIONS

This script takes its input as a URL from the command line. The URL is processed, and the relevant details of the URL are extracted into their component parts. Using this information, we call the corresponding function, which downloads the file to the machine. By splitting the actual processing down into functions, we allow for additional protocols to be added later.

```
1    #!/usr/local/bin/perl5
2
3    use Ssockets;
4    use FileHandle;
5    use File::Basename;
6    use Net::FTP;
7    use Getopt::Std;
8
```

We need a lot of modules in this script. Lines 3 to 7 incorporate the simple sockets module so we can connect to a TCP server, **FileHandle** to control buffering, **Basename**, **Net::FTP** for FTP access, and the standard (short) **Getopt** module.

```
9    getopts('d');
10
11   die "Usage: $0 [-d (debug)] URL" unless (@ARGV == 1);
12   my $url = shift;
13
14   my ($protocol, $user, $password, $machine, $port, $path)
15       = decipher_url($url);
16
```

Line 9 extracts the command-line options. This script uses just one: **-d** to specify the use of debug mode. We check for the number of arguments on the command line on line 11, reporting an error if no URL is specified. We shift the first option off the command line in line 12. Lines 14 and 15 use the **decipher_url** function to extract the individual elements from the URL on the command line.

```
17   unless ($protocol)
18   {
19       die "Couldn't decipher URL $url";
20   }
21
22   unless($port)
23   {
24       $port = 80 if ($protocol =~ /http/i);
25       $port = 21 if ($protocol =~ /ftp/i);
26   }
27
```

If a protocol cannot be extracted by the **decipher_url** function, we report an error on line 19. Line 22 checks to see if a specific port was requested; if it wasn't, we set the default ports according to the specified protocol in lines 24 and 25. The HTTP protocol uses port 80, while FTP uses port 21. These lines are a quick way of hand coding the two protocols we support in this script. You may want to consider using **getservbyname**, which returns the server's numerical value, based on a name you supply. See the **Simple Sockets** module, **Ssockets.pm**, which we viewed at the start of this chapter.

```
28   print <<EOF if $opt_d;
29   Retrieving: $path
30   Machine:    $machine
31   Protocol:   $protocol
32   Port:       $port
33   User:       $user
34   Password:   $password
35   EOF
36
```

If debugging was switched on in the command line, then we print a summary of what we are about to do in lines 28 to 35.

```
37  if ($protocol =~ /http/i)
38  {
39      get_http_document($machine, $port, $path);
40  }
41  elsif ($protocol =~ /ftp/i)
42  {
43      get_ftp_document($machine, $user, $password, $path);
44  }
45  else
46  {
47      die "Protocol type not recognized/not supported\n";
48  }
49
```

Lines 37 to 48 decide which function to call, if the protocol is recognized, or they report an error. Note the difference between the two calls to the two protocol functions. An HTTP request consists of the server, port, and path, but an FTP server consists of only the machine, user, password, and path.

```
50  sub decipher_url
51  {
52      my ($url) = @_;
53      my ($matched, $protocol, $host, $path);
54      my ($user, $password, $machine);
55
```

The **decipher_url** function is designed to identify the individual elements of an entire URL in all of its different guises. Unfortunately for us, a URL can be specified in a number of different ways. For example:

`http://twinspark:8081/patch.html`

and

`ftp://foo@bar:twinspark/pub/foo.txt`

are equally valid, but they mean two different things. If we tried to develop a single match statement to identify the line, we would come unstuck. Although URLs follow a specific format, it doesn't transfer very easily over to a regular expression match statement. Therefore, instead of using one statement, we extract elements from the original URL and then extract further elements from previous extractions until we have built a complete picture of the URL in the form of individual variables.

```
56      $matched = $url =~ m#(\S+)://([^/ ]+)(.*)#;
57
58      return(undef) unless($matched);
59
```

We're specifically expecting a URL with a leading protocol specification in line 56. The regular expression is looking for a string, followed by the :// separator, another string that can be composed of any characters except a space or forward slash, and finally the path and filename specification. Although the match statement will not match URLs like "mailto:mc@whoever.com," we don't expect this issue when searching for HTTP or FTP URLs. If we don't match the statement, then we return a single undefined entry. I've specified the **undef** value here, although it could be ignored; **return** automatically returns a undefined value in a scalar context and () in an array context.

```
60        $protocol = $1;
61        $host = $2;
62        $path = $3;
63
```

If the match succeeded, the protocol, host, and path information will have already been extracted. Now we need to further extract the host information to identify a user name, password, or protocol.

```
64        $user = 'anonymous';
65        $password = 'me@foo.bar';
66
67        $_ = $host;
68
```

We set the defaults for the user and password in lines 64 and 65. The defaults will be relayed back if we can't match these elements. To make life easier for us, on line 67 we set the default buffer to the host name we extracted above.

```
69        if (m#(\S+):(\d+)#)
70        {
71            $_ = $1;
72            $port = $2;
73        }
```

The match statement in line 69 matches a simple "host:port" reference. Note that because we specify a number after the colon, this regular expression will extract the correct element from a URL of the type "user:password@host:port"—the host information will be extracted as "user@host:machine." A more simple match of "host:port" will also return the values we expect. Either way, if the match worked, then we set the value of the default buffer to the host information so that we can process it further, and we set the port information in line 72.

```
74        if (m#(\S+):(\S+)@(\S+)#)
75        {
76            $user = $1;
77            $password = $2;
```

```
78              $machine = $3;
79         }
```

This match extracts the user, password, and host information from a URL of the type "user:password@host." If the match fails, we proceed to line 80.

```
80      elsif (m#(\S+)@(\S+)#)
81      {
82          $user = $1;
83          $machine = $2;
84      }
```

The last regular expression for the host information extracts references like "user@machine." If the line still doesn't match, then we proceed to line 85.

```
85      else
86      {
87          $machine = $host;
88      }
89
```

If we haven't been able to extract any more information from the host portion of the URL, then it's safe to assume that the final machine address equals that of the original host information.

```
90      return($protocol, $user, $password, $machine, $port, $path);
91   }
92
```

Line 90 returns the information we extracted back to the calling script. Here is another major advantage of Perl over single-variable return languages like C: we are able to return a list containing the individual elements of the URL that we have been able to identify.

If you want a more extensive URL identifier/extractor, you may want to get the libwww Perl package from the CPAN archives. One of the included modules in this comprehensive package is the **URI::URL** module, which accepts any URL as input and allows you extract the individual elements from the URL as methods within the URL object you create from the URL string. For example, the following code would extract the same basic information as our **decipher_url** function:

```
Use URI::URL;
$url       = new URI::URL $ARGV[0];
$path      = $url->path;
$user      = $url->user;
$password  = $url->password;
$machine   = $url->host;
$port      = $url->port;   # returns default if not defined
```

The **URI::URL** module interfaces with the rest of the libwww package and may make a more suitable replacement for the previous function if you are using URLs in a Web-based context.

```
93   sub get_http_document
94   {
95       my ($machine, $port, $path) = @_;
96       my ($localfile);
97       unless (connectsocket(*SERVERHANDLE,
98                               $machine,
99                               $protocol,
100                              'tcp'))
101      {
102          die $Ssockets::error;
103      }
104
```

Line 93 is the start of the **get_http_document** function. This function opens a connection to a Web server, sends a simple GET request to the server, and writes the results to a local file based on the filename contained within the URL. The function accepts three arguments: the machine and port to connect to, as well as the path name of the file to receive.

An open connection is made to the server on line 97; we **die** if the connection cannot be made. Since we're using a single function within a single script, we do not need to worry about its return value. If we were going to include the function within a package, then it would make sense to return an error to the caller, instead of simply **die**-ing and escaping from the entire script.

```
105      autoflush SERVERHANDLE 1;
106
107      print SERVERHANDLE "GET $path\n";
108
109      $localfile=basename($path);
110
111      open(D, ">$localfile") || die "Can't write $localfile, $!";
112
113      while(<SERVERHANDLE>)
114      {
115          print D $_;
116      }
117
118      close(D);
119      close(SERVERHANDLE);
120  }
121
```

Lines 105 to 120 are quite straightforward. We set the buffer to autoflush on line 105 and then send the GET request on line 107. The local filename is extracted on line 109, and then a new file is opened on line 111. The **while** loop in lines 113 to 116 takes input from the socket and writes it straight out to the file. Once the file has completed being read, we close the file on line 118, and we close the network socket on the following line.

Using a **while** loop and relying on Perl to split the input on the record separator is not an ideal way to proceed. We could undefine the input record separator, causing Perl to place the entire server response into the input buffer. However, when downloading a large file, this might cause Perl to exhaust the available memory, and that wouldn't be much of a solution to the problem of downloading the file in the first place. The method I've used above should work for all HTML files and most binary files. If you find you are having problems, you might want to use **sysread** and **syswrite**. These read and write functions set numbers of bytes from and to files into temporary buffers, completely ignoring any record or field separation in the source, bypassing the stdio buffering.

```
while ($nread = sysread SERVERHANDLE, $buffer, 4096)
{
    syswrite D, $buffer, $nread;
}
```

The **sysread** function in this example will read up to 4,096 bytes into the variable **$buffer** from the network socket. The return value is the number of bytes actually read from the source. This number of bytes read is then used to specify the number of bytes to write out to the local file. Using the method, reading a 4,096-byte block will write 4,096 bytes out to the destination as easily as it will read and write 1 byte.

If you want a more robust solution, get the **LWP** module from your local CPAN archive. This module works much like the **Net::FTP** module we will use below. The LWP module is now part of the libwww package, which we looked at to resolve some of the issues surrounding the identification of URL elements.

```
122 sub get_ftp_document
123 {
124     my ($machine, $user, $password, $path, $port) = @_;
125
126     my $file = basename($path);
127     my $dir = dirname($path);
128
129     my $ftp = Net::FTP->new("$machine", "Port" => $port);
130     die "Could not connect to $machine" unless $ftp;
131     $ftp->login($user, $password)
132         || die "Couldn't login to $machine";
133     $ftp->cwd($dir)
134         || die "Invalid directory ($dir) on FTP Server";
```

```
135      $ftp->get($file)
136          || die "File ($path) on $machine is not accessible";
137      $ftp->quit();
138  }
```

The **get_ftp_document** on line 122 retrieves an FTP file from the specified host using the user, password, port, and path information extracted from the URL. The function uses the **Net::FTP** module to access the server, which eliminates the need for us to handle low-level communication with the server. Instead, we call individual functions that handle the communication on a command-by-command basis with the host.

The **Net::FTP** module works by creating a new object. Within this object, a number of methods perform the communication between the two ends of the network connection, allowing us to access and use the various commands provided by the FTP server. This module simplifies the communication process and, aside from the error checking, reduces the process to a few lines.

Line 129 creates a new FTP connection object, using a minimum of the host address. The **Net::FTP->new** method allows us to specify additional options in a hash. In this example, I've also specified a specific port, which will equal either the value extracted from the URL if it was present or the default port of 23 if one wasn't specified. We could also specify that debugging be switched on to print progress information as the link is used. We'll look at an example of this output when we try out this script.

If the connection fails, the method returns undefined, so the test on line 130 will fail and **die** with a suitable message. We log in with the information from the URL, or the defaults, on line 131. The **Net::FTP** module handles the real communication, which consists of sending the strings "user ..." and "pass ..." to the server, including handling the response and ensuring it works correctly.

Line 133 changes the server directory to the directory extracted with the **dirname** function in line 127. Line 135 retrieves the file. Again, the **Net::FTP** module handles the communication with the server, and this time it also reads the response (which should be the file), creates the local file, and then writes out the contents. If the transfer completed successfully, then line 136 won't generate an error. Finally, line 137 closes the connection to the FTP server.

Using the script is simply a case of providing a URL on the command line. For example, the following code retrieves the index.html file from the www.mcslp.com Web server:

```
$ grfile.pl http://www.mcslp.com/index.html
```

Alternatively, this command downloads the file filelist.txt in the /pub directory of the ftp.mcslp.com server using anonymous FTP:

```
$ grfile.pl ftp://ftp.mcslp.com/pub/src.tar.gz
```

Here is the same request, this time using a login and password and with debugging switched on in the **Net::FTP** module:

```
grfile.pl ftp://martinb:foo@twinspark.mcslp.com/pub/filelist.txt
Net::FTP: Net::FTP(2.33)
Net::FTP:   Exporter
Net::FTP:     Net::Cmd(2.11)
Net::FTP:     IO::Socket::INET
Net::FTP:       IO::Socket(1.1603)
Net::FTP:         IO::Handle(1.1504)

Net::FTP=GLOB(0xb68ec)<<< 220 twinspark FTP server (UNIX(r) System V
Release 4.0) ready.
Net::FTP=GLOB(0xb68ec)>>> user martinb
Net::FTP=GLOB(0xb68ec)<<< 331 Password required for martinb.
Net::FTP=GLOB(0xb68ec)>>> PASS ....
Net::FTP=GLOB(0xb68ec)<<< 230 User martinb logged in.
Net::FTP=GLOB(0xb68ec)>>> CWD /pub
Net::FTP=GLOB(0xb68ec)<<< 250 CWD command successful.
Net::FTP=GLOB(0xb68ec)>>> PORT 193,122,10,132,128,13
Net::FTP=GLOB(0xb68ec)<<< 200 PORT command successful.
Net::FTP=GLOB(0xb68ec)>>> RETR filelist.txt
Net::FTP=GLOB(0xb68ec)<<< 150 ASCII data connection for filelist.txt
(193.122.10.132,32781) (1328 bytes).
Net::FTP=GLOB(0xb68ec)<<< 226 ASCII Transfer complete.
Net::FTP=GLOB(0xb68ec)>>> QUIT
Net::FTP=GLOB(0xb68ec)<<< 221 Goodbye.
```

After the initial preamble containing the version number of various reliant modules, the debug option shows outgoing ">>>" commands and incoming "<<<" responses.

expmail.pl

The E-mail Address Expander

When you send an e-mail to somebody, the address is decoded in two ways. First of all, a request is made to a DNS (Domain Name System) server, which returns the mail exchange (MX) hosts for the domain specified after the @ sign. Then, when the mail server has been discovered, you need to discover whether the mail server further expands the portion before the @ sign based on a number of local aliases. For example, your e-mail address to the world might be mbrown@foo.bar, but the server the mail is sent to is actually mail.foo.bar, and a local alias on that machine actually expands mbrown@foo.bar to be Martin_Brown@mail.bar.foo. This latter process is called expansion, and it exists as an option to clients on many mail servers to enable clients to verify that the specified user can be sent mail.

This expansion can also prove invaluable when you want to check an address that fails when you send e-mail to it. However, don't expect the script, or indeed the EXPN or VRFY functions of the mail server, to work as you expect. Many sites turn them off or even return a canned reply that may mean nothing. The process is two-fold: first we must discover the mail server, and then we have to communicate with that server to run the expansion command on the address. In this script, we use the **Net::DNS** module from Michael Fuhr in combination with the **Net::SMTP** module from Graham Barr.

```perl
1   #!/usr/local/bin/perl5
2
3   use Net::SMTP;
4   use Net::DNS;
5
6   while (@ARGV)
7   {
8       my $email = shift;
9       my ($user, $host) = split '@', $email;
10      my $res = new Net::DNS::Resolver;
11      my @mx = mx($res, $host);
12
13      if (@mx)
14      {
15          print "Expansions for $email\n";
16          foreach my $rr (@mx)
17          {
18              my ($mxhost) = $rr->exchange;
19              print "Checking $mxhost\n";
20              my $smtp = Net::SMTP->new($mxhost);
21              unless($smtp)
22              {
23                  warn "Couldn't open connection to $host";
24                  next;
25              }
26              my $realrecipient = $smtp->expand($email);
27              print "$realrecipient\n" if $realrecipient;
28              $smtp->quit();
29          }
30          print "\n";
31      }
32      else
33      {
34          warn "Couldn't find any MX hosts for $host\n";
35      }
36  }
```

ANNOTATIONS

As discussed earlier, the sequence in determining an e-mail address is to first discover the MX hosts for the domain name specified and then to communicate with each host and ask it to expand the e-mail address.

```
1    #!/usr/local/bin/perl5
2
3    use Net::SMTP;
4    use Net::DNS;
5
```

We incorporate the two required modules in lines 1 to 5.

```
6    while (@ARGV)
7    {
8        my $email = shift;
9        my ($user, $host) = split '@', $email;
10       my $res = new Net::DNS::Resolver;
11       my @mx = mx($res, $host);
12
```

By specifying **@ARGV** within the **while** statement, we enable the user to specify multiple e-mail addresses on the command line. Each one will be processed individually, in sequence.

Line 8 shifts the next argument off the command line, and this argument is then split into its component parts by line 9. You could also use the line:

```
foreach $email (@ARGV)
```

to condense lines 6 and 8 down to one line.

A new resolver object is created on line 10. Line 11 requests the list of MX hosts for the specified host portion of the e-mail address, using the previously opened resolver connection.

```
13       if (@mx)
14       {
15           print "Expansions for $email\n";
16           foreach my $rr (@mx)
```

Presuming we get a response from the resolver (line 13), then we print the e-mail address we are checking on line 15, and then start a **foreach** loop to go through each host returned in the **@mx** array. The resulting variable, **$rr**, is split into two parts that contain the preference number for that host and the host name, accessible by using the reference **$rr->preference** and **$rr->exchange**, respectively.

PROGRAMMER'S NOTE   *If you have a version of Perl earlier than 5.004, you may have trouble with line 16. You can remove the **my** reference and declare the $rr variable elsewhere before the start of the **foreach** loop.*

```
17          {
18              my ($mxhost) = $rr->exchange;
19              print "Checking $mxhost\n";
20              my $smtp = Net::SMTP->new($mxhost);
21              unless($smtp)
22              {
23                  warn "Couldn't open connection to $host";
24                  next;
25              }
26              my $realrecipient = $smtp->expand($email);
27              print "$realrecipient\n" if $realrecipient;
28              $smtp->quit();
29          }
```

Line 18 obtains the MX host name, which is used on line 20 to create a new SMTP connection to the specified server. On line 23, we report if the connection to the server couldn't be made, but only as a warning (using **warn**, which is like **die** except that the program does not quit) before skipping to the next host on line 24. We then run the expansion command on the MX host, which returns the full recipient information into the **$realrecipient** variable on line 26. If the response returns, anything then we print it out on line 27. We are not worried about the class of the error, only whether there was a response or not. Finally, we close the SMTP connection on line 28.

```
30          print "\n";
31      }
```

Once we have cycled through all the MX hosts, we print a separator line on line 30, leaving us ready to start printing the results of the next e-mail address from the command line.

```
32      else
33      {
34          warn "Couldn't find any MX hosts for $host\n";
35      }
36  }
```

If the domain name resolver couldn't find any MX hosts for the specified e-mail address, we print a warning on line 34 before moving on to the next e-mail address from the command line at the end of the loop statement on line 36.

The results of this script can be quite interesting. Running it on my own local machine reports my name (from the /etc/passwd file) and the real e-mail address the requested address points to.

```
$ expmail.pl mc@twinspark
Expansions for mc@twinspark
```

```
Checking twinspark.mcslp.com
Martin C Brown <martinb>
```

However, not all hosts support the expn command, so it isn't a foolproof way to discover someone's real e-mail address.

popbiff.pl

Getting a Summary of POP Mail

Like our previous script, this one was designed specifically to find a quicker, simpler, neater solution to a problem. In this case, the goal was to find a quick and easy way to get the list of senders and subjects from the e-mail messages stored on a POP server. Both my work and personal e-mail systems use POP3 (version 3 of the Post Office Protocol) servers to supply messages to client applications. I'm often in a situation where an e-mail client is not available, or I'm logged into the work system and want to check my personal mailbox, or vice versa.

The solution is to use the **Net::POP** module from Graham Barr, which comes as part of the **libnet** module available from CPAN. Like the previous FTP example, the connection is made and processed using an object that encapsulates the connection to the remote server.

```perl
1   #!/usr/local/bin/perl5
2
3   use Net::POP3;
4   use Getopt::Std;
5
6   getopts('q');
7
8   my ($host, $login, $password) = ('pop', 'foo', 'bar');
9
10  $host = shift || $host;
11  $login = shift || $login;
12  $password = shift || $password;
13
14  my $server = Net::POP3->new($host);
15  die "Couldn't connect to server $host" unless $server;
16  my $nomsgs = $server->login($login, $password);
17
18  die "Could not login" unless defined($nomsgs);
19
20  my $msglist = $server->list();
21  $nomsgs = keys %$msglist;
22
23  print "There are $nomsgs messages on $host\n";
```

```
24
25  unless ($opt_q)
26  {
27      foreach my $msg_id (sort { $a <=> $b } keys %$msglist)
28      {
29          printf "Msg %3s ", $msg_id;
30          my $msgcontent = $server->top($msg_id, 20);
31          summarize(@$msgcontent);
32      }
33  }
34
35  $server->quit();
36
37  sub summarize
38  {
39      my (@lines) = @_;
40      my ($from, $line, $subject);
41
42      foreach $line (@lines)
43      {
44          if ($line =~ m/^From: (.*)/)
45          {
46              $from = $1;
47              $from =~ s/"|<.*>//g;
48              $from = substr($from, 0, 39);
49          }
50          elsif ($line =~ m/^Subject: (.{1, 30})/)
51          {
52              $subject = $1;
53          }
54          last if (defined($subject) && defined($from));
55      }
56      printf "%-40s %s\n", $from, $subject;
57      undef($subject);
58      undef($from);
59  }
```

ANNOTATIONS

This script makes a connection to the POP server, then it reads the first 20 lines of each message, which should provide us with enough lines to identify the sender and the subject. An e-mail message is composed of two main sections, the header and the body. The header contains the fields that specify the sender, recipient, date, and so on; this information is used by mail clients and servers to respond and route e-mail around the network and the Internet. The body is the actual mail message, and for our purposes it can be ignored.

```
1    #!/usr/local/bin/perl5
2
3    use Net::POP3;
4    use Getopt::Std;
5
6    getopts('q');
7
8    my ($host, $login, $password) = ('pop', 'foo', 'bar');
9
10   $host = shift || $host;
11   $login = shift || $login;
12   $password = shift || $password;
13
```

On line 6 we extract a command-line argument if it exists. The **-q** option will print the number of messages on the server, acting as a quick check for new mail.

The defaults for the host, user name, and password are set in line 8. By setting defaults, we can get away with issuing the command without any specific settings. If the user wants to specify an alternative host, login, and password, we extract that information from the command line using **shift** on lines 10 to 12.

```
14   my $server = Net::POP3->new($host);
15   die "Couldn't connect to server $host" unless $server;
16   my $nomsgs = $server->login($login, $password);
17
18   die "Could not login" unless defined($nomsgs);
19
20   my $msglist = $server->list();
21   $nomsgs = keys %$msglist;
22
23   print "There are $nomsgs messages on $host\n";
24
```

Lines 14 to 24 log in to the server and obtain the number of messages waiting for the specified user. Line 14 creates a new object that will be used for the remainder of the script to supply the methods required to access the message file. On line 16 we actually log in to the server. The **login** method returns the number of available messages. However, due to a discrepancy with some of the servers available on the Internet, we have to introduce a workaround at this point. Most servers will return the number of messages in a user's mailbox at the point of login. Some don't, such as the POP server supplied with Sun's Netra server. We could trap the value returned and decide whether the value returned was valid. A server with no messages in the users mailbox will return zero, *but* a server that doesn't return the number of messages will also return zero, which makes the difference impossible to verify.

Instead, the solution is to extract the message numbers available from the server using the **list** method. The result of this is a hash of the message IDs, and reporting the number of entries in the hash is a more reliable method of returning the number of available messages. Unfortunately, it's also slower because it requires the server to go away and read the user's mailbox. Because it's more reliable, and because we need this information when we report the e-mail details, we do it anyway on line 20. The result of assigning a scalar variable to the keys in a hash that is returned is the number of keys in the hash, and therefore the number of messages. This is reported in line 23.

```
25   unless ($opt_q)
26   {
27       foreach my $msg_id (sort { $a <=> $b } keys %$msglist)
28       {
29           printf "Msg %3s ", $msg_id;
30           my $msgcontent = $server->top($msg_id, 20);
31           summarize(@$msgcontent);
32       }
33   }
34
35   $server->quit();
36
```

If the user hasn't specified the quick option on the command line (checked on line 25 via **unless**), then we proceed to read in each message and extract the subject and sender information. Line 27 uses a **foreach** loop to extract the message ID from the message list. The keys are sorted, numerically (using <=>) before they are assigned in each iteration.

On line 29 we use **printf** to display a formatted version of the message ID; note that there is no new-line character at the end of the string, so we can append information to the same line before ending with a new-line character.

On line 30, the **top** method returns the specified number of lines from the top of the message referred to by **$msgid**. Twenty lines should be enough to obtain the sender and subject information. The result is an array containing the top 20 lines of the message. This result is then passed as an array to the **summarize** function, before the loop ends on line 32 and the "quick" test ends on line 33. Before leaving the script, we close the connection to the server.

```
37   sub summarize
38   {
39       my (@lines) = @_;
```

```
40        my ($from, $line, $subject);
41
42        foreach $line (@lines)
43        {
44            if ($line =~ m/^From: (.*)/)
45            {
46                $from = $1;
47                $from =~ s/"|<.*>//g;
48                $from = substr($from, 0, 39);
49            }
```

The **summarize** function works through each line of the passed array looking for lines beginning with "Subject:" and "From:". We use match statements to identify the lines so that we can use the match references to extract the real data from the line. Once the From: line has been identified on line 44, we string any double-quotes or e-mail addresses from the field. An e-mail address is generally in two forms; either it will be

```
From: mc@foo.bar
```

or

```
From: Martin Brown <mc@foo.bar>
```

Since displaying a user's real name is friendlier than their address, it's safe to remove the e-mail address entirely from the field data. If no name is specified, we'll just end up displaying the e-mail address, provided it hasn't been incorrectly enclosed in the angle brackets. We'll look at more advanced ways of extracting and cleaning up address fields in Chapter 6.

Because we are outputting this information to the screen, it's best to try to restrict the width of the output to a maximum of 80 characters. Stripping an entire line down to this size might strip information the user wants to see, so we strip the individual elements down to preset sizes. We use the **substr** function to extract 39 characters from the start of the **$from** string, placing the result back into the **$from** variable.

```
50            elsif ($line =~ m/^Subject: (.{1, 30})/)
51            {
52                $subject = $1;
53            }
54            last if (defined($subject) && defined($from));
55        }
```

In line 50 we identify a Subject: string. The **(.{1, 30})** element of the regular expression extracts between 1 and 30 characters from the input line if it started with the word "subject." Since a subject field will contain nothing except text, we can get away with this method here. It saves us from using **substr** to perform the same action, and it is quicker and neater to boot.

This method wouldn't have worked on the previous example, since the e-mail address string could have contained information we wanted to print. We had to extract the useless information first, and then trim the field down to size.

Line 54 escapes from the loop if both fields have been found, another time-saving tactic. If the from and subject fields are the first two lines in the message, there is no need to process the remaining 18 lines in the array.

```
56    printf "%-40s %s\n", $from, $subject;
57    undef($subject);
58    undef($from);
59  }
```

Line 56 prints out the data we have obtained, formatting it to a maximum width of 40 characters in the case of the e-mail address. We don't need to worry about formatting the subject field data, since that is the last element of the line that we print, and we already know that the maximum size that will have been extracted is 30 characters (see line 50). Then, to make sure line 54 works the next time the function is called, we ensure that the **$subject** and **$from** variables are undefined. If we don't undefine the variables, then the next call may contain the value from a previous call. We could also get around this by initializing the variables on line 40 for each invocation of the function.

Here is some sample output from the script:

```
$ popbiff.pl
There are 2 messages on pop.foo.bar
1    Terry Jones                        Meeting
2    Dorothy Smith                      Your Holiday
```

I find it an invaluable tool and generally much quicker than, say, Netscape or Outlook at giving me a quick rundown of the mail waiting for me.

autonntp.pl

Automatic Newsgroup Downloader

In spite of the controversy that exists over Usenet, the discussion service on the Internet, there is still a lot of very useful information on it. Some of the most useful newsgroups are those that are not actually discussion groups at all but rather moderated newsgroups, often used for announcing new products, releases, or pieces of general news.

Using a news reading program for reading these items seems an obvious choice. But if you want to keep the text of the message, perhaps to redistribute it internally to another group of people, or just as a record of the message to store on your machine, then sequentially reading each message and manually saving it to a file is quote a chore. A better solution is to have some form of automatic system with which to read individual messages and save them to a file.

The **autonntp.pl** script does precisely this. Newsgroups are added to a local file that stores the newsgroup name and the highest message downloaded. When run, the script works through the file, reading each newsgroup, before updating the file with the new highest message number at the time the script exits. The script is completely self-contained: we can add or delete groups from the group file. Messages are stored individually, by newsgroup and message number, either within the current directory or within a directory structure.

```perl
1    #!/usr/local/bin/perl5
2
3    use Getopt::Long;
4    use Net::NNTP;
5
6    $SIG{'INT'} = $SIG{'QUIT'} = \&clean_exit;
7
8    my ($newgroup, $debug, $oldgroup, $server, $usage, $annotate);
9    my ($force, $directory, $recurse);
10
11   GetOptions("n=s" => \$newgroup,
12              "g"   => \$debug,
13              "r=s" => \$oldgroup,
14              "s=s" => \$server,
15              "h"   => \$usage,
16              "a"   => \$annotate,
17              "d=s" => \$directory,
18              "c"   => \$recurse,
19              "f"   => \$force
20             );
21
22   print_usage() if $usage;
23
24   $annotate = 1 if $debug;
25   $directory = $directory || "./";
26   $server = $server || "news.foo.bar";
27
28   my $nntp = Net::NNTP->new($server, Debug => $debug ? 1 : 0);
29   die "Couldn't open connection" unless $nntp;
30
31   my (%groups);
32
33   init_group_table();
34
35   init_new_group($newgroup) if $newgroup;
```

```perl
36    delete $groups{$oldgroup} if $oldgroup;
37
38    foreach my $group (sort keys %groups)
39    {
40        get_group_mesgs($group, $groups{$group}, $directory, $recurse);
41    }
42
43    update_group_table();
44
45    sub get_group_mesgs
46    {
47        my ($group, $first, $directory, $recurse) = @_;
48        my @groupinfo = $nntp->group($group);
49        my $last=$groupinfo[2];
50
51        print "Retrieving $group (messages $first to $last)\n"
52            if $annotate;
53
54        if (($recurse) && ($last-$first++))
55        {
56            mkdir ("$directory/$group", 0700)
57                unless (-d "$directory/$group");
58        }
59
60        for (my $id=($first);$id<=$last;$id++)
61        {
62            print "Getting article $id\n" if $annotate;
63            my $lines = $nntp->article($id);
64            next unless $lines;
65            my ($filespec) = $recurse ? ">$directory/$group/$id" :
66                ">$directory/$group.$id";
67
68            if (open(D, $filespec))
69            {
70                print D @$lines;
71                close(D);
72            }
73            else
74            {
75                warn "Couldn't create $filespec\n";
76            }
77            $groups{$group} = $id;
78        }
```

```
79   }
80
81   sub init_new_group
82   {
83       my ($group) = @_;
84
85       if (exists($groups{$group}))
86       {
87           warn "$group is already in table\n" if $annotate;
88           return unless ($force);
89           warn "Resetting $group\n" if $annotate;
90       }
91       my @groupinfo = $nntp->group($group);
92       if (@groupinfo)
93       {
94           $groups{$group} = $groupinfo[1]-1;
95           print "Added $group starting msgno $groupinfo[1]\n"
96               if $annotate;
97       }
98       else
99       {
100          warn "Group $group is not available on this server";
101      }
102  }
103
104  sub init_group_table
105  {
106      unless (open(GROUPS, "<autonntp.rc"))
107      {
108          warn "Couldn't open an existing group file\n";
109          warn "A new file will be created\n";
110          return;
111      }
112      while(<GROUPS>)
113      {
114          chomp;
115          my ($group, $lastid) = split ', ';
116          $groups{$group} = $lastid;
117      }
118      close(GROUPS);
119  }
120
121  sub update_group_table
```

```
122 {
123
124     open(GROUPS, ">autonntp.rc")
125         || die "Couldn't update the group table\n";
126
127     foreach my $key (sort keys %groups)
128     {
129         print GROUPS "$key, $groups{$key}\n";
130     }
131     close(GROUPS);
132 }
133
134 sub clean_exit
135 {
136     my ($sig) = @_;
137
138     $SIG{'INT'} = $SIG{'QUIT'} = 'IGNORE';
139     update_group_table();
140     $nntp->quit() if (defined($nntp));
141     die "Asked to quit on $sig";
142 }
143
144 sub print_usage
145 {
146     print <<EOF
147 Usage:
148         $0 [-d] [-n|-r group] [-s server] [-h] \
149             [-f] [-c] [-d directory]
150 Where:
151
152 -a              Annotate download
153 -g              Show debugging information (implies annotate)
154 -n group        Add new group to the download list
155 -r group        Delete group from the download list
156 -f              Resets the message ids for an existing group
157 -d directory Save files/structure in specified directory
158 -c              Store messages as group/msgid not group.msgid
159 -s server       Specify a different NNTP server
160
161 -h              Show this help information
162 EOF
163     ;
```

```
164      exit(0);
165  }
```

ANNOTATIONS

Once again, this script uses the **libnet** module from the CPAN archives. This time we make use of the **Net::NNTP** module to directly access and use an NNTP (Network News Transfer Protocol) server, the servers that supply other clients and servers with their news feeds. The actual process of extracting the individual messages is fairly straightforward, and it is made significantly easier through the use of the **Net::NNTP** module.

```
1    #!/usr/local/bin/perl5
2
3    use Getopt::Long;
4    use Net::NNTP;
5
6    $SIG{'INT'} = $SIG{'QUIT'} = \&clean_exit;
7
```

We'll need the extended version of **Getopt** to extract the required fields from the command line. Except for the newsgroup file, all control is handled by the command-line options given to the script. On line 6 we set the interrupt and quit signals to call the **clean_exit** function. This function reliably closes the connection to the server and updates the newsgroup file before exiting.

```
8    my ($newgroup, $debug, $oldgroup, $server, $usage, $annotate);
9    my ($force, $directory, $recurse);
10
11   GetOptions("n=s"  => \$newgroup,
12             "g"    => \$debug,
13             "r=s"  => \$oldgroup,
14             "s=s"  => \$server,
15             "h"    => \$usage,
16             "a"    => \$annotate,
17             "d=s"  => \$directory,
18             "c"    => \$recurse,
19             "f"    => \$force
20             );
21
```

The command-line options are extracted on lines 11 to 20. Specifying **-n group** adds the group to the newsgroup file and to the current execution cycle of the script.

To remove a group, you use **-r group**. This option immediately removes the group from the hash used to store the group list. No updates take place, but the existing messages downloaded are not be deleted. An alternative server from the default is specified via **-s server**.

The script's progress can be monitored by specifying **-a**. This option annotates the progress, but it doesn't output all the debugging information, which is available with the **-g** option. You can specify a directory other than the current one to download the messages to by specifying **-d directory**. In addition, messages can be stored as "group/msgid" as opposed to "group.msgid" by specifying the recurse option, **-c**. The force option, **-f**, resets the newsgroup's highest message ID to the *lowest* message number available on the server if the group is specified via the **-n group** option. Resetting the ID is useful when you want to re-download messages that you have deleted, provided they still exist on the server.

```
22  print_usage() if $usage;
23
24  $annotate = 1 if $debug;
25  $directory = $directory || "./";
26  $server = $server || "news.foo.bar";
27
28  my $nntp = Net::NNTP->new($server, Debug => $debug ? 1 : 0);
29  die "Couldn't open connection" unless $nntp;
30
```

The final option on the command line is to display the usage instructions by specifying **-h** on the command line; the option is processed on line 22. Line 24 switches annotation messages on if we have selected debugging. Line 25 sets the default directory for storing the messages or selects the directory specified on the command line. Line 26 does the same for the news server.

A new connection is made to the NNTP server on line 28. Like the other **libnet** modules, the process creates a new object, and the methods defined in the NNTP object execute the necessary commands with the server. If the user selected to switch on debugging on the command line, we pass this information on to the **Net::NNTP** module. The output is similar to that provided by the **Net::FTP** module in the **grfile.pl** script, except that the content is NNTP related, not FTP related. If the connection fails for any reason, then the **$nntp** variable will be undefined, and line 29 will print an error and drop us out of the script.

```
31  my (%groups);
32
33  init_group_table();
34
35  init_new_group($newgroup) if $newgroup;
36  delete $groups{$oldgroup} if $oldgroup;
37
```

A new hash is created in line 31 to hold the group list. The keys of the hash are the newsgroup names, and the values are the current highest-read message. The table is initialized from the file by the **init_group_table** function that we call in line 33. If the user has specified a new group on the command line, we add it to the group hash via the **init_newgroup** function on line 35, while a group deletion is processed by line 36. We use the **delete** function to remove the specified group from the hash.

```
38   foreach my $group (sort keys %groups)
39   {
40       get_group_mesgs($group, $groups{$group}, $directory, $recurse);
41   }
42
43   update_group_table();
44
```

Lines 38 to 41 form the loop that will work through each key in the hash, downloading the messages. The actual download process is conducted by the **get_group_mesgs** function. Once the loop has completed, we update the group table by writing the updated group hash back to the file again.

```
45   sub get_group_mesgs
46   {
47       my ($group, $first, $directory, $recurse) = @_;
48       my @groupinfo = $nntp->group($group);
49       my $last=$groupinfo[2];
50
51       print "Retrieving $group (messages $first to $last)\n"
52           if $annotate;
53
54       if (($recurse) && ($last-$first++))
55       {
56           mkdir ("$directory/$group", 0700)
57               unless (-d "$directory/$group");
58       }
59
```

The first command called to process the newsgroup is on line 48. The **group** method selects the current newsgroup from which to read messages. It has the added benefit of reporting the current newsgroup parameters, including the lowest and highest message numbers available. The highest message number in the group is actually the third element of the array that is returned, and we extract that information to the **$last** variable for later use.

If the progress of the download is to be annotated, we announce the progress of the download on line 51. On line 54 we check if the newsgroup is to be stored as files or within its own directory. To save us from creating a directory that already exists, we also check that the current message number is not higher than the highest message number in the group. Lines 56 and 57 then create the directory, if it doesn't already exist. The directory name is based on the directory (the default or one specified on the command line) and the group name. Because the highest message number recorded in the hash will be the highest number *read*, not the next number to read, we increment the message pointer first.

```
60      for (my $id=($first);$id<=$last;$id++)
61      {
62          print "Getting article $id\n" if $annotate;
63          my $lines = $nntp->article($id);
64          next unless $lines;
65          my ($filespec) = $recurse ? ">$directory/$group/$id" :
66              ">$directory/$group.$id";
67
```

Line 60 sets the **for** loop to work through the messages, from the last highest message reference (note that it will have been incremented on line 54, setting it to the correct value to use here) to the highest message available on the server. If the progress is to be annotated, then we print the article number being downloaded on line 62. Line 63 retrieves all the lines from the article number **$id**. In this script, we are retrieving the entire article from the server. If you want to be more selective about the articles you download, the **Net::NNTP** module allows you to download the two elements of an article: the header, using

```
my $lines = $nntp->head($id);
```

and the body, using

```
my $lines = $nntp->body($id);
```

Using the same extraction system as in the previous script, **popbiff.pl**, you could retrieve the header of the article, then identify the sender or the subject of the article before downloading the body of the article.

If the server has "expired" the message, and it doesn't exist on the server anymore, then we simply skip to the next message (line 64). There is no point in quitting the process; it is quite normal for individual messages within the entire message base to be unavailable.

On lines 65 and 66 we set the name of the file in which to store the message, based on whether we have opted to store the messages in files in the current directory or as files within a directory named after the newsgroup. We can do this quickly with a simple test.

```
68      if (open(D, $filespec))
69      {
70          print D @$lines;
71          close(D);
```

```
72              }
73              else
74              {
75                  warn "Couldn't create $filespec\n";
76              }
```

Lines 70 writes the message lines out to the file we opened on line 68, based on the filename we created on lines 65 and 66. Note that the return type of the **article** method is an array, so we must explicitly de-reference the **$lines** variable as an array instead of a scalar. This will print out the article lines in one go. It's also worth noting that the lines stored in the array have a new-line character at the end, so we don't need to worry about setting the field separator to reproduce the articles as readable text files. If the file creation failed, we report the error on line 75. As before, we don't **die**, just in case there is a legitimate reason for the failure.

```
77              $groups{$group} = $id;
78          }
79      }
80
```

Line 77 updates the group hash to the last message processed. This information will be written back to the newsgroup file at the end of the newsgroup download process.

```
81  sub init_new_group
82  {
83      my ($group) = @_;
84
85      if (exists($groups{$group}))
86      {
87          warn "$group is already in table\n" if $annotate;
88          return unless ($force);
89          warn "Resetting $group\n" if $annotate;
90      }
```

The **init_new_group** function accesses the server and sets the highest message read to the lowest message available on the server. First of all, we check if the newsgroup already exists in the hash. If it does, we print a warning on line 87 if the connection is to be annotated. If the intention of the user is to reset the newsgroup to the lowest message number available on the server, then they will have specified the force option on the command line. If they didn't specify this option, we return from this function on line 88. If they did specify the force option, the function will not return, and a message will be printed on line 89, provided annotation is switched on.

```
91      my @groupinfo = $nntp->group($group);
92      if (@groupinfo)
```

```
93          {
94               $groups{$group} = $groupinfo[1]-1;
95               print "Added $group starting msgno $groupinfo[1]\n"
96                    if $annotate;
97          }
98          else
99          {
100              warn "Group $group is not available on this server";
101         }
102 }
103
```

Line 91 extracts new newsgroup information from the server. As was noted earlier, the **group** method reports the newsgroup name, the lowest message number available, and the highest message number available. We set the default message number within the hash to one lower than the lowest number available. Since the hash contains the highest message read, setting the value to lowest number available would cause the program to skip the first message (see the **get_group_mesgs** function, above). The process is annotated on line 95, if appropriate. If the newsgroup cannot be found, then we warn the user on line 100.

```
104 sub init_group_table
105 {
106     unless (open(GROUPS, "<autonntp.rc"))
107     {
108         warn "Couldn't open an existing group file\n";
109         warn "A new file will be created\n";
110         return;
111     }
112     while(<GROUPS>)
113     {
114         chomp;
115         my ($group, $lastid) = split ', ';
116         $groups{$group} = $lastid;
117     }
118     close(GROUPS);
119 }
120
```

Initializing the group table is a simple case of reading in a file and extracting the newsgroups and message numbers from it. The result will be an updated group hash.

In lines 106 to 111 we attempt to open an existing file. If the file cannot be opened, then we only warn the user that it does not exist and that a new one will be created. By returning from the function on line 110, we avoid reading from a file that doesn't exist, and we allow the script to continue to the next stage in the main execution cycle. It might be the first time the script was executed: a newsgroup specified on the command line will be added to the hash, with a new newsgroup file created at the end of the download.

If the file does exist, then lines 112 to 117 read in the lines, strip the new-line character off the end (line 114), extract the newsgroup name and message number (line 115) before creating an entry in the hash (line 116).

```
121 sub update_group_table
122 {
123
124     open(GROUPS, ">autonntp.rc")
125         || die "Couldn't update the group table\n";
126
127     foreach my $key (sort keys %groups)
128     {
129         print GROUPS "$key, $groups{$key}\n";
130     }
131     close(GROUPS);
132 }
133
```

Updating the group table is even easier than importing it. The file is opened or created on line 124. If the file cannot be overwritten or created, then we **die**—it's a serious fault that will need rectification. Then lines 127 to 130 print out each entry in the group hash, using the same format required by the import process.

```
134 sub clean_exit
135 {
136     my ($sig) = @_;
137
138     $SIG{'INT'} = $SIG{'QUIT'} = 'IGNORE';
139     update_group_table();
140     $nntp->quit() if (defined($nntp));
141     die "Asked to quit on $sig";
142 }
143
```

If the script is running and the user presses CTRL-C, or the script receives an interrupt or quit signal, then we need to exit gracefully by updating the group table. If we didn't update the group table before finally exiting, the next time the script is run it may re-download an entire newsgroup before reading in the new messages. Our top priority, in line 138, is to switch off any further signal handling. If we left the handling switched on, then further interruptions could occur within the signal handling functions.

Line 140 closes the connection to the server if the connection has been made, before we finally quit on line 141. The only argument passed to a signal handle is the signal that was received, so we include that information in the message to the **die** function.

```
144 sub print_usage
145 {
146     print <<EOF
147 Usage:
148         $0 [-d] [-n|-r group] [-s server] [-h] \
149              [-f] [-c] [-d directory]
150 Where:
151
152 -a           Annotate download
153 -g           Show debugging information (implies annotate)
154 -n group     Add new group to the download list
155 -r group     Delete group from the download list
156 -f           Resets the message ids for an existing group
157 -d directory Save files/structure in specified directory
158 -c           Store messages as group/msgid not group.msgid
159 -s server    Specify a different NNTP server
160
161 -h           Show this help information
162 EOF
163     ;
164     exit(0);
165 }
```

The **print_usage** function uses a here document to print the usage instructions when requested on the command line. Since requesting the instructions implicates that the user does not know how to use the program, we also quit on line 164.

Let's look at a typical session with the script by adding a new newsgroup. I've specified the annotate option so you can see what the script is doing:

```
$ autonntp.pl -a -n rec.humor.funny -d /usr/local/news -c
Couldn't open an existing group file
A new file will be created
Added rec.humor.funny starting msgno 7742
Retrieving rec.humor.funny (messages 7742 to 7756)
Getting article 7742
Getting article 7743
Getting article 7744
Getting article 7745
Getting article 7746
Asked to quit on INT at ./autonntp.pl line 141
```

You can see on this last line that I interrupted the download. Here's the result if I run the script again, without specifying any new groups:

```
$ autonntp.pl -a -d /usr/local/news -c
Retrieving rec.humor.funny (messages 7748 to 7756)
Getting article 7748
Getting article 7749
Getting article 7750
Getting article 7751
Getting article 7752
Getting article 7753
Getting article 7754
Getting article 7755
Getting article 7756
```

I've used this script for a few years now for everything from downloading software updates from newsgroups, to reading the news newsgroups and republishing the information onto a Web interface. The key part of the process is downloading the messages in the first place and managing the list of messages that have already been read.

The only problem with the script is that it works with one server at a time. This is because we use message numbers, rather than message IDs. The reason for using message numbers is speed: we can obtain the lowest and highest message numbers at the point we enter a group; obtaining message IDs would require an additional call to the NNTP server and further processing. It would also require a different storage mechanism for recording the progress within a group. You can obtain a list of message IDs by requesting a list of all the new messages since a specific date and time. For example, the line:

```
$nntp->newnews('199808011200','rec.humor');
```

results in a list of message IDs that you can then pass on to the **article** function to download the entire article contents. In my experience, the time taken to produce the list by the average server is prohibitive if it's the only server you are using to download articles. Of course, if you use multiple servers, or want to use Perl to manage the "sucking" of news from other servers to your own, you will need to use the message ID system to avoid duplication.

Using message IDs will involve a lot of changes to the code. The structure of the group file will need to be updated. When adding a new group you will need to decide what is a suitable date to download messages from, and you will need to update the message download code (in **get_group_mesgs**) to something like this:

```
@msgids = $nntp->newnews($group,$date);
($min,$hour,$mday,$mon,$year) = (localtime(time))[1-5];
$mon++;
$year += 1900;
foreach $id (@msgids)
{
```

```
    print "Getting article $id\n" if $annotate;
    my $lines = $nntp->article($id);
    next unless $lines;
    my ($filespec) = $recurse ? ">$directory/$group/$id" :
        ">$directory/$group.$id";

    if (open(D, $filespec))
    {
        print D @$lines;
        close(D);
    }
    else
    {
        warn "Couldn't create $filespec\n";
    }
}
$groups{$group} = sprintf("%04d%02d%02d%02d%02d",
                          $year,$mon,$mday,$hour,$min);
```

This code obtains the list of message IDs in the first line from the group, downloads the messages by message ID, and then updates the group table with the date the download was started. Note the date is taken from the point just after we've got a list of message IDs. This is because the time taken to download the newsgroup could be in hours—or even days—so we must ensure that the value recorded is relative to the last time a message list was recovered.

Summary

Using Perl to facilitate networking tasks involves two different interacting layers. The bottom layer is related to the actual communication between two machines at a protocol level. In this chapter, we created networking sockets over a TCP/IP network, and then we sent and received the data by using familiar file handle commands, such as **print**. The top layer is more complicated, and it revolves around the application-level protocols used to control the communication of the application information between two machines. In this chapter, we looked at a very simple protocol that was developed for a specific purpose, as well as the more commonly found protocols used on the Internet for services such as HTTP and FTP.

Creating and using these protocols ourselves is a complex process that relies on a number of variables, processes, and assumptions that we must master before we get them to work correctly. When using pre-existing protocols, an existing module, such as **libnet**, makes the process easier and allows you to concentrate on writing the script to solve the problem, instead of introducing new problems such as using protocols.

Working with E-mail

As e-mail becomes ever more a general communication tool, it becomes harder and harder for us to imagine a world without it. For most people, e-mail is a practical tool for sending messages quickly and easily almost anywhere in the world. For some, it is a purely social medium; others mix business with pleasure; and other people need e-mail as a vital link with the outside world.

Many people have used e-mail as a business communication tool for a number of years, but the explosion of the Internet has hugely changed our use of e-mail. I years ago lost track of the number of mailing lists I subscribe to. Each mailing list is either an information resource that sends one message at a time to a large number of people, or it is a discussion list where everybody can contribute, and each person's message is automatically relayed to all members of the list.

As with many useful things, there is a downside to e-mail. On many mailing lists, you receive much more information than you want or than is useful. Junk e-mail is also becoming more of a problem. Like its snail-mail (postal) equivalent, junk e-mail is often mass-mailed to thousands, or probably hundreds of thousands, of people at a time. The actual number of people interested in the content is very small, and most people simply delete the mail without reading it. For these situations, it is helpful to have some form of mail filtering, where you can choose to screen out messages based on the sender, recipient, subject, or even message body.

Before we look at the sample scripts, it's worth taking a few minutes to go over what an e-mail message looks like and how e-mail is transferred between machines. An e-mail message is composed of two parts, the header and the body. The header information contains all of the meta-information about the mail message, including the sender, recipient, and return addresses, as well as the route taken by the mail message to reach its destination and many other fields too numerous to mention. The most basic message is composed of the following lines:

```
From: mc@foo.bar
To: mc@foo.bar
Subject: Meeting
```

Each line in the header is a field of information. The field name is specified before the colon; the field data is the text after the colon. There is, however, one exception to this rule when parsing a local mailbox file under Unix. In this case, the first line of an e-mail message is the "origination" line. It is inserted by the local mail transfer agent (MTA), and it specifies where the e-mail originated from and acts as a separator when messages are concatenated together into one file. Let's look at a complete header from a real e-mail message:

```
Return-Path: <martinb>
Received: by whoever.com (5.x/SMI-SVR4)
        id AA00413; Sun, 2 Aug 1998 11:20:27 +0100
Date: Sun, 2 Aug 1998 11:20:27 +0100
From: martinb (Martin C Brown)
```

```
Message-Id: <9808021020.AA00413@whoever.com>
Apparently-To: martinb
Content-Type: text
Content-Length: 7
```

PROGRAMMER'S NOTE   *An e-mail requires at a minimum the Date, From, and To fields.*

You can see the first line is the origination line. Different e-mail systems represent this information in different ways, some without seconds (as in this example), others with; some include the time zone (as here), and others don't. This variety can add to the difficulty of identifying this line. The rest of the fields are self explanatory. There is one item missing from this example: there is no To field. However, there is an Apparently-To field, which contains the local e-mail address that this message was actually sent to, rather than the mail address entered by somebody on the command line. Since addresses can be expanded by the e-mail server (see **expmail.pl** in Chapter 5), the To and Apparently-To fields won't necessarily match, but if the To field doesn't exist, then the Apparently-To field can be used in its place.

The body of the message comes immediately after the header; a single blank line separates the two elements. The body of the message continues until the end of the message is reached, which is signified either by an end-of-file character (in the case of a single message) or by the origination line in the next message (under Unix). Now that we know the format of a message, we'll just need to identify the appropriate lines to extract the necessary information. We'll look at examples of this when we start looking at e-mail–parsing scripts, such as **mailfilt.pl**.

Now that we've looked at the basic format of e-mail messages, let's go over how e-mail is transferred between machines: SMTP (Simple Mail Transfer Protocol). This application-level protocol is similar in some respects to the FTP or NNTP protocols we looked at in Chapter 5. When a connection is made to an SMTP server, commands are issued that specify the recipient and the sender, and then they supply the rest of the message, including any additional header fields, as a block of text. An individual's e-mail is either accessed directly via a mail user agent (MUA), such as elm or mailx, or via a client protocol, such as the Post Office Protocol (POP).

Within a typical Unix installation, access to e-mail is generally direct: the e-mail for a user is stored in a single file in a "mailbox" within the directory structure of the machine. Reading the e-mail is a case of opening the file and identifying the individual messages using the techniques outlined above. Indirect client access is generally handled by a protocol, such as POP, to transfer your mail from a server to your local machine. (We saw an example of this in Chapter 5 in **popbiff.pl**.) The messages are downloaded individually, but the content remains the same; the mail message is a block of text that includes the header fields and body text.

Sending e-mail is a little more complex. Under Unix, a suite of programs connect the e-mail server and the local mailbox. Simple tools such as mail and mailx exist to send and read messages. Sending e-mail using the mail program automatically implies the sender, based on the user ID of the person invoking the program, which makes it impossible to include your "real" e-mail address, unless it matches your Unix user name and machine name. A better solution is to send mail using the application sendmail, which handles SMTP requests directly and also has the ability to take preformatted input and parse it to obtain the sender and recipient information. Versions of sendmail are available for NT, but there are no useful programs for the MacOS that would allow for sending e-mail using the same techniques.

The last option is really the only one available on all platforms and has some additional advantages. By communicating with the SMTP server directly, you can specify the recipient and sender of a message without this information being included in the text of the actual message sent. This trick is used by many mailing lists. The To address contains the name of the mailing list, not the names of the recipients; the text of the mail message contains the fake To, From, and other header fields, and the SMTP servers exchange the real recipient information as the message is sent around the Internet. In this way the individual recipients on the mailing list are unaware of who the other recipients are, while still obtaining what appears to be a personalized message. Unfortunately, this method is also used by junk e-mailers, sometimes making it impossible to track the message origin.

PROGRAMMER'S NOTE   *The SMTP server you use depends on your local setup. It may be your machine, your local mail server, or the mail server of your Internet service provider.*

This information can be used by mail programs, including the **mailfilt.pl** script in this chapter, to automatically file, forward, or otherwise process e-mail as it comes in by something more specific than the sender and recipient addresses.

In this chapter we'll start by looking at how to send e-mail, both by using local programs and by talking directly to an STMP server. We will then look at ways to use mail sending techniques to write a simple mailing list program for mailing a single message to an unlimited number of people. As an extension to this idea, I've included a mailbot, a program that studies the contents of an e-mail, sending back any files that the user has specified.

Nonstandard E-mail Header Fields

There are a number of nonstandard (that is, unofficial) headers used within messages to define additional information about the message, its contents and its origins. These extended header fields start with an X, and they can include such things as X-Mailer, which specifies the mailing program used to send the e-mail, and X-Mailing-List, so that a message can be identified as originating from, and therefore part of, a mailing list.

The ability to filter out undesirable e-mail, or even automatically file the messages into predefined folders, is the job of our mail filtering script. A simple version specially designed to send back an "I am on vacation" message is also supplied. Finally, the last part of this chapter is set aside for ways to monitor and manage e-mail at server and individual levels.

Smail.pm

Compiling a Simple E-mail Module

As I've already explained, there are a number of different ways to send e-mail. All of them can be implemented within Perl, but there is no such thing as a "standard" interface within the base Perl package for sending e-mail. Even if there were, it would have to be implemented separately for each platform, since neither MacOS nor NT supports a standard method for sending e-mail within the OS. There are modules on CPAN that are platform independent, and we shall use one of them, **Net::SMTP** from Graham Barr's libnet package, in the **smtpwrap** module later in this chapter.

Our first script, **Smail.pm**, shows some examples of how to send e-mail within Perl under Unix, along with some tricks for extracting some useful information from preprocessed mail messages; we'll use these same tricks in many of the scripts in this chapter.

The first two methods use sendmail as the mail application. By using an open file handle to send information directly to the input of the sendmail application, we can support the process used by a typical Unix user to send e-mail.

```
1    package Smail;
2
3    use strict;
4    use vars qw(@ISA @EXPORT $error);
5    require Exporter;
6    @ISA = 'Exporter';
7    @EXPORT = qw (simple_send_message
8                  set_msg_address
9                  set_msg_body
10                 set_msg_subject
11                 send_msg);
12
13   sub simple_send_message
14   {
15       my ($to, $from, $subject, $message) = @_;
16
17       unless (open(MAIL,"|/usr/lib/sendmail -oi -t"))
18       {
```

```
19          $error = "Couldn't open sendmail, $!";
20          return(0);
21      }
22
23      print MAIL "To: $to\n";
24      print MAIL "From: $from\n";
25      print MAIL "Subject: $subject\n\n";
26      print MAIL $message;
27      unless (close(MAIL))
28      {
29          $error = "Couldn't close sendmail pipe, $!";
30          return(0);
31      }
32      1;
33  }
34
35  sub set_msg_address
36  {
37      my ($message,$to,$from,$cc,$bcc) = @_;
38      my ($addressfields);
39
40      if (defined($$message) &&
41          (($$message =~ /^To:/mi) && $to) &&
42          (($$message =~ /^From:/mi) && $from))
43      {
44          $error = "This message already has To/From fields\n";
45          return(0);
46      }
47
48      $addressfields .= "To: $to\n" if $to;
49      $addressfields .= "From: $from\n" if $from;
50      $addressfields .= "CC: $cc\n" if $cc;
51      $addressfields .= "BCC: $bcc\n" if $bcc;
52
53      if ($$message)
54      {
55          $$message = $addressfields . $$message;
56      }
57      else
58      {
59          $$message = $addressfields;
60      }
61      return(1);
```

```
62    }
63
64    sub set_msg_subject
65    {
66        my ($message,$subject) = @_;
67
68        if ($$message)
69        {
70            $$message = "Subject: $subject\n" . $$message;
71        }
72        else
73        {
74            $$message .= "Subject: $subject\n";
75        }
76    }
77
78    sub set_msg_body
79    {
80        my ($message,@body) = @_;
81
82        $$message .= "\n";
83
84        foreach my $line (@body)
85        {
86            chomp $line;
87            $$message .= $line;
88            $$message .= "\n";
89        }
90        $$message .= "\n";
91    }
92
93    sub send_msg
94    {
95        my $message = shift;
96
97        unless (($$message =~ /^To:/mi)
98                && ($$message =~ /^From:/mi))
99        {
100           $error = "Bad message, no To/From fields\n";
101           return(0);
102       }
103
104       unless (open(MAIL,"|sendmail -oi -t"))
```

```
105     {
106         $error = "Couldn't open sendmail, $!";
107         return(0);
108     }
109
110     print MAIL $$message;
111
112     unless (close(MAIL))
113     {
114         $error = "Couldn't close sendmail pipe, $!";
115         return(0);
116     }
117     return(1);
118 }
119
120 1;
```

ANNOTATIONS

This module supports the two basic e-mail methods: a single function or a suite of functions to create a message. Both techniques use a pipe to the sendmail program.

```
1   package Smail;
2
3   use strict;
4   use vars qw(@ISA @EXPORT $error);
5   require Exporter;
6   @ISA = 'Exporter';
7   @EXPORT = qw (simple_send_message
8                 set_msg_address
9                 set_msg_body
10                set_msg_subject
11                send_msg);
12
```

Line 1 sets the default name space to **Smail**. Line 3 sets the **strict** pragma that makes Perl more specific about how variables, functions, and other constructs are required. As a result of using this pragma, we must explicitly define the **@EXPORT** and **@ISA** arrays we use to export the functions from the package. We employ **use vars** to define them as global variables, and additionally we define **$error**, which will define our error messages, as global. Lines 5 to 9 first import the **Exporter** module and then set the functions from this package that we will export. We use the **qw** quoting system so that we can use bare words without quotes or commas.

```
13   sub simple_send_message
14   {
15       my ($to, $from, $subject, $message) = @_;
16
17       unless (open(MAIL,"|/usr/lib/sendmail -oi -t"))
18       {
19           $error = "Couldn't open sendmail, $!";
20           return(0);
21       }
22
```

The **simple_send_message** function supports the sending of a message by passing all the required information to the function as arguments. There are four basic elements to a message: the sender, recipient, subject, and message body. We extract these elements from the arguments in line 15.

To actually send the message, we are going to use the sendmail application. The sendmail application sends e-mail over the Internet by examining the e-mail addresses of the recipients and intelligently routing the e-mail to the required servers. By default, sendmail requires the recipient information on the command line, and it formulates the rest of the message based on your local environment. Unfortunately, the default option also fails to specify a subject within the message text. However, the **-t** option to sendmail forces it to examine the standard input from the From and To fields, which it then uses to transfer the e-mail. The **-oi** option forces sendmail to accept an end-of-file signal as the end of the message, and it ignores a single period, the normal method for accepting e-mail.

We open a pipe to the **sendmail** command on line 17. By placing the pipe symbol in front of the command, Perl sends any data printed to the open file handle to the standard input of the command. We use the full path name to the sendmail program rather than relying on the **PATH** to contain the directory that contains the application. This is doubly important if you are using this method within a CGI script with "tainting" switched on. (See Chapter 9 for more information on taint checking.) Under most Unix flavors, sendmail can be found under /usr/lib.

If the command failed for any reason, we set the error message in line 19 and return from the function with a false result on line 20.

```
23       print MAIL "To: $to\n";
24       print MAIL "From: $from\n";
25       print MAIL "Subject: $subject\n\n";
26       print MAIL $message;
```

Lines 23 to 26 formulate the message text, which is composed of the header fields and the message body separated by a single blank line, specified within the subject specified on line 25. Because we are printing to the **MAIL** file handle, the information is being passed verbatim on to the standard input of the sendmail application.

```
27    unless (close(MAIL))
28    {
29        $error = "Couldn't close sendmail pipe, $!";
30        return(0);
31    }
32    1;
33 }
34
```

We close the handle on line 27, which will send an end-of-file character to the sendmail application; sendmail will then process the message contents and send the message. If the operation failed for any reason, then the error message is created on line 29, and the return value from the function is set to false (line 30). If everything worked okay, we return a positive (true) value to the calling script in line 32.

```
35 sub set_msg_address
36 {
37     my ($message,$to,$from,$cc,$bcc) = @_;
38     my ($addressfields);
39
40     if (defined($$message) &&
41         (($$message =~ /^To:/mi) && $to) &&
42         (($$message =~ /^From:/mi) && $from))
43     {
44         $error = "This message already has To/From fields\n";
45         return(0);
46     }
47
```

The **set_msg_address** function allows us to set the recipient, sender, carbon copy, and blind carbon copy recipients of the e-mail. Lines 40 to 42 check if the message text scalar has already been defined and whether it has already had To and From fields imported into the text. This check ensures that we do not repeat, or supercede, information already in the message text. The **/^To:/** regular expression checks for a multiline (with the **/m** option) string based on the header field name, starting at the beginning of the line. Note that we also ignore the case, although it's probably a better idea to ensure the case is correct.

```
48     $addressfields .= "To: $to\n" if $to;
49     $addressfields .= "From: $from\n" if $from;
```

```
50      $addressfields .= "CC: $cc\n" if $cc;
51      $addressfields .= "BCC: $bcc\n" if $bcc;
52
```

Lines 48 to 51 set the address fields. For each argument to the function, we check if it has been defined before setting the address field label and value into a temporary **$addressfields** variable.

```
53      if ($$message)
54      {
55          $$message = $addressfields . $$message;
56      }
57      else
58      {
59          $$message = $addressfields;
60      }
61      return(1);
62  }
63
```

Lines 53 to 60 set the address fields before the existing message if it already has text in it on line 55, or after the message text on line 59. You can see now why we specified the address field information in a separate variable first. We could shorten this to

```
$$message = $$message   ? "$addressfields$$message"
                  : $addressfields;
```

This change is purely aesthetic; it makes no difference to the code operation or speed.

```
64  sub set_msg_subject
65  {
66      my ($message,$subject) = @_;
67
68      if ($$message)
69      {
70          $$message = "Subject: $subject\n" . $$message;
71      }
72      else
73      {
74          $$message .= "Subject: $subject\n";
75      }
76  }
77
```

The **set_msg_subject** function puts a subject field into the message string. It accepts only two arguments, the message and the subject. If the message text field already has entries in it, then we prepend the subject field to the message text on line 70. If not, we append the subject to the existing message text to ensure that the subject appears in the message header, not after, or perhaps within, the message body.

```
78   sub set_msg_body
79   {
80       my ($message,@body) = @_;
81
82       $$message .= "\n";
83
84       foreach my $line (@body)
85       {
86           chomp $line;
87           $$message .= $line;
88           $$message .= "\n";
89       }
90       $$message .= "\n";
91   }
92
```

The **set_msg_body** function appends the message body array onto the message text scalar. First we insert the separator line on line 82 before using a **foreach** loop to strip any end-of-line characters from each element of the array (line 86) before appending the element and a new new-line character on lines 87 and 88. Line 90 adds an additional new-line character to ensure the message ends with one.

There are two cleaner options than the preceding method. The code fragment

```
$$message .= "\n";
chomp @body;
$$message .=  join "\n", @body;
$$message .= "\n\n";
```

first adds the blank, then **chomps** the end-of-line character off every element of the **@body** array, before using **join** to concatenate the individual lines from **@body** to the message body, using a new-line character as the separator. The shorter fragment

```
chomp @body;
$$message .= join ("\n", '', @body, '', '');
```

performs the same operation, except that we are introducing the blank lines as additional elements of the entire array, supplied to the **join** functions.

```
93   sub send_msg
94   {
95       my $message = shift;
96
97       unless (($$message =~ /^To:/mi)
```

```
98              && ($$message =~ /^From:/mi))
99      {
100         $error = "Bad message, no To/From fields\n";
101         return(0);
102     }
103
```

The **send_msg** function checks and then sends the message to the sendmail application. We extract the message variable using **shift** on line 95. Because the message variable will be passed as a reference, we'll need to specify the variable type each time we use it.

Lines 97 and 98 check that the message incorporates, at a minimum, To and From fields. The regular expression we use checks for To and From fields at the start of each line. The **/mi** option allows us to match multiline regular expressions and to ignore the case. If the check fails, then we set the error and return from the function with a false result on line 101.

```
104     unless (open(MAIL,"|sendmail -oi -t"))
105     {
106         $error = "Couldn't open sendmail, $!";
107         return(0);
108     }
109
110     print MAIL $$message;
111
112     unless (close(MAIL))
113     {
114         $error = "Couldn't close sendmail pipe, $!";
115         return(0);
116     }
117     return(1);
118 }
119
120 1;
```

Lines 104 to 117 execute the sending process by opening a file handle to the sendmail application, printing the message text to the file handle, and then closing it. We incorporate the same error checking, setting the error message and returning from the function with a false value. Remember that a package must return a true value to the script that is **use**-ing the module, so we specify a 1 on line 120.

We'll look in the next two scripts at ways of ways of using this module.

If you want a tidier and more robust way of achieving a similar result, you may want to modify the preceding functions to use a hash as the storage medium instead of the simple scalar we used before. When using a hash, attributing information for the message is as simple as specifying the field name as the hash key and the field value as the hash value. For example:

```
$msgtext{To} = "mc\@foo.bar";
$msgtext{From} = "mc\@foo.bar";
$msgtext{Subject} = "Testing...";
$msgtext{Body} = "This is a test";
```

PROGRAMMER'S NOTE *Because double quotes force Perl to check for variables, expanding them as necessary, we need to backslash the @ signs to ensure they are treated as text.*

All the fields are given their standard names, but the special one is Body. We'll use it in the following function to actually send the e-mail:

```
sub send_message
{
my $hashref = shift;
my %message = %$hashref;

    unless (open(MAIL,"|sendmail -t"))
    {
        $error = "Couldn't open sendmail";
        return(0);
    }

    foreach $field (keys %message)
    {
        next if (uc($field) eq 'BODY');
        print MAIL uc(field),": $message{$field}\n";
    }

    print MAIL "\n$message{Body}\n";
    unless (close(MAIL))
    {
        $error = "Couldn't close sendmail pipe";
        return(0);
    }
    return(1);
}
```

This function takes a hash as argument, using every key except Body as a field name. The field names (in uppercase) and their values form the message header. The Body value is used as the body text for the message. The formatted output is sent, as before, directly to a sendmail process; the basic effect is the same as before. This method provides greater flexibility when it comes to the message header, although we gain nothing else over the previous example, aside from the obvious simplicity.

Using a Single Function to Send Mail

sendmsg.pl

Using the module we created in the first section, let's reproduce the basic functionality of the Unix mail program, available on most Unix machines. These programs typically specify the recipients on the command line, sometimes with an optional subject and sender's address, and then take input from the terminal until an end-of-file character or a single period on a line is received.

```perl
1   #!/usr/local/bin/perl5
2
3   use Smail;
4   use Getopt::Long;
5
6   my ($subject,$from,$message);
7
8   GetOptions("s=s" => \$subject,
9              "f=s" => \$from);
10
11  if (@ARGV < 1)
12  {
13      die "No recipient specified";
14  }
15
16  while(<STDIN>)
17  {
18      last if (/^\.$/);
19      $message .=$_;
20  }
21
22  unless (simple_send_message(join(',',@ARGV),
23                              $from ? $from : $ENV{USER},
24                              $subject ? $subject : "<no subject>",
25                              $message))
26  {
27      die $Smail::error;
28  }
```

ANNOTATIONS

Because we have farmed out the core functionality involved in sending the actual message to a separate program, all we need to do is identify the command-line elements and then pass the information on to the mail sending function.

```perl
1    #!/usr/local/bin/perl5
2
3    use Smail;
4    use Getopt::Long;
5
6    my ($subject,$from,$message);
7
8    GetOptions("s=s" => \$subject,
9              "f=s" => \$from);
10
```

We use the Simple Mail module from the last example, and we need the Long version of **Getopt** to get the command-line arguments. As we've seen, there are four basic elements to an e-mail message: subject, sender, recipient, and message. We defined variables for three of these elements in line 6. The recipients will be specified on the command line.

The GetOptions function extracts two options from the command line, if they exist, on lines 8 and 9. Using **-s** allows us to specify a subject, and **-f** will enable us to specify an alternative sender.

```perl
11   if (@ARGV < 1)
12   {
13       die "No recipient specified";
14   }
15
```

If, after separating out any specified command-line options, we don't get any further arguments, this result constitutes an error, which is reported using the **die** function in line 13.

```perl
16   while(<STDIN>)
17   {
18       last if (/^\.$/);
19       $message .= $_;
20   }
21
```

Lines 16 to 20 read in the standard input. A special file handle exists for reading the standard input and is automatically provided when the script is invoked along with STDOUT, the default output device, and STDERR, the default error-reporting device. Because they are standard file handles, aside from their automatic creation, they can be read, opened, and closed in the same way as any other file handle.

In this instance, we are reading the standard input using a **while** loop until an end-of-file character is reached. On line 18, we also check whether a line contains a single period, which is the alternative method for ending message input that is supported by the standard **mail** program. Individual lines are then appended to the **$message** variable. Note that we don't remove the end-of-line character(s)—we can assume the user wants those in the message.

```
22  unless (simple_send_message(join(',',@ARGV),
23                  $from ? $from : $ENV{USER},
24                  $subject ? $subject : "<no subject>",
25                  $message))
26  {
27      die $Smail::error;
28  }
```

Lines 22 to 25 call the mail sending function **simple_send_message**. If you refer back to the **Smail.pm** module at the start of this chapter, you will see that it uses sendmail to send e-mail. The arguments to the function are recipient(s), sender, subject, and message body.

The recipients will have been specified on the command line as individual arguments. We join them together, using **join**, with commas as separators. This will produce a single string of all the recipients that will be passed to the function. Line 23 selects either the sender specified on the command line, or, if none is specified, we take the value of the **$USER** environment variable. The shell sets this variable by default to the value of the login name used to log in to the machine. This is not a failsafe mechanism for discovering the sender; it doesn't include any host or domain information for example. We will see better examples later in this chapter when we cover mailing lists and mailbots.

We repeat the same style quick-test on the subject in line 24. The message body, which we extracted from the command line into a single variable, can be specified directly to the function. If the command failed for any reason, then we print an error on line 27, using the **$Smail::error** variable generated by the **Smail** module.

To use the script, you can use it in place of the mail command:

```
$ sendmsg.pl -s Testing martinb
This is a test message.
.
$
```

The Environment

The environment is a set of variables that are generated by the OS (Unix and NT), usually as part of the shell or parent process that called the script. The environmental variables provide a way to make information about the environment in which programs are executed available to the programs. This information is important, in that it supplies information such as the **PATH** and other variables, but it is not used to store user information because of its dynamic nature. Both Unix and NT support an environment, but the Mac does not. On the Mac, you can use the preferences of the MacPerl application to set environment variables.

Some of the standard environmental variables include **$HOME**, which specifies the user's home directory, and **$LANG**, which specifies the language or locality to be used when displaying numbers, dates, and times. One variable which many people will be familiar with is **$PATH**, which specifies the list of directories to be searched when executing an application.

Accessing the environment within Perl is made easy through the use of a hash. The key is the environment variable name; the value is the value of the environment variable. From within Perl you can also set the values of the environment variables. Any programs you call from the script will use this information, but it will not affect the parent process the script was called from.

The reason for this is that the environment is copied from the parent into the called program. Although you can make changes to the copy of the parent, you cannot change the parent. However, when you execute a program from within Perl, the environment that is copied is that of the Perl script, so changing the environment for the script will affect the programs called.

It should also be noted that the environment is a separate entity to the global variables within the Perl script. You are not publishing the Perl variables when you access the environment variables.

Or, if we want to specify a different sender:

```
$ sendmsg.pl -s Testing -f fred martinb
This is a test message. Supposedly from Fred.
.
$
```

This latter trick will place a different From line into the message, but it doesn't hide the real sender from the recipient. This information will still be a part of the From field specified at the start of the message fields that incorporate the route taken by the message on its journey.

sendmsg2.pl

Using Multiple Functions to Send Mail

Using our sample module, we can create an alternative way to generate an e-mail message: section by section. The same basic method is used, in that a message is composed and then handed off to a mail application (sendmail, in our case). But rather than supplying the recipient, sender, subject, and message body as part of a single function, we instead supply components to individual functions that build a string containing the message.

This method can be useful if you build up the components of a message over a period of time, or if you want to generate an entire message (header and body) to display on screen before sending the final version.

```perl
1    #!/usr/local/bin/perl5
2
3    use Smail;
4    use Getopt::Long;
5    my ($subject,$from,$message,$msgbody);
6
7    GetOptions("s=s" => \$subject,
8               "f=s" => \$from);
9
10   if (@ARGV < 1)
11   {
12       die "No recipient specified";
13   }
14
15   while(<STDIN>)
16   {
17       last if (/^\.$/);
18       $message .=$_;
19   }
20
21   unless (set_msg_address(\$msgbody,
22                           shift,
23                           $from ? $from : $ENV{USER}))
24   {
25       die $Smail::error;
26   }
27
28   set_msg_subject(\$msgbody,
29                   $subject ? $subject : "<no subject>");
30
```

```
31   set_msg_body(\$msgbody,$message);
32
33   unless(send_msg(\$msgbody))
34   {
35       die $Smail::error;
36   }
```

ANNOTATIONS

The **sendmsg2.pl** script is largely identical to the previous **sendmsg.pl**. The difference is in the last few lines, where we compose the obtained elements into the final message.

```
1    #!/usr/local/bin/perl5
2
3    use Smail;
4    use Getopt::Long;
5    my ($subject,$from,$message,$msgbody);
6
7    GetOptions("s=s" => \$subject,
8               "f=s" => \$from);
9
10   if (@ARGV < 1)
11   {
12       die "No recipient specified";
13   }
14
15   while(<STDIN>)
16   {
17       last if (/^\.$/);
18       $message .=$_;
19   }
20
```

Lines 1 to 20 are almost identical to the previous script. The only difference is that we have introduced a new variable, **$msgbody**, that we will use to contain the final e-mail message in its formatted state, ready to be passed to the **send_msg** function.

```
21   unless (set_msg_address(\$msgbody,
22                           shift,
23                           $from ? $from : $ENV{USER}))
24   {
```

```
25       die $Smail::error;
26  }
27
```

Lines 21 to 23 set the message sender and recipients. The first argument is the variable that will be used to store the message body text. Next, in line 22, we extract the first e-mail address specified on the command line, and line 23 sets the sender, either from the command-line option or the **$USER** environment variable. If the process fails for any reason, then we report an error in line 25.

```
28  set_msg_subject(\$msgbody,
29                      $subject ? $subject : "<no subject>");
30
```

Lines 28 and 29 add a message subject or a default subject if none is specified.

```
31  set_msg_body(\$msgbody,$message);
32
```

Line 31 sets the body of the message.

```
33  unless(send_msg(\$msgbody))
34  {
35       die $Smail::error;
36  }
```

Line 33 sends the message using the message body we composed in the previous lines. An error message is printed on line 35 if the process fails for any reason. Remember that the functions in **Smail** return false if the function fails, placing the error into the **$error** variable within the package.

The method and result of using the script is the same:

```
$ sendmsg2.pl -s "Testing 2" martinb
This is a test message.
.
$
```

Or, if we want to specify a different sender:

```
$ sendmsg2.pl -s "Testing 2" -f fred martinb
This is a test message. Supposedly from Fred.
.
$
```

Notice in these examples, because we want a subject with titles in it, that we have quoted the subject text in double quotes on the command line. This will cause the shell to pass the "Testing 2" string as a single argument.

Using a Direct SMTP Connection to Send Mail

There are a number of problems with the previous two examples relating—mostly—to the method employed to send the message. Both rely on the **Smail** package we created in the first script in this chapter, and that package in turn relies on the functionality provided by the sendmail program. The sendmail program, when used with the **-t** option, studies the message body for From and To lines in order to identify who sent and who should receive the message. This implies that we put the e-mail addresses of the recipients within the body of the message.

This is not always the desired behavior. For example, examine the latest message from a mailing list, and you are bound to spot that the To entry probably matches a generic "mailing-list@domain" style address and not your e-mail address at all. This format isn't just a nicety: the mailing list may have been sent to thousands of people, and the distributors don't want to send out thousands of individual messages or a single message with thousands of e-mail addresses in it.

In addition to this annoyance, the scripts have also relied on the functionality of an external program in order to do the real work. While this isn't a major problem—many of the external programs are relatively bug-free and provide better performance through the use of C code—it does limit our Perl application's cross-platform abilities.

A better solution, therefore, is to talk directly to a mail server using SMTP, so you can specify recipient and sender information separately from the actual message body, and thus format the message how you like, while still ensuring that the intended recipients will get the message they expect. Being a remote service, we can use our existing skills in network programming (see Chapter 5) to access an SMTP server directly. In fact, we'll use the **Net::SMTP** module provided as part of Graham Barr's **libnet** module collection.

```perl
1    #!/usr/local/bin/perl5
2
3    use Net::SMTP;
4    use Getopt::Long;
5    my ($subject,$from,$message,$msgbody,$smtp,$realsubject);
6
7    GetOptions("s=s" => \$subject,
8               "f=s" => \$from);
9
10   if (@ARGV < 1)
11   {
12       die "No recipients specified";
13   }
14
```

```
15   while(<STDIN>)
16   {
17       last if (/^\.$/);
18       $message .=$_;
19   }
20
21   $smtp = Net::SMTP->new('mail');
22   die "Couldn't open connection to server" unless $smtp;
23
24   $smtp->mail(defined($from) ? $from : $ENV{USER})
25       || die "Bad 'from' address";
26   foreach my $recipient (@ARGV)
27   {
28       warn "Couldn't set recipient $recipient"
29           unless($smtp->to($recipient));
30   }
31
32   $realsubject = "Subject: ";
33   $realsubject .= defined($subject) ? $subject : "<no subject>";
34   $realsubject .= "\n\n";
35   $smtp->data();
36   $smtp->datasend($realsubject);
37   $smtp->datasend($message);
38   die "Connection wouldn't accept data"
39       unless($smtp->dataend());
40
41   die "Couldn't close connection to server"
42       unless($smtp->quit());
```

ANNOTATIONS

The format follows that of the previous two scripts. We set up the environment in which to work, obtaining the subject, sender, recipient, and message body information from a combination of the command line and standard input. We then use the **Net::SMTP** module to send the actual message.

```
1    #!/usr/local/bin/perl5
2
3    use Net::SMTP;
4    use Getopt::Long;
5    my ($subject,$from,$message,$msgbody,$smtp,$realsubject);
6
```

```
7   GetOptions("s=s" => \$subject,
8              "f=s" => \$from);
9
10  if (@ARGV < 1)
11  {
12      die "No recipients specified";
13  }
14
15  while(<STDIN>)
16  {
17      last if (/^\.$/);
18      $message .=$_;
19  }
20
```

Again, lines 1 to 20 are largely identical to our previous example. We need to specify further variables for this example, but otherwise this section of the script is identical.

```
21  $smtp = Net::SMTP->new('mail');
22  die "Couldn't open connection to server" unless $smtp;
23
```

We create a new object on line 21 based on the **Net::SMTP** module. The only argument to the function is the mail server. I've specified a fairly generic host in this example; you may want to change the value to your local SMTP server or to that of your ISP. Assuming the creation of the new object completed successfully, the **$smtp** variable will be the new object. If the operation failed (for example, if the mail server couldn't be reached), then a false value will be returned to **$smtp**, which is checked and report on in line 22.

```
24  $smtp->mail(defined($from) ? $from : $ENV{USER})
25      || die "Bad 'from' address";
```

We have to specify the sender of the e-mail to the SMTP server. Note that this is the "real" sender, not the sender we want to appear in the message the recipient receives.

```
26  foreach my $recipient (@ARGV)
27  {
28      warn "Couldn't set recipient $recipient"
29          unless($smtp->to($recipient));
30  }
31
```

Lines 26 to 30 step through each argument on the command line and set the recipient. Again, these are the real recipients of the e-mail—their names will appear only in the e-mail body that they receive if we don't specify an explicit recipient as part of the message body. There are often limits on the maximum number of recipients that can be specified in a single e-mail. Since it's unlikely that anybody would specify any more than, say, 10 recipients on the command line, we can ignore this limit. We'll look at a way of handling this limit in the next script, **ml.pl**.

If the recipient function returns an error, we report the error as a warning to the user. Note that this is a warning—we don't **die**, just in case the user wants to ignore bad e-mail addresses.

```
32   $realsubject = "Subject: ";
33   $realsubject .= defined($subject) ? $subject : "<no subject>";
34   $realsubject .= "\n\n";
```

Line 32 sets the subject line, which is composed of the Subject header line. Then line 33 sets the subject text. The separation between the message header and the message body is a single empty line. We end the subject line, and then we insert the blank line by concatenating two end-of-line characters to the subject string on line 34.

```
35   $smtp->data();
36   $smtp->datasend($realsubject);
37   $smtp->datasend($message);
38   die "Connection wouldn't accept data"
39       unless($smtp->dataend());
40
```

You can specify a block of data or, in this case, the message body to the SMTP server by specifying the start of the data on line 35, the message contents on line 36 and 37, and then setting the end of the data stream on line 38. The function returns false if it fails, and we report an error on line 39.

Incidentally, in this example we have not specified alternative values for the sender or recipient, so the SMTP server will automatically insert the values into the message body. How they are represented is entirely dependent on the SMTP server.

```
41   die "Couldn't close connection to server"
42       unless($smtp->quit());
```

We close the connection using the **quit** method on the **$smtp** object. Provided there is no error, this method will tell the SMTP server to deliver the message, or queue the message ready for delivery later. If it fails, a false value will be returned, and we report the error on line 42.

As has already been noted, operation is identical to the previous sample mail sending scripts. The biggest difference with this example is that it should work as well under NT or MacOS as it does under any Unix flavor—provided, of course, you have installed the **libnet** package.

ml.pl

Creating a Mailing List Sender

Building on our previous example, let's take a look at a very quick, large-scale e-mailing system. I have called it a mailing list, and it is targeted at mailing lists, although it could be used to send any bulk e-mail. (Unfortunately, the method used by many bulk e-mailers to distribute unsolicited and junk e-mail is identical to the method used in the script I am going to demonstrate.)

We use SMTP again, like last time, but we can now specify a "ghost" sender and recipient, while still sending the e-mail to the intended real recipients. The list of recipients is taken from a source file composed of the recipients' names and their e-mail addresses.

For more ideas, you may want to look at the **majordomo** package, which used Perl 4 to provide an entire mailing list solution.

```perl
1   #!/usr/local/bin/perl5
2
3   use Net::SMTP;
4   use Getopt::Long;
5   my ($subject,$from,$message,$msgbody,
6       $smtp,$realsubject,$recipients,$hide,
7       $debug,$name,$address,@addlist);
8
9   GetOptions("s=s" => \$subject,
10             "f=s" => \$from,
11             "r=s" => \$recipients,
12             "h=s" => \$hide,
13             "d"   => \$debug);
14
15  die <<EOF
16  Usage: $0 -r file -f from [-h toaddress]
17                  [-s subject] [-d(ebug)]
18  EOF
19      unless ($recipients && $from);
20
21  open(RECP,"<$recipients")
22      || die "Couldn't open mailing list file, $!";
23
24  while(<>)
25  {
26      last if ($_ =~ /^\./);
27      $message .=$_;
28  }
```

```
29
30   while(<RECP>)
31   {
32       chomp;
33       ($name,$address) = split /,/;
34
35       print "Sending to $name, $address\n" if $debug;
36
37       if ($hide)
38       {
39           push @addlist,$address;
40           if (@addlist >16)
41           {
42               warn "$0: Could not send message"
43                   unless(mail_a_message($subject,$from,$hide,
44                                           $message,$name,@addlist));
45               undef @addlist;
46           }
47       }
48       else
49       {
50           warn "$0: Could not send message"
51               unless(mail_a_message($subject,$from,0,
52                                       $message,$name,$address));
53       }
54   }
55   close(RECP);
56
57   if ((@addlist))
58   {
59       warn "$0: Could not send message"
60           unless(mail_a_message($subject,$from,$hide,
61                                   $message,$name,@addlist));
62   }
63
64   sub mail_a_message
65   {
66       my ($subject,$from,$hide,$message,$name,@recipients) = @_;
67       my ($address);
68
69       $smtp = Net::SMTP->new('mail');
70       die "Cannot open mail server" unless $smtp;
71       $smtp->mail($from ? $from : $ENV{USER});
```

```
72
73      foreach $address (@recipients)
74      {
75          $smtp->to($address);
76      }
77
78      $realsubject = "Subject: ";
79      $realsubject .= $subject ? $subject : "<no subject>\n";
80
81      $smtp->data();
82      if ($hide)
83      {
84          $smtp->datasend("To: $hide\n");
85      }
86      else
87      {
88          $smtp->datasend("To: $name <$recipients[0]>\n");
89      }
90      $smtp->datasend($realsubject);
91      $smtp->datasend("\n");
92      $smtp->datasend($message);
93      $smtp->dataend();
94
95      $smtp->quit();
96  }
```

ANNOTATIONS

This script employs the direct SMTP method we saw in the last script to send e-mail to multiple recipients. The script will handle both normal "named" recipients and the more usual "masked" recipient and sender used by many mailing list services. The principles shown here could be used for any mass-mailing system. The script doesn't support adding people to the list; we'll look at ways to do that when we look at the mailbot script, **mailbot.pl**.

```
1   #!/usr/local/bin/perl5
2
3   use Net::SMTP;
4   use Getopt::Long;
5   my ($subject,$from,$message,$msgbody,
6       $smtp,$realsubject,$recipients,$hide,
7       $debug,$name,$address,@addlist);
```

```
8
9    GetOptions("s=s" => \$subject,
10             "f=s" => \$from,
11             "r=s" => \$recipients,
12             "h=s" => \$hide,
13             "d"   => \$debug);
14
```

All we need to use is the **Net::SMTP** module and the extended **Getopt** module. Options on the command line allow us to specify whether to hide the recipient and the sender and which address to use. We also extract the subject and sender and the file used to specify the recipients. Finally, we have a debug option that prints out an annotated run-down of what the script is doing. Note that I haven't trapped any errors from **GetOptions** even though I've specified required strings after each option. This is because we need to check separately for the existence and combination of some of the elements. This method of checking is not tidy, but it is effective for our purposes.

```
15   die <<EOF
16   Usage: $0 -r file -f from [-h toaddress]
17                    [-s subject] [-d(ebug)]
18   EOF
19       unless ($recipients && $from);
20
```

The minimum you can specify on the command line is the list of recipients and who the message is to be sent from. Because we are sending from a mailing list, using the user's current e-mail address might not be appropriate. A simple test in line 19 makes sure both options have been specified. The test ignores the possibility that the options may be naturally negative; we are expecting a filename and a mail address, both of which are unlikely to make much sense as false values (such as zero) anyway.

```
21   open(RECP,"<$recipients")
22       || die "Couldn't open mailing list file, $!";
23
```

We open the recipients file on line 21, or report an error on line 22 if the file failed to open.

```
24   while(<>)
25   {
26       last if ($_ =~ /^\./);
27       $message .=$_;
28   }
29
```

Like our simple message senders, we read input from the standard input, unless a file is specified on the command line. The end of the message will be taken as when the end-of-file character is received or if a single period is found on the command line.

```
30   while(<RECP>)
31   {
32       chomp;
33       ($name,$address) = split /,/;
34
```

The format of the recipient file can be seen in the following example:

```
Martin Brown,mc@foo.com
Mike Smith,mike@bar.com
```

A single comma separates the name and e-mail address.

Line 32 strips the record separator off the end-of-line character (the new-line character under Unix, carriage return under MacOS, and new-line character under Windows NT) only because Perl automatically strips it (see Appendix A for more information). Line 33 splits the e-mail recipients' files by a comma. The first field is the recipient's full name, and the second field is the user's e-mail address.

```
35       print "Sending to $name, $address\n" if $debug;
36
```

If debugging is switched on in the command line, then we report whom the e-mail is being sent to. This is a simple commentary, but it can prove invaluable when you are trying to find an error.

```
37       if ($hide)
38       {
39           push @addlist,$address;
40           if (@addlist >16)
41           {
42               warn "$0: Could not send message"
43                   unless(mail_a_message($subject,$from,$hide,
44                                                 $message,$name,@addlist));
45               undef @addlist;
46           }
47       }
```

A "normal" message header might look like this:

```
To: john@foo.bar
From: mailing-list-errors@foo.bar
Subject: New Mailing
```

In comparison, a hidden e-mail message might look like this:

```
To: mailing-list@foo.bar
From: mailing-list-errors@foo.bar
Subject: New Mailing
```

The specification of the hidden recipient comes from the command line and is specified as the e-mail address to be used in the e-mail text. Because of the way SMTP works, the text of a message is separate from the information used to send the mail message to its targeted recipient. This means that even though the headers contain address information, SMTP ignores them.

Assuming the sender wants to hide the real recipient, we check on line 37 and then execute lines 38 to 47. If a message is being hidden, then we can send the same body text to a theoretically unlimited number of recipients. To keep the number of e-mail addresses specified to a suitable limit, both for the benefit of the SMTP server (some limit the numbers) and to keep the array sizes down within Perl, we chop the recipient lists into manageable chunks. I've used a figure of 16 here; it's a bit low, so you may want to experiment with a larger number. Line 39 pushes the e-mail address onto an address stack. We then check on line 40 for 16 addresses on the stack, before sending the message in line 43 to the recipients on the stack. We then undefine the address stack in line 45, ready for it to be refilled with the next group of addresses.

We warn the user if the mail sending failed for any reason; this allows the process to continue if minor glitches occur, without it causing the script to fail completely. The **ml.pl** script takes all the inputs supplied, both from the command line and from the standard input of the message body.

```
48      else
49      {
50          warn "$0: Could not send message"
51              unless(mail_a_message($subject,$from,0,
52                                     $message,$name,$address));
53      }
54  }
55  close(RECP);
56
```

If the message recipient is not to be hidden, we send an e-mail on line 51. This time we specify a static zero for the value of the **$hide** option to the **mail_a_message** function. This time we haven't packaged up the recipient list because each message must be composed individually to contain an individual's e-mail address in the message text.

Line 55 closes the recipient file. I haven't checked that the **close** operation failed, but if you use this script within a live mailing list situation, you may want to add a logical **or** and a **die** or **warn** statement. If e-mail addresses are being added to the recipient file, you should check that the file has been closed properly. Better still, you may want to read the file into a hash or array before sending the individual e-mails. This should help prevent the problems connected with updating the recipient file when another Perl script is reading from it.

The sample code for putting the recipient list straight into a hash might look like this:

```perl
open(RECP,"<$recipient");
while(<RECP>)
{
    my ($name, $email) = split /,/;
    $recipients{$email} = $name;
}
close(<RECP>);
```

There is an added benefit to this method: we can sort the recipient list alphabetically before sending. This benefit may not sound like much, but with a little modification to the preceding script, the mailing list could be sorted by the recipients' domains. Consider the following lines of code:

```perl
my ($name, $email) = split /,/;
my $token = join('@',reverse(split(/@/,$email)));
$recipients{$email} = $name;
```

The preceding code reverses the "split" elements of the e-mail address, changing, for example, mc@foo.bar to foo.bar@mc. When we came to sort the hash, the recipient e-mail list would be sorted in the order of the recipients' domains, which would speed up transfer rates for e-mail messages because the host handling the domain should only have to be contacted once or twice for a large number of recipients to be e-mailed. Of course, you will need to remember to swap the values around again when its time to send the e-mail!

```perl
57  if ($hide && (@addlist>1))
58  {
59      warn "$0: Could not send message"
60          unless(mail_a_message($subject,$from,$hide,
61                                $message,$name,@addlist));
62  }
63
```

Because we put e-mail addresses onto an address stack and only clear the stack when we reach 16 addresses, we need to make sure we clear the stack when there are less than 16 addresses on it. Lines 57 to 62 sort out this problem. We check that there are values on the stack, and that there would have been values placed on it because we are in hide mode.

```perl
64  sub mail_a_message
65  {
66      my ($subject,$from,$hide,$message,$name,@recipients) = @_;
```

```
67        my ($address);
68
```

We extract the arguments for the **mail_a_message** function on line 66. Note that the last argument is an array, not a scalar. All of the arguments supplied after the **$name** argument are placed into the **@recipients** array, allowing us to accept either just one address (from a nonhidden message) or up to the figure specified in the sending loop (16, in this example) placed directly into the array (for a hidden message).

```
69        $smtp = Net::SMTP->new('mail');
70        die "Cannot open mail server" unless $smtp;
71        $smtp->mail($from ? $from : $ENV{USER});
72
```

We create a new SMTP object on line 69. I've used the name **mail** here, which is the name of my local machine. You will need to change this value to your local SMTP server, or perhaps specify it as a variable earlier in the function to make it slightly more flexible. If the connection to the server fails, we **die** on line 70. Remember that earlier we only gave a warning if the **mail_a_message** function failed. A connection failure is a serious enough error to warrant a full exit, instead of just warning the user; it's likely to be a problem for all connections, not just a single e-mail message.

On line 71, just in case the From detail from the command line has not come through correctly, we specify the sender as either the From address or the user's login.

```
73        foreach $address (@recipients)
74        {
75            $smtp->to($address);
76        }
77
```

Lines 73 to 76 work through the recipient array and set the recipients. This is where we set the e-mail addresses of the real recipients of the e-mail. What we put here will not affect the message body, nor will the information be seen by the recipient(s).

```
78        $realsubject = "Subject: ";
79        $realsubject .= $subject ? $subject : "<no subject>\n";
80
```

Lines 78 and 79 set the subject line, either from the one supplied on the command line or from a default value if none is specified. We add a new-line character to the subject field to ensure that there is a blank line between the message headers, which end with the subject field, and the message body.

```
81        $smtp->data();
82        if ($hide)
```

```
83      {
84          $smtp->datasend("To: $hide\n");
85      }
86      else
87      {
88          $smtp->datasend("To: $name <$recipients[0]>\n");
89      }
```

Line 81 sets the e-mail object to accept the data, or body, of our e-mail message. Lines 82 to 89 then set the recipient address that will appear in the e-mail text the recipients receive. If the recipient is to be hidden, then we put the hide address into the To field on line 84, or we put the recipient's name and e-mail address into the To field on line 88.

```
90      $smtp->datasend($realsubject);
91      $smtp->datasend("\n");
92      $smtp->datasend($message);
93      $smtp->dataend();
94
```

Lines 90 to 94 then set the subject, the separator between body and subject, and finally the message body in line 93. Line 94 ends the data input and actually sends the message.

```
95      $smtp->quit();
96  }
```

Line 95 then closes the connection to the SMTP server. Note that because this is the last line of the function, the result will be passed back to the calling line. If the send fails, a false result will be passed back to the main part of the script, which will produce a warning.

To use this script on an unhidden message, create a file of the form:

Name, E-mail Address

Then, on the command line, type

$ ml.pl -r file -f mailing-list

Type in your message and send it. The e-mail will be sent to all the recipients in your file.

If you want to hide the recipients' addresses and masquerade as the mailing list address, use the following:

$ ml.pl -r file -f mailing-list -h mailing-list

and check the result!

Building an SMTP Wrapper Module

The first script in this chapter demonstrated two ways of sending e-mail using the sendmail application. These sections were followed by the **sendmsg3.pl** script, which used the **Net::SMTP** module to talk directly to an SMTP server in order to send mail. There are advantages to this method, not least of which is that we have significantly more control over the message contents, irrespective of the message recipients. Our next few scripts need this flexibility to work effectively, although it's safe to say that we could do without it if we had to.

To make our lives easier, and to eliminate code replication, we'll generate a quick module that provides a wrapper around the **Net::SMTP** functionality that simulates the functionality we saw in the first script of this chapter. We'll also supply two new functions, **return_address**, which returns the correct return address from a mail header hash, and **clean_address**, which removes the name, punctuation, and other characters to return a plain e-mail address.

```
1    package smtpwrap;
2
3    require Net::SMTP;
4    require Exporter;
5    @ISA = 'Exporter';
6    @EXPORT = qw (send_smtp
7                    mail_a_message
8                    return_address
9                    clean_address);
10   use vars qw($error);
11
12   sub send_smtp
13   {
14       my ($to,$from,$message) = @_;
15       my $smtp = Net::SMTP->new('mail');
16       unless($smtp)
17       {
18           $error = "Couldn't open connection to mail server";
19           return 0;
20       }
21       unless($smtp->mail($from))
22       {
23           $error = "Bad 'From' address specified";
24           return 0;
25       }
26       unless($smtp->to($to))
```

```
27        {
28            $error = "Bad 'To' address specified";
29            return 0;
30        }
31        unless($smtp->data())
32        {
33            $error = "Not ready to accept data";
34            return 0;
35        }
36        $smtp->datasend($message);
37        unless($smtp->dataend())
38        {
39            $error = "Bad response when sending data";
40            return 0;
41        }
42        unless($smtp->quit())
43        {
44            $error = "Error closing SMTP connection";
45            return 0;
46        }
47        1;
48    }
49
50    sub mail_a_message
51    {
52        my ($subject,$to,$from,$message) = @_;
53        my ($newmessage);
54
55        $newmessage .= "To: $to\n";
56        $newmessage .= "From: $from\n";
57        $newmessage .= "Subject: $subject\n";
58        $newmessage .= "\n" . $message;
59
60        send_smtp($to,$from,$newmessage);
61    }
62
63    sub return_address
64    {
65        my ($hash) = shift;
66
67        $$hash{'reply-to'} || $$hash{'from'} ||
68            $$hash{'return-path'} || $$hash{'apparently-from'};
69    }
```

```
70
71   sub clean_address
72   {
73       local($_) = @_;
74       s/\s*\(.*\)\s*//;
75       1 while s/.*<(.*)>.*/$1/;
76       s/^\s*(.*\S)\s*$/$1/;
77       $_;
78   }
79
80   1;
```

ANNOTATIONS

The bulk of the package is the **send_smtp** function. It uses the **Net::SMTP** module and checks for errors at each stage of the process. The function is simple and takes the delivery information and a precomposed message text made up of headers and message body. The **mail_a_message** function allows us to supply the message header and body. The function then assembles the mail body before calling the **send_smtp** function.

We employ the same techniques we have already used for other packages. We use the **Exporter** module to automatically import the functions into the calling script. A global variable is used to record an error message, and where necessary the functions return a false result on failure, setting the error message accordingly.

```
1    package SMTPwrap;
2
3    require Net::SMTP;
4    require Exporter;
5    @ISA = 'Exporter';
6    @EXPORT = qw (send_smtp
7                  mail_a_message
8                  return_address
9                  clean_address);
10   use vars qw($error);
11
```

Lines 1 to 10 follow the same basic format we have used before. The difference here is that we have specified that we require the **Net::SMTP** module. By using **require** instead of **use**, any functions within **Net::SMTP** will be available to all the scripts that use the **SMTPwrap** package. In this instance, **Net::SMTP** uses objects that are automatically imported when we create a new **SMTP** object on line 15.

Incidentally, many people prefer to use **@EXPORT_OK** in place of **@EXPORT**. The **@EXPORT_OK** array specifies the list of functions that it is safe to export (or import) into the calling script. Since we only have four functions in this example, we don't need to worry too much about this, but it's worth noting if you start creating larger modules.

```perl
12  sub send_smtp
13  {
14      my ($to,$from,$message) = @_;
15      my $smtp = Net::SMTP->new('mail');
16      unless($smtp)
17      {
18          $error = "Couldn't open connection to mail server";
19          return 0;
20      }
```

We open a connection to an SMTP server in line 15. I've hard-coded the address here, but it might be useful to support another global package variable that allows the user to specify the host to use. Adding this support would involve changing line 10 to something like

```perl
use vars qw($error $mailhost);
```

and line 15 to

```perl
my $smtp = Net::SMTP->new($mailhost);
```

From the script we would then specify the host as part of the initialization process:

```perl
$SMTPwrap::$mailhost = 'mail';
```

If the connection to the SMTP server failed, we trap it on line 16, set the error message, and then return a failure on line 19. You might also want to specify a default value within the package, just in case the user does not specify a host.

```perl
21      unless($smtp->mail($from))
22      {
23          $error = "Bad 'From' address specified";
24          return 0;
25      }
26      unless($smtp->to($to))
27      {
28          $error = "Bad 'To' address specified";
29          return 0;
30      }
```

Lines 21 to 30 send the sender and recipient information to the server, accounting for and reporting on errors if we have problems.

```
31    unless($smtp->data())
32    {
33        $error = "Not ready to accept data";
34        return 0;
35    }
36    $smtp->datasend($message);
37    unless($smtp->dataend())
38    {
39        $error = "Bad response when sending data";
40        return 0;
41    }
```

Lines 31 to 41 then send the message text. Line 31 tells the **Net::SMTP** package to start accepting data, then line 36 sends the message body. We stop the data sending process on line 37, which also causes the SMTP server to queue and send the message, accounting for an error if the method reports one.

```
42    unless($smtp->quit())
43    {
44        $error = "Error closing SMTP connection";
45        return 0;
46    }
47    1;
48 }
49
```

Line 42 closes the connection with the SMTP server. Again, we report an error if there is a problem; or, if the function worked, then we return a true value indicating success on line 47.

```
50 sub mail_a_message
51 {
52    my ($subject,$to,$from,$message) = @_;
53    my ($newmessage);
54
55    $newmessage .= "To: $to\n";
56    $newmessage .= "From: $from\n";
57    $newmessage .= "Subject: $subject\n";
58    $newmessage .= "\n" . $message;
59
60    send_smtp($to,$from,$newmessage);
61 }
62
```

The **mail_a_message** function, which starts on line 50, takes the subject, sender, recipient, and message body information, formulates it into a formatted message with the required fields, and then calls the **send_smtp** function. To compose the new message body, we create a new scalar, **$newmessage,** and then concatenate the field titles and values on lines 55 to 58. We then send the message on line 60. Remember that the last result from a line is sent back to the calling script, so if the **send_smtp** function returns false, the **mail_a_message** function will also return false.

```
63   sub return_address
64   {
65       my ($hash) = shift;
66
67       $$hash{'reply-to'} || $$hash{'from'} ||
68           $$hash{'return-path'} || $$hash{'apparently-from'};
69   }
70
```

Line 63 defines the **return_address** function. This function extracts, in order, either the Reply-To, From, Return-Path, and finally Apparently-From fields from the mail header hash passed to it on line 65 as a reference. Since a return address can be defined by any of these fields, we need to check each one. The standard is to check the Reply-To field if it has been defined in preference to From, which should be used in preference to Return-Path, and so on. Because by default a function returns the value of the last line from the function, we don't need to specify the return value; it is implied by lines 67 and 68.

```
71   sub clean_address
72   {
73       local($_) = @_;
74       s/\s*\(.*\)\s*//;
75       1 while s/.*<(.*)>.*/$1/;
76       s/^\s*(.*\S)\s*$/$1/;
77       $_;
78   }
79
80   1;
```

A standard e-mail address as sent by most mailers contains all sorts of additional pieces of information beyond the e-mail address itself. This information often includes the sender's or recipient's full name, quotation marks, spaces, and other spurious characters. An e-mail address is usually encapsulated within a pair of angle brackets:

```
Martin C Brown <mc@foo.bar>
```

To clean out the spurious information, we need to run the e-mail address through a number of regular expression operations until we end up with, simply, the e-mail address itself. This is the purpose behind the **clean_address** function. We assign the default buffer to the argument passed to the function on line 73.

Line 74 removes leading and trailing spaces around a parenthesized string, for example:

```
(Martin C Brown) <mc@foo.bar>
```

Line 75 repeats the action of extracting the string between a pair of angle brackets, discarding everything else. Remember that the result of a regular expression substitution is the number of times the substitution took place, so using it in combination with a **while** loop will cause the process to continue until there are no angle brackets left in the buffer space.

Line 76 removes any leading or trailing spaces from the e-mail address. The result is returned to the caller on line 77 by simply specifying the default buffer space.

Passing an address like

```
"MC" <mc@foo.bar>
```

returns

```
mc@foo.bar
```

Passing the above address would simply send it straight back. This is an incredibly quick and dirty solution to what is a very complex process. It should catch about 95 percent of the e-mail address inconsistencies. I don't guarantee that it will solve all problems with all addresses, however.

Compiling a Vacation Responder

vacation.pl

One of the simplest and most practical automatic mail tools you will find on your Unix system is the vacation responder, which sends an e-mail to each person who mails you, telling them that you are on holiday. In fact, the message sent back by the program can be anything, but it was designed primarily for returning those "I'm not here" messages.

The **vacation.pl** script simulates this functionality entirely within Perl. This script is simpler than the standard equivalent; we respond to all e-mail with a message, whereas the Unix tool keeps a record of the e-mail addresses it has replied to and only sends vacation messages back to addresses not already in the database. We'll take a look at how to code this functionality within Perl, as well.

```
1   #!/usr/local/bin/perl5
2
3   use SMTPwrap;
```

```perl
 4
 5   my (%mailheader,$message);
 6   my ($user) = $ENV{'USER'} || $ENV{'LOGNAME'} ||
 7                 getlogin || (getpwuid($>))[0];
 8
 9   close(STDERR);
10   close(STDOUT);
11
12   while(<STDIN>)
13   {
14       chomp;
15       my ($keyword,$value) = m/^(.*):\s*(.*)\s*$/;
16       $mailheader{lc($keyword)} = $value;
17   }
18
19   unless($mailheader{to})
20   {
21       $mailheader{to} = ($mailheader{'apparently-to'}
22                          || $ENV{USER});
23   }
24
25   my $to   = clean_address(return_address(\%mailheader));
26   my $from = clean_address($mailheader{to});
27
28   my ($homedir) = (getpwnam($user))[7];
29
30   if (open(MSG,"<$homedir/.vacation.msg"))
31   {
32       my $rs = $/;
33       undef $/;
34       $message = <MSG>;
35       close(MSG);
36       $/ = $rs;
37   }
38   else
39   {
40       $message = $from . " is on vacation.";
41   }
42
43   unless(mail_a_message("On Vacation",$to,$from,$message))
44   {
45       mail_a_message("Vacation Error",$from,$from,$SMTPwrap::error);
46   }
```

ANNOTATIONS

The vacation system works because it is listed within the user's .forward file as one of the "recipients" of the user's mail. In fact, the e-mail contents are sent to the standard input of any application listed. Because the script will be called by the sendmail or equivalent application directly, we have to create a safe environment to work within. We also need to read the standard input as the source for the message. For the safe environment, we must ensure that the standard output and standard error mail handles are closed to prevent any spurious messages being returned to sendmail.

Beyond these requirements, the script is fairly straightforward. We read in the message text, identify the senders return address, clean it, and then send a message back.

```
1   #!/usr/local/bin/perl5
2
3   use SMTPwrap;
4
5   my (%mailheader,$message);
6   my ($user) = $ENV{'USER'} || $ENV{'LOGNAME'} ||
7                getlogin || (getpwuid($>))[0];
8
```

The **%mailheader** hash holds the message header fields, and the **$message** scalar holds the message, imported from the user's home directory, that is sent back to the sender. Lines 6 and 7 obtain the user login. Because the script will be called from within sendmail, it is unlikely that the USER or LOGNAME environment variables will be set. The usual method is for sendmail to fork a new process, change to the recipient's ID, and then call the program. The recipient's ID is therefore likely to be obtained from either the **getlogin** system call or the array extraction of the first element from the password file based on the script's effective user ID.

```
9   close(STDERR);
10  close(STDOUT);
11
```

We are being called from within another program that will take printed output as an error message. To ensure we don't accidentally generate any output that could be misconstrued as a header, we close the standard output and standard error file handles. Attempting to print to these closed file handles will produce an error if we decide to trap it but will not produce any output. If you are worried about the errors that might be produced, you could reopen the **STDOUT** and **STDERR** file handles with the output pointing to the /dev/null device.

```
12  while(<STDIN>)
13  {
14      chomp;
```

```
15        my ($keyword,$value) = m/^(.*):\s*(.*)\s*$/;
16        $mailheader{lc($keyword)} = $value;
17    }
18
```

We read in the standard input, which will be the message text, stripping the new-line character off the end (line 14) and then extracting the field label and value information in line 15. The regular expression I've used here sets the value of the first match to be all text up to the first colon, and the value of the second match is all the text after the colon, not including any leading or trailing spaces. We are not interested in the message contents or body or in distinguishing the difference between the two, so we don't need to worry about checking that the field values are in the actual message header. The field name and value are assigned to the hash on line 16. We naturalize the header name by making sure it is recorded as lowercase within the hash.

```
19    unless($mailheader{to})
20    {
21        $mailheader{to} = ($mailheader{'apparently-to'}
22                          || $ENV{USER});
23    }
24
```

If we haven't found a To field in the message, then we set the value of the To entry in the hash to equal either Apparently-To, which is an optional field often used by mailing list programs, or to the USER environment variable. It is unlikely that we will not obtain a To field, and even less likely that we will not obtain an Apparently-To field. We need this information to supply a From address as part of the vacation message.

```
25    my $to   = clean_address(return_address(\%mailheader));
26    my $from = clean_address($mailheader{to});
27
```

Line 25 sets up the variable to contain a cleaned version of the address as received from the original mail. We'll send the vacation e-mail to this address. Line 26 cleans our address for inclusion in the mail message.

```
28    my ($homedir) = (getpwnam($user))[7];
29
```

We get the recipient's home directory by making a call to the **getpwnam** function, which extracts the data from the /etc/passwd file keyed on the user's login name. In this case, we want field 7, the user's home directory.

```
30    if (open(MSG,"<$homedir/.vacation.msg"))
31    {
```

```
32        my $rs = $/;
33        undef $/;
34        $message = <MSG>;
35        close(MSG);
36        $/ = $rs;
37     }
```

On line 30 we attempt to open the .vacation.msg file within the recipient's home directory. If we can open it, then we set the vacation message to equal the contents. Rather than using a **while** loop to read in the file, we use a simple trick. Usually, the default record separator automatically separates reads from a file handle. By remembering the value in line 32, and then undefining it in line 33, we allow line 34 to read the entire file contents into the **$message** variable in one go. Once imported, we close the file handle and reset the default separator to its original value.

```
38     else
39     {
40        $message = $from . " is on vacation.";
41     }
42
```

If we couldn't open the vacation file from the user's home directory, we set a default message based on the address the e-mail was sent to on line 40.

```
43     unless(mail_a_message("On Vacation",$to,$from,$message))
44     {
45        mail_a_message("Vacation Error",$from,$from,$SMTPwrap::error);
46     }
```

By now, we have identified the sender and the recipient, and we've generated a message to send back. Line 43 attempts to send the message using the **mail_a_ message** function. If this function fails for any reason, we try to send a message, based on the error from the **mail_a_message** package, to the original recipient. If this attempt fails, there is not a lot we can do!

To use this script, create a .forward file like this:

`\martinb,"|vacation.pl"`

The leading backslash on the user name specifies that the e-mail should be copied directly to the user's mailbox, ignoring any expansion within either the aliases or the .forward file. All messages are also copied to the **vacation.pl** script. You will need to make sure that the **vacation.pl** script is in a standard location. Alternatively, you can specify the location of the script absolutely. If you send e-mail to it, you should get a canned response. If you create the .vacation.msg file, you should get that back instead.

If you want to emulate the functionality whereby a vacation message is sent only once to a sender, then you need to modify the script to create and update a DBM file. The keys of the DBM file should be the sender's cleaned e-mail address, and the value can either be left blank or you could increment the value to show how many times that person has e-mailed you. This latter option can be useful if you want to send a vacation message for every 20 e-mails you have received. Before what is currently line 30, check the database for the sender's e-mail address. If it exists, simply exit. If it doesn't exist, then set the vacation message and send it before adding their details to the database. If you use **tie** (see Chapter 4), the script should be quick to use and easy to maintain.

You may need to employ some form of file locking to ensure that addresses aren't added to the database simultaneously by two different invocations of the **vacation.pl** script. The easiest method is to create a temporary file of a fixed name; if it exists, then another script will pause and try again before performing its own update. Make sure you set the pause value to something suitable: if it's too long, the scripts may be waiting around just long enough for another script to open, update, and close the database. If the pause is too short, your script will be forever testing the existence of the file if there are lots of messages being received simultaneously. In theory, the update should take less than a second, but on a busy system it may take longer.

This addition will also ensure that the script does not get into long conversations with mailing lists or mailer daemons. Imagine the situation where you receive an e-mail from a mailing list and the message is parsed by **vacation.pl**, which returns a message to the list. That message then gets rebroadcast to everybody on the mailing list, including yourself, so the script returns a message to the "I'm not here message," which gets rebroadcast, and so it goes on. By keeping a log within a DBM file of who you have already sent to, only one e-mail message will be sent back to the mailing list—even if it receives another message.

mailbot.pl

Creating a Mailbot

Another way in which the **vacation.pl** program can be used is to automatically send a file back to a specified e-mail address. This can be useful if you want to supply information automatically to people via e-mail: they send an e-mail to an address, and the system automatically responds with the information they requested.

The only problem with using **vacation.pl** this way is that you must set up individual e-mail accounts and users to supply more than one document back to the sender. The solution to this problem is to expand the functionality of the **vacation.pl** script. Instead of ignoring the body contents, you parse them just like a list of instructions. Each line can request a file, a list of available files, help—in fact anything that you can program in Perl.

This type of application is called a *mailbot*, a mail-handling robot that performs jobs based on the contents of the mail message. Mailbots are in place all over the Internet, where they are used for tasks ranging from simple file delivery, as in this example, to the more complex jobs of updating mailing list databases and the seemingly impossible task of automatically processing the forms that organizations like InterNIC use to manage their databases. The biggest advantage with this method is that requests can be queued, which may be advantageous if you have a busy or overloaded Web server.

```perl
1    #!/usr/local/bin/perl5
2
3    use SMTPwrap;
4
5    my %mailheader;
6    my $mailbotaddress = "mailbot\@foo.bar";
7
8    close(STDERR);
9    close(STDOUT);
10
11   my %commandlist = (
12                       'send'  => 'send_file',
13                       'list'  => 'send_list',
14                       'help'  => 'send_help',
15                       );
16
17   chdir("/users/martinb/sub/mail");
18
19   my $state=1;
20
21   while(<STDIN>)
22   {
23       chomp;
24       if (length($_) eq 0)
25       {
26           $state=0;
27           next;
28       }
29       if ($state)
30       {
31           if ( m/^From\s/)
32           {
33               next;
34           }
35           elsif ( m/(^[\w\-\.]+):\s*(.*\S)\s*$/)
36           {
37               $keyword = $1;
38               $value = $2;
```

```perl
39              $mailheader{$keyword} = $value;
40          }
41          else
42          {
43              $mailheader{$keyword} .= "\n" . $_;
44          }
45      }
46      else
47      {
48          my ($command, @opts) = split;
49          my $to = clean_address(return_address(\%mailheader));
50          next if /^\s*$/;
51          unless ($commandlist{lc($command)})
52          {
53              send_error($to,"Unknown command, $command.\n" .
54                          "Rest of Message ignored.\n",1);
55          }
56          my $function = $commandlist{lc($command)};
57          &$function($to,$opts[0]);
58      }
59 }
60 sub send_error
61 {
62      my ($to,$error,$fatal) = @_;
63      mail_a_message("Mailbot Error",$to,$mailbotaddress,$error);
64      exit(1) if $fatal;
65 }
66
67 sub send_list
68 {
69      my $to = shift;
70      send_file($to,"list");
71 }
72
73 sub send_help
74 {
75      my $to = shift;
76      send_file($to,"help");
77 }
78
79 sub send_file
80 {
81      my ($to,$filename) = @_;
```

```
82    $filename =~ s#^.*/##;
83    $filename =~ s/[^\w\.\-]//g;
84    send_error($to,"Cannot open $filename",0)
85        unless (open(D, "<$filename"));
86    my $message  = "Attached below is the file $filename\n";
87    $message .= "--------------------------------------\n\n";
88
89    $mailheader{subject} = "" unless $mailheader{subject};
90    {
91        local $/;
92        $message .= <D>;
93    }
94    close(D);
95    send_error($to,"Error: $SMTPwrap::error",0)
96        unless(mail_a_message("Mailbot Reply to job, " .
97                              "$mailheader{subject}",
98                              $to,$mailbotaddress,$message));
99  }
```

ANNOTATIONS

Our mailbot script uses the same principles as the **vacation.pl** script above, but it adds the dispatch system we saw in Chapter 5, where we invented our own communications protocol. The basic process is to read in the message, identify the sender so we know where to send the information back to, and then process the message body by parsing each line, and running the corresponding local function to service the request. The **mailbot.pl** script works in the same way as the **vacation.pl** script; we'll create an entry in either the .forward file or the alias database, and incoming e-mail for the user will be piped to the standard input of the script. We therefore need to incorporate the same security and safety measures as before.

Security is of paramount importance here—we are creating a script that allows users to request files from the machine. We must ensure that we don't allow the user to specify absolute filenames, or we risk providing unrestricted access to the machine—including the /etc/passwd file. If you are concerned, you may also want to change the start line so that taint checking is switched on. See Chapter 9 for more information on tainted Perl scripts.

```
1    #!/usr/local/bin/perl5
2
3    use SMTPwrap;
4
5    my %mailheader;
```

```
6    my $mailbotaddress = "mailbot\@foo.bar";
7
```

We only require the **SMTPwrap** module to send e-mail back to the user. We could use the **Smail.pm** package and **send_message** to send messages back, but using SMTP is more portable and efficient. The **%mailheader** hash (line 5) will store the mail header information. To save us from trying to extract and identify the address the incoming mail was sent to, we'll set the address in line 6.

```
8    close(STDERR);
9    close(STDOUT);
10
```

We close the standard error and standard output in lines 8 and 9.

```
11   my %commandlist = (
12                      'send'  => 'send_file',
13                      'list'  => 'send_list',
14                      'help'  => 'send_help',
15                      );
16
```

Lines 11 to 15 define the dispatch table. We support three basic commands, send, list, and help. These commands refer to three functions that send back the specified file, send back a list of files, and send back help on how to request files, respectively.

```
17   chdir("/users/martinb/sub/mail")||die "Can't chdir";
18
```

We change the directory on line 17, which is part of the security measures. I've changed the directory to the location of the file people will request. You'll probably want to change this name to something more practical. If you are really worried about security, you should also double-check that the **chdir** command works correctly.

```
19   my $state=1;
20
```

We are about to start the process of identifying the mail header and body. The **$state** variable will be set to true for the duration that we are within the mail header. The script performs different actions depending on our location within the message text (header and body).

```
21   while(<STDIN>)
22   {
23       chomp;
24       if (length($_) eq 0)
25       {
```

```
26          $state=0;
27          next;
28      }
```

We start reading in the message text on line 21. First we take off the end-of-line character(s) on line 23. The separation line between header and body is a single, empty line that we identify on line 24. This line switches the message processing state from true (within the header) to false (within the body) on line 26. Since there is no useful information on this line, we skip to the next input line on line 27.

```
29      if ($state)
30      {
31          if ( m/^From\s/)
32          {
33              next;
34          }
```

If we are currently processing the mail header, then we need to extract information from the message. Lines 31 to 34 skip the origination line if it exists—it contains no information of use to us.

```
35          elsif ( m/(^[\w\-\.]+):\s*(.*\S)\s*$/)
36          {
37              $keyword = $1;
38              $value = $2;
39              $mailheader{$keyword} = $value;
40          }
```

If there's no origination line, then we extract the field name and value from the header line. I've used a different regular expression here for the match, although the result should be mostly identical. Since we are interested in only two header entries, From and Subject, we can afford to be a little less picky about the header line format. We assign the name and values to the **%mailheader** hash on line 39.

```
41          else
42          {
43              $mailheader{$keyword} .= "\n" . $_;
44          }
45      }
```

If the regular expression on line 35 failed to match, then since we are still within the message header the line must be a continuation line, in which case, we append the line contents to the existing hash entry based on the value of the previous field name.

```
46      else
47      {
```

```
48      my ($command, @opts) = split;
49      my $to = clean_address(return_address(\%mailheader));
```

If we are not within the mail header, then we are within the message body, and
we need to service the commands that have been supplied. We split the command
and options from the source line on line 48. The mail address we'll be sending the
result to is extracted and cleaned on line 49.

```
50      next if /^\s*$/;
51      unless ($commandlist{lc($command)})
52      {
53          send_error($to,"Unknown command, $command.\n" .
54                          "Rest of Message ignored.\n",1);
55      }
56      my $function = $commandlist{lc($command)};
57      &$function($to,$opts[0]);
58      }
59  }
```

Line 50 skips the line if it is composed of just spaces. Line 51 ensures that the
specified command exists within the command dispatch table. If it doesn't, we call
the **send_error** function to send a failure message back to the sender on lines 52 and
53. Line 55 gets the function name from the command dispatch table, and then line
56 calls the function specifying the return address and first value from the argument
array. Note that we specify the function explicitly by specifying the ampersand
before the **$function** variable.

Because we don't exit after reading in one line, the script should process all the
commands for as long as the files that are requested exist. This makes the script more
flexible and more efficient than the single-request mechanisms available elsewhere.

```
60  sub send_error
61  {
62      my ($to,$error,$fatal) = @_;
63      mail_a_message("Mailbot Error",$to,$mailbotaddress,$error);
64      exit(1) if $fatal;
65  }
66
```

The **send_error** function makes a call to the **mail_a_message** function, with the
error information supplied as the arguments. We have the option to exit if the error
has been specified as being fatal. A true value will cause the script to exit on line 64.

```
67  sub send_list
68  {
69      my $to = shift;
70      send_file($to,"list");
```

```
71  }
72
```

The **list** command refers to the **send_list** function, which actually just calls the **send_file** function with a fixed filename of "list."

```
73  sub send_help
74  {
75      my $to = shift;
76      send_file($to,"help");
77  }
78
```

Similarly, the **send_help** function calls **send_file**, with a fixed filename of "help."

```
79  sub send_file
80  {
81      my ($to,$filename) = @_;
82      my ($rs) = ($/);
83      $filename =~ s#^.*/##;
```

The **send_file** function on line 79 checks the filename for any insecure characters, imports the specified file, and then composes an e-mail based on the contents to send back to the user. We extract the mail address and filename from the argument list on line 81. We'll be using the same default input separator trick as the **vacation.pl** script, so we record the current value on line 82.

Line 83 strips any preceding directory specification from the filename. You might also want to check for the pipe character (|) to prevent people from running programs via this script. Remember that this script could, potentially, send back any file requested by the sender, so we must make checks here to ensure that the file requests are legitimate.

```
84      send_error($to,"Cannot open $filename",0)
85          unless (open(D, "<$filename"));
```

We send a nonfatal error message to the user if the file they request does not exist. This type of error will allow the processing of the incoming message to continue, even if the file cannot be found. I personally can't stand systems where a missing file causes your whole job to be ignored!

```
86      my $message  = "Attached below is the file $filename\n";
87      $message .= "-------------------------------------\n\n";
88
```

Lines 86 and 87 specify the start of the message that will be sent back to the user.

```
89      $mailheader{subject} = "" unless $mailheader{subject};
```

Line 89 creates an empty subject line if the **%mailheader** hash, and therefore the original message, didn't define one.

```
90        {
91            local $/;
92            $message .= <D>;
93        }
94        close(D);
```

Line 90 defines a new anonymous code block, which means that the name space is different. On line 91 we localize the record separator variable, effectively setting it to empty, which means that line 92 imports the entire file into the **$message** variable.

```
95        send_error($to,"Error: $SMTPwrap::error",0)
96            unless(mail_a_message("Mailbot Reply to job, " .
97                                  "$mailheader{subject}",
98                                  $to,$mailbotaddress,$message));
99    }
```

Lines 95 to 98 then send the message, and therefore the requested file, back to the requester. If there was an error sending the e-mail, then we send the requester an e-mail detailing the error!

To use the script, the best method is to create a new entry in the alias database pointing to the **mailbot.pl** script:

```
mailbot:   "|/usr/local/etc/mailbot.pl"
```

Then all you need to do is create the help and list files and populate your directory with information files. If you want to expand on the available commands, add an entry to the dispatch table and add the corresponding function to the script. The possibilities are endless; you could use the same basic structure I've outlined here to manage a mailing list, provide status information (see **statclnt.pl** in Chapter 5), or provide files in the same way I've described here.

Whatever you use it for, remember that the security of your machine and your site relies on the security of the script, so make sure any requests that allow files to be accessed or applications to be executed are filtered and checked. Although I haven't specified it here, simply by switching on warnings and taint checking and by using the **use strict** pragma you can eliminate most of the common errors.

mailfilt.pl

Building a Mail Filter

So far we have looked at ways of automatically dealing with vacation messages and responding to requests for information files. Our next script uses a similar sequence, but this time we will use the script to filter incoming e-mail, automatically replying, forwarding, deleting, or filing mail as it reaches a recipient's mailbox.

There are many e-mail filtering programs available. For those of you who use MacOS or Windows, you will already be aware that many programs incorporate the technology. Under Unix, the process is slightly different, but applications such as procmail have for years provided mail-filtering capabilities to the Unix community.

My only complaint about all of the different systems available is that they insist on using their own programming languages to define the rules. This is fine for the average user, who perhaps doesn't want to learn how to program just to get the best out of his mail filter. For me, though, I have always found myself constricted by the lack of options and flexibility inherent in the mail filtering programs.

For this reason, I wrote the following script. It identifies the necessary information from the incoming mail message that we need to process the contents. Where it differs is that the programming language used to define the filtering rules is Perl. This means that I cannot only delete and forward the e-mail, I can also run a mailing list, all from within the same script and all within the confines of a single e-mail address.

```perl
1   #!/usr/local/bin/perl5
2
3   use SMTPwrap;
4
5   my (%mailheader,@message,@mailbody);
6   my ($filtscript);
7   my ($user) = $ENV{'USER'} || $ENV{'LOGNAME'} ||
8               getlogin || (getpwuid($>))[0];
9   my ($homedir) = (getpwnam($user))[7];
10
11  close(STDERR);
12  close(STDOUT);
13  my $state=1;
14
15  while(<STDIN>)
16  {
17      chomp;
18      push @message,$_;
19      if (length($_) eq 0)
20      {
21          $state=0;
22          next;
23      }
24      if ($state)
25      {
26          if ( m/^From\s/)
27          {
```

```
28            next;
29        }
30        elsif ( m/(^[\w\-\.]+):\s*(.*\S)\s*$/)
31        {
32            $keyword = lc($1);
33            $value = $2;
34            $mailheader{$keyword} = $value;
35        }
36        else
37        {
38            $mailheader{$keyword} .= "\n" . $_;
39        }
40    }
41    else
42    {
43        push @mailbody,$_;
44    }
45 }
46 close(STDIN);
47
48 $filtscript = read_parse_script("$homedir/.mailfilt.cfg");
49
50 eval $filtscript;
51
52 if ($@)
53 {
54     write_local_mail(join("\n",@message));
55     write_local_error($@);
56 }
57
58 sub read_parse_script
59 {
60     my($file) = @_;
61     my $permissions = (stat($file))[2];
62
63     unless ($permissions & 00600)
64     {
65         write_local_error("Bad permissions on config file $file");
66         return(undef);
67     }
68     unless(open(D,"<$file"))
69     {
70         write_local_error("Can't open config $file, $!");
```

```perl
 71            return(undef);
 72        }
 73        {
 74            local $/;
 75            $file=<D>;
 76        }
 77        close(D)
 78            || write_local_error("Can't close config $file, $!");
 79        $file;
 80    }
 81
 82    sub write_local_error
 83    {
 84        my ($error) = @_;
 85
 86        my $message  = "To: $user\n";
 87        $message .= "From: Mailfilter (local program) <$user>\n";
 88        $message .= "Subject: Mail Filter Error\n\n";
 89        $message .= "$error\n";
 90        write_local_mail($message);
 91    }
 92
 93    sub write_local_mail
 94    {
 95        my ($message) = @_;
 96        my ($sec,$min,$hour,$mday,$mon) = (localtime(time))[0-4];
 97        my $tempfile = "/tmp/ml.$user.$mday$mon$hour$min$sec.$$";
 98        open(T,">$tempfile") || die "Cant open temp file,$!";
 99        print T $message,"\n";
100        close(T);
101        system('/bin/rmail -d $user < $tempfile');
102        unlink("/tmp/ml.$$");
103    }
104
105    sub forward_mail
106    {
107        my ($to) = @_;
108        $mailheader{to} = $mailheader{'apparently-to'}
109                        unless $mailheader{to};
110        my $subject = $mailheader{subject} ?
111            "FWD: $mailheader{subject}" : "FWD: <no subject>";
112
113
```

```
114      unless(mail_a_message($subject,$to,
115                           clean_address($mailheader{to}),
116                           join("\n",@message)))
117      {
118          write_local_mail(join("\n",@message));
119          write_local_error("Forwarding mail, $SMTPwrap::error");
120      }
121  }
122
123  sub anonymous_forward
124  {
125      my ($toaddress) = @_;
126      my $message;
127      my @fields = qw(Date From Reply-To Organization
128                      X-Mailer Mime-Version Subject
129                      Content-Type Content-Transfer-Encoding);
130
131      foreach $field (@fields)
132      {
133          $message .= "$field: " . $mailheader{$field}
134                    . "\n" if defined($mailheader{$field});
135      }
136
137      $message .= "\n";
138      $message .= join("\n",@mailbody);
139      $message .= "\n";
140
141      unless(send_smtp($toaddress,$mailheader{from},$message))
142      {
143          write_local_mail(join("\n",@message));
144          write_local_error("Anonymous Forward, $SMTPwrap::error");
145      }
146  }
```

ANNOTATIONS

This script is almost identical to the **mailbot.pl** script in most respects. The trick is
that once the message text has been read in and split into a combination of the entire
message and the mail header, we import the rule file and parse it with an **eval**
statement within the Perl script.

```
1    #!/usr/local/bin/perl5
2
3    use SMTPwrap;
4
5    my (%mailheader,@message,@mailbody);
6    my ($filtscript);
7    my ($user) = $ENV{'USER'} || $ENV{'LOGNAME'} ||
8                 getlogin || (getpwuid($>))[0];
9    my ($homedir) = (getpwnam($user))[7];
10
```

The **%mailheader** hash will store the header fields and values. The **@message** array will be used to store the entire message, while the **@mailbody** will store only the body of the e-mail message. We need the entire message in case we want to write it out to the local mail file, or forward on the entire message, in its entirety, to a new e-mail address. The mail filter rules will be imported into the **$filtscript** scalar.

Lines 7 to 9 obtain the recipient's user ID and then home directory. We need to know the home directory because the rule file is stored there.

```
11   close(STDERR);
12   close(STDOUT);
13   my $state=1;
14
```

As before, we close the standard output and error file handles, and we set the message parsing state to 1, within the header.

```
15   while(<STDIN>)
16   {
17       chomp;
18       push @message,$_;
```

We start reading the message text on line 15; when the message is output by the MTA to a program, it sends the message to the standard input of the called program. We strip off the end-of-line character on line 17. The message line is first pushed onto the **@message** array—remember that this variable stores the entire message text.

```
19       if (length($_) eq 0)
20       {
21           $state=0;
22           next;
23       }
24       if ($state)
```

```
25          {
26              if ( m/^From\s/)
27              {
28                  next;
29              }
30              elsif ( m/(^[\w\-\.]+):\s*(.*\S)\s*$/)
31              {
32                  $keyword = lc($1);
33                  $value = $2;
34                  $mailheader{$keyword} = $value;
35              }
36              else
37              {
38                  $mailheader{$keyword} .= "\n" . $_;
39              }
40          }
```

Lines 19 to 40 are identical to the previous script. They identify the mail header fields and values, placing the information into the **%mailheader** hash.

```
41          else
42          {
43              push @mailbody,$_;
44          }
45  }
46  close(STDIN);
47
```

Once we reach line 42, instead of running commands based on the message body, we just put the line onto the **@mailbody** stack on line 43. To ensure we don't suddenly start reading the wrong thing later on in the script, we close the standard input on line 46.

```
48  $filtscript = read_parse_script("$homedir/.mailfilt.cfg");
49
```

We use the **read_parse_script** function to import the text of the mail filter rules into the **$filtscript** variable.

```
50  eval $filtscript;
51
```

We then execute the Perl script within the **$filtscript** variable using an **eval** statement. We have seen this function before. In essence, it allows you to parse and execute the Perl script contained within a script block or variable. In our previous examples, we have used it as a way to introduce a user-driven substitution on a filename (see Chapter 2: **lwrename.pl**, Larry Wall's Rename Script). In this instance we are again using it to process some user-supplied code; however, this time the code will use the variables containing the mail header, body, and entire message in combination with the functions we have defined in this script in order to process incoming e-mail.

By using **eval** we make the script infinitely configurable and expandable, so a user can use the script as supplied without any need for modification, and yet they can still program their mail handling rules in Perl.

```
52  if ($@)
53  {
54      write_local_mail(join("\n",@message));
55      write_local_error($@);
56  }
57
```

The result of the **eval** operation is stored in the **$@** variable. If the parsing failed for any reason, then we write the received mail message to the user's mailbox in line 55 via the **write_local_mail** function, and then we also add an error message using the same function. This is in effect the end of the script: the remainder of the script is devoted to the functions that support the mail parsing and initialization process.

```
58  sub read_parse_script
59  {
60      my($file) = @_;
61      my $permissions = (stat($file))[2];
62
63      unless ($permissions & 00600)
64      {
65          write_local_error("Bad permissions on config file $file");
66          return(undef);
67      }
```

The **read_parse_script** imports the specified file into a variable for processing by **eval**. We check that the permissions on the configuration script are read and write by the user only, to prevent the script from executing commands from a file that may be available to everybody to use. This small security feature is very effective.

```
68      unless(open(D,"<$file"))
69      {
70          write_local_error("Can't open config $file, $!");
71          return(undef);
72      }
73      {
74          local $/;
75          $file=<D>;
```

```
76          }
77          close(D)
78              || write_local_error("Can't close config $file, $!");
79          $file;
80      }
81
```

We open the input file, then import the entire file in the **$file** variable on line 75 by defining a localized (undefined) input record separator. Note that we return an undefined value if the import failed or the file could not be read. We don't return an undefined value if the **close** function failed, since this is a nonfatal error. Incidentally, if there is a failure and **undef** is returned, then the **eval** function will fail and will be trapped by line 52.

```
82      sub write_local_error
83      {
84          my ($error) = @_;
85
86          my $message  = "To: $user\n";
87          $message .= "From: Mailfilter (local program) <$user>\n";
88          $message .= "Subject: Mail Filter Error\n\n";
89          $message .= "$error\n";
90          write_local_mail($message);
91      }
92
```

The **write_local_error** function on line 82 formulates an error message from the mail filter program to the user's mailbox. In essence, all it does is create a new message body based on the error message supplied, before calling the **write_local_mail** function.

```
93      sub write_local_mail
94      {
95          my ($message) = @_;
96          my ($sec,$min,$hour,$mday,$mon) = (localtime(time))[0-4];
97          my $tempfile = "/tmp/ml.$user.$mday$mon$hour$min$sec.$$";
98          open(T,">$tempfile") || die "Cant open temp file,$!";
99          print T $message,"\n";
100         close(T);
101         system('/bin/rmail -d $user < $tempfile');
102         unlink("/tmp/ml.$$");
103     }
```

There are a number of ways in which you can append an e-mail message to a user's mailbox. The most obvious is just to open the mailbox, append the mail message, and then close it again. However, this method is unfriendly and fails to follow the sort of discipline required when writing to what is effectively a shared mail file. Instead, the solution is to use the rmail program, which you can find (in one form or another) on all Unix systems, and it's the program used by sendmail and other mail transfer agents to append incoming e-mail to a user mailbox. You specify the user to receive the mail message, and then text of the message is imported by the application from the standard input.

In our function, we write the mail message out to a file first, and then call the rmail program with a redirection from the temporary file we just created. I've found this sequence to be more reliable than writing directly to the standard input of the rmail application. Note that the filename we use is based on a fixed string and the user name and the current date and time. This is to protect us from entering "race" conditions where multiple instances of the same script try to open, read, write, and close the same filename.

If we are unable to create the temporary file, then we **die** on line 98. Remember that we have closed standard error, so the message won't be printed. If you find you are having problems, you might want to comment out line 11 until you have identified the error.

```
105  sub forward_mail
106  {
107      my ($to) = @_;
108      $mailheader{to} = $mailheader{'apparently-to'}
109                        unless $mailheader{to};
110      my $subject = $mailheader{subject} ?
111          "FWD: $mailheader{subject}" : "FWD: <no subject>";
112
113
```

The **forward_mail** function allows us to forward a mail message onto a new recipient. It forwards the entire message, re-specifying the recipient and subject. We set the original recipient to match the value of the Apparently-To field if the To field has not been set. The new subject field, with the FWD string preceding the original contents, is set on line 110.

```
114      unless(mail_a_message($subject,$to,
115                            clean_address($mailheader{to}),
116                            join("\n",@message)))
117      {
118          write_local_mail(join("\n",@message));
119          write_local_error("Forwarding mail, $SMTPwrap::error");
120      }
121  }
122
```

The actual message is sent on lines 114 to 116. If the process caused an error, we write a copy of the message to the local mailbox coupled with an error message.

```
123  sub anonymous_forward
124  {
125      my ($toaddress) = @_;
126      my $message;
127      my @fields = qw(Date From Reply-To Organization
128                      X-Mailer Mime-Version Subject
129                      Content-Type Content-Transfer-Encoding);
130
```

The previous **forward_mail** function forwarded the mail using the original recipient's address as the new sender. The **anonymous_forward** function sends the message to a new recipient as if it had been directly sent from the original sender. This requires a slightly different method. Because we are hiding the original message header contents, we need to select fields from the message header, enclosing them in the new message and then appending the original message body onto the new message. The list of fields specified on lines 127 to 129 is by no means exhaustive, but it should be adequate enough to forward most messages without losing any vital information.

```
131      foreach $field (@fields)
132      {
133          $message .= "$field: " . $mailheader{$field}
134                      . "\n" if defined($mailheader{$field});
135      }
136
```

Lines 131 to 135 set the message header information, using the mail header fields specified earlier. Note that we check on line 134 that the original message contains the field before we include it in the new message.

```
137      $message .= "\n";
138      $message .= join("\n",@mailbody);
139      $message .= "\n";
140
```

Line 137 inserts the blank separation line before we incorporate the message body with a **join**, using new-line characters on line 138. Just to make sure the message is finished off properly, we append a new-line character on line 139.

```
141      unless(send_smtp($toaddress,$mailheader{from},$message))
142      {
143          write_local_mail(join("\n",@message));
144          write_local_error("Anonymous Forward, $SMTPwrap::error");
145      }
146  }
```

Because we are sending a special e-mail with predefined fields from elsewhere, we cannot use the **mail_a_message** function. Instead, we use the **send_smtp** function directly. Again, a failure to send the message is handled by recording the message in the user's mailbox, coupled with an error message describing the problem.

To use the script, you need to write some Perl that identifies the message contents before either writing the message to the local mail file or forwarding it elsewhere. You also need to specify the script as the mail handler within your .mailfilt.cfg file:

```
"|/usr/local/bin/mailfilt.pl"
```

If you specify nothing else, or if you don't want your mail to be filtered, then you must at least specify that a message be written to your mailbox; otherwise all incoming mail will be deleted:

```
write_local_mail(join("\n",@message));
```

If you want to specify an option, you can just use standard Perl. For example, to forward all mail with a subject of "Win," you would put the following line into your mail filter configuration file:

```
forward_mail('mc@foo.bar') if ($mailheader{subject} eq 'Win');
```

Of course, because the mail filtering rules are based on Perl, you can put any Perl code into the mail filter configuration. This doesn't restrict you to a list of available options when an e-mail is received. You could use this script to automatically print e-mail when it arrives, or even to automatically forward failure warnings on your network to your home e-mail address when you receive e-mail outside of normal working hours. The possibilities are, quite literally, limitless.

mailq.pl

Using a Sendmail Queue Summary

Within Unix there is a command that displays the queue for the sendmail program. The queue lists waiting messages on a message-by-message basis, showing the date and time an e-mail was sent, as well as the sender and recipient e-mail addresses. When dealing with large-volume e-mail servers, such as those used by ISPs and other large organizations, the output can be very long, and it displays a lot of data that you have to study before you can distill any useful information. For example, here is the sample output from the mailq program on my Solaris machine:

```
% mailq
Mail Queue (3 requests)
--QID--    --Size-- ----Q-Time----- ------------Sender/Recipient-----------
AA00208*   7         Sun Aug  9 15:3 martinb
                                        johann@martinb
AA00214    4         Sun Aug  9 15:3 martinb
                     (Deferred: Connection refused by atuin)
                                        martinb@atuin
AA00202    7         Sun Aug  9 15:3 martinb
                     (Deferred: Connection refused by insentient)
                                        martinb@atuin
                                        johnb@insentient
```

The output shows two messages, both of which are destined for the machine "atuin," and one that is also destined for "insentient." Now imagine a server that handles thousands of messages a day. At an ISP, many of the dial-up customers would have messages waiting in the sendmail queue, so the eventual output could be thousands of lines long.

If you are trying to find out why a particular site or machine is not receiving e-mail, it could take a lot of reading to find out why the service is broken. Furthermore, the mailq output gives us information we don't really need. For example, the queue ID is not useful information; it's just a reference number to a message that can't be sent. A more useful report would show the number of messages destined for a host or domain and the reason why the message(s) could not be sent. This data would give an immediate overview of why specific hosts or domains are not receiving their e-mail—and the **mailq.pl** script attempts to create such a summary.

PROGRAMMER'S NOTE   *This script, which I wrote some time ago, is used by a number of ISPs as a replacement for the* **mailq** *program.*

```perl
1    #!/usr/local/bin/perl5
2
3    my $queuelen = 0;
4    my (@recipient,$error,$time);
5    my (%rec,%recerr,%rectime);
6    die "Can't access queue, need root access" if ($>);
7
8    foreach my $file (glob("/usr/spool/mqueue/qf*"))
9    {
10       next unless(open(MSG,"<$file"));
11
12       while(<MSG>)
13       {
14           chomp;
15           if (m/^M(.*)/)
16           {
17               $error = $1;
18           }
19           elsif (m/^R(.*)/)
20           {
21               push @recipient,$1;
22           }
23           elsif (m/^T(.*)/)
24           {
25               $time = $1;
```

```
26              }
27          }
28      close(MSG);
29      $queuelen++;
30
31      foreach my $recipient (@recipient)
32      {
33          $recipient = (split /@/,$recipient)[1];
34          $rec{$recipient}++;
35          $recerr{$recipient} = $error;
36          $rectime{$recipient} = 0 unless ($rectime{$recipient});
37          $rectime{$recipient} = time-$time
38              if ((time-$time)>=$rectime{$recipient});
39      }
40      @recipient = ();
41  }
42
43  printf("%-20s %5s %5s %s\n",'Domain','Qty','HrsQd','Error');
44
45  foreach my $recipient
46      (sort { $rec{$b} <=> $rec{$a}; } keys %rec)
47  {
48      my $hours = ($rectime{$recipient}/ (60*60));
49      printf("%-20s %5d %5d %s\n",$recipient,$rec{$recipient},
50                                  $hours,$recerr{$recipient});
51  }
52  print "$queuelen messages in total\n";
```

ANNOTATIONS

The mail queue on a Unix machine is generally held within a directory called /usr/spool/mqueue. For each message there are at least two files. One, starting with "qf," contains the message sender, recipient, and other header information; the other, starting with "df," contains the message body. The individual files are not available to be read by anybody but the systems administrator (root), to prevent other users from examining other people's e-mail.

In nearly all implementations, the mailq program is just a renamed version of the sendmail application. When executed, sendmail checks the name used to invoke it and performs different functions based on the invocation name. The same trick is used with the newaliases program we discussed in Chapter 4 when we looked at DBM files. The sendmail program has the **setuid** permission bit set, so that the application executes as root, giving sendmail unrestricted access to the mail queue files.

We could import the output of the mailq program, but this would involve a significant amount of processing, albeit in memory, before we achieved our goal. Instead, this script opens and reads in the qf files directly, identifying the individual elements. In order to use this script, you must either run it as root (the best option) or set the permissions of the script to the same **setuid** permissions. We use the same trick as before: hashes will be used to store the summary information using the same key for each element, and once all the queued message files have been processed, the hashes will be sorted and printed out.

```perl
1   #!/usr/local/bin/perl5
2
3   my $queuelen = 0;
4   my (@recipient,$error,$time);
5   my (%rec,%recerr,%rectime);
```

This script doesn't require any external modules. The script uses the basic ability of Perl to open files and process text to produce the report. Line 2 defines the variable that will be used to contain the number of messages in the mail queue. We initialize it to zero so that the reporting later on in the script works when we check the number of parsed messages. Line 3 defines the variables we will use to store the summary information.

```perl
6   die "Can't access queue, need root access" if ($>);
7
8   foreach my $file (glob("/usr/spool/mqueue/qf*"))
9   {
```

On line 6 we use the special variable $>, which contains the effective user ID of the executor of the script. The user ID is an integer, so unless the effective user ID is zero, that of root, the test will return true and **die** with an appropriate error. We use the **glob** function in line 8 to get a list of the available queue files. Under Solaris (used here) and most other System V–based Unix variants, the directory should be the same. If your queue is not in this directory, then check your manual page on sendmail, which should tell you the real location.

```perl
10      next unless(open(MSG,"<$file"));
11
```

Because of the speed and method in which sendmail processes the queue, it's quite possible that a file returned by **glob** on line 8 may have already been processed by the time we try to open it and summarize the details. Therefore, if we can't open the file, we just skip the rest of the loop and go on to process the next file.

```perl
12      while(<MSG>)
13      {
14          chomp;
```

```
15          if (m/^M(.*)/)
16          {
17              $error = $1;
18          }
19          elsif (m/^R(.*)/)
20          {
21              push @recipient,$1;
22          }
23          elsif (m/^T(.*)/)
24          {
25              $time = $1;
26          }
27      }
```

If we take a look at one of the queue files from the sample mailq output above, we can see that each line starts with a single letter that denotes the contents of the line:

```
P46098
T902065368
DdfAA00556
L10,2,0
MDeferred: Connection refused by atuin
Smartinb
Rmartinb@atuin
H?P?return-path: <martinb>
Hreceived: by whoever.com (5.x/SMI-SVR4)
        id AA00556; Sun, 2 Aug 1998 14:42:48 +0100
H?D?date: Sun, 2 Aug 1998 14:42:48 +0100
H?F?From: martinb (Martin C Brown)
H?x?full-name: Martin C Brown
H?M?message-id: <9808021342.AA00556@whoever.com>
Hcontent-type: text
Hcontent-length: 11
Happarently-to: martinb@atuin
```

All lines beginning with "H" are the lines used to construct header lines within the e-mail message. Lines with first letters other than "H" contain queue information that will be used only by the local sendmail or other MTA application. The lines we are interested in start with "T," "R," and "M." The "T" lines denotes the time the message was originally placed in the queue. The time is stored as the number of seconds from the epoch, the standard time format used internally by Unix, and something that can be processed directly by Perl. "R" lines specify the recipients; there can be more than one "R" line in a queue file. The error message denoting why the message is held in the queue is contained in lines beginning with "M." Lines 15 to 26 extract this information for us into some temporary variables while we are reading the file contents. Because the message may be destined for multiple recipients, we push the recipient information onto the **@recipient** stack.

```
28     close(MSG);
29     $queuelen++;
30
```

If we've made it this far, we must have identified a queue mail message, so we increment the total messages counter.

```
31     foreach my $recipient (@recipient)
32     {
33         $recipient = (split /@/,$recipient)[1];
34         $rec{$recipient}++;
35         $recerr{$recipient} = $error;
36         $rectime{$recipient} = 0 unless ($rectime{$recipient});
37         $rectime{$recipient} = time-$time
38             if ((time-$time)>=$rectime{$recipient});
39     }
```

Line 31 sets up a loop to process through each of the recipients. The recipient's domain is the key on which we store the summary information, and the domain is extracted on line 33 by taking the second element of the array returned by splitting an e-mail address by @. If none is specified, then the key will be blank, which is still something that can be keyed within a hash.

Line 34 increments the message counter for the domain; the counter will be used to report the number of messages. The error recorded for the message is placed into a hash on line 35. We could set this up as an array, rather than a scalar, hash. Then we could record the different error messages recorded. However, this method is relatively pointless for this exercise. It is unlikely that a single domain will produce more than one type of error.

Lines 36 initializes the time the message was originally queued to zero if the domain does not already have a time set. We need to set the value to zero because on line 37 we extract the longest time that a domain has had a message waiting. We use the value of the current time (stored in the special variable **time**) minus the time stored in the queue file. This calculation gives us the difference between the two, which we can then report on using **localtime**.

```
40     @recipient = ();
41   }
42
```

Finally, at the end of reading in and recording the information from one queue file, we empty the **@recipient** array by assigning a new, empty array list to it. The end of the queue file processing is line 41.

```
43    printf("%-20s %5s %5s %s\n",'Domain','Qty','HrsQd','Error');
44
45    foreach my $recipient
46        (sort { $rec{$b} <=> $rec{$a}; } keys %rec)
47    {
48        my $hours = ($rectime{$recipient}/ (60*60));
49        printf("%-20s %5d %5d %s\n",$recipient,$rec{$recipient},
50                                    $hours,$recerr{$recipient});
51    }
52    print "$queuelen messages in total\n";
```

Lines 43 to 53 print out the summary information. We start by printing a header on line 43. We then work through a sorted list of domain keys (lines 45 and 46), printing out the time (extracted on lines 48 with a simple calculation, and converted to hours in line 49) before printing out the formatted report in lines 50 and 51. Finally, we print out the total number of messages in the queue on line 53.

The output from script, using the same data used to demonstrate the mailq command, looks like this:

```
% mailq.pl
Domain               Qty HrsQd Error
atuin                  2     1 Deferred: Connection refused by atuin
insentient             1     1 Deferred: Connection refused by insentient
martinb                1     1 Deferred: Connection refused by insentient
3 messages in total
```

The output is much more useful for detecting faults and monitoring problems. It shows the problem exhibited with each host, and we know the number of messages this problem affects. For an ISP or busy mail host, this summary provides invaluable information to the postmaster.

splitml.pl

Creating an E-mail Splitter

The mail filtering script we saw earlier (**mailfilt.pl**) does a very good and very flexible job of extracting and sorting incoming mail on the fly into other folders, forwarding messages on to other hosts or simply ignoring a message, thereby ensuring it never reaches the human recipient.

Sometimes, though, what we want to do is simply split a Unix mail file into individual files, where each file contains one or more messages. The **splitml.pl** script does exactly this. In its supplied form, it reads in the user's current mailbox file and splits the messages up by subject and an arbitrary number to ensure that subsequent messages with the same subject don't overwrite each other. We'll look at alternatives to this method as we work through the script.

```perl
1   #!/usr/local/bin/perl5
2
3   my (%mailheader,@maillist);
4   my ($user) = $ENV{'USER'} || $ENV{'LOGNAME'} ||
5               getlogin || (getpwuid($>))[0];
6   my ($maildir) = "/usr/mail";
7
8   open(MAIL,"<$maildir/$user")
9       || die "Couldn't open mail file (no mail?)";
10
11  my $state = 1;
12
13  while(<MAIL>)
14  {
15      chomp;
16      $state = 0 if (length($_) eq 0);
17      if (($_ =~ m/^From\s/) && ($. >1))
18      {
19          file_message($mailheader{subject},@maillist);
20          undef (@maillist);
21          undef (%mailheader);
22      }
23      elsif (( m/(^[\w\-\.]+):\s*(.*\S)\s*$/) && $state)
24      {
25          my ($keyword,$value) = ($1,$2);
26          $mailheader{lc($keyword)} = $value
27              if (defined($keyword) && defined($value));
28      }
29      push @maillist,$_;
30  }
31  close(MAIL);
32
33  file_message($mailheader{subject},@maillist) if (@maillist);
34
35  sub file_message
36  {
37      my ($basename,@lines) = @_;
38      $basename =~ tr:/:_:;
39      $basename = $basename || "None";
40      my ($subid,$basefile) = (1,$basename);
41      while (-e $basefile)
42      {
43          $basefile = sprintf("%s.%03d",$basename,$subid++);
```

```
44        }
45
46        $, = $/;
47        open(MSG,">$basefile")
48            || die "Couldn't write message to $basefile,$!";
49        print MSG @lines;
50        close(MSG) || die "Couldn't close message $basefile,$!";
51    }
```

ANNOTATIONS

This script uses a simpler version of the mail parsing routine we have already used. Since we are not interested in the contents of the message or in logically splitting a message into header and body parts within Perl, we can skip much of the "intelligence" we used previously, making for a much simpler, leaner, and quicker parser. The rest of the script uses techniques we have already seen to create a file and write out of contents of variables—albeit with a slightly different twist.

```
1     #!/usr/local/bin/perl5
2
3     my (%mailheader,@maillist);
4     my ($user) = $ENV{'USER'} || $ENV{'LOGNAME'} ||
5                  getlogin || (getpwuid($>))[0];
6     my ($maildir) = "/usr/mail";
7
```

There are two internal sources of information used by the script. The **%mailheader** hash stores the mail header information; we need this information so we can pick a field to use as a key for the split filenames. The **@maillist** array stores the lines for each message. Lines 4 to 6 set the user ID and mail directory. The user's name is extracted by selecting, in order, the value of the **USER** and **LOGNAME** environment variables and the result from **getlogin** and finally by extracting the first element of the password entry based on the user's effective user ID. You may need to change the mail directory location, although the one I've specified here should work with most Unix flavors.

```
8     open(MAIL,"<$maildir/$user")
9         || die "Couldn't open mail file (no mail?)";
10
```

We open the user's mail file, based on the user and mail directory information discovered on lines 4 to 6. You may want to change this to something like
```
open(MAIL,"<$ARGV[0]")
```

to use a file specified on the command line.

```
11  my $state = 1;
12
13  while(<MAIL>)
14  {
15      chomp;
16      $state = 0 if (length($_) eq 0);
17      if (($_ =~ m/^From\s/) && ($. >1))
18      {
19          file_message($mailheader{subject},@maillist);
20          undef (@maillist);
21          undef (%mailheader);
22      }
```

We set the message parsing state on line 11. We chop off the end-of-line character on line 15. Line 16 flips the state from being within the header to being within the body. Line 17 then checks for the existence of a standard From separation line. Remember that different mailers use a different format: some ignore and some specify the locality and time zone, and some use four-digit years.

```
From martinb Sat Aug 22 11:53 BST 1998
```

The regular expression string we could use would be

```
m/^From\s\S+\s\S+\s\S+\d{2}\s\d{2}:\d{2}\s\S\S{2}\s\d{4}$/
```

To save us all the agony of this, we can in fact just check for From at the beginning of a line. The MTA will insert > at the start of any lines that begin with From, which makes the regular expression and processing significantly simpler.

We couple this regular expression check with a line number check. The $. special variable refers to the number of lines read in from the current file. Because this check causes the last mail message to be written out to disk, running it on the first line will produce an empty file without a reference to use as a name. If a message boundary had been found, then we call the **file_message** function to write the entire message out to disk. We only supply two details; the first argument specifies the value to be used as the basis for the filename; the second argument is the array that contains the entire message text. I've used the message subject in this example, and we'll see later how this is used as the basis for a filename. You may want to use a static string, or even the sender of the message, as the file base.

To ensure that we start with a clean slate for the next e-mail message, we undefine the message text array on line 20 and the mail header hash on line 21.

```
23      elsif (( m/(^[\w\-\.]+):\s*(.*\S)\s*$/) && $state)
24      {
25          my ($keyword,$value) = ($1,$2);
26          $mailheader{lc($keyword)} = $value
```

```
27              if (defined($keyword) && defined($value));
28          }
```

Line 23 checks for a valid header line, if we are specified as being within the header by the **$state** variable. The regular expression extracts a field name composed of multiple alphanumeric strings, hyphens, and periods. The field value is simply all the text between leading and trailing spaces. Line 25 assigns the field value to the field name within the **%mailheader** hash, but it does so only if both a keyword and value could be extracted from the source line. Not all lines (namely those of the message body) will contain a colon. Without this test, we risk putting undefined values into hash keys, which is both wasteful of space and also dangerous. The script could extract a blank field from a message just because the line contains a colon, which this could, for example, overwrite the value of the field we want to use as the message filename.

```
29      push @maillist,$_;
30  }
31  close(MAIL);
32
33  file_message($mailheader{subject},@maillist) if (@maillist);
34
```

Line 29 puts the message line to the message text array. This is done whether we are in the message body or header—we want to record the entire message for writing to the file. Once the input file has finished on line 30, we close the file on line 31 and then run the **file_message** function again if there are any lines within **@maillist** array. In theory, the **@maillist** array will contain a message at this point, whatever has happened. The **undef** in line 20 only lasts until line 29. There is no way the previous call to **file_message** will be called unless a new message boundary has been identified.

```
35  sub file_message
36  {
37      my ($basename,@lines) = @_;
38      $basename = tr:/:_:;
39      $basename = $basename || "None";
40      my ($subid,$basefile) = (1,$basename);
41      while (-e $basefile)
42      {
43          $basefile = sprintf("%s.%03d",$basename,$subid++);
44      }
45
```

The **file_message** function uses the message text array to write a message out to a file based on the base name supplied as the first argument. Line 38 uses the **tr** (transform) function to convert any forward slashes into underscores, which helps eliminate problems where the subject field contains forward slashes that would otherwise separate the elements of a path name.

On line 39 we make sure a base name has actually been specified by assigning a default value to **$basename** unless it already has a valid value. Note, again, that this sequence would not allow a false value to be passed. A base name of zero is false, so the default value will be used even if the zero is what the user intended.

Line 40 sets up the sequence ID and base filename, using initial values of 1 and the base name. We check on line 43 if the base file already exists. If it does then we re-specify it using **sprintf** to generate a new base filename based on the base name and an incremented version of the sequence ID. This quick method for creating a file based on a particular name avoids overwriting an existing file. For example, if a base name of "message" was specified and it already existed, then lines 38 to 41 would try "message.001." If that existed, too, then it would try "message.002," and so on.

If you wanted to use a different format for the filenames, you would need to change this section. For example, if you wanted to use a sequential number, then you could change lines 41 to 44 to

```
my $subid = 1;
$basefile = sprintf("%03d",$subid++) while (-e $basefile);
```

You would also need to remove the lines referring to the **basename** variable and change the calls earlier in this script.

```
46      $, = $/;
47      open(MSG,">$basefile")
48          || die "Couldn't write message to $basefile,$!";
49      print MSG @lines;
50      close(MSG) || die "Couldn't close message $basefile,$!";
51  }
```

To save us working through the array and printing each element as an individual element, we'll change the default separator for array elements to a new-line character, and then print the entire array. This separator will have the same effect, but it is quicker and shorter. The default output field separator is specified by the special **$,** variable. Remember that the individual elements of our message text array are the lines of the original message. Therefore, we need to set the output separator to a new-line character. In fact, to make sure we get the same result, we set the output separator to match the input separator in line 46.

Line 47 then opens the file, line 49 prints the message text, and then we close the file on line 50. On both the open and close, we **die** if the process failed for any reason, remembering to specify the filename in the error message—since it is automatically generated, it may not be immediately apparent what the problem is.

As another alternative, you might want to use the base name and put all the messages with the same base name into a single file. In this case, you could remove lines 40 to 44 entirely, and then change line 47 to

```
open(MSG,"+>$basename") || die "Couldn't write message $basefile,$!";
```
This sets the open mode to append to the existing file.

To use it, just call the script on the command line:
```
$ splitml.pl
$ ls
None          None.001    None.002
```
This result shows the output after splitting a mailbox with e-mail messages that didn't contain a subject line so the default was used.

mailsumm.pl

Compiling a Quick Mailbox Summary

In Chapter 5, we looked at a script, **popbiff.pl**, that showed a summary of the mail stored on a POP server. The script was quite straightforward because the **Net::POP** module automatically handed back the top few lines from each message. The script was also made easier because the server automatically provided individual messages back to the **Net::POP** module.

With this new script, we are going to perform the same basic operation, only this time we're going to read in the contents of the user's local mail file on a Unix server. The script could equally be used to summarize the contents of any mail file.

```
1    #!/usr/local/bin/perl5
2
3    use SMTPwrap;
4
5    my (%mailheader,@maillist);
6    my ($user) = $ENV{'USER'} || $ENV{'LOGNAME'} ||
7                 getlogin || (getpwuid($>))[0];
8    my ($maildir) = "/usr/mail";
9    my ($state) = 1;
10
11   open(MAIL,"<$maildir/$user")
12       || die "Couldn't open mail file (no mail?)";
13
14   while(<MAIL>)
15   {
16       chomp;
17       $state=0 if (length($_)==0);
18
19       if (($_ =~ m/^From\s/) &&
20           ($. >1))
21       {
22           push(@maillist,
```

```
23              [@mailheader{qw/from subject content-length/}]);
24          $state=1;
25          undef %mailheader;
26      }
27      if ($state)
28      {
29          if ( m/^From\s/)
30          {
31              next;
32          }
33          elsif ( m/(^[a-zA-Z0-9-._]+):\s*(.*)$/)
34          {
35              $keyword = $1;
36              $value = $2;
37              $mailheader{lc($keyword)} = $value;
38          }
39          else
40          {
41              $mailheader{lc($keyword)} .= "\n" . $_;
42          }
43      }
44  }
45
46  close(MAIL);
47
48  push @maillist, [@mailheader{qw/from subject content-length/}]
49      if (defined($mailheader{from}) &&
50          defined($mailheader{subject}));
51  if (@maillist)
52  {
53      printf "%3s  %-30s  %-39s  %6s\n",'ID','From',
54                                        'Subject','Size';
55      for(my $i=0;$i<@maillist;$i++)
56      {
57          print_message_summary($i + 1,@{$maillist[$i]});
58      }
59  }
60  else
61  {
62      print "No mail at this time\n";
63  }
64
```

```
65   sub print_message_summary
66   {
67       my ($msgno,$from,$subject,$length) = @_;
68
69       $subject = "<none>" unless ($subject);
70       $subject = substr($subject,0,39);
71       $from    = substr(clean_address($from),0,30);
72       printf("%3d  %-30s  %-39s  %6d\n",
73               $msgno,$from,$subject,$length);
74   }
```

ANNOTATIONS

This script is an amalgamation of some of the techniques we have used in the previous scripts in this chapter. Essentially, we are identifying the header portions of the mail messages, placing selected fields from the header into an array that we then print, formatted, at the end of the script.

```
1    #!/usr/local/bin/perl5
2
3    use SMTPwrap;
4
5    my (%mailheader,@maillist);
6    my ($user) = $ENV{'USER'} || $ENV{'LOGNAME'} ||
7                    getlogin || (getpwuid($>))[0];
8    my ($maildir) = "/usr/mail";
9    my ($state) = 1;
10
```

The first part of the script is the same basic initialization process as the previous script. The **%mailheader** hash will hold the message header details temporarily, and we'll use the **@maillist** array to hold the summary information before printing. Lines 6 and 7 obtain the user's login, and line 8 sets the mail directory. The **$state** variable will be used to identify whether we are within the message header or the body.

```
11   open(MAIL,"<$maildir/$user")
12       || die "Couldn't open mail file (no mail?)";
13
14   while(<MAIL>)
15   {
16       chomp;
17       $state=0 if (length($_)==0);
18
```

We open the default user mail file based on the mail directory and user name we extracted earlier. Line 16 **chomps** off the end-of-line character(s). Line 17 identifies if the message contents have switched from the header section to the body—a single blank line, or one of zero length separates the two. This switch causes a change of state: if we were in the header, the state now defines that we have moved to the body. If we are already in the body, then it makes no difference.

```
19      if (($_ =~ m/^From\s/) &&
20          ($. >1))
21      {
22          push(@maillist,
23              [@mailheader{qw/from subject content-length/}]);
24          $state=1;
25          undef %mailheader;
26      }
```

Lines 19 and 20 perform the same test as the last script to identify the start of a new message. Note, again, that we ensure we are not already on the first line of the source file. Lines 22 and 23 push an anonymous array containing the sender's details, message subject, and the message size onto the **@maillist** array. The trick in line 23 returns, as an array, the elements referred to by the **qw** quoted words. This creates a list of lists, the main list being the message and the sublist being composed of the summary information. Because we have found the start of a new message, we switch the state back to 1 to signify we are back in the message header. We then undefine the **%mailheader** hash so that the next message will put fresh values into the keys. If we didn't do this, a message without a subject may inherit the subject from the previous message.

```
27      if ($state)
28      {
29          if ( m/^From\s/)
30          {
31              next;
32          }
33          elsif ( m/(^[a-zA-Z0-9-._]+):\s*(.*)$/)
34          {
35              $keyword = $1;
36              $value = $2;
37              $mailheader{lc($keyword)} = $value;
38          }
39          else
40          {
41              $mailheader{lc($keyword)} .= "\n" . $_;
```

```
42                }
43          }
44    }
45
```

Lines 27 to 45 identify the header information. Lines 29 to 32 skip over a From line without a colon; otherwise we will create an entry in the hash that is formed from the From line up to, and including, the hour of the time.

Line 33 matches against a field line from the message header. I've used a slightly different regular expression here, although the basic result is the same—the three values we need, From, Subject, and Content-Length. Line 37 puts the field value into the hash. The key is based on a lowercase version of the field name. Line 41 appends data to the current header field, accounting for fields that stretch over more than one physical line. This can be useful for subject and sender details; although the chance of multiline entries is remote, it is better to account for it than ignore it entirely.

```
46    close(MAIL);
47
```

By the time we reach line 46 we should have an array, **@maillist**, which contains the summary information we want to print out.

```
48    push @maillist, [@mailheader{qw/from subject content-length/}]
49        if (defined($mailheader{from}) &&
50            defined($mailheader{subject}));
51    if (@maillist)
52    {
```

We push the last message information on to the summary stack (line 48), provided the sender's information had been extracted (line 49 and 50). Line 51 checks that there are entries in the summary array; we want to avoid printing out a summary header if there is no information to report on.

```
53        printf "%3s  %-30s  %-39s  %6s\n",'ID','From',
54                                          'Subject','Size';
```

Lines 53 and 54 print out the header information for the message summary. This summary uses the same format that will be used to print out the message detail.

```
55        for(my $i=0;$i<@maillist;$i++)
56        {
57            print_message_summary($i + 1,@{$maillist[$i]});
58        }
59    }
```

We use a **for** loop in line 55 to work through the summary array. Remember that we have put three pieces of summary information into an anonymous array that is the value of the main array. Line 57 therefore passes the array returned by the anonymous reference to the **print_message_summary** function.

```
60   else
61   {
62       print "No mail at this time\n";
63   }
64
```

If there aren't any values in the array, then the script hasn't read any detail from the mail file. We report this on line 65.

```
65   sub print_message_summary
66   {
67       my ($msgno,$from,$subject,$length) = @_;
68
69       $subject = "<none>" unless ($subject);
70       $subject = substr($subject,0,39);
71       $from    = substr(clean_address($from),0,30);
72       printf("%3d  %-30s  %-39s  %6d\n",
73               $msgno,$from,$subject,$length);
74   }
```

Lines 68 to 77 print out an individual message summary, formatted into a columnar report. This format involves setting the subject, trimming the lengths to fit the screen width, and cleaning the field data before finally printing it out. We set a default subject, if none is already specified in line 72. Line 73 trims the subject down to a maximum of 39 characters, using the **substr** function. Line 74 sets the sender information. We've enclosed a call to the **clean_address** function from the **SMTPwrap** module into a call to **substr** to trim the sender data down to a maximum of 30 characters. Lines 75 and 76 print out the line using a fixed field–width format to the **printf** function.

If we run the script on the same collection of messages as we used for the previous script, we get this result:

```
$ mailsumm.pl
ID   From                 Subject            Size
 1   martinb              <none>                4
 2   martinb              <none>               14
```

Summary

There are two sides to e-mail within Perl: either we are sending it (or monitoring the status of the mail we have sent) or processing the contents of received e-mail. In this chapter, I've demonstrated a number of different methods for sending e-mail. The most practical and efficient of these methods is to use the **SMTPwrap** module to talk directly to a mail server. This method doesn't require us to call external programs, a technique that is both slow and unreliable if the platform we are using does not support a command-line mail interface. It is also platform independent—an important point since the MacOS doesn't support a standard mail sending program or even a command-line interface. Under NT, versions of sendmail are available, but generally they support limited sending ability, and even then they use the same method as the **SMTPwrap** module anyway. The real flexibility from using an SMTP server directly comes when you want to support more complex options, such as mailing lists and anonymous forwarding.

However, there are situations where the Perl you write does not have access to the **SMTPwrap** module, or where you are not allowed to communicate using network sockets directly from within the Perl script. In these situations, the only option available to you is to use the sendmail techniques I covered at the start of this chapter.

When processing incoming e-mail, the most complex process is identifying the message header and body. Once we have that information, though, the possibilities are endless, and scripts such as the **mailfilt.pl** filtering script demonstrate the effects that we can achieve once we have overcome the hurdle of parsing the message text.

## PART 3

World Wide Web

Creating and Managing HTML
Common Gateway Interface
CGI Security

Creating and Managing HTML

I t is more than likely that your first exposure to Perl was as a solution for creating and executing CGI (Common Gateway Interface) programs within a Web server. While obviously one of Perl's more common application areas, it is not necessarily a design feature. For this chapter, we will ignore the intricacies of dealing with CGI data and instead concentrate on the production and checking and manipulation of the HTML that exists on your Web server.

Despite what design agencies and professional Web authors tell you, HTML, which stands for Hypertext Markup Language, is not difficult to use and learn. What is difficult, however, is ensuring that the HTML you have generated does what you want and displays correctly. A lot of the complexity comes from the coding required to produce the format and layout of the HTML you are writing. A much smaller but perhaps more significant proportion comes from the semantics of the HTML itself.

I don't really want to get into the precise details on how HTML is formed—if you want more information on how to write good HTML refer to the www.w3c.org Website that gives full details, or visit your local bookstore. It is sufficient for our purposes that you understand that HTML uses *tags* to format and structure the document; for example, the HTML fragment

`<b>Hello World!</b>`

would produce a boldfaced "Hello World!" within a Web browser window. The tags are the <b> at the beginning of the text section and the </b> at the end. This format is used throughout HTML coding, so the fragment

`<i>Hello World!</i>`
`<u>This is a test message</u>`

would produce "Hello World!" in italics and "This is a test message" with an underline.

One very useful tag is <a>, which is short for "anchor" or "address." It denotes the hypertext links that allow you to jump from one HTML document to another. Another significant tag is <img…, which allows you to incorporate graphics into your pages. Unlike the other links we have discussed so far, there is no closing tag since we are simply inserting another element into the Web page.

While this has been a very quick introduction to HTML, it covers enough of the basics for us to look at ways of checking and verifying a single HTML page. If we "follow" and process the links and image references, we can also verify the content of an entire Web site.

We will look in this chapter at a simple method for checking the validity of an HTML page (**chkhtml.pl**), using the **HTMLQC.pm** module, also in this chapter. We'll then move on to checking entire Web sites, both locally with **chklinks.pl** and remotely with **chkrlink.pl**. These scripts use a personally developed, simple parsing system in the first instance and the more extensive parsing engine supported by the LWP library by Gisle Aas. Still dealing with HTML, we will then take a look at script I use to extract the fields and elements from an HTML form.

In the latter part of this chapter, we concentrate on mirroring and distributing sites. The **singmirr.pl** mirrors a single HTML document from a Web server, ensuring that the local copy is as up to date as the remote version. At the other end of the scale, the **sitemirr.pl** script can copy the entire HTML and graphics structure and files from a remote site. For the reverse option we'll look at **uplsite.pl**, which uses FTP and the libnet library from Graham Barr to upload a local site to a remote server.

The last script demonstrates how to generate static HTML pages using Perl. The **wwwlogs.pl** script generates a single page of HTML based on a file/directory structure, in this instance one used to store the processed and formatted HTML logs from a Web server. We will look at more complex examples of HTML generation in our next chapter, which covers the use of Perl as a CGI programming language.

HTMLQC.pm

HTML Quick Check Module

There are a number of different issues surrounding the validity of an HTML page. Without developing the same sort of parsing engine as used in a Web browser it's impossible to check everything. However, that said, there are things we can check very quickly and easily that will help highlight, if not completely fix, many of the common errors.

If you refer to the introduction of this chapter, you will note that some HTML tags come in pairs. A number of the common HTML errors that cause problems are caused by mismatched start and end tags. In order to check for complete pairs, we need to parse the HTML and search for these tags, keeping a record of which tag has been opened and when that tag was correctly closed. As an extra verification, we should also ensure that each tag has the correct start and end brackets (< >) around each tag name.

The **HTMLQC.pm** module supports a single function, **htmlqc**, which checks for start tags, end tags, and mismatched brackets. The result, if there was an error, is the list of tags that have not been closed, a list of close tags that have not been opened, and a list of tags that do not have an open or close bracket around them.

PROGRAMMER'S NOTE *Although I've used regex searches and matches in this and other scripts, it is not always the most reliable or efficient way to check the validity of HTML scripts. HTML is much more complex, and has far more nuances that affect the code operation. Furthermore, the term "correct" HTML is automatically a misnomer—different browsers interpret the same HTML in different ways and this can cause all kinds of problems.*

```
1    package HTMLQC;
2
3    use strict;
4    use vars qw/@ISA @EXPORT $error/;
```

```
5    require Exporter;
6    @ISA = 'Exporter';
7    @EXPORT = qw (htmlqc);
8    use SHTML;
9
10   my %tagpair = (
11                  'A',            1,
12            'ADDRESS',            1,
13                  'B',            1,
14        'BLOCKQUOTE',            1,
15                 'BQ',            1,
16             'CENTER',            1,
17               'CITE',            1,
18               'CODE',            1,
19                'DFN',            1,
20                'DIR',            1,
21                 'DL',            1,
22                 'EM',            1,
23                'FIG',            1,
24               'FONT',            1,
25               'FORM',            1,
26                 'H1',            1,
27                 'H2',            1,
28                 'H3',            1,
29                 'H4',            1,
30                 'H5',            1,
31                 'H6',            1,
32               'HEAD',            1,
33               'HTML',            1,
34                  'I',            1,
35                'KBD',            1,
36            'LISTING',            1,
37               'MATH',            1,
38               'MENU',            1,
39                 'OL',            1,
40                'PRE',            1,
41                  'S',            1,
42               'SAMP',            1,
43             'SELECT',            1,
44             'STRONG',            1,
45              'STYLE',            1,
46              'TABLE',            1,
47           'TEXTAREA',            1,
```

```
48              'TITLE',           1,
49                'TD',            1,
50                'TR',            1,
51                'TT',            1,
52                 'U',            1,
53                'UL',            1,
54               'VAR',            1,
55               'XMP',            1,
56         'BLOCKQUOTE',           1,
57  );
58
59  sub htmlqc
60  {
61      my ($html) = @_;
62      my $lineno = 0;
63
64      my %taghistory = ();
65      $html = striptohtml($html);
66
67      for $_ (split(/\n/,$html))
68      {
69          unless (anglematch($_))
70          {
71              $error .= "  Mismatched < and >, line: $_\n";
72          }
73          if (my ($starttag) = m#<\s*([^/\s]+)[^>]*>#)
74          {
75              $starttag =~ tr/a-z/A-Z/;
76              $taghistory{$starttag}++ if ($tagpair{$starttag});
77          }
78          elsif (my ($endtag) = m#</\s*([^\s]+)[^>]*>#)
79          {
80              $endtag =~ tr/a-z/A-Z/;
81              if ($tagpair{$endtag})
82              {
83                  if ($taghistory{$endtag})
84                  {
85                      $taghistory{$endtag}--;
86                  }
87                  else
88                  {
89                      $error .= "  Endtag </$endtag> mismatch\n";
90                  }
```

```
91                       }
92                   }
93               }
94           for my $tag (keys %taghistory)
95           {
96               $error .=
97                   "  Tag <$tag> has $taghistory{$tag} tags to close\n"
98                   if $taghistory{$tag};
99           }
100          $error ? 0 : 1;
101  }
102
103  sub anglematch
104  {
105      return 1 if (/<!--/ or /-->/);
106      return 0 if /<[^>]*</m;
107      return 0 if />[^<]*>/m;
108      return 0 if /<[^>]*$/m;
109      return 0 if /^[^<]*>/m;
110      1;
111  }
112
113  1;
```

ANNOTATIONS

The reference material for the script is contained within the **%tagpair** hash. This contains a list of the tag pairs—that is, those tags that require both a start and end tag to work correctly. The main function, **htmlqc**, transforms the text passed to it into a range of lines where each consists of a single HTML tag, using **striptohtml** function. This is then parsed by first checking that each tag has a start and end bracket. We then record the existence of an opening tag if it exists, using the **%tagpair** table as a reference. If we find an end tag, then we decrement the tag counter for the document. We report errors by a combination of too many end tags and by the recorded list of start tags with a value greater than zero.

```
1    package HTMLQC;
2
3    use strict;
4    use vars qw/@ISA @EXPORT $error/;
5    require Exporter;
6    @ISA = 'Exporter';
7    @EXPORT = qw (htmlqc);
```

```
8    use SHTML;
9
```

The package is called **HTMLQC**, and we set the name space on line 1. In deference to our previous modules, I've specifically used the **strict** pragma within the module. Although it's not vital for a "finished" module, it can be useful to highlight bugs and problems not yet encountered or handled—and to ensure the module is not incorrectly updated or modified. Because the **strict** pragma is switched on, we need to pre-declare the global variables within this package with the **use vars** pragma. Because we are using the **Exporter** module, we need to include the @ISA and @EXPORT variables in the declaration. The last variable, $error, will be used to record the errors we find in the HTML code we are supplied.

Lines 5 and 6 set us up for the **Exporter** module so that the function we want to export, **htmlqc**, is automatically imported by a calling script or module. Although there is another function in this package, it is local to this package and will not be published and imported into the calling scripts namespace via the **Exporter**. Line 8 incorporates the **SHTML** package, which we will look at later in this chapter.

```
10   my %tagpair = (
11                     'A',          1,
12              'ADDRESS',          1,
13                     'B',          1,
14           'BLOCKQUOTE',          1,
15                    'BQ',          1,
16               'CENTER',          1,
17                 'CITE',          1,
18                 'CODE',          1,
19                  'DFN',          1,
20                  'DIR',          1,
21                   'DL',          1,
22                   'EM',          1,
23                  'FIG',          1,
24                 'FONT',          1,
25                 'FORM',          1,
26                   'H1',          1,
27                   'H2',          1,
28                   'H3',          1,
29                   'H4',          1,
30                   'H5',          1,
31                   'H6',          1,
32                 'HEAD',          1,
33                 'HTML',          1,
34                    'I',          1,
35                  'KBD',          1,
36              'LISTING',          1,
```

```
37                'MATH',          1,
38                'MENU',          1,
39                  'OL',          1,
40                 'PRE',          1,
41                   'S',          1,
42                'SAMP',          1,
43              'SELECT',          1,
44              'STRONG',          1,
45               'STYLE',          1,
46               'TABLE',          1,
47             'TEXTAREA',         1,
48               'TITLE',          1,
49                  'TD',          1,
50                  'TR',          1,
51                  'TT',          1,
52                   'U',          1,
53                  'UL',          1,
54                 'VAR',          1,
55                 'XMP',          1,
56          'BLOCKQUOTE',          1,
57    );
58
```

Lines 10 to 57 define the contents of the **%tagpair** variable. The hash is defined by specifying the key and then the value. Perl automatically places pairs of comma-separated elements into the necessary key/value. We could, arguably, have used a simple array rather than a hash to store this information. However, an array would have required a separate lookup function, slowing down the process. By using a hash, we simplify the lookup process and instead rely on Perl to do the lookups using the built-in hash algorithms.

```
59    sub htmlqc
60    {
61        my ($html) = @_;
62
63        $error = '';
64        my %taghistory = ();
65        $html = striptohtml($html);
66
```

Line 59 is the start of the **htmlqc** function, the main function in this package. It takes a single argument, extracted on line 61 into the **$html** scalar. This argument should be an HTML document. By accepting a scalar with the HTML contained within it rather than a filename or reference, we can support the checking of any HTML element, even that generated within a Perl script, without having to rely on an external file to import the HTML from. This makes the function and package more practical long term, and it allows us to support the checking of HTML within a number of other scripts that may not necessarily rely on a local file for their HTML source.

Line 63 empties the **$error** variable; because it's a global package variable, it will not be initialized for each function invocation. There is a danger that multiple calls to the function will simply append errors to the existing error list, creating erroneous error entries and highlighting problems in files that don't actually have problems.

The **%taghistory** hash stores the number of start and end tags in the document. Line 65 uses the **striptohtml** function from the **SHTML** package to convert the document to a simpler format for us to work with. See the **SHTML.pm** package later in this chapter for more information.

```
67      for $_ (split(/\n/,$html))
68      {
69          unless (anglematch($_))
70          {
71              $error .= "  Mismatched < and >, line: $_\n";
72          }
```

Line 67 sets up a **for** loop, which will iterate through each line of the document, as supplied by the **split** function. Lines 69 to 72 check for start *and* end tags on the line with the **anglematch** function, which is part of this package. It returns a zero if there was a mismatch between the start and end tags. If an error is found, we add it to the **$error** variable. Note that the error starts with a space to help with indentation when reporting the fault. Also note that the error message is self contained and terminated to be a single line. This means that subsequent errors will be new, additional lines to the scalar.

```
73      if (my ($starttag) = m#<\s*([^/\s]+)[^>]*>#)
74      {
75          $starttag =~ tr/a-z/A-Z/;
76          $taghistory{$starttag}++ if ($tagpair{$starttag});
77      }
```

Line 73 checks if the line is a start tag. The regular expression looks for an opening bracket and a string of text that isn't composed of a leading slash (which would signify an end tag) or white space. If there is a match for the tag label (the value without the brackets), it is assigned to the **$starttag** variable. Line 75 uses the **tr** regular expression to transform any lowercase characters to uppercase. Line 76 then increments the value of the tag against the keyed value in the **%taghistory** hash if the tag is recognized as a paired tag, based on the contents of the **%tagpair** reference hash we generated at the start of this script.

This fragment of code basically counts and totals up the number of start tags within the document. We'll need this information, in combination with the number of end tags, to decide if there are any errors in the code. Of course, it would be foolish to count up the start tags and go through the document again and count the end tags to compare the results. We do it in a single pass by decrementing the corresponding key/value pair in the **%taghistory** hash.

```
78        elsif (my ($endtag) = m#</\s*([^\s]+)[^>]*>#)
79        {
80            $endtag =~ tr/a-z/A-Z/;
```

Line 78 uses a regular expression to identify if the line has an end tag. This regular expression is similar to the start tag expression, except that it has the leading slash as a required element. If it matches the tag name (without the brackets or slash), then it's assigned to the **$endtag** variable, which is converted to uppercase on line 80.

```
81        if ($tagpair{$endtag})
82        {
83            if ($taghistory{$endtag})
84            {
85                $taghistory{$endtag}--;
86            }
87            else
88            {
89                $error .= "  Endtag </$endtag> mismatch\n";
90            }
91        }
92        }
93    }
```

The matching system for the end tag is slightly more complicated than for the start tag. This is because we need to ensure that the tag exists and has a nonzero value in the **%taghistory** hash (line 81). If it doesn't, we need to report it as an error (line 89). If it does exist, then we just decrement the tag count in the hash (line 85).

```
94    for my $tag (keys %taghistory)
95    {
96        $error .=
97            "  Tag <$tag> has $taghistory{$tag} tags to close\n"
98            if $taghistory{$tag};
99    }
```

Lines 94 to 99 check the tags recorded in the **%taghistory** hash that still register a non-zero value. This would indicate that the start tag never had a matching end tag. We report it as such on lines 96 to 98. Although it is rather fragmented here because of the line length restrictions on the printed page, these lines are in fact a single line that appends a suitable error message to the **$error** scalar if the tag entry in the hash is other than zero.

```
100        $error ? 0 : 1;
101 }
102
```

Line 100 returns a zero if the **$error** variable has any reported errors, or 1 if there were no problems.

```
103 sub anglematch
104 {
105        return 1 if (/<!--/ or /-->/);
106        return 0 if /<[^>]*</m;
107        return 0 if />[^<]*>/m;
108        return 0 if /<[^>]*$/m;
109        return 0 if /^[^<]*>/m;
110        1;
111 }
112
113 1;
```

The **anglematch** function on line 103 checks for matching start and end tag brackets on a supplied string. Line 105 accounts for HTML comments; they do not follow the same format as a standard tag, and they can cross multiple lines. To get around this being reported as an error by the function, we return a 1 (no errors) if a comment tag (whether open or close) is found.

Line 106 checks for strings that have an opening bracket but no close bracket before another opening bracket. For example, this line of the form:

```
<b<i>
```

would report an error. Line 107 checks for a close bracket followed by another close bracket without an intervening opening bracket. So the following line would trigger an error:

```
<b>i>
```

Lines 108 and 109 check for open and close brackets, respectively, without a matching bracket on the same line. This would return a failure for the following lines:

```
<b
i>
```

Note for all the regular expressions the multiline argument is given. Within this package, we shouldn't get multiline strings containing tags—this is the reason for the **striptohtml** function—but that doesn't mean it's not worth accounting for. As I stated at the start of the script, the process is quick and dirty, but I've used it successfully to check all my sites, including production sites for blue chip company Web sites with few failures or problems.

Checking HTML Validity

The **chkhtml.pl** script uses the **HTMLQC** module to check the validity of the files specified on the command line. The **HTMLQC** module performs most of the work, so this script simply becomes a wrapper around the outside to give the script a friendly user interface.

```perl
1   #!/usr/local/bin/perl5
2
3   use HTMLQC;
4   die "No files specified\n" unless (@ARGV);
5   for my $file (@ARGV)
6   {
7       open(D,"<$file") or die "Couldn't open $file, $!";
8       { local $/; $_ = <D>; }
9       close(D) or die "Couldn't close $file correctly, $!";
10      htmlqc($_) ?
11          print "As far as I can tell, $file appears OK\n" :
12          print "In file $file:\n$HTMLQC::error\n";
13  }
```

ANNOTATIONS

This script is incredibly simple, but only because the work is almost entirely passed on to the **htmlqc** function. We open the file, import its contents into the default pattern space, execute the **htmlqc** function, and print any errors it produces.

```perl
1   #!/usr/local/bin/perl5
2
3   use HTMLQC;
4   die "No files specified\n" unless (@ARGV);
5   for my $file (@ARGV)
6   {
7       open(D,"<$file") or die "Couldn't open $file, $!";
8       { local $/; $_ = <D>; }
9       close(D) or die "Couldn't close $file correctly, $!";
```

We import the exported functions from the **HTMLQC** module into the current namespace in line 3. We check for a valid list of files from the command line on line 4. By sequentially working through the elements of the **@ARGV** array, which contains the arguments specified on the command line, we can accept a number of files as input.

Line 7 opens the file, reporting a suitable error and the reason via the $! special variable. Line 8 then uses the trick we saw in the last chapter: By localizing the end-of-record (or line) separator variable, we undefine it within the block created by the curly brackets, {}. This allows us to assign the entire contents of the file to the default IO buffer. I've included what could be written on four lines into a single line here for brevity and clarity—there is no difference in the operation.

Line 9 checks that we can close the file properly. In theory this should never fail, since we have correctly opened the file (or the script would have died on line 7) and we haven't been writing to the file. However, it's good practice to introduce as much error checking as possible, however unlikely a failure may seem.

```
10      htmlqc($_) ?
11          print "As far as I can tell, $file appears OK\n" :
12          print "In file $file:\n$HTMLQC::error\n";
13      }
```

Lines 10 to 12 print a success or failure message. We use the quick test operator, where the format of the test is

```
test ? result if true : result if false
```

The test can be any of the normal tests you might use; there are no restrictions, limitations, or additions. The first fragment after the question mark and before the colon is executed if the test is true, and then everything after the colon is executed if the test result was false. The test is executed as an entire statement in its own right, so the values or results of operations can be used as return values. In our example, they simply print two different results using separate print statements, but it's also valid to use a statement like this:

```
print "Hello ",(($world) ? "World!" : "Mars!"),"\n";
```

This line would print "Hello World!" if the value of **$world** was true, or "Hello Mars!" if it was false. Note that we have to enclose it in brackets to ensure that it is executed as a separate statement within the entire **print** statement.

In our case, if the result of **htmlqc** is true, the check completed successfully, and so we print a suitable message on line 11. Remember that we could be dealing with multiple files, so we need to include the filename in the message. If the check failed, we print the error message from the **HTMLQC** package, remembering to prefix the filename to the error.

If we run the script on a deliberately faulty test file that looks like this:

```
<iThis is in italics</i>
b>This is in bold</b>
<a href=#here>This is a broken anchor tag
<h1 And here is a mismatched header tag </h1>
```

we get the following results:

```
% chkhtml.pl test.html
In file /users/martinb/t.html:
  Mismatched < and >, line: <iThis is in italics
  Endtag </I> mismatch
  Mismatched < and >, line: b>
  Endtag </B> mismatch
  Mismatched < and >, line: <h1 And here is a mismatched header tag
  Endtag </H1> mismatch
  Tag <A> has 1 tags to close
```

Although this only tests the basics of the HTML code, it highlights many of the most common problems you will see on Web sites. Despite assurances by Netscape and Microsoft that the minor errors that would be picked up by this script do not always mean the page looks wrong, I know that some page bugs are caused by such errors.

As an extension to this script, it would be very easy to expand the script to perform more in-depth checks on some HTML tags. For example, the anchor tag, used to define links on the pages, is composed of a number of different elements; all we need to do is identify an anchor tag, check for the required and optional arguments, and then check that the entire tag has been correctly formatted. We'll look in more detail at how to extract information from a tag when we look at extracting the form fields from an HTML document in the **extform.pl** script.

SHTML.pm

HTML Support Module

We've already seen some of the basics surrounding the processing of HTML. The **SHTML** module is intended to support the processing of HTML, first by supplying the **striptohtml** function, used in the first module in this chapter, and also to supply two further functions already seen in this book in function form.

```
1   package SHTML;
2
3   use strict;
4   use vars qw/@ISA @EXPORT/;
5   require Exporter;
6   @ISA = 'Exporter';
7   @EXPORT = qw (striptohtml
8                 decipher_url
9                 expand_path);
10
11  sub striptohtml
12  {
```

```
13         ($_) = @_;
14         s/\n//g;
15         s/\t//g;
16         s/\s\s+/ /g;
17         s/\</\n\</sg;
18         s/\>/\>\n/sg;
19         return($_);
20     }
21
22     sub decipher_url
23     {
24         my ($url) = @_;
25         my ($matched, $protocol, $host, $path);
26         my ($user, $password, $machine, $port);
27
28         $matched = $url =~ m#(\S+)://([^/ ]+)(.*)#;
29
30         return unless($matched);
31
32         $protocol = $1;
33         $host = $2;
34         $path = $3;
35
36         $user = 'anonymous';
37         $password = 'me@foo.bar';
38
39         $_ = $host;
40
41         if (m#(\S+):(\d+)#)
42         {
43             $_ = $1;
44             $port = $2;
45         }
46         if (m#(\S+):(\S+)@(\S+)#)
47         {
48         $user = $1;
49             $password = $2;
50             $machine = $3;
51         }
52         elsif (m#(\S+)@(\S+)#)
53         {
54             $user = $1;
55             $machine = $2;
```

```
56          }
57      else
58      {
59          $machine = $host;
60      }
61      return($protocol, $user, $password, $machine, $port, $path);
62  }
63
64  sub expand_path
65  {
66      my ($old) = @_;
67      local (*_, *dir);
68      $old =~ s#^#/# unless $old =~ m#^/#;
69      my @dir = split(/\//, $old);
70      shift(@dir);
71      $_ = '';
72      foreach my $dir (@dir)
73      {
74          next if $dir eq '.';
75          if ($dir eq '..')
76          {
77              s#/[^/]+$##;
78              next;
79          }
80          $_ .= '/' . $dir;
81          while (my $r = readlink)
82          {
83              if ($r =~ m#^/#)
84              {
85                  $_ = &expand_path($r);
86                  s#^/tmp_mnt## && next dir;
87              }
88              else
89              {
90                  s#[^/]+$#$r#;
91                  $_ = &expand_path($_);
92              }
93          }
94      }
95      ($_ eq '') ? '/' : $_;
96  }
97
98  1;
```

ANNOTATIONS

The **SHTML** package introduces only one function that we haven't already seen. The **striptohtml** function uses a number of regular expression matches in order to convert an HTML document so that individual HTML tags are on separate lines. This makes the processing of the forms significantly easier. The other two functions are **decipher_url**, which extracts the elements of a URL into its component parts (it was first introduced in Chapter 5), and **expand_path**, which converts a local file reference into a full file reference (it was first seen in Chapter 2).

```
1    package SHTML;
2
3    use strict;
4    use vars qw/@ISA @EXPORT/;
5    require Exporter;
6    @ISA = 'Exporter';
7    @EXPORT = qw (striptohtml
8                  decipher_url
9                  expand_path);
10
```

Once again, the package follows the typical package style. We've defined the **use strict** pragma to restrict unsafe code and variable constructs, and we use the **Exporter** module so the functions will automatically be imported into a calling script.

```
11   sub striptohtml
12   {
13       ($_) = @_;
```

The **striptohtml** function was designed as a quick way to convert HTML formatted like this:

```
<font size=+1><b>Title</b></font>
```

into a more processing friendly format:

```
<font size=+1>
<b>
Title
</b>
</font>
```

This saves us from having to do unnecessarily complex matching to identify faults and the start and end tags in an HTML document. There is a trade-off: we no longer have any knowledge of the format of the original document. This makes references to the original layout impossible, so pinpointing a specific error for the user is more difficult, but this is a relatively minor inconvenience when compared to the speed improvements and the simplicity of the parsing engine required to perform the checks.

```
14      s/\n//g;
```

The first substitution removes all new lines from the document. We'll replace them with reference to the start and end tags.

```
15      s/\t//g;
```

Now we remove any tabs. We don't need them, and the browser does not interpret them anyway.

```
16      s/\s\s+/ /g;
```

Line 16 replaces multiple spaces with a single space.

```
17      s/\</\n\</sg;
```

Line 17 inserts a new-line character before the start bracket of a tag.

```
18      s/\>/\>\n/sg;
```

Line 18 appends a new-line character after the end bracket of a tag.

```
19      return($_);
20  }
21
```

Line 19 very simply ensures that the return value is the pattern buffer we have been working on.

```
22  sub decipher_url
23  {
24      my ($url) = @_;
25      my ($matched, $protocol, $host, $path);
26      my ($user, $password, $machine, $port);
27
28      $matched = $url =~ m#(\S+)://([^/ ]+)(.*)#;
29
30      return unless($matched);
31
32      $protocol = $1;
33      $host = $2;
34      $path = $3;
35
36      $user = 'anonymous';
37      $password = 'me@foo.bar';
```

```
38
39        $_ = $host;
40
41        if (m#(\S+):(\d+)#)
42        {
43            $_ = $1;
44            $port = $2;
45        }
46        if (m#(\S+):(\S+)@(\S+)#)
47        {
48      $user = $1;
49            $password = $2;
50            $machine = $3;
51        }
52        elsif (m#(\S+)@(\S+)#)
53        {
54            $user = $1;
55            $machine = $2;
56        }
57        else
58        {
59            $machine = $host;
60        }
61        return($protocol, $user, $password, $machine, $port, $path);
62    }
63
```

Because we have already seen the **decipher_url** function, I will refer to the Universal File Downloader (**grfile.pl**) script in Chapter 5. Also, for a more robust system, you'll want to check out the **URI::URL** module by Gisle Aas. We have used this module before, and will be using it late in this chapter.

A simple explanation of the function is that it takes a URL as a single argument, and, using a progressive selection of regular expression and programmed intelligence, it returns the protocol, user, password, machine, port, and path that have been extracted.

```
64    sub expand_path
65    {
66        my ($old) = @_;
67        local (*_, *dir);
68        $old =~ s#^#/# unless $old =~ m#^/#;
69        my @dir = split(/\//, $old);
70        shift(@dir);
71        $_ = '';
```

```
72      foreach my $dir (@dir)
73      {
74          next if $dir eq '.';
75          if ($dir eq '..')
76          {
77              s#/[^/]+$##;
78              next;
79          }
80          $_ .= '/' . $dir;
81          while (my $r = readlink)
82          {
83              if ($r =~ m#^/#)
84              {
85                  $_ = &expand_path($r);
86                  s#^/tmp_mnt## && next dir;
87              }
88              else
89              {
90                  s#[^/]+$#$r#;
91                  $_ = &expand_path($_);
92              }
93          }
94      }
95      ($_ eq '') ? '/' : $_;
96  }
97
98  1;
```

The **expand_path** function is simply a copy of the function that is part of the Link Expander (**explink.pl**) script at the end of Chapter 2. Please refer to that script for more detailed information.

The function takes a file as an argument and returns the full path to the file by expanding and resolving the references and directories in which the file exists.

Verifying Local Links and Images

One of the most tedious jobs in the world is checking and verifying a project. This could never be truer than for a Web site. It can take hours, if not days, to manually work through a Web site, verifying that every image and every link on every page works. Surely there is an easier way?

Well, there is. The trick is to build on the methods we have already used to identify the link and image references in the documents. We then need to expand the references so that we can relate the relative references made in the HTML to the real locations of the files on the local Web server.

The **chklinks.pl** script is just such a solution. It involves two main parts: the main body of the script works through a list of files, verifies their existence, runs the **htmlqc** function to verify the code quality, and then runs a separate function to parse the contents to identify any more links that need to be checked. Once the entire HTML has been parsed, we generate a list of the files that exist within the Web site directory but that are not referenced (as far we can tell) within the HTML.

The result is a list of missing links and faulty HTML for the entire Web site, as well as the list of files in the directory structure that are not referenced in the Web site.

```perl
1   #!/usr/local/bin/perl5
2
3   use HTMLQC;
4   use SHTML;
5   use File::Basename;
6   use Cwd;
7   use Getopt::Long;
8   use File::Find;
9   my ($webroot,$single,$fileroot,$confine,$gethelp);
10
11  unless(GetOptions("r=s" => \$webroot,
12                    "s"   => \$single,
13                    "d=s" => \$fileroot,
14                    "c"   => \$confine,
15                    "h"   => \$gethelp
16                    ))
17  {
18      warn "Bad options\n";
19      usage_summary();
20  }
21
22  if ($gethelp)
23  {
24      usage_summary();
25      exit;
26  }
27
28  chdir($fileroot);
29
30  my (@urls,%procurls,%fullurl);
31  (push @urls,$ARGV[0]) || die "No URL specified";
32  $procurls{$ARGV[0]} = "root";
33
34  while (defined(my $url = pop @urls))
35  {
```

```perl
36      unless(open(D,"<$fileroot/$url"))
37      {
38          print "Couldn't open ($url) <- ($procurls{$url}): $!\n";
39          next;
40      }
41
42      next if ($url =~ /gif|jpg|jpeg|pdf$/i);
43      next if ($confine and $url !~ m#$webroot/#);
44      { local $/; $_ = <D>; }
45      close(D);
46      $_ = striptohtml($_);
47      extract_urls($_,$url) unless($single);
48      unless(htmlqc($_))
49      {
50          print "In file $url:\n$HTMLQC::error\n";
51      }
52  }
53
54  unless ($single)
55  {
56      print "\n\nFiles in directory ($webroot) not in HTML\n\n";
57      chdir($fileroot);
58      find(\&vrfyfile,"$webroot");
59
60      print "\n\nFiles/Images/References found in HTML\n\n";
61
62      for my $url (keys %fullurl)
63      {
64          print "$url\n";
65      }
66  }
67
68  sub vrfyfile
69  {
70      return if (-d "$fileroot/$File::Find::name");
71      my $file = $File::Find::name;
72      $file =~ s#^#/# unless ($file =~ m#^/#);
73      print "$file is not referenced in HTML\n"
74          unless(defined($fullurl{$file}));
75  }
76
77  sub extract_urls
78  {
```

```perl
79      my ($file,$topurl) = @_;
80
81      foreach $_ (split "\n",$file)
82      {
83          if (m/<a.*href=(.*)[> ].*/i or m/<img.*src=(.*)[> ].*/i)
84          {
85              my $url = $1;
86              $url =~ s/\"//g;
87              $url =~ s/>.*//g;
88              $url =~ s/^\s+//;
89              $url =~ s/\ .*//g;
90              next if ($url =~ /cgi-bin/i);
91              next if ($url =~ /\.map/i);
92              next if ($url =~ /\.zip/i);
93              next if ($url =~ /^\S+:/i);
94              my ($protocol,$machine,$path)
95                  = (decipher_url($url))[0,3,5];
96              next if (defined($protocol));
97
98              $path = $url unless $path;
99              next if ($path =~ /\#.*/);
100             print "Line $_ looks bad\n" if (length($path) <1);
101             $path .= "/index.html" if ($path =~ /.*\/$/);
102             unless ($path =~ m#^/#)
103             {
104                 $path = dirname($topurl) ."/". $path;
105             }
106             $path = expand_path($path);
107             $path =~ s#//#/#g;
108             push(@urls,$path) unless $procurls{$path};
109             $fullurl{$path} = 1 unless $procurls{$path};
110             $procurls{$path} = $topurl;
111         }
112     }
113 }
114
115 sub usage_summary()
116 {
117     print <<EOF
118 Usage: chklinks [-s] [-r root] [-d fileroot] [-c] [-h] htmlfile
119
120 Extracts links from HTML (<IMG> and <A> tags only) and checks
121 for destination links and HTML validity.
```

```
122
123  Where:
124
125  s  -  Check a single page for link and HTML validity
126
127  r  -  Specify the root directory for the website
128        eg. To check all files beneath http://www.foo.com/bar
129            you would set the root to bar
130
131  d  -  Specify the physical directory for the website
132        eg. /usr/local/etc/httpd/service
133
134  c  -  Confine checks to within the root directory
135        eg. Using: chklinks.pl -r bar -c
136            /bar/index.html would be expanded
137            /index.html wouldn't
138
139  h  -  Show this help
140
141  EOF
142      ;
143  }
```

ANNOTATIONS

This script uses a form of recursion to achieve its aim. A single array, **@urls**, contains a list of the URLs that need to be processed. A corresponding hash, **%fullurls** will be used to store the list of URL's that have already been processed. We'll use the information in the hash to prevent us from processing the same file more than once. The act of processing may or may not add new URLs to the array. Since we use a **while** loop, URLs will continue to be taken and processed until popping a value off the array fails. Because we have to read the file into memory in order to parse it (to find more links), we can also use the opportunity to run the file through the **HTMLQC** module to verify the quality of the HTML.

Finally, in the act of processing the file, we also obtain a list of all the links within the Web site. We can use this information to make a comparison with the files in the Web site directory and to make a list of links, or files, contained within the Web site.

```
1  #!/usr/local/bin/perl5
2
3  use HTMLQC;
4  use SHTML;
```

```
5   use File::Basename;
6   use Cwd;
7   use Getopt::Long;
8   use File::Find;
9   my ($webroot,$single,$fileroot,$confine,$gethelp);
10
```

We need a large number of modules in order to support all of the functionality for this script. The **HTMLQC** and **SHTML** packages are the ones included in this chapter. The **File::Basename** module is needed to extract the file element from a path, and the **CWD** package is needed to identify the current directory, which acts as a reference point when we start identifying the true location of the linked files.

Line 9 defines a number of variables that hold the command-line information.

```
11  unless(GetOptions("r=s" => \$webroot,
12                     "s"   => \$single,
13                     "d=s" => \$fileroot,
14                     "c"   => \$confine,
15                     "h"   => \$gethelp
16                     ))
17  {
18      warn "Bad options\n";
19      usage_summary();
20  }
21
```

Lines 11 to 16 extract the command-line options. The **$webroot** variable is the root directory of the Web site. If you are checking an entire Web site, then the value is .;, if you want to check a single directory within a Web site, then you can specify the directory here. This information is in reference to the file root, specified in the **$fileroot** variable. For example, to examine the files beneath the directory foo on a Web site stored locally under the /usr/local/http directory you would use

```
-r foo -d /usr/local/http
```

The **$webroot** variable automatically expands values to be within the physical /usr/local/http/foo directory.

The **$single** option confines the check to verify the links within a single page. This checks that links exist in the specified document, but it doesn't parse the documents it finds to extract additional URLs. The **$confine** variable specifies that only links within **$webroot** are parsed through the URL extractor function. If this is not specified, then all local links within and above the Web root directory will be checked.

Finally, the **$gethelp** option identifies whether the user wants to get help on using the script.

```
22    if ($gethelp)
23    {
24        usage_summary();
25        exit;
26    }
27
```

If the user asked for help on the command line, then we print out the usage information via the function on line 24 before exiting the script on line 25.

```
28    chdir($fileroot);
29
```

Line 28 changes the current directory to the Web site directory specified on the command line. This will make identifying and expanding the link locations easier, as well as simplifying the process of opening and checking the existence of files within the Web site. Remember that Web sites are generally referenced from within a single directory, so although you access a Web site home page as /index.html the Web site actually holds the page under a directory like /usr/local/etc/httpd/htdocs. By changing the directory here, we allow ourselves to specify files by the local references that would be used when accessing the file remotely.

This assumes a simple Web server configuration with all the files for one Web site being contained in a single directory. This is not unusual, but you may need to modify the script or run it multiple times if your Web server directory layout is more complex.

```
30    my (@urls,%procurls,%fullurl);
31    (push @urls,$ARGV[0]) || die "No URL specified"
32    $procurls{$ARGV[0]} = "root";
33
```

Line 30 defines the array and hashes that store information on the URLs to be visited (**@urls**), the list of URLs that have been processed and the page the link was extracted from (**%procurls**), and the full list of URLs that are referenced within the HTML (**%fullurl**).

Line 31 pushes the URL onto the URL array, **die**-ing if the operation fails. Line 32 adds it to the list of URLs and where they were referenced.

```
34    while (defined(my $url = pop @urls))
35    {
36        unless(open(D, "<$fileroot/$url"))
37        {
38            print "Couldn't open ($url) <- ($procurls{$url}): $!\n";
39            next;
40        }
41
```

Line 34 starts the **while** loop that will progress through the array containing the list of URLs to check. We ensure a valid value by checking that the value returned to us by the array has been defined. We attempt to open the URL on line 36. The URL as supplied within the **@urls** array is a file path that has been expanded within the scope of the current Web site. We add **$webroot** to the path we are trying to open.

If the attempt fails, then we print an error on line 38, including the URL that the current URL was referenced from for more information. If the file cannot be opened, then we cannot extract any further links from the file or perform any other form of check on the document. We can therefore skip to the next URL from the array, which we do on line 39.

```
42      next if ($url =~ /gif|jpg|jpeg|pdf$/i);
```

Line 42 skips over the URL if we identify the file as being a graphic or other file format that does not contain further HTML links. An alternative to this solution is to decide what files to let through— for example specifying only **.htm** or **.html** files.

```
43      next if ($confine and $url !~ m#$webroot/#);
```

Line 43 skips any further processing of the file if its path does not match that of the Web root directory specified on the command line. This allows the links found in a file within the Web root directory structure to be tested for their existence, but they will not be parsed to extract more URLs. The test here restricts the checks to only those files, wherever referenced, to the Web root directory.

```
44      { local $/; $_ = <D>; }
45      close(D);
```

Line 44 uses the localized input record separator trick to import the file into the default pattern space, before closing the file on line 45.

```
46      $_ = striptohtml($_);
```

Line 46 uses the **striptohtml** function to reduce the file to a more usable format.

```
47      extract_urls($_,$url) unless($single);
```

Line 47 calls the local **extract_urls** function. This will extract any links from the file, adding them to the URL arrays and hashes accordingly. The function takes two arguments: the text of the file and the URL of the file. We'll look at how the URL information is used shortly. The only exception to the rule is when the user has requested a single file check: checking a single file does not extract additional URLs. Note that the function is not actually called recursively— it is just called continuously on the elements of a list that it adds elements to. The call is repetitive but not recursive.

```
48      unless(htmlqc($_))
49          {
```

```
50          print "In file $url:\n$HTMLQC::error\n";
51     }
52 }
53
```

Lines 48 to 51 call the **htmlqc** function, which we have already seen, and print out the errors produced by the checking function.

```
54 unless ($single)
55 {
56     print "\n\nFiles in directory ($webroot) not in HTML\n\n";
57     chdir($fileroot);
58     find(\&vrfyfile,"$webroot");
59
60     print "\n\nFiles/Images/References found in HTML\n\n";
61
62     for my $url (keys %fullurl)
63     {
64         print "$url\n";
65     }
66 }
67
```

Lines 54 to 66 check the list of extracted URLs against the directory structure, provided we haven't been asked to check only a single file. Line 56 prints a title, before changing to the root of the Web server directory. Line 58 then calls the **find** function, which traverses through the Web root directory, calling the **vrfyfile** function for each file or directory found.

Finally, as a sanity and reference check, we print out a list of the URLs extracted by the script on lines 62 to 65.

```
68 sub vrfyfile
69 {
70     return if (-d "$fileroot/$File::Find::name");
71     my $file = $File::Find::name;
72     $file =~ s#^#/# unless ($file =~ m#^/#);
73     print "$file is not referenced in HTML\n"
74         unless(defined($fullurl{$file}));
75 }
76
```

The **vrfyfile** function checks if the file that has been found in the directory structure exists in the list of URLs extracted from the HTML files. We skip the function checks if the directory entry found is indeed a directory. Line 71 assigns a local variable to the full path of the found file, and line 72 adds a leading forward slash if the file path does not include one. Line 73 prints out a suitable error, if the test in line 74 is false.

The result of this function should be a list of files in the local directory that do not exist in the hash. The validity of the hash contents is only as good as the parsing function and the files that we decide to skip at parsing time.

```
77   sub extract_urls
78   {
79       my ($file,$topurl) = @_;
80
81       foreach $_ (split "\n",$file)
82       {
83           if (m/<a.*href=(.*)[> ].*/i or m/<img.*src=(.*)[> ].*/i)
84           {
```

Line 79 extracts the two arguments passed to the function. Line 81 then sets up a **for** loop to work through the HTML file that we imported earlier. Remember that this file has been converted to our preferred format, which places individual HTML tags on each of the lines in the string that contains the file.

Line 83 identifies a link. There are two types of links: links to other HTML pages and URLs specified by the <a> tag, and links to images referenced by the <img> tag. Note that I've specified two match strings here, which define as much information as would be required to identify the real piece of information we want—the URL the links point to.

```
85           my $url = $1;
86           $url =~ s/\"//g;
87           $url =~ s/>.*//g;
88           $url =~ s/^\s+//;
89           $url =~ s/\ .*//g;
```

By the time we reach line 85, we should have a variable from one of the match strings in line 83. Lines 86 to 89 then process the string to make sure we have only the URL and not any additional characters that are not part of the link itself. Line 86 removes double quotes; line 87 removes end tags and the information that follows them; line 88 removes leading spaces; and line 89 removes any spaces within the URL.

```
90           next if ($url =~ /cgi-bin/i);
91           next if ($url =~ /\.map/i);
92           next if ($url =~ /\.zip/i);
93           next if ($url =~ /^\S+:/i);
```

Lines 90 to 94 skip URLs that we know we don't want to reference or check. We skip any references to the programs that would normally be part of the cgi-bin directory. We then skip "map" and "zip" files, before line 93 skips files that have any form of protocol specified (this script deals only with local files).

```
94          my ($protocol,$machine,$path)
95              = (decipher_url($url))[0,3,5];
96          next if (defined($protocol));
97
```

Line 94 and 95 extract the protocol, machine, and path from the URL. Line 96 skips the link if a protocol has been defined.

```
98          $path = $url unless $path;
99          next if ($path =~ /\#.*/);
```

Line 98 makes the **$path** variable equal the **$url** variable if there was no path specified in the link. Line 99 then checks if the link includes a hash sign, which signifies an anchor within a file, something we do not check.

```
100         print "Line $_ looks bad\n" if (length($path) <1);
```

Line 100 reports a bad line if the length is less than 1—this highlights references to a directory that are not specified, including a filename.

```
101         ..$path .= "/index.html" if ($path =~ /.*\/$/);
```

Line 101 adds the default value of "index.html" for the filename if the path ends with a slash.

```
102         unless ($path =~ m#^/#)
103         {
104             $path = dirname($topurl) ."/". $path;
105         }
```

If the path does not include the full reference, which is identifiable by a leading forward slash, then we add the directory name of the file that the current page text was imported from. This accounts for local references (that is, no directory is contained within the path) within the directory of the current URL.

```
106         $path = expand_path($path);
```

Line 106 uses the **expand_path** function to expand the current filename, stored within the **$path** variable, to a full directory name.

```
107         $path =~ s#//#/#g;
108         push(@urls,$path) unless $procurls{$path};
109         $fullurl{$path} = 1 unless $procurls{$path};
110         $procurls{$path} = $topurl;
111     }
112   }
113 }
114
```

We strip out any double slashes in line 107 for clarity more than anything else. Line 108 then adds the URL to the list of URLs to be processed, if the URL has not already been added. That decision is based on whether the URL has been defined within the **%procurls** hash. Line 109 updates the list of the URLs extracted. Because we use a hash, the list of URLs extracted will automatically be de-duped. Line 110 then updates the list of found URLs, with the key being the URL just extracted and the reference URL being the URL of the current page.

The result, by line 113, is that a list of URLs will have been added to the list of URLs to be processed. If another file is processed and it references URLs that have already been added, they won't be added to the list of URLs to be checked, therefore optimizing the process of checking the site by only checking individual files once, not each time they are referenced.

```
115 sub usage_summary()
116 {
117     print <<EOF
118 Usage: chklinks [-s] [-r root] [-d fileroot] [-c] [-h] htmlfile
119
120 Extracts links from HTML (<IMG> and <A> tags only) and checks
121 for destination links and HTML validity.
122
123 Where:
124
125 s   -   Check a single page for link and HTML validity
126
127 r   -   Specify the root directory for the website
128         eg. To check all files beneath http://www.foo.com/bar
129             you would set the root to bar
130
131 d   -   Specify the physical directory for the website
132         eg. /usr/local/etc/httpd/service
133
134 c   -   Confine checks to within the root directory
135         eg. Using: chklinks.pl -r bar -c
136             /bar/index.html would be expanded
137             /index.html wouldn't
138
139 h   -   Show this help
140
141 EOF
142     ;
143 }
```

Lines 115 to 143 specify the usage instructions. I cannot stress how useful built-in documentation is, whether in the form of usage instructions as we have here, or in the form of a POD document within the Perl script. We'll take a closer look at POD documentation in Appendix C.

When using the script to specify the local directory, Web root directory, and base URL, remember that all directories and files are in reference to the local file directory. For example, to check the links on the home page of a Web site stored under /usr/local/http, you would use this line:

```
$ chklinks.pl -d /usr/local/http -r . index.html
```

There are a few problems with this script. For instance, we rely very heavily on the ability of the parsing function, **extract_urls**, to obtain the list of links and therefore files to check. To prevent the script from running away from itself, we also have to make a number of decisions about what to include in the link list, and what to ignore. Since a Web site is mostly composed of HTML and graphics files, we concentrate on them and ignore everything else.

chkrlink.pl

Verifying Remote Links and Images

Checking the local version of a Web site is fine, if you have access to the site locally. If you are checking a site on behalf of somebody else, your only access may be over the Web. You could copy the site locally using a number of different tools, including the **sitemirr.pl** script described later in this chapter, and then run the previous script on the local copy. But that method seems both excessive and messy for a language that we know is capable of networking and accessing remote sites (refer to Chapter 5).

One possible solution is to use the **libwww-perl**, or **LWP**, package by Gisle Aas. The package incorporates almost everything you need to create and extract information to and from HTML files, as well as the ability to download those files from remote sites by simply supplying a URL. We'll be using the package extensively for the rest of this chapter, so it's worth familiarizing yourself with the package elements.

```perl
1   #!/usr/local/bin/perl5
2
3   use LWP::UserAgent;
4   use HTML::LinkExtor;
5   use URI::URL;
6   use Getopt::Std;
7
8   my (%fullurl,$opt_d);
9
10  getopts('d');
```

```
11
12  unless (@ARGV)
13  {
14      die "Usage: chkrhtml.pl [-d] url\n\n";
15  }
16
17  my $url = $ARGV[0];
18  print "Checking Website $url\n" if $opt_d;
19
20  my $ua = new LWP::UserAgent;
21  my @urlstack = ();
22  my @urls = ($url);
23  my $p = HTML::LinkExtor->new(\&callback);
24
25  my $res = $ua->request(HTTP::Request->new(GET => $url),
26                      sub {$p->parse($_[0])});
27
28  die "Couldn't open $url\n" unless ($res->status_line eq '200 OK');
29
30  my $base = $res->base;
31  $fullurl{$base} = 1;
32  @urls = map { $_ = url($_, $base)->abs; } @urls;
33
34  addtostack($base,@urls);
35
36  while ($url = pop(@urlstack))
37  {
38      print "Checking URL $url\n" if $opt_d;
39      $res = $ua->request(HTTP::Request->new(GET => $url),
40                      sub {$p->parse($_[0])});
41
42      unless ($res->status_line eq '200 OK')
43      {
44          print("Couldn't open $url (",
45                $res->status_line,
46                ")\n   from: $fullurl{$url}\n");
47          next;
48      }
49      @urls = map { $_ = url($_, $base)->abs; } @urls;
50      addtostack($url,@urls);
51  }
52
53  sub addtostack
```

```
54   {
55       my ($refurl, @urllist) = @_;
56
57       for my $url (@urllist)
58       {
59     next unless($url =~ /^$base/);
60     push(@urlstack,$url) unless(defined($fullurl{$url}));
61     $fullurl{$url} = $refurl;
62       }
63   }
64
65   sub callback
66   {
67       my($tag, %attr) = @_;
68       push(@urls, values %attr);
69   }
```

ANNOTATIONS

This script uses a complex selection of objects and object methods to download and parse a Web page. The output of the parsing process is a list of the links contained within the file. Because the UserAgent object allows for functions to be called against the methods that download the file, the core of the script is actually relatively short. There is a lot of surrounding code that supports the setup and initialization of the objects and methods that will be used to parse and extract further links and references from the HTML.

```
1   #!/usr/local/bin/perl5
2
3   use LWP::UserAgent;
4   use HTML::LinkExtor;
5   use URI::URL;
6   use Getopt::Std;
7
```

We incorporate the necessary modules in lines 3 to 6. The **LWP::UserAgent** module allows us to download files directly from a Web site, while the **HTML::LinkExtor** function provides a set of utilities that extract the links from a Web page into an array. We need both modules in order to identify the links and site structure.

```
8    my (%fullurl,$opt_d);
9
10   getopts('d');
11
```

```
12   unless (@ARGV)
13   {
14       die "Usage: chkrhtml.pl [-d] url\n\n";
15   }
16
17   my $url = $ARGV[0];
18   print "Checking Website $url\n" if $opt_d;
19
```

Lines 8 to 18 parse and process the command-line options. The exception to this is that line 8 defines the hash that will store the list of URLs that have already been accessed. There is only one command-line option, **-d**, that switches on more extensive output during the checking process. We also require just one other argument, the URL, to use as the base for checking the entire Web site. It must be a full URL, including the protocol and server information. However, unlike the **chklinks.pl** script, we do not need to specify a file—we can rely on the LWP package and the remote Web server to sort out that information.

```
20   my $ua = new LWP::UserAgent;
21   my @urlstack = ();
22   my @urls = ($url);
23   my $p = HTML::LinkExtor->new(\&callback);
24
```

Line 20 creates a new UserAgent object. A *UserAgent* is an object that stores the information about a remote Web site, and it provides the methods to access and process a remote file. Line 21 defines the array that stores the list of URLs that need to be accessed and parsed. The **@urls** stack is a temporary list of URLs that have been extracted from the remote Web page.

We create a new parsing object, **$p**, one line 23 using the **LWP::LinkExtor** module. In this script, the object is configured so that calling the **parse** method for the object calls the **callback** function for each link type discovered. For example, we have already seen in the last script two basic link types, anchor, <a>, and image, <img>. The information passed to the **callback** function is the link type and a hash, the values of which are the URLs extracted from the document.

```
25   my $res = $ua->request(HTTP::Request->new(GET => $url),
26                          sub {$p->parse($_[0])});
27
```

Lines 25 and 26 are probably the most complicated we have seen up to now. Looking at the component elements, we can see that we are calling the **request** method on the UserAgent we created on line 20 and the URL of the site we want to access. The arguments to this method are the request (the URL we want to access) and the function to be called once the document has been received. In our case, we create an anonymous subroutinate that calls the **parse** of the parse object **$p** we created on line 23 using the **HTML::LinkExtor** module.

The result of the entire line is that a document is accessed, downloaded, and parsed by the link extract. The link extraction process, in turn, extracts the links, parsing the list of links to the **callback** function, as defined when we created the **HTML::LinkExtor** object.

```
28  die "Couldn't open $url\n" unless ($res->status_line eq '200 OK');
29
```

The result code of the access by the **request** method is stored in the resulting object, **$res**, and it can be obtained by accessing the **status_line** element. Assuming the access was successful, the Web server should return a value of 200. This result is verified in line 28. Any failure is reported to the user via the **die** function since it probably indicates a Web server failure.

```
30  my $base = $res->base;
31  $fullurl{$base} = 1;
```

The base URL of the URL accessed can be obtained by accessing the **base** variable within the **$res** object. We'll need the base URL information in order to reconstruct the full URL of a URL extracted from a Web page. We must extract this information now, before we start accessing further pages, otherwise later URLs may be incorrectly interpreted. Line 31 adds the full URL to the list of URLs that have already been downloaded and processed.

```
32  @urls = map { $_ = url($_, $base)->abs; } @urls;
33
```

The map function applies the expression within the curly brackets to each element of the array **@urls**. Each element of the array is assigned to the default pattern space, and the result should be stored back in the IO buffer. In line 32, the effect is to assign the array elements the **abs** method of the **url** object. This expands a relative URL to a full URL, using the base URL as a template. Using this method, the entire array of URLs has been converted from a combination of full and relative URLs into full URLs; this gives us a common base to work from when checking which URLs have already been accessed and downloaded. (In our last script, we used the **expand** function to perform the same task.)

```
34  addtostack($base,@urls);
35
```

Line 34 then adds the list of URLs from the base document specified on the command line to the list of documents that need to be downloaded and parsed. The process is carried out by the **addtostack** function, which takes account of any URLs that have already been specified. We'll be looking at this function shortly.

```
36   while ($url = pop(@urlstack))
37   {
38       print "Checking URL $url\n" if $opt_d;
39       $res = $ua->request(HTTP::Request->new(GET => $url),
40                           sub {$p->parse($_[0])}};
41
42       unless ($res->status_line eq '200 OK')
43       {
44           print("Couldn't open $url (",
45                 $res->status_line,
46                 ")\n    from: $fullurl{$url}\n");
47           next;
48       }
49       @urls = map { $_ = url($_, $base)->abs; } @urls;
50       addtostack($url,@urls);
51   }
52
```

Lines 36 to 51 follow the same basic process of events as lines 25 to 34. We download a file to a variable and extract the URLs, report any access errors, and convert the URLs extracted into full URLs so they can be added to the list of URLs to be processed.

The major difference is that we do not need to discover the base URL, because we have already extracted that. The only other difference is that an error accessing a subfile is treated as a piece of information, rather than causing the script to exit completely.

```
53   sub addtostack
54   {
55       my ($refurl, @urllist) = @_;
56
57       for my $url (@urllist)
58       {
59           next unless($url =~ /^$base/);
60           push(@urlstack,$url) unless(defined($fullurl{$url}));
61           $fullurl{$url} = $refurl;
62       }
63   }
64
```

The **addtostack** function very simply adds the URLs supplied to it to the list of URLs to be downloaded, provided they haven't already been processed. We set up a **for** loop to work through each URL in the list provided on line 57. Line 59 ensures that the URL is within the base specification of the original URL. Without it, the script would add any link on any page to the list of links to be downloaded. This would include pages from other sites, which may in turn include links to other sites, and so on. In an extreme case, the script could go on downloading the entire Internet!

Line 60 adds the URL to the download queue, provided it hasn't already been added. The check is performed by verifying whether a particular key exists in the **%fullurl** hash, which itself is updated on line 61. The value associated with the key is the URL that the URL list was extracted from. We use this information to help the user track down the problem when we print an error on lines 44 to 46.

```
65  sub callback
66  {
67      my($tag, %attr) = @_;
68      push(@urls, values %attr);
69  }
```

The **callback** function is very simple: it converts the vales of the hash of extracted URLs into a list for adding the download queue.

To use the script, simply specify the URL on the command line:

```
$ chkrlink.pl http://www.prluk.demon.co.uk
```

The script will download the first page, process any links, including images and other files, adding any URLs from those files to the list of files to download. Eventually, the entire list of links will have been added and then processed by the script, at which point it will stop. Note that the script downloads the remote pages to a variable within the script, not to a local file. For the method required to do this, look at the **sitemirr.pl** script later in this chapter.

extform.pl

Extracting Form Elements

If, like me, you have to manage and help develop Web sites, then you will have come across the problem I'm about to solve. There is nothing worse for a programmer than having a designer supply an HTML form without any information about what the form's elements are. A form is composed of a number of fields, checkboxes, and pop-ups defined directly within the HTML code. Extracting the information from the HTML is a tedious but necessary process, because not knowing what the fields are called and what data they might contain makes it impossible to process the form contents.

PROGRAMMER'S NOTE   *We'll cover the processing of Web forms in Chapter 8.*

To make life easier for me, I wrote a small script in Perl to extract the form field information directly from an HTML file. I include all of the information that could be included with the form, including any predefined lengths, sizes, or values. Although all the script does is provide information on the form contents, it speeds up the development of a suitable processing script so much that it's hard to imagine anymore life without the script!

```perl
1    #!/usr/local/bin/perl5
2
3    use SHTML;
4
5    open(D,"<" . $ARGV[0])
6        || die "Couldn't open $ARGV[0], $!";
7    {
8        local $/;
9        $_ = <D>;
10   }
11   close(D) || die "Couldn't close $ARGV[0], $!";
12
13   $_ = striptohtml($_);
14   my ($fieldref,$inform) = (0,0);
15   my (@forminfo,%fieldlist,@fieldlist);
16
17   for my $line (split(/\n/))
18   {
19       if ($line =~ /<form/i)
20       {
21           $inform=1;
22           next;
23       }
24       elsif ($inform)
25       {
26           if (($line =~ /<input.*/i) || ($line =~ /<textarea.*/i))
27           {
28               for my $element (split / /,$line)
29               {
30                   $element =~ s/[<>\"]//g;
31                   my ($formfield,$vinfo) = split /=/,$element;
32                   $formfield = lc($formfield);
33
34                   if ($formfield =~ /textarea/i)
35                   {
36                       $fieldlist{type} = 1;
37                       $forminfo[$fieldref]{type} = $formfield;
38                   }
```

```
39                    else
40                    {
41                        $fieldlist{$formfield} = 1;
42                        $forminfo[$fieldref]{$formfield} = $vinfo;
43                    }
44                }
45                $fieldref++;
46            }
47        }
48  }
49
50  push @fieldlist,'name',grep(!/name/,sort keys %fieldlist);
51
52  foreach $_ (@fieldlist)
53  {
54      printf("%-8s",lc($_));
55  }
56  print "\n";
57  for($fieldref=0;$fieldref<@forminfo;$fieldref++)
58  {
59      foreach $_ (@fieldlist)
60      {
61          printf("%-8s",defined($forminfo[$fieldref]{lc($_)}) ?
62                  "$forminfo[$fieldref]{lc($_)}" : '');
63      }
64      print "\n";
65  }
```

ANNOTATIONS

Once the script has read in the HTML document, it's a case of processing the lines of the HTML, looking first for a form and then for the fields defined within the form. Once we have collated all of the information, we print it out using a simple **printf** statement. This is slightly restrictive, as you will see, but we'll look at a way of expanding the script that makes the use of **printf** slightly more flexible.

```
1   #!/usr/local/bin/perl5
2
3   use SHTML;
4
5   open(D,"<" . $ARGV[0])
6       || die "Couldn't open $ARGV[0], $!";
```

```
7    {
8        local $/;
9        $_ = <D>;
10   }
11   close(D) || die "Couldn't close $ARGV[0], $!";
12
```

We're going to be using the **striptohtml** function to separate the HTML tag elements from the text, so we import the functions from the **SHTML** package. Lines 5 to 11 open and import the first file specified on the command line. We're only going to be dealing with one file at a time, so the **die** statement in line 6 should be enough to highlight any problems to the user. Lines 7 to 10 import the document using the localized input record separator trick. We close the file on line 11, as usual checking to make sure we can close the file correctly.

⌐PROGRAMMER'S NOTE   *As an exercise you may want to investigate the **HTML::TokeParse** module which is part of the **LWP** kit.*

```
13   $_ = striptohtml($_);
14   my ($fieldref,$inform) = (0,0);
15   my (@forminfo,%fieldlist,@fieldlist);
16
```

Line 13 converts the HTML document to a format that is easier to work with. We can assign the default pattern space with the result of the function call on the pattern space to make our lives easier. Line 14 defines the **$fieldref** variable, which will be used to refer to the element of the summary array we will create. The **$inform** variable is used to identify whether we are within a form or not. Both variables are set to an initial value of zero.

The variables **@forminfo, %fieldlist**, and **@fieldlist** will hold the summary information and help print out the final report.

```
17   for my $line (split(/\n/))
18   {
19       if ($line =~ /<form/i)
20       {
21           $inform=1;
22           next;
23       }
```

Line 17 starts the **for** loop that works through the document. Remember that the document has been converted so that tags are on separate, individual lines with the $_ variable. Line 19 checks if the current line is the start of a form. We do a simple regular expression search to verify the fact, remembering to ignore the case of the tag—HTML tags can be upper- or lowercase. If we identify a form, then we set the

$inform variable to true, and skip the line with **next** on line 22. (The **next** function simply skips to the next iteration of the loop.)

```
24      elsif ($inform)
25      {
26          if (($line =~ /<input.*/i) || ($line =~ /<textarea.*/i))
27          {
28              for my $element (split / /,$line)
29              {
```

Line 24 checks to see if we are in a form. If we are, then we identify the two main types of form elements. The input tag allows you to define input text boxes, checkboxes, and lists. The textarea tag allows you to incorporate multiline text fields into a document. In either case, additional options are specified as key/value pairs, separated by a space. Here's an example:

```
<input type=text name=surname>
```

We split the entire option list using a space as the separator, putting each key/value pair into the **$element** scalar on line 28.

```
30              $element =~ s/[<>\"]//g;
31              my ($formfield,$vinfo) = split /=/,$element;
32              $formfield = lc($formfield);
33
```

On line 30 we string the tag brackets, backslash, and double-quotes from the element, before splitting it by the equals sign on line 31 into the **$formfield** and **$vinfo** scalars. The **$formfield** variables holds the field name, and **$vinfo** holds the value information for the field name. We then convert the **$formfield** to lowercase using the **lc** function.

```
34              if ($formfield =~ /textarea/i)
35              {
36                  $fieldlist{type} = 1;
37                  $forminfo[$fieldref]{type} = $formfield;
38              }
```

If the form field element is textarea, then we need to treat it slightly differently, so we check for it on line 34. We add the field name to the list of the fields stored in the **%fieldlist** hash. We could have used an array, but we would have had to manually de-dupe the field list; by using a hash, the list of fields is automatically de-duped. If the field name has already been defined in line 36, then the value for that key is just updated to be 1 again.

WARNING   *The script currently takes no action on duplicate fields within a form—the information will simply be overwritten.*

Line 37 creates an anonymous hash within the **@forminfo** element referred to by the current **$fieldref** counter. An anonymous hash is like a normal hash, except that it has no name because it is part of another variable—in this instance, a standard array—it has no direct name. In fact, we create a reference to an anonymous hash within the named array; Perl just provides us with the ability to directly assign and access the hash like any named hash. The field type within an HTML form is specified by the type value in the definition. A textarea field does not have a type value: its type is inherent from its name. We therefore assign the type to be textarea directly.

```
39                    else
40                    {
41                         $fieldlist{$formfield} = 1;
42                         $forminfo[$fieldref]{$formfield} = $vinfo;
43                    }
44                }
45              $fieldref++;
46          }
47      }
48  }
49
```

Line 39 handles all the other field information from a form field. Line 41 adds the form field key to the field list, while line 41 adds the value of the current element of the current field to the name of the element key of the anonymous array that is referenced by the current field specified by the **$fieldref**.

Line 44 is the end of the processing required for a single field in the HTML form, so we can increment the field reference variable. Because storing the information within a hash requires us first to identify the elements from the field specification, we have to use an array to store the information on a single field before placing it into the hash.

The result of the entire processing, which ends on line 48, is an array (**@forminfo**) that contains a list of the field definitions. The actual field elements and values are stored within an anonymous hash for each array element, and therefore each HTML form field. We also have a list of field element names stored within a hash (**$fieldlist**).

```
50  push @fieldlist,'name',grep(!/name/,sort keys %fieldlist);
51
```

In order to print out the information, we need to create a list of the elements within the form fields. The field name is stored within the name element, and it would obviously be useful to print this information first in the list. Line 50 sorts this out for us. We create a new array, **@fieldlist**, the first element of which is name, and the subsequent elements are taken from the **%fieldlist** hash we generated while reading the form in. By using **grep** with an inverse regular expression, which extracts all of the fields *not* matching name, we ensure we capture all of the remaining fields from the field list.

```
52   foreach $_ (@fieldlist)
53   {
54       printf("%-8s",lc($_));
55   }
56   print "\n";
```

Lines 52 to 56 print out the field titles, using a string format eight characters wide. The result should be a single line with the field element list, so we need to add a new-line character to the list on line 56.

```
57   for($fieldref=0;$fieldref<@forminfo;$fieldref++)
58   {
59       foreach $_ (@fieldlist)
60       {
61           printf("%-8s",defined($forminfo[$fieldref]{lc($_)}) ?
62                   "$forminfo[$fieldref]{lc($_)}" : '');
63       }
64       print "\n";
65   }
```

Lines 57 to 65 print out the field information. Line 57 sets up a **for** loop that works through the array. Line 59 works through the preordered list of element fields within the individual form field. Line 61 then prints out the value. We check first that the form field element has been defined on line 61, printing the value if it exists, or doing nothing if it has not been defined.

Running the script on an HTML form produces output similar to this:

```
$ extform.pl feedback.html
```

name	cols	form	input	rows	size	type	value
comments	50			10		textarea	
name					30	text	
title					30	text	
email					30	text	
company					45	text	
city						text	
state						text	
postcode					11	text	
country						text	
reason	50			5		textarea	
						submit	Send
						reset	Reset

The output provides us with enough information that we should be able to write the necessary handling script for processing the form.

The biggest problem with this script is that the field output uses a fairly small fixed width. To get around this, we could create a new entry in the anonymous hash designed to specify the maximum width of the element field in question. To do this, we can insert the following line before line 44:

```
$forminfo[$fieldref]{'width-$formfield'} = length($vinfo)
    if length($vinfo > $forminfo[$fieldref]{'width-$formfield'});
```

The list of fields will not be updated, so the new references we have created—for example, those starting with "width-"—will not be included in the field titles. All we need to do is modify the **printf** format we use by adding these lines before each **printf** statement:

```
$forminfo[$fieldref]{'width-$formfield'} = length($formfield)
    unless (defined($forminfo[$fieldref]{'width-$formfield'});
my $format = sprintf("%%-%ds",
                     ($forminfo[$fieldref]{'width-$formfield'} + 1));
```

Finally, you need to change the **printf** statement to include the new **$format** variable as the first argument. For example, we could change line 54 to

```
printf($format,lc($_));
```

The result would be a list formatted with widths matching at least the width of the element name, and at most the maximum width of the element value.

Mirroring a Single Page

Earlier in this chapter, we saw the **LWP** package being used to retrieve files remotely and then parse those files to extract the links and recursively repeat the process until the entire site had been checked.

The core of that script was the UserAgent object, which allowed us to specify a URL to be downloaded and then what to do with the file that was retrieved. The **LWP** package also includes a simpler method of retrieving a file from a remote server to a local file. The **mirror** function copies a remote file to a local file if the remote file is more recent than the local version. The script can be used to quickly copy a remote file to a local server, either to speed up access or because you want a copy of the remote file.

This **singmirr.pl** script is a renamed version of the lwp-mirror script that is supplied as a demonstration in the bin directory of the LWP distribution. The only other changes I have made to this script are for line length, to incorporate it into the book, and to remove the built-in POD documentation.

```perl
1   #!/usr/local/bin/perl -w
2
3   use LWP::Simple;
4   use Getopt::Std;
5
6   $progname = $0;
7   $progname =~ s,.*/,,;
8   $progname =~ s/\.\w*$//;
9
10  $VERSION = sprintf("%d.%02d",
11                      q$Revision: 1.18 $ =~ /(\d+)\.(\d+)/);
12
13  $opt_h = undef;
14  $opt_v = undef;
15  $opt_t = undef;
16
17  unless (getopts("hvt:")) {
18      usage();
19  }
20
21  if ($opt_v) {
22      require LWP;
23      my $DISTNAME = 'libwww-perl-' . LWP::Version();
24      die <<"EOT";
25  This is lwp-mirror version $VERSION ($DISTNAME)
26
27  Copyright 1995-1996, Gisle Aas.
28
29  This program is free software; you can redistribute it and/or
30  modify it under the same terms as Perl itself.
31  EOT
32  }
33
34  $url  = shift or usage();
35  $file = shift or usage();
36  usage() if $opt_h or @ARGV;
37
38  if (defined $opt_t) {
39      $opt_t =~ /^(\d+)([smh])?/;
40      die "$progname: Illegal timeout value!\n" unless defined $1;
41      $timeout = $1;
42      $timeout *= 60   if ($2 eq "m");
43      $timeout *= 3600 if ($2 eq "h");
```

```
44        $LWP::Simple::ua->timeout($timeout);
45  }
46
47  $rc = mirror($url, $file);
48
49  if ($rc == 304) {
50      print STDERR "$progname: $file is up to date\n"
51  } elsif (!is_success($rc)) {
52      print STDERR ("$progname: $rc ",
53                     status_message($rc),
54                     "    ($url)\n");
55      exit 1;
56  }
57  exit;
58
59
60  sub usage
61  {
62      die <<"EOT";
63  Usage: $progname [-options] <url> <file>
64      -v            print version number of program
65      -t <timeout>  Set timeout value
66  EOT
67  }
```

ANNOTATIONS

Because the bulk of the work is performed by a single, external function, **mirror**, the script is actually shorter than it looks. The bulk of the rest of the script is devoted to parsing and configuring the values specified by the user on the command line.

```
1   #!/usr/local/bin/perl -w
2
3   use LWP::Simple;
4   use Getopt::Std;
5
```

We need the **LWP::Simple** module for the **mirror** function. This is a cut down version of the full **LWP** module that supplies enough information for us to download a file, while excluding a lot of the overhead associated with the much larger **LWP::UserAgent** module. We also use the standard **Getopt** module to extract user options from the command line.

```
6    $progname = $0;
7    $progname =~ s,.*/,,;
8    $progname =~ s/\.\w*$//;
9
```

The name of the script being executed is contained in the **$0** special variable, which we extract to a globally accessible variable name in line 6. To make sure we just have the program name, we strip any characters up to, and including, the last forward slash on line 7, and then we strip any extension off the end of the file on line 8. This ensures that names like

`./singmirr.pl`

and

`/usr/local/bin/singmirr.pl`

are interpreted and printed as "singmirr."

```
10   $VERSION = sprintf("%d.%02d",
11                      q$Revision: 1.18 $ =~ /(\d+)\.(\d+)/);
12
```

Gisle has also specified a version number for the script. The **Revision** text block will have been automatically inserted by a source code management system, such as RCS (Revision Control System), as part of the package release process. The regular expression on line 11 returns the version number as an array to the **sprintf** function. The result of lines 10 and 11 is that **$VERSION** equals 1.18.

```
13   $opt_h = undef;
14   $opt_v = undef;
15   $opt_t = undef;
16
17   unless (getopts("hvt:")) {
18       usage();
19   }
20
```

The command-line options are initialized to undefined values on lines 13 to 15 before we extract the options on line 17. We check the result of the **getopts** function to ensure that no extra options are specified that are not supported, and that the value required by the **t** option is actually supplied. Any failure in extracting the command-line options is handled by the **usage** function, which prints the usage instructions to the user before exiting.

```
21   if ($opt_v) {
22       require LWP;
23       my $DISTNAME = 'libwww-perl-' . LWP::Version();
```

```
24      die <<"EOT";
25  This is lwp-mirror version $VERSION ($DISTNAME)
26
27  Copyright 1995-1996, Gisle Aas.
28
29  This program is free software; you can redistribute it and/or
30  modify it under the same terms as Perl itself.
31  EOT
32  }
33
```

The **v** command-line option specifies that the script should work in verbose mode. If specified, lines 21 to 32 print out extended information about the script and package it uses. Unlike a **use** statement, a **require** statement is processed only when the line is actually executed. This means that the full **LWP** package will only be imported when the verbose option has been specified on the command line. In fact, the verbose option only requires the version information from the **LWP** package.

```
34  $url  = shift or usage();
35  $file = shift or usage();
36  usage() if $opt_h or @ARGV;
37
```

Line 34 **shift**s the first argument off the command-line argument stack (after the options have been removed by **getopts**), or prints the usage message if none is specified. Line 35 gets the local filename from the command line, again printing an error if none is specified. The usage message is printed if there are any more arguments on the command line or if the help option is specified.

```
38  if (defined $opt_t) {
39      $opt_t =~ /^(\d+)([smh])?/;
40      die "$progname: Illegal timeout value!\n" unless defined $1;
41      $timeout = $1;
42      $timeout *= 60   if ($2 eq "m");
43      $timeout *= 3600 if ($2 eq "h");
44      $LWP::Simple::ua->timeout($timeout);
45  }
46
```

The **t** command-line option specifies the default timeout value to be used for retrieving the file. If it has been specified, then line 38 identifies this. Line 39 performs a regular expression on the option value: remember that the **t** option required a string. The regular expression allows for a number that is followed, optionally, by one of three letters: *s*, *m*, or *h*. The letters correspond to seconds, minutes, and hours. This allows the user to specify a timeout value of "2h," which equates to two hours, or "7m," which equates to seven minutes.

We check whether the regular expression on line 39 worked. If the regular expression did not match (which we test by examining the value of the first match) then we **die** on line 40. The timeout specified is set on line 41. The specified value is multiplied by 60, if the user specified minutes, to convert the value into seconds. If the user specified hours, then we multiply by 3,600 (60 minutes per hour × 60 seconds per minute). Note that we don't need to make any calculation if the user did not specify a modifier—we'll assume the value is in seconds, which is what we want anyway.

The timeout value is controlled via the **timeout** method of the UserAgent object ua. We set the value, based on our earlier calculations, on line 44.

```
47   $rc = mirror($url, $file);
48
```

Once we reach line 47, we are ready to actually request the file from the remote server. This is performed by the single **mirror** function. We specify the URL and local filename we extracted from the command line. The result is the standard return code given by the Web server.

```
49   if ($rc == 304) {
50       print STDERR "$progname: $file is up to date\n"
51   } elsif (!is_success($rc)) {
52       print STDERR ("$progname: $rc ",
53                     status_message($rc),
54                     "   ($url)\n");
55       exit 1;
56   }
57   exit;
58
59
```

If the return code from the **mirror** function is 304, it signifies that the local file is up to date compared to the remote file. The check is performed against the modification times of the two files, taking into account any time zone differences. Another function supplied by the **LWP** toolkit identifies whether a return code is within the list of successful codes. The opposite (a failure), is identified on line 51. The result is an error message, printed out by lines 51 to 54. The **status_message** function converts the numerical return code into a human-friendly string. Finally, if there was an error, then we exit with a nonzero value on line 55. Within Unix, a zero return code from a called program signifies success, so line 55 ensures that the calling program knows there was an error executing the script. Line 57 quits with a zero exit code and closes the script.

```
60    sub usage
61    {
62        die <<"EOT";
63    Usage: $progname [-options] <url> <file>
64        -v             print version number of program
65        -t <timeout> Set timeout value
66    EOT
67    }
```

Lines 60 to 67 format the **usage** function, which just uses a here document to output the usage instructions.

To use, specify the URL you want to download and the local file you want to store the returned document in. For example:

```
$ singmirr.pl http://www.omh.com omh-index.html
```

If the local file exists, and it is older than the remote version, or if the local file does not exist, then it will be downloaded. If it is up to date, you'll receive the "up to date" message, and no downloading will occur.

sitemirr.pl

Mirroring an Entire Site

It is unlikely that you want to download only a single page from the site; usually you'll want to download an entire site, either for offline browsing, or for updating or modifying it on behalf of a client.

Using the **singmirr.pl** script, this would be a very long process, especially when you consider that we already know how to extract the URLs from a Web page using the LWP library. However, there are some extra levels of complication. First of all, we need to be able to download a file to a local copy; secondly we need to identify the links in a page and then update a list of links to be downloaded before repeating the process again.

The two scripts that we need to keep in mind are **chkrlink.pl** and **singmirr.pl**. The **chkrlink.pl** script uses the built-in methods and abilities of the LWP library to download the file into a temporary variable; we never really see the file that is downloaded. The **singmirr.pl** script uses the **mirror** function to copy the remove file to the local hard disk. If we employ the methods in these two scripts, in combination with some of the manual tricks we examined within the **chklinks.pl** script, we should be able to write a script that downloads the entire Web site from a remote Web server.

PROGRAMMER'S NOTE   *This script works for static sites. For the newer dynamic sites you may get mixed results. They use CGI scripts to generate pages dynamically and the **LWP** toolkit may or may not follow these correctly.*

```
1   #!/usr/local/bin/perl
2
3   use LWP::Simple;
4   use LWP::UserAgent;
5   use HTML::LinkExtor;
6   use URI::URL;
7   use Getopt::Long;
8   use File::Basename;
9
10  my ($file,$host,$localdir,$curhost);
11  my ($url, $specdir, $quiet, $silent, $inchost, $unrestrict)
12      = (undef, undef, undef, undef, undef);
13
14  usage() unless(GetOptions("d=s" => \$specdir,
15                            "s"   => \$silent,
16                            "q"   => \$quiet,
17                            "h"   => \$inchost,
18                            "u"   => \$unrestrict
19                            ));
20
21  usage() unless($url=shift);
22  $specdir = '.' unless defined($specdir);
23  $specdir = "$specdir/" unless ($specdir =~ m#/$#);
24  $quiet = 1 if ($silent);
25
26  my %fullurl;
27  my @urlstack = ($url);
28  my @urls = ();
29  my $p = HTML::LinkExtor->new(\&callback);
30
31  my $ua = new LWP::UserAgent;
32  my $res = $ua->request(HTTP::Request->new(GET => $url));
33  my $base = $res->base;
34  $curhost = $host = url($url,'')->host;
35
36  print "Retrieving from $url to $specdir",
37        ($inchost ? "$host\n" : "\n")
38            unless ($silent);
39
40  while ($url = pop(@urlstack))
41  {
42      $host = url($url,'')->host;
43      if ($host ne $curhost)
44      {
```

```
45          my $ua = new LWP::UserAgent;
46          my $res = $ua->request(HTTP::Request->new(GET => $url));
47          my $base = $res->base;
48          $host = url($url,'')->host;
49          $curhost = $host;
50          print "Changing host to $host\n" unless $quiet;
51      }
52      $localdir = ($inchost ? "$specdir$host/" : "$specdir/");
53
54      $file = url($url,$base)->full_path;
55      $file .='index.html' if ($file =~ m#/$#);
56      $file =~ s#^/#$localdir#;
57
58      print "Retrieving: $url to $file\n" unless ($quiet);
59      my $dir = dirname($file);
60      unless (-d $dir)
61      {
62          mkdirhier($dir);
63      }
64      getfile($url,$file);
65      if (-e $file)
66      {
67          $p->parse_file($file);
68          @urls = map { $_ = url($_, $base)->abs; } @urls;
69          addtostack(@urls);
70      }
71  }
72
73  sub addtostack
74  {
75      my (@urllist) = @_;
76
77      for my $url (@urllist)
78      {
79          next if ($url =~ /#/);
80          next unless ($url =~ m#^http#);
81          my $urlhost = url($url,$base)->host;
82          unless (defined($unrestrict))
83              { next unless ($urlhost eq $host); };
84          push(@urlstack,$url) unless(defined($fullurl{$url}));
85          $fullurl{$url} = 1;
86      }
87  }
```

```perl
88
89  sub callback
90  {
91      my($tag, %attr) = @_;
92      push(@urls, values %attr);
93  }
94
95  sub getfile
96  {
97      my ($url,$file) = @_;
98      my $rc = mirror($url, $file);
99
100     if ($rc == 304)
101     {
102         print "File is up to date\n" unless ($quiet);
103     }
104     elsif (!is_success($rc))
105     {
106         warn "sitemirr: $rc ", status_message($rc), " ($url)\n"
107             unless ($silent);
108         return(0);
109     }
110 }
111
112 sub mkdirhier
113 {
114     my ($fullpath) = @_;
115     my $path;
116
117     for my $dir (split(m#/#,$fullpath))
118     {
119         unless (-d "$path$dir")
120         {
121             mkdir("$path$dir",0777)
122                 or die "Couldn't make directory $path/$dir: $!";
123         }
124         $path .= "$dir/";
125     }
126 }
127
128 sub usage
129 {
130     die <<EOF;
```

```
131 Usage:
132     sitemirr.pl [-d localdir] [-s] [-q] URL
133
134 Where:
135
136 localdir is the name of the local directory you want
137          files copied to (default: .)
138 h        Include host in local directory path
139 q        Retrieve quietly (show errors only)
140 s        Retrieve silently (no output)
141 u        Unrestrict site match (will download ALL
142          URL's, including those from other hosts)
143 EOF
144 }
```

ANNOTATIONS

The bulk of this script is actually identical to the **chkrhtml.pl** script. The same methods and processes are used; the difference lies in the fact that the file is downloaded to a local file, using the **mirror** function, and then the page parser to extract the links is executed on the local file, instead of the remote file.

```
1   #!/usr/local/bin/perl
2
3   use LWP::Simple;
4   use LWP::UserAgent;
5   use HTML::LinkExtor;
6   use URI::URL;
7   use Getopt::Long;
8   use File::Basename;
9
```

This script requires a lot of modules. We need the **LWP::Simple** and **LWP::UserAgent** modules to support the ability to download and access remote pages.

```
10  my ($file,$host,$localdir,$curhost);
```

Line 10 defines some global variables that are used throughout the rest of the script. The **$file** variable stores the location of the local file to which URLs will be downloaded. The **$host** variable stores the host of the current URL, while the **$curhost** stores the host of the current base URL.

```
11  my ($url, $specdir, $quiet, $silent, $inchost, $unrestrict)
12      = (undef, undef, undef, undef, undef);
13
14  usage() unless(GetOptions("d=s" => \$specdir,
15                            "s"   => \$silent,
16                            "q"   => \$quiet,
17                            "h"   => \$inchost,
18                            "u"   => \$unrestrict
19                            ));
20
21  usage() unless($url=shift);
22  $specdir = '.' unless defined($specdir);
23  $specdir = "$specdir/" unless ($specdir =~ m#/$#);
24  $quiet = 1 if ($silent);
25
```

Lines 11 to 24 sort out the command-line options. Lines 11 and 12 define the variables that hold the configuration information. They are all defaulted to undefined values to ensure that tests later in the script will work as expected. Lines 14 to 19 use the **GetOptions** function to extract the entries from the command line. We print the usage instructions if the options could not be deciphered correctly.

The variables, in order, define the local download directory specification, silent mode, quiet mode, whether to include the host name in the local directory, and whether to unrestrict the remote hosts to allow any extracted URL to be downloaded.

Line 21 attempts to get a URL off the command line, printing usage instructions if it fails. Line 22 defines the current directory as the download directory unless the user has specified one on the command line. Line 23 adds a trailing forward slash to the directory if the user didn't add one. Line 24 defines that the script will ignore messages that are not printed when working in quiet mode if the user has specified silent mode. Silent mode has precedence, and it implies quiet mode if specified. The differences of what will be printed will become apparent as we work through the script.

```
26  my %fullurl;
27  my @urlstack = ($url);
28  my @urls = ();
29  my $p = HTML::LinkExtor->new(\&callback);
30
```

Lines 26 to 29 set up the last few variables we will need. The **%fullurl** records the URLs added to the list of URLs to download and the location of the URL that referenced it. Line 27 is the array containing the list of URLs to download. We initialize it with the URL extracted from the command line. Line 28 is the array that stores the temporary list of URLs to be downloaded between the link extractor and the **addtostack** function.

```
31   my $ua = new LWP::UserAgent;
32   my $res = $ua->request(HTTP::Request->new(GET => $url));
33   my $base = $res->base;
34   $curhost = $host = url($url,'')->host;
35
```

The next four lines, from 31 to 34, are used to obtain the base URL and host for the URL specified on the command line. Although doing this requires downloading the original URL twice, it ensures that the base URL information is correct. Since this is required and relied upon heavily by the rest of the script, it's an important part of the entire download process.

Line 31 creates a new UserAgent object, while line 32 creates a new request object based on the UserAgent object **$ua**. The call to the **http::Request** function handles the retrieval of the URL. Lines 33 and 34 extract the base URL and base URL host respectively.

```
36   print "Retrieving from $url to $specdir",
37           ($inchost ? "$host\n" : "\n")
38               unless ($silent);
39
```

Lines 36 to 38 print out the summary information of the URL and site being downloaded, and where it is being downloaded to, provided we are not working in silent mode. Remember that silent mode implies quiet mode.

```
40   while ($url = pop(@urlstack))
41   {
42       $host = url($url,'')->host;
43       if ($host ne $curhost)
44       {
45           my $ua = new LWP::UserAgent;
46           my $res = $ua->request(HTTP::Request->new(GET => $url));
47           my $base = $res->base;
48           $host = url($url,'')->host;
49           $curhost = $host;
50           print "Changing host to $host\n" unless $quiet;
51       }
```

Line 40 is the start of the **while** loop that will download the URLs specified in the download queue that is the **@urlstack** array. The host for the current URL is extracted on line 42. If the host for the URL does not equal the host for the current base URL, then we need to redefine the base URL and the current base host information. This is carried out by lines 45 to 50 in much the same way as the original discovery at the start of this script.

This update of the base URL occurs only if we are working in unrestricted mode; we don't test for that here because URLs outside of the original URL will only be added to the download queue by the **addtostack** function. This takes account of the unrestricted option as part of the tests it carries out on the extracted URLs.

```perl
52      $localdir = ($inchost ? "$specdir$host/" : "$specdir/");
53
54      $file = url($url,$base)->full_path;
55      $file .='index.html' if ($file =~ m#/$#);
56      $file =~ s#^/#$localdir#;
57
```

Lines 52 to 56 select the local filename and path to use for downloading the file. On line 52 we select the local directory, based on whether we are including the host name in the directory specification or not. Note that we need to compute this for every URL. Since each URL could have a different host, and obviously a different directory, the host part is especially significant if we are working in unrestricted mode.

Line 54 obtains the full path of the file, by using the **full_path** method against an anonymous **url** object. Line 55 adds a filename of index.htm if no filename is available. We check this by looking for a slash at the end of the current filename. Finally, line 56 inserts the local directory specified on the command line if the current path starts with a single forward slash.

```perl
58      print "Retrieving: $url to $file\n" unless ($quiet);
59      my $dir = dirname($file);
60      unless (-d $dir)
61      {
62          mkdirhier($dir);
63      }
```

Line 58 prints a progress message, provided were not working in quiet mode. The directory element of the path we have created is extracted on line 59 so that we can verify that the directory exists on line 60. If it doesn't exist, then we call the **mkdirhier** function to make the entire directory structure for the specified directory path.

```perl
64      getfile($url,$file);
```

Line 64 calls the **getfile** function, which is a special wrapper around the **mirror** function. We pass two arguments to it: the URL of the file we want downloaded and the full path of the location and file to download it to.

```
65      if (-e $file)
66      {
67          $p->parse_file($file);
68          @urls = map { $_ = url($_, $base)->abs; } @urls;
69          addtostack(@urls);
70      }
71  }
72
```

Lines 66 to 70 verify that the file that should have been downloaded by the **getfile** function exists before parsing the file to extract the links on line 67. On line 67, we are calling the **parse** method and specifying the location of the local file, instead of relying on the variable passed to it by the UserAgent object. Line 68 maps the returned URLs to full URLs based on the current base URL, before the URLs are added to the download stack on line 69. This code fragment will work regardless of whether the file was downloaded in this session or a previous session. The **for** loop and the main part of the script end on line 71.

```
73  sub addtostack
74  {
75      my (@urllist) = @_;
76
77      for my $url (@urllist)
78      {
79          next if ($url =~ /#/);
80          next unless ($url =~ m#^http#);
81          my $urlhost = url($url,$base)->host;
82          unless (defined($unrestrict))
83              { next unless ($urlhost eq $host); };
84          push(@urlstack,$url) unless(defined($fullurl{$url}));
85          $fullurl{$url} = 1;
86      }
87  }
88
```

The **addtostack** function adds the list of URLs to the main download queue. We work through each URL, checking for anchor links within a document (line 79), and we ensure the protocol is http on line 80. In both cases, a mismatch will skip to the next URL.

Line 81 extracts the host information from the URL by creating a new **url** object using the current URL and the base URL information and then calling the **host** method on the new object. Lines 82 and 83 skip the URL unless we are working in unrestricted mode and the host of the URL is different from the host of the base URL. Note that I've concatenated a full block onto a single line for space and clarity;

it still makes sense, even though it appears to be a bit cramped. It's important to remember that Perl ignores line breaks, taking only semicolons as the real breaks between different executable lines.

If we get to it, line 84 then adds the URL to the download queue if it has not already been added, and line 85 updates the list of URLs added to the download queue.

```
89  sub callback
90  {
91      my($tag, %attr) = @_;
92      push(@urls, values %attr);
93  }
94
```

The **callback** function adds the URLs that are contained in the values of the **%attr** hash passed to the function by the **parse** method to the temporary **@urls** array.

```
95   sub getfile
96   {
97       my ($url,$file) = @_;
98       my $rc = mirror($url, $file);
99
100      if ($rc == 304)
101      {
102          print "File is up to date\n" unless ($quiet);
103      }
104      elsif (!is_success($rc))
105      {
106          warn "sitemirr: $rc ", status_message($rc), " ($url)\n"
107              unless ($silent);
108          return(0);
109      }
110  }
111
```

Line 95 starts the **getfile** function, a special wrapper around the **mirror** function that takes into account files that may already be up to date on the local server. The function takes two arguments: the URL of the remote file and the local filename to download the file to. Line 98 then attempts to download the file.

The result, stored in **$rc**, is then checked. If the file is up to date, the result code is 304, which is trapped on line 100. A suitable message is printed on line 102, unless we are working in silent mode. Line 104 ensures that the result code indicated a success. Because the result of the test is inverted by the exclamation mark, an error will be printed by the **warn** function on line 106. This reports the problem, reason, and URL, unless we are working in silent mode.

```
112 sub mkdirhier
113 {
114     my ($fullpath) = @_;
115     my $path;
116
117     for my $dir (split(m#/#,$fullpath))
118     {
119         unless (-d "$path$dir")
120         {
121             mkdir("$path$dir",0777)
122                 or die "Couldn't make directory $path/$dir: $!";
123         }
124         $path .= "$dir/";
125     }
126 }
127
```

The **mkdirhier** script creates an entire directory path. It works by splitting the supplied path by a forward slash (line 117). Line 119 checks if the filename and current path name exist and refer to a directory; if the directory doesn't exist, then it attempts to make the directory, using a mode of 777 (read, write, and execute for all) on line 121, **die**-ing and reporting an error if the creation failed. The path name is the current directory tree, actually defined later in this function.

Line 124 adds the new directory to a temporary variable, and then the **for** loop repeats until all of the directory elements have been created.

For example, when calling the function with a directory of foo/bar, the first iteration checks for a directory called foo, based on the first split element and the empty path variable. At the end of the first iteration, foo/ is added to the path variable. The second iteration sets **$dir** to bar, but the check and creation on lines 119 and 121 respectively use a directory name of foo/bar.

```
128 sub usage
129 {
130     die <<EOF;
131 Usage:
132     sitemirr.pl [-d localdir] [-s] [-q] URL
133
134 Where:
135
136 localdir is the name of the local directory you want
137         files copied to (default: .)
138 h       Include host in local directory path
139 q       Retrieve quietly (show errors only)
140 s       Retrieve silently (no output)
```

```
141 u          Unrestrict site match (will download ALL
142            URL's, including those from other hosts)
143 EOF
144 }
```

The **usage** function on line 128 simply prints out the usage instructions using a here document.

Using the script is largely identical to how you use the **singmirr.pl** script, except that the whole site is downloaded, and you have more control over where the files are downloaded. For example, to download the Osborne/McGraw-Hill site to your local machine, you might use this command line:

```
$ sitemirr.pl -h www.mcgraw-hill.com
```

This would download the entire site to the current directory, within a directory called www.mcgraw-hill.com.

uplsite.pl

Uploading an Entire Web Site Using FTP

The typical process for developing and publishing a Web site is to first design the site, then check it, and finally release it. Unless you are hosting your site on a one of your own servers, chances are you are using a Web hosting service provided by an Internet service provider. The process for getting your site uploaded to the site usually involves using FTP to transfer the files over to a secure directory on the remote server.

Although there are tools that help in the process of uploading sites, the programs are often limited to copying over the selected set of files in a single directory. Even if they do support the option of uploading an entire directory structure, you have to copy the entire directory structure to the destination. To speed up the process of updating an existing Web site, it would make sense to copy to the server only any items that have changed.

This is effectively the reverse of the **sitemirr.pl** script we have already seen. The **uplsite.pl** script attempts to fill this gap. It uses the **Net::FTP** module from Graham Barr to do the actual uploading, using the same FTP protocol that we would use if we were uploading the site manually. The difference is that the process is automatic, and the destination and local files are compared against each other, so only the changed files are uploaded.

When uploading files with FTP there are two basic transfer modes. The ASCII mode is used to transfer text files. The ASCII mode automatically accounts for any differences in line termination across different platforms. The BINARY mode is required when transferring pure binary files, such as graphics, programs, or even compressed files. We also automatically account for the two transfer modes supported by FTP, binary and ASCII, by checking the file type before the file is sent, intelligently changing the mode accordingly.

```perl
1    #!/usr/local/bin/perl5
2
3    use Net::FTP;
4    use Getopt::Long;
5    use File::Find;
6    use Cwd;
7
8    my $debug      = 1;
9    my $remserver  = undef;
10   my $remport    = '21';
11   my $user       = 'anonymous';
12   my $password   = 'me@foo.bar';
13   my $dir        = '.';
14   my $localdir   = './';
15   my $curxfermode = 'ASCII';
16
17   unless (GetOptions("d" => \$debug,
18                      "s=s" => \$remserver,
19                      "r=s" => \$dir,
20                      "p=i" => \$remport,
21                      "u=s" => \$user,
22                      "w=s" => \$password,
23                      "l=s" => \$localdir
24                      ))
25   {
26       usage();
27   }
28
29   usage() unless $remserver;
30
31   $localdir = './' unless ($localdir);
32   my $ftp = Net::FTP->new($remserver, 'Port' => $remport);
33   die "Could not connect to $remserver" unless $ftp;
34   $ftp->login($user, $password)
35       or die "Couldn't login to $remserver";
36   $ftp->cwd($dir)
37       or die "Invalid directory ($dir) on FTP Server";
38   $ftp->ascii()
39       or warn "Couldn't change default xfer mode, continuing";
40
41   chdir($localdir);
42   my $currentdir = getcwd();
43   find(\&sendfile,'.');
```

```perl
44
45  $ftp->quit();
46
47  sub sendfile
48  {
49      my $file      =   $File::Find::name;
50      $file         =~  s#^\./##g;
51      my $localfile =   "$currentdir/$file";
52      $localfile    =~  s#//#/#g;
53      my $remfile   =   $file;
54
55      print "Processing $localfile rem($remfile)\n" if $debug;
56
57      if (-d $localfile)
58      {
59          my $remcurdir = $ftp->pwd();
60          unless($ftp->cwd($remfile))
61          {
62              unless ($localfile eq '..')
63              {
64                  print "Attempting to make directory $remfile\n";
65                  $ftp->mkdir($remfile,1) or
66                      die "Couldn't make directory $remfile";
67              }
68          }
69          else
70          {
71              $ftp->cwd($remcurdir) or
72                  die "Couldn't change to directory $currentdir";
73          }
74      }
75      else
76      {
77          my ($remtime,$localtime,$upload) = (undef,undef,0);
78          unless($remtime = $ftp->mdtm($remfile))
79          {
80              $remtime = 0;
81          }
82          $localtime = (stat($file))[9];
83          if (defined($localtime) and defined($remtime))
84          {
85              if ($localtime > $remtime)
86              {
```

```
87                    $upload=1;
88                }
89            }
90            else
91            {
92                $upload=1;
93            }
94            if ($upload)
95            {
96                if (-B $localfile)
97                {
98                    if ($curxfermode eq 'ASCII')
99                    {
100                       if ($ftp->binary())
101                       {
102                           $curxfermode = 'BIN';
103                           print "Changed mode to BINary\n"
104                               if $debug;
105                       }
106                       else
107                       {
108                           warn "Couldn't change transfer mode";
109                       }
110                   }
111               }
112               else
113               {
114                   if ($curxfermode eq 'BIN')
115                   {
116                       if ($ftp->ascii())
117                       {
118                           $curxfermode = 'ASCII';
119                           print "Changed mode to ASCII\n"
120                               if $debug;
121                       }
122                       else
123                       {
124                           warn "Couldn't change transfer mode";
125                       }
126                   }
127               }
128               print "Uploading $localfile to $remfile\n" if $debug;
129               $ftp->put($localfile,$remfile)
```

```
130                   or warn "Couldn't upload $remfile";
131            }
132        else
133        {
134            print "File $remfile appears to be up to date\n"
135                if $debug;
136        }
137    }
138 }
139
140 sub usage
141 {
142     print <<EOF;
143 Usage:
144
145     uplsite.pl [-d] [-r remdir] [-p remport] [-u user]
146               [-w password] [-l localdir] -s server
147
148 Description:
149
150 Uploads a directory structure to the server using FTP.
151
152 Where:
153
154 -d  Switch on debugging output
155 -r  Remote directory to upload to (defaults to .)
156 -p  The remote port to use (defaults to 21)
157 -u  The user name to login as (defaults to anonymous)
158 -w  The password to use (defaults to me\@foo.bar)
159 -l  The local directory to upload from (defaults to .)
160 -s  The remote server address to upload to (required)
161
162 EOF
163     exit 1;
164 }
```

ANNOTATIONS

Using the **File::Find** module, we work through the specified directory checking the file type and then the remote file's modification time. If the file is older than the local copy, or if the remote file does not exist, then we upload it. We use a state variable to record the current transfer mode, changing the mode to match the file we are uploading—but only if the required mode does not match the current mode.

```
1   #!/usr/local/bin/perl5
2
3   use Net::FTP;
4   use Getopt::Long;
5   use File::Find;
6   use Cwd;
7
```

We'll need the **File::Find** module to supply us with a mechanism for traversing a directory tree. We also need the long version of the **Getopt** system to extract complex selections from the command-line arguments.

```
8    my $debug      = 1;
9    my $remserver  = undef;
10   my $remport    = '21';
11   my $user       = 'anonymous';
12   my $password   = 'me@foo.bar';
13   my $dir        = '.';
14   my $localdir   = './';
```

Lines 8 to 14 set the default configuration values for the script. By presetting them here, we negate the need to make any kind of decision based on the information supplied on the command line. Any command-line selections simply replace whatever value we have configured here as a default with the specified value.

The variables control whether debugging information is printed, the remote server and port, and the login and password to gain access to the site. Line 13 defines the **$dir** scalar, which is the name of the remote directory to use a base for uploading files to. Line 14 specifies the local directory that contains the files we want to upload.

```
15   my $curxfermode = 'ASCII';
16
```

Line 15 sets up the variable we will use to hold the current transfer mode. We initially set this file to ASCII. We could, arguably, use a simple toggle with a zero for ASCII and 1 for BINARY.

```
17   unless (GetOptions("d" => \$debug,
18                      "s=s" => \$remserver,
19                      "r=s" => \$dir,
20                      "p=i" => \$remport,
21                      "u=s" => \$user,
22                      "w=s" => \$password,
```

```
23                          "l=s" => \$localdir
24                          ))
25   {
26       usage();
27   }
28
```

Lines 17 to 24 extract the command-line options. Because we are using the **Getopt::Long** module, we can ensure that we get an integer for the remote port while getting strings for the remainder of the options. If there is any error in extracting the options, then we call the **usage** function to print out the usage instructions.

```
29   usage() unless $remserver;
30
```

Line 29 checks to ensure that we get a remote server specified on the command line. This is the only option that does not have a predefined value, so we must check for it specifically.

```
31   $localdir = './' unless ($localdir);
```

We double-check that the local directory specification has been specified; we need this information for the **find** function that is a part of the **File::Find** module.

```
32   my $ftp = Net::FTP->new($remserver, 'Port' => $remport);
33   die "Could not connect to $remserver" unless $ftp;
```

The **Net::FTP** module uses objects to specify and use an FTP connection. We create a new FTP object, using the remote server and port specified earlier as the base. The new object is referenced by the **$ftp** scalar. If the open failed, then the value of the **$ftp** variable is undefined, which will trip an error in the test on line 33. We report a suitable error and then **die** if the connection failed.

```
34   $ftp->login($user, $password)
35       or die "Couldn't login to $remserver";
36   $ftp->cwd($dir)
37       or die "Invalid directory ($dir) on FTP Server";
38   $ftp->ascii()
39       or warn "Couldn't change default xfer mode, continuing";
40
```

We log in to the remote server on line 34, again using the login and password supplied, either by the user or from the default values we initialized at the start of the script. If the login failed, then we quit with an error on line 35. Note that we've used the word "or" instead of the logical-OR operator (| |). The **or** is a keyword and is a lower precedence version of the logical OR operator. In single tests like this there is little difference between the two, although you should be careful if using the keyword in more complex situations.

Line 36 changes to the remote server directory specified. The **cwd** method within an FTP object changes the directory. A failure can be detected by the return value of the method call; a false return value refers to a failure, which can be checked and reported on. The directory we are changing to will be used as the base reference for all files that are uploaded. All files and folders within the specified local directory will be uploaded to a structure within this remote directory.

Line 38 changes the transfer mode to the default specified on line 15. Although most servers will set the transfer mode to ASCII by default, changing it here gives us a point of reference for the rest of the script.

```
41  chdir($localdir);
42  my $currentdir = getcwd();
```

One line 41 we change to the specified local directory, and then we get the current working directory on line 42. By changing directory and then using the new value of the current working directory, we can support relative directory selections as well as full path names.

```
43  find(\&sendfile,'.');
44
45  $ftp->quit();
46
```

At this point in the script, we hand the execution over to the **find** function. This will work through the current directory and its entire subtree, calling the **sendfile** function for each directory entry found. Once the **find** has completed, we close the FTP connection on line 45 before exiting the script.

```
47  sub sendfile
48  {
49      my $file      =  $File::Find::name;
50      $file         =~ s#^\./##g;
51      my $localfile =  "$currentdir/$file";
52      $localfile    =~ s#//#/#g;
53      my $remfile   =  $file;
54
```

The **sendfile** function does the bulk of the processing. The filename, including the path name relative to the directory specification used on the **find** function, is contained within the **$File::Find::name** scalar variable. We assign this value to a local variable on line 50 before stripping off the leading *./*. Since we always use the same file reference to the **find** function, the filename always includes this information. We don't want or need it, so it's safe to remove it from the file specification.

The name of the local file needs to be specified exactly. Since the relative directory supplied by the **find** function is the current directory we extracted on line 42, we can prefix the filename with the current directory name. Line 52 ensures there are no double-forward-slashes in the name. The name of the remote file is the same as the stripped filename we formatted on line 50. Remember that we are uploading a local file, which may be buried deep in a directory structure, to a server where we want the file to be referenced from an equivalent of the root directory.

For example, your Web site home page may be located in the /usr/local/etc/httpd/ htdocs directory, but when we upload it, we want to upload it to the / directory of the Web server. Lines 49 to 53 convert the locally referenced file (that is, one without the /usr/local/etc/httpd/htdocs prefix) to its full path name while retaining the basic filename and its relative path when the file is uploaded to the remote server.

```
55      print "Processing $localfile rem($remfile)\n" if $debug;
56
```

If debugging is switched on, then we print out a progress message on line 55.

```
57      if (-d $localfile)
58      {
59          my $remcurdir = $ftp->pwd();
60          unless($ftp->cwd($remfile))
61          {
62              unless ($localfile eq '..')
63              {
64                  print "Attempting to make directory $remfile\n";
65                  $ftp->mkdir($remfile,1) or
66                      die "Couldn't make directory $remfile";
67              }
68          }
```

If the file supplied to this function by the **find** function is a directory, then we need to think about creating the remote directory, if it does not already exist. We record the current remote directory in a variable on line 59. Line 60 checks if we can change to the new directory. If we can't, then we create the new remote directory on line 65; if we fail to make the new directory then we **die**, since without it we will be unable to upload the remote site. The **mkdir** method includes the option to create the entire directory path, allowing us to make the directory pub/html/graphics, even if the pub and pub/html directories don't already exist—the **Net::FTP** module does the work for us. Note that we ensure the directory we are trying to create is not the parent directory, **..** by checking on line 62.

```
69          else
70          {
71              $ftp->cwd($remcurdir) or
72                  die "Couldn't change to directory $currentdir";
```

```
73              }
74          }
```

If we can change to the new directory, then we change back to the old current directory on line 71. Since we don't need to be in the remote directory to upload the file, we change back to our original location. If this operation fails, then it denotes another significant error, which we trap with a **die** function on line 72.

```
75          else
76          {
77              my ($remtime,$localtime,$upload) = (undef,undef,0);
78              unless($remtime = $ftp->mdtm($remfile))
79              {
80                  $remtime = 0;
81              }
82              $localtime = (stat($file))[9];
```

It the file is not a directory, it must be a standard file that requires uploading. Before we needlessly upload the file, we check the modification time of the remote version, if it exists, against the modification time of the local version. We initialize the values of the remote time, local time, and whether to upload the file on line 77.

Line 78 attempts to get the modification time of the remote file. If it fails, then we set the modification time variable to zero: since this equates to the epoch, any file we are attempting to upload should be older than the remote version. Line 82 uses the **stat** command with a subscript to get the local file's modification time.

```
83              if (defined($localtime) and defined($remtime))
84              {
85                  if ($localtime > $remtime)
86                  {
87                      $upload=1;
88                  }
89              }
90              else
91              {
92                  $upload=1;
93              }
```

On line 83, provided we have values for both the local and remote modification times, then we compare the values on line 85, setting the **$upload** variable to one. This variable decides whether the file needs uploading or not. If neither of the two values could be determined, we assume this means that the file needs uploading (line 92).

```
94              if ($upload)
95              {
```

```
96              if (-B $localfile)
97              {
98                  if ($curxfermode eq 'ASCII')
99                  {
100                     if ($ftp->binary())
101                     {
102                         $curxfermode = 'BIN';
103                         print "Changed mode to BINary\n"
104                             if $debug;
105                     }
106                     else
107                     {
108                         warn "Couldn't change transfer mode";
109                     }
110                 }
111             }
```

If the file does require uploading, then the final step is to check the file type and
the method in which it should be transferred. Line 96 tests whether the local file is
binary. If it is, and the current transfer mode is ASCII (line 98), then we attempt to
change transfer modes on line 100. If it succeeds, then we update the current transfer
mode and report an error to the user if they have specified the debug option. If the
mode change fails, we print an error on line 108. Note that we only warn the user;
the file could have erroneously been identified as a binary file when it was text. The
final online QC should highlight any problems.

```
112             else
113             {
114                 if ($curxfermode eq 'BIN')
115                 {
116                     if ($ftp->ascii())
117                     {
118                         $curxfermode = 'ASCII';
119                         print "Changed mode to ASCII\n"
120                             if $debug;
121                     }
122                     else
123                     {
124                         warn "Couldn't change transfer mode";
125                     }
126                 }
127             }
```

The same test is then repeated. If the file is not binary, it's assumed to be ASCII, and we attempt to check the current transfer mode in lines 116 to 125.

```
128              print "Uploading $localfile to $remfile\n" if $debug;
129              $ftp->put($localfile,$remfile)
130                  or warn "Couldn't upload $remfile";
```

Finally, line 128 announces the upload (if debugging is on) and then line 29 attempts to send the file using the local filename and the composed remote filename. If the transfer failed, we warn the user instead of **die**-ing—there may be a perfectly legitimate reason for the failure.

```
131          }
132          else
133          {
134              print "File $remfile appears to be up to date\n"
135                  if $debug;
136          }
137      }
138  }
139
```

If the modification time of the remote file is equal to or greater than that of the local file, then there is no need to upload it, which we report on line 134.

```
140  sub usage
141  {
142      print <<EOF;
143  Usage:
144
145      uplsite.pl [-d] [-r remdir] [-p remport] [-u user]
146              [-w password] [-1 localdir] -s server
147
148  Description:
149
150  Uploads a directory structure to the server using FTP.
151
152  Where:
153
154  -d  Switch on debugging output
155  -r  Remote directory to upload to (defaults to .)
156  -p  The remote port to use (defaults to 21)
157  -u  The user name to login as (defaults to anonymous)
158  -w  The password to use (defaults to me\@foo.bar)
159  -1  The local directory to upload from (defaults to .)
160  -s  The remote server address to upload to (required)
```

```
161
162 EOF
163     exit 1;
164 }
```

Lines 140 to 164 are the **usage** function, which simply prints how best to use the script.

For example, if you wanted to upload the directory of your local Web server to one provided by an Internet service provider, you might use this command line:

```
$ uplsite.pl -r public_html -l /usr/local/etc/httpd/htdocs
            -s web.foo.bar -u user -w password
```

Although I've marketed this as a script for uploading Web sites, it could in fact be used to duplicate any structure on any remote machine acting as an FTP server.

wwwlogs.pl

Static Web Log Listing

Here is a very simple script that I've used many times in different forms on my own Web sites. In this instance, it's being used to generate a list of Web server logs that have been filed on a Web server. They are filed in a directory structure that defines the machine, Web site, and the date of the Web log in question. I've included it here as a very simple demonstration of how to generate an HTML page within Perl.

The format of the directories and Web files looks like this:

```
sparc
    www
        199804
        199805
        199806
    intranet
        199805
        199806
mac
    clients
        199805
```

All we need to do is traverse the directory. We could use the **File::Find** module to produce the output, but this wouldn't give us a structured and ordered list. Instead, we use the **glob** function and check directories, subdirectories, and files within the subdirectories sequentially in order to produce the static page.

The actual HTML generation is simply a case of printing the raw HTML to the standard output. It's redirected to the desired file at the time the script is executed.

This is actually a modified version of a script in use on an intranet and is part of the network management and monitoring toolkit I've developed that will be discussed in detail in Chapter 11.

```perl
1   #!/usr/local/bin/perl5
2
3   my @months = qw (JUNK Jan Feb Mar Apr May
4                    Jun Jul Aug Sep Oct Nov Dec );
5   my $logdir = '/usr/local/etc/wwwlogs';
6
7   print <<EOF;
8   <html>
9   <head>
10  <title>WWW Server Logs</title>
11  </head>
12  <body>
13  <font size=+2><b>WWW Server Logs</b></font>
14  <dl>
15  EOF
16
17  chdir("$logdir");
18  for my $dir (grep (/^[a-zA-Z0-9]/,glob("*")))
19  {
20      print "<dt>$dir\n";
21      chdir("$logdir/$dir");
22      for my $server (grep(/^[a-zA-Z0-9]/,glob("*")))
23      {
24          chdir("$logdir/$dir/$server");
25          print "<dl><dt>$server\n";
26          for my $date (grep (/^[a-zA-Z0-9]/, glob("*")))
27          {
28              my ($dateonly) = (split (/\./,$date))[0];
29              my $mon = substr($dateonly, 5, 2);
30              my $year = substr($dateonly, 0, 4);
31              print("<dd><a href=\"/wwwlogs/$dir/$server/$date\">",
32                    " $months[$mon] $year</a>\n");
33          }
34          print "</dl>\n";
35      }
36  }
37  print "</dl>\n</body>\n";
```

ANNOTATIONS

By using nested loops we can easily traverse through a sequence of directories and subdirectories. By using a pre-populated array of month names, we can also very quickly label and list the available Web logs using the more friendly English language. This does, of course, require that the logs are recorded and stored with a predefined name.

We could, theoretically, have used the **stat** function to identify the date and time the log was generated. Unfortunately this method is not a reliable way of identifying the Web log dates because the reporting program could have been executed at any time.

```
1   #!/usr/local/bin/perl5
2
3   my @months = qw (JUNK Jan Feb Mar Apr May
4                    Jun Jul Aug Sep Oct Nov Dec );
5   my $logdir = '/usr/local/etc/wwwlogs';
6
```

Line 3 defines the month names' array. We use the **qw** quoting system to define a list of strings specifying the months into an array in sequence starting from zero. Because arrays start with a index of zero and months start at 1 (for January), we need to insert an empty value into the first element of the array. We can do this using the special value **JUNK**. The result of this line is that **$months[1]** equals Jan, **$months[2]** equals Feb, and so on.

Line 5 specifies the Web log directory. I've specified a fairly typical location here, but you could use any directory.

```
7   print <<EOF;
8   <html>
9   <head>
10  <title>WWW Server Logs</title>
11  </head>
12  <body>
13  <font size=+2><b>WWW Server Logs</b></font>
14  <dl>
15  EOF
16
```

Lines 7 to 15 use a here document to specify the header information for the HTML page. Note that we've simply quoted the HTML directly within the here document; this will print to standard output and will become part of the final HTML document. The **<dl>** tag on the last line sets up a definition list, which is an indented list without numbers or bullet points that is composed of two elements: the detail title, **<dt>**, and the detail description, **<dd>**. We'll be using a definition list to indent the different levels of the directories and logs within the directory structure.

```
17   chdir("$logdir");
18   for my $dir (grep (/^[a-zA-Z0-9]/,glob("*")))
19   {
```

Line 17 changes to the log directory we set on line 5 to enable us to reference directories locally without having to strip information off the front of a full path. Line 18 sets up a **for** loop to work through the contents of the log directory. We use the **glob** function to get a list of files based on the directory name. The **glob** function returns a list to the **grep** function, which ensures that the filename starts with an alphanumeric character. This strips out the **.** and **..** directories. The result is a list, the values of which are passed to the **$dir** variable on each cycle of the **for** loop.

```
20       print "<dt>$dir\n";
21       chdir("$logdir/$dir");
22       for my $server (grep(/^[a-zA-Z0-9]/,glob("*")))
23       {
```

Line 20 prints out the directory as a detail title element. Line 21 then changes the directory to the machine directory under the main log directory before we execute identical **glob** and **grep** functions to generate a list of the Web servers within the top-level directories. This is extracted and processed by yet another **for** loop.

```
24           chdir("$logdir/$dir/$server");
25           print "<dl><dt>$server\n";
26           for my $date (grep (/^[a-zA-Z0-9]/, glob("*")))
27           {
```

We change directories yet again in line 24 to the Web server directory within the machine directory. This directory should contain a list of the Web logs that are available for this Web server/machine combination. Line 25 prints out the Web server name by defining a new detail list, with the server name being defined within the detail title. The last **for** loop on line 26 reports the individual logs based on the year and month they report on.

```
28               my ($dateonly) = (split (/\./,$date))[0];
29               my $mon = substr($dateonly, 5, 2);
30               my $year = substr($dateonly, 0, 4);
```

Line 28 extracts the date information from the Web log. This is the name up to the first period, and we use **split** with a subscript to get the date info. Lines 28 and 29 extract the month and year from the data information. I've used **substr** in this example, but we could have easily used a regular expression. The format of **substr** is the variable or string to extract from, the character to start from, and the number of characters to extract. So, line 29 takes characters 5 and 6 from the date (the month), while line 30 takes the first four characters from the date (the year).

```
31            print("<dd><a href=\"/wwwlogs/$dir/$server/$date\">",
32                  " $months[$mon] $year</a>\n");
```

Lines 31 and 32 print out the detail description, which in our case is the server log file for the current month/year on the current machine. Line 31 introduces a link to the log report, which is in HTML format. Line 32 extracts the month name by using the array we created back on line 3.

```
33          }
34        print "</dl>\n";
35      }
36  }
37  print "</dl>\n</body>\n";
```

Line 34 ends the detail list for the current Web server, and line 37 ends the top detail list, which specifies the machines supporting Web services on the network.

If you try the script on the sample directory I outlined at the start of this section, the output it generates should look like the screen shown in Figure 7-1.

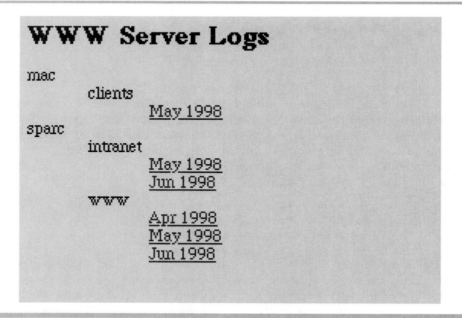

FIGURE 7-1. Sample output from the **wwwlogs.pl** script

The significant part of this demonstration is that if you know how to write HTML, then you know how to produce it within Perl. If you want to further guarantee the quality of the HTML you produce, you should consider using the LWP toolkit to produce the HTML. Unfortunately it doesn't guarantee that the HTML produced will give you the effect you want!

Static versus Dynamic Web Pages

Although it is more usual to use a CGI script to serve up information, there are times when using static pages has its advantages. If you are not modifying the information regularly or if there is a large amount of technical or otherwise static information that makes up a page, then serving dynamically what is effectively static text can be a painful experience. Your clients and visitors may get tired of waiting if the Web server you are running the script on is not up to providing the pages at a suitable rate.

In these situations, using a script to automate the process of converting the static database information into static HTML pages with all the necessary links can provide a real benefit. Your pages and information are still available, but because they are static, the scripting load on your server is reduced. The information can still be up to date; you could set the generation script to work automatically each night, but the method of delivery is significantly quicker.

If you are developing a database-sourced Web site for somebody else, then this method can be employed at a significantly cheaper rate than a fully developed and scripted dynamic site, while still providing a large number of the benefits and information they require. Of course, this doesn't suit everybody. Some sites, notably e-commerce sites and those updated throughout the day, require at least some, if not all, of their components to be dynamically served and scripted to keep the update and flow of information at a suitable level.

A dynamically created site also allows for changes within individual pages, and even within individual calls by clients to the same page. It also puts more pressure on the Web server, and it requires stricter checking to ensure that bugs in the code do not break or disable access to the site. We'll look at some of the details surrounding this in the next chapter.

Summary

To check and validate your HTML, you must have a fundamental understanding of how it is formatted and how to get an HTML file into a format that can be easily parsed and processed. Of course, a better method is to use an external module to do the work for you.

All that you need, then, is the wrap-around code that turns the simplicity of the function into a tool that can become a practical solution for a number of different problems. In this chapter, we have seen both how to make use of Perl's text processing features to do the checking for us and how to use the LWP package to achieve the same result.

It should also be clear by now that creating HTML within Perl is as easy as writing the HTML within a text editor. The difference is that because the HTML can be generated pragmatically, we can use any source of information to create the HTML and textual contents. Although it's possible to use Perl to create static pages, it's much more likely that you will be creating HTML for use within a CGI program. That's the topic of our next chapter.

Common Gateway Interface

I n our last chapter, we saw how you could use Perl to generate and check static HTML pages. Another, more advanced method of generating HTML is to create it "on the fly," or dynamically, alternatively, you may want to accept input and supply data and information back to the user. This last method is used to process Web-based forms that submit information to a site. Once you know how to process the information, the same system can be used to provide all sorts of dynamic content, from simple interactive forms to more complex e-commerce sites.

This interaction requires some cooperation between the Web server and the programs being used to process and provide the interactive content. The Web server needs to be able to pass on the information to the external program that is supplied by the browser, using the format of the online form. In reverse, the external program needs to be able to pass information directly back to the Web server, so that it can then be passed on back to the browser.

The Common Gateway Interface (CGI) handles this communication between the browser and external programs. (If you have visited Web sites before and noticed the URLs at the top of page, you may have seen a directory called /cgi-bin, which is often the default location for the CGI programs that make up a Web site.) There are two ways for the information from a browser form to be passed to a CGI program: POST and GET. The POST method transfers the information from a web form to the CGI script via the standard input, hence "POST" because the information is sent to the CGI program. With GET, the information is placed by the web server into an environment variable, and the CGI program must access the correct environment variable to obtain the information, hence "GET" because the program must get the information.

PROGRAMMER'S NOTE   *A program that is being used for CGI is referred to either as a CGI program or a CGI script but not simply as a CGI, which refers to a number of different protocols and systems.*

In both cases, the information is formatted in the same way, as a list of name/value pairs, separated by ampersands (&). Each name/value pair is separated by an equal sign. For example, the following string shows two variables, **name** and **mode**:

```
name=Martin&mode=edit
```

To add more complication, the information is encoded so that special characters that make up the URL are not misinterpreted. The encoding consists of nonalphanumeric characters being converted to their hexadecimal equivalent, preceded by a percent sign. For example, the string "Martin Brown" would be converted to "Martin%20Brown."

PROGRAMMER'S NOTE   *Although "escaping" is the preferred method for encoding the space character, it's often the case that plus signs are used instead. Most parsing systems, including the ones we look at here, account for this.*

There are advantages and disadvantages of using POST and GET, and depending on what you are trying to achieve, you may want to choose different methods even within the confines of the same application.

The GET method's main advantage is that the form data can be encapsulated within a URL. This means that you can bookmark GET requests or even introduce them as links directly within HTML without having to generate a separate form. Its major disadvantage is that data size is limited because the information is exchanged via an environment variable. Although this limitation should not cause a major problem in many situations, in e-mail, news, or other high-volume text applications it can become a problem.

When using the POST method, almost the opposite is true: because the information is transferred as a data stream to the standard input of the CGI application, there are no theoretical limits on the amount of information that can be transferred this way. However, there are practical and security limitations that we will discuss later in this and the next chapter. The biggest disadvantage for the POST method is that you must create a form in order for the information to be sent to the host. It's not possible to POST information as part of the URL.

We'll be looking in this chapter at a number of examples that employ these two methods, but we will start by looking at the environment that a CGI script is executed within (**webenv.pl**). We will then examine the processes that are involved in extracting the data from GET and POST requests, both individually (**cgiget.pl** and **cgipost.pl**) and through dynamic selection during the execution of the script (**SCGI.pm**).

The two scripts **phone.pl** and **webnews.pl** will be examined in detail, using the principles we have examined in the earlier part of this chapter. Both demonstrate the use of CGI scripts as an interface to simple database systems; one is read only and supports a simple phone number system, and the second is more complex and demonstrates the use of a single script to manage a Web-based news page that could be employed on a public or private site.

The next part of this chapter covers the use of HTTP directly and how the return codes and protocol can be used to communicate directly with a browser. Our first script in this section, **sendfile.pl**, sends back a file, using the correct file type as extracted from the MIME (Multipurpose Internet Mail Extensions) information supplied with the Apache Web server. The second script, **redirect.pl**, demonstrates the ability to redirect the browser to a different page when a request is made.

Finally, the last part of this chapter examines the principles behind an online bookstore using the BookWare scripts (**bookstor.pl**) from GlassCat Software. The BookWare system implements the major aspects of the e-commerce process in Perl, although we will concentrate on the store-specific features rather than covering the entire BookWare system.

webenv.pl

The CGI Environment

Our first script, which itself should be run as a CGI script, shows the environment information that is available to all CGI programs. Some of this data is purely for information purposes; other parts are more useful and hold the information supplied by GET requests, and support information for handling POST requests.

```perl
1    #!/usr/local/bin/perl5
2
3    print "Content-type: text/html\n\n";
4
5    print "<font size=+1>Environment</font><p>\n";
6
7    for $_ (keys %ENV)
8    {
9        print "$_: $ENV{$_}<br>\n";
10   }
```

ANNOTATIONS

The script is, understandably, very simple: all we need to do is print out the environment variables, which as we know are stored in the **%ENV** hash. There are some minor requirements, however, that are CGI-script specific.

```perl
1    #!/usr/local/bin/perl5
2
3    print "Content-type: text/html\n\n";
4
```

When a Web server sends back a file to the browser, it precedes the actual file with HTTP header data. This includes at a minimum the success or otherwise of the request and the data type being returned. When a CGI program is executed, the Web server does not supply the header information; instead, the CGI program must generate the necessary fields. For scripts that are returning HTML, as we are in this case, the content type is "text/html." This is a MIME file type as defined by the MIME specification (see RFC1341 for more information on MIME). The end of the HTTP header is identified by a single blank line.

Line 3 therefore prints out the content type header, with the MIME type, followed by the single blank line.

```perl
5    print "<font size=+1>Environment</font><p>\n";
6
```

Line 5 very simply prints out a header for the HTML document that will be formatted by the browser.

```
7   for $_ (keys %ENV)
8   {
9       print "$_: $ENV{$_}<br>\n";
10  }
```

Lines 7 to 10 then print out the environment hash.

If you install this script on your Web server (see the following sidebar, "Installing CGI Scripts") and then access the script via your browser, you should get an environment list within your browser window similar to this:

```
SERVER_SOFTWARE: Apache/1.2.6
GATEWAY_INTERFACE: CGI/1.1
DOCUMENT_ROOT: /usr/local/http/service
REMOTE_ADDR: 198.112.10.130
SERVER_PROTOCOL: HTTP/1.0
REQUEST_METHOD: GET
REMOTE_HOST: f.foo.bar
QUERY_STRING:
HTTP_USER_AGENT: Mozilla/4.5b2 (Macintosh; I; PPC)
PATH: /bin:/usr/bin:/usr/lib:/etc
TZ: GMT0BST
HTTP_CONNECTION: Keep-Alive
HTTP_ACCEPT: image/gif, image/x-xbitmap, image/jpeg, image/pjpeg,
image/png, */*
REMOTE_PORT: 1994
HTTP_ACCEPT_LANGUAGE: en
SCRIPT_NAME: /cgi-bin/webenv.pl
HTTP_ACCEPT_ENCODING: gzip
SCRIPT_FILENAME: /usr/local/http/cgi-bin/webenv.pl
SERVER_NAME: twinspark.foo.bar
REQUEST_URI: /cgi-bin/webenv.pl
HTTP_ACCEPT_CHARSET: iso-8859-1,*,utf-8
SERVER_PORT: 80
HTTP_HOST: twinspark
SERVER_ADMIN: webmaster@foo.bar
```

The exact output depends on your Web server and the browser you used to access the information. Table 8-1 explains the purpose and contents of the different variables. There is a wealth of information available from the environment. Some of this information we need when processing CGI information; other parts can help you produce more friendly and advanced scripts.

Installing CGI Scripts

To install a CGI script on a Unix machine, you must first install a Web server such as Apache (www.apache.org). The server has a configuration setting for the location of the CGI script directory, which is usually a directory called cgi-bin under the main installation directory for the Web server.

Make sure that your script has the correct permissions (0555, or read and execute for all) and then ensure that the first line of the script refers to the correct Perl executable and version. You should then be ready to run the script via your Web browser.

For MacOS and NT this installation depends largely on the application you are using to support Web services. You will need to refer to the documentation for your Web server software. In addition, on the Mac, you will need to save the script as a MacPerl CGI Script. See Appendix A for more information on Mac script formats.

Environment Variable	Description
SERVER_SOFTWARE	The name and version number of the server software that is being used. This can be useful if you want to introduce a single script that makes use of specific features of multiple Web servers.
GATEWAY_INTERFACE	The interface name and version number.
DOCUMENT_ROOT	The root document directory for this Web server.
REMOTE_ADDR	The IP address of the browser.
SERVER_PROTOCOL	The protocol (usually HTTP) and version number.
REQUEST_METHOD	The request method, for example, GET or POST.
REMOTE_HOST	The resolved name of the browser.
QUERY_STRING	The query string, used with GET requests.
QUERY_LENGTH	The length of the query information. It's available both for GET and POST requests, and it can help with the security of the scripts you produce.
HTTP_USER_AGENT	The name, version number, and platform of the remote browser. In our preceding example, this was Mozilla (Netscape) v4.5b2, for Macintosh PPC. Don't be fooled into thinking that the name Mozilla applies only to Netscape; other browsers, including Microsoft Internet Explorer, also report themselves as being Mozilla browsers.

TABLE 8-1.   Web Server Environment Variables for CGI Scripts

Environment Variable	Description
PATH	The PATH for the CGI script.
TZ	The time zone of the Web server.
HTTP_CONNECTION	Any HTTP connection directives. In our example, the only directive was "Keep-Alive," which forces the server to keep a Web server process and the associated network socket dedicated to this browser until a defined period of inactivity.
HTTP_ACCEPT	The formats accepted by the browser. This information is optionally supplied by the browser when it first requests the page from the server. In our example, the default types accepted include all of the major graphics types (GIF, JPEG, X bitmap), as well as all other MIME types (*/*).
REMOTE_PORT	The remote port of the browser machine.
HTTP_ACCEPT_LANGUAGE	The languages accepted by this browser. If supported by the server, then only documents of a specific language will be returned to the browser.
SCRIPT_NAME	The name of the CGI script.
HTTP_ACCEPT_ENCODING	Any special encoding formats supported by the browser. In our example, Netscape supports Gzip encoded documents; they will be decoded on the fly at the time of receipt.
SCRIPT_FILENAME	The full path to the CGI script.
SERVER_NAME	The fully qualified name of the server.
REQUEST_URI	The requested URI (uniform resource identifier).
HTTP_ACCEPT_CHARSET	The character sets accepted by the browser.
SERVER_PORT	The server port number.
HTTP_HOST	The server host (without domain).
SERVER_ADMIN	The e-mail address of the Web server administrator.

TABLE 8-1.   Web Server Environment Variables for CGI Scripts *(continued)*

cgiget.pl

Processing a GET Request

The GET request system passes the information supplied from a browser form, via the Web server, in the format of a formatted query string contained in an environment variable. Parsing the query string is a case of importing the query, separating the individual field/value pairs, and then creating a data structure to hold the information. It should be immediately apparent that the ideal structure for holding the information is a hash, where the hash key is the form's field name, and the corresponding hash value is the value of the form field.

The following script is a very simple demonstration of extracting information from a GET request. It uses the **SMTPwrap** module we generated in Chapter 6 to send a subscription e-mail to a mailing list server, using the e-mail address and name supplied from the form.

```perl
1   #!/usr/local/bin/perl5
2
3   use SMTPwrap;
4
5   my $length = $ENV{CONTENT_LENGTH};
6   my $query = $ENV{QUERY_STRING};
7   my (@assign,%formlist);
8
9   if ( defined($query) and $length > 0 )
10  {
11      @assign = split(/&/,$query);
12  }
13
14  for (my $i=0; $i<@assign; $i++)
15  {
16      my ($name,$value) = split(/=/,$assign[$i]);
17      $value =~ tr/+/ /;
18      $value =~ s/%([a-fA-F0-9][a-fA-F0-9])/pack("C", hex($1))/eg;
19      if (defined($formlist{$name}))
20      {
21          $formlist{$name} .= ",$value";
22      }
23      else
24      {
25          $formlist{$name} = $value;
26      }
27  }
28
39  if (scalar keys %formlist)
30  {
31      if (defined($formlist{name}) and
32          defined($formlist{email}))
33      {
34          if (length($formlist{email}) eq 0 or
35              length($formlist{name}) eq 0)
36          {
37              respond('Error: You must complete all fields');
38          }
```

```
39          mail_a_message('subscribe list',
40                         'listproc@foo.bar',
41                         "$formlist{email}",
42                         "subscribe list $formlist{name}");
43          respond('Your form has been submitted');
44      }
45      else
46      {
47          respond('Error: Fields are badly defined');
48      }
49  }
50  else
51  {
52      respond('Error: Your form didnt submit any information');
53  }
54
55  sub respond
56  {
57      my $message = shift;
58      print "Content-type: text/html\n\n";
59      print <<EOF;
60  <head>
61  <title>$message</title>
62  </head>
63  <body>
64  $message
65  </body>
66  EOF
67      exit;
68  }
```

ANNOTATIONS

The fundamental part of this script, as far as we are concerned, is comprised of lines 5 to 29. These lines extract the information from the query string that has been generated by the Web server, via the user's Web browser, and that is passed on to the CGI script as an environment variable. Once we have the information in a format we want, a hash, we can then start checking the form contents before acting on it accordingly.

```
1   #!/usr/local/bin/perl5
2
3   use SMTPwrap;
4
```

We need to include the **SMTPwrap** function from Chapter 6; it will provide us with the **mail_a_message** function that we need to e-mail information on to a specified user.

```perl
5    my $length = $ENV{CONTENT_LENGTH};
6    my $query = $ENV{QUERY_STRING};
7    my (@assign,%formlist);
8
```

The query information from a browser form that is sent via the GET method is help within the **QUERY_STRING** environment variable. As I've already discussed, the format of this variable is an ampersand-separated list of field names and values. As a verifier, we'll also record the value of the query's length. This value is calculated by the Web server and should be a reliable sanity check on the quality and validity of the information. See the next chapter for more details about securing your CGI script.

Lines 5, 6, and 7 set up the variables we need to process the query information. The **@assign** array stores the name/value pairs, while **%formlist** the field/value information.

```perl
9    if ( defined($query) and $length > 0 )
10   {
11       @assign = split(/&/,$query);
12   }
13
```

Line 9 ensures that the information we are going to attempt to extract actually exists. We check both the existence of the actual query string and the Web browser–supplied length of that string. Checking both should cover us for most eventualities.

Line 11 splits the individual field/value pairs and places them in the **@assign** array. At this point, the information is stored within each element of the array in its original field=value format.

```perl
14   for (my $i=0; $i<@assign; $i++)
15   {
16       my ($name,$value) = split('=',$assign[$i]);
17       $value =~ tr/+/ /;
18       $value =~ s/%([a-fA-F0-9][a-fA-F0-9])/pack("C", hex($1))/eg;
```

Line 14 sets up a **for** loop to work through the elements of the array. Line 16 splits up the name/value elements into their respective parts by splitting the strings by an equal sign. Lines 17 and 18 then convert the "escaped" string back to a nonescaped format. First we convert plus signs into spaces on line 18. Then line 18 converts encoded characters, which are referenced by a two-digit hex value preceded by a percent sign, back into their original characters. This conversion is handled by a regular expression substitution on a matching string. The replacement value is a function, in this case **pack**, with a format string of "C," which converts a hexadecimal number back into its character equivalent. This is possible because we grouped the two-digit specification in the search regular expression and used that as the argument for the replacement. The **/e** option to the regular expression allows you to use a function, rather than a string, as the replacement.

```
19      if (defined($formlist{$name}))
20      {
21          $formlist{$name} .= ",$value";
22      }
23      else
24      {
25          $formlist{$name} = $value;
26      }
27  }
28
```

If the field name already exists within the **%formlist** hash, then we append the information to the field, using a comma as a separator on line 21. Otherwise, line 25 sets the hash key matching the field name to the value of the field from the browser. By the time we reach line 28, we have extracted all of the useful information from the form. There are only two variables passed from the browser that we now need to make sense of: **$formlength**, which contains the number of fields on the form, and **%formlist**, which is the hash that contains the field names and values.

```
29  if (scalar keys %formlist)
30  {
31      if (defined($formlist{name}) and
32          defined($formlist{email}))
33      {
```

Line 29 checks to ensure that we have received some information from the browser form; we can do a quick test by checking the number of items processed from the request using **scalar** to obtain the number of keys in the hash. We're looking for at least one in this example, but it's easier just to check if there are any form fields, and then look for and process the individual fields to ensure their content is correct. This is the purpose of lines 31 and 32, which check that "name" and "email" fields were in the original form.

```
34      if (length($formlist{email}) eq 0 or
35          length($formlist{name}) eq 0)
36      {
37          respond('Error: You must complete all fields');
38      }
```

Lines 34 and 35 check to see if the length of the values of the "name" and "email" fields are greater than zero. If they aren't, then we haven't received the information

required to send an e-mail, so we report an error to the user via the **respond**
function on line 37.

```
39          mail_a_message('subscribe list',
40                         'listproc@foo.bar',
41                         "$formlist{email}",
42                         "subscribe list $formlist{name}");
43          respond('Your form has been submitted');
```

Provided the form fields exist, and contain information, then we'll assume the
information in the form is correct and go ahead and send the e-mail message to the
mailing list processor and have the person's e-mail address added. This is a security
risk—we've made an assumption about the quality and contents of the form fields,
without actually checking those details.

It would be quite possible for an unscrupulous user to submit a suspect e-mail
address. Although this doesn't affect us directly (since we're not actually sending
e-mail *to* that address, only from it), it is still something we should be aware of. It
should be noted that because the address is being added to a mailing list it could
still cause a problem. We'll look in the next script at ways of checking that the field
values contain the sort of information we expect.

Once the e-mail has been sent, we respond with a success message on line 43.

```
44      }
45      else
46      {
47          respond('Error: Fields are badly defined');
48      }
49  }
```

Line 45 catches any failures of the test for field contents, which reports a suitable
error to the browser.

```
50  else
51  {
52      respond('Error: Your form didnt submit any information');
53  }
54
```

Line 52 reports an error only if there were no fields defined on the form.

```
55  sub respond
56  {
57      my $message = shift;
58      print "Content-type: text/html\n\n";
59      print <<EOF;
60  <head>
61  <title>$message</title>
62  </head>
```

```
63    <body>
64    $message
65    </body>
66    EOF
67        exit;
68    }
```

Lines 55 to 68 form the **respond** function, which takes the message passed to it and formulates an HTML reply. We must send back the MIME type of the information we are sending (line 58) before formulating the actual HTML that makes up the response.

If you try this script with the corresponding HTML page supplied on the CD-ROM, you can see how the process works. You may want to change the e-mail address that the e-mails are sent to.

cgipost.pl

Processing a POST Request

The format of the information within GET and POST requests is identical—the only difference is the method by which you obtain the query information. GET requests store information in an environment variable; POST requests pipe information to the standard input of the CGI program. This difference presents one, probably not-so-obvious problem: we need to ensure that the size of the data that we receive is of a suitable size.

I've already discussed the security aspects of CGI scripts and touched on a number of the problems with the last script. One of the most fundamental failures with CGI scripts is that people blindly trust, and use, the information that has been sent to them without first checking that it matches the format we expect.

We'll look at some of these problems with our next script, which provides a Web-based e-mail form to allow you to send an e-mail with a sender, recipient, subject, and message body.

```
1    #!/usr/local/bin/perl5
2
3    use SMTPwrap;
4    my $length = $ENV{CONTENT_LENGTH};
5    my (@assign,%formlist);
6
7    if (defined($length) and $length > 0 )
8    {
9        sysread(STDIN, $_, $length);
10       chomp;
11       @assign = split('&');
12   }
13
```

```perl
14   for (my $i=0; $i<@assign; $i++)
15   {
16       my ($name,$value) = split('=',$assign[$i]);
17       $value =~ tr/+/ /;
18       $value =~ s/%([a-fA-F0-9][a-fA-F0-9])/pack("C", hex($1))/eg;
19       if (defined($formlist{$name}))
20       {
21           $formlist{$name} .= ",$value";
22       }
23       else
24       {
25           $formlist{$name} = $value;
26       }
27   }
28
29   if (scalar keys %formlist)
30   {
31       my @errfields;
32       for $_ (keys %formlist)
33       {
34           push(@errfields,$_) unless(length($formlist{$_}) > 0);
35       }
36       if (@errfields)
37       {
38           respond("Error: The fields " . join(', ',@errfields)
39                   . " must be completed");
40       }
41       respond("The email address $formlist{email} is invalid")
42           unless ($formlist{email} =~ /^[\w@\.\-]+$/);
43       respond("The from address $formlist{from} is invalid")
44           unless ($formlist{from} =~ /^[\w@\.\-]+$/);
45       mail_a_message('$formlist{subject}',
46                      '$formlist{from}',
47                      "$formlist{email}",
48                      "$formlist{message}");
49       respond('Your email has been sent');
50   }
51   else
52   {
53       respond('Error: Your form didn't submit any information');
54   }
55
56   sub respond
```

```
57   {
58       my $message = shift;
59       print "Content-type: text/html\n\n";
60       print <<EOF;
61   <head>
62   <title>$message</title>
63   </head>
64   <body>
65   $message
66   </body>
67   EOF
68       exit;
69   }
```

ANNOTATIONS

You should have noticed immediately that the lead-in to the script is different from the previous example. Instead of accessing the **QUERY_STRING** environment variable, we read in a set number of bytes from the standard input. Once it's read in, we parse the information as before. The remainder of the script checks the form fields and their contents (length and format) before accepting the information and calling **mail_a_message** to send the e-mail.

```
1    #!/usr/local/bin/perl5
2
3    use SMTPwrap;
4    my $length = $ENV{CONTENT_LENGTH};
5    my (@assign,%formlist);
6
```

We import the **SMTPwrap** module on line 3; this is the one we generated in Chapter 6. Line 4 extracts the length, in bytes, of the query from the environment. We'll need this information shortly. Line 5 sets up the same set of variables as before: **@assign** contains the form information temporarily until we place it into the **%formlist** hash.

```
7    if (defined($length) and $length > 0 )
8    {
9        sysread(STDIN, $_, $length);
10       chomp;
11       @assign = split('&');
12   }
13
```

Lines 7 to 13 read in the form data from the standard input, provided, of course, the length of the query has been defined and is greater than zero. We use **sysread,** a built-in Perl function, to read a set number of bytes from a file handle. Line 9 imports a maximum of **$length** bytes into the $_ variable from the standard input. Line 10 then strips any trailing line termination, before splitting the field/value pairs by an ampersand in line 11.

```
14   for (my $i=0; $i<@assign; $i++)
15   {
16       my ($name,$value) = split('=',$assign[$i]);
17       $value =~ tr/+/ /;
18       $value =~ s/%([a-fA-F0-9][a-fA-F0-9])/pack("C", hex($1))/eg;
19       if (defined($formlist{$name}))
20       {
21           $formlist{$name} .= ",$value";
22       }
23       else
24       {
25           $formlist{$name} = $value;
26       }
27   }
28
```

Lines 14 to 27 are identical to the previous script's lines. We process each field/value pair, splitting the pair by equal sign, unescaping any escaped characters, before assigning the field/value pair to the key and value of a hash, respectively.

```
29   if (scalar keys %formlist)
30   {
31       my @errfields;
32       for $_ (keys %formlist)
33       {
34           push(@errfields,$_) unless(length($formlist{$_}) > 0);
35       }
```

By line 29 we have finished extracting the form information and can now start to examine the fields and field contents and process the information. Line 31 sets up an array that will hold a list of field names that do not contain information. For this form, which will be used to send e-mail, we need all four fields filled. Line 32 works through all the keys of **%formlist** hash, and therefore the list of fields on this form, adding empty fields to the array (line 34).

```
36       if (@errfields)
37       {
38           respond("Error: The fields " . join(', ',@errfields)
39                   . " must be completed");
40       }
```

If there are any fields that are empty, then we report an error back to the user on lines 38 and 39. We use **join** to format the list of fields correctly, with each field being separated by a comma and a space. Note that because the **respond** function, which appears later in this script, accepts only a single argument, we must concatenate the elements, using a period rather than using commas which would indicate separate arguments to the function.

```
41    respond("The email address $formlist{email} is invalid")
42        unless ($formlist{email} =~ /^[\w@\.\-]+$/);
43    respond("The from address $formlist{from} is invalid")
44        unless ($formlist{from} =~ /^[\w@\.\-]+$/);
```

Lines 41 to 44 check the format of the e-mail addresses supplied by testing the fields against a regular expression that contains only valid characters. In this instance, I've chosen a fairly standard regular expression, which allows any number of characters, from the start to the end of the expression, made up from a set of valid words, periods, hyphens, and the obligatory "at" sign. If the e-mail address does not match the expression, then we respond with an error to user via the **respond** function.

Invalid e-mail addresses are the scourge of Web forms, along with any other information that is supplied to an external program or that is used as a filename. Consider, for example, a Web form that allows you to view files from the system. Without any checking, an unscrupulous user could request the /etc/passwd file. Also, it's possible to set an e-mail address to respond with the contents of a specific file; the contents of the /etc/passwd file could be retrieved this way, too. Chapter 9 contains a more detailed discussion on the security breaches and concerns that you need to be aware of when writing CGI scripts.

```
45    mail_a_message('$formlist{subject}',
46                   '$formlist{from}',
47                   "$formlist{email}",
48                   "$formlist{message}");
49    respond('Your email has been sent');
50  }
```

By line 45, we have finished the checks we need to make. There is no point in checking the format of the subject and message body fields; they don't contain any information that will be used in anything but static text. Lines 45 to 48 send the e-mail message, and then line 49 sends a "success" message to the user.

```
51  else
52  {
53    respond('Error: Your form didn't submit any information');
54  }
55
```

Line 51 handles the instance where no form fields were found in the information supplied to the script. In this example, this could be because the script was called with the GET method, not the POST method. We could have checked for this by examining the contents of the REQUEST_FORM environment variable. (Coping with a script that needs to handle both formats is the subject of our next script.) Line 53 reports the error if there are no defined form fields.

```
56  sub respond
57  {
58      my $message = shift;
59      print "Content-type: text/html\n\n";
60      print <<EOF;
61  <head>
62  <title>$message</title>
63  </head>
64  <body>
65  $message
66  </body>
67  EOF
68      exit;
69  }
```

Lines 56 to 69 form the **respond** function and are identical to the previous script, so I won't go into detail here.

The **cgipost.htm** file on the CD-ROM is the HTML form to be used with this script. You can try it out by following the installation instructions in the sidebar "Installing CGI Scripts" earlier in this chapter. Alternatively, use the method supplied in the sidebar "Testing CGI Scripts Without a Web Server" later in this chapter.

SCGI.pm

Simple CGI Module

It is often impractical to impose a specific method on the process of accepting information from a form. What many people use depends largely on a personal preference and what they are used to. More experienced Web programmers who understand the differences between the two systems, and their advantages and disadvantages, tend to be more careful about which system they choose. Indeed, it's sometimes useful for the same script to be able to use either method, depending on the operation being performed.

What we need, therefore, is a way of identifying the type of request being made before we obtain the information that is then processed by the parsing system. There are two ways we can do this. The first is to try to obtain the information from one request, and if that fails, try the alternative method. The second is to access the **REQUEST_METHOD** environment variable that will contain GET or POST accordingly. Personally, I prefer the former rather than the latter solution because it actually attempts to get the information regardless of what the Web server software thinks the request type is. This is the purpose of the **SCGI.pm** module we will look at next.

PROGRAMMER'S NOTE *If you want to use a more standard and stress-tested solution for your CGI needs, then you should examine the CGI module that comes with the Perl distribution.*

Also in this module is a function to import and print templates and other documents by opening a file and replacing fixed strings with alternatives supplied at run time. I've been using this method for importing header, body, and footer templates for a number of years, and its prime purpose is much like the concept of modules: using a single source for a particular function. In this case, we can make managing the site easier by using a core set of files to supply the header and body styles, while still retaining the flexibility of adding other information and customization to the body of the HTML page.

```perl
1   package SCGI;
2
3   use strict;
4   use vars qw/@ISA @EXPORT/;
5   require Exporter;
6   @ISA = 'Exporter';
7   @EXPORT = qw(
8                   init_cgi
9                   template
10                  show_debug
11                  );
12  use vars qw(
13                  %formlist
14                  $formlength
15                  );
16
17  sub init_cgi
18  {
19      my $length = $ENV{CONTENT_LENGTH};
20      my $query = $ENV{QUERY_STRING};
21      my (@assign);
22
23      if ( defined($query) and $length > 0 )
24      {
25          @assign = split(/&/,$query);
26          $formlength = @assign;
27      }
28      elsif (defined($length) and $length > 0 )
29      {
30          sysread(STDIN, $_, $length);
31          chomp;
32          @assign = split('&');
```

```
33            $formlength = @assign;
34        }
35        else
36        {
37            $formlength=0;
38            return;
39        }
40        for (my $i=0; $i<$formlength; $i++)
41        {
42            my ($name,$value) = split('=',$assign[$i]);
43            $value =~ tr/+/ /;
44            $value =~
45                s/%([a-fA-F0-9][a-fA-F0-9])/pack("C", hex($1))/eg;
46            if (defined($formlist{$name}))
47            {
48                $formlist{$name} .= ",$value";
49            }
50            else
51            {
52                $formlist{$name} = $value;
53            }
54        }
55        return;
56    }
57
58    sub template
59    {
60        my ($template,$range,%options) = @_;
61
62        open(WRAPPER,"</usr/local/http/templates/$range/$template")
63            or return '';
64
65        { local $/; $_ = <WRAPPER> }
66        close (WRAPPER);
67        for my $key (keys %options)
68        {
69            s/REPLACE_KEY_$key/$options{$key}/;
70        }
71        return $_;
72    }
73
74    sub show_debug
75    {
76        print("//Debug<br>\n",
```

```
77              "Form length is: $formlength<br>\n");
78      for my $key (sort keys %formlist)
79      {
80          print "Key $key = $formlist{$key}<br>\n";
81      }
82      print "Debug//<p>\n";
83  }
84
85  1;
```

ANNOTATIONS

This module is, as the name suggests, very simple. All we've done is merge the two sequences for processing the different methods into a single function. Note here that we are not using the **REQUEST_METHOD** environment variable to discover the request method; you may want to place a wrapper around lines 23 to 34 that use this variable.

```
1   package SCGI;
2
3   use strict;
4   use vars qw/@ISA @EXPORT/;
5   require Exporter;
6   @ISA = 'Exporter';
7   @EXPORT = qw(
8                   init_cgi
9                   template
10                  show_debug
11                  );
12  use vars qw(
13                  %formlist
14                  $formlength
15                  );
16
```

Lines 1 to 15 set up the package environment. I've specified the **strict** pragma for this module, which places more strict usage on the module. The pragma works for each name space, so even if we define it in a calling script, unless it was defined within the package the tests and restrictions would not be in place.

Because of the **strict** pragma, we have to define the variables used by the **Exporter** module using the **vars** pragma, which is then also used to define the two variables we will export, **formlength** and **%formlist**, which store the number of elements and the hash of field/value pairs, respectively.

```
17   sub init_cgi
18   {
19       my $length = $ENV{CONTENT_LENGTH};
20       my $query = $ENV{QUERY_STRING};
21       my (@assign);
22
```

We start off the **init_cgi** function with a set of variables similar to our previous examples. The **$length** variable should be the number of bytes in the query regardless of the method used. We set up the **$query** variable, based on the environment variable, because we'll check for information via a GET request first. If that fails, then we'll try POST, and if that fails we'll assume there is no information and set the **$formlength** and **%formlist** variables to be empty.

```
23       if ( defined($query) and $length > 0 )
24       {
25           @assign = split(/&/,$query);
26           $formlength = @assign;
27       }
```

Lines 23 to 27 attempt to process the information from a GET request. Line 23 checks that the query string has been defined and that the query length is greater than zero; then we split the query by ampersands and set the **$formlength** variable to the number of elements in the array.

```
28       elsif (defined($length) and $length > 0 )
29       {
30           sysread(STDIN, $_, $length);
31           chomp;
32           @assign = split(/&/);
33           $formlength = @assign;
34       }
```

If the GET request does not work, we try to read **$length** bytes from the standard input as if we were processing a POST request. As before, we use **sysread** to read in a specified number of bytes from the standard input before splitting the query string into the **@assign** array.

```
35       else
36       {
37           $formlength=0;
38           return;
39       }
```

If we determine the query length was zero (since that's what we essentially test for in lines 23 to 28), it's safe to assume there isn't any form information at all, in which case we set the **$formlength** variable to be zero, and then return to the calling script. Note that we don't do any form of error handling here—it is entirely up to the calling script to cope with an empty request. This is partly because the module has no way of knowing what information has already been sent back to the browser. We can't use **die** since those error strings are reported to the STDERR file handle, which is not redirected to the browser.

```
40      for (my $i=0; $i<$formlength; $i++)
41      {
42          my ($name,$value) = split('=',$assign[$i]);
43          $value =~ tr/+/ /;
44          $value =~
45              s/%([a-fA-F0-9][a-fA-F0-9])/pack("C", hex($1))/eg;
```

If we've made it this far, it means there is information to be parsed from the **@assign** array into the **%formlist** hash. This section is identical to our previous examples, so I won't go into any detail. Suffice it to say that the array elements are split and then the values unescaped.

```
46          if (defined($formlist{$name}))
47          {
48              $formlist{$name} .= ",$value";
49          }
50          else
51          {
52              $formlist{$name} = $value;
53          }
54      }
55      return;
56  }
57
```

The URI::Escape Module

Part of the LWP package by Gisle Aas, the **URI::Escape** module provides a standard way of both "escaping" and "unescaping" characters. Converting special characters to their escaped equivalents is more complicated, and I often use the **URI::Escape** module when formatting URLs that include a GET request. We'll see an example of this type of URL later in this chapter as part of the **webnews.pl** script. If you want more information on the **URI::Escape** module, please check the manual page.

Lines 48 and 52 then append, or place the value against the field name specified by the key of the hash. This is the end of the **init_cgi** module. To use it, import the **SCGI** module and then call the **init_cgi()** function. It doesn't return anything, but if any fields were supplied as part of a GET or POST request, then the number of fields will be in the **$formlength** variable. We'll be using this module for all of the CGI examples from now on, so there will be plenty of opportunity to examine how to use the system.

It's also important to note that the function does not return the MIME header to the browser. This remains the responsibility of the calling script, which allows us greater flexibility when it comes to the header data we return. We'll see an example of this in the **sendfile.pl** script later in this chapter.

```
58  sub template
59  {
```

If you are developing a site that has a particular house style, and you are implementing a number of different CGI or even static scripts that need to follow the format, there are very few options open to you. One option is Server Side Includes (SSI), which allows you to reference other HTML files within the file that is processed by the Web server. There are two problems with this method.

First of all, the many Web servers do not parse information from CGI scripts on the way to the user's browser, so SSIs don't work on these systems. Secondly, SSIs impose additional loading on your server when you have already taken a performance hit by calling an external CGI program. A better method, therefore, is to use the text processing capabilities of Perl to import the page templates and output the result as part of the information sent back to the browser by the script.

This is the principle behind the **template** function. Also built in to the script is the ability to make selective replacements on the imported code, based on a predefined format. In this way we can use the same template for, for example, the header information but still have the Perl script introducing a different header and title for the HTML document.

```
60      my ($template,$range,%options) = @_;
61
62      open(WRAPPER,"</usr/local/http/templates/$range/$template")
63          or return '';
64
```

The function takes three arguments: **$template** is the name of the template to be imported, **$range** is the name of a subdirectory in the main structure, and **%options** is the hash that contains the strings to be replaced and their replacements. The use of both **$template** and **$range** means that we can use this module in scripts on a multihomed server, where multiple Web sites are supported on one machine.

Lines 62 and 63 attempt to open the template file based on the range and template name. If the operation fails, then it just returns to the calling script, without an empty string.

```
65      { local $/; $_ = <WRAPPER> }
66      close (WRAPPER);
```

Line 65 uses a localized record separator within a new block to import the entire file into the default variable space. Because the size of the HTML is unlikely to be very large, it's relatively safe to do this without worrying about the amount of memory required. Line 66 then closes the file. We don't bother checking the success of the close operation since we are not writing to the file.

```
67      for my $key (keys %options)
68      {
69          s/REPLACE_KEY_$key/$options{$key}/;
70      }
```

Lines 67 to 70 process the default variable, making replacements for a string matching the **REPLACE_KEY_$key**, where **$key** is the key from the hash, and replacing it with the value of the corresponding hash key.

```
71      return $_;
72  }
73
```

Line 71 then returns the template, with the substitutions that were made to the calling script. We'll see examples of using this function in many of the remaining scripts.

```
74  sub show_debug
75  {
76      print("//Debug<br>\n",
77              "Form length is: $formlength<br>\n");
78      for my $key (sort keys %formlist)
79      {
80          print "Key $key = $formlist{$key}<br>\n";
81      }
82      print "Debug//<p>\n";
83  }
84
85  1;
```

The **show_debug** script that starts on line 74 prints out the list of fields and corresponding values; it can be very useful to print the information if you are having trouble processing the contents of the form. The information is printed to the browser, so you must ensure that the main script has already sent the correct HTTP header before calling the function.

phone.pl

Phone List

Our first real CGI script using the Simple CGI module from this chapter is a simple phone list system. It's designed to search a NDBM database that contains names, phone numbers, and references to the memory number in which the contact's number is stored within your phone system.

The script introduces another of the basic CGI principles, which is the connection of a Web form with an online database. Although this script does not update the information (we'll leave that for the next script), it demonstrates many of the principles behind database access with a browser.

```perl
1   #!/usr/local/bin/perl5
2
3   use SCGI;
4   use NDBM_File;
5   use Fcntl;
6
7   my $pagetitle = "Phone Memory List";
8   my $pageheader = "Phone Memory Numbers";
9
10  init_cgi();
11
12  print "Content-type: text/html\n\n";
13  print template('header','www',
14                  'pagetitle' => $pagetitle,
15                  'pageheader' => $pageheader,
16                  );
17  print template('main','www','pageheader' => $pageheader);
18
19  unless (tie(my %phone, 'NDBM_File', '/usr/local/http/data/phone',
20      O_CREAT|O_RDWR, 0666))
21  {
22      print "Help, can't open database!!!! $!\n";
23      print template('footer','www');
24      exit;
25  }
26
27  if ($SCGI::formlength == 0)
28  {
```

```
29       print <<EOF;
30   <form method=POST action="/cgi-bin/phone.pl">
31   <b>Name:</b><input type=text name=name size=20><p>
32   <input type="submit" value="Show Me">
33   <input type="reset" value="Reset">
34   EOF
35   }
36   else
37   {
38       unless(defined($SCGI::formlist{name}))
39       {
40           print "Error: Query supplied is invalid\n";
41           print template('footer','www');
42           exit;
43       }
44       my @list = grep(/$SCGI::formlist{name}/i,keys %phone);
45       if (@list)
46       {
47           print <<EOF
48   <p><table border=0>
49   <tr>
50   <td width=300><font size+1><b>Name</b></font></td>
51   <td width=80><font size+1><b>Memory No.</b></font></td>
52   <td width=300><font size+1><b>Number</b></font></td>
53   </tr>
54   EOF
55           foreach my $name (sort @list)
56           {
57               my ($memoryno,$phone) = split(/,/,$phone{$name});
58               print("<tr><td>$name</td><td>$memoryno</td>",
59                   "<td>$phone</td></tr>\n");
60           }
61           print <<EOF;
62   </table>
63   <hr>
64   <form method=POST action="/cgi-bin/phone.pl">
65   <b>Name:</b><input type=text name=name size=20><p>
```

```
66   <input type="submit" value="Show Me">
67   <input type="reset" value="Reset">
68   <p>
69   EOF
70       }
71       else
72       {
73           print("<h2>No Match Found</h2>",
74                   "<a href=/cgi-bin/phone.pl>Try Again!</a>\n");
75       }
76   }
77
78   print template('footer','www');
```

ANNOTATIONS

This script is entirely self contained; we use the ability to check for the number of form elements to decide what to do. If there are no fields passed to the script, then we provide the search form to the browser. Once the user has filled in the script, we can use the same script to perform the search and respond with the results.

I'm a great believer in using single scripts wherever possible because it reduces the number of files that need to be managed. A single script also makes the introduction of the scripts functionality that much easier to integrate—we have a single point of reference for the script's functionality. There is, of course, a downside to this technique: your Web server takes an unnecessary hit each time someone simply goes to the search form. Since this is an intranet, rather than the Internet, this issue is possibly of little consequence, but it remains a consideration all the same.

```
1    #!/usr/local/bin/perl5
2
3    use SCGI;
4    use NDBM_File;
5    use Fcntl;
6
7    my $pagetitle = "Phone Memory List";
8    my $pageheader = "Phone Memory Numbers";
9
```

We need the **SCGI** module from this chapter to support the CGI interface, as well as the **NDBM_File** and **Fcntl** modules so we can access the NDBM file that will store the phone memory information. Lines 7 and 8 set up the variables that store the HTML title and the header that will be printed at the top of the page. These are two of the values that I've configured in my templates to be replaced.

```
10   init_cgi();
11
```

Line 10 calls the **init_cgi** function from the **SCGI** module. As we already know, this places the number of elements and the field/value pairs into two public variables within the **SCGI** namespace, **$formlength** and **%formlist**.

```
12   print "Content-type: text/html\n\n";
13   print template('header','www',
14                    'pagetitle' => $pagetitle,
15                    'pageheader' => $pageheader,
16                    );
17   print template('main','www','pageheader' => $pageheader);
18
```

Lines 12 to 17 print out first the MIME type for the browser and then the templates for the header and the main body of the HTML document. This is based on the templates I use, where the header defines only the HTML title and the body color. The "main" template is a button bar on the left-hand side contained within a table; the body of the document is on the right-hand side in the remainder of the window. By splitting the two elements, I can introduce custom button bars at the top of the main button bar to allow for context. You'll see an example of the layout at the end of this script.

If you remember, the **SCGI** script defined the **template** function to accept values from a hash to act as replacements in the template text. Rather than creating a new hash and passing that to the function, we can specify the hash elements, using the => notation we have seen before, directly within the function call.

```
19   unless (tie(my %phone, 'NDBM_File', '/usr/local/http/data/phone',
20       O_CREAT|O_RDWR, 0666))
21   {
22       print "Help, can't open database!!!! $!\n";
23       print template('footer','www');
24       exit;
25   }
26
```

Lines 19 and 20 open the NDBM file that contains the phone memory database. Note that here we have to print an error to the user with a **print** call because only the standard output is passed back to the user's browser. It's safe to do this now because we have already sent the document's MIME type and header information. Note that in this example, because of the template and design I have used, we need to remember to print the footer before finally quitting from the script.

```
27   if ($SCGI::formlength == 0)
28   {
```

```
29      print <<EOF;
30  <form method=POST action="/cgi-bin/phone.pl">
31  <b>Name:</b><input type=text name=name size=20><p>
32  <input type="submit" value="Show Me">
33  <input type="reset" value="Reset">
34  EOF
35  }
```

Line 27 checks the number of fields supplied to the script from the query. If the script has just been called blindly (that is, without a query), then the number of fields will be zero, and we'll print out the form required to search the database (lines 29 to 34). There is only one form field, name, that is for the contact's name. The text entered in this field is the string used to search the database.

```
36  else
37  {
38      unless(defined($SCGI::formlist{name}))
39      {
40          print "Error: Query supplied is invalid\n";
41          print template('footer','www');
42          exit;
43      }
```

If there are form elements, then we start processing them on line 38 by checking that we were actually supplied the field name we were expecting. If it has not been specified, we report an error, again remembering to print the footer to keep the house style.

```
44      my @list = grep(/$SCGI::formlist{name}/i,keys %phone);
```

Line 44 searches the keys of the phone database, based on the contents of the name field. We use **grep** on the keys of the tied NDBM database. The **keys** function returns an array of keys for the database, and **grep** returns an array of matching entries from the keys array using the regular expression as a filter.

The keys contain the contact name, so if the user enters "Martin" on the form, then **grep** returns a list of all the keys containing "Martin." There are two things of importance to note here, too. Firstly, we ensure the regular expression is not case sensitive. Secondly, an empty expression matches all elements of the array, so we've automatically provided an extra level of functionality without even trying to. If the user clicks on the Show Me button on the form without entering anything to search by, the script will return all the phone numbers in the array.

```
45      if (@list)
46      {
47          print <<EOF
48  <p><table border=0>
49  <tr>
```

```
50   <td width=300><font size+1><b>Name</b></font></td>
51   <td width=80><font size+1><b>Memory No.</b></font></td>
52   <td width=300><font size+1><b>Number</b></font></td>
53   </tr>
54   EOF
```

If there are any matching elements from the search, then we print out an HTML table, with a suitable header row, to display the results. There are three fields to the database—the name, the memory number, and the phone number—all of which can display very cleanly in three columns.

```
55       foreach my $name (sort @list)
56       {
57           my ($memoryno,$phone) = split(/,/,$phone{$name});
58           print("<tr><td>$name</td><td>$memoryno</td>",
59                   "<td>$phone</td></tr>\n");
60       }
```

Lines 55 to 60 work through the list of names, and therefore keys, from the phone database, printing out each entry as a new row in the table. The memory number and phone number are stored as a comma-separated list in the value of the corresponding hash key. We split the details out on line 57 before printing the actual HTML table row on lines 58 and 59.

```
61       print <<EOF;
62   </table>
63   <hr>
64   <form method=POST action="/cgi-bin/phone.pl">
65   <b>Name:</b><input type=text name=name size=20><p>
66   <input type="submit" value="Show Me">
67   <input type="reset" value="Reset">
68   <p>
69   EOF
70       }
```

Once we reach line 61, we have finished printing out the matching entries. We can therefore close the HTML table before printing out another copy of the search form in case the user didn't find what they were looking for.

```
71   else
72   {
73       print("<h2>No Match Found</h2>",
74               "<a href=/cgi-bin/phone.pl>Try Again!</a>\n");
75   }
76   }
77
```

Lines 71 to 75 cope with the situation when there are no matching records in the database: we just print an error message and provide a link back to the nonsearch version of the form. We could have supplied another copy of the search form here by replicating the HTML code in lines 64 to 67.

```
78  print template('footer','www');
```

By line 78, we have reached the end of the script, and we need to print out the template footer. Although we've called this function before, it has only been as part of an error-trapping situation. To make sure we include all of the output information in the main body, we make this the last thing we execute before we finally exit.

You can see the result of a search in Figure 8-1.

You may want to consider an extension to this script to make it slightly more flexible. At the moment, entries are sorted alphabetically by the name of the person in the phone list. Sometimes it can be helpful to view the data by phone number (perhaps if you can remember the person's number but not their name) or by the memory (in case you want to update the list).

Probably the best way to alter the searching capabilities is to change the way the information is stored internally by the script before being regurgitated to the user. We'll also need to add a new field to hold the sort information, as well as decide on some simple way to make the sort selection.

Let's cover the last item first. You may remember that at the beginning of this chapter, when discussing the differences between GET and POST requests, I mentioned one of the advantages of GET—field elements can be referenced as part of the URL. This means we can set, for example, the column headers of the results table to be the "buttons" that change the sort order of the output. The method required for incorporating a GET request in the URL is to place a question mark after the base URL of the script, and then put the query string after that as part of the whole URL. We'll need to escape any special characters on the command line, so we use the **URI::Escape** module from the LWP toolkit.

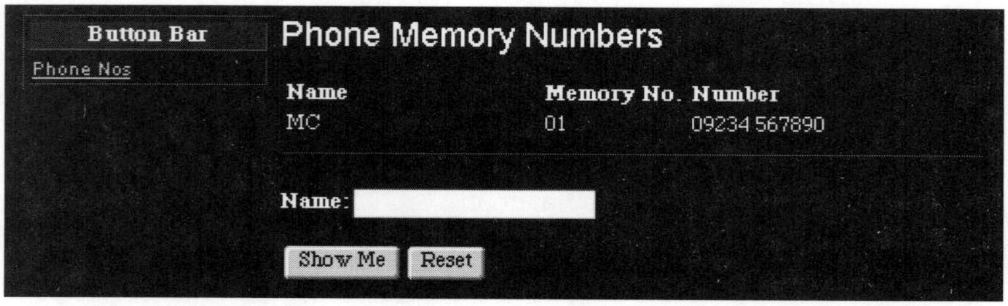

FIGURE 8-1. The result of a phone number search

The code we need follows:

```
my $sortby = $USP::SCGI::formlist{sortby} || 'id';
my $resortby = uri_escape($USP::SCGI::formlist{name});

print <<EOF;
<tr>
<td width=300><font size+1><b>
<a href="/cgi-bin/ssd.cgi?name=$resortby&sortby=id">Name</a>
</b></font></td>
<td width=80><font size+1><b>
<a href="/cgi-bin/ssd.cgi?name=$resortby&sortby=mem">Memory No.</a>
</b></font></td>
<td width=300><font size+1><b>
<a href="/cgi-bin/ssd.cgi?name=$resortby&sortby=phone">Number</a>
</b></font></td></tr>
EOF
```

The first line sets the **$sortby** variable, which we'll use later, either to that specified by the query or to a default value of "id," which refers to the keys and therefore the names from the database. The second line generates an escaped version of the name field so that the search information can be included as part of the URL. The here document then prints out the new table header row with the links set on the column titles. Clicking on one of these titles will call the script again, with the same name value as before combined with a different "sort by" field.

The data search works in the same way as before, but rather than printing the information directly from the table, we place the information into a hash of hashes and then sort out a printed version of that. To explain this further, let's have a look at the code, starting with the code for creating the hash structure:

```
foreach my $name (sort @list)
{
    my ($memoryno,$phone) = split(',',$phone{$name});
    $phonehash{$name}{id}    = $name;
    $phonehash{$name}{phone} = $name;
    $phonehash{$name}{mem}   = $name;
}
```

This generates a hash called **%phonehash**. Its keys are the contact's name, just as before, but rather than containing the comma-separated fields, each element contains a new hash. The keys are hardcoded as id, phone, and mem, and these represent the fields of the new internal database of contacts, memory, and phone numbers. What we have effectively done is create a new record; each record of information has its own field structure, and the records themselves can be referenced by a key, just as before.

Testing CGI Scripts Without a Web Server

Although it sounds like a bit of an impossible task, sometimes you need to test a script without requiring or using a browser and Web server. Certainly, if you switch warnings and use the **strict** pragma, then your script may well **die** before reporting any information to the browser, or even to the Web server's error log. Worse, you may find yourself in a situation where you do not have privileges or even the software to support a Web service on which to do your testing. Any or all of these situations require another method for supplying a query to a CGI script.

In fact, the principle is very simple. Because we know that the information can be supplied to the script via an environment variable, all we have to do is create the environment variable with a properly formatted string in it. For example, for the **phone.pl** script you might use the following lines for a Bourne Shell:

```
QUERY_STRING='name=MC'
export QUERY_STRING
```

This is easy if the query data is simple, but what if the information needs to be escaped because of special characters? In this instance, the easiest thing is to grab a GET-based URL from the browser, or get the script to print out a copy of the escaped query string, and then assign that to the environment variable.

As another alternative, if you use the SCGI script at the beginning of this chapter (**webenv.pl**), it will wait for input from the keyboard before continuing if no environment query string has been set. Here, too, you can enter the query string at the time of execution.

All of these methods assume that you cannot (or do not want) to make modifications to the script. If you can make modifications to the script, then it's easier, and sometimes clearer, just to assign sample values to the form variables directly, for example:

```
$SCGI::formlist{name} = 'MC';
```

Just remember to unset them, or the environment query strings, before you use the script, otherwise you may have trouble using the script effectively!

The main hash is still accessible as usual, so we can write terms like

```
keys %phonehash
```

and still obtain a list of the keys, or, in our case, record numbers from the database. You will have noticed, I hope, that the three field names match the names we used when creating the header row in the table. This is significant because we need the information for sorting the table. Remember that the **$sortby** variables contains this reference, and we'll use this for sorting the information before we print it. The next code fragment demonstrates this more fully.

```
foreach my $name
    (sort { $phonehash{$a}{$sortby} cmp
            $phonehash{$b}{$sortby}; } keys %phonedata)
{
    print("<tr><td>$name</td>",
          "<td>$phone{$name}{mem}</td>",
          "<td>$phone{$name}{phone}</td></tr>\n");
}
```

This sets up a **foreach** loop that will go through the keys of the **%phonedata** hash. The **sort** runs a comparison against the values of the **$sortby** field of the subhash of each element, returning the list of keys for the main hash sorted by the corresponding field values.

This means that if **$sortby** is id, then the data is sorted by the contact names, like before; if it's mem, then the sort is by the memory numbers; and so on. This internal hash of hashes structure can be used to model just about any data record you want, and we'll use it again in Chapter 11.

webnews.pl

Web News Page Management Interface

Our phone list was a simple one-way (read-only) interface to a pre-created database of phone memories and numbers. In this script, we'll look at a complete creation and editing system for creating a Web-based news page. Many of the principles behind this script are the same as in the previous example. The biggest difference is that we will be introducing pre-filled forms and update processes into the body of the script, as well as creating a static HTML page as part of the process of generating the Web page.

Once again, this script is entirely self contained, which should make any management and updates to the process much easier. I've also separated many of the features that were duplicated in the last script into individual functions, including some tricks to reduce the number of functions required to support the different operations of adding and updating the database via a form.

The basis for the script is fairly simple. We have a database, using NDBM, that contains news stories. The key for the NDBM database is a combination of the date, time, and a random number. The database contents include the title and the news text. A single screen provides an outline of the stories available. Clicking on a story title allows you to edit it, and links provide the ability to add new stories to the database. There are two checkboxes against each news story: one allows you to mark the story for deletion, and the other allows you to set the story to be included or excluded in the final news page. Finally, another link at the bottom of the page allows you to create the static news page that the user will see. You can see a sample screen in Figure 8-2.

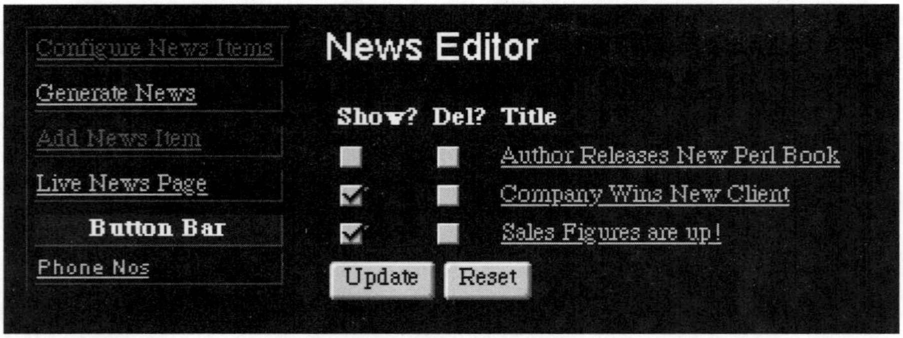

FIGURE 8-2. The main Web News interface screen

```
1   #!/usr/local/bin/perl5
2
3   use SCGI;
4   use NDBM_File;
5   use Fcntl;
6
7   my $packtemplate = 'IA80A800';
8   my %news;
9
10  init_cgi;
11
12  print "Content-type: text/html\n\n";
13  print template('header','www','pagetitle' => 'News Editor');
14
15  print <<EOF;
16  <tr><td>
17  <a href="/cgi-bin/webnews.pl">Configure News Items</a><br>
18  </td></tr>
19  <tr><td>
20  <a href="/cgi-bin/webnews.pl?mode=generate">Generate News</a><br>
21  </td><tr>
22  <tr><td>
23  <a href="/cgi-bin/webnews.pl?mode=add">Add News Item</a><br>
```

```
24  </td><tr>
25  <tr><td>
26  <a href="/news.html">Live News Page</a>
27  </td><tr>
28  EOF
29
30  print template('main','www','pageheader' => 'News Editor');
31
32  unless(tie(%news, 'NDBM_File', '/usr/local/http/data/news',
33          O_CREAT|O_RDWR, 0666))
34  {
35      print "Help, can't open database!!!! $!\n";
36      print template('footer','www');
37      die;
38  }
39
40  if ($SCGI::formlength == 0)
41  {
42      summary_list();
43  }
44  else
45  {
46      if ($SCGI::formlist{mode} eq 'add')
47      {
48          my ($sec,$min,$hour,$mday,$mon,$year)
49              = (localtime(time))[0..5];
50          $mon += 1;
51          $year += 1900;
52          srand $sec;
53          my $refrnd = rand 32768;
54          my $ref=sprintf("%d%02d%02d.%02d%02d%02d.%d",
55                          $year,$mon,$mday,$hour,$min,$sec,$refrnd);
56          printform('addupdate',"$ref",'','');
57      }
58      elsif ($SCGI::formlist{mode} eq 'addupdate')
59      {
60          $news{$SCGI::formlist{id}} = pack($packtemplate,1,
61                                           $SCGI::formlist{title},
62                                           $SCGI::formlist{desc});
```

```perl
63          print "News item has been added/updated.<p>\n";
64          print("<a href=/cgi-bin/webnews.pl>",
65              "Back to News Summary</a>");
66      }
67      elsif ($SCGI::formlist{mode} eq 'edit')
68      {
69          my ($active,$title,$desc)
70              = unpack($packtemplate,
71                      $news{$SCGI::formlist{id}});
72          printform('addupdate',$SCGI::formlist{id},$title,$desc);
73      }
74      elsif ($SCGI::formlist{mode} eq 'generate')
75      {
76          generate_page();
77      }
78      elsif ($SCGI::formlist{mode} eq 'update')
79      {
80          foreach my $key (grep(/^del-/,keys %SCGI::formlist))
81          {
82              my $realkey = $key;
83              $realkey =~ s/^del-//;
84              delete $news{$realkey};
85          }
86          foreach my $key (keys %news)
87          {
88              my ($active,$title,$desc)
89                  = unpack($packtemplate,$news{$key});
90              defined($SCGI::formlist{"mode-$key"}) ?
91                  $active=1 :
92                      $active=0;
93              $news{$key} =
94                  pack($packtemplate,$active,$title,$desc);
95          }
96          summary_list();
97      }
98      elsif ($SCGI::formlist{mode} eq 'approve')
99      {
100         unlink("/usr/local/http/news.html");
101         rename("/usr/local/http/newstemp.html",
102                 "/use/local/http/news.html");
103         print("Live News page updated.<br>",
104             "You can view it <a href=/news.html>here</a>\n");
105     }
```

```
106 }
107
108 untie(%news);
109 print template('footer','www');
110
111 sub summary_list
112 {
113     print <<EOF;
114 <form method=POST action=/cgi-bin/webnews.pl>
115 <input type=hidden name=mode value=update>
116 <table>
117 <tr><td><b>Show?</b></td><td><b>Del?</b></td>
118 <td><b>Title</b></td></tr>
119 EOF
120     for my $key (sort keys %news)
121     {
122         my ($active,$title)
123             = (unpack($packtemplate,$news{$key}))[0,1];
124         if ($active)
125         {
126             print("<tr><Td><input type=checkbox",
127                 " name=mode-$key value=$key checked></td>\n");
128         }
129         else
130         {
131             print("<tr><Td><input type=checkbox",
132                 " name=mode-$key value=$key></td>\n");
133         }
134         print <<EOF;
135 <td><input type=checkbox name=del-$key value=$key></td>
136 <td><a href="/cgi-bin/webnews.pl?mode=edit&id=$key">
137 $title</a></td>
138 </tr>
139 EOF
140     }
141     print("</table><input type=submit value=Update>",
142         "<input type=reset value=Reset><p>\n");
143 }
144
145 sub printform
146 {
147     my ($mode,$id,$title,$desc) = @_;
148     print <<EOF;
```

```
149  <form method=POST action=/cgi-bin/webnews.pl>
150  <input type=hidden name=mode value=$mode>
151  <input type=hidden name=id value=$id>
152  <table>
153  <tr>
154  <td><b>ID: </b></td><td>$id</td>
155  </tr>
156  <tr>
157  <td><b>Title</b></td>
158  <td>
159  <input type=text name=title size=50 maxlength=80 value="$title">
160  </td>
161  </tr>
162  <tr valign=top>
163  <td><b>Description</b></td>
164  <td>
165  <textarea name=desc rows=20 cols=40 maxlength=800>
166  $desc</textarea></td>
167  </tr>
168  </table>
169  <input type=submit value=Update>
170  <input type=reset value=Reset><p>
171  </form>
172  EOF
173  }
174
175  sub generate_page()
176  {
177      open(TMPPAGE,">/usr/local/http/newstemp.html")
178          or warn "Panic: $!";
179
180      print TMPPAGE template('header','www',
181                             'pagetitle' => 'News');
182      print TMPPAGE template('header','www',
183                             'pageheader' => 'News');
184
185      for my $key (reverse sort keys %news)
186      {
187          my ($active,$title,$desc) =
188              unpack($packtemplate,$news{$key});
189          my $realdate = (split(/\./,$key))[0];
190          $realdate =~ s:(\d{4})(\d{2})(\d{2}):$3/$2/$1:;
191          if ($active)
192          {
```

```
193            $desc =~ s/\n/<p>/g;
194            print("<font size=+2><b>$title, ",
195                  "$realdate</b></font><p>",
196                  "$desc<hr>");
197        }
198    }
199    open(WRAPPER,
200    print TMPPAGE template('footer','www');
201    close (TMPPAGE);
202    print <<EOF
203 Page Generated<p>
204 <A href=/newstemp.html>
205 You can view the page here</a><br>
206 <A href=/cgi-bin/webnews.pl?mode=approve>
207 Approve the page here</a>
208 EOF
209 }
```

ANNOTATIONS

About half of the script is given over to the HTML and related formatting for the interface elements. An equal amount is given to the actual code of the script that handles the communication link between the Web forms and the backend NDBM database.

It's worth noting as you read through that the script makes some assumptions about the queries being made. A special field variable in the query, mode, is responsible for telling the CGI script what mode it's in and what it should do with the information that is provided. If there is no mode variable, then the list of news stories is printed out; if a mode is specified, then the script responds differently, updating the database, adding to it, or reporting from it accordingly.

```
1   #!/usr/local/bin/perl5
2
3   use SCGI;
4   use NDBM_File;
5   use Fcntl;
6
7   my $packtemplate = 'IA80A800';
8   my %news;
9
10  init_cgi;
11
```

Lines 3 to 10 are the initialization. Because the news information is going to be stored in an NDBM database, we need the **NDBM_File** and **Fcntl** modules. The template on line 7 will be used with the **pack** and **unpack** functions to store the information in the value part of the NDBM database. We use **pack** so that we don't have to worry about selecting a specific field separator, which may interfere with the actual text of the title and body of the news item. There are three fields: the first is an unsigned integer that specifies whether the item should be included in the news page. The two strings that follow, of 80 and 800 characters in length, are the title and body of the news item.

Line 8 defines the hash that will be tied to the NDBM database, and then line 10 initializes the form variables based on the supplied query information (if there is any).

```
12   print "Content-type: text/html\n\n";
13   print template('header','www','pagetitle' => 'News Editor');
14
15   print <<EOF;
16   <tr><td>
17   <a href="/cgi-bin/webnews.pl">Configure News Items</a><br>
18   </td></tr>
19   <tr><td>
20   <a href="/cgi-bin/webnews.pl?mode=generate">Generate News</a><br>
21   </td><tr>
22   <tr><td>
23   <a href="/cgi-bin/webnews.pl?mode=add">Add News Item</a><br>
24   </td><tr>
25   <tr><td>
26   <a href="/news.html">Live News Page</a>
27   </td><tr>
28   EOF
29
30   print template('main','www','pageheader' => 'News Editor');
31
```

Lines 12 to 30 print out the necessary http and then HTML header information, using the template files where appropriate. You'll notice that the links in lines 17 to 26 are intended to be quick connections to different parts of the main script; they make use of the GET query method, specifying the mode of operation as part of the URL. This information will be printed for every invocation of the script, acting as a sort of toolbar for the Web news tool.

```
32   unless(tie(%news, 'NDBM_File', '/usr/local/http/data/news',
33           O_CREAT|O_RDWR, 0666))
34   {
```

```
35      print "Help, can't open database!!!! $!\n";
36      print template('footer','www');
37      die;
38  }
39
```

Lines 32 to 38 tie the NDBM file to the **%news** hash, reporting an error if the tie fails. Note that in the error we must also print the footer template to ensure the format of the entire page remains the constant. Furthermore, we **die** on line 37 so that the Web server identifies a problem with the execution of the script.

```
40  if ($SCGI::formlength == 0)
41  {
42      summary_list();
43  }
```

If there is no query element, then we call the **summary_list** function to print out the list of available stories that you saw in Figure 8-2.

```
44  else
45  {
46      if ($SCGI::formlist{mode} eq 'add')
47      {
48          my ($sec,$min,$hour,$mday,$mon,$year)
49              = (localtime(time))[0..5];
50          $mon += 1;
51          $year += 1900;
52          srand $sec;
53          my $refrnd = rand 32768;
54          my $ref=sprintf("%d%02d%02d.%02d%02d%02d.%d",
55                          $year,$mon,$mday,$hour,$min,$sec,$refrnd);
56          printform('addupdate',"$ref",'','');
57      }
```

If there are form elements, then it's safe to assume that there is information for us to work with. Lines 46 to 57 handle the situation where we are expecting to add new information to the database. This section is specifically interested in printing the form responsible for adding the information, rather than actually adding the information itself.

All database entries have a unique key, which is actually generated within this section of the script and then supplied to the browser as part of the add form. The key is generated by extracting the date via the **localtime** function (lines 48 and 49). We then account for the date information ranges. Remember that months start at 0, for January, so we need to add 1 to the value (line 50), and dates are specified as the number of years since 1900, so we add 1900 to the year value (line 51).

Lines 52 and 53 first seed (initialize) the random number generator and then obtain a random number with a value range of 0 to 32768. Lines 54 and 55 then produce a string based on the date, time, and random number. This string is the record number that is stored as the NDBM key. The string produced with this method will be fairly unique—it's unlikely even on a busy database that this method would generate two identical IDs.

Line 56 calls the **printform** function, which outputs the necessary form to add to or update the database. It takes four arguments: the mode and the three main database elements—the key, title, and description. Because this is a new record, the only piece of information we have is the key; the other two fields will be filled in by the user once the form has been supplied. The mode information (the first argument to the function) is actually the data to be specified in the **mode** field of the query that controls how the form is handled when it is submitted.

```
58    elsif ($SCGI::formlist{mode} eq 'addupdate')
59    {
60        $news{$SCGI::formlist{id}} = pack($packtemplate,1,
61                                          $SCGI::formlist{title},
62                                          $SCGI::formlist{desc});
63        print "News item has been added/updated.<p>\n";
64        print("<a href=/cgi-bin/webnews.pl>",
65              "Back to News Summary</a>");
66    }
```

Lines 58 to 66 handle addupdate mode. This mode is specified by the browser forms when you are adding or updating the database. The two options are actually identical; in both cases you are assigning a value in the database to a particular key. All of the information is supplied by the browser form (see the **printform** function below), so all we need to do is pack the value string using the pack template and then report the success back to the user.

Lines 60 to 62 perform the actual update, which uses the ID supplied by the browser as the key. This is either the date/time/random number that we generated in lines 54 and 55, or one already stored in the database if this form has come from an update request. We then pass the result of the **pack** function as the key's value.

The 1, which is the second argument to the function and the first field of the record, specifies that the record should be displayed in the static version of the file. This value is set each time you add or update the information—I've made the assumption that if you are updating a particular story it's because you want to include it in the news page. You can change this setting very easily as part of the management page, and the actual page generation is also a separate command to the CGI script, so it is a fairly safe assumption to make.

Lines 63 to 65 report success to the user and then provide a link back to the main news management page, by specifying a link without any query information.

```
67      elsif ($SCGI::formlist{mode} eq 'edit')
68      {
69          my ($active,$title,$desc)
70              = unpack($packtemplate,
71                      $news{$SCGI::formlist{id}});
72          printform('addupdate',$SCGI::formlist{id},$title,$desc);
73      }
```

If the user clicks on a news item in the management interface, the mode is set to edit, the data is retrieved from the database.The Web form is generated, this time based not on blank fields, or a new database record ID, but with the existing record ID instead.

Lines 69 to 71 extract the specified record from the database, using **unpack** to return an array of the field data, which is then assigned to the three variables, **$active**, **$title**, and **$desc**. We then make a call to the **printform** function, this time supplying the real field data of the record we are going to edit. Note that the mode is still addupdate—this is required because it is the name of the mode which will be placed into a hidden field in the form to define how the form information should be processed.

```
74      elsif ($SCGI::formlist{mode} eq 'generate')
75      {
76          generate_page();
77      }
```

If the user clicks on the Generate Page link on any of the Web news pages, the mode specified is generate, which is trapped for in line 74. The result is a simple call to the **generate_page** function, which we'll examine shortly.

```
78      elsif ($SCGI::formlist{mode} eq 'update')
79      {
```

On the news management page, the Update button uses the information supplied in the list of stories to select and/or delete the checked stories. A hidden field in the form, which is what the list is, specifies the mode, which is caught by line 78. First we delete the stories that have been marked for deletion, and then we update the display status for the remainder of the stories. We delete first because there is no point in updating the status of stories that are shortly to be deleted.

```
80          foreach my $key (grep(/^del-/,keys %SCGI::formlist))
81          {
82              my $realkey = $key;
83              $realkey =~ s/^del-//;
84              delete $news{$realkey};
85          }
```

Lines 80 to 85 delete the checked records from the database. The form fields that define whether a story should be deleted start with "del-," so we use **grep** on the keys of the form field hash. Each key found is then stripped of its prefix in lines 82 and 83, before being deleted from the hash, and therefore from the database, on line 84 using the **delete** function.

```
86        foreach my $key (keys %news)
87        {
88            my ($active,$title,$desc)
89                = unpack($packtemplate,$news{$key});
```

Lines 86 to 97 are responsible for updating the status of the story: either it remains in the database but is not included when the static news page is generated, or it's both in the database and on the generated page. Since all of the stories will be on the management page, and to save us from filtering out the other fields on the browser form, we simply step through all of the records in the database (line 86). Lines 88 and 89 extract the existing information for the current record from the database.

```
90            defined($SCGI::formlist{"mode-$key"}) ?
91                $active=1 :
92                    $active=0;
```

The checkboxes responsible for specifying whether to include or exclude the story are prefixed by "mode-." If it has been defined on the form, it means the box was checked, and we set the value of the **$active** field to 1 on line 91. If the form field has not been specified, then the box is not checked, and we switch off the display by setting the field to zero in line 92.

```
93            $news{$key} =
94                pack($packtemplate,$active,$title,$desc);
95        }
96        summary_list();
97    }
```

Lines 93 and 94 write the updated fields back to the database using **pack** to format the data. Line 96 then calls the **summary_list** function to redisplay the updated information.

```
98     elsif ($SCGI::formlist{mode} eq 'approve')
99     {
100        unlink("/usr/local/http/news.html");
101        rename("/usr/local/http/newstemp.html",
102            "/use/local/http/news.html");
103        print("Live News page updated.<br>",
104            "You can view it <a href=/news.html>here</a>\n");
105    }
106 }
107
```

Lines 98 to 105 approve the static news page that has been generated. The generation process actually creates a temporary news page that can be viewed and checked before it finally replaces the real news page. These lines move the temporary page to the real news page location. First we delete the existing real page (line 100), then we rename the temporary page (lines 101 and 102). Lines 103 and 104 print a success message and a link to the real news page for final verification.

Line 106 is the end of the main script test.

```
108 untie(%news);
109 print template('footer','www');
110
```

The final two lines close the NDBM database and then print the page footer to the browser.

It should have been apparent that throughout the script there is a distinct lack of checks on the quality of the information. This is not an oversight, just an appreciation of the fact that with a self-contained script, it is unlikely that incorrect, missing, or badly formatted fields and queries will be sent back to the same script that generated them.

```
111 sub summary_list
112 {
113     print <<EOF;
114 <form method=POST action=/cgi-bin/webnews.pl>
115 <input type=hidden name=mode value=update>
116 <table>
117 <tr><td><b>Show?</b></td><td><b>Del?</b></td>
118 <td><b>Title</b></td></tr>
119 EOF
```

Line 111 starts the **summary_list** function. The purpose of this function is to provide the list of available stories in the database in a format that allows for controlling their status, deleting them, and editing individual stories. The first few lines, 114 to 119, print out the main management form and print the header information for the table that will list the stories.

Note that line 114 specifies that we will use the POST method for updates; there is no particular reason for using this over GET, except that I find it cleaner for forms. GET requests make more sense when used within URLs. Line 115 specifies the hidden field that will specify the mode, in this case update, which will define how the script handles the information it is sent.

```
120     for my $key (sort keys %news)
121     {
```

The next part of the process is to work through the contents of the database, printing out the title and the boxes that allow you to update the individual records. We sort the database by sorting the keys, which as we already know are stored as dates/times, in a format that allows for easy sorting. By placing the year, month, and day together as a number, of sorts, the data will be sorted in date order, with the most recent items at the bottom of the page. If you want to reverse the order, you can use the **reverse** function, which inverts any array passed to it. In this example, changing line 120 to

```
120     for my $key (reverse sort keys %news)
```

would sort the news items in reverse order, with the most recent items first.

```
122         my ($active,$title)
123             = (unpack($packtemplate,$news{$key}))[0,1];
```

We are interested only in two pieces of information, the item status and title, which we extract using subscript notation on lines 122 and 123.

```
124         if ($active)
125         {
126             print("<tr><Td><input type=checkbox",
127                 " name=mode-$key value=$key checked></td>\n");
128         }
```

Lines 124 to 128 print out an already checked checkbox if the status of the story is active—that is, it has a value of 1 in the first field. These are the fields that were used on lines 86 to 95 to update the story status.

```
129         else
130         {
131             print("<tr><Td><input type=checkbox",
132                 " name=mode-$key value=$key></td>\n");
133         }
```

Lines 129 to 133 print out an unchecked checkbox if the value of **$active** is false.

```
134         print <<EOF;
135 <td><input type=checkbox name=del-$key value=$key></td>
136 <td><a href="/cgi-bin/webnews.pl?mode=edit&id=$key">
137 $title</a></td>
138 </tr>
139 EOF
140     }
```

Lines 134 to 140 print out the remainder of the record information. Line 135 prints the delete checkboxes, using, if you will notice, the "del-" prefix on the field name as required by the update mode. Lines 136 and 137 print out the title as a link—the link address specifies edit mode and the ID of the record.

```
141     print("</table><input type=submit value=Update>",
142         "<input type=reset value=Reset><p>\n");
```

```
143 }
144
```

Finally, lines 141 to 143 print out the two buttons, Update and Reset.

```
145 sub printform
146 {
147     my ($mode,$id,$title,$desc) = @_;
148     print <<EOF;
149 <form method=POST action=/cgi-bin/webnews.pl>
150 <input type=hidden name=mode value=$mode>
151 <input type=hidden name=id value=$id>
152 <table>
153 <tr>
154 <td><b>ID: </b></td><td>$id</td>
155 </tr>
156 <tr>
157 <td><b>Title</b></td>
158 <td>
159 <input type=text name=title size=50 maxlength=80 value="$title">
160 </td>
161 </tr>
162 <tr valign=top>
163 <td><b>Description</b></td>
164 <td>
165 <textarea name=desc rows=20 cols=40 maxlength=800>
166 $desc</textarea></td>
167 </tr>
168 </table>
169 <input type=submit value=Update>
170 <input type=reset value=Reset><p>
171 </form>
172 EOF
173 }
174
```

Lines 145 to 173 print out the Web form. I won't go into detail here, since the bulk of the function is just the HTML that makes up the form, but I'll cover some specific highlights. First of all, the arguments to the function contain the mode and field data. This is incorporated into the form as it is printed. In the case of adding a record, the information will be blank, but if we are editing a file, then it will contain the existing record information. In either case, the principle should be obvious: this

single function is dual purpose, allowing you to use it either for printing a new
record form or an update form.

```
175  sub generate_page()
176  {
177      open(TMPPAGE,">/usr/local/http/newstemp.html")
178          or warn "Panic: $!";
179
```

Line 175 starts the **generate_page** function, which generates the static news page
based on the active records in the database. Lines 177 and 178 attempt to open the
temporary news page file. If it fails, then we use **warn** to report an error to the Web
server, which will then write an error to the Web log, but we don't report the error
to the user. Again, this decision is largely based on the knowledge that the system
will be correctly configured. If you want a more robust system, I suggest you copy
the code from the **tie** statement earlier in this script.

```
180      print TMPPAGE template('header','www',
181                                  'pagetitle' => 'News');
182      print TMPPAGE template('header','www',
183                                  'pageheader' => 'News');
184
```

Lines 180 to 183 print out the templates to the news page. These are the same
templates used with this script, allowing you to keep the same format and style
throughout the Web site. Of course, you could change the template names and
generate a different template to create a completely different page style for the news
page. Using the templates gives you flexibility.

```
185      for my $key (reverse sort keys %news)
186      {
187          my ($active,$title,$desc) =
188              unpack($packtemplate,$news{$key});
```

Line 185 starts a **for** loop to work through the keys in the database. Note that we
work in reverse order, so the most recent news items are at the top of the news page.
Lines 187 and 188 then extract the field data from the database record.

```
189          my $realdate = (split(/\./,$key))[0];
190          $realdate =~ s:(\d{4})(\d{2})(\d{2}):$3/$2/$1:;
```

Lines 189 and 190 convert the first element of the database key, which is the date,
into a more familiar (in this case British) date format. First, line 189 assigns the first
element of the key, split by periods, to the **$realdate** variable. Remember that the

date is formatted in universal format, with year then month then day, without any form of separator.

Line 190 then uses a regular expression to convert this single string into the British format. This is used by specifying groups around each of the four elements, which are themselves specified, and a specific number of digits. This regular expression converts the date string "19980813" into "13/08/1998." If you want a USA formatted date, you just swap the group elements around; for instance, you would change line 190 to read

```
190        $realdate =~ s:(\d{4})(\d{2})(\d{2}):$2/$3/$1:;
```

This method is much more efficient than using multiple **substr** functions to extract each character string from the original string, and then recombining them to form the formatted version.

```
191        if ($active)
192        {
193            $desc =~ s/\n/<p>/g;
194            print("<font size=+2><b>$title, ",
195                "$realdate</b></font><p>",
196                "$desc<hr>");
197        }
198    }
```

Lines 191 to 197 print out a formatted version of the news item—provided, of course, that the item has been marked for inclusion in the final page. Line 193 converts new-line characters from the Web form into HTML paragraph breaks, and then lines 194 to 196 print out the item date, title, and body.

```
199    open(wrapper,
200    print TMPPAGE template('footer','www');
201    close (TMPPAGE);
202    print <<EOF
203 Page Generated<p>
204 <A href=/newstemp.html>
205 You can view the page here</a><br>
206 <A href=/cgi-bin/webnews.pl?mode=approve>
207 Approve the page here</a>
208 EOF
209 }
```

Line 200 prints the footer to the temporary page, before the file is finally closed on line 201. The very final action is to print out the "success" page to the user in lines 202 to 208. Remember to include details on how to view the temporary page and how to approve it once you've seen it.

To use the entire script, first visit the management screen and then add a new record, filling in the title and body text. We return to the management screen and request that the page be generated. Once generated, we view it and then approve it.

If we want to edit a news item, we can click on the title in the management page, which will take us to the editing form. If we want to delete an item, we check the delete checkbox on the management screen and click the Update button. The best way to understand how it works is, of course, to play with the form yourself!

PROGRAMMER'S NOTE   *You may remember in Chapters 3 and 4 the discussion of record and database locking when using databases in a multi-user context. Because the database is actually open for updating and even reading from for only a short period of time, we can safely ignore the issue in this script. Even on a slow machine the entire script process takes seconds to execute, and it is not likely to be simultaneously updated by hundreds or even tens of people during a typical day.*

Sending a File Directly via HTTP

sendfile.pl

You may remember that at the start of this chapter we looked at the script **webenv.pl**, where we looked at the response header that needs to be sent by the script in order for the browser to know how to interpret the file it is being sent. That original example was an HTML file that we sent back to the browser, although I did mentioned that it was possible to send back a file in any format. This method of responding with non-HTML files from a script is used in many Web sites to implement more dynamic content.

Since an image or other URL can be incorporated "inline" into HTML as an element, we can reference a script that sends back a random image or page element instead of a static file. This is how the banner advertisements on many Web sites work: the HTML code at the top of each page is identical, but because the URL that is referred to at that point is in fact a CGI script, the contents of the window are controlled by the script.

The trick is to send an alternative MIME type in the header information that is sent back to the user's browser and then send back the data stream of the file. You can see a list of some of the HTTP headers supported by HTTP version 1.0 in Table 8-2. For a full list, refer to RFC2068, which is available from http://www.w3.org.

Our example script is simply a toolkit for sending back a file using a different MIME format. It reads in the MIME file type information supplied by the Apache Web server to identify the type of the file requested via a standard Web form before sending back the file itself.

```perl
1    #!/usr/local/bin/perl5
2
3    use SCGI;
4
5    my %mimetypes;
6    my $file_directory = "/users/martinb";
7
8    init_cgi();
```

```
9     init_mime('/usr/local/http/apache/conf/mime.types');
10
11    my $filename;
12
13    defined($SCGI::formlist{filename}) ?
14        $filename = $SCGI::formlist{filename} :
15        respond("Error: Didn't get the info I was expecting");
16
17    respond("Error: File $filename isn't valid")
18        if ($filename =~ /[!|\/\\$()]/);
19    my ($filext) = ($filename =~ /\.(.*)$/);
20
21    defined($mimetypes{$filext}) ?
22        send_file($filename,$mimetypes{$filext}) :
23        send_file($filename,'application/octet-stream');
24
25    sub init_mime()
26    {
27        my ($file) = @_;
28        open(MIME,"<$file")
29            or respond('Error: Couldn't get any mime types');
30        while(<MIME>)
31        {
32            next if (/^\#/);
33            next if (length eq 0);
34            my ($mime,@ext) = split(/\s+/);
35            for my $ext (@ext)
36            {
37                $mimetypes{$ext} = $mime;
38            }
39        }
40        close(MIME);
41    }
42
43    sub send_file
44    {
45        my ($filename,$mimetype) = @_;
46        my $buffer;
47        open(FILE,"<$file_directory/$filename")
48            or respond("Error: Can't find file");
49        print "Content-type: $mimetype\n\n";
50        while(sysread(FILE,$buffer,1024))
51        {
```

```
52          print $buffer;
53       }
54       close(FILE);
55  }
56
57  sub respond
58  {
59      my $message = shift;
60      print "Content-type: text/html\n\n";
61      show_debug();
62      print <<EOF;
63  <head>
64  <title>$message</title>
65  </head>
66  <body>
67  $message
68  </body>
69  EOF
70      exit;
71  }
```

ANNOTATIONS

The script follows the same basic layout as before, except that the point at which we return header information to the browser is much later in the script, and in fact the information sent depends on what we're doing. Once we've read in the MIME information table, we identify the file, and then send back the header and the file contents.

Field	Meaning
Allow: list	A comma-delimited list of the HTTP request methods supported by the requested resource (script or program). Scripts generally support GET and POST; other methods include HEAD, PUT, DELETE, LINK, and UNLINK.
Content-Encoding: string	The encoding used in the message body. Currently the only supported formats are gzip and compress. If you want to encode data this way, make sure you check the value of **HTTP_ACCEPT_ENCODING** from the environment variables.

TABLE 8-2.   HTTP Request Header Fields

Field	Meaning
Content-length: string	The length, in bytes, of the data being returned. The browser uses this value to report the estimated download time for a file.
Date: string	The date and time the message is sent. It should be in the format 01 Jan 1998 12:00:00 GMT. The time zone should be GMT for reference purposes; the browser can calculate the difference for its local time zone if it has to.
Expires: string	The date the information becomes invalid. This should be used by the browser to decide when a page needs to be refreshed.
Last-modified: string	The date of last modification of the resource.
Location: string	The URL that should be returned instead of the URL requested.
MIME-version: string	The version of the MIME protocol supported.
Server: string/string	The Web server application and version number.
Title: string	The title of the resource.
URI: string	The URI that should be returned instead of the requested one.

TABLE 8-2.   HTTP Request Header Fields (*continued*)

I've used a slightly modified version of this script to automatically send back special files, such as Macromedia Flash animations and even sounds based on a configuration set by an HTML designer.

```
1   #!/usr/local/bin/perl5
2
3   use SCGI;
4
5   my %mimetypes;
6   my $file_directory = "/users/martinb";
7
```

We need the **SCGI** module to accept a filename from the browser. It's likely that this script will called as part of a URL within an HTML file, so a GET request is expected. To us, this doesn't matter; the **SCGI** module selects the information whichever method is used. Lines 5 and 6 set up the two main variables we use. The **%mimetypes** table contains the extension/MIME-type mapping information. The **$file_directory** variable is the location of the files that we'll be sending back to the user.

```
8    init_cgi();
9    init_mime('/usr/local/http/apache/conf/mime.types');
10
```

Line 8 grabs the information from the query by calling the **init_cgi** function. The MIME table is populated by calling the **init_mime** function and specifying the location of the Apache MIME-type file. I've included a copy on the CD-ROM, in case you don't have MIME.

```
11   my $filename;
12
13   defined($SCGI::formlist{filename}) ?
14       $filename = $SCGI::formlist{filename} :
15       respond("Error: Didn't get the info I was expecting");
16
```

The **$filename** variable stores the filename from the query. Although we could specify it directly, doing so makes code more complex and difficult to follow and leaves more margin for error. Lines 13 to 15 extract the filename from the query (line 14) or report an error (line 15) if the filename field has not been specified in the query.

```
17   respond("Error: File $filename isn't valid")
18       if ($filename =~ /[!|\/\\$()]/);
19   my ($filext) = ($filename =~ /\.(.*)$/);
20
```

Lines 17 and 18 report an error to the user if the filename specified contains any special characters. Basically, we expect to see only valid characters for a filename, not additional directories, pipes, and so on. This is a security measure to make sure the script is not open to abuse by allowing any file to be sent back to the user.

Line 19 extracts the file extension from the filename by extracting all the text after the period after the end of the line.

```
21   defined($mimetypes{$filext}) ?
22       send_file($filename,$mimetypes{$filext}) :
23       send_file($filename,'application/octet-stream');
24
```

Lines 21 to 23 do the final sending of the file. We assume that if we've made it this far, the file specification and location are okay, although there is still margin for error. If the file extension exists within the internal MIME table, then we call the **sendfile** function with the corresponding MIME type in line 22. If the MIME type could not be found, then we call the same function with a fixed MIME type of "application/octet-stream"; that is the default binary file MIME type. Incidentally, it's worth noting that even if the MIME table didn't initialize properly, we can still send the file back, just without the special MIME type.

```
25   sub init_mime()
26   {
27       my ($file) = @_;
28       open(MIME,"<$file")
29           or respond('Error: Couldn't get any mime types');
```

The **init_mime** function imports the MIME-type file from Apache into the **%mimetypes** hash. MIME-type information is used to convert file extensions into MIME types, which are then set back to the browser so that the browser knows whether to handle them internally or with an external plug-in, or whether to just save the file to disk. The format of the MIME-type file from Apache is organized into two columns, MIME type and extension(s). Here's a fragment from the real file:

```
application/x-cpio          cpio
application/x-csh           csh
application/x-director      dcr dir dxr
application/x-dvi           dvi
application/x-gtar          gtar
application/x-gzip          gz
```

The format of the hash is that the keys are the file extensions, and the corresponding key value is the MIME type. We therefore need to first process the file to extract the line and then work through the file extensions to build the table.

Lines 28 and 29 ensure that we can open the file; if we can't, we exit via the **respond** function, which reports the error to the user.

```
30       while(<MIME>)
31       {
32           next if (/^\#/);
33           next if (length eq 0);
34           my ($mime,@ext) = split(/\s+/);
```

Line 32 skips the line if it begins with a hash sign, which signifies a comment and is a standard Unix platform trick for including comments in configuration files so the lines can be safely ignored. Line 33 skips blank lines, and line 34 splits the line into its MIME type and an array of all the extensions.

```
35           for my $ext (@ext)
36           {
37               $mimetypes{$ext} = $mime;
38           }
```

Lines 35 to 38 then step through each element of the array, updating the hash key and values as it goes.

```
39       }
40       close(MIME);
41   }
42
```

Lines 39 to 41 close the file and then the function.

```
43   sub send_file
44   {
45       my ($filename,$mimetype) = @_;
46       my $buffer;
47       open(FILE,"<$file_directory/$filename")
48            or respond("Error: Can't find file");
```

The **send_file** function does the important work. It takes the filename and MIME type and sends the information to the browser. Line 45 extracts the arguments, and line 46 sets up the variable we'll use to buffer the file data we send back to the user. Lines 47 and 48 open the file, reporting an error to the user if the access fails.

```
49       print "Content-type: $mimetype\n\n";
50       while(sysread(FILE,$buffer,1024))
51       {
52            print $buffer;
53       }
54       close(FILE);
55   }
56
```

Line 49 prints out the MIME type to the browser. The format of the MIME specification follows the lines we have previously hardcoded into the script. Note that as before we must terminate the HTTP header with a blank line.

Lines 50 to 53 then read 1K (1,024 bytes) from the file, using **sysread**, before printing that information back to the user's browser. By using **sysread**, we ensure we are reading actual data from the file, rather than relying on Perl to split by the input record separator. The return value of the **sysread** function is the number of bytes read from the file, so when it reaches zero, the loop will complete.

```
57   sub respond
58   {
59       my $message = shift;
60       print "Content-type: text/html\n\n";
61       show_debug();
62       print <<EOF;
63   <head>
64   <title>$message</title>
65   </head>
66   <body>
67   $message
68   </body>
69   EOF
70       exit;
71   }
```

The **respond** function works here as it does in the scripts at the start of this chapter. The only addition is that line 60 now prints out the familiar HTML MIME header before printing the message. This ensures that an error will always be printed correctly.

Note that we still had not responded with any information to the user until we were sure we had all the information we needed; line 49 was the cutoff point for errors on sending the file, and the next line (50) started the loop to send the file contents back. This is important because we were not responding with the traditional static header of an HTML file.

To use the script, specify the file you want within the URL you call. For example, to retrieve the ZIP file chapter.zip from the Web server, you would use this URL:

`http://www.foo.bar/cgi-bin/sendfile.pl?chapter.zip`

This script is an effective means of responding with non-HTML information to the browser. Unfortunately, it suffers one failing, which is not really the script's fault. It is not possible to set the name of the file that you are returning to the Web browser. You can specify the URL and location of the file (see Table 8-2), but the browser will ignore this information. This script is therefore only really useful for sending inline information back to the browser—such as files that will be displayed within the browser window, rather than those intended to be saved to disk.

redirect.pl

Redirecting URL Requests

It doesn't matter how good your Web site is, there will inevitably be a point when people will leave your site. Depending on *how* they leave your site, you can opt to track the site they went off to visit. Obviously, if they type in a new URL in the browser, or choose one of their bookmarked sites, there is no way to identify where they have gone. However, if they leave your site from a link on one of your pages, then it is possible to track the information, which can then be used to gauge how your site is being used and which links are raising the most interest.

The method of tracking is to replace a standard URL link with a link to a script that records the user's selection in a log file, and then points their browser in the direction of the URL they thought they were selecting. I've seen this done a number of different ways, including a rather unwieldy Perl script that actually had the server read the Web site page from the remote site and then regurgitate it to the user.

The more straightforward method is to return a customized header to the user that specifies the site the browser should actually load. The header field to use is the Location field, which returns a redirected URL to the browser, which then causes the browser to retrieve the specified Web page, just as if that was the location of the link they had originally selected. Its normal use is to redirect users to a new page or site when a Web site has moved, but it can steal it to implement our redirect logging script.

```
1   #!/usr/local/bin/perl5
2
3   use SCGI;
4
5   init_cgi();
6
7   respond("Error: No URL specified")
8       unless(defined($SCGI::formlist{url}));
9
10  open(LOG,">>/usr/local/http/logs/jump.log")
11      or respond("Error: A config error has occured");
12
13  print LOG (scalar(localtime(time)),
14           " $ENV{REMOTE_ADDR} $SCGI::formlist{url}\n");
15  close(LOG)
16      or respond("Error: A config error has occured");
17
18  print "Location: $SCGI::formlist{url}\n\n";
19
20  sub respond
21  {
22      my $message = shift;
23      print "Content-type: text/html\n\n";
24      show_debug();
25      print <<EOF;
26  <head>
27  <title>$message</title>
28  </head>
29  <body>
30  $message
31  </body>
32  EOF
33      exit;
34  }
```

ANNOTATIONS

Aside from the usual error checking, the script is incredibly simple. We extract the URL from the query, write out some information to the log, and then send the redirect header back to the user. Pathetically simple, but on a busy Web site it's also extremely useful because the information can be invaluable in tracking your users and their interests and tastes beyond your own site.

```
1    #!/usr/local/bin/perl5
2
3    use SCGI;
4
5    init_cgi();
6
7    respond("Error: No URL specified")
8        unless(defined($SCGI::formlist{url}));
9
```

There is only one field we expect, url, which we first obtain from the query by calling the **init_cgi()** function, before checking for its existence in line 8. An error is printed if we don't find the information we want.

```
10   open(LOG, ">>/usr/local/http/logs/jump.log")
11       or respond("Error: A config error has occured");
12
13   print LOG (scalar(localtime(time)),
14               " $ENV{REMOTE_ADDR} $SCGI::formlist{url}\n");
15   close(LOG)
16       or respond("Error: A config error has occured");
17
```

Lines 10 to 16 open, update, and close the log file. We report an error if the log file cannot be opened or closed. Provided you configure the machine properly, this shouldn't occur too many times. Lines 13 and 14 print out the date and time, IP address of the browser machine, and the URL that was requested. We use the **scalar** keyword to precede the **localtime** function which will force the value returned by **localtime** to be a scalar value, not an array. In the case of **localtime**, this forces it to return a formatted time string of the form

```
Sun Oct 18 10:02:05 1998
```

You can include any amount of information in the log that is produced at this point. For example, you might want to track the page the user was on when they selected the link, and therefore this script.

```
18   print "Location: $SCGI::formlist{url}\n\n";
19
```

Line 18 sends back the header field to the browser. All the information after the Location: string is taken as a URL by the browser, and it will try to access this URL without the user being aware of the change of location.

```
20   sub respond
21   {
22       my $message = shift;
23       print "Content-type: text/html\n\n";
24       show_debug();
25       print <<EOF;
```

```
26  <head>
27  <title>$message</title>
28  </head>
29  <body>
30  $message
31  </body>
32  EOF
33      exit;
34  }
```

Line 20 is the now familiar **respond** function. Once again, it's important to note that the content type header field must be printed out before the error message, and that this is the first point that information is returned to the browser, aside from line 18.

In addition, you may want to consider inserting the URL that the user thought they were accessing, just in case the reason for the failure is a misconfiguration of the log file location. This will ensure that the user gets where they expected to go the first time. On the other hand, you may want to hide the fact that the logging failed and not produce an error if the **open** operation in line 10 failed, but simply send back the redirection URL.

Incidentally, if you specify a local URL—that is, a page or script within the scope of the same server as the **redirect.pl** script—then you can identify information about the page and environment from which the user linked. The environment variables starting **REDIRECT** contain the previous access information. You can see this better if you specify the URL for the **webenv.pl** script we used at the start of this chapter to demonstrate the execution environment of CGI scripts. For example, accessing the URL

`http://198.112.10.135/cgi-bin/redirect.pl?url=/cgi-bin/webenv.pl`

on my own Web server produces the following list of information:

```
DOCUMENT_ROOT: /usr/local/http/prluk
GATEWAY_INTERFACE: CGI/1.1
HTTP_ACCEPT: image/gif, image/x-xbitmap, image/jpeg, image/pjpeg,
image/png, */*
HTTP_ACCEPT_CHARSET: iso-8859-1,*,utf-8
HTTP_ACCEPT_ENCODING: gzip
HTTP_CONNECTION: Keep-Alive
HTTP_HOST: 198.112.10.135
HTTP_USER_AGENT: Mozilla/4.5b2 (Macintosh; I; PPC)
PATH: /usr/sbin:/usr/bin
QUERY_STRING:
REDIRECT_DOCUMENT_ROOT: /usr/local/http/prluk
REDIRECT_HTTP_ACCEPT: image/gif, image/x-xbitmap, image/jpeg,
image/pjpeg, image/png, */*
REDIRECT_HTTP_ACCEPT_CHARSET: iso-8859-1,*,utf-8
REDIRECT_HTTP_ACCEPT_ENCODING: gzip
```

```
REDIRECT_HTTP_CONNECTION: Keep-Alive
REDIRECT_HTTP_HOST: 198.112.10.135
REDIRECT_HTTP_USER_AGENT: Mozilla/4.5b2 (Macintosh; I; PPC)
REDIRECT_PATH: /usr/sbin:/usr/bin
REDIRECT_QUERY_STRING: url=/cgi-bin/webenv.pl
REDIRECT_REMOTE_ADDR: 198.112.10.130
REDIRECT_REMOTE_HOST: b
REDIRECT_REMOTE_PORT: 1203
REDIRECT_SCRIPT_FILENAME: /usr/local/http/cgi-bin/redirect.pl
REDIRECT_SERVER_ADMIN: martinb@mchome.com
REDIRECT_SERVER_NAME: www.mchome.com
REDIRECT_SERVER_PORT: 80
REDIRECT_SERVER_SOFTWARE: Apache/1.2.6
REDIRECT_STATUS: 200
REDIRECT_URL: /cgi-bin/redirect.pl
REMOTE_ADDR: 198.112.10.130
REMOTE_HOST: b
REMOTE_PORT: 1203
REQUEST_METHOD: GET
REQUEST_URI: /cgi-bin/redirect.pl?url=/cgi-bin/webenv.pl
SCRIPT_FILENAME: /usr/local/http/cgi-bin/webenv.pl
SCRIPT_NAME: /cgi-bin/webenv.pl
SERVER_ADMIN: martinb@mchome.com
SERVER_NAME: www.mchome.com
SERVER_PORT: 80
SERVER_PROTOCOL: HTTP/1.0
SERVER_SOFTWARE: Apache/1.2.6
TZ: GB
```

This information isn't available to remote servers, since it's the Web server that is identifying and providing this information to the user. Processing the information produced is an exercise that I will leave up to you.

bookstor.pl

The Bookware Online Book Shop

E-commerce is the hottest topic on the Internet at the moment, and for an obvious reason: the target market for shopping on the Internet increases every day, and many people prefer the anonymity it provides.

There are many different sites that use Perl as their CGI scripting language, including probably the most well-known Internet shopping Web site, Amazon.com. Keeping with the theme of books, the Bookware Online Book Shop from Glasscat Software is another Perl-based CGI bookstore. I haven't included the full system here, since it runs to thousands of lines, but we will take a close at the core of the system, the library module that provides many of the glue functions for the rest of the CGI scripts.

The principles behind any Web store revolve around a simple "shopping basket" idea. The user selects products, and this information is recorded somehow so that once the user has finished shopping, the information can be regurgitated in order to formulate the final order. The methods for recording the selections vary; some sites use frames that that have hidden fields to record the information, while others use cookies, and others use a unique identifier and a completely dynamically generated site.

This last method stores the order on the server with the information uniquely attached to the user's login details. This is the method employed by Amazon.com, and although it requires a hefty server investment, it places fewer restrictions and requirements on the quality of the Web browser required to browse and use the site.

The Bookware scripts use cookies, which store information in a format similar to a CGI query. The Bookware cookie stores the user's book selections and then exports the details into e-mail when the user purchases the books.

You can find out more information about the Bookware system, including the sites that already use it as their CGI backend, on the Glasscat Web site, www.glasscat.com. The latest version of the script can be found in the **original** directory for this chapter on the CD-ROM. Please note that I've shortened the filename from **bookstore.pl** to **bookstor.lib**.

You can find out more information about the Bookware system, including the sites that already use it as their CGI backend, on the Glasscat Web site, www.glasscat.com. The latest version of the script can be found in the **original** directory for this chapter on the CD-ROM. Please note that I've shortened the filename from **bookstore.pl** to **bookstor.lib**.

```perl
1    $bookstorename = "Your Bookstore";
2    $cookiename = "bookware";
3    $topstring =
4           "you can change this text to anything you want";
5    $bottomstring =
6           "you can change this text to anything you want";
7    $bottomshoppingcart =
8           "this text on the shopping cart can also be changed";
9    $bookstorehomepage =
10          "http://www.glasscat.com/bookdemo";
11   $bookwarebaseurl =
12          "http://www.glasscat.com/bookdemo";
13   $upclink="yes";
14   $searchpageurl = "http://www.glasscat.com/bookdemo";
15   $bookstoreemail = "simon\@glasscat.com";
16   $mailerpath = "/usr/sbin/sendmail";
17   $emailsubjectline = "BookWare Test Email";
```

```
18   $formtype = "complex";
19   $by = "10";
20   $dosort = "title";
21   $security = "on";
22   $topquan = "5";
23   $isbegin = "1";
24   $islength = "10";
25   $tbegin = "13";
26   $tlength = "30";
27   $abegin = "45";
28   $alength = "15";
29   $pubegin = "62";
30   $pulength = "6";
31   $catbegin = "80";
32   $catlength = "3";
33   $prbegin = "72";
34   $prlength = "6";
35
36   sub upc
37   {
38       $_[0] =~ /^006|^014|^0345|^0375|^0385|^0394|^0399|^0440|^0449|
39                ^0452|^0517|^0553|^0590|^0609|^0670|^0671|^0679|
40                ^0684|^0689|^0691|^0690|^07139|^08037|^08041|^08052|
41                ^087156|^087637|^09129|^155611|^157322|^1576|
42                ^185744|^185828|^1884/x;
43   }
44
45   sub printtop
46   {
47       print <<EOF;
48   <!DOCTYPE HTML PUBLIC "-//W3C//DTD HTML 4.0 Transitional//EN"
49    "http://www.w3.org/TR/REC-html140/loose.dtd">
50   <HTML><HEAD><TITLE>$bookstorename $_[0]</TITLE></HEAD>
51   <BODY BGCOLOR="WHITE">
52
53   <table border=0 width="100\%" cellspacing=0 cellpadding=0>
54   <tr><td bgcolor="black" height=10 colspan=6
55   align="center" valign="bottom">
56   <font color="black">.</font></td></tr>
57
58   <tr><td colspan=2 align="left" valign="top">
59   <font size="+2" face="Helvetica, Arial, San-serif">
60   $bookstorename $_[0]</font>
```

```
61  EOF
62          if ($topstring ne "none") { print "<br>", $topstring;}
63          print <<EOF;
64  </td><td valign="top" align="right">
65  <form ACTION="$bookwarebaseurl/invoice.cgi" METHOD=post>
66  <input type=submit value="View Shopping Cart">
67  <input type="hidden" name="cart" value="view"></form>
68
69  </td><td valign="top" align="left">
70  <FORM ACTION="$searchpageurl" METHOD="get">
71  <input type="submit" value="Search"></form>
72  </td><td valign=top align=right>
73
74  <FORM ACTION="$bookwarebaseurl/mailer.cgi" method="get">
75  <input type="hidden" name="command" value="drawform">
76  <input type="submit" value="Mail"></form>
77  </td><td valign="top" align="right">
78  EOF
79
80  if ($_[0] eq "Search Results")
81  {
82      if ($upclink eq "yes")
83      {
84          print("<font size=-1 color=red face=\"San-serif\">",
85                "UPC Link<br> Enabled</font>");
86      }
87      print <<EOF;
88  <form action="$bookwarebaseurl/invoice.cgi" method="post">
89  <input type="hidden" name="cart" value="add">
90  </td></tr>
91
92  <tr bgcolor="#8FBC8F">
93  <td valign="top" align="left"><b>Title</b></td>
94  <td valign="top" align="left"><b>Author</b></td>
95  <td valign="top" align="left"><b>Publisher</b></td>
96  <td valign="top" align="left"><b>Price</b></td>
97  <td valign="top" align="left"><b>Category</b></td>
98  <td valign="top" align="right"><b>Order Books</b></td>
99  </tr>
100 EOF
101     }
102   elsif ($_[0] eq "Shopping Cart")
```

```
103      {
104          print <<EOF;
105  <FORM ACTION="$bookwarebaseurl/invoice.cgi" METHOD=POST>
106  <input type="hidden" name="cart" value="change">
107  </td></tr>
108
109  <tr bgcolor="\#8FBC8F">
110  <td valign="top" align="left"><b>Quantity</b></td>
111  <td valign="top" align="left"><b>Title</b></td>
112  <td valign="top" align="left"><b>Author</b></td>
113  <td valign="top" align="left"><b>Unit Price</b></td>
114  <td colspan=2 valign="top" align="right"><b>Sub Total</b></td>
115  </tr>
116  EOF
117      }
118      elsif ($_[0] =~ "mailer")
119      {
120          print <<EOF;
121  <FORM ACTION="$bookwarebaseurl/mailer.cgi" METHOD=POST></td></tr>
122  EOF
123      }
124  }
125
126  sub printbottom
127  {
128      if ($_[0] =~ "plain")
129      {
130          print <<EOF;
131  <tr><td bgcolor="black" colspan=6 align="left" valign="middle">
132  <font color=white><a href="http://www.glasscat.com/bookstores">
133  <img
134  src="http://www.glasscat.com/bookstores/pics/bookbanner.gif"
135  alt="Technology for BookStores" border=0></a></font></td></tr>
136  </table>
137  </BODY></HTML>
138  EOF
139      }
140      elsif ($_[0] =~ "Search")
141      {
142          print <<EOF;
143  <tr><td align=left valign=top colspan=6>
144  <form action="$bookwarebaseurl/bookware.cgi" method=get>
145  <b>Title </b>
```

```
146  <br>
147  <input type="text" size=30 name="title">
148  <br>
149  <b>Author </b>
150  <br>
151  <input type="text" size=30 name="author">
152  <br>
153  <b>ISBN</b>
154  <br>
155  <input type="text" size=30 name="ISBN">
156  <p>
157
158  <select name="sort_by">
159  <option selected>Sort Results by:
160  <option>Title
161  <option>Author
162  <option>Publisher
163  </select>
164
165  <select name="searching">
166  <option selected>Match my search:
167  <option>anywhere
168  <option>as_a_complete_keyword
169  <option>only_from_the_beginning
170  </select>
171
172  <select name="bool">
173  <option selected>Treat multiple fields as:
174  <option>and
175  <option>or
176  </select>
177  <P>
178  EOF
179          if ($bottomstring ne "none")
180          {
181                  print "<center>", $bottomstring, "</center>";
182          }
183          print <<EOF;
184  </td></tr>
185
186  <tr><td bgcolor="black" align="left" valign="middle" colspan=3>
187  <font color="white">
```

```
188 <a href="http://www.glasscat.com/bookstores">
189 <img
190 src="http://www.glasscat.com/bookstores/pics/bookbanner.gif"
191 alt="BookWare: Technology for BookStores" border=0></a>
192 </font></td>
193 <td bgcolor="black" align="right" colspan=3>
194 <input type="reset" value="clear form">
195 <INPUT TYPE="submit" value="$_[0]"></td></tr>
196 </form></table>
197 </BODY></HTML>
198 EOF
199     }
200    else
201    {
202        print <<EOF;
203 <tr><td bgcolor="black" align="left" valign="middle" colspan=3>
204 <font color=white><a href="http://www.glasscat.com/bookstores">
205 <img
206 src="http://www.glasscat.com/bookstores/pics/bookbanner.gif"
207 alt="BookWare: Technology for BookStores" border=0></a>
208 </font></td>
209 <td bgcolor="black" align=right colspan="3">
210 EOF
211        if ($_[0] =~ "Send")
212        { print "<input type=\"reset\" value=\"clear form\">"; }
213        print <<EOF;
214        <INPUT TYPE="submit" value="$_[0]"></td></tr>
215        </form></table>
216        </BODY></HTML>
217 EOF
218    }
219 }
220
221 #############################################
222 # ERRORS ####################################
223
224 sub cgi_noluck
225 {
226    print "Content-type: text/html\n\n";
227    if ($_[0] eq "no search string" ||
228        $_[0] eq "no selection" ||
229        $_[0] =~ "mailer")
230    {
```

```
231         print <<EOF;
232 <HTML><HEAD><TITLE>BookWare User Error</TITLE></HEAD>
233 <BODY BGCOLOR="WHITE">
234 <center>
235 <h1>BookWare has encountered an error.</h1>
236 <font size="+1">The error message is:</FONT><P>
237 <font color=red size="+1"><code> $_[0] </code></font><p>
238 <font size="+1">
239 Hopefully you will be able to figure out what happened from the
240 message above. Please use the back button and try your action
241 again, If you feel you should not be getting this error,
242 please contact the site administrator.<P> Find out more about
243 <a href="http://www.glasscat.com/bookstores">Bookware</a>
244 </font></center></BODY></HTML>
245 EOF
246         exit;
247         }
248         else
249         {
250             &printtop("$_[0]");
251             if ($_[0] eq "Empty Cart")
252             {
253                 print <<EOF;
254  </td></tr><tr><td bgcolor="#8FBC8F" colspan=6 align=left>
255 <font size="+1" face="Helvetica, Arial, San-serif">
256 Oh No! There are no books in your cart. What can we do to
257 change that situation? Please search again, or use your
258 browser's 'back' button to return to your previous
259 search.</font></td></tr>
260 EOF
261             }
262             else
263             {
264                 print <<EOF;
265  </td></tr><tr><td bgcolor="#8FBC8F" colspan=6 align=left>
266 <font size="+1" face="Helvetica, Arial, San-serif">No results.
267 There were no books which matched your query. Please try
268 your search again</font></td></tr>
269 EOF
270             }
271         &printbottom("Search");
272     }
```

```
273      exit;
274  }
275
276  sub cgi_die
277  {
278      print <<EOF;
279  Content-type: text/html\n\n
280  <HTML><HEAD><TITLE>BookWare Script Error</TITLE></HEAD>
281  <BODY BGCOLOR="WHITE">
282  <center>
283  <h1>BookWare has encountered an error.</h1>
284  <font size="+1">The error message is:</FONT><P>
285  <font color=red size=+1><code> $_[0] </code></font><p>
286  <font size="+1">
287  Please try your action again, or email the site administrator
288   with this error message.<p>
289  Find out more about
290  <a href="http://www.glasscat.com/bookstores">Bookware</a>.
291  </font></center></BODY></HTML>
292  EOF
293      exit;
294  }
295
296  ############################################
297  # INTERFACE ################################
298
299  sub quanbutton
300  {
301      local($quantity);
302      local(@return);
303      local($isbn);
304      $isbn = $_[0];
305      $quantity = $_[1];
306
307      push(@return,"<select name=$isbn>\n");
308      for ($vv=0; $vv<=$topquan; $vv++)
309      {
310          if ($vv == $quantity)
311          {
312              push(@return, "<option selected>".$quantity."\n");
313          }
314          else
315          {
```

```perl
316                 push(@return, "<option>".$vv."\n");
317         }
318     }
319     push(@return, "</select>\n");
320     @return;
321 }
322
323 sub mailerform
324 {
325     print <<EOF;
326 <tr><td colspan=6 valign="top" align="left" bgcolor="#8FBC8F">
327 <font color=red face="Helvetica, Arial, San-serif">
328 EOF
329     if ($_[0] =~ "order")
330     {
331         print("Please complete all fields of this ",
332                 "form to send in your order.\n");
333     }
334     if ($_[0] =~ "mail")
335     {
336         print("Please fill out all fields of this ",
337                 "form to send email to $bookstorename.\n");
338     }
339     print <<EOF;
340 </font></td></tr>
341 EOF
342
343     if ($formtype eq "complex")
344     {
345         print <<EOF;
346 <tr><td colspan=1 valign="top" align="right">
347         <input type="text" name="name" size=50></td>
348 <td colspan=4 valign="top" align="left"> Name</td></tr>
349
350 <tr><td colspan=1 valign="top" align="right">
351         <input type="text" name="email" size="50"></td>
352 <td colspan=5 valign="top" align="left"> Email Address</td></tr>
353
354 <tr><td colspan=6 bgcolor="#8FBC8F">
355 <font color=red face="Helvetica, Arial, San-serif">
356 Contact Information</font></td></tr>
357
```

```
358  <tr><td colspan=1 valign="top" align="right">
359         <input type="text" name="address" size=50></td>
360  <td colspan=5 valign="top" align="left"> Address</td></tr>
361
362  <tr><td colspan=1 valign="top" align="right">
363         <input type="text" name="city" size=15></td>
364  <td colspan=5 valign="top" align="left"> City</td></tr>
365
366  <tr><td colspan=1 valign="top" align="right">
367         <input type="text" name="state" size=4></td>
368  <td colspan=5 valign="top" align="left"> State</td></tr>
369
370  <tr><td colspan=1 valign="top" align="right">
371         <input type="text" name="zip" size=9></td>
372  <td colspan=5 valign="top" align="left"> Zip</td></tr>
373
374  <tr><td colspan=1 valign="top" align="right">
375         <input type="text" name="country" size=15></td>
376  <td colspan=5 valign="top" align="left"> Country</td></tr>
377
378  <tr><td colspan=1 valign="top" align="right">
379         <input type="text" name="phone" size=15></td>
380  <td colspan=4 valign="top" align="left"> Phone Number</td></tr>
381
382  <tr><td colspan=6 align="left" bgcolor="#8FBC8F"><font
383  color=red face="Helvetica, Arial, San-serif">
384  Question, Inquiry or Comment?</font></td></tr>
385
386  <tr><td colspan=2 valign="top" align="right">
387         <textarea rows=10 cols=45 name="other"></textarea>
388  <td colspan=4 valign="top" align="left"> Comments?</td></tr>
389  EOF
390      }
391      elsif ($formtype eq "simple")
392      {
393          print <<EOF;
394  <p>
395  <tr><td colspan=1 valign="top" align="right">
396         <input type="text" name="name" size=45></td>
397  <td colspan=5 valign="top" align="left"> Name</td></tr>
398
399  <tr><td colspan=1 valign="top" align="right">
400         <input type="text" name="email" size=45></td>
```

```
401  <td colspan=5 valign="top" align="left"> Email Address</td></tr>
402
403  <tr><td colspan=6 align="left" bgcolor="#8FBC8F"><font
404  color=red face="Helvetica, Arial, San-serif">
405  Question, Inquiry or Comment?</font></td></tr>
406
407  <tr><td colspan=1 valign="top" align="right">
408          <textarea rows=10 cols=45 name="other"></textarea>
409  <td colspan=5 valign="top" align="left"> Comments?</td></tr>
410  EOF
411      }
412  }
413
414  $date = `date`;
415
416  sub by_title
417  {
418      substr($a, $tbegin, $tlength)
419          cmp substr($b, $tbegin, $tlength);
420  }
421
422  sub by_author
423  {
424      substr($a, $abegin, $alength)
425          cmp substr($b, $abegin, $alength);
426  }
427
428  sub by_publisher
429  {
430      substr($a, $pubegin, $pulength)
431          cmp substr($b, $pubegin, $pulength);
432  }
433
434  sub parse_form
435  {
436      if ($ENV{'REQUEST_METHOD'} eq "GET")
437      {
438          $buffer = $ENV{'QUERY_STRING'};
439      }
440      else
441      {
442          read(STDIN, $buffer, $ENV{'CONTENT_LENGTH'})
443              || &cgi_die('Not a POST, must be called from form.');
```

```
444         }
445
446         @pairs = split(/&/, $buffer);
447         foreach $pair (@pairs)
448         {
449             ($name, $value) = split(/=/, $pair);
450             $value =~ tr/+/ /;
451             $value =~
452                 s/%([a-fA-F0-9][a-fA-F0-9])/pack("C", hex($1))/eg;
453             $value =~ s/~!/ ~!/g;
454             $FORM{$name} = $value;
455         }
456
457         if ($security == "on")
458         {
459             while (($f, $l) = each(%FORM))
460             {
461                 if ($l =~ /;|\||\~|\`|\!|\+|\*|\%|\$/ig)
462                 {
463                     &cgi_die("bad character $&");
464                 }
465             }
466         }
467 }
468
469 sub cookiename
470 {
471     $cookiename = $bookstorename;
472     $cookiename =~ s/\s| //ig;
473 }
474
475 sub get_cookie
476 {
477     if ($ENV{'HTTP_COOKIE'})
478     {
479         $ENV{'HTTP_COOKIE'} =~ s/$cookiename=//;
480         $ENV{'HTTP_COOKIE'} =~ s/ //ig;
481         @books = split(/-/, $ENV{'HTTP_COOKIE'});
482         foreach $d (@books)
483         {
484             ($cisbn, $cquan) = split(/_/, $d);
485             $cisbn =~ tr/+/ /;
486             $cisbn =~
```

```
487                    s/%([a-fA-F0-9][a-fA-F0-9])/pack("C", hex($1))/eg;
488            $cisbn =~ s/~!/ ~!/g;
489            $cquan =~ tr/+/ /;
490            $cquan =~
491                    s/%([a-fA-F0-9][a-fA-F0-9])/pack("C", hex($1))/eg;
492            $cquan =~ s/~!/ ~!/g;
493            $FORM2{$cisbn} = $cquan;
494        }
495    }
496 }
```

ANNOTATIONS

As with many CGI scripts, a significant amount of the code is given over to introducing HTML into the user's browser form. This library provides all of the core functions used by the other scripts in the toolkit, including the ones that create and access the cookie that stores the user's book selections before they buy them.

The script is Perl 4 compatible, so many of the constructs we have become familiar with when dealing with Perl 5 are not available, and therefore not incorporated in this script. The library will be imported using **require**, so the variables defined within this file will be available within the calling script directly; there has been no name space change.

```
1  $bookstorename = "Your Bookstore";
2  $cookiename = "bookware";
3  $topstring =
4          "you can change this text to anything you want";
5  $bottomstring =
6          "you can change this text to anything you want";
7  $bottomshoppingcart =
8          "this text on the shopping cart can also be changed";
9  $bookstorehomepage =
10          "http://www.glasscat.com/bookdemo";
11 $bookwarebaseurl =
12          "http://www.glasscat.com/bookdemo";
```

Lines 1 to 12 set up the core variables that specify the name and associated details for the bookstore. Most of this information will be used to build the pages for the site—the entire HTML for the bookstore is generated by one of the CGI scripts that make up the Bookware toolkit. Personally, I find that large quantities of HTML within a script can slow down execution, since the parser still has to read and verify the text strings as part of the Perl interpretation cycle. In this instance, there is not enough to make a big difference, and it does allow a certain amount of flexibility not seen in a template system, such as that described by the **SCGI** module at the beginning of this chapter.

```
13   $upclink="yes";
14   $searchpageurl = "http://www.glasscat.com/bookdemo";
15   $bookstoreemail = "simon\@glasscat.com";
16   $mailerpath = "/usr/sbin/sendmail";
17   $emailsubjectline = "BookWare Test Email";
18   $formtype = "complex";
19   $by = "10";
20   $dosort = "title";
21   $security = "on";
22   $topquan = "5";
```

Lines 13 to 22 specify more of the configuration information that will be used when running the Bookware scripts. The **$upclink** variable specifies that the site allow UPC-linked book information, which is an initiative that allows information about a book to be linked between the book's ISBN number and the publisher's Web site. By switching this on, it will force the use of the **upc** function below.

```
23   $isbegin = "1";
24   $islength = "10";
25   $tbegin = "13";
26   $tlength = "30";
27   $abegin = "45";
28   $alength = "15";
29   $pubegin = "62";
30   $pulength = "6";
31   $catbegin = "80";
32   $catlength = "3";
33   $prbegin = "72";
34   $prlength = "6";
35
```

Lines 23 to 34 specify the start character and length for the different fields that make up the book database. This is a longer method of specifying a pack string, and it will allow us, with the **substr** function, to pull information directly out of the lines that make up the stock database of the bookstore.

```
36   sub upc
37   {
38       $_[0] =~ /^006|^014|^0345|^0375|^0385|^0394|^0399|^0440|^0449|
39               ^0452|^0517|^0553|^0590|^0609|^0670|^0671|^0679|
```

```
40                    ^0684|^0689|^0691|^0690|^07139|^08037|^08041|^08052|
41                    ^087156|^087637|^09129|^155611|^157322|^1576|
42                    ^185744|^185828|^1884/x;
43    }
44
```

The **upc** function strips the specified numbers from the start of the first element of the @_ array. This highlights something that you may have overlooked up to now when programming with Perl. We are all familliar with using the **$_** variable as the pattern space and @_ as the array to store arguments supplied to functions. Line 39 looks like a typo, but in fact we are accessing the first element of the @_ array using the same notation as we would with any other array variable.

```
45    sub printtop
46    {
```

The **printtop** function prints the header at the top of each page produced by the Bookware system.

```
47        print <<EOF;
48    <!DOCTYPE HTML PUBLIC "-//W3C//DTD HTML 4.0 Transitional//EN"
49     "http://www.w3.org/TR/REC-html40/loose.dtd">
50    <HTML><HEAD><TITLE>$bookstorename $_[0]</TITLE></HEAD>
51    <BODY BGCOLOR="WHITE">
52
53    <table border=0 width="100\%" cellspacing=0 cellpadding=0>
54    <tr><td bgcolor="black" height=10 colspan=6
55    align="center" valign="bottom">
56    <font color="black">.</font></td></tr>
57
58    <tr><td colspan=2 align="left" valign="top">
59    <font size="+2" face="Helvetica, Arial, San-serif">
60    $bookstorename $_[0]</font>
61    EOF
62            if ($topstring ne "none") { print "<br>", $topstring;}
63            print <<EOF;
64    </td><td valign="top" align="right">
65    <form ACTION="$bookwarebaseurl/invoice.cgi" METHOD=post>
66    <input type=submit value="View Shopping Cart">
67    <input type="hidden" name="cart" value="view"></form>
68
69    </td><td valign="top" align="left">
70    <FORM ACTION="$searchpageurl" METHOD="get">
71    <input type="submit" value="Search"></form>
72    </td><td valign=top align=right>
```

```
73
74   <FORM ACTION="$bookwarebaseurl/mailer.cgi" method="get">
75   <input type="hidden" name="command" value="drawform">
76   <input type="submit" value="Mail"></form>
77   </td><td valign="top" align="right">
78   EOF
79
```

Lines 47 to 77 use a here document to print out the actual header. The next lines will be used to identify the type of header being printed, generating a different response accordingly. The type is extracted by the same trick as used by the **upc** function: we extract the first argument from the argument list directly, rather than using a separate assignation statement.

```
80   if ($_[0] eq "Search Results")
81   {
82       if ($upclink eq "yes")
83       {
84           print("<font size=-1 color=red face=\"San-serif\">",
85                 "UPC Link<br> Enabled</font>");
86       }
```

In lines 80 to 85, if the site manager has designated it as a UPC supporting site then we print out a "UPC Enabled" message.

```
87       print <<EOF;
88   <form action="$bookwarebaseurl/invoice.cgi" method="post">
89   <input type="hidden" name="cart" value="add">
90   </td></tr>
91
92   <tr bgcolor="#8FBC8F">
93   <td valign="top" align="left"><b>Title</b></td>
94   <td valign="top" align="left"><b>Author</b></td>
95   <td valign="top" align="left"><b>Publisher</b></td>
96   <td valign="top" align="left"><b>Price</b></td>
97   <td valign="top" align="left"><b>Category</b></td>
98   <td valign="top" align="right"><b>Order Books</b></td>
99   </tr>
100  EOF
101      }
```

If we're dealing with a list of search results, then in lines 87 to 100 we print out the table header that will report the result of the search.

```
102      elsif ($_[0] eq "Shopping Cart")
103      {
104          print <<EOF;
105  <FORM ACTION="$bookwarebaseurl/invoice.cgi" METHOD=POST>
106  <input type="hidden" name="cart" value="change">
107  </td></tr>
108
109  <tr bgcolor="\#8FBC8F">
110  <td valign="top" align="left"><b>Quantity</b></td>
111  <td valign="top" align="left"><b>Title</b></td>
112  <td valign="top" align="left"><b>Author</b></td>
113  <td valign="top" align="left"><b>Unit Price</b></td>
114  <td colspan=2 valign="top" align="right"><b>Sub Total</b></td>
115  </tr>
116  EOF
117      }
```

Lines 102 to 115 print out the header that will display the contents of their shopper's shopping cart.

```
118      elsif ($_[0] =~ "mailer")
119      {
120          print <<EOF;
121  <FORM ACTION="$bookwarebaseurl/mailer.cgi" METHOD=POST></td></tr>
122  EOF
123      }
124  }
125
```

Lines 118 to 122 print out the FORM header for an e-mail. The Bookware system uses e-mail to communicate orders, invoices, and other enquiries to the bookstore managers. The same CGI script, **mailer.cgi**, is used for all communication.

```
126  sub printbottom
127  {
128      if ($_[0] =~ "plain")
129      {
```

```
130        print <<EOF;
131 <tr><td bgcolor="black" colspan=6 align="left" valign="middle">
132 <font color=white><a href="http://www.glasscat.com/bookstores">
133 <img
134 src="http://www.glasscat.com/bookstores/pics/bookbanner.gif"
135 alt="Technology for BookStores" border=0></a></font></td></tr>
136 </table>
137 </BODY></HTML>
138 EOF
139    }
140    elsif ($_[0] =~ "Search")
141    {
142        print <<EOF;
143 <tr><td align=left valign=top colspan=6>
144 <form action="$bookwarebaseurl/bookware.cgi" method=get>
145 <b>Title </b>
146 <br>
147 <input type="text" size=30 name="title">
148 <br>
149 <b>Author </b>
150 <br>
151 <input type="text" size=30 name="author">
152 <br>
153 <b>ISBN</b>
154 <br>
155 <input type="text" size=30 name="ISBN">
156 <p>
157
158 <select name="sort_by">
159 <option selected>Sort Results by:
160 <option>Title
161 <option>Author
162 <option>Publisher
163 </select>
164
165 <select name="searching">
```

```
166 <option selected>Match my search:
167 <option>anywhere
168 <option>as_a_complete_keyword
169 <option>only_from_the_beginning
170 </select>
171
172 <select name="bool">
173 <option selected>Treat multiple fields as:
174 <option>and
175 <option>or
176 </select>
177 <P>
178 EOF
179         if ($bottomstring ne "none")
180         {
181             print "<center>", $bottomstring, "</center>";
182         }
183         print <<EOF;
184 </td></tr>
185
186 <tr><td bgcolor="black" align="left" valign="middle" colspan=3>
187 <font color="white">

188 <a href="http://www.glasscat.com/bookstores">
189 <img
190 src="http://www.glasscat.com/bookstores/pics/bookbanner.gif"
191 alt="BookWare: Technology for BookStores" border=0></a>
192 </font></td>
193 <td bgcolor="black" align="right" colspan=3>
194 <input type="reset" value="clear form">
195 <INPUT TYPE="submit" value="$_[0]"></td></tr>
196 </form></table>
197 </BODY></HTML>
198 EOF
199     }
200     else
201     {
202         print <<EOF;
203 <tr><td bgcolor="black" align="left" valign="middle" colspan=3>
204 <font color=white><a href="http://www.glasscat.com/bookstores">
205 <img
206 src="http://www.glasscat.com/bookstores/pics/bookbanner.gif"
207 alt="BookWare: Technology for BookStores" border=0></a>
```

```
208 </font></td>
209 <td bgcolor="black" align=right colspan="3">
210 EOF
211         if ($_[0] =~ "Send")
212         { print "<input type=\"reset\" value=\"clear form\">"; }
213         print <<EOF;
214         <INPUT TYPE="submit" value="$_[0]"></td></tr>
215         </form></table>.
216         </BODY></HTML>
217 EOF
218     }
219 }
220
```

Lines 126 to 219 handle printing the bottom of the page. The same basic rules apply, and depending on the mode of the Web site, and the parent CGI script being called, different footer information will be printed. The bulk of the code is HTML, with a few tests to identify the current mode.

```
221 ###########################################
222 # ERRORS ##################################
223
224 sub cgi_noluck
225 {
226     print "Content-type: text/html\n\n";
227     if ($_[0] eq "no search string" ||
228         $_[0] eq "no selection" ||
229         $_[0] =~ "mailer")
230     {
231         print <<EOF;
232 <HTML><HEAD><TITLE>BookWare User Error</TITLE></HEAD>
233 <BODY BGCOLOR="WHITE">
234 <center>
235 <h1>BookWare has encountered an error.</h1>
236 <font size="+1">The error message is:</FONT><P>
237 <font color=red size="+1"><code> $_[0] </code></font><p>
238 <font size="+1">
239 Hopefully you will be able to figure out what happened from the
240 message above. Please use the back button and try your action
241 again, If you feel you should not be getting this error,
242 please contact the site administrator.<P> Find out more about
243 <a href="http://www.glasscat.com/bookstores">Bookware</a>
244 </font></center></BODY></HTML>
245 EOF
```

```
246          exit;
247          }
248          else
249          {
250               &printtop("$_[0]");
251               if ($_[0] eq "Empty Cart")
252               {
253                    print <<EOF;
254  </td></tr><tr><td bgcolor="#8FBC8F" colspan=6 align=left>
255 <font size="+1" face="Helvetica, Arial, San-serif">
256 Oh No! There are no books in your cart. What can we do to
257 change that situation? Please search again, or use your
258 browser's 'back' button to return to your previous
259 search.</font></td></tr>
260 EOF
261               }
262               else
263               {
264                    print <<EOF;
265  </td></tr><tr><td bgcolor="#8FBC8F" colspan=6 align=left>
266 <font size="+1" face="Helvetica, Arial, San-serif">No results.
267 There were no books which matched your query. Please try
268 your search again</font></td></tr>
269 EOF
270               }
271          &printbottom("Search");
272     }
273     exit;
274 }
275
```

Lines 224 to 275 print an error message back to the browser. This is a noncritical error, so at the end of the error message, on line 271, we print the search information again to allow the user to search for a different book.

```
276 sub cgi_die
277 {
278     print <<EOF;
279 Content-type: text/html\n\n
280 <HTML><HEAD><TITLE>BookWare Script Error</TITLE></HEAD>
281 <BODY BGCOLOR="WHITE">
282 <center>
283 <h1>BookWare has encountered an error.</h1>
284 <font size="+1">The error message is:</FONT><P>
```

```
285 <font color=red size=+1><code> $_[0] </code></font><p>
286 <font size="+1">
287 Please try your action again, or email the site administrator
288  with this error message.<p>
289 Find out more about
290 <a href="http://www.glasscat.com/bookstores">Bookware</a>.
291 </font></center></BODY></HTML>
292 EOF
293     exit;
294 }
295
```

Lines 276 to 294 form the **cgi_die** function, the Bookware equivalent of the standard Perl **die** function.

```
296 #############################################
297 # INTERFACE ###############################
298
299 sub quanbutton
300 {
301     local($quantity);
302     local(@return);
303     local($isbn);
304     $isbn = $_[0];
305     $quantity = $_[1];
306
```

The **quanbutton** function prints out a pop-up list, up to the maximum number specified by the **$topquan** variables specified at the start of this library. Line 304 extracts the ISBN number from the arguments to the function, and line 305 extracts the currently selected quantity, based on the user's shopping basket.

```
307     push(@return,"<select name=$isbn>\n");
308     for ($vv=0; $vv<=$topquan; $vv++)
309     {
310         if ($vv == $quantity)
311         {
312             push(@return, "<option selected>".$quantity."\n");
313         }
314         else
315         {
316             push(@return, "<option>".$vv."\n");
317         }
318     }
```

Line 307 pushes the "select" tag string onto the **@return** array—each element of the array will be a part of the pop-up definition. Lines 308 to 318 then step through each possible value from zero to **$topquan**, adding the necessary HTML tag to the **@return** array. If the quantity value matches the current quantity for the matching ISBN number, we mark the pop-up as selected.

```perl
319     push(@return, "</select>\n");
320     @return;
321 }
322
```

Line 319 pushes the "end" pop-up tag onto the array before we return the whole array to the caller.

```perl
323 sub mailerform
324 {
325     print <<EOF;
326 <tr><td colspan=6 valign="top" align="left" bgcolor="#8FBC8F">
327 <font color=red face="Helvetica, Arial, San-serif">
328 EOF
329     if ($_[0] =~ "order")
330     {
331         print("Please complete all fields of this ",
332               "form to send in your order.\n");
333     }
334     if ($_[0] =~ "mail")
335     {
336         print("Please fill out all fields of this ",
337               "form to send email to $bookstorename.\n");
338     }
339     print <<EOF;
340 </font></td></tr>
341 EOF
342
```

Line 323 starts the **mailerform** function, which prints out the form for e-mailing the Bookware site's manager.

```
343     if ($formtype eq "complex")
344     {
345         print <<EOF;
346 <tr><td colspan=1 valign="top" align="right">
347         <input type="text" name="name" size=50></td>
348 <td colspan=4 valign="top" align="left"> Name</td></tr>
349
350 <tr><td colspan=1 valign="top" align="right">
351         <input type="text" name="email" size="50"></td>
352 <td colspan=5 valign="top" align="left"> Email Address</td></tr>
353
354 <tr><td colspan=6 bgcolor="#8FBC8F">
355 <font color=red face="Helvetica, Arial, San-serif">
356 Contact Information</font></td></tr>
357
358 <tr><td colspan=1 valign="top" align="right">
359         <input type="text" name="address" size=50></td>
360 <td colspan=5 valign="top" align="left"> Address</td></tr>
361
362 <tr><td colspan=1 valign="top" align="right">
363         <input type="text" name="city" size=15></td>
364 <td colspan=5 valign="top" align="left"> City</td></tr>
365
366 <tr><td colspan=1 valign="top" align="right">
367         <input type="text" name="state" size=4></td>
368 <td colspan=5 valign="top" align="left"> State</td></tr>
369
370 <tr><td colspan=1 valign="top" align="right">
371         <input type="text" name="zip" size=9></td>
372 <td colspan=5 valign="top" align="left"> Zip</td></tr>
373
374 <tr><td colspan=1 valign="top" align="right">
375         <input type="text" name="country" size=15></td>
376 <td colspan=5 valign="top" align="left"> Country</td></tr>
377
378 <tr><td colspan=1 valign="top" align="right">
379         <input type="text" name="phone" size=15></td>
380 <td colspan=4 valign="top" align="left"> Phone Number</td></tr>
```

```
381
382 <tr><td colspan=6 align="left" bgcolor="#8FBC8F"><font
383 color=red face="Helvetica, Arial, San-serif">
384 Question, Inquiry or Comment?</font></td></tr>
385
386 <tr><td colspan=2 valign="top" align="right">
387         <textarea rows=10 cols=45 name="other"></textarea>
388 <td colspan=4 valign="top" align="left"> Comments?</td></tr>
389 EOF
390     }
391     elsif ($formtype eq "simple")
392     {
393         print <<EOF;
394 <p>
395 <tr><td colspan=1 valign="top" align="right">
396         <input type="text" name="name" size=45></td>
397 <td colspan=5 valign="top" align="left"> Name</td></tr>
398
399 <tr><td colspan=1 valign="top" align="right">
400         <input type="text" name="email" size=45></td>
401 <td colspan=5 valign="top" align="left"> Email Address</td></tr>
402
403 <tr><td colspan=6 align="left" bgcolor="#8FBC8F"><font
404 color=red face="Helvetica, Arial, San-serif">
405 Question, Inquiry or Comment?</font></td></tr>
406
407 <tr><td colspan=1 valign="top" align="right">
408         <textarea rows=10 cols=45 name="other"></textarea>
409 <td colspan=5 valign="top" align="left"> Comments?</td></tr>
410 EOF
411     }
412 }
413
```

Lines 343 to 410 print out the complex and simple versions of the comment form.

```
414 $date = `date`;
415
```

We extract the date, in local format, from the system's **date** command on line 414.

```
416 sub by_title
417 {
418     substr($a, $tbegin, $tlength)
```

```
419            cmp substr($b, $tbegin, $tlength);
420 }
421
```

Lines 416 to 420 sort the book database. This function can be included within a sort statement like this:

@FINAL = sort by_title @RESULTS;

The **substr** functions extract a string based on the character positions specified by **$tbegin**, the start of the title field, and **$tlength**, the length of the title field. The **cmp** function then compares adjoining values in the array.

```
422 sub by_author
423 {
424     substr($a, $abegin, $alength)
425         cmp substr($b, $abegin, $alength);
426 }
427
```

In lines 422 to 425, the **by_author** function performs the same function, but by author.

```
428 sub by_publisher
429 {
430     substr($a, $pubegin, $pulength)
431         cmp substr($b, $pubegin, $pulength);
432 }
433
```

In lines 428 to 431, the **by_publisher** function performs the same function, but by publisher.

```
434 sub parse_form
435 {
436     if ($ENV{'REQUEST_METHOD'} eq "GET")
437     {
438         $buffer = $ENV{'QUERY_STRING'};
439     }
440     else
441     {
442         read(STDIN, $buffer, $ENV{'CONTENT_LENGTH'})
443             || &cgi_die('Not a POST, must be called from form.');
444     }
445
```

Line 433 is the **parse_form** function. It performs the same action as the **init_cgi** function in our **SCGI** module earlier in this chapter. Line 436 checks the value of the

REQUEST_METHOD environment variable. It specifies the method by which the request was sent to the server, and therefore the CGI script. If GET is specified, then we recover the contents of the **QUERY_STRING** environment variables. Otherwise, on line 442, we attempt to read a POST request from the standard input.

```
446     @pairs = split(/&/, $buffer);
447     foreach $pair (@pairs)
448     {
449         ($name, $value) = split(/=/, $pair);
450         $value =~ tr/+/ /;
451         $value =~
452             s/%([a-fA-F0-9][a-fA-F0-9])/pack("C", hex($1))/eg;
453         $value =~ s/~!/ ~!/g;
454         $FORM{$name} = $value;
455     }
456
```

Line 446 splits the request with an ampersand; these separate the key/value pairs into the **pairs** array, where they are further processed and separated in lines 447 to 454, almost identically to the method used within our **SCGI** module.

```
457     if ($security == "on")
458     {
459         while (($f, $1) = each(%FORM))
460         {
461             if ($1 =~ /;|\||\~|\`|\!|\+|\*|\%|\$/ig)
462             {
463                 &cgi_die("bad character $&");
464             }
465         }
466     }
467 }
468
```

If security has been switched on, then line 461 checks that the values of the **FORM** hash do not contain any nonstandard or potentially lethal characters.

```
469 sub cookiename
470 {
471     $cookiename = $bookstorename;
472     $cookiename =~ s/\s| //ig;
473 }
474
```

Lines 469 to 473 set the name of the cookie that will be used by the Bookware system to store the user's book selections. We'll see how this is used by the rest of the Bookware system shortly.

```
475  sub get_cookie
476  {
477      if ($ENV{'HTTP_COOKIE'})
478      {
479          $ENV{'HTTP_COOKIE'} =~ s/$cookiename=//;
480          $ENV{'HTTP_COOKIE'} =~ s/ //ig;
481          @books = split(/-/, $ENV{'HTTP_COOKIE'});
```

The cookie is extracted by reading the cookie environment variable, which is created by the Web server, via the Web browser, and contains a list of matching cookies for this site that are known to the browser.

A cookie is composed of the cookie's name, followed by an equal sign, which we strip out on line 479. We then strip out any spaces from the cookie on line 480, before splitting the individual elements, which are separated by hyphens in line 481. Note that we are still accessing the original cookie environment, not a copy, when we make these changes.

```
482          foreach $d (@books)
483          {
484              ($cisbn, $cquan) = split(/_/, $d);
```

Line 482 sets up the loop to process each of the books and quantities, which we separate on line 484.

```
485              $cisbn =~ tr/+/ /;
486              $cisbn =~
487                  s/%([a-fA-F0-9][a-fA-F0-9])/pack("C", hex($1))/eg;
488              $cisbn =~ s/~!/ ~!/g;
```

Line 485 converts any plus signs to spaces, and lines 486 and 487 unescape any escape characters from the string.

```
489              $cquan =~ tr/+/ /;
490              $cquan =~
491                  s/%([a-fA-F0-9][a-fA-F0-9])/pack("C", hex($1))/eg;
492              $cquan =~ s/~!/ ~!/g;
493              $FORM2{$cisbn} = $cquan;
494          }
495      }
496  }
```

Lines 489 to 492 perform the same regular expression and unescape replacements on the quantity field, before the final ISBN and quantity values are placed into a new hash, along the same lines as the main form element hash.

The main **bookware.cgi** script contains, mostly, lines for extracting data from the database and the necessary HTML display it. The core of the code, as far as e-commerce is concerned, can be found in the **invoice.cgi** script, which composes and updates the shopping cart and therefore the cookie used to store the user's chopping cart information.

Cookies are added to or updated in the browser's own cookie database by printing a **Set-Cookie** string as part of the header fields sent back to the browser before the HTML is printed, in much the same way as our earlier examples. Following is the code fragment that updates the cookie value and contents based on the invoice form. Modifications are written straight back to the cookie when the Submit button is clicked from the invoice view.

```perl
elsif ($FORM{"cart"} eq "add") {
  while (($first,$last) = each(%FORM)) {
   if ($last eq 0) {
   delete $FORM{$first};
  }}
  while (($is, $qa) = each(%FORM)) {
    $FORM2{$is} = $qa;
  }
  while (($first,$last) = each(%FORM2)) {
   if ($last eq 0) {
   delete $FORM2{$first};
  }}
  while (($first,$last) = each(%FORM2)) {
    $item = $first."_".$last."-";
   push(@COOKIESTRING, $item);
}
print "Set-Cookie: $cookiename=@COOKIESTRING\n";
```

If you remember, the **get_cookie** function at the end of the **bookstor.lib** file recovered the browser cookie from the environment, placing the variables into the **%FORM2** hash. This information is first updated, based on the form contents, before being written back out again into the hyphen- and underscore-separated list. This is then printed back as part of the HTTP header information sent back to the browser.

Again, what is interesting to note is that the most significant part of the script is almost one of the smallest: setting and recovering a cookie is easy, and it's entirely up to you how you store the information with the cookie string. Everything else related to the e-commerce process follows the same line as other CGI scripts and other Perl scripts in general.

Summary

Although often portrayed as a black art, programming with Perl and the Common Gateway Interface is actually relatively easy. Once you have processed the query details into a format you can use—and a Perl hash is an ideal form—you can more or less do anything you like within, or without, the confines of the HTML-based browser interface.

There are, of course, some things to remember when programming CGI scripts. First and foremost, you must remember that communication with the user must be via the browser interface. This requirement means you cannot use tools such as **die** and **warn** and complicates the process of communicating errors, problems, and even real information back to the user. The second thing to remember is that Perl's flexibility can also be its greatest weakness in that it can provide methods that allow crackers and unscrupulous users to access and overwrite information they wouldn't otherwise be able to access.

However you implement your e-commerce system, security is of the utmost importance, and you should take care to ensure that the quality of your scripts, and the information they provide and use, is of a suitable quality—and achieving such quality is the topic of our next chapter.

CGI Security

There are two types of security when using CGI scripts, Web server security and script security. The first, Web server security, uses a CGI script to validate a user and add them to the Web server's own list of secure users. This makes use of the Web server's own security mechanism and enables you to support the sort of login services that you find on many personalized news systems and e-commerce sites.

Although it is possible to develop a "front-page" login-style system within Perl—therefore bypassing the Web server security systems—I've found this system to be less than satisfactory from a security point of view because information posted from a form is sent as clear text to the server, so any password would also be sent as clear text at the time of login. It can form part of a more secure SSL server installation but this is more complex and has greater implications than we can discuss in this book.

The second form of CGI security is that of the individual scripts. Attackers can use the loopholes and gaps in CGI scripts to gain access to important files and, in some cases, access to your machine. Most of the time, simply checking the information supplied to the script from the Web form can very quickly eliminate these problems. However, in more secure situations, you may want to look at using Perl with "taint" switching turned on, which is much stricter about the use and quality of the information provided, based on the information's origin.

We will look at all three systems in this chapter, first by examining the password and authorization system employed by the Apache Web server. We'll examine a registration script to update the authorization files, as well as a script that mails the user's password to them if they forget it. Then we'll take a look at the specifics of CGI security and the use of "tainting" Perl to improve security when using CGI scripts.

Apache Registration System

register.pl

Apache, the most popular free Web server, is available in both Unix and NT versions. Among its many features is the ability to restrict access to a directory or subdirectory structure using an access control file and a corresponding password file. This allows you to restrict access to a selection of pages using a login and password system just as access to the machine is restricted.

Access control is managed by a file called .htaccess in the directory you want to control access to. This file specifies the authorization name, type, and user or group password file that should be used to validate the user. Here's an example of this file:

```
AuthName Extranet
AuthType Basic
AuthUserFile /usr/local/http/etc/AuthUser-Public-Extranet
<Limit GET POST PUT>
satisfy any
order deny,allow
allow from usp.co.uk
require valid-user
</Limit>
```

The password file is straightforward, containing only the user's name and password. Like the main /etc/passwd file under Unix, the password is encrypted using the system function **crypt**. Here's a brief snippet from a text version of the corresponding authorization file to the previous example:

```
martinb:TauUVkjRjyXPM
```

When you try to access a secured directory on the Web server, the browser presents you with a login window requesting the login name and password. Once you have entered the information and it has been validated you then have unrestricted access to the directory. For the remainder of the "session" you will continue to have access to the secure directory. However, if you exit your browser you will have to log in again next time you want access to the directory. The security works on entire directories, and you can secure different directories with the same login and password or different ones—the browser and server key on the 'AuthName' field from the access control file.

The registration script uses a predefined HTML form that supplies the necessary information—login, password (twice), and e-mail address.

The following script is a modified version of a real registration script in use on an extranet server.

```
1   #!/usr/local/bin/perl5 -w
2
3   use Fcntl;
4   use NDBM_File;
5   use SCGI;
6   use Encrypt;
7
8   print "Content-type: text/html\n\n";
9   init_cgi;
10
11  my $basedir  = "/usr/local/http/etc/";
12  my $group    = uc($SCGI::formlist{group});
13  $group      =~ s/[;\|~`!+*%$]//g;
14  my $clientpackage = "$group-extras.pm";
15  my $authfile = "$basedir/AuthUser-$group";
16  my $userfile = "$basedir/UserInfo-$group";
17  my (%userdb);
18
19  if (-e $clientpackage)
20  {
21      require $clientpackage;
22  }
23  else
24  {
```

```
25        print "<h1>Fatal Error!: Can't load required module</h1>\n";
26        die "Can't load module ($group)";
27    }
28
29    group_print_header();
30
31    if ((length($SCGI::formlist{login}) <6) or
32        (length($SCGI::formlist{login})>20) or
33        ($SCGI::formlist(login) !~ /^[A-Za-z0-9]+$/))
34    {
35        print <<EOF;
36    <h1>Error!: Invalid login name</h1>
37    You must specify a login name between 8 and 20 characters
38    long. Your login can consist only of letters and numbers,
39    no punctuation (including spaces) are allowed.
40    EOF
41        webdie("Bad login name");
42    }
43
44    if (($SCGI::formlist{passwda}) cmp ($SCGI::formlist{passwdb}))
45    {
46        print <<EOF;
47    <h1>Error!: Passwords don't match</h1>
48    Please respecify your passwords, ensuring that they match.
49    EOF
50        webdie("Mismatched Passwords");
51    }
52
53    if ((length($SCGI::formlist{email})>0) and
54        ($SCGI::formlist{email} !~ /^[-\@\w_.]+$/))
55    {
56        print <<EOF;
57    <h1>Error!: Bad email address</h1>
58    Your email address does not seem to be correctly formatted. You
59    should enter your email address including your domain, e.g.
60    first_last\@domain.com. Please re-submit.
61    EOF
62        webdie("Bad email address");
63    }
64
65    unless (open(D,"<$authfile"))
66    {
67        print <<EOF;
```

```
 68  <h1>Error!: Couldn't open the password file</h1>
 69  A fatal error has occurred which means I can't open the
 70  authorisation file - please email webmaster\@foo.bar
 71  EOF
 72      webdie("Couldn't open the auth file, $authfile");
 73  }
 74
 75  my @lines;
 76  { local $/; @lines = <D>; }
 77
 78  unless(close(<D>))
 79  {
 80      print <<EOF;
 81  <h1>Error!: Couldn't close the password file properly</h1>
 82  A fatal error has occurred which means I can't close the
 83  authorisation file properly - please email webmaster\@foo.bar
 84  EOF
 85      webdie("Couldn't open the auth file, $authfile");
 86  }
 87
 88  if (grep(/^$SCGI::formlist{login}/i,@lines))
 89  {
 90      print <<EOF;
 91  <h1>Error!: Login already exists</h1>
 92  Please use a different login name.<br>
 93  EOF
 94      webdie("Login, $SCGI::formlist{login} already exists");
 95  }
 96
 97  unless(open(D,">>$authfile"))
 98  {
 99      print <<EOF;
100  <h1>Error!: Couldn't append to the authorisation file</h1>
101  Please email webmaster\@foo.bar.
102  EOF
103      webdie("Couldn't append to the authfile, $authfile: $!\n");
104  }
105
106  unless(tie %userdb, 'NDBM_File', $userfile, O_RDWR|O_CREAT, 0666)
107  {
108      print <<EOF;
109  <h1>Error!: Couldn't access the user database</h1>
110  Please email webmaster\@foo.bar.
```

```
111 EOF
112     webdie("Couldn't open user info file\n");
113 }
114
115 my $salt = substr($SCGI::formlist{passwda},0,2);
116 my $encrypt = encryptword($SCGI::formlist{passwda},
117                          $SCGI::formlist{email});
118 my $decrypt = decryptword($encrypt,$SCGI::formlist{email});
119
120 if ($decrypt != $SCGI::formlist{passwda})
121 {
122     print <<EOF;
123 <h1>Error!: Password Registration failure</h1>
124 A problem has occurred in the registration process regarding
125 registering your password. Please report to the
126 <a href="mailto:webmaster\@foo.bar">webmaster</a> immediately,
127 stating the time at which the error occurred.<p>
128 EOF
129     webdie("Password Reg failure - encryptions don't match");
130 }
131
132 my $login = $SCGI::formlist{login};
133
134 print D ("$SCGI::formlist{login}:",
135         crypt($SCGI::formlist{passwda},$salt),"\n");
136 $userdb{$login} = "$encrypt:$SCGI::formlist{email}";
137
138 close(D);
139 untie %userdb;
140
141 print <<EOF;
142 <h1>Registration Successful!</h1>
143 User $SCGI::formlist{login} created successfully<br>
144 We have your email as $SCGI::formlist{email}<br>
145 You can enter the site <a href=/clients/pages/home.html>
146 Here</a><p>
147 In the future you will not need to register in order to gain
148 access to the site, please bookmark whichever page in the
149 extranet is most appropriate for your needs. Should you forget
150 your password, please click <a href="/clients/forgot.html">
151 here</a> to have your password sent to your registered email
152 address.<p>
153 EOF
```

```
154
155  group_print_footer();
156
157  sub webdie
158  {
159      my ($message) = @_;
160      group_print_footer();
161      die $message;
162  }
```

ANNOTATIONS

As should be apparent from the scripts in the previous chapter, a significant amount of the script is given to error checking and reporting. Because HTML and Web browsers are not able to support simple raw text as an error message, we are unable to use **die**. The actual working part of the code is very small; it's limited, in fact, to lines 134 to 136.

```
1    #!/usr/local/bin/perl5 -w
2
3    use Fcntl;
4    use NDBM_File;
5    use SCGI;
6    use Encrypt;
7
```

We need the **Fcntl** and **NDBM_File** modules to store the user information (we'll use an NDBM database for speed and practicality); it makes little difference in this script, but its advantages will become apparent in the next script. The **SCGI** module is the one we examined in our last chapter. The **Encrypt** module provides us with an encryption and decryption function that we'll need to record the user's password for use by the **forgot** script. It uses an identical algorithm to the one we looked at in Chapter 1 and is included in this chapter directory on the CD-ROM.

```
8    print "Content-type: text/html\n\n";
9    init_cgi;
10
```

As before, we must print the content type back to the browser so that it interprets our text correctly. The **init_cgi** function processes the fields from the Web form into a hash.

```
11   my $basedir    = "/usr/local/http/etc/";
12   my $group       = uc($SCGI::formlist{group});
13   $group         =~ s/[;\|~`!+*%$]//g;
14   my $clientpackage = "$group-extras.pm";
15   my $authfile = "$basedir/AuthUser-$group";
16   my $userfile = "$basedir/UserInfo-$group";
17   my (%userdb);
18
```

Lines 11 to 17 set up some variables for use in the rest of the script. The **$basedir** variable specifies the directory that will hold the real Apache password file, as well as the user information file that will store all the user's information. The **$group** variable contains the value of the **group** field from the registration form, and line 13 ensures the value of the field contains only valid characters. This is a very simple way of ensuring that the value from a field contains the sort of information you expect. In this case, the **$group** variable will be used as part of a filename, and so we ensure that it does not consist of any characters that might be interpreted otherwise by the shell.

Line 14 uses the **$group** variable to specify the name of the package that will be incorporated later on in this script. Lines 15 and 16 specify the authorization and user filenames.

```
19   if (-e $clientpackage)
20   {
21       require $clientpackage;
22   }
23   else
24   {
25       print "<h1>Fatal Error!: Can't load required module</h1>\n";
26       die "Can't load module ($group)";
27   }
28
```

Lines 19 to 28 attempt to incorporate the client package. You may remember from the last chapter that we used template files and a function from the **SCGI** module to print customized information to the browser, depending on the specification within the script. The script you see here was used within a multiple-client extranet system. Different registration forms were available for each client company, and the specification for the client was made via a hidden **group** field in the form.

To further complicate matters, different clients often require additional information and even additional programming as part of the registration process. To save myself from duplicating and managing multiple code sets, I used the **require** function to allow modules to be incorporated into the main script at run time, based on the group field value. If the package exists, then we include it on line 21.

Remember that the **require** function loads the module at run time, not at compile time as the **use** function does.

If the package cannot be found—and it should be placed in the same directory as the original script—then we report a fatal error to the user before exiting on line 26.

```
29    group_print_header();
30
```

Line 29 calls the **group_print_header** function, which should have been imported from the group module we imported with the **require** statement on line 21. Although the name implies that it simply prints information, in fact it could do any form of initialization.

```
31    if ((length($SCGI::formlist{login}) <6) or
32        (length($SCGI::formlist{login})>20) or
33        ($SCGI::formlist(login) !~ /^[A-Za-z0-9]+$/))
34    {
35        print <<EOF;
36    <h1>Error!: Invalid login name</h1>
37    You must specify a login name between 8 and 20 characters
38    long. Your login can consist only of letters and numbers,
39    no punctuation (including spaces) are allowed.
40    EOF
41        webdie("Bad login name");
42    }
43
```

Lines 31 to 33 check that the login entered via the form is within the required parameters. In this instance, the length is between 6 and 20 characters, and the login consists of only letters or numbers. If there is a fault, then an error is reported to the user; this must be done by printing the error as HTML, which will then be passed on to the user's browser. We then call the **webdie** function, defied at the end of this script. This calls the **group_print_footer** function, as defined by the earlier **required** module, before calling **die** and quitting.

```
44    if (($SCGI::formlist{passwda}) cmp ($SCGI::formlist{passwdb}))
45    {
46        print <<EOF;
47    <h1>Error!: Passwords don't match</h1>
48    Please respecify your passwords, ensuring that they match.
49    EOF
50        webdie("Mismatched Passwords");
51    }
52
```

Line 44 compares the two passwords supplied by the user to ensure they match. This is a fairly standard test for all password entry systems to ensure that the user is able to type in the password twice correctly.

```
53  if ((length($SCGI::formlist{email})>0) and
54      ($SCGI::formlist{email} !~ /^[-\@\w_.]+$/))
55  {
56      print <<EOF;
57  <h1>Error!: Bad email address</h1>
58  Your email address does not seem to be correctly formatted. You
59  should enter your email address including your domain, e.g.
60  first_last\@domain.com. Please re-submit.
61  EOF
62      webdie("Bad email address");
63  }
64
```

Lines 53 and 54 ensure that the e-mail address supplied by the user is greater than 1 character and is composed of only words, hyphens, underscores, periods, or the obligatory @ sign.

```
65  unless (open(D,"<$authfile"))
66  {
67      print <<EOF;
68  <h1>Error!: Couldn't open the password file</h1>
69  A fatal error has occurred which means I can't open the
70  authorisation file - please email webmaster\@foo.bar
71  EOF
72      webdie("Couldn't open the auth file, $authfile");
73  }
74
```

We attempt to open the user authorization file in line 65. We open it as read only first of all so we can verify that the login specific does not already exist. An error is reported if there is a problem.

```
75  my @lines;
76  { local $/; @lines = <D>; }
77
```

Line 75 creates a new array to hold the lines from the authorization file, and line 76 populates the array with the contents of the file using the localized record separator trick we have used before. This script assumes that the size of the file is relatively small—it should be clear that a large authorization file would consume a lot of memory at this point. You may want to update this section to use a loop to work through the contents of the file, something like:

```
while (<D>)
{
    my ($user) = (split(/:/))[0];
    if ($SCGI::formlist{login} eq $user)
    {
     print <<EOF;
<h1>Error!: Login already exists</h1>
Please use a different login name.<br>
EOF
    webdie("Login, $SCGI::formlist{login} already exists");
    }
}
```

This updated code eliminates the need to read in the entire file for checking.

```
78  unless(close(<D>))
79  {
80      print <<EOF;
81  <h1>Error!: Couldn't close the password file properly</h1>
82  A fatal error has occurred which means I can't close the
83  authorisation file properly - please email webmaster\@foo.bar
84  EOF
85      webdie("Couldn't open the auth file, $authfile");
86  }
87
```

Line 78 checks that the **close** function on the file operates correctly.

```
88  if (grep(/^$SCGI::formlist{login}/i,@lines))
89  {
90      print <<EOF;
91  <h1>Error!: Login already exists</h1>
92  Please use a different login name.<br>
93  EOF
94      webdie("Login, $SCGI::formlist{login} already exists");
95  }
96
```

Line 88 checks whether the login already exists by using **grep** on the user array, reporting an error if it exists.

```
97  unless(open(D,">>$authfile"))
98  {
99      print <<EOF;
```

\

```
100 <h1>Error!: Couldn't append to the authorisation file</h1>
101 Please email webmaster\@foo.bar.
102 EOF
103     webdie("Couldn't append to the authfile, $authfile: $!\n");
104 }
105
```

Line 97 opens the authorization file for appending; we'll need to add the user information to the authorization file.

```
106 unless(tie %userdb, 'NDBM_File', $userfile, O_RDWR|O_CREAT, 0666)
107 {
108     print <<EOF;
109 <h1>Error!: Couldn't access the user database</h1>
110 Please email webmaster\@foo.bar.
111 EOF
112     webdie("Couldn't open user info file\n");
113 }
114
```

Line 106 uses **tie** to open the NDBM database that will be used to store the user information. The **tie** function associates a DBM file with a hash making it significantly easier to use. If the operation fails, then we report an error to the user. Note that we still haven't actually updated any information—we must ensure that we *can* update the information before we actually proceed.

```
115 my $salt = substr($SCGI::formlist{passwda},0,2);
116 my $encrypt = encryptword($SCGI::formlist{passwda},
117                           $SCGI::formlist{email});
118 my $decrypt = decryptword($encrypt,$SCGI::formlist{email});
119
```

Line 115 creates a **$salt** variable, which will be used as the source reference string for the encryption. Line 116 uses the **encryptword** function from the **Encrypt** module to generate an encrypted version of the password based on the e-mail address. This encrypted password will be stored in the user information file that we'll need with the **forgot.pl** script. Line 118 decrypts the encrypted version of the password created in line 116.

```
120 if ($decrypt != $SCGI::formlist{passwda})
121 {
122     print <<EOF;
123 <h1>Error!: Password Registration failure</h1>
124 A problem has occurred in the registration process regarding
125 registering your password. Please report to the
126 <a href="mailto:webmaster\@foo.bar">webmaster</a> immediately,
```

```
127  stating the time at which the error occurred.<p>
128  EOF
129      webdie("Password Reg failure - encryptions don't match");
130  }
131
```

Line 120 verifies that the encryption and decryption of the password match. This is really a test to ensure that the encryption algorithm works correctly, rather than a test of the information supplied by the user. If we cannot reliably encrypt the same password twice then there is a serious problem with the encryption system. As usual, an error is reported if the decrypted version does not match the original.

```
132  my $login = $SCGI::formlist{login};
133
134  print D ("$SCGI::formlist{login}:",
135           crypt($SCGI::formlist{passwda},$salt),"\n");
136  $userdb{$login} = "$encrypt:$SCGI::formlist{email}";
137
```

Line 132 creates a local version of the **login** field from the form. It serves no useful purpose, other than to make the next few lines look less complex!

Line 134 adds the user's login and an encrypted version of the password (taken directly from the output of **crypt)** to the Apache user file. Line 136 then creates an entry in the **%userdb** hash, which is tied to the NDBM user information database. I've used a colon to separate the encrypted password and the e-mail address; the information is unlikely to contain either (we've checked both for their contents already) so this is a safe option.

```
138  close(D);
139  untie %userdb;
140
```

Lines 138 and 139 close the user authorization and user information file accordingly. I haven't checked that the files could be closed correctly, you may want to add similar tests for errors to the script, perhaps using the lines below:

```
unless(close(D))
{
    print <<EOF;
<h1>Error!: Couldn't close the user database</h1>
Please email webmaster\@foo.bar.
EOF
    webdie("Couldn't close user db \n");
}
unless(untie %userdb)
{
```

```
    print <<EOF;
<h1>Error!: Couldn't close the user information database</h1>
Please email webmaster\@foo.bar.
EOF
    webdie("Couldn't close user info file\n");
}
```

In both cases we report an error to the user—you may want to adjust this.

```
141 print <<EOF;
142 <h1>Registration Successful!</h1>
143 User $SCGI::formlist{login} created successfully<br>
144 We have your email as $SCGI::formlist{email}<br>
145 You can enter the site <a href=/clients/pages/home.html>
146 Here</a><p>
147 In the future you will not need to register in order to gain
148 access to the site, please bookmark whichever page in the
149 extranet is most appropriate for your needs. Should you forget
150 your password, please click <a href="/clients/forgot.html">
151 here</a> to have your password sent to your registered email
152 address.<p>
153 EOF
154
```

If we've got this far, then the operation must have been successful, and we report this information to the user in the form of a Web page. We incorporate the necessary links onto protected portions of the Web site; this will enable the user to log in with the ID and password they have just generated, a good test of the validity of the update.

```
155 group_print_footer();
156
```

Line 155 prints the footer for the page, according to the group module we imported at the start of the script.

```
157 sub webdie
158 {
159     my ($message) = @_;
160     group_print_footer();
161     die $message;
162 }
```

Line 157 defines the **webdie** function. It accepts one argument, the message to be used in the **die** function. Because we cannot report an 'error' from the standard error output and the **die** or **warn** functions we must use a separate system for reporting an error to the user. This is the HTML we have already seen. The purpose of the **webdie** function is to report an error to the Web server error log (via **die**), and print out any required footer to the browser before finally **dieing**. Line 160 prints the page footer, and line 161 **dies** with the specified message. This message will be the one reported to the Web server and should appear in the Web server's log file.

The execution of the script is fairly straightforward; ignoring the verification and validation of the form information the script does the following:

1. Checks that the login does not already exist.

2. Encrypts the password for internal use only.

3. Adds the user to the Apache password file.

4. Adds the user, encrypted password, and e-mail address to the user information file.

We can ignore steps 2 and 4 if we do not need to store the information elsewhere. In practice, however, step 2 is probably the only one that is uncommon. With step 4, most registration systems usually record some additional information for the user; this may be name and address details for an e-commerce site or simply an e-mail address so the user can be kept abreast of developments on the site via e-mail.

forgot.pl

Apache Password Reminder

However simple a password is, many users still manage to forget it the next time they come back to visit a site. It is therefore quite common to see a "reminder" facility to allow users to receive their chosen password back via e-mail.

There is obviously a security hazard here. Storing unencrypted passwords so they can be broadcast back to the user poses a problem if people gain access to your machine. It's therefore advisable to store an encrypted version as part of the registration process—we saw how this was implemented in the previous script.

In our example, we've used my own encryption algorithm, but as we'll see later in this chapter, this is not generally a good idea. If you want to store information about a user, then a tried and tested system, such as the DES module, available from CPAN, may be more sensible.

```perl
1   #!/usr/local/bin/perl5 -w
2
3   use Fcntl;
4   use NDBM_File;
5   use SCGI;
6   use Encrypt;
7
8   print "Content-type: text/html\n\n";
```

```perl
9    init_cgi;
10
11   my $basedir = '/usr/local/http/etc/';
12   my $group = uc($SCGI::formlist{group});
13   $group    =~ s/[;\|~`!+*%$]//g;
14   my $authfile = "$basedir/AuthUser-$group";
15   my $userfile = "$basedir/UserInfo-$group";
16   my $clientpackage = "$group-extras.cgi";
17   my $login = $SCGI::formlist{login}
18      if (defined($SCGI::formlist{login}));
19
20   my (%userdb);
21
22   if (-e $clientpackage)
23   {
24       require $clientpackage;
25   }
26   else
27   {
28       print "<h1>Fatal Error!: Can't load required module</h1>\n";
29       die("Can't load module ($group)");
30   }
31
32   group_print_header();
33
34   if ((length($login) <6) or
35       (length($login)>20) or
36       ($login !~ /[A-Za-z0-9]*/))
37   {
38       print <<EOF;
39   <h1>Error!: Invalid login name</h1>
40   You must specify a login name between 8 and 20 characters
41   long. Your login can consist only of letters and numbers,
42   no punctuation (including spaces) are allowed.
43   EOF
44       webdie("Invalid login, $SCGI::formlist{login}");
45   }
46
47   if ((length($SCGI::formlist{email})>0) and
48       ($SCGI::formlist{email} !~ /^[-\@\w_.]+$/))
49   {
50       print <<EOF;
51   <h1>Error!: Bad email address</h1>
```

```
52  Your email address does not seem to be correctly formatted.
53  You should enter your email address including your domain,
54  e.g. first_last\@domain.com. Please re-submit.
55  EOF
56      webdie("Bad Email Address");
57  }
58
59  open(D,"<$authfile") or webdie "Couldn't open the password file";
60  my @loginlines;
61  { local $/; @loginlines = <D>; }
62  close(<D>);
63
64  unless ((grep(/^$SCGI::formlist{login}/,@loginlines)))
65  {
66      print <<EOF;
67  <h1>Error!: Login does not exist</h1>
68  Please enter the correct login name.<br>
69  EOF
70      webdie("Login $SCGI::formlist{login} does not exist");
71  }
72
73  (tie %userdb, 'NDBM_File', $userfile, O_RDWR|O_CREAT, 0666) or
74      webdie("Couldn't open user info file\n");
75
76  unless (defined($userdb{$login}))
77  {
78      print <<EOF;
79  <h1>Error!: Couldn't find user in database</h1>
80  Couldn't find your details in the user DB. Please report to <a
81  href="mailto:webmaster\@foo.bar">webmaster</a>.<br>
82  EOF
83      webdie("Couldn't find user $userdb{$login} in DB");
84  }
85
86  my ($passwd,$email) = split /:/,$userdb{$login};
87  my $decrypt = decryptword($passwd,$email);
88
89  open(MAIL,"|/usr/lib/sendmail -t") or
90      webdie("Couldn't open a pipe to the email program");
91
92  $SCGI::formlist{email} =~ s/[;\|~`!+*%$]//g;
93
94  print MAIL <<EOF;
```

```
 95   To: $SCGI::formlist{email}
 96   From: webmaster\@foo.bar
 97   Subject: $group Intranet Login
 98
 99   This is an email reminder of your password for login
100
101   $SCGI::formlist{login}
102
103   We have your password recorded as:
104
105   $decrypt
106
107   Please note that passwords are case sensitive.
108   EOF
109
110   close(MAIL) or webdie("Couldn't close mail pipe");
111
112   print <<EOF;
113   <h1>Reminder Sent</h1>
114   You should receive your email reminder shortly.<br>
115   You can enter the site
116   <a href=/secure/home.html>Here</a>
117   EOF
118
119   untie %userdb;
120
121   group_print_footer();
122
123   sub webdie
124   {
125       my ($message) = @_;
126       group_print_footer();
127       die $message;
128   }
```

ANNOTATIONS

This script follows the same basic layout of the previous example, except that the user supplies the login and e-mail address, and their login and password information is e-mailed back to them.

```
1    #!/usr/local/bin/perl5 -w
2
3    use Fcntl;
4    use NDBM_File;
5    use SCGI;
6    use Encrypt;
7
```

We need the **Fcntl** and **NDBM_File** modules to store the user information—we need to read the NDBM database created in the last script. Using an NDBM file will be much quicker than attempting to read in a text file line by line. The **SCGI** module is the one we examined in the last chapter.

```
8    print "Content-type: text/html\n\n";
9    init_cgi;
10
```

As before, we must print the content type back to the browser so that it interprets our HTML correctly. The **init_cgi** subroutine processes the fields from the Web form into a hash.

```
11   my $basedir = '/usr/local/http/etc/';
12   my $group = uc($SCGI::formlist{group});
13   $group       =~ s/[;\|~`!+*%$]//g;
14   my $authfile = "$basedir/AuthUser-$group";
15   my $userfile = "$basedir/UserInfo-$group";
16   my $clientpackage = "$group-extras.cgi";
17   my $login = $SCGI::formlist{login}
18       if (defined($SCGI::formlist{login}));
19
20   my (%userdb);
21
```

Lines 11 to 18 set up some variables for use in the rest of the script. The **$basedir** variable specifies the directory that will hold the real Apache password file, and it specifies the user information file that will store all the user's information. The **$group** variable contains the value of the **group** field from the registration form, and line 13 ensures the value of the field contains only valid characters. Lines 14 and 15 specify the authorization and user filenames. Line 16 uses the **$group** variable to specify the name of the package that will be incorporated later on in this script. Lines 17 and 18 define the **$login** variable, which will hold the user's login name. We will be using the login a number of times, so we define it early here for clarity. Line 20 sets up the **%userdb** hash that will be tied to the user information NDBM database.

```
22  if (-e $clientpackage)
23  {
24      require $clientpackage;
25  }
26  else
27  {
28      print "<h1>Fatal Error!: Can't load required module</h1>\n";
29      die("Can't load module ($group)");
30  }
31
```

We incorporate the group Perl module for printing group specific headers and footers, reporting an error if the package does not exist.

```
32  group_print_header();
33
```

Line 32 prints out the group header from the group module.

```
34  if ((length($login) <6) or
35      (length($login)>20) or
36      ($login !~ /[A-Za-z0-9]*/))
37  {
38      print <<EOF;
39  <h1>Error!: Invalid login name</h1>
40  You must specify a login name between 8 and 20 characters
41  long. Your login can consist only of letters and numbers,
42  no punctuation (including spaces) are allowed.
43  EOF
44      webdie("Invalid login, $SCGI::formlist{login}");
45  }
46
```

Lines 34 to 36 check the size and format of the login name to ensure they match the required parameters.

```
47  if ((length($SCGI::formlist{email})>0) and
48      ($SCGI::formlist{email} !~ /^[-\@\w_.]+$/))
49  {
50      print <<EOF;
51  <h1>Error!: Bad email address</h1>
52  Your email address does not seem to be correctly formatted.
53  You should enter your email address including your domain,
54  e.g. first_last\@domain.com. Please re-submit.
55  EOF
56      webdie("Bad Email Address");
57  }
58
```

Lines 47 to 58 verify that the e-mail address supplied by the user is of an appropriate size and that it consists of valid characters.

```
59  open(D,"<$authfile") or webdie "Couldn't open the password file";
60  my @loginlines;
61  { local $/; @loginlines = <D>; }
62  close(<D>);
63
```

Line 69 opens the authorization file, or else it does an unceremonious exit. We then import the file into the **@loginlines** array so that we can check that the user login actually exists in the database.

```
64  unless ((grep(/^$SCGI::formlist{login}/,@loginlines)))
65  {
66      print <<EOF;
67  <h1>Error!: Login does not exist</h1>
68  Please enter the correct login name.<br>
69  EOF
70      webdie("Login $SCGI::formlist{login} does not exist");
71  }
72
```

We verify the existence of the login in line 64, reporting an error to the user if the login they have entered does not exist in the authorization file.

```
73  (tie %userdb, 'NDBM_File', $userfile, O_RDWR|O_CREAT, 0666) or
74      webdie("Couldn't open user info file\n");
75
```

Line 73 ties the **%userdb** hash to the NDBM database of user information.

```
76  unless (defined($userdb{$login}))
77  {
78      print <<EOF;
79  <h1>Error!: Couldn't find user in database</h1>
80  Couldn't find your details in the user DB. Please report to <a
81  href="mailto:webmaster\@foo.bar">webmaster</a>.<br>
82  EOF
83      webdie("Couldn't find user $userdb{$login} in DB");
84  }
85
```

Line 76 performs a second check on the existence of the user's login by verifying that a corresponding record exists in the user information database.

```
86   my ($passwd,$email) = split /:/,$userdb{$login};
87   my $decrypt = decryptword($passwd,$email);
88
```

Line 86 extracts the password and e-mail address stored in the user information database against the supplied login information—remember that a colon separated the information. Line 87 then decrypts the password, using the e-mail address as the keyword.

```
89   open(MAIL,"|/usr/lib/sendmail -t") or
90       webdie("Couldn't open a pipe to the email program");
91
```

Line 89 then opens a pipe to the **sendmail** program so that we can e-mail the user their password. We use the **-t** option so that we can specify the address as part of the e-mail body.

```
92   $SCGI::formlist{email} =~ s/[;\|~`!+*%$]//g;
93
```

Line 92 strips any invalid characters from the users e-mail address. See "Common CGI Security Traps" later in this chapter for more information on parsing and checking HTML form fields.

```
94   print MAIL <<EOF;
95   To: $SCGI::formlist{email}
96   From: webmaster\@foo.bar
97   Subject: $group Intranet Login
98
99   This is an email reminder of your password for login
100
101  $SCGI::formlist{login}
102
103  We have your password recorded as:
104
105  $decrypt
106
107  Please note that passwords are case sensitive.
108  EOF
109
```

Line 94 starts a here document for the e-mail message that will report the password and login information to the user.

```
110 close(MAIL) or webdie("Couldn't close mail pipe");
111
```

Line 110 quits if the **close** operation on the e-mail pipe fails.

```
112 print <<EOF;
113 <h1>Reminder Sent</h1>
114 You should receive your email reminder shortly.<br>
115 You can enter the site
116 <a href=/secure/home.html>Here</a>
117 EOF
118
119 untie %userdb;
120
```

Lines 112 to 117 report the success of the e-mail report to the user via the browser. Line 119 **untie**s the **%userdb** hash from the user information file.

```
121 group_print_footer();
122
123 sub webdie
124 {
125     my ($message) = @_;
126     group_print_footer();
127     die $message;
128 }
```

Line 121 prints the footer, based on the function defined by the group module. Line 123 defines the **webdie** function, which is identical to the version in the previous script.

This script works largely in reverse to the previous one. It accepts a login and e-mails the already recorded password back to the user. As has already been mentioned, it only uses a simple encryption algorithm to store the password; a more secure encryption system should be used if you want to use this script in a commercial situation.

Common CGI Security Traps

Surprisingly few sites are actually aware of the very real problems that a badly written CGI script can cause. I've personally come across "Blue Chip" companies and even Internet service providers who do not take the matter of CGI security seriously. In fact, it's incredibly easy to ensure that your scripts are secure if you follow some simple guidelines. However, before we look at solutions, let's look at the types of scripts that are vulnerable to attack:

- Any script that passes form input to a mail address or mail message

- Any script that passes information that will be used within a subshell

- Any script that blindly accepts unlimited amounts of information during the form processing

The first two danger zones should be relatively obvious: anything that is potentially executed on the command line is open to abuse if the attacker supplies the right information. For example, imagine an e-mail address passed directly to **sendmail** that looks like this:

```
mc@foo.bar;(mail mc@foo.bar </etc/passwd)
```

If this were executed on the command line as part of a **sendmail** line, the command after the semicolon would mail the password file to the same user—a severe security hazard if not checked.

If there were a simple rule to follow when using CGI scripts and form elements, it would be this: don't trust the size, content, or organization of the data supplied.

For some more specific things to watch out for, use this checklist:

- Double-check the field names, values, and associations before you use them. For example, make sure an e-mail address looks like an e-mail address, and that it's part of the right field you are expecting from the form.

- Don't automatically process the field values without checking them.

- Check the input size of the variables, or better still, of the form data. You can use the **$ENV{CONTENT_LENGTH}** field, which is calculated by the Web server to check the length of the data being accepted.

- Don't assume that field data exists or is valid before use; a blank field can cause as many problems as a field filled with bad data.

- Don't ever return the content of a file unless you can be sure of its content.

- Don't accept that the path information sent to your script is automatically valid.

- If you are going to accept paths or filenames, make sure that they are relative, not absolute, and that they don't contain .., which leads to the parent directory. An attacker could easily specify a file of ../../../../../../../../etc/passwd, which would reference the password file from even a deep directory.

- Always validate information used with **open**, **system**, **fork**, or **exec**. If nothing else, ensure any variables passed to these functions don't contain the characters ; | ().

◆ Ensure your Web server is not running as **root**, which opens up your machine to all sorts of attacks. Run your Web server as **nobody** or create a new user specifically for the Web server, ensuring that scripts are readable and executable only by the Web server owner, and not writable by anybody.

◆ Use Perl in place of **grep** where possible. This will negate the need to make a system call to search file contents.

◆ Don't assume that hidden fields are really hidden—the user will still see them if they view the file source. And don't rely on your own encryption algorithms to encrypt the information supplied in these hidden fields. Use an existing system that has been checked and is bug free, like the **DES** module available from your local CPAN archive.

◆ Consider using taint checking (see "Taint Checking" next).

If you follow these guidelines, you will at least reduce your risk from attacks, but there is no way to completely guarantee your safety. A determined attacker will use a number of different tools and tricks to achieve his goal.

Taint Checking

Perl provides a facility called *taint checking*. This option forces Perl to examine the origin of the variables used within a script. Information gleaned from the outside world is tainted, or marked as possibly unsafe, depending on the context in which it's used. Further, variables that are derived from tainted variables are also tainted. Perl then examines where the variables are used, and in what context, to decide whether the code breaks any of the pre-built rules.

Some of the checks are relatively simple, such as verifying that the directories within a given path are not writable by others. Some are more complex and rely on Perl's compiler and syntax checker to accept or reject the statement.

The rule is straightforward: you cannot use any data from the outside world that may directly or indirectly affect something outside of your program. In essence, this means that you can use external variables internally for everything except specific system calls, subshell executions, or destinations for data files. The following code fragment shows the results of running some statements with taint checking switched on:

```
1   $cmd = shift;                # tainted - its origin is the command line
2   $run = "echo $cmd";          # Also tainted - derived from $cmd
3   $alsoran = "echo Hello";     # Not tainted
4   system "echo $cmd";          # Insecure - external shell with $cmd
5   system "$alsoran";           # Insecure - until $PATH set
6   system "/bin/echo", $cmd;    # Secure - doesn't use shell to execute
```

If you try to execute this as a script, with taint checking switched on you will received errors similar to "Insecure dependency" or "Insecure $ENV{PATH}" for lines 4 and 5.

To switch on taint checking, you must specify the **-T** option on the command line. This works for Unix and Windows NT. Taint checking with MacPerl is not strictly available, and even if it were, it wouldn't make a huge difference since the MacOS is not capable of executing external programs—and even if it were, it is not prone to the same security breaches as a Unix or NT system.

To detect if a variable is tainted, you can use the function **is_tainted** from the **tainted.pl** script supplied in the standard library of the Perl distribution. The only way to untaint variables is to reference substring regular expression matches. For example, for an e-mail address you might use the following code fragment to extract an untainted version of the e-mail address:

```
If ($addr =~ /^([-\@\w.]+)$/)
{
    $addr = $1;
}
else
{
    die "Bad email address";
}
```

Obviously, running an unspecific and all-encompassing regular expression on the data provided defeats the object of taint checking in the first place! If you use taint checking you must ensure that the regular expressions filter and validate the information provided.

Because variables from CGI scripts are tainted (they come from either an external environment variable or the standard), tainting Perl CGI scripts is a good idea. On the whole, using some of the programming techniques we have already looked at in this chapter for validating and protecting CGI data and scripts will protect you from most mishaps and attacks. Adding taint checking to the process provides a mental check and ensures the security of the script.

For more information on taint checking, refer to the **perlsec** manual page that comes the Perl distribution, or to the "camel" book (that is, *Programming Perl*—see Appendix B for more information).

If you want to check the validity of supplied Perl code, or protect the execution of supplied Perl code, then you might want to examine the documentation for the **Safe** and **Opcode** modules. The **Safe** module allows you to create an environment in which scripts can be run. Only those functions that are specified as part of the environment creation can be executed. In essence, the system is like a safe, except that it keeps bad code in, not bad code out.

The **Safe** module makes use of the fact that Perl is compiled into a collection of opcodes at the time of execution. An opcode is the smallest executable module within the code that makes up the Perl language. They can be small, such as the opcode to add two numbers together, or more complex, like the code to handle hash variable manipulation. The Safe module uses the **Opcode** module to specify which opcodes, and therefore which functions can be executed within a special **eval** statement. For further information on the modules, refer to the module code, manual pages, or "camel" book. For further information on Perl internals and opcodes, refer to *Advanced Perl Programming* by Sriram Srinivasan (see Appendix B for more details).

Summary

Because it's likely that the CGI scripts you produce will be available to the public via the Internet and a Web site, you should ensure that the security of your scripts, and indeed your Web server, is of the highest standard. Attacks are on the increase, and anything you can do to improve your safety and position is only a good thing.

The security of pages on your Web site can be managed manually through the use of the tools supplied with the Apache Web server. However, the interactive nature of Web sites implies that you must provide a more interactive method of allowing registered users access to your site. The two scripts in this chapter should provide you with a suitable mechanism for supporting such a system.

Securing your scripts involves verifying and double-checking the information supplied to you. If you don't trust your programming expertise, then using taint checking will help you isolate any problem areas in your script.

However if you decide to secure your Web site and scripts, I think it is best to complete this chapter by reiterating the basic rule of CGI script security:

Don't trust the size, content, or organization of the data supplied by a Web browser or form.

Administrator's Toolkit

Systems Administration
Network Administration

Systems Administration

Although there is a wide range of programs and utilities available for managing the individual machines in your network, you're virtually certain at some point to be unhappy with your system's toolkit, even on "grown-up" operating systems like Unix. Shellscripts and some C programming can fill some of the holes, but much of the configuration information—behind Unix particularly—is stored in text files that could be more easily processed by Perl.

Better still, because Perl has access to all of the same system functions as C—and the same external programs, like Shellscript—it can become a quick and easy solution to all your systems headaches. Personally, I have never found a user creation script as good as the visual tools that are available on most modern systems. When a new staff member starts, I go around and manually create users on each system, usually because the different machines provide different services and have different rules and requirements. The bulk of my systems administration involves monitoring and checking different aspects of the server environment, including everything from managing aliases for the Unix mail server to verifying and reporting the disk space and usage of different files and folders on Mac-based file servers.

In this chapter we're going to take a look at some of the scripts that I use (mine and those of others) that fill in some of the gaps in my toolkit. We'll start off by looking at a script that checks the validity of the Unix alias file that provides better checks than the usual manual checks that can be performed by sendmail. The **wtmp.pl** and **lastlog.pl** scripts examine the extraction of information from the logs generated by Unix to record login information; both follow the same basic principles to extract information from a preformatted file that uses a C structure, rather than following the normal text-delimited structure.

Analyzing the volume of e-mail traffic being processed by your server can provide invaluable information on the load and requirements of the mail server. The **mlsyslog.pl** script extracts the information from the syslog file; it follows a specific format, but on a line-by-line basis that requires more careful extraction. The next three scripts cover the checking of user password and login information, both on Unix (**uxckpw.pl** and **uxugrps.pl**) and Windows NT (**ntpwck.pl**). The **cron2nt.pl** script fills the compatibility gap between NT and Unix time-based automation.

Our last script is a df-type tool for monitoring file sizes on the Mac. The **macfbf.pl** script provides a familiar, file-size-by-folder report, sorted largest first so you can find the largest folder on a Mac volume or within another Mac folder.

chkalias.pl

Checking Unix Aliases

If you manage a Unix mail server, it's likely you have an alias file that maps e-mail addresses to groups of people or to alternative e-mail addresses. Once you have edited the file, you then have to verify that your modifications work. Because alias entries can refer to other aliases within the file, it's not a simple case of checking that the lines you have edited make sense. Instead you must somehow verify the alias you updated and all of the aliases that it may refer to.

This process could be incredibly time consuming if you did it manually. However, help is at hand. The sendmail program has a command-line option, **-bt**, that allows you to test the alias file. For example, if you wanted to check the alias for MC_Team, you would enter

```
$ sendmail -bt MC_Team
```

It will come as no surprise to you that there is a disadvantage to this system. The tests use the generated DBM file, which means you must replace your old and presumably working file with your newly modified version. This replacement could have disastrous effects on your mail server if you receive any mail that uses one of the modified aliases.

What we need, therefore, is a way of verifying the text file that is used to generate the DBM file before the "live" version is created. This is the purpose of the **chkalias.pl** script. It reads in the alias text file, then resolves and recursively expands the aliases before reporting on any problems. Because the process of parsing the alias file is quite complex, we take the opportunity to check individual aliases and the entire alias file, and to report on which users are members of which aliases.

```perl
1   #!/usr/local/bin/perl5 -w
2
3   use strict;
4   use FileHandle;
5   use Getopt::Std;
6   my $usage = "Usage: [-r | [-e|m alias...]] [-f aliasfile]";
7   use vars qw/$opt_e $opt_f $opt_m $opt_r/;
8   die $usage unless (getopts('merf:'));
9   $opt_e = 1 unless($opt_r || $opt_m);
10  $opt_f = '/etc/aliases' unless ($opt_f);
11  die $usage unless @ARGV or $opt_r;
12
13  my %alias = readaliases($opt_f);
14  expand_aliases(\%alias) if $opt_e;
15  member_of(\%alias) if $opt_m;
16  report_bad_aliases(\%alias) if $opt_r;
17
18  sub member_of
19  {
20      local *alias = shift;
21      my %members = memberalias(\%alias);
22
23      for $_ (@ARGV)
24      {
```

```
25              if ($members{$_})
26              {
27                  print "$_ is a member of $members{$_}\n";
28              }
29              else
30              {
31                  print "$_ isn't a member of anything\n";
32              }
33          }
34      }
35
36      sub expand_aliases
37      {
38          local *alias = shift;
39          for $_ (@ARGV)
40          {
41              my @expand=expandalias(\%alias,$_);
42              if ($expand[-1])
43              {
44                  print "$_ expands to @expand\n";
45              }
46              else
47              {
48                  print "$_ not found in alias DB\n";
49              }
50          }
51      }
52
53      sub report_bad_aliases
54      {
55          local *alias = shift;
56          my %erroralias;
57          for my $aliasname (keys %alias)
58          {
59              my @members = expandalias(\%alias,$aliasname);
60              for my $member (@members)
61              {
62                  if ($member)
63                  {
64                      unless (($member =~ /.*@.*/) ||
65                              ($member =~ /^\/.*/) ||
66                              ($member =~ /["!|]/))
```

```
67                    {
68                         $erroralias{$aliasname} .=
69                              "$member " unless getpwnam(lc($member));
70                    }
71               }
72          }
73     }
74     if (keys %erroralias)
75     {
76          for my $aliasname (keys %erroralias)
77          {
78               print("Alias $aliasname has missing members:",
79                    $erroralias{$aliasname},"\n");
80          }
81     }
82     else
83     {
84          print "No problems found";
85     }
86 }
87
88 sub readaliases
89 {
90     my $file = shift;
91     my (%alias,$aliasname,$members);
92     open(D,"<$file") || die "Cannot open $file, $!";
93     while (<D>)
94     {
95          next if /^#/;
96          chomp;
97          ($aliasname,$members) = split /:\s+/;
98          $alias{(lc($aliasname))} = lc($members);
99     }
100    close(D) || return 0;;
101    return(%alias);
102 }
103
104 sub expandalias
105 {
106    *alias = shift;
107    my $expand = shift;
108    my @expanded;
109    my @toexpand = split /\s*,\s*/,$expand;
```

```
110
111      return(0) unless $alias{$expand};
112
113    OUTEXPAND:
114      {
115          while ($#toexpand >= 0)
116          {
117              my $toexpand = pop @toexpand;
118            EXPAND:
119              {
120                  if (defined($alias{$toexpand}))
121                  {
122                      if (defined($alias{$alias{$toexpand}}))
123                      {
124                          $toexpand = $alias{$alias{$toexpand}};
125                          redo EXPAND;
126                      }
127                      $toexpand = $alias{$toexpand};
128                  }
129              }
130              if ($toexpand =~ /,/)
131              {
132                  push @toexpand,split(/\s*,\s*/,$toexpand);
133                  redo OUTEXPAND;
134              }
135              else
136              {
137                  push @expanded,$toexpand;
138              }
139          }
140      }
141      my %dedupe;
142      for (@expanded)
143      {
144          $dedupe{$_} = 1;
145      }
146      return (keys %dedupe);
147 }
148
149 sub memberalias
150 {
151      *alias = shift;
152      my %mteams;
```

```
153
154     for my $aliasname (keys %alias)
155     {
156         for my $member (split /,/,$alias{$aliasname})
157         {
158             $mteams{$member} .= "$aliasname ";
159         }
160     }
161     return %mteams;
162 }
```

ANNOTATIONS

This script is very long, and it certainly looks more complicated than the principles that are involved. The process involved is to read in the file, the contents of which we place into an ever useful hash. Then, depending on the command-line option specified, the aliases are optionally expanded, recursively to take account of the recursive nature of the alias file, before finally being reported on.

```
1    #!/usr/local/bin/perl5 -w
2
3    use strict;
4    use FileHandle;
5    use Getopt::Std;
6    my $usage = "Usage: [-r | [-e|m alias...]] [-f aliasfile]";
7    use vars qw/$opt_e $opt_f $opt_m $opt_r/;
8    die $usage unless (getopts('merf:'));
9    $opt_e = 1 unless($opt_r || $opt_m);
10   $opt_f = '/etc/aliases' unless ($opt_f);
11   die $usage unless @ARGV or $opt_r;
12
```

The first 11 lines set up the environment for the script and parse the command-line options so that we know what we are doing. Line 6 defines a scalar variable to hold the usage instructions. Line 7 then initializes the variables that hold the command-line options. Line 8 uses the simple version of the **getopts** function to parse the command-line options into the variables we set up in line 7.

There are four command-line options: **-r** resolves and reports on all aliases; **-e** and **-m** take the remainder of the arguments off the command line to expand and report the membership of the specified aliases, respectively; and **-f** allows you to specify an alternate aliases file. Line 9 sets the default mode to expand aliases unless the user has already specified the **-r** or **-m** option. Line 10 sets the default location for the alias text file. The setting I've used here works for Solaris and most other Unix flavors.

Finally, line 11 causes the script to **die** if the user has failed either to specify the **-r** option, which needs no further arguments, or to specify any arguments for the **-e** or **-m** options.

```perl
13  my %alias = readaliases($opt_f);
14  expand_aliases(\%alias) if $opt_e;
15  member_of(\%alias) if $opt_m;
16  report_bad_aliases(\%alias) if $opt_r;
17
```

Line 13 calls the **readaliases** function, which returns a hash in which each alias is the key and the alias members are the corresponding value. We remember to pass the **$opt_f** variable, which contains the location of the alias file.

Lines 14 to 16 then call different functions based on the command-line options specified. In each case, we pass the **%alias** hash as a reference to the function.

```perl
18  sub member_of
19  {
20      local *alias = shift;
21      my %members = memberalias(\%alias);
22
```

We take the alias hash reference into a typeglob on line 20. Line 21 then calls the **memberalias** function, which returns a reversed version of the **%alias** hash from the alias-to-members format to a members-to-alias format.

```perl
23      for $_ (@ARGV)
24      {
25          if ($members{$_})
26          {
27              print "$_ is a member of $members{$_}\n";
28          }
```

To print out the results, all we need do is access the reverse hash and, using each argument on the command line as a key, print out the hash value. Line 23 sets up the required **for** loop using the **@ARGV** array as the list of elements to check. Provided the specified member exists within the reverse hash, we print out the list on line 27.

```perl
29          else
30          {
31              print "$_ isn't a member of anything\n";
32          }
33      }
34  }
35
```

If the specified entry does not exist, then we print an error on line 31. There is no point in quitting the script at this point, as the user may genuinely not be a member of any aliases in the file. This is the end of this function.

```
36  sub expand_aliases
37  {
38      local *alias = shift;
39      for $_ (@ARGV)
40      {
41          my @expand=expandalias(\%alias,$_);
42          if ($expand[-1])
43          {
44              print "$_ expands to @expand\n";
45          }
```

The **expand_aliases** function expands individual aliases from the command line, reporting the expansions back to the user. Line 38 extracts the **%alias** hash, which will have been passed as a reference by assigning the alias to a local typeglob. Line 39 then starts the loop to work through the aliases specified on the command line. Line 41 calls the **expandalias** function, which expands a single specified alias, returning an array. Line 42 checks that there is a value in the last element of the array, and then line 44 reports the list of expanded aliases.

```
46          else
47          {
48              print "$_ not found in alias DB\n";
49          }
50      }
51  }
52
```

Line 48 reports an error if the alias specified on the command line cannot be found in the alias database. Again, exiting at this point by using **die** instead of **print** is unnecessary: the fact that the alias does not exist may be the error the user is looking for.

```
53  sub report_bad_aliases
54  {
55      local *alias = shift;
56      my %erroralias;
```

The **report_bad_aliases** function parses the entire alias file, expanding and resolving all aliases, and then checks each element of the aliases to ensure the alias is valid. We extract the alias hash on line 55, and we set up a new hash to contain the error messages on line 56.

```
57    for my $aliasname (keys %alias)
58    {
59        my @members = expandalias(\%alias,$aliasname);
```

Line 57 uses a **for** loop to work through the entire list of keys of the main **%alias** hash. We are checking the whole file, so there is no point in using specific aliases from the command line. Line 59 uses the **expandalias** function to resolve all of the elements of the current alias. The return value of the function is the expanded array of alias members.

```
60        for my $member (@members)
61        {
```

Line 60 then starts the loop to work through the list of expanded alias members.

```
62            if ($member)
63            {
64                unless (($member =~ /.*@.*/) ||
65                        ($member =~ /^\/.*/) ||
66                        ($member =~ /["!|]/))
67                {
68                    $erroralias{$aliasname} .=
69                        "$member " unless getpwnam(lc($member));
70                }
71            }
72        }
73    }
```

If the current member of the alias member list is defined, we check the value of the aliases in lines 64 to 66. Line 64 checks for a "user@host" e-mail address. Line 65 checks for a file specification in the alias member, and line 66 checks for a program specification in the alias. In all three cases they can be safely ignored, as they are valid aliases. Line 69 checks whether the alias is a user from the local /etc/passwd file. The **getpwnam** function returns false if the member cannot be found. Since users on a Unix should have lowercase user names we encapsulate the **$member** variable in a call to the **lc** function which will return a lowercase version of the variable.

The result of all the tests is an error message, based on the key of the alias name, with the error being placed in the corresponding hash value.

```
74    if (keys %erroralias)
75    {
76        for my $aliasname (keys %erroralias)
77        {
78            print("Alias $aliasname has missing members:",
79                $erroralias{$aliasname},"\n");
80        }
81    }
```

Line 74 checks for errors in the **%erroralias** hash. If there are entries, then we need to print out the errors, which is the purpose of the **for** loop on lines 76 to 80. The result will be a list of errors for the corresponding list of faulty aliases.

```
82      else
83      {
84          print "No problems found";
85      }
86  }
87
```

If there are no entries in the **%erroralias** hash, then we report a success message on line 84.

```
88  sub readaliases
89  {
90      my $file = shift;
91      my (%alias,$aliasname,$members);
92      open(D,"<$file") || die "Cannot open $file, $!";
```

The **readaliases** file imports the **alias** file into a hash, returning the hash. Line 90 extracts the filename from the function arguments, and line 91 sets up the variables, including the hash, that we need for this function.

Line 92 attempts to open the alias file, **die-**ing if the operation fails: if we cannot open the alias file, there is no point in continuing.

```
93      while (<D>)
94      {
95          next if /^#/;
96          chomp;
97          ($aliasname,$members) = split /:\s+/;
98          $alias{(lc($aliasname))} = lc($members);
99      }
```

Lines 93 to 99 work through the file, first ignoring any comments (line 95) and stripping any end-of-line characters off the end (line 96). We then assign the **$aliasname** and **$members** scalars to the values from the alias file, which are separated by a colon and multiple spaces. Line 98 creates the entries in the hash; note that in both cases we convert the strings to lowercase to ensure that tests of other operations work without us having to check the case of an element. By converting everything to lowercase, we ensure that everything is at the same level and the same common denominator; it does not affect the operation of the script, since aliases are not case sensitive anyway.

```
100     close(D) || return 0;;
101     return(%alias);
102 }
103
```

Once the file has been imported, we close it on line 100, and then we return the local hash to the caller. Note that we return zero to the caller if the close fails; this is less serious than **die**-ing and will cause the script to fail anyway.

```
104  sub expandalias
105  {
106      *alias = shift;
107      my $expand = shift;
108      my @expanded;
109      my @toexpand = split /\s*,\s*/,$expand;
110
111      return(0) unless $alias{$expand};
112
```

The process of expanding an alias is quite simple, although difficult to envision at first. Remember that an alias can contain a list of elements, and each element can itself be an alias, which, in turn, can be made up of further aliases with further expansions. We therefore need to recursively process the alias member list, and all the aliases to which it refers, until the element can no longer be expanded.

The alias hash is extracted into a typeglob on line 106, and the alias to be expanded is extracted on line 107. The **@expanded** array contains the list of aliases that have been completely expanded. The **@toexpand** array is defined on line 109, and it is initialized to contain the list of aliases from the function arguments, split by commas and optional multiple white space on either side of the comma. The array will also be used during the expansion process to hold the list of further aliases to be expanded.

The final part of initialization is to check that the alias to be expanded actually exists: we return zero (false) if it doesn't on line 111.

```
113      OUTEXPAND:
114      {
115          while ($#toexpand >= 0)
116          {
117              my $toexpand = pop @toexpand;
```

We name the block between lines 114 and 140 **OUTEXPAND**. We will see how it is used later. Line 115 sets up a loop, provided the list of aliases to be expanded contains more than one entry. Line 117 then pops the last value off of the **@toexpand** array and into a corresponding scalar variable.

```
118              EXPAND:
119              {
120                  if (defined($alias{$toexpand}))
121                  {
```

We name the next block of lines 119 to 129 **EXPAND**. On line 120, if the current alias to be expanded is defined within the hash, we go on to check if the alias contained within the alias to be expanded is also defined.

```
122                     if (defined($alias{$alias{$toexpand}}))
123                     {
124                         $toexpand = $alias{$alias{$toexpand}};
125                         redo EXPAND;
126                     }
```

Line 122 checks if the value of the aliases to be expanded is defined within the list of aliases; this accounts for aliases that specify only one member. If they specify only one member, then the alias (and its expansion) will be found in the alias hash. The expansion for this alias is therefore the value of the alias to be expanded. So we set the value to the **$toexpand** variable in line 124. Since the new alias may also be a reference to another alias or list of aliases, we must also expand the new alias to be expanded. The **redo** function moves the program execution to the specified block, which in this case is **EXPAND**, the name of the current block.

To describe this better, let's look at an alias file fragment:

```
MC_Team: martinb, johnd
mc-team: mc_team
mc.team: mc-team
```

In this fragment, expanding **mc.team** would expand the single element **mc-team**, but that alias also expands to a single element, the **MC_Team** alias. This would cause the test on line 122 to return true, signifying that the alias needed further expansion. We therefore expand the original alias to the expanded value of a new alias, which requires reparsing by the **EXPAND** code block.

```
127                     $toexpand = $alias{$toexpand};
128                 }
129             }
```

If the value of the alias cannot be found in the hash, that means the value is either the destination or it is a further list of aliases. In this case, we set the **$toexpand** variable to equal the alias list, corresponding to the alias value. For example, using our previous example, if we were expanding **MC_Team**, then the value of **MC_Team** would not be found in the alias hash because it is a list of new aliases.

```
130             if ($toexpand =~ /,/)
131             {
132                 push @toexpand,split(/\s*,\s*/,$toexpand);
133                 redo OUTEXPAND;
134             }
```

If the value of **$toexpand** contains commas (which we check for in line 130), then the value is an alias list, which means we must add the list of aliases to the **@toexpand** array (line 132). Then we need to start back at the beginning of the expansion process, which was defined by the **OUTEXPAND** block name. This block takes the next value of the list of aliases to be expanded and repeats the process just executed.

```
135                    else
136                    {
137                        push @expanded, $toexpand;
138                    }
```

If the value of the expanded alias was not a list, and was not itself a reference to a single further alias, then it's safe to assume that it can no longer be expanded. What we need to do, on line 137, is to add the fully expanded alias to the list of expanded aliases held in the **@expanded** array.

```
139            }
140        }
141        my %dedupe;
142        for (@expanded)
143        {
144            $dedupe{$_} = 1;
145        }
146        return (keys %dedupe);
147    }
148
```

Line 140 is the end of the outer expansion block. Once we exit from that block, the original alias must have been completely expanded, but the list of expanded aliases may contain duplicate values since different aliases could have specified the same user twice. The easiest way to de-duplicate is to use a hash to store the list of alias members. Since a hash cannot contain duplicate keys, the resulting hash keys will contain a de-duplicated list of alias members. The final list of alias members is returned as an array on line 146 by returning the list of keys from the **%dedupe** hash.

```
149 sub memberalias
150 {
151     *alias = shift;
152     my %mteams;
153
```

The **memberalias** function reverses the original **%alias** hash so that the relationship of keys containing alias names, with the values containing the list of members instead returns a new hash that contains a list of members and the aliases to which they belong. This requires a very simple nested loop to work first through the list of aliases and then the list of members.

```
154     for my $aliasname (keys %alias)
155     {
```

Line 154 sets the loop for the aliases in the main hash.

```
156         for my $member (split /,/,$alias{$aliasname})
157         {
158             $mteams{$member} .= "$aliasname ";
159         }
```

Line 156 then sets the loop to work through the alias members (separated by commas), creating a new hash in line 158 and appending the current alias name to the hash key of the current member name.

```
160     }
161     return %mteams;
162 }
```

Once the hash has been reversed into the new hash, we can return the hash on line 161.

As I said at the start of the annotations, the most complicated part of the process is the recursion involved in expanding a single alias from a list of members through to expanding the individual members of the original alias, and all the aliases they may refer to. Once you understand the process involved, you can achieve the expanded list, on which you can perform any check or report.

We'll try the script on the fairly simple alias file that follows (and is included on the CD as **alias.txt**):

```
Postmaster: root
MAILER-DAEMON: postmaster
nobody: /dev/null
staff: mcslp
mc: martinb
mcslp: martinb, slp
martin_brown: martinb
root: martinb
```

Trying the "report" option, we get this result:

```
$ chkalias.pl -r -f alias.txt
Alias staff has missing members:slp
Alias mcslp has missing members:slp
```

The errors have been reported because the user slp does not exist within the /etc/passwd file. Trying to expand a specific alias returns the final expansion:

```
$ chkalias.pl -f alias.txt -e postmaster
postmaster expands to martinb
```

You can verify this if you follow the original file. It's best if you try it on a much larger alias file; you can verify the results by checking the alias database with the sendmail trick I outlined at the start of the chapter.

PROGRAMMER'S NOTE *In spite of the advantages of processing the text file, we would still have had to parse the aliases within the final DBM file generated by sendmail because the DBM file holds only the original alias definitions, not expanded versions.*

Extracting the Lastlog

lastlog.pl

Each time a user logs in, either directly on the machine or remotely via telnet or rlogin, the information is recorded in the *lastlog*. To make the information easy to retrieve, it is located within the file using a reference based on the byte location within the file. To calculate the location of a specific log entry for a user, you multiply the user's numerical ID by the size of each record. Like our previous example, the record format is specified by a standard C structure, which we can extract with a standard **pack** string. This script works through the entire lastlog, printing out the date, time, and device used the last time each user logged in.

This script is a slightly modified version of the CPAN version, originally contributed by Mike Stok.

```
1   #!/usr/local/bin/perl5 -w
2
3   use strict;
4   require 'ctime.pl';
5
6   my $utTemplate = 'l A8 A16';
7   my $utSize = length(pack($utTemplate));
8   my $utBuffer = ' ' x $utSize;
9
10  my $uid = 0;
11  open (LASTLOG, '</var/adm/lastlog')
12      or die "can't open lastlog ($!)\n";
13  while (sysread (LASTLOG, $utBuffer, $utSize) == $utSize)
14  {
15      my ($time, $line, $host) = unpack ($utTemplate, $utBuffer);
16      if ($time != 0)
17      {
```

```
18        my $user = (getpwuid ($uid))[0];
19        print "$user on $line ";
20        print $host eq '' ? "(local)" : "from $host";
21        print " at ", &ctime ($time);
22      }
23      $uid++;
24    }
25  close (LASTLOG) or die "can't close lastlog ($!)\n";
```

ANNOTATIONS

The **lastlog.pl** script first creates the **pack** string to extract the information, then uses a simple **while** loop to report on the information. There are no tricks here—it's just a very simple demonstration of how to access a system file.

```
1   #!/usr/local/bin/perl5 -w
2
3   use strict;
4   require 'ctime.pl';
5
```

Both warnings and strict usage have been switched on, and we incorporate the **ctime.pl** script, which is an interface to the C **ctime** function. With Perl 5, this is largely redundant, since it outputs the date and time in a format identical to the scalar version of **localtime**.

```
6   my $utTemplate = 'l A8 A16';
7   my $utSize = length(pack($utTemplate));
8   my $utBuffer = ' ' x $utSize;
9
```

The format for the lastlog structure is the date/time of logout (calculated as the number of seconds from the epoch), the user's login name, and the device or terminal that they logged out from. This information is specified as a **pack** string in line 6, before calculating the **pack** string size in line 7. Line 8 fills the **$utBuffer**, which stores each record as it is extracted from the file. We use a method here that places **$utSize** spaces in the buffer; it may make it clearer if you read it as "**$utBuffer** equals **$utSize** spaces."

```
10  my $uid = 0;
11  open (LASTLOG, '</var/adm/lastlog')
12      or die "can't open lastlog ($!)\n";
```

The **$uid** variable stores the user's ID number—remember that the information for a single user is located at the value of the user's ID multiplied by the record size. Therefore, to work out the current ID when working through the entire file, we need only count the number of records that have been read. The file will start with the entry for root, which as we know has an ID of zero. Lines 11 and 12 then open the lastlog. The location, and indeed the **pack** string we are using here, is compatible with SunOS 4.x and Solaris 2.x; other Unix flavors may have different settings, and some may not even support a lastlog of any sort.

```perl
13   while (sysread (LASTLOG, $utBuffer, $utSize) == $utSize)
14   {
15       my ($time, $line, $host) = unpack ($utTemplate, $utBuffer);
```

Line 13 sets up the loop to work through the file handle that refers to the lastlog file. Note that we check that the return value from the **sysread** function (which returns the actual number of bytes read) matches the size of the lastlog structure. Line 15 then unpacks the values from the current record into some temporary variables.

```perl
16       if ($time != 0)
17       {
18           my $user = (getpwuid ($uid))[0];
19           print "$user on $line ";
20           print $host eq '' ? "(local)" : "from $host";
21           print " at ", &ctime ($time);
22       }
```

If the **time** value does not equal zero, we print out the results. Any entries that have never been made, or that do no exist because there is no matching user ID, will have a zero **time** element. Line 18 uses the **getpwuid** function to obtain the name matching the current user ID. The function accesses the /etc/passwd file to work out this information. Lines 19 to 20 then print out the information. Line 20 incorporates a quick test to print out either that the login was "local" to the machine or that it was from a remote machine. Line 21 prints out the formatted time. Note that we could have used **localtime**, replacing line 21 with

```perl
print " at ", scalar localtime($time), "\n";
```

Note that we have to append a new-line character to the value—the **ctime** function includes this information.

```perl
23       $uid++;
24   }
25   close (LASTLOG) or die "can't close lastlog ($!)\n";
```

Line 23 then increments the user ID counter since we have finished processing a record, before the loop ends on line 24. Then we close the file handle, ensuring that we report an error if the close operation failed.

Running the script on my SPARC box running Solaris 2.4 reports

```
root on console (local) at Mon Oct  5 11:39:09 GB 1998
martinb on pts/2 from a at Sun Oct 25  9:40:10 GB 1998
```

wtmp.pl

Reporting from wtmp

In addition to recording an entry in the lastlog file, which records only the last time a user logged in, every login is also recorded in the *wtmp* file. Other system events are also recorded within the wtmp file, including changes to the current run (*init*) level, and reboots and shutdowns. This file stores the login information that is held within a C structure straight out to a file as a binary string of information. Extracting the information from the wtmp file is straightforward, provided you know the format of the wtmp structure. If you examine the wtmp manual page, you should see the C structure definition, and from that we can compose a string to pass to **unpack** so we can extract the information. You can see here the structure of a Solaris 2.4 wtmp file:

```
struct utmp
{
    char   ut_user[8];
    char   ut_id[4];
    char   ut_line[12];
    short  ut_pid;
    short  ut_type;
    struct exit_status
    {
        short e_termination;
        short e_exit;
    } ut_exit;
    time_t ut_time;
};
```

Even if you don't know how to program in C, you should be able to extract the layout and therefore the string required for **unpack** to be able to extract the information from the wtmp file. A wtmp file is composed of the user who logged in, the /etc/inittab ID, and the real or pseudo device on which the user logged in, the ID of the process created to service the user and the wtmp entry type. There is then a substructure that defines the termination status and the exit code of the process started by the user when they logged in. Finally, the time the entry was recorded is stored as a long number. The value specifies the number of seconds that have elapsed since the epoch, so it will be easy to print an English version using the **localtime** function.

The script here very simply reads in the file and outputs a formatted, readable version to the standard output to describe the basic principles.

```
1   #!/usr/local/bin/perl5 -w
2
3   use strict;
4
5   my $packstring = "a8a4a12ssssl";
6   my $reclength = length(pack($packstring));
7   my @ut_types = qw(EMPTY RUN_LVL BOOT_TIME OLD_TIME
8                     NEW_TIME INIT_PROCESS LOGIN_PROCESS
9                     USER_PROCESS DEAD_PROCESS ACCOUNTING);
10
11  open(D,"</var/adm/wtmp") or die "Couldn't open wtmp, $!";
12  my $rec;
13
14  while(sysread(D,$rec,$reclength))
15  {
16      my ($user,$userid,$line,$pid,$type,$eterm,$eexit,$time)
17          = unpack($packstring,$rec);
18      print("$user, $userid, $line, $pid, $ut_types[$type], ",
19            "$eterm, $eexit, ", scalar localtime($time),"\n");
20  }
21  close(D) or die "Couldn't close file properly, $!";
```

ANNOTATIONS

Once we have initialized some core variables, we open the wtmp file, read in a record (or the number of bytes that make up a single structure within the file), **unpack** it, and then print the result.

```
1   #!/usr/local/bin/perl5 -w
2
3   use strict;
4
```

I've switched on warnings and defined the **strict** pragma. Although specifying strict handling will make little difference on this script, it is a very good habit to permanently use these two options—it certainly instills additional vigilance when creating code and often highlights errors or other things you have overlooked that may cause problems.

```
5   my $packstring = "a8a4a12ssssl";
```

Line 5 defines the string that will be used to **unpack** the structure data from the file. If you compare this **pack** string against the structure we saw at the start of this script, you should see the correlation between the string and the structure. To summarize the pack format, we have three strings: one of 8, one of 4, and one of 12 characters. Four short numbers and one long number follow the strings. The difference between a short and a long number is that a "short" is composed of 16 bits, whereas a "long" is 32 bits.

```
6    my $reclength = length(pack($packstring));
```

We extract the length of the **pack** string, and therefore the size in bytes of the structure as it will be stored within the wtmp file.

```
7    my @ut_types = qw(EMPTY RUN_LVL BOOT_TIME OLD_TIME
8                      NEW_TIME INIT_PROCESS LOGIN_PROCESS
9                      USER_PROCESS DEAD_PROCESS ACCOUNTING);
10
```

Lines 7 to 9 define the wtmp entry types in an array. Within the Unix header file used to define the wtmp structure, there are also a number of "defines" that allow you to specify a name instead of the number when recording an entry. The **#define** list follows:

```
#define   EMPTY          0
#define   RUN_LVL        1
#define   BOOT_TIME      2
#define   OLD_TIME       3
#define   NEW_TIME       4
#define   INIT_PROCESS   5
#define   LOGIN_PROCESS  6
#define   USER_PROCESS   7
#define   DEAD_PROCESS   8
#define   ACCOUNTING     9
```

For the report, we want to convert the numbers back into strings, which we can easily do by creating an array in the same order as the numbers above. Perl automatically assigns the values quoted by the **qw** function to sequential numbers within the **@ut_types** array. When we want to print the string, we just use the type as the reference to the **@ut_types** array.

```
11   open(D,"</var/adm/wtmp") or die "Couldn't open wtmp, $!";
12   my $rec;
13
```

Line 11 opens the default wtmp file for Sun Solaris 2.4. You may want to modify this for your own system. Line 12 defines the scalar variable that stores the structure data being imported from the file and then **unpacked**.

```
14   while(sysread(D,$rec,$reclength))
15   {
16       my ($user,$userid,$line,$pid,$type,$eterm,$eexit,$time)
17           = unpack($packstring,$rec);
18       print("$user, $userid, $line, $pid, $ut_types[$type], ",
19              "$eterm, $eexit, ", scalar localtime($time),"\n");
20   }
21   close(D) or die "Couldn't close file properly, $!";
```

Lines 14 to 20 do the actual extraction from the file. In line 14, we read in **$reclength** bytes from the open file handle. The return value from **sysread** is the actual number of bytes read from the file; we don't bother to check the specific value since we have made the assumption that the file will contain complete records all the way through the file. Once the loop reaches the end, the return value will be zero, since there will be no further information to read, and the loop will exit.

Lines 16 and 17 **unpack** the structure data we have just read from the file before we print it out on lines 18 and 19. You should be able to spot the point where the **@ut_types** array is referenced, and also that the time is printed as a time string using the **localtime** function. We ensure that a formatted time is printed, rather than an array of the individual elements, by using the **scalar** prefix to the **localtime** function.

If you run this script, you should get a result similar to this output:

```
martinb, co, console, 211, USER_PROCESS, 0, 0, Fri Jun 12 19:25:15 1998
martinb, co, console, 211, DEAD_PROCESS, 0, 0, Fri Jun 12 19:26:42 1998
ttymon, co, console, 221, INIT_PROCESS, 0, 0, Fri Jun 12 19:26:42 1998
LOGIN, co, console, 221, LOGIN_PROCESS, 0, 0, Fri Jun 12 19:26:42 1998
.telnet, tn10, /dev/pts/0, 225, LOGIN_PROCESS, 0, 0, Fri Jun 12 19:38:42 1998
martinb, tn10, pts/0, 225, USER_PROCESS, 0, 0, Fri Jun 12 19:38:55 1998
sac, sc, , 206, DEAD_PROCESS, 15, 0, Fri Jun 12 21:21:51 1998
LOGIN, co, console, 221, DEAD_PROCESS, 15, 0, Fri Jun 12 21:21:51 1998
, , run-level 0, 0, RUN_LVL, 48, 51, Fri Jun 12 21:21:51 1998
rc0, s0, , 577, INIT_PROCESS, 0, 0, Fri Jun 12 21:21:51 1998
rc0, s0, , 577, DEAD_PROCESS, 0, 0, Fri Jun 12 21:22:15 1998
uadmin, fw, , 690, INIT_PROCESS, 0, 0, Fri Jun 12 21:22:15 1998
, , system boot, 0, BOOT_TIME, 0, 0, Sat Jun 13 11:24:53 1998
, , run-level 3, 0, RUN_LVL, 51, 83, Sat Jun 13 11:24:53 1998
rc2, s2, , 41, INIT_PROCESS, 0, 0, Sat Jun 13 11:24:53 1998
rc2, s2, , 41, DEAD_PROCESS, 0, 0, Sat Jun 13 14:23:30 1998
rc3, s3, , 177, INIT_PROCESS, 0, 0, Sat Jun 13 14:23:30 1998
rc3, s3, , 177, DEAD_PROCESS, 0, 0, Sat Jun 13 14:23:35 1998
```

This script shows a very simple dump of the data, although it would be possible to use this information once you have extracted it to report on when the system was rebooted or to report on the dates and times different users had logged in.

Although very basic, the script demonstrates the principles behind extracting information from system files whose format is governed by C structures. Luckily, the data was in a straightforward format, and therefore easy to extract using the built-in features of Perl. For more complex structures, it's necessary to write "glue" routines that interface Perl structures and the underlying C structures. This method is used by the Perl distribution to include the data structures returned by the C function, such as **getpwuid** and even the network socket interface.

If you want to develop extensions to the Perl system that rely on external C code, then you should take a closer look at the Perl XS system. XS is short for *eXtension Subroutines*. It is a language that creates an extension interface between Perl and a C library. The XS interface enables you to create an XSUB function, which is actually just a C function. An XS compiler then adds the wrapper code to allow the code to map and access Perl variables. Typemaps are then employed to allow conversion between the Perl variables and types and the underlying C variables and types.

Using the XS system is relatively straightforward, provided you know how to program in C, and it is flexible enough to handle interfaces and data types to any underlying C code. The XS system is, in fact, used for many of the core interfaces to the underlying OS by the base Perl distribution; examine the ext directory for more information and some examples of the XS system in action.

For more details on the XS system, you should view the perlxs manual page. A tutorial, in the perlxstut manual page, is also available. For a more general discussion on interfacing with Perl, and the Perl internal structures that you need to be aware of in order to make more sense of the process, I can heartily recommend *Advanced Perl Programming* by Sriram Srinivasan (see Appendix B for more information).

If you would rather avoid the vagaries of the XS system in favor of just getting an interface working, you may want to take a look at Dave Beazley's SWIG system. It still generates XS glue code, but it requires fewer steps and less understanding of the underlying Perl structures. See the Web site at http://www.cs.utah.edu/~beazley/SWIG for more information.

Analyzing Mail Traffic via syslog

mlsyslog.pl

Understanding the amount of e-mail traffic on your system can be an important part of optimizing the system and introducing load balancing and distribution into your network. There is a built-in system with sendmail that records e-mail statistics for later use; however, the information it provides really isn't very useful. It consists of a summary of the number and size of messages sent, summarized by the sendmail rule that sent them. In addition, it summarizes the information into a single file that has to be manually reset periodically to enable you to extract historical information. To top it all, the information is not stored in a format that can be researched and analyzed separately: the data is stored within C structures in summary form in a single file, but the source of the information is not recorded within the same file. You can see some sample output from the sendmail statistics file:

```
Statistics from Mon Feb  5 11:30:13 1996
 M msgsfr bytes_from  msgsto    bytes_to
 0   4868    219097K   12655      61823K
 1      0        0K     333        425K
 2  13272     25019K    7399     178190K
 6      0        0K       1         1K
```

Some good news, however, is that the source information is recorded in the Unix *syslog*, the same system that records most system events according to the rules and configuration of the syslog daemon. The format of the syslog log file is different, depending on the program that has made an entry in the log, which means we must first process the individual lines so we can identify their contents before going on and identifying the individual elements of the sendmail entries.

As with the previous two examples, we'll look at the processes involved in reporting and extracting the information from the file, and then reporting the basic details. We'll also look at ways in which we can expand and improve upon the information that is reported.

```perl
1   #!/usr/local/bin/perl5 -w
2   use strict;
3
4   die "Usage: $0 syslogfile..." unless (@ARGV);
5
6   for my $file (@ARGV)
7   {
8       my (%qids,$nmsgs,$fullsize,$fullnrcpts);
9       open(D,"<$file") or die "Couldn't open $file: $!";
10      while(<D>)
11      {
12          my ($prog, $qid, @info) = (split)[4..10];
13          next if ($prog !~ /^sendmail/);
14          if ($info[0] =~ /^from=/)
15          {
16              my ($size, $nrcpts)
17                  = (split(/,/,join(' ',@info)))[1,4];
18              if (defined($qids{$qid}))
19              {
20                  next;
21              }
22              else
23              {
24                  $qids{$qid} = 1;
```

```
25              $nmsgs++;
26              $size = (split(/=/,$size))[1];
27              $fullsize += $size
28                  if (defined($size));
29              $nrcpts = (split(/=/,$nrcpts))[1];
30              $fullnrcpts += $nrcpts
31                  if (defined($nrcpts));
32          }
33      }
34  }
35  close(D) or die "Couldn't close $file: $!";
36  print("$file: $nmsgs total size: $fullsize ",
37      "recipients: $fullnrcpts\n");
38  if ($nmsgs > 0 )
39  {
40      print("        Average Message Size: ",
41          int(($fullsize/$nmsgs))," bytes\n");
42  }
43  }
```

ANNOTATIONS

This script allows you to specify multiple syslog files on the command line and have the summary results for each file reported. I wrote it this way to allow me to batch the reporting of the log files. Most Unix systems employ a script that regularly (via **cron**) "rotates" the log files, deleting the old ones and renaming the new ones.

An extract from the log file of a Solaris 2.5 machine looks like this:

```
Aug  2 11:20:27 twinspark sendmail[413]: AA00413: from=martinb,
size=42, class=0, pri=0, nrcpts=1, proto=SMTP, received from local
Aug  2 11:20:28 twinspark sendmail[415]: AA00413: to=martinb,
delay=00:00:01, stat=Sent
Aug  2 14:42:48 twinspark sendmail[556]: AA00556:
message-id=<9808021342.AA00556@whoever.com>
Aug  2 14:42:48 twinspark sendmail[556]: AA00556: from=martinb,
size=48, class=0, pri=0, nrcpts=1, proto=SMTP, received from local
Aug  2 14:42:48 twinspark sendmail[558]: AA00556: to=martinb@atuin,
delay=00:00:00, stat=Deferred: Connection refused by atuin
Aug  2 14:43:15 twinspark sendmail[562]: AA00562:
message-id=<9808021343.AA00562@whoever.com>
Aug  2 14:43:15 twinspark sendmail[562]: AA00562: from=martinb,
size=45, class=0, pri=0, nrcpts=2, proto=SMTP, received from local
Aug  2 14:43:16 twinspark sendmail[564]: AA00562: to=martinb,
delay=00:00:01, stat=Sent
```

```
Aug   2 14:43:31 twinspark sendmail[570]: AA00570: to=jhonny,
delay=00:00:00, stat=User unknown
Aug   2 14:43:31 twinspark sendmail[570]: AA00570:
message-id=<9808021343.AA00570@whoever.com>
```

As you can see, for each individual message in the sendmail queue there are two lines. One specifies the details of who the message is from, its size and class, and where it was received from. The other specifies who the message was sent to, how long it was delayed (between receiving it for processing and it finally being accepted at its destination), and its status. For this script, we'll emulate the sendmail statistics output—I've never had to be aware of anything more than the number of message sent and their size. Anything more than this information is overkill, even for an ISP. Active monitoring of the queue often proves much more valuable, and we have already looked at that functionality in Chapter 6 with the **mailq.pl** script.

```
1    #!/usr/local/bin/perl5 -w
2    use strict;
3
4    die "Usage: $0 syslogfile..." unless (@ARGV);
5
```

Line 4 prints out an error if there are no syslog files specified on the command line. Note that I've used **$0** as the name of the program; should the script name change, it will still report the name of the script called.

```
6    for my $file (@ARGV)
7    {
8        my (%qids,$nmsgs,$fullsize,$fullnrcpts);
9        open(D,"<$file") or die "Couldn't open $file: $!";
```

Line 6 sets up a **for** loop to work through the argument list, making the assumption that each argument is the name of a syslog file. Line 8 defines the variables that store information about the statistics of the syslog file. By specifying them here, within the **for** loop, we ensure that the details will be re-initialized for each **syslog** file that we open.

```
10       while(<D>)
11       {
12           my ($prog, $qid, @info) = (split)[4..10];
13           next if ($prog !~ /^sendmail/);
```

Line 10 sets up the **while** loop to work through the lines of the file. Line 12 extracts fields 4 to 10 from the syslog file. Remember that the format of the file is the date, machine, and program making the log entry, followed by program-specific fields. By extracting the line's main field body, we can process the individual elements separately.

Line 13 skips the syslog entry if the name of the program that made the entry is not sendmail.

```
14          if ($info[0] =~ /^from=/)
15          {
16              my ($size, $nrcpts)
17                  = (split(/,/,join(' ',@info)))[1,4];
```

If we look at a sendmail entry from the syslog again, you can see that the second field contains the specification of whether the remainder of the detail is about the sender or the recipient:

```
Aug  2 14:43:15 twinspark sendmail[562]: AA00562: from=martinb,
size=45, class=0, pri=0, nrcpts=1, proto=SMTP, received from local
```

Because we are interested only in the **from** line (field 2), to extract the message size, and the number of recipients (field 5) from the program fields, we do a test on line 14. If we are within a **from** line, then we extract the two pieces of information on lines 16 and 17. Note that at this point, the variables still contain the field names and the equal sign.

Note the trick we use on line 17. The data was originally split by spaces, but we now need to split it by commas, so we **join** the old data together again before re-splitting it to provide the information we want.

If we wanted to report on other information—for example, to provide a summary of who was sending the e-mail message—we could also extract that information at this point, before processing it in the following lines.

```
18          if (defined($qids{$qid}))
19          {
20              next;
21          }
```

If we have processed the queue entry before, then we skip to the next line. This prevents us from counting the same message multiple times if it has been "requeued" because the remote server cannot be reached.

```
22          else
23          {
24              $qids{$qid} = 1;
25              $nmsgs++;
26              $size = (split(/=/,$size))[1];
27              $fullsize += $size
28                  if (defined($size));
29              $nrcpts = (split(/=/,$nrcpts))[1];
30              $fullnrcpts += $nrcpts
31                  if (defined($nrcpts));
32          }
33      }
34  }
```

If we haven't processed the queue entry before, we make sure we record the queue ID in the hash on line 24. Line 25 increments the number of messages we have processed. Line 26 sets the new value of the **$size** variable to the value after the equal sign of the old **$size** variable, again using **split** to make the separation.

This process is repeated for the number of recipients field on line 29, and then lines 27 and 28 and 30 and 31 add the values to the summary variables specified at the beginning of the syslog file loop, provided, of course, the two values contain valid information.

```
35    close(D) or die "Couldn't close $file: $!";
36    print("$file: $nmsgs total size: $fullsize ",
37          "recipients: $fullnrcpts\n");
```

Line 25 closes the syslog file or reports an error if the operation fails. Lines 36 and 37 report the summary information totals.

```
38    if ($nmsgs > 0 )
39    {
40        print("      Average Message Size: ",
41            int(($fullsize/$nmsgs))," bytes\n");
42    }
43  }
```

As a better indication of the loading, lines 40 and 41 print out the average message size, provided we have found one or more messages when processing. We have to do this because dividing by zero is an error, and it would cause Perl to exit if we tried the operation.

Running the script on some sample log files gives a fairly good indication of the message processing and handling of the machine. The output here is taken from a Solaris 2.5 machine, and the logs go back, in order, from last week's log to eight weeks ago (the logs are autorotated by a **cron** job on a Saturday night).

```
$ mlsyslog.pl syslog.*
syslog.0: 952 total size: 24316148 recipients: 1122
      Average Message Size: 25542 bytes
syslog.1: 994 total size: 17487593 recipients: 1173
      Average Message Size: 17593 bytes
syslog.2: 868 total size: 20642377 recipients: 1163
      Average Message Size: 23781 bytes
syslog.3: 1023 total size: 59456070 recipients: 1397
      Average Message Size: 58119 bytes
syslog.4: 854 total size: 42602868 recipients: 1185
      Average Message Size: 49886 bytes
syslog.5: 825 total size: 22249840 recipients: 1189
      Average Message Size: 26969 bytes
```

```
syslog.6: 856 total size: 13976644 recipients: 1283
     Average Message Size: 16327 bytes
syslog.7: 698 total size: 20121554 recipients: 893
     Average Message Size: 28827 bytes
```

uxckpw.pl

Checking the Unix Password File

One of the lesser known, and therefore less used, programs supplied with most Unix systems is pwck, the /etc/passwd checker. It was designed to perform a consistency check on the password file to ensure that the number of fields, name format, and the program to use as the shell exist. However, like all of these programs, there is often a gap in the information they check. Most significantly for me, the pwck program fails to check the security aspects of the entries in the login file. Here's a sample report from the pwck program:

```
$ pwck

uucp:x:5:5:0000-uucp(0000):/usr/lib/uucp:
        Login directory not found

nuucp:x:9:9:0000-uucp(0000):/var/spool/uucppublic:/usr/lib/uucp/uucico
        Login directory not found
        Optional shell file not found

MC:x:1000:1001:MC Shared Files:/users/MC:/sbin/sh
        Logname contains no lower-case letters

SLP:x:1001:1001:SLP Shared Files:/users/SLPL:/sbin/sh
        Logname contains no lower-case letters
        Login directory not found
```

To give an example of the things the script overlooks, let's look at the login directory. It has identified in a number of cases that the login directory does not exist, but what about the login directories that do exist but are not actually owned by the user they are supposed to be owned by?

Here's another example: it verifies the existence of the user's shell (or more correctly the name and location of the program to use as the user's shell), which is a potential security risk because the file could have been modified to reference a setuid program, giving the user access to somebody else's files or even super-user access to the entire system. The **uxckpw.pl** script aims to plug some of these gaps by performing more extensive checks on the directory and the shell-specified /etc/passwd file.

```perl
1    #!/usr/local/bin/perl5 -w
2
3    use strict;
4
5    my %shells = loadshells();
6    while ( my ($user, $accountuid, $accountgid,
7                $home, $shell) = (getpwent())[0,1,2,3,7,8])
8    {
9        if (length($shell) == 0)
10       {
11           printf("Error: %-8s : User's shell " .
12                   "not specified\n",$user);
13       }
14       else
15       {
16           if(!defined($shells{$shell}))
17           {
18               printf("Error: %-8s : User's shell, $shell, " .
19                       "not in approved list\n",$user);
20           }
21           if (-e $shell)
22           {
23               my ($mode, $uid) = (stat ($shell))[2,4];
24               if (($mode & 04000) == 04000 && $uid == 0)
25               {
26                   printf("Error: %-8s : Shell $shell, " .
27                           "is setuid root.\n",$user);
28               }
29           }
30           else
31           {
32               printf("Error: %-8s : Shell $shell, " .
33                       "does not exist.\n",$user);
34           }
35       }
36
37       unless (-e $home)
38       {
39           printf("Error: %-8s : Home directory, " .
40                   "$home, does not exist.\n",$user);
41           next;
42       }
43
```

```
44      my ($mode, $uid, $gid) = (stat (_))[2,4,5];

45

46      if (! -d $home)

47      {

48          printf("Error: %-8s : Home directory, " .

49                  "$home, is not a dirctory.\n",$user);

50      }

51      elsif ($accountuid != $uid)

52      {

53          printf("Error: %-8s : Home directory is " .

54                  "actually owned by %s\n",$user,

55                  (getpwuid($uid))[0]);

56      }

57      elsif ($accountgid != $gid)

58      {

59          printf("Error: %-8s : Home directories group " .

60                  "is %s instead of %s\n",

61                  $user,(getgrgid($gid))[0],

62                  (getgrgid($accountgid))[0]);

63      }

64      elsif ( ($mode & 0022) != 0)

65      {

66          printf("Error: %-8s : Home directory is " .

67                  "insecure\n",$user);

68      }

69      elsif ( ($mode & 0700) != 0700)

70      {

71          printf("Error: %-8s : User doesn't have " .

72                  "access to their own directory!\n",$user);

73      }

74  }

75

76  sub loadshells

77  {

78      my %shells;

79      if (open(SHELLS,"</etc/shells"))

80      {

81          while(<SHELLS>)

82          {

83              chomp;

84              $shells{$_} = 1;

85          }
```

```
 86          close(SHELLS);
 87      }
 88      else
 89      {
 90          %shells = {'/bin/sh',
 91                      '/sbin/sh',
 92                      '/usr/bin/sh',
 93                      '/usr/sbin/sh',
 94                      '/bin/ksh',
 95                      '/sbin/ksh',
 96                      '/sbin/csh',
 97                      '/bin/csh',
 98                      '/usr/local/bin/bash'
 99                      };
100      }
101      return(%shells);
102 }
```

ANNOTATIONS

We use the **getpwent** function to retrieve the information from the /etc/passwd file. The first call reads the first entry from the password file, and progressive calls read the next entry from the file until eventually we reach the end of the file. Through each entry we check the shell information first, using a predefined hash to identify the list of valid shells. Then we check the owner, group, permissions, and location of the user's home directory.

```
1  #!/usr/local/bin/perl5 -w
2
3  use strict;
4
5  my %shells = loadshells();
```

The **loadshells** function, defined at the end of this script, imports the information from the /etc/shells file, or it uses a built-in list of valid shells. The return value is a hash to make identifying the shell quicker.

```
6  while ( my ($user, $accountuid, $accountgid,
7              $home, $shell) = (getpwent())[0,1,2,3,7,8])
8  {
```

Lines 6 and 7 start the **while** loop, which works through the file. We only need the user, ID, primary group ID, home directory, and the shell.

```
9        if (length($shell) == 0)
10       {
11           printf("Error: %-8s : User's shell " .
12                   "not specified\n",$user);
13       }
```

Line 9 checks that the shell has been specified in the file. If it hasn't, we report an error. Depending on the Unix flavor, a blank shell may allow the user to log in using the default shell, /bin/sh. This is a potential security risk—you should specify /bin/false or something equally useless as the user's shell if you want to prevent them from logging in. Note that I've used **printf** to format the user's login name to a set width. The first argument is the format to be used, so we must use concatenation—with a period—since the second argument to **printf** fills the **%-8s** field format specification.

```
14       else
15       {
16           if(!defined($shells{$shell}))
17           {
18               printf("Error: %-8s : User's shell, $shell, " .
19                       "not in approved list\n",$user);
20           }
```

If a shell has been specified, then we go on to check that it exists in line 16. Lines 18 and 19 print out an error if the shell specified is not contained within the hash we initialized at the start of the script.

```
21           if (-e $shell)
22           {
23               my ($mode, $uid) = (stat ($shell))[2,4];
24               if (($mode & 04000) == 04000 && $uid == 0)
25               {
26                   printf("Error: %-8s : Shell $shell, " .
27                           "is setuid root.\n",$user);
28               }
29           }
```

Regardless of whether the shell is in an approved list, we go on to check if the shell exists on line 21. If it exists, we then check the mode of the shell to ensure that the shell does not unwittingly give the user super-user access to the system. The information is extracted using **stat** to obtain the file's mode and user ID on line 23. Line 24 then makes a comparison.

Modes are stored as octal values; the setuid bit has a value of 04000. The mode of the shell is bitwise ANDed with the setuid value and then compared with the setuid value. If the shell has the setuid bit set, then the value of the bitwise expression will be 04000—and will hence return a true value from the entire test. We logical AND the result with a test that checks if the user ID is zero, that of root. If the result of line 24 is true, we report a warning on lines 26 and 27.

```
30          else
31          {
32              printf("Error: %-8s : Shell $shell, " .
33                      "does not exist.\n",$user);
34          }
35      }
36
```

Line 30 is the other half of the test for the existence of the file. If it does not exist, then lines 32 and 33 report the error. This ends the tests for the shell's location, mode, and existence in the list of valid shells.

```
37      unless (-e $home)
38      {
39          printf("Error: %-8s : Home directory, " .
40                  "$home, does not exist.\n",$user);
41          next;
42      }
43
```

Line 37 checks that the user's home directory exists. Because we've used **unless**, if the result of the test is false, then lines 39 to 41 will be executed. They report the missing directory before moving on to the next entry using the **next** function, which skips the remainder of the loop code. This is because the remainder of the tests pertains to the home directory that has been specified; if it doesn't exist, there is no point in continuing the checks.

```
44      my ($mode, $uid, $gid) = (stat (_))[2,4,5];
45
```

We extract the directory mode, owner, and group owner information using **stat** on line 44.

```
46      if (! -d $home)
47      {
48          printf("Error: %-8s : Home directory, " .
49                  "$home, is not a dirctory.\n",$user);
50      }
```

Lines 46 to 50 test and then print out an error if the location specified is not a directory.

```
51      elsif ($accountuid != $uid)
52      {
53          printf("Error: %-8s : Home directory is " .
54                  "actually owned by %s\n",$user,
55                  (getpwuid($uid))[0]);
56      }
```

Line 51 checks that the owner of the directory matches the current password entry, reporting an error on lines 53 to 55. We use the **getpwuid** function to obtain the password name of the user who actually owns the directory, which could provide clues as to why the owner is different.

```
57      elsif ($accountgid != $gid)
58      {
59          printf("Error: %-8s : Home directories group " .
60                  "is %s instead of %s\n",
61                  $user,(getgrgid($gid))[0],
62                  (getgrgid($accountgid))[0]);
63      }
```

Line 57 checks the directories group against the primary group of the current password entry. The two should match if we want a secure system. An error is reported on lines 59 to 62 if they don't match. Line 61 and 62 obtain the group name of the directory's group and the user's group ID, respectively, again acting as a useful mental reminder for the user.

```
64      elsif ( ($mode & 0022) != 0)
65      {
66          printf("Error: %-8s : Home directory is " .
67                  "insecure\n",$user);
68      }
```

Line 64 verifies that the mode of the directory does not include write privileges for the group owner and everybody else. Allowing other people to have write access to someone's group directory is potentially dangerous: anybody with directory ownership can delete and recreate files in the directory.

```
69      elsif ( ($mode & 0700) != 0700)
70      {
71          printf("Error: %-8s : User doesn't have " .
72                  "access to their own directory!\n",$user);
73      }
74  }
75
```

The last test checks that the user has complete access (read, write, and execute) to their own directory, reporting an error on lines 71 and 72 if this is not the case.

```perl
76    sub loadshells
77    {
78        my %shells;
79        if (open(SHELLS,"</etc/shells"))
80        {
81            while(<SHELLS>)
82            {
83                chomp;
84                $shells{$_} = 1;
85            }
86            close(SHELLS);
87        }
```

The **loadshells** function imports the list of valid shells from a file. In this instance, I've specified the /etc/shells file, which is traditionally used to specify valid shells for FTP access to the machine. You could replace the file with another if you want a different list than that allowed for FTP access. Line 78 sets up the hash that will store the list. Then line 79 attempts to open the shell list file. If the file could be opened, then lines 81 to 85 strip the end-of-line character from each line and create an entry in the hash, using the shell name as the key. Line 86 closes the file handle.

```perl
88        else
89        {
90            %shells = {'/bin/sh',
91                       '/sbin/sh',
92                       '/usr/bin/sh',
93                       '/usr/sbin/sh',
94                       '/bin/ksh',
95                       '/sbin/ksh',
96                       '/sbin/csh',
97                       '/bin/csh',
98                       '/usr/local/bin/bash'
99                       };
100       }
```

If the file containing the list of valid shells could not be opened, we create the list of shells manually. The list shown here includes the most common location for the standard Bourne, C, and Korn shells, along with the BASH shell from GNU. Note that I've just listed the entries here without specifying a corresponding value; Perl initiates the value to zero. This doesn't bother us, since we only check that the shell has been defined within the list; we are not concerned with its value.

```
101  return(%shells);
102  }
```

Line 101 returns the **%shells** hash to the caller.

Running the script on a fairly standard system will highlight a number of missing elements and possible security holes:

```
Error: root     : Home directories group is root instead of other
Error: daemon   : User's shell not specified
Error: daemon   : Home directory is actually owned by root
Error: bin      : User's shell not specified
Error: bin      : Home directory is actually owned by root
Error: sys      : User's shell not specified
Error: sys      : Home directory is actually owned by root
Error: adm      : User's shell not specified
Error: adm      : Home directory is actually owned by root
Error: lp       : User's shell not specified
Error: lp       : Home directory is insecure
Error: smtp     : User's shell not specified
Error: uucp     : User's shell not specified
Error: uucp     : Home directory, /usr/lib/uucp, does not exist.
Error: nuucp    : User's shell, /usr/lib/uucp/uucico, not in approved list
Error: nuucp    : Shell /usr/lib/uucp/uucico, does not exist.
Error: nuucp    : Home directory, /var/spool/uucppublic, does not exist.
Error: listen   : User's shell not specified
Error: listen   : Home directory is actually owned by root
Error: nobody   : User's shell not specified
Error: nobody   : Home directory is actually owned by root
Error: noaccess : User's shell not specified
Error: noaccess : Home directory is actually owned by root
Error: martinb  : Home directories group is other instead of
Error: MC       : Home directory is insecure
Error: SLP      : Home directory, /users/SLPL, does not exist.
```

Running the script on a secured system where all of the problems have been resolved shouldn't return any errors at all.

uxugrps.pl

Checking Unix Groups

Even for relatively small sites, tracking which users are members of which groups can be a headache. On my own systems, I tend to group people by the resources they need to access, which means that a single machine can have 30 or 40 groups, even though there may be fewer users than that who are members of those groups. Tracking which user is a member of which group usually involves running grep on the /etc/group file and checking the list—not the friendliest or most reliable method.

I wrote this script to fill a gap: I wanted to know, categorically, which groups a single user was a member of when I had to recreate the FTP directory structure for remote users to retrieve files from. Although I could have just duplicated the group structure, I wanted to take the opportunity to update the list. Some of the people had moved to different departments and needed to be updated, while others no longer needed access to the FTP system at all.

```perl
1   #!/usr/local/bin/perl5 -w
2
3   use strict;
4   my (@logins,%groups);
5
6   while (my ($group, $members) = (getgrent())[0,3])
7   {
8       for my $login (split / /,$members)
9       {
10          $groups{$login} .= "$group ";
11      }
12  }
13
14  if (@ARGV)
15  {
16      @logins = @ARGV;
17  }
18  else
19  {
20      @logins = keys %groups;
21  }
22
23  for my $key (@logins)
24  {
25      if (defined($groups{$key}))
26      {
27          printf("%-8s: %s\n", $key, $groups{$key});
28      }
29      else
30      {
31          printf("%-8s: No groups\n",$key);
32      }
33  }
```

ANNOTATIONS

Working on similar principles to the **chkalias.pl** script at the beginning of this chapter, the **uxugrps.pl** script imports the /etc/group file. Each member of each group has their own entry in a hash; their login is the key, and the value is a space-separated list of the groups to which they are a member.

Since the purpose of the script is to work out which groups a user is a member of, there is no quick way of selecting the groups: we must import the entire file for processing. Reporting the information back is then as simple as pulling the corresponding key/value pair out of the hash.

```
1   #!/usr/local/bin/perl5 -w
2
3   use strict;
4   my (@logins,%groups);
5
```

The **@logins** array holds the list of users that are to be reported on. Note that we cannot define the array with **my** inside the blocks on lines 14 to 21; this would localize the array to that block, making it unavailable by the time we reached line 22. The same is true of the **%groups** hash, which contains the list of groups (in the value) to which a user is a member of (the key).

```
6   while (my ($group, $members) = (getgrent())[0,3])
7   {
8       for my $login (split / /,$members)
9       {
10          $groups{$login} .= "$group ";
11      }
12  }
13
```

Line 6 extracts the group and list of members from the group file using the **getgrent** function. By using a C function, instead of reading the file directly, we automatically make this script cross-platform. Even though different Unix flavors implement the group file in different places, the script will work. The **getgrent** function returns the Perl equivalent of a **group** structure, which is actually composed of the group's name, password, group ID, and the list of members. Note that when the return value of the **getgrent** function fails, the loop will exit, because the entire statement defining the **$group** and **$members** variable will also fail.

Lines 8 to 11 then work through the member list. The list is separated by spaces and therefore requires the **split** function to extract the array for use with the **for** loop. Line 10 then reverses the association of group to members by adding the group name (and a space) to the hash entry for the current member name. For example, the group list

```
groupa: martinb johnd
groupb: martinb johnd
```

would generate a hash of the form

```
martinb: groupa groupb
johnd: groupa groupb
```

We now have the information we are looking for, and for all of the users specified as members of groups within the group file. All we need to do now is report on the users requested by the script user on the command line.

```
14  if (@ARGV)
15  {
16      @logins = @ARGV;
17  }
18  else
19  {
20      @logins = keys %groups;
21  }
22
```

Lines 14 to 21 decided which users to report on. If there are any names specified as arguments to the script, we make the **@logins** array match the command-line arguments array **@ARGV**. However, if none were specified, then we assume the user wants to report all users in the group file, so we assign the keys of the **%groups** hash to the **@logins** array instead.

```
23  for my $key (@logins)
24  {
25      if (defined($groups{$key}))
26      {
27          printf("%-8s: %s\n", $key, $groups{$key});
28      }
```

Line 23 now works through the list of requested logins on which to report. In line 25, we check if the specified login exists within the **%groups** hash. If it does, then we print out the list on line 27. Note that because we used a space to separate the group list, we can print the value of the hash key straight out without formatting it with a **join** and **split** combination. I've used **printf** here so that we can format the login name to appear within the first eight characters of the line, followed by a colon. This format just makes the reported list easier to understand.

```
29        else
30        {
31            printf("%-8s: No groups\n",$key);
32        }
33  }
```

If the specified user does exist, we report that they are not, as far as we can tell, a member of any groups on line 31.

To use this script, simply call it, specifying the users:

```
$ uxugrps.pl martinb
martinb : root other
```

If no users are specified, then the entire file is reported:

```
$ uxugrps.pl
MC       : shared
tty      : tty
adm      : sys adm tty lp
daemon   : bin adm daemon
root     : root bin sys adm uucp mail tty lp nuucp daemon
bin      : bin sys
nuucp    : nuucp
dummy    : root other
lp       : lp
martinb  : root other
uucp     : uucp
SLP      : shared
sys      : sys
```

ntpwck.pl

Verifying Windows NT Users

NT user information is stored differently than in Unix, and in fact NT stores different information than the Unix equivalents, as well. We therefore have to check for different problems when looking for errors, as well as obtaining the information differently in the first place.

Most significant of all is the fact that NT automatically checks and verifies much of the information that we've checked for in the Unix equivalent. It's impossible, for example, to have a user be a member of a group that does not exist, or for a group to have a member that does not exist. This is because the information is stored in proper databases and is controlled via a proper interface that performs the checks at the time the information is added. We are not relying on the administrator to update a text file correctly.

This script uses the Win32 libraries to access the user details and report on the discrepancies between the user's status and their abilities, along with warnings about expired passwords and incorrect password entries. Because of the nature of the Windows NT environment, this script can work with the user database stored on the domain controller for the domain of the current machine, or the domain controller and user database from a different domain.

```perl
1    #!perl
2
3    use Win32::AdminMisc;
4    use Win32::NetAdmin;
5    use Getopt::Long;
6
7    my ($machine,$domain,@users,%attribs);
8
9    GetOptions("d=s" => \$domain);
10
11   $machine = Win32::NodeName();
12
13   $domain =Win32::DomainName()
14       unless (defined($domain));
15
16   if (@ARGV)
17   {
18       @users = @ARGV;
19   }
20   else
21   {
22     Win32::NetAdmin::GetUsers(Win32::AdminMisc::GetDC($domain),
23                                 '',\@users);
24   }
25
26   if (@users)
27   {
28       print "Domain: $domain\n";
29   }
30
31   for $user (sort @users)
32   {
33       unless(Win32::AdminMisc::UserGetMiscAttributes($domain,
34                                                      $user,
35                                                      \%attribs))
36       {
37           opstatus();
38       }
```

```
39   else
40   {
41       if ($attribs{"USER_PASSWORD_EXPIRED"} == 1)
42       {
43           print "Error: $user : Password has expired\n";
44       }
45       if ($machine eq Win32::AdminMisc::GetDC($domain))
46       {
47           unless(-d $attribs{"USER_HOME_DIR"})
48           {
49               print("Error: $user : Home directory, ",
50                     $attribs{"USER_HOME_DIR"},
51                     " does not exist\n");
52           }
53       }
54       if ($user !~ /Administrator/)
55       {
56           if ($attribs{"USER_PRIV"} == 2)
57           {
58               print("Warning: $user : User has ",
59                     "administrator privileges\n");
60           }
61           else
62           {
63               if ($attribs{"USER_AUTH_FLAGS"} & 1)
64               {
65                   print("Warning: $user : User does not have ",
66                         "administrator privileges but does ",
67                         "have Print Admin privileges\n");
68               }
69               if ($attribs{"USER_AUTH_FLAGS"} & 4)
70               {
71                   print("Warning: $user : User does not have ",
72                         "administrator privileges but does ",
73                         "have Server Admin privileges\n");
74               }
75               if ($attribs{"USER_AUTH_FLAGS"} & 8)
76               {
77                   print("Warning: $user : User does not have ",
78                         "administrator privileges but does ",
79                         "have Accounts Admin privileges\n");
80               }
81           }
```

```
82              }
83              if ($attribs{"USER_PASSWORD_AGE"} > (31*24*60*60))
84              {
85                  print("Error: $user : Password is more than ",
86                      "one month (31 days) old\n");
87              }
88              if ($attribs{"USER_BAD_PW_COUNT"} > 0)
89              {
90                  print("Warning: $user : User has had ",
91                      $attribs{"USER_BAD_PW_COUNT"},
92                      " bad password attempts\n");
93              }
94          }
95      }
96
97  sub opstatus
98  {
99      my $error=Win32::GetLastError();
100     if ($error ne 0)
101     {
102         print("\nERROR: ", Win32::FormatMessage($error),"\n");
103     }
104     else
105     {
106         print "OK\n";
107     }
108 }
```

ANNOTATIONS

Aside from the method in which we obtain the information in the first place, the basic outline is similar to the **uxpwck.pl** script. There are a few important things to highlight in the script, including how errors from the Win32 system have to be obtained and reported on. We'll look at those individual elements as we work through the script.

```
1   #!perl
2
3   use Win32::AdminMisc;
4   use Win32::NetAdmin;
5   use Getopt::Long;
6
```

The **Win32::AdminMisc** module I have used here comes from Dave Roth, who has developed his own toolkit to augment the administration of Win32 (specifically NT) systems within the Win32 environment. See Appendix B for more information about how to obtain the **Win32::AdminMisc** module. The **Win32::NetAdmin** module provides access to the domain servers and the information sorted on them, including the user details.

```
7   my ($machine,$domain,@users,%attribs);
8
9   GetOptions("d=s" => \$domain);
10
```

The **$machine** scalar holds the name of the local machine—we'll need this when we check the user's directory. If the machine we are using matches the primary domain controller (PDC), then we check the location of the directory. The **$domain** scalar holds the name of the domain we are checking, which can be specified on the command line with the **-d** option; or it can be obtained by getting the domain of the current machine.

The **@users** array stores the list of user names we are trying to verify, either taken from the command line or, like the Unix version of this script, by extracting all of the names from the database. Finally, the **%attribs** hash stores the information about the user's attributes; we'll see how this is used later in this script.

```
11  $machine = Win32::NodeName();
12
13  $domain =Win32::DomainName()
14      unless (defined($domain));
15
```

Line 11 gets the name of the current machine by using the standard **Win32** module. This is purely the name of the machine; the domain and full path of the machine are not included. Line 13 obtains the NT domain name of the current machine, unless, by the test of line 14, the user has specified a different domain on the command line.

```
16  if (@ARGV)
17  {
18      @users = @ARGV;
19  }
20  else
21  {
22    Win32::NetAdmin::GetUsers(Win32::AdminMisc::GetDC($domain),
23                              '',\@users);
24  }
25
```

If there are any additional arguments on the command line, they are assumed to be the names of users that we want to check. If there are no users specified on the command line, then we obtain a list of users from the domain controller on lines 22 and 23. The function that gets the user list is **Win32::NetAdmin::GetUsers**, and its arguments are the machine to obtain the user list from, a filter to restrict the user list with, and a reference to the array you want to store the list in.

We've specified for the first argument another Win32 function, **Win32::AdminMisc::GetDC**, which is short for Get Domain Controller. This function takes a single argument, the domain, and then interrogates the network to find out which machine is the domain controller for the domain. Because we have specified a blank filter, the result should be a list of all the valid users in the **@users** array for the default domain, or the domain specified on the command line.

```
26    if (@users)
27    {
28        print "Domain: $domain\n";
29    }
30
```

Rather than checking for any errors in the process of obtaining the list, we just check on line 26 if the **@users** array contains any entries. If it does, we print out a title, which is the name of the domain specified, before continuing on to perform the checks.

```
31    for $user (sort @users)
32    {
33        unless(Win32::AdminMisc::UserGetMiscAttributes($domain,
34                                                       $user,
35                                                       \%attribs))
36        {
37            opstatus();
38        }
```

Line 31 sets up a **for** loop to work through a sorted list of users from the **@users** array. Lines 33 to 35 make a call to the **Win32::AdminMisc::UserGetMiscAttributes** function, which places information on a key/value basis in the **%attribs** hash, which we pass as a reference. Following you can see the full list of information provided by this function. We'll use some of it to perform the different checks we'll be making:

```
USER_ACCT_EXPIRES: 4294967295
USER_AUTH_FLAGS: 13
USER_BAD_PW_COUNT: 0
USER_CODE_PAGE: 0
USER_COMMENT:
USER_COUNTRY_CODE: 0
```

```
USER_FLAGS: 66049
USER_FULL_NAME: Martin Brown
USER_HOME_DIR: C:\WinNT\Profiles\MC
USER_HOME_DIR_DRIVE:
USER_LAST_LOGOFF: 909383709
USER_LAST_LOGON: 909383709
USER_LOGON_HOURS: 255
USER_LOGON_SERVER: \\*
USER_MAX_STORAGE: 4294967295
USER_NAME: MC
USER_NUM_LOGONS: 97
USER_PARMS:
USER_PASSWORD:
USER_PASSWORD_AGE: 18976857
USER_PASSWORD_EXPIRED: 0
USER_PRIMARY_GROUP_ID: 513
USER_PRIV: 2
USER_PROFILE:
USER_SCRIPT_PATH:
USER_UNITS_PER_WEEK: 168
USER_USER_ID: 1050
USER_USR_COMMENT:
USER_WORKSTATIONS:
```

If the command fails, then we call **opstatus**, a function that obtains errors from the Win32 system; these errors have to be extracted and reported on outside of the normal use of the **die** function and the **$!** special variable.

```
39      else
40      {
41          if ($attribs{"USER_PASSWORD_EXPIRED"} == 1)
42          {
43              print "Error: $user : Password has expired\n";
44          }
```

Provided the command succeeded, we start checking the details of the user information. The first thing we report on the expiration of the password. It is possible with NT to specify that users must change their password periodically. When a password expires, the user must enter a new one before they can continue using the machine. For a busy server in a large organization, this can provide a mental reminder that a user has left, or that they no longer need access to the machine in question. The value of the **USER_PASSWORD_EXPIRED** hash has a value of 1 if the password has expired.

```
45        if ($machine eq Win32::AdminMisc::GetDC($domain))
46        {
47            unless(-d $attribs{"USER_HOME_DIR"})
48            {
49                print("Error: $user : Home directory, ",
50                      $attribs{"USER_HOME_DIR"},
51                      " does not exist\n");
52            }
53        }
```

If we identify, on line 45, that the name of the machine we are running the script on and the name of the domain controller are identical, we can verify the location and existence of the user's home directory. Line 47 checks that the directory exists and is a directory, printing an error on lines 49 to 51 if there is a problem.

```
54        if ($user !~ /Administrator/)
55        {
```

The next few checks verify the user's abilities, if the user is *not* the administrator. It is possible with NT to give other users administrator status, as well as individual abilities for managing different resource and services. Line 54 checks that the current user is not the administrator.

```
56            if ($attribs{"USER_PRIV"} == 2)
57            {
58                print("Warning: $user : User has ",
59                      "administrator privileges\n");
60            }
```

Line 56 checks to the see if user has administrator privileges. This information is stored against the **USER_PRIV** key in the **%attribs** hash. A value of zero specifies that this person has guest privileges; a 1 means they are a normal user; and a 2 indicates administrator privileges.

```
61            else
62            {
```

If the user does not have administrator privileges, then we need to check individual abilities. This information is stored as a bitmask in the **USER_AUTH_FLAGS** key of the **%attribs** hash.

```
63                if ($attribs{"USER_AUTH_FLAGS"} & 1)
64                {
65                    print("Warning: $user : User does not have ",
66                          "administrator privileges but does ",
67                          "have Print Admin privileges\n");
68                }
```

A value of 1 (bit 0) in the bitmask means that the user has the ability to manage the print queues of the domain controller. We check this by bitwise ANDing the value of the **USER_AUTH_FLAGS** key with a value of 1; if the result is greater than zero, Perl takes it as a true value, and an error is printed on lines 65 to 67.

```
69          if ($attribs{"USER_AUTH_FLAGS"} & 4)
70          {
71              print("Warning: $user : User does not have ",
72                      "administrator privileges but does ",
73                      "have Server Admin privileges\n");
74          }
```

Lines 69 to 74 perform the same check, this time against server administration privileges, which allow the user to start and stop servers and services within the domain.

```
75          if ($attribs{"USER_AUTH_FLAGS"} & 8)
76          {
77              print("Warning: $user : User does not have ",
78                      "administrator privileges but does ",
79                      "have Accounts Admin privileges\n");
80          }
81      }
82  }
```

Finally, lines 75 to 80 check for the account's administrator privilege, which allows a user to modify users and groups within the domain.

```
83      if ($attribs{"USER_PASSWORD_AGE"} > (31*24*60*60))
84      {
85          print("Error: $user : Password is more than ",
86                  "one month (31 days) old\n");
87      }
```

The **USER_PASSWORD_AGE** value is the age, in seconds, since the password was last changed. Line 83 checks this value against a calculation of 31 days multiplied by the number of seconds in a day. If the age of the NT password is older than this calculated value, we print an error on lines 85 and 86.

```
88      if ($attribs{"USER_BAD_PW_COUNT"} > 0)
89      {
90          print("Warning: $user : User has had ",
91                  $attribs{"USER_BAD_PW_COUNT"},
92                  " bad password attempts\n");
93      }
94  }
95 }
96
```

The **USER_BAD_PW_COUNT** contains the number of times that a password of the current user has been entered badly since the last valid login. This can help highlight attempted cracks into the system, both of the normal users and administrators.

```
97   sub opstatus
98   {
99       my $error=Win32::GetLastError();
100      if ($error ne 0)
101      {
102          print("\nERROR: ", Win32::FormatMessage($error),"\n");
103      }
104      else
105      {
106          print "OK\n";
107      }
108  }
```

Line 97 starts the **opstatus** function, which extracts the error from the Win32 system and prints out the error.

Line 99 gets the last error generated by the Win32 system; this is a number, like most errors; if the value is greater than zero, there was a genuine error produced by the last Win32 call. If so, we print out an error message, using the **Win32::FormatMessage** function to convert the error number into a message string. Otherwise, we print "OK" if there wasn't a definable error returned by the last call. Win32 errors can be misleading: a function could return an undefined or false value, but that does not necessarily indicate an error, so we must account for such returns in the error-checking function.

The result of running the function on a typical server is a list of problems and possible security problems in the user list and permissions:

```
Domain: DOMAIN_USP
Error: Administrator : Password is more than one month (31 days) old
Error: JonN : Password has expired
Error: MarionC : Password has expired
Warning: MC : User has administrator privileges
Error: MC : Password is more than one month (31 days) old
Error: Win95 : Password is more than one month (31 days) old
```

cron2nt.pl

Converting Unix cron Entries to Windows NT

One of my own personal bugbears with NT is that some elements of the system are difficult to control and manage. This is especially true if you are integrating an NT server into a mixed-platform network: you find yourself looking for a specific tool or capability that you are used to using elsewhere. Even if the job is possible, there are usually some pitfalls and traps that make the process more complex or difficult than it needs to be.

A perfect example is the cron utility. Under Unix, you can use the crontab and at commands to schedule different jobs to take place at different times. The specification is via six fields: the first five specify the date and time to schedule a command to be run; the command is specified in the sixth field. The fields are specified as follows:

```
minute (0-59)
hour (0-23)
day of the month (1-31)
month of the year (1-12)
day of the week (0-6 with 0=Sunday)
```

Each of these patterns can be either an asterisk (meaning all legal values) or a list of elements separated by commas. An element can be a single number, or two numbers separated by a hyphen (meaning an inclusive range). For example, the specification

```
0 9 * * 1-5 backup
```

would run a backup at 9:00 A.M. every Monday through Friday. Note that two fields (the day of the month and the day of the week) are able to specify the days. If both are specified, then both will be adhered to. For example:

```
0 9 1,10,20,30 * 6 backup
```

would run the backup program on day 1, 10, 20, and 30 of each month, as well as every Saturday, regardless of whether those dates fall on Saturday.

Windows NT, on the other hand, uses a different specification. The at command allows you to specify a time and the day of the week or day of the month for the command to be executed. For example, to emulate our first crontab example above, you would enter

```
C:\> at 09:00 /every:m,t,w,th,f backup
```

If you wanted to emulate our second example, you would have to do it in two steps:

```
C:\> at 09:00 /every:s backup
C:\> at 09:00 /every:1,10,20,30 backup
```

Also, you cannot specify ranges: you must list each option, and it is impossible to specify a particular month because commands are executed every specified day of the week and/or day of the month every month.

To get around this limitation, I created a script that parses the normal cron specification and outputs, to the standard output, a batch file that can be executed to update the Windows NT scheduled execution tables.

PROGRAMMER'S NOTE *It is possible to use the **Win32::AdminMisc** toolkit to place entries directly from Perl into the Windows NT scheduling system. However, I wrote a standalone program for two main reasons. Firstly, I can hand-edit the batch file that is created, just in case I want to fine-tune the entries. The second reason is that I can create this file on any machine (even a Mac, if I wanted to) before moving the batch file to the NT machine, which means I can refer directly to the source crontab entries from a Unix machine, and I can also generate a single batch file that could be executed on a number of machines, instead of retyping the cron specification each time.*

```perl
1   #!/usr/local/bin/perl5 -w
2
3   use strict;
4
5   if (@ARGV < 6)
6   {
7       die "Not enough args";
8   }
9
10  my @days = qw/Su M T W Th F S/;
11
12  my @minutes = parse($ARGV[0],0,59);
13  my @hours   = parse($ARGV[1],0,23);
14  my @mday    = parse($ARGV[2],1,31);
15  my @month   = parse($ARGV[3],1,12);
16  my @wday    = parse($ARGV[4],0,6);
17  my $command = $ARGV[5];
18
19  if (@month < 12)
20  {
21      die "NT does not support scheduling for specific months";
22  }
23
24  for my $hour (sort @hours)
25  {
26      for my $minute (sort @minutes)
27      {
28          if ((@wday == 7 and @mday == 31) or
29              (@wday < 7 and @mday == 31) or
30              (@wday < 7 and @mday < 31))
```

```
31              {
32                  for my $day (sort @wday)
33                  {
34                      print("at $hour:$minute ",
35                            "/every:$days[$day] $command\n");
36                  }
37              }
38              if ((@wday == 7 and @mday < 31) or
39                  (@wday < 7 and @mday < 31))
40              {
41                  for my $day (sort @mday)
42                  {
43                      print "at $hour:$minute /every:$day $command\n";
44                  }
45              }
46          }
47      }
48
49  sub parse
50  {
51      my ($string,$lowrange,$highrange) = @_;
52
53      my @return;
54
55      if ($string =~ /^\*$/)
56      {
57          push(@return,range($lowrange,$highrange));
58          return(@return);
59      }
60      else
61      {
62          unless ($string =~ /[\d-,]+/)
63          {
64              die "Bad format $string";
65          }
66          for my $element (split(/,/,$string))
67          {
68              if (my ($low,$high) = ($element =~ m/^(\d+)-(\d+)$/))
69              {
70                  push @return,range($low,$high);
71              }
72              else
73              {
```

```
74                    push @return,$element;
75                }
76            }
77        }
78        if (((sort @return)[0] < $lowrange) or
79            ((sort @return)[-1] > $highrange))
80        {
81            die "Out of range (should be $lowrange-$highrange)\n";
82        }
83        @return;
84   }
85
86   sub range
87   {
88       my ($low,$high) = @_;
89       my @return;
90       for(my $i=$low;$i<=$high;$i++)
91       {
92            push(@return,$i);
93       }
94       return(@return);
95   }
```

ANNOTATIONS

The essence of this script is the **parse** function, which accepts a cron specification and a range, producing, as a result, an array of the expanded options. We can then use the array within a **for** loop to produce the actual batch file.

```
1    #!/usr/local/bin/perl5 -w
2
3    use strict;
4
5    if (@ARGV < 6)
6    {
7        die "Not enough args";
8    }
9
```

We're dealing with arrays and number ranges, so switching on warnings and the **strict** pragma should help us catch any problems with badly specified array elements, or with undefined values that might cause problems when it comes to generating the batch file. Line 5 checks the command-line arguments. Remember we're looking for six fields—five specifying the date and time and one specifying the program to be executed.

```
10    my @days = qw/Su M T W Th F S/;
11
```

NT takes day names, rather than numbers, as arguments to the function. The **@days** function is initialized with the day names NT is expecting in the same order that cron expects—meaning that element zero equals Sunday.

```
12    my @minutes = parse($ARGV[0],0,59);
13    my @hours   = parse($ARGV[1],0,23);
14    my @mday    = parse($ARGV[2],1,31);
15    my @month   = parse($ARGV[3],1,12);
16    my @wday    = parse($ARGV[4],0,6);
17    my $command = $ARGV[5];
18
```

Lines 12 to 16 parse the field specification via the **parse** function, placing the result into corresponding arrays. For example, line 12 asks the **parse** function to process the first field, using a possible range of between 0 and 59, relating to the number of minutes in an hour. Note that we process the month specification, even though we cannot use the information. This is to check that the specification is valid; it should be an asterisk to specify the entire month range.

The resulting array from each of these calls contains elements matching the corresponding specification. For example, if someone has requested a job to be run every hour, the **@hours** array will contain 24 entries, from zero to 23. If, on the other hand, they have only requested it to run every six hours, it will contain only four entries: 0, 6, 12, and 18.

By using a set of nested **for** loops, with the outer loop being used for the smallest element, we then build up a complete list of the days, hours, and minutes that match the full specification supplied on the command line.

Line 17 obtains the command that should be executed from the sixth argument to the script.

```
19    if (@month < 12)
20    {
21        die "NT does not support scheduling for specific months";
22    }
23
```

Lines 19 to 22 check and report an error if the month specification does not equal the full 12 months. By processing the option, and checking the size of the array here, we allow people to select month ranges of "1–12" or "1,2,3,4,5,6,7,8,9,10,11,12" and still have the script work. Anything less than 12 months reports an error.

```
24   for my $hour (sort @hours)
25   {
```

Line 24 sets up the **for** loop to work through the list of hours.

```
26       for my $minute (sort @minutes)
27       {
```

Line 26 sets up the **for** loop for working through the list of specified minutes.

```
28           if ((@wday == 7 and @mday == 31) or
29               (@wday < 7 and @mday == 31) or
30               (@wday < 7 and @mday < 31))
```

We now get to the point where we have to make a decision about which days the command should be executed on. We can specify the day by two ranges: numerically by the day of the month or numerically by the day of the week. For this block, lines 30 to 36, we are specifically interested in the days of the week.

The logic here works as follows. On line 28, if the user has specified that the command be run on all days of the month and all days of the week, then we need to specify the days of the week. This will not cause duplicate entries because the same test is not part of the "days of the month" block below. This is also quicker, since every day of the week is only 7 days, but every day of the month is 31 days. Line 29 accounts for situations where specific days of the week have been requested on any day of the month. Line 30 accounts for the situation where both days of the week and days of the month have been specified, and the specification is less than the maximum number.

```
31           {
32               for my $day (sort @wday)
33               {
34                   print("at $hour:$minute ",
35                       "/every:$days[$day] $command\n");
36               }
37           }
```

Lines 31 to 35 then work through the day range, printing out the individual command for the NT batch file. We have to work through the days individually because we must access the **@days** array in order to print out the day name, rather than the day number.

```
38           if ((@wday == 7 and @mday < 31) or
39               (@wday < 7 and @mday < 31))
```

The logic here compliments the earlier logic. Line 37 prints accounts for all of the days of the week being specified, in combination with a specific list of days of the month. Specifications of both week and month days are handled by line 38.

```
40              {
41                  for my $day (sort @mday)
42                  {
43                      print "at $hour:$minute /every:$day $command\n";
44                  }
```

Lines 40 to 43 then work through and print the days of the month entries for the command. Incidentally, we could have shortened this line to

```
print "at $hour:$minute /every:",join(',',@mday)," $command\n";
```

The day specification can be a comma-separated list, and since we can specify numbers here, we can very quickly use the **join** command to generate the list.

```
45              }
46          }
47      }
48
```

Lines 44 to 46 finish off the **for** loops for the days, minutes, and hours. The result of this nested **for** loop section can be seen at the end of this chapter.

```
49  sub parse
50  {
51      my ($string,$lowrange,$highrange) = @_;
52
53      my @return;
54
```

Line 48 starts the **parse** function, which processes an individual field specification, specified in the **$string** argument, using, if appropriate, a range between **$lowrange** and **$highrange**. The list is stored in **@return** until it is ready to be returned to the caller.

```
55      if ($string =~ /^\*$/)
56      {
57          push(@return,range($lowrange,$highrange));
58          return(@return);
59      }
```

If the string just contains an asterisk, checked for here on line 54, then we can call the **range** function, pushing the resulting range specification onto the **@return** variable and then returning it on line 57. We could shorten this to a single line, by directly returning the result of the **range** function, but that is sometimes more difficult to decipher since it's not obvious what the function is returning.

```
60      else
61      {
62          unless ($string =~ /[\d-,]+/)
63          {
64              die "Bad format $string";
65          }
```

Line 61 checks that the remainder of the string is composed only of digits, hyphens, or commas. A failure here causes the entire script to **die** on line 63. It's sensible to **die** here, since the function is self contained within the script.

```
66          for my $element (split(/,/,$string))
67          {
```

Line 65 sets up a **for** loop to work through the individual, comma-separated elements of the string.

```
68              if (my ($low,$high) = ($element =~ m/^(\d+)-(\d+)$/))
69              {
70                  push @return,range($low,$high);
71              }
```

If the regular expression match on line 67 is successful, then the element is a range, in which case we need to **push** the results of the **range** function onto the **@result** array.

```
72              else
73              {
74                  push @return,$element;
75              }
76          }
77      }
```

If the element is just a number, we can **push** the number directly onto the **@return** array.

```
78      if (((sort @return)[0] < $lowrange) or
79          ((sort @return)[-1] > $highrange))
80      {
81          die "Out of range (should be $lowrange-$highrange)\n";
82      }
```

Now that we have generated the final array, we check to make sure that none of the values are lower or higher than the lower and upper ends of the range supplied to the function. We check this by sorting the array elements with **sort** and then using subscript notation to check the lowest number in the array against the **$lowrange** variable. Line 78 uses the same trick, only this time we use a negative index value, which returns the element referenced from the end of the array—that is, –1 means the last element. If the values are out of the specified range, then we print an error on line 80. Note that I don't print a specification: since the ranges are all different, it should be obvious which range has been badly specified, if we print the low and high range values.

```
83        @return;
84    }
85
```

Line 82 references the **@return** array. The result of the last expression is the value returned to the caller.

```
86    sub range
87    {
88        my ($low,$high) = @_;
89        my @return;
90        for(my $i=$low;$i<=$high;$i++)
91        {
92            push(@return,$i);
93        }
94        return(@return);
95    }
```

The **range** function is incredibly straightforward. It takes a high and a low value and returns an array matching the values between the low and high values.

The result of the script should be a batch file with a list of NT at commands that match the cron specification you entered on the command line. For example, the specification we saw earlier,

```
0 9 * * 1-5 backup
```

should create a batch file that runs at 9 A.M. Monday to Tuesday:

```
$ cron2nt.pl 0 9 \* \* 1-5 backup
at 9:0 /every:M backup
at 9:0 /every:T backup
at 9:0 /every:W backup
at 9:0 /every:Th backup
at 9:0 /every:F backup
```

PROGRAMMER'S NOTE *We have to specify the asterisks with preceding slashes to ensure the Unix shell does not expand them.*

macfbf.pl

Reporting Macintosh File Sizes by Folder

It's hard to deny that the Mac has an easy-to-use and intuitive interface. There are times, though, when its ease of use means a lack of features in other areas. One of these holes, as far as I am concerned, is reporting directory sizes. Although it's possible to switch on Show Folder Sizes in the Views control panel, the process is slow. There is also no way of extracting the information provided, short of copying it by hand.

What would be nice to have is a Mac version of the Unix df command, which is exactly what this script, **macfbf.pl**, is designed to emulate. Although it uses fairly basic principles for extracting the information, it gives you a good introduction to using Perl on the Mac. It plugs the all-important gap in the MacOS facilities that I've needed before now to report on disk usage for different departments on AppleShare servers.

To give you an example of the limitations of the standard MacOS directory size information, look at Figure 10-1. We'll look at the output of this script on the same folder after the annotations.

Apple Extras		
22 items, 286.7 MB available		
Name	**Size**	
▷ About the Mac™ OS	128K	
▽ Apple IR File Exchange	620K	
Apple IR File Exchange	396K	
Apple IR File Exchange Guide	224K	
▷ Apple LaserWriter Software	2.4 MB	
▷ AppleCD Audio Player	268K	
▷ AppleScript™	480K	
▷ Assistants	440K	
▷ Disk Copy 6.1.3	792K	
Disk First Aid	156K	
▷ Drive Setup folder	564K	
▷ Mac OS Info Center	2 MB	
▷ Mac OS Runtime For Java	3.6 MB	
▷ Monitors Extras Folder	228K	
▷ Movie Player	288K	
▷ Portables	364K	
▷ QuickDraw™ 3D 1.5 Folder	4.2 MB	
▷ QuickTime™ Folder	820K	
▷ Remote Access Client Folder	336K	
▷ Sample Desktop Pictures	304K	
SimpleText	120K	
▷ Sound Control Panel	56K	

FIGURE 10-1. Standard Mac directory size information

This script is a reformatted version of the FindBiggestFolder script by Bruce Barnett.

```perl
1   #!/bin/perl
2
3   require "GUSI.ph" ;
4   require "StandardFile.pl";
5
6
7   if ($#ARGV < 0)
8   {
9       die "No input, no output"
10          unless $file = &StandardFile'GetFolder("Which folder?");
11      $ARGV[0] = $file;
12  }
13
14  $command_line_options = 1;
15  $select_outfile = 0;
16
17  if ($command_line_options)
18  {
19          &getArgs();
20          &getOptions();
21  }
22  $select_outfile && &selectOutfile();
23
24  $dirname = $ARGV[0];
25
26  &listDirectory($dirname);
27  &printSizes();
28
29  exit 0;
30
31  sub listDirectory
32  {
33      local($dirname) = @_;
34
35      local(@fnames,@subDirs);
36      local($fname,$pathname,$size,$creator,%type,$pname);
37      if ($dirname !~ /:$/)
38      {
39          $dirname =~ s/$/:/;
40      }
```

```
41
42        $dirsize{$dirname}=0;
43        opendir(DIR,$dirname);
44        @fnames = readdir(DIR);
45        closedir(DIR);
46
47        foreach $fname (@fnames)
48        {
49            $pathname = $dirname.$fname;
50            $size = -s $pathname;
51            $pname = $fname ; $pname =~ s/[\000-\037]/\377/g;
52            $dname = $dirname; $dname =~ s/[\000-\037]/\377/g;
53            $dirsize{$dirname}+=$size;
54            if (-d $pathname)
55            {
56                &listDirectory($pathname);
57            }
58        }
59    }
60
61    sub printSizes
62    {
63        @a=();
64        foreach $d (keys %dirsize)
65        {
66            push(@a,sprintf("%15d %s\n", $dirsize{$d}, $d));
67        }
68        print sort {$b <=> $a;} @a;
69    }
70
71    sub getArgs
72    {
73        require 'shellwords.pl';
74        local( $args ) = &MacPerl'Ask( 'Enter command line options:' );
75        unshift( @ARGV,&shellwords( $args ));
76    }
77
78    sub getOptions
79    {
80        while($ARGV[0] =~ /^-/)
81        {
```

```
82          $ARGV[0] =~ /-v/ && ($verbose++,shift ( @ARGV ),next);
83          $ARGV[0] =~ /-o/
84              && ($select_outfile++,shift ( @ARGV ),next);
85          print "Ignoring option $ARGV[0]\n";
86          last;
87      }
88  }
89
90  sub selectOutfile
91  {
92      $output = &MacPerl'Choose(&GUSI'AF_FILE, 0, "", "",
93          &GUSI'CHOOSE_NEW + &GUSI'CHOOSE_DEFAULT, $dirname." dir");
94      open(OUT,">".$output);
95      &MacPerl'SetFileInfo("ALFA", "TEXT", $output);
96      select(OUT);
97  }
```

ANNOTATIONS

Aside from the obvious Mac interface issues, this script follows a very simple process. We open a directory, read the files, and add up the file sizes, branching off to calculate the size of another directory if one is found. The results are all stored in a hash, with the keys representing the directory names and the values containing the directory sizes. The information can be output to the standard output (a window within the MacPerl environment) or to a separate file if required.

```
1   #!/bin/perl
2
3   require "GUSI.ph" ;
4   require "StandardFile.pl";
5
6
```

We use two of the standard MacPerl modules. GUSI provides additional information for the Mac networking types, and it also provides an interface to the Mac toolbox, allowing us to select and specify Mac files. We'll need this to enable the user to specify an alternate file to the standard output in which to store the directory size listing. The **StandardFile** module is a more generalized Mac interface module that supports the standard MacOS file and folder dialog boxes.

```
7   if ($#ARGV < 0)
8   {
```

```
9      die "No input, no output"
10         unless $file = &StandardFile'GetFolder("Which folder?");
11     $ARGV[0] = $file;
12  }
13
```

Lines 7 to 12 get the name of the directory that we want to summarize by calling the **GetFolder** function. This returns a Mac version of the path to the specified directory. The dialog box itself is different from standard dialog boxes in that a Directory button is used to return the selected directory, rather than the usual Open button that returns a selected file. Any files are grayed-out to ensure that the user selects a directory and not a file. You can see a sample directory dialog in Figure 10-2.

An error is reported, via the standard **die** function, if the user clicks Cancel in the dialog box. The directory name is then placed into the command-line arguments array on line 11.

```
14  $command_line_options = 1;
15  $select_outfile = 0;
16
```

Line 14 sets the value of the **$command_line_options** variable to 1. By setting the value here, it's possible to disable the ability to set command-line options without

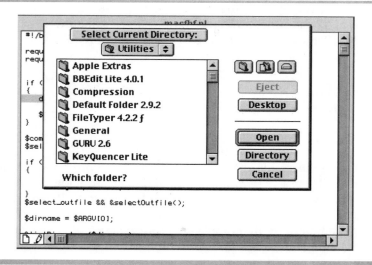

FIGURE 10-2. The Select Current Directory dialog box

having to modify such a significant part of the code. Line 15 then sets the value of the **$select_outfile** variable, which decides whether we need to select and use a separate file to report the results to.

```
17   if ($command_line_options)
18   {
19           &getArgs();
20           &getOptions();
21   }
22   $select_outfile && &selectOutfile();
23
```

Lines 17 to 21 extract the command-line options, provided that's what we are supposed to do according to the test in line 17. The **getArgs** function produces a dialog box requesting command-line options to be specified in much the same way as you would with Unix. Line 20 parses the standard command-line argument list, looking for options and setting them accordingly. There are only two: one specifies verbose output (which actually does nothing in this script), and the other extracts the output filename.

Line 22 performs a logical AND between the **$select_outfile** variable and the corresponding function. This works in an identical manner to the logical OR constructs we have seen before for error reporting. If the **$select_outfile** variable is true (nonzero), then the function will be executed.

```
24   $dirname = $ARGV[0];
25
26   &listDirectory($dirname);
27   &printSizes();
28
29   exit 0;
30
```

Line 24 re-extracts the directory name from the command-line arguments. The **listDirectory** function does the bulk of the work, working through the directory list and recursively calling itself to build up the hash. Line 27 calls the function that prints out the information to the standard output or the selected output file. Line 29 closes the script with an **exit** call, specifying a value of zero to show that the script exited normally.

```
31   sub listDirectory
32   {
33       local($dirname) = @_;
34
35       local(@fnames,@subDirs);
36       local($fname,$pathname,$size,$creator,%type,$pname);
```

Line 31 starts the **listDirectory** function, taking the first argument (extracted on line 33), which is the name of the directory to be reported on. Lines 35 and 36 localize the variables we will use in the rest of the function. Some of these are not used in this script, but I've left them in to remain consistent with the original. By localizing them, rather than letting Perl create them in the main name space, we ensure that they will not be overwritten or added to when the function calls itself to process an additional directory.

```
37      if ($dirname !~ /:$/)
38      {
39          $dirname =~ s/$/:/;
40      }
41
```

Line 37 checks that the directory name ends with a colon, the standard path separator under MacOS. If it doesn't, then we add it on line 39.

```
42      $dirsize{$dirname}=0;
43      opendir(DIR,$dirname);
44      @fnames = readdir(DIR);
45      closedir(DIR);
46
```

Line 42 initializes the directory entry in the hash to zero. Although Perl should do this automatically, it's a good idea to ensure against the possibility of a spurious value. Lines 43 to 45 use the **opendir** and **readdir** functions to place a list of the files and folders in the current directory. This is possibly dangerous, since it requires making an array to contain the entire list, even though that list may exceed the size of the memory allocated to MacPerl. On the other hand, it also ensures that the list remains constant, even though the processing and recursion involved may introduce additional files and folders if we made the **readdir** call as part of a loop.

```
47      foreach $fname (@fnames)
48      {
49          $pathname = $dirname.$fname;
50          $size = -s $pathname;
```

We start processing the filenames on line 47 via a **for** loop. Line 49 sets the name of the file being examined to contain the entire path, based on the current directory name and filename. Line 50 then extracts the file's size using the **-s stat** test.

```
51          $pname = $fname ; $pname =~ s/[\000-\037]/\377/g;
52          $dname = $dirname; $dname =~ s/[\000-\037]/\377/g;
```

Lines 51 and 52 are spurious, obviously left over from another script.

```
53              $dirsize{$dirname}+=$size;
54              if (-d $pathname)
55              {
56                  &listDirectory($pathname);
57              }
58          }
59      }
60
```

Line 53 adds the size of the current file to the size of the current directory, totaling up the file sizes for the current directory. If the file is a directory, which is checked for via the test on line 54, then we call the **listDirectory** function again, specifying the full path name as the argument to the function. By doing this, we recursively call the function on all the directories within the original directory tree, totaling up the directory sizes in the **%dirsize** hash.

```
61  sub printSizes
62  {
63      @a=();
64      foreach $d (keys %dirsize)
65      {
66          push(@a,sprintf("%15d %s\n", $dirsize{$d}, $d));
67      }
68      print sort {$b <=> $a;} @a;
69  }
70
```

The **printSizes** function prints out a sorted list of the directories and sizes. First the information is taken from the hash and placed, as formatted strings, into a new array via the **for** loop in lines 64 to 67. Then line 68 prints out a sorted version of the array, with the sort working in reverse order. This is simpler to understand than our previous one-line examples, but it requires more memory and process to achieve. We could get away with removing line 68 and change line 64 to

```
foreach $d (sort {$dirsize{$b} <=> $dirsize{$a}; } keys %dirsize)
```

This achieves the same goal but without all the memory and processing requirements.

```
71  sub getArgs
72  {
73      require 'shellwords.pl';
74      local( $args ) = &MacPerl'Ask( 'Enter command line options:' );
75      unshift( @ARGV,&shellwords( $args ));
76  }
77
```

The **getArgs** function produces a dialog box into which we can type arguments just as we would if we were calling the function on the command line. The **shellwords.pl** script checks the validity of a string to ensure the user has entered the options correctly. Line 74 then calls the **Ask** function to obtain the program arguments. Line 75 uses **unshift** to put the argument list supplied by the **Ask** function back onto the standard argument array.

```
78    sub getOptions
79    {
80        while($ARGV[0] =~ /^-/)
81        {
82            $ARGV[0] =~ /-v/ && ($verbose++,shift ( @ARGV ),next);
83            $ARGV[0] =~ /-o/
84                && ($select_outfile++,shift ( @ARGV ),next);
85            print "Ignoring option $ARGV[0]\n";
86            last;
87        }
88    }
89
```

The **getOptions** function demonstrates some of the principles behind processing the command-line arguments without using the standard **GetOpt** module. Line 80 starts a **while** loop to process the first argument of the array, provided it starts with a hyphen. Line 82 then tries to match the argument to "-v," signifying that the user wants verbose mode on. If this is this case, then we logical AND the test with a new statement that increments the **$verbose** counter and shifts the current (first) argument off the argument stack, before skipping to the next argument with the **next** function.

The operation is repeated with lines 83 and 84 when identifying the command-line option for selecting a different output file. If we cannot find a match, then the **next** function is not called and line 85 reports an error before exiting the loop via the **last** function on line 86.

```
90    sub selectOutfile
91    {
92        $output = &MacPerl'Choose(&GUSI'AF_FILE, 0, "", "",
93            &GUSI'CHOOSE_NEW + &GUSI'CHOOSE_DEFAULT, $dirname." dir");
94        open(OUT,">".$output);
95        &MacPerl'SetFileInfo("ALFA", "TEXT", $output);
96        select(OUT);
97    }
```

The **selectOutfile** function is called when the user has opted to store the output from the command in a separate file, rather than report it to the standard output.

Lines 92 and 93 call the **Choose** function, from the **GUSI** module we incorporated at the start of the script. The **Choose** function is called as follows:

```
&MacPerl'Choose(DOMAIN,TYPE,PROMPT,CONSTRAINT,FLAGS,DEFAULT)
```

The result is a dialog box requesting the file. The **DOMAIN** is the communication domain. This is intended to support access of different files over different communication domains, in much the same way as the **socket** call requires a communications domain. The **TYPE** is currently unused. **PROMPT** is the title and prompt to be used in the dialog. Using **CONSTRAINT** allows you to restrict the selection to specific address, or in our case, particular types of files. The MacOS uses type and creator attributes for each file to enable the application and file type to be identified, a more advanced and extensive system than the Windows's three-letter extensions.

The **FLAGS** specify what the dialog can support. In our script, we can either create a new file by typing the name in the box or use the default filename, supplied by the **DEFAULT** function argument. The result is a dialog box, with a box at the bottom for a filename pre-filled with the default name we give in line 93.

Line 94 opens the file using the standard **open** command. Note that we don't check for success or failure—we assume that **Choose** returned with a valid entry. This isn't always the case, and it cannot be guaranteed, either, so you may want to check the value. Line 95 ensures that the type and creator of the file just opened is set correctly. Then line 96 uses the **select** command to switch the default file handle from **STDOUT** to the recently created output file. This is an underused command that makes outputting results to different files significantly easier.

If we run the script, either from within the MacPerl environment or as a droplet (see Appendix A), we first get prompted for a directory to choose and then for any command-line arguments. If we use the same directory we tried earlier within the MacOS environment, we get the following results:

```
2110209 MacOS HD:Utilities:Apple Extras:Apple LaserWriter Software:
1428563 MacOS HD:Utilities:Apple Extras:QuickDraw™ 3D 1.5 Folder:3DMF
Models Folder:Viewpoint Datalabs Intl.:
1274122 MacOS HD:Utilities:Apple Extras:QuickDraw™ 3D 1.5 Folder:3DMF
Models Folder:Zygote:
 542455 MacOS HD:Utilities:Apple Extras:QuickDraw™ 3D 1.5 Folder:3DMF
Models Folder:Plastic Thought Inc.:
 391205 MacOS HD:Utilities:Apple Extras:Assistants:
 371552 MacOS HD:Utilities:Apple Extras:QuickDraw™ 3D 1.5 Folder:3DMF
Models Folder:Model Masters:
 333083 MacOS HD:Utilities:Apple Extras:Disk Copy 6.1.3:
 256154 MacOS HD:Utilities:Apple Extras:Sample Desktop Pictures:
 220672 MacOS HD:Utilities:Apple Extras:Drive Setup folder:
 220539 MacOS HD:Utilities:Apple Extras:Mac OS Info Center:Mac OS
Info Center Files:os:osqtv:
 204718 MacOS HD:Utilities:Apple Extras:Mac OS Runtime For Java:Apple
```

```
Applet Runner:Applets:Internationalization:code:
 169530 MacOS HD:Utilities:Apple Extras:QuickTime™ Folder:
 142171 MacOS HD:Utilities:Apple Extras:Mac OS Runtime For Java:Apple
Applet Runner:
 135211 MacOS HD:Utilities:Apple Extras:Mac OS Runtime For Java:Apple
Applet Runner:Applets:ImageMap:images:
 109353 MacOS HD:Utilities:Apple Extras:Mac OS Runtime For Java:Apple
Applet Runner:Applets:Animator:images:Beans:
 107447 MacOS HD:Utilities:Apple Extras:Mac OS Runtime For Java:Apple
Applet Runner:Applets:ImageMap:
 102912 MacOS HD:Utilities:Apple Extras:Apple IR File Exchange:
  92076 MacOS HD:Utilities:Apple Extras:Mac OS Runtime For Java:Apple
Applet Runner:Applets:WireFrame:models:
  84716 MacOS HD:Utilities:Apple Extras:Mac OS Info Center:Mac OS
Info Center Files:ks:
  81619 MacOS HD:Utilities:Apple Extras:Mac OS Info Center:Mac OS
Info Center Files:mn:
  78336 MacOS HD:Utilities:Apple Extras:AppleCD Audio Player:
  75814 MacOS HD:Utilities:Apple Extras:Mac OS Info Center:Mac OS
Info Center Files:wn:wneou:
  65177 MacOS HD:Utilities:Apple Extras:Mac OS Runtime For
Java:License Agreement:
  64572 MacOS HD:Utilities:Apple Extras:Mac OS Runtime For Java:Apple
Applet Runner:Applets:GraphLayout:audio:
  61161 MacOS HD:Utilities:Apple Extras:About the Mac™ OS:
  58163 MacOS HD:Utilities:Apple Extras:Mac OS Runtime For Java:Apple
Applet Runner:Applets:Animator:audio:
  54502 MacOS HD:Utilities:Apple Extras:Mac OS Info Center:Mac OS
Info Center Files:os:osfin:
  53487 MacOS HD:Utilities:Apple Extras:Mac OS Info Center:Mac OS
Info Center Files:os:osqd3:
...
```

I've shortened the list here for brevity (the full list is significantly longer). You can see that it provides a lot more detailed information, and—best of all—the information is in a format that I can report on and print out much more easily than the standard MacOS tool.

There is a similar tool, **macbycrt.pl**, by the same author that I have supplied on the CD but not included in the book text. That script enables you to report on the total file size used on a volume by a specific creator (application). This can be enormously helpful when you want to track down what variety of files are using the most space. I've used it to support recommendations for a separate server for a department. The script supported my impression that the department's artwork files were using more than 80 percent of what was supposed to be an administration server's file space.

Summary

As I said at the start of this chapter, the bulk of systems administration work comes from monitoring and checking the existing configuration rather than producing the configuration in the first place. Systems rarely change and mutate, but ensuring that systems work, and reporting on their current status, is a laborious process that can be eased and improved through the use of Perl. Our first script is an excellent example of this: it checks the alias file, a file that *is* frequently modified, before the changes you make to it affect your e-mail systems.

Other systems administration problems relate to the differences that exist between different systems. I work with Macs and NT and Unix systems every day and the small differences between each system slow me down when I am trying to do even simple tasks. Scripts like **cront2nt.pl** and **macfbf.pl** resolve these problems by using Perl to emulate the functionality and abilities of one platform on another.

Network Administration

Like systems administration, network administration involves editing and managing network-based information and resources. Network administration also involves a significant amount of monitoring to ensure that your network is working correctly, which involves not only monitoring the status and availability of machines, but also requires you to study the status of individual components, such as disk space and the memory of the machines within your network.

In all cases, anything that simplifies the process of managing a network, and particularly the information and resources that are used on your network, must be a benefit. Our first script manages the information used by the Domain Name System within your network. Building the file that controls and configures the domain name server is a lengthy job, as individual parts of the configuration must be obtained by examining the information about individual domains. The **bnamed.pl** script simplifies the process by obtaining the information required automatically, and then it builds the required configuration file ready for you to use.

The next script, **ntserv.pl**, allows you to monitor and manage NT services from the command line. The services can be either on the local machine or on a remote machine that you have the permissions and abilities to control. This tool has been a huge help for managing an NT system remotely: I can telnet into an NT machine on my network and start or stop services on any other NT machine using this script.

For the last five scripts in this chapter, I have indulged myself and included some main scripts for a management and monitoring system that is still in development. As a network administrator, I need some way of reducing the amount of time I spend keeping an eye on the availability and status of different machines in the network. To complicate matters, I need the system to monitor different types of network entities, such as FTP services and AppleTalk services all on the same network.

I also want to be able to remotely monitor the available disk space, memory, and load average of the different servers within my network. The result is a system that not only monitors all of these factors, but also provides the flexibility to allow other systems and factors to be monitored using the same core components and information gathering system.

bnamed.pl

Automatically Building named.boot

If you manage a number of domains, and a number of machines that cache details on secondary domain names, then you will have experienced the problems of resolving and updating the details in the /etc/named.boot file that stores the configuration information for the **named** domain name server. The format of the file is simple. Each line specifies a different domain or configuration option in the file. For example:

```
directory /var/named
cache . fake/cache
primary 0.0.127.in-addr.arpa primary/0.0.127.in-addr.arpa
```

```
primary 10.112.198.in-addr.arpa primary/10.112.198.in-addr.arpa
primary mchome.com primary/mchome.com
secondary mcwords.com 207.240.118.18 207.155.127.155
secondary/mcwords.com
```

Each field in each line is separated by a space, and depending on the value of the first field, the format of the line is different. In this sample, you can see four different types. The **directory** line specifies the base directory for the **named** system. The **cache** line specifies the root point and path name (within the directory specified above) for the root domain name server file.

The **primary** entries are those domains that you manage on your local machine; the remainder of the fields are the domain name and the path to the primary domain file. The **secondary** entries specify the domains that you hold details on but do not manage, either in an official or unofficial capacity. The remainder of the fields specify the domain name, the IP addresses of the official domain name servers for the domain, and the path in which to store the domain file. The **named** daemon refreshes the contents of these secondary files by contacting, in order, the list of hosts specified by each address.

The first three types—directory, cache, and primary—are easy to manage, since you have all of the information at hand. The secondary entries are more difficult to build since you need to find out the IP addresses of the servers before you list them in the **named.boot** configuration file. Furthermore, if you are officially holding the domains as a secondary domain name server, you need to ignore your own IP address from the list. It's also a good idea, if you have a number of servers holding secondary information on your site, that you list them last in the list of servers from which to obtain the latest copy of the domain file.

The **bnamed.pl** script makes the process easier by automatically building the **named.boot** file. The script automates the process by interrogating the local domain name server to obtain the list of domain name servers for a specified domain. It then builds the list of IP addresses, taking account of local servers and the current machine in order to produce the final configuration information for the domain, and eventually the entire file.

This script uses the **Net::DNS** module from Michael Fuhr and the **libnet** module from Graham Barr.

```
1   #!/usr/local/bin/perl5 -w
2
3   use strict;
4
5   use Net::DNS;
6   use Net::Domain;
7
8   my $hostfqdn = Net::Domain::hostfqdn();
9   my ($dnsdir,$cache,@secondaries,@primaries,%dnshosts);
```

```perl
10
11   open(DNSCONF,"<$ARGV[0]") or die "Couldn't open $ARGV[0], $!";
12
13   while(<DNSCONF>)
14   {
15       chomp;
16       s/\s+//g;
17       my ($type,$opt) = split(/:/,$_,2);
18       if ($type eq 'dir')
19       {
20           $dnsdir = $opt;
21       }
22       elsif ($type eq 'cache')
23       {
24           $cache = $opt;
25       }
26       elsif ($type eq 'primary')
27       {
28           push(@primaries,$opt);
29       }
30       elsif ($type eq 'secondary')
31       {
32           push(@secondaries,$opt);
33       }
34   }
35   close(DNSCONF) or die "Couldn't close $ARGV[0], $!";
36
37   open(NAMED,">$ARGV[0].boot")
38       or die "Couldn't open $ARGV[0].boot, $!";
39
40   print NAMED "directory $dnsdir\n";
41   print NAMED "cache . $cache";
42
43   for my $primary (sort @primaries)
44   {
45       print NAMED "primary $primary primary/$primary\n";
46   }
47
48   my $res = new Net::DNS::Resolver;
49   unless ($res)
50   {
51       die "Error creating resolver";
```

```
52   }
53
54
55   for my $domain (sort @secondaries)
56   {
57       my $query = $res->query($domain,"NS");
58       unless ($query)
59       {
60           print("Error processing query for $domain: ",
61                   $res->errorstring,"\n");
62           next;
63       }
64       my (@remote,@local);
65
66       for my $rr ($query->answer)
67       {
68           next unless($rr->type eq 'NS');
69           next if ($rr->nsdname eq $hostfqdn);
70           my $islocal = 0;
71           for my $dom (@primaries)
72           {
73               if ($rr->nsdname =~ /$dom$/)
74               {
75                   $islocal=1;
76                   last;
77               }
78           }
79           if ($islocal)
80           {
81               push(@local,$rr->nsdname);
82           }
83           else
84           {
85               push(@remote,$rr->nsdname);
86           }
87       }
88       print NAMED "secondary $domain ";
89       for my $host (@local,@remote)
90       {
91
92           unless(defined($dnshosts{$host}))
93           {
94               $dnshosts{$host} =
```

```
95                  join('.',
96                      unpack('C4',
97                          gethostbyname($host)));
98          }
99          print NAMED "$dnshosts{$host} "
100             if(defined($dnshosts{$host}));
101     }
102     print NAMED " secondary/$domain\n";
103 }
104
105 close(NAMED)
106     or die "Couldn't close $ARGV[0].boot, $!";
```

ANNOTATIONS

The script uses a file specified on the command line, reading in each line to process the information. We process the file first, which enables us to specify the configuration information in any order within the file and allows us to use the list of primary domains extracted from the file in order to decide which of the domain name servers to use. Machines within one of the local domains that are specified as secondary servers are polled for updated information first, followed by external servers; you may want to reverse this operation depending on how your site and configuration work.

Once we have a list of name servers, in the required order, we obtain the IP addresses for each server in order to build the corresponding line in the **named.boot** file.

```
1   #!/usr/local/bin/perl5 -w
2
3   use strict;
4
5   use Net::DNS;
6   use Net::Domain;
7
8   my $hostfqdn = Net::Domain::hostfqdn();
9   my ($dnsdir,$cache,@secondaries,@primaries,%dnshosts);
10
```

The **Net::Domain** module is new to us; it is part of the **libnet** package, and it provides a better alternative to the **hostname.pl** script we have previously used. We use one of the supplied functions in line 8 to obtain the full, qualified domain name (that is, the host name and domain) of the current machine. We need this information to exclude the current host from any domain name server lists—we cannot ask ourselves for the latest version of a domain!

Line 9 sets up the variables that store the information about the secondary and primary hosts before the data is formatted to produce the final **named.boot** file.

```perl
11    open(DNSCONF,"<$ARGV[0]") or die "Couldn't open $ARGV[0], $!";
12
```

The script takes only one command-line argument: the configuration file to be used to create the **named.boot** file. We open it on line 11, or **die** if the file cannot be opened.

```perl
13    while(<DNSCONF>)
14    {
15        chomp;
16        s/\s+//g;
17        my ($type,$opt) = split(/:/,$_,2);
```

We start processing the configuration file in line 13. The format of the file is as follows:

```
section:value
```

There are only two fields: the first specifies the section of the **named.boot** file, and the second specifies the value to be used or processed by the script to build the **named.boot** file.

Line 15 strips the input record separator (new-line) character off the end of the current line, and line 16 removes any multiple spaces from the input line; they are not required in the output file. Line 17 splits the line into a maximum of two fields, using the **split** function. The third argument to the function specifies the number of fields that should be extracted—the last field returned will contain the remainder of the fields in their separated form.

Note, you may want to expand the procedure here to account for blank lines, or for comments in the configuration script. You can do this very easily by using **next** and a couple of tests. The lines

```perl
next if (s/^#/);
next if (length($_) == 0);
```

would be enough.

```perl
18        if ($type eq 'dir')
19        {
20            $dnsdir = $opt;
21        }
22        elsif ($type eq 'cache')
23        {
24            $cache = $opt;
25        }
```

The first two options in the **named.boot** file are simply strings that require no processing of any sort; we detect and extract the information for these fields in lines 18 to 25. Note that in both cases, the test is case sensitive. You may want to consider changing the lines to be a regular expression test, for example:

```
if ($type =~ /^dir$/i)
```

I prefer lowercase since it is the format of the final file, but it really doesn't matter.

```
26      elsif ($type eq 'primary')
27      {
28          push(@primaries,$opt);
29      }
30      elsif ($type eq 'secondary')
31      {
32          push(@secondaries,$opt);
33      }
34  }
35  close(DNSCONF) or die "Couldn't close $ARGV[0], $!";
36
```

For the primary and secondary domain definitions there will be multiple entries, so we build a list of the entries by adding the value of the second field to a suitably named array in lines 28 and 32, using the **push** function. Line 34 is the end of the loop, and line 45 closes the input file since we have finished processing.

```
37  open(NAMED, ">$ARGV[0].boot")
38      or die "Couldn't open $ARGV[0].boot, $!";
39
```

We open a new file to hold the generated **named.boot** configuration in line 37, remembering to check and report an error on failure in line 38.

```
40  print NAMED "directory $dnsdir\n";
41  print NAMED "cache . $cache";
42
43  for my $primary (sort @primaries)
44  {
45      print NAMED "primary $primary primary/$primary\n";
46  }
47
```

We print the first two configuration lines out on lines 40 and 41. We already know the format of the output, and we know the format of the input file, although we haven't checked it for valid entries.

For the primary domain information, we need to work through the list of primary domains, printing out the definition lines. There is no further processing here, since we have all the information we need. We do make some assumptions: first of all we assume that the primary domain information will be stored within a directory called **primary** within the directory definition we printed on line 41.

```
48  my $res = new Net::DNS::Resolver;
49  unless ($res)
50  {
51      die "Error creating resolver";
52  }
53
54
```

We create a new domain name resolver in line 48; the **$res** scalar holds a reference to the object that is created. We use the new object to resolve the domain name servers for each of the secondary domains. We can reuse the same resolver object, so we create it outside of the loop that processes the secondary domains; this improves performance, although by only a marginal amount for most sites. The **$res** variable will contain a false value if the resolver object failed to be created correctly.

```
55  for my $domain (sort @secondaries)
56  {
57      my $query = $res->query($domain,"NS");
```

Line 55 sets up the loop to work through each of the domains in the array of secondary domains we populated when processing the configuration file. On line 57 we query the domain name server, via the **$res** DNS resolver object, using a DNS type of NS, which is short for Name Servers. The result is a query object that contains a list of the domain name servers for the domain specified in the first argument of the **$query** method.

```
58      unless ($query)
59      {
60          print("Error processing query for $domain: ",
61              $res->errorstring,"\n");
62          next;
63      }
```

Once again we check the value of the object that has just been created. It will have a false value if the information could not be obtained or if the domain was invalid. If this is the case, we print an error on lines 60 and 61. The **errorstring** method to the **$resobject** returns an error string containing the reason for the failure. We don't quit at this point, since it could be a transient error that may disappear with further use. Line 62 then skips right on to the next domain, ignoring any further processing of the domain.

```
64      my (@remote,@local);
65
```

The **@remote** and **@local** arrays hold the list of remote domain name servers for the current domain—that is, any machine not within one of the primary domains specified within the configuration file. The **@local** array stores the servers that are within the primary domains.

```
66      for my $rr ($query->answer)
67      {
68          next unless($rr->type eq 'NS');
69          next if ($rr->nsdname eq $hostfqdn);
70          my $islocal = 0;
```

Line 66 starts a loop through the answer from the earlier name server query. Each element of the array that is returned will be yet another object from which we can extract the name and type of the entry. Line 68 checks that the type returned is a name server, skipping to the next element of the loop if it isn't. Line 69 then skips the current entry if the server matches the host and domain name of the current machine that we extracted in line 8. There is no point in adding ourselves to the list of secondary servers: we need to obtain a copy of the file from another server. Line 70 initializes the variable that specifies whether the server is local or not.

```
71          for my $dom (@primaries)
72          {
73              if ($rr->nsdname =~ /$dom$/)
74              {
75                  $islocal=1;
76                  last;
77              }
78          }
```

Lines 71 to 78 set up a **for** loop to work through the list of primary domains, as extracted from the configuration file. If the end of the server name matches the domain via the regular expression test on line 73, then the server is local, so we set the **$islocal** variable to a positive value and exit the loop via the **last** function on line 76.

```
79          if ($islocal)
80          {
81              push(@local,$rr->nsdname);
82          }
83          else
84          {
85              push(@remote,$rr->nsdname);
86          }
87      }
```

If the server was local, as defined by the value of the **$islocal** variable, we push the server name onto the **@local** server array. If not, then we push the value onto the **@remote** array. Remember that at this point we are still working with the names, rather than the IP addresses, of the domain name servers. The last step, therefore, is to obtain the IP addresses and then output the lines for the **named.boot** file.

```
88     print NAMED "secondary $domain ";
89     for my $host (@local,@remote)
90         {
91
```

Line 88 prints out the start of the secondary domain line. The format of the line is
`secondary domainname domain_server_ip… pathname_to_file`
Because Perl does not automatically append a new-line character to everything printed, we can use different print statements to build the individual lines. The first part prints out the first two fields, and the loop that starts on line 89 prints out the list of IP addresses. Note that we have specified both the local and remote arrays in line 89, separating them with a comma. Perl treats the result as one big array, which will then be processed element by element. Note that to change the precedence of the local servers over the remote servers, you should swap the two arrays around in line 89.

As a general rule, if the secondary domains you are hosting are secondary to your own local domains, then you should list the local domain name servers first to prevent individual machines going offsite to discover what is local information. If the secondary domains are official and for external sites, or they are unofficial, then you should list the remote servers first.

```
92         unless(defined($dnshosts{$host}))
93             {
94             $dnshosts{$host} =
95                 join('.',
96                     unpack('C4',
97                         gethostbyname($host)));
98             }
```

To avoid looking up the IP address of the same server more than once, the information is stored, as a string, in a hash. The key of the hash is the domain name, with the value containing the IP address. If the current domain name server does not exist in the hash, we add it on lines 94 to 97.

The **gethostbyname** function returns the IP address of a host based on the name supplied. The information is returned as a packed quad of unsigned characters that we **unpack** directly on line 96. The returned array is joined by periods on line 95, with the resulting string being placed directly into the hash. (The command actually fits onto a single line, but I used four lines here due to the book's line length constraints.)

```
99          print NAMED "$dnshosts{$host} "
100              if(defined($dnshosts{$host}));
101      }
102      print NAMED " secondary/$domain\n";
103  }
104
```

Lines 99 and 100 print out the IP address of the host, provided it has been defined within the hash. Note that this sequence prints out both existing and new hosts, since lines 92 to 98 have resolved the IP address. Line 102 prints out the last field of the **named.boot** line; remember this time to include the new-line character.

```
105  close(NAMED)
106      or die "Couldn't close $ARGV[0].boot, $!";
```

Once the secondary domain loop has ended on line 103, we close the resulting file on lines 105 and 106, and the script is finished.

Let's try it out on the sample file supplied, **bnamed.cnf**, which looks like this:

```
dir:/var/named
cache:fake/cache
primary:0.0.127.in-addr.arpa
primary:mcslp.com
primary:mcwords.com
primary:10.112.198.in-addr.arpa
secondary:mcgraw-hill.com
secondary:stok.co.uk
```

The resulting file, **bnamed.conf.boot** looks like this:

```
directory /var/named
cache . fake/cacheprimary 0.0.127.in-addr.arpa
primary/0.0.127.in-addr.arpa
primary 10.112.198.in-addr.arpa primary/10.112.198.in-addr.arpa
primary mcslp.com primary/mcslp.com
primary mcwords.com primary/mcwords.com
secondary mcgraw-hill.com 199.221.47.8 207.24.245.179 207.24.245.178
199.221.47.7   secondary/mcgraw-hill.com
secondary stok.co.uk 194.207.0.129 194.207.13.1   secondary/stok.co.uk
```

This result can be renamed and copied directly into the /etc/named.boot file. I've used this script for a number of years to manage the 60 secondary domains that we host in collaboration with another site. It has yet to fail on me, and in fact it normally highlights differences between domains—especially those that no longer exist—long before a notification e-mail arrives.

ntserv.pl

Windows NT Services Manager

Windows NT services are the individual components and functions of an NT machine. They do everything from providing network access all the way to supporting file sharing and Web and other Internet services. Services can be started or stopped at will on an NT machine, and they can be configured to start up automatically when a machine boots or to be started manually by the user or another program.

Managing NT services is easy if you have access to the Services control panel. It can be more difficult if you prefer the command-line interface or if you want to control the services remotely from a local NT machine. The **ntserv.pl** script aims to fill the gap by allowing you to monitor, start, and stop NT services from the command line on a local or remote machine within the current domain.

Although produced here as a command-line utility, this script could be easily converted into a Web-based interface, providing the same functionality and allowing you to control the services of a machine from anywhere in the world—provided, of course, the machine was on the Internet and that you had access to it!

```perl
1   #!perl -w
2   use Win32::Service;
3   use Getopt::Long;
4
5   my ($upserv,$downserv,$server,%services);
6
7   GetOptions("u=s" => \$upserv,
8              "d=s" => \$downserv
9              );
10  if (@ARGV)
11  {
12      $server = $ARGV[0];
13  }
14  else
15  {
16      $server = Win32::NodeName();
17  }
18
19  Win32::Service::GetServices($server,\%services);
20
21  print "Server $server\n";
22
23  if ($upserv)
24  {
```

```
25        startservices(split(/,/,$upserv));
26  }
27  elsif ($downserv)
28  {
29        stopservices(split(/,/,$downserv));
30  }
31  else
32  {
33        listservices();
34  }
35
36  sub startservices
37  {
38        my (@servicelist) = @_;
39        for my $service (@servicelist)
40        {
41            if (defined($services{$service}))
42            {
43                print "Starting the $service service...";
44                Win32::Service::StartService($server,$service);
45                opstatus("start $service");
46                sleep 5;
47                print "$service: ",chkstatus($service);
48            }
49            else
50            {
51                print "ERROR: Service $service does not exist\n";
52            }
53        }
54  }
55
56  sub stopservices
57  {
58        my (@servicelist) = @_;
59        for my $service (@servicelist)
60        {
61            if (defined($services{$service}))
62            {
63                print "Stopping the $service service...";
64                Win32::Service::StopService($server,$service);
65                opstatus("stop $service");
66                sleep 5;
67                print "$service: ",chkstatus($service);
68            }
```

```
69          else
70          {
71              print "ERROR: Service $service does not exist\n";
72          }
73      }
74  }
75
76  sub opstatus
77  {
78      my ($opname) = @_;
79      my $error=Win32::GetLastError();
80      if ($error ne 0)
81      {
82          print("\n$opname: ", Win32::FormatMessage($error),"\n");
83      }
84      else
85      {
86          print "OK\n";
87      }
88  }
89
90  sub chkstatus
91  {
92      my ($service) = @_;
93      my %status;
94      Win32::Service::GetStatus($server,$service,\%status);
95      if (defined($status{CurrentState})
96          and $status{CurrentState} eq 4)
97      {
98          return "Started";
99      }
100     else
101     {
102         return "Stopped";
103     }
104 }
105
106 sub listservices
107 {
108     for my $service (sort keys %services)
109     {
110         print "$service: ",chkstatus($service),"\n";
111     }
112 }
```

ANNOTATIONS

This script makes use of the **Win32::Service** module, which is part of the base distribution of the Perl package on Windows NT. It allows you to monitor and control the services of a local or remote machine, provided you have the access and authority to do so. The script is fairly straightforward: it either reports on all services or allows a single service to be started or stopped. We have to make some allowances for the Windows environment and the implementation of modules within the Win32 Perl package.

```
1   #!perl -w
2   use Win32::Service;
3   use Getopt::Long;
4
5   my ($upserv,$downserv,$server,%services);
6
```

The **$upserv, $downserv**, and **$server** scalar variables store the options from the command line. These variables store the service to be started, the service to be stopped, and the server on which to start/stop services, respectively. The **%services** hash stores the list of active services on the specified machine.

```
7   GetOptions("u=s" => \$upserv,
8              "d=s" => \$downserv
9             );
10  if (@ARGV)
11  {
12      $server = $ARGV[0];
13  }
14  else
15  {
16      $server = Win32::NodeName();
17  }
18
```

The command-line arguments are extracted using the **GetOptions** function from the **GetOpt::Long** module on lines 7 to 9. Line 7 extracts the service to be started, and line 8 extracts the service to be stopped. In both cases they accept the name of the service to be started or stopped, placing the value into the corresponding variable. The result of the argument extraction is not checked, but you could easily add a test to the result of the **GetOptions** function.

Lines 10 to 17 attempt to extract the name of an NT machine from the remaining command-line arguments. If specified, we take the first argument as a server name on line 12; otherwise we take the name of the current machine on line 16 from the result of the **Win32::NodeName** function.

```
19   Win32::Service::GetServices($server,\%services);
20
21   print "Server $server\n";
22
```

Line 19 gets a list of the valid services from the required machine. The list of services and their status are placed into the hash passed as a reference in the second argument. The result is not checked, although it might be a good idea to add a test to this line to ensure that the machine specified is correct. Line 21 prints out the name of the machine being reported on or controlled.

```
23   if ($upserv)
24   {
25       startservices(split(/,/,$upserv));
26   }
27   elsif ($downserv)
28   {
29       stopservices(split(/,/,$downserv));
30   }
31   else
32   {
33       listservices();
34   }
35
```

Lines 23 to 35 decide what we are going to do, depending on the command-line options supplied. If the user specified that services were to be started (which we test for on line 23), then we call the **startservices** function. Note that the function takes an array as the argument; if the user specifies more than one service, separated by commas, then we pass this on as an array, using **split** to separate the elements on line 25.

If the user wants to stop services, we identify this on line 27, calling a similar function with similar arguments on line 29. We use **elsif** so that the user can specify both services to be started and stopped in a single line. If neither option has been specified, then we call the **listservices** function on line 33 to report on the services and their status.

```
36   sub startservices
37   {
38       my (@servicelist) = @_;
39       for my $service (@servicelist)
40           {
```

```
41          if (defined($services{$service}))
42          {
43              print "Starting the $service service...";
44              Win32::Service::StartService($server,$service);
45              opstatus("start $service");
46              sleep 5;
47              print "$service: ",chkstatus($service);
48          }
49          else
50          {
51              print "ERROR: Service $service does not exist\n";
52          }
53      }
54  }
55
```

The **startservices** function accepts a list of services to be started. The list is extracted from the function arguments as an array on line 38, and line 39 sets up the loop to work through each service, provided the service name exists within the list of services we obtained from the machine in line 19. Line 43 prints out a progress message, and line 44 calls the function that will attempt to start the service on line 45. Note that the function just requests that the machine attempt to start the services.

We then wait 5 seconds in line 46 via the **sleep** function before checking the status on line 47. We won't know until this line whether the request to start the service was successful. The reason for waiting before reporting the status is that it can take a few seconds for the service to stop. If you find that the service has been stopped even though the result from this line shows otherwise, then you may want to increase the waiting time; the value specifies the number of seconds to wait. I know from experience that a number of services, particularly Internet Information Server (IIS) and Microsoft Exchange, can take almost a minute to come to a complete stop.

```
56  sub stopservices
57  {
58      my (@servicelist) = @_;
59      for my $service (@servicelist)
60      {
61          if (defined($services{$service}))
62          {
63              print "Stopping the $service service...";
64              Win32::Service::StopService($server,$service);
65              opstatus("stop $service");
66              sleep 5;
67              print "$service: ",chkstatus($service);
68          }
```

```
69          else
70          {
71              print "ERROR: Service $service does not exist\n";
72          }
73      }
74  }
75
```

The **stopservice** function on lines 56 to 74 is identical in format to the **startservice** function, except that we call the **Win32::Service::StopService** function to stop the required service from the list supplied.

```
76  sub opstatus
77  {
78      my ($opname) = @_;
79      my $error=Win32::GetLastError();
80      if ($error ne 0)
81      {
82          print("\n$opname: ", Win32::FormatMessage($error),"\n");
83      }
84      else
85      {
86          print "OK\n";
87      }
88  }
89
```

The **opstatus** function, which starts on line 76, obtains an error message from the Win32 system. It accepts a single argument that will be used to report an error. The **Win32::GetLastError** function gets the number of the last error from the Win32 system; if the error equals zero, there is no problem, and we print a success message on line 86. If there is an error, then we use the **Win32::FormatMessage** function to return a string that will form part of the error message reported on line 82.

```
90  sub chkstatus
91  {
92      my ($service) = @_;
93      my %status;
94      Win32::Service::GetStatus($server,$service,\%status);
```

The **chkstatus** function obtains the status information for a specified service name and returns a string specifying the status of the individual service. Line 92 extracts the service from the function arguments. Line 93 initializes a hash in which to store the information about a particular service, and is passed as a reference in the third

argument to the function on line 94. The **GetStatus** function also accepts the name of
the NT machine and the name of the service.

```
95      if (defined($status{CurrentState})
96          and $status{CurrentState} eq 4)
97      {
98          return "Started";
99      }
100     else
101     {
102         return "Stopped";
103     }
104 }
105
```

The current status of the specified service is defined within the CurrentState
element of the **$status** hash. The value of the element defines the status, and a value
of 4 signifies that the server has been started, which we check for in lines 95 and 96.
If the element is not defined, or if the value is not equal to 4, then the test will fail,
and we'll return "Stopped" to the caller. If the value does equal 4, then we return a
"Started" string to the caller.

```
106 sub listservices
107 {
108     for my $service (sort keys %services)
109     {
110         print "$service: ",chkstatus($service),"\n";
111     }
112 }
```

Lines 106 to 112 form the **listservices** function, which reports on the status of all
the functions available on an NT machine. Line 108 sets up the loop to work through
a sorted list of keys (service names) and the name and status, as extracted by the
chkstatus function line 110.

If you run the script from the command line without any options, you should get
a list of the services that are currently running, such as:

```
Alerter: Started
ClipBook Server: Stopped
Computer Browser: Stopped
DHCP Client: Stopped
Directory Replicator: Stopped
EventLog: Started
MGACtrl: Started
McAfee Alert Manager: Started
```

```
McAfee VirusScan Task Manager: Started
Messenger: Started
NT LM Security Support Provider: Started
Net Logon: Stopped
Network DDE: Stopped
Network DDE DSDM: Stopped
Norton SpeedDisk: Started
Norton Unerase Protection: Started
Plug and Play: Stopped
Protected Storage: Started
Remote Access Autodial Manager: Stopped
Remote Access Connection Manager: Stopped
Remote Access Server: Stopped
Remote Procedure Call (RPC) Locator: Stopped
Remote Procedure Call (RPC) Service: Stopped
Retrospect Remote Client: Started
Schedule: Stopped
Server: Stopped
Spooler: Started
TCP/IP NetBIOS Helper: Started
Telephony Service: Stopped
UPS: Stopped
Workstation: Started
```

If we try to start a service, we get this result:

```
C:\> ntserv.pl -u
Server INSENTIENT
Starting the Server service...

Server: Starter
```

Of course, this command could fail if you don't have the right permissions or authority to make any changes.

nstatus.pl

Monitoring Network Status

Our next five scripts relate to the status monitoring system. There are three parts to the system: the information-gathering scripts, the "collector" that processes the information from the gathering scripts into a hierarchy of log files, and the reporting system that extracts the information from the log files. In this book we'll look at two types of reporting, the network status monitor and the machine status monitor. See the "MediaWeb" sidebar for more information on the principles behind the status monitoring system.

MediaWeb

As a network manager, I understand the pressures and demands on a network manager's time. One of the network manager's most time-consuming tasks is monitoring the network and processing and filing the various logs and reports that are produced by the system. In order to get around this, I started developing a modular monitoring system that would be flexible enough to handle all types of information, including monitoring the status of the network and individual machines in the network and handling the logs and reports that individual machines might produce.

What I produced was a quasi-client/server system that was capable of reporting a variety of different pieces of information. The "quasi" element is the collection process. A single machine, running an FTP server, collects the data from other machines in the network. The process is only one-way; the machines transfer information to the collection server, not the other way around. The other side to this is that any machine, given the right access, can obtain the details from the Web server, perpetuating the client/server model, even though the method of sharing information between the two entities uses different methods, depending on the direction the information is traveling.

The system is still in development. There are lots of different aspects that require further work. In fact, for those of you who haven't skipped to this last chapter, we saw an early version of the status monitoring system in Chapter 5, in the **statserv.pl** and **statclnt.pl** scripts. In the end, it became apparent that developing a new communications system to exchange files was re-engineering the wheel: FTP could serve the same purpose. FTP is a well-established system, with security built in, and it's supported by virtually every platform.

The list of supported modules in the current system provides monitoring for Unix and NT machines, network availability, automatic log file clearing and reporting, and a network administrator's task list. In all cases, the provision of information comes from a number of sources, always delivered by FTP to the collection machine. To make the reporting process easy, we follow the current trend in intranet technology and use CGI scripts and Web servers to provide information to the user.

You can find more information on the MediaWeb system via my Web site (see the Introduction for more details).

The information-gathering scripts run on a variety of different machines, creating status files with a specific format that are then transferred to the collector machine, using FTP, into an "incoming" directory. The collection script then processes the files in the incoming directory, adding the information to the log files. Reporting on this information is just a case of accessing the log files and reporting on the stored information. The collector is actually a shell script and is not therefore included here or on the CD. You should be able to find the latest version of the collector script on my Web site (see the Introduction).

This script, **nstatus.pl**, is the network status monitor. It uses a configuration file and network status functions to check the availability of the different servers and services within the configuration. We check the status by using a combination of ping, which tests TCP/IP availability; the **Ssockets** module from Chapter 5 to check specific services on machines; and an external program, **aecho1**, to check AppleTalk hosts on an Apple network. This last program is a modified version of the **aecho** program that is part of the **atalkd** toolkit for supporting AppleTalk services on a Unix machine.

The status of each machine is recorded for historical information and is also reported straight into an HTML file, which can be accessed via a Web server. Furthermore, the server list file can also specify that the network manager be automatically notified by e-mail when a machine is unavailable; this is probably the most useful feature because the network manager will know, almost instantaneously, that a particular machine or service is down.

```perl
1   #!/usr/local/bin/perl5 -w
2
3   use strict;
4   use Net::Ping;
5   use SCGI;
6   use Ssockets;
7   use SMTPWrap;
8   use MCConfig;
9
10  my ($min,$hour,$mday,$mon,$year) = (localtime(time))[1..5];
11  $year += 1900;
12  $mon += 1;
13  my $date = "$year$mon$mday";
14  my $time = "$hour$min";
15
16  open(SRVRLIST,"<$serverlist")
17      or status_die("PANIC: Can't open $serverlist, $!",1);
18  open(STATUS,">$nstatusloc.temp")
19      or status_die("PANIC: Can't open $nstatusloc.temp, $!",1);
20  open(STATLOG,">>$nstatuslog/$year$mon")
21      or status_die("PANIC: Can't open $nstatuslog/$year$mon, $!",1);
22
23  print STATUS template('header','systems',
```

```
24                              'pagetitle' => 'Network Status',
25                              );
26  print STATUS template('main','systems',
27                              'pageheader' => 'Network Status',
28                              );
29
30  while(<SRVRLIST>)
31  {
32      next if (/^\#/);
33      chomp;
34      next unless (length($_) > 0);
35      my ($mode,$name,$address,$port,$report) = split /,/;
36      if ($mode =~ /^HEADER/)
37      {
38          print STATUS "</table><p>\n";
39          print STATUS "<font size=+1><b>$name</b></font><br>\n";
40          print STATUS "<table border=1>\n";
41          next;
42      }
43      else
44      {
45          if ($mode eq 'IP')
46          {
47              if ($port)
48              {
49                  record($name,$report,
50                      connectsocket(*IPTEMP,$address,
51                                      $port,'tcp'));
52                  close(IPTEMP);
53              }
54              else
55              {
56                  record($name,$report,pingecho($address));
57              }
58          }
59          elsif ($mode eq 'APPLE')
60          {
61              record($name,$report,
62                  !system("/usr/local/etc/atalk/bin/aecho1",
63                          "$address:$port"));
64          }
65      }
```

```perl
66  }
67  print STATUS "</table>\n";
68  print STATUS template('footer','www');
69
70  close(SRVRLIST)
71      or status_die("WARN: Couldn't close $serverlist, $!",0);
72  close(STATUS)
73      or status_die("WARN: Couldn't close $nstatusloc.temp, $!",0);
74  close(STATLOG)
75      or status_die("WARN: Couldn't close " .
76                    "$nstatuslog/$year$mon, $!",0);
77
78  unlink($nstatusloc);
79  rename("$nstatusloc.temp",$nstatusloc);
80
81  sub record
82  {
83      my ($host, $email, $success) = @_;
84      if ($success)
85      {
86          print STATUS ("<tr><Td>$host</td>",
87                        "<Td><font color=\"#00ff00\">",
88                        "Up</font></td></tr>\n");
89          print STATLOG "$date:$time:$host:1\n";
90      }
91      else
92      {
93          print STATUS ("<tr><td>$host</td>",
94                        "<td><font color=\"#ff0000\">",
95                        "Down</font></td></tr>\n");
96          print STATLOG "$date:$time:$host:0\n";
97          if ($email =~ /^yes$/i)
98          {
99              status_die("$host Down");
100         }
101     }
102  }
103
104  sub status_die
105  {
106      my ($message,$fatal) = @_;
```

```
107     mail_a_message("NS Warn:$message",
108                   "$colluser\@$collector",
109                   "$colluser\@$collector",
110                   $message);
111     exit if $fatal;
112 }
```

ANNOTATIONS

This script should be executed automatically on the collector machine every 5 minutes. It checks the status of the machines in order, writing the information both to the log file that stores historical information and to a static HTML page that can be accessed via a Web server to give the network administrator an immediate view of the status of the network. Each machine or service is polled in order, and failure to respond indicates that a machine or service is down; a valid response indicates success. This makes the script look significantly more complex than it actually is, as we write the same information to a number of files, including one HTML page.

```
1   #!/usr/local/bin/perl5 -w
2
3   use strict;
4   use Net::Ping;
5   use SCGI;
6   use Ssockets;
7   use SMTPWrap;
8   use MCConfig;
9
```

We need a lot of modules for this script. The **Net::Ping** module is part of the standard Perl distribution and supports a functional equivalent of the system ping command. The **SCGI** module, from this book, is required because I use the **template** function to produce the headers and footers for the HTML status page.

The **Ssockets** module will be used to test individual TCP/IP services on the network, such as Web and STMP mail servers. To report errors, we use the **SMTPWrap** module from Chapter 6. The last module, **MCConfig** on line 8, is supplied on the CD. It very simply defines the variables that we will user later in this and other scripts that form the status monitoring system. By defining the variables in a central location, we can change the configuration once, and all scripts will be aware of the change—and anything that avoids the effort of making multiple changes is worth some additional work.

```
10  my ($min,$hour,$mday,$mon,$year) = (localtime(time))[1..5];
11  $year += 1900;
```

```
12   $mon += 1;
13   my $date = "$year$mon$mday";
14   my $time = "$hour$min";
15
```

Lines 10 to 14 obtain the date and time and create formatted versions to be used later in the script. The format of the log file is

`date:time:hostname:status`

The status is either 1 or zero, signifying that the machine is up or down, respectively.

```
16   open(SRVRLIST,"<$serverlist")
17       or status_die("PANIC: Can't open $serverlist, $!",1);
18   open(STATUS,">$nstatusloc.temp")
19       or status_die("PANIC: Can't open $nstatusloc.temp, $!",1);
20   open(STATLOG,">>$nstatuslog/$year$mon")
21       or status_die("PANIC: Can't open $nstatuslog/$year$mon, $!",1);
22
```

Lines 16 to 21 open the files for reading and writing that we will require throughout the script. The first file is the list of servers that we need to check. The format of this file is

`Mode,name,address,port,report`

The mode is the type of host to check. We recognize two in this script, IP and APPLE, which specify a TCP/IP host or service or an AppleTalk host or service. The name is the name of the host that will appear in the reports. The address is the network address of the machine, which can either be a TCP/IP host name or IP address, or an AppleTalk name. The port is the TCP/IP service port or the AppleTalk type (the equivalent of a TCP/IP port). If it is the former, we use the **Ssockets** module to try accessing the specified service. The last field has a value of "yes" or "no" and defines whether a failure to reach the specified machine or service should be reported by e-mail to the network manager.

PROGRAMMER'S NOTE   *We use commas to separate the fields because the colon is used by AppleTalk to separate machine names and the zone they are in. If we had used a colon, we would have been unable to specify a machine within a specified zone.*

The **STATUS** file handle refers to the HTML file that will show the current network status. Line 20 opens the status file for appending; we will write the historical status information to this file. In each case, we ensure that the file can be opened, reporting an error via the **status_die** function. An error sends an e-mail to the network administrator. The second argument specifies whether the status message should be fatal or not; a zero indicates nonfatal.

Note that in line 18 we open a temporary file. We deliberately do not write directly to the active status page so that the page is permanently available, even when the information is being updated. Also note that in line 20 the name of the log file is based on the current year and month; historical information is split up by each month. This affects how the information is reported on when we come to do daily, monthly, and yearly reports. We'll see the effect of this in the next script, **dr.pl**.

```
23   print STATUS template('header','systems',
24                          'pagetitle' => 'Network Status',
25                          );
26   print STATUS template('main','systems',
27                          'pageheader' => 'Network Status',
28                          );
29
```

Lines 23 to 28 print out the header for the HTML page, using the **template** function that we have used previously in Chapter 8.

```
30   while(<SRVRLIST>)
31   {
32       next if (/^\#/);
33       chomp;
34       next unless (length($_) > 0);
35       my ($mode,$name,$address,$port,$report) = split /,/;
```

We start processing the server list on line 30. Line 32 skips the line if it starts with a hash, which is the standard comment character and allows the user to include comments in the server list file. We take the new-line character off the end of the current line on line 33. Line 34 skips over blank lines. It's worth noting that we must check the line length after we have taken the new-line character off; otherwise the length of the current line will be at least 1—that one character being the new line. We then split up the fields of the input line on line 35.

```
36       if ($mode =~ /^HEADER/)
37       {
38           print STATUS "</table><p>\n";
39           print STATUS "<font size=+1><b>$name</b></font><br>\n";
40           print STATUS "<table border=1>\n";
41           next;
42       }
```

The server list file includes the ability to support the separation of the report into different sections. A mode of HEADER specifies that the machine name should be used as the title for a new section. Lines 38 to 41 end the previous table (if there was one) and start a new table, before skipping the processing of the rest of the input line via the **next** function on line 41.

```
43      else
44      {
45          if ($mode eq 'IP')
46          {
47              if ($port)
48              {
49                  record($name,$report,
50                          connectsocket(*IPTEMP,$address,
51                                          $port,'tcp'));
52                  close(IPTEMP);
53              }
```

If the line is not a header definition, then we need to identify what type the entry is, and perform the necessary tests to check the availability of the machine. Line 45 identifies an IP test. If a TCP/IP port has been specified, lines 49 to 52 try to connect to the specified port at the specified address using the **connectsocket** function from the **Ssockets** module. The **connectsocket** function returns true if the connection was successful, and the result of the call passes directly to the **record** function.

The **record** function writes the necessary report information both to the HTML status file and the historical log file. The **record** function takes two other arguments: **$name** is the name that will be recorded, and **$report** decides whether the unavailability of a machine is to be reported by e-mail. This value is taken directly from the server list file.

```
54              else
55              {
56                  record($name,$report,pingecho($address));
57              }
58          }
```

If the TCP/IP port has not been specified, then we just need to ping the address of the machine we are checking. We use the simple **pingecho** function from the **Net::Ping** module, which emulates the system equivalent entirely within Perl. It returns a true value if the machine answers correctly.

```
59          elsif ($mode eq 'APPLE')
60          {
61              record($name,$report,
62                      !system("/usr/local/etc/atalk/bin/aecho1",
63                              "$address:$port"));
64          }
65      }
66  }
```

Line 59 checks if the machine type we are checking is an AppleTalk host. Lines 61 to 63 then call the **record** function to record the result of the call to the **aecho1** program. Unlike the **aecho** program, **aecho1** returns a zero if the specified host could be found on the AppleTalk network. This emulates the normal operation of the **ping** program. The **aecho** program, on the other hand, persistently checks for a machine's availability, which is not the functionality we want. You can find out more details on this program on my Web site.

The **system** Perl function allows you to run an external program, and the resulting code of the program is used as the return value of the function. In our case, the **aecho1** function returns zero on success. Since we expect a nonzero value to indicate success, we must invert the return value of the **system** function, and therefore the external program.

This ends the main loop of the script, and in fact all that remains is to print the footer to the HTML status page and then close the open files.

```
67   print STATUS "</table>\n";
68   print STATUS template('footer','www');
69
70   close(SRVRLIST)
71       or status_die("WARN: Couldn't close $serverlist, $!",0);
72   close(STATUS)
73       or status_die("WARN: Couldn't close $nstatusloc.temp, $!",0);
74   close(STATLOG)
75       or status_die("WARN: Couldn't close " .
76                     "$nstatuslog/$year$mon, $!",0);
77
```

We print the footer for the HTML status page on line 68, before closing each file on lines 70 to 76, remembering, in each case, to report an error if there is a problem. Unlike our previous failures, we mark them as nonfatal by specifying a zero as the second argument to the **status_die** function.

```
78   unlink($nstatusloc);
79   rename("$nstatusloc.temp",$nstatusloc);
80
```

Now that the HTML status page has been completed, we need to replace the active status page with the version we have just created. The **unlink** function deletes the old file, and then we use **rename** to move the new version to the active location. In both cases, the value of **$nstatusloc** is defined by the **MCConfig** module.

```
81   sub record
82   {
83       my ($host, $email, $success) = @_;
84       if ($success)
85       {
```

```
86          print STATUS ("<tr><Td>$host</td>",
87                          "<Td><font color=\"#00ff00\">",
88                          "Up</font></td></tr>\n");
89          print STATLOG "$date:$time:$host:1\n";
90       }
```

The **record** function accepts three arguments: the machine name, whether to e-mail the network administrator if the machine is down, and the success or otherwise of the machine test. This function is called as part of the test for the machine or service availability. The value of **$success** should be zero if the machine is unavailable, or 1 if the machine or service could be contacted.

If the machine could be contacted (according to the value of **$success**), then we print out a table row on lines 86 to 89 showing the name of the host and the fact the machine is available, highlighted in green. Line 89 then reports the status to the historical log, recording the date, time, host, and a status value of 1, indicating that the machine was available.

```
91       else
92       {
93          print STATUS ("<tr><td>$host</td>",
94                          "<td><font color=\"#ff0000\">",
95                          "Down</font></td></tr>\n");
96          print STATLOG "$date:$time:$host:0\n";
97          if ($email =~ /^yes$/i)
98          {
99              status_die("$host Down",0);
100          }
101      }
102 }
103
```

If the machine was unavailable, we print out the same table row on lines 93 to 95, except that this time we highlight the machine as down by specifying the value in red text. Line 96 prints a corresponding failure entry to the historical log. Lines 97 to 100 then report a status failure, by e-mail, if the option was specified in the server configuration list. We use the same **status_die** function, only this time the second argument is zero, indicating that this is a nonfatal error.

```
104 sub status_die
105 {
106     my ($message, $fatal) = @_;
107     mail_a_message("NS Warn:$message",
108                     "$colluser\@$collector",
109                     "$colluser\@$collector",
110                     $message);
111     exit if $fatal;
112 }
```

The **status_die** function formats and sends an e-mail message to the user at the collector machine. This should be set, via the **MCConfig** module, to the value of the administrator and collection machine. The **$fatal** argument specifies whether the error is fatal—if it is then we **exit** on line 111. This allows us to use the same function to report warnings and fatal errors.

Using the script is a case of setting up the necessary crontab entry and populating the server list. With the following example, we get an HTML page like the one shown in Figure 11-1.

```
#
# Net Tester Configuration File
#
# Lines beginning # are ignored
#
# Sequence is:
#
# Protocol
# Name
# Host to search for
# Port to identify
# Email on failure
#
HEADER,TCP/IP Services
IP,Internet Connectivity,158.152.1.65,,yes
IP,Internet Router,198.112.10.128,,yes
IP,NT Server,198.112.10.131,,yes
IP,Client FTP Server,ftp.mcwords.com,ftp,yes
#
HEADER,Appleshare Services
APPLE,MC Server,MC Server,AFPServer,yes
```

In the next script, we'll look at how to analyze this information to provide daily, monthly, or yearly reports of the availability of different servers and services.

dr.pl

Network Status Daily Report

The name "daily report" is a bit of a misnomer—the report will report on the availability of all of the machines that have been reported on, per day, month, or year, or the exact day month or year can be specified. It's a CGI script, and we use techniques we saw back in Chapter 8 to create a self-standing script that provides the form to be used and the formatted information, depending on whether the script is called with or without options.

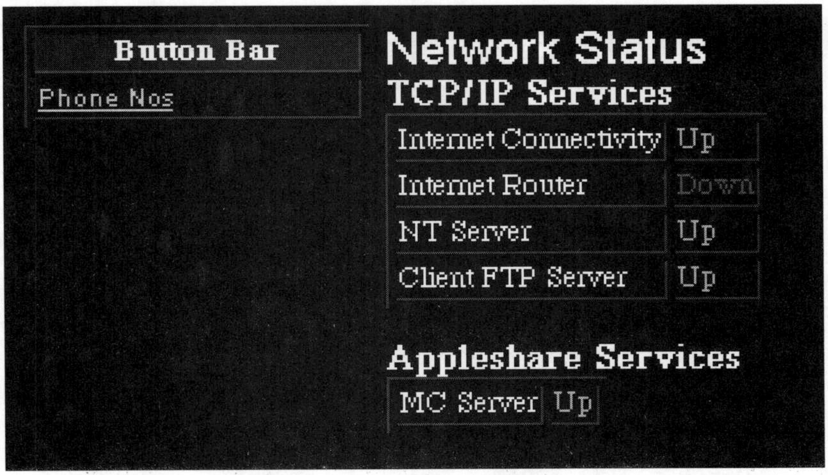

FIGURE 11-1. The network status report

The script takes the information reported by the previous script. It uses a calculation, based on the expected number of entries against the actual number of success entries in the log file, to display the availability as a percentage.

```perl
1   #!/usr/local/bin/perl5 -w
2
3   use strict;
4   use SCGI;
5   use MCConfig;
6
7   print "Content-type: text/html\n\n";
8
9   init_cgi;
10
11  my $pagetitle = "Daily Report";
12  my $pageheader = "Daily Report";
13
14  print template('header','www',
15                 'pagetitle' => $pagetitle,
16                 );
17  print template('main','www',
18                 'pageheader' => $pageheader,
19                 );
```

```perl
20
21  my ($mday,$mon,$year) = (localtime(time))[3,4,5];
22  $year += 1900;
23  $mon++;
24
25  if ( $SCGI::formlength < 1 )
26  {
27      print <<EOF;
28  <form method=GET method="/cgi-bin/dr.pl">
29  <b>Report type:</b><select name=type>
30  <option value=day>Day
31  <option value=month>Month
32  <option value=year>Year
33  </select><br>
34  <b>Date to Review:</b>
35  <input type=text size=2 name=day value=$mday>/
36  <input type=text size=2 name=mon value=$mon>/
37  <input type=text size=4 name=year value=$year><br>
38  <input type="submit" value="send">
39  </form>
40  EOF
41  }
42  else
43  {
44      print("<font size=+1><b>",
45              "Report for $SCGI::formlist{day}/",
46              "$SCGI::formlist{mon}/",
47              "$SCGI::formlist{year}<p>\n");
48      print <<EOF;
49  <table border=1>
50  <tr><td><b>Server</b></td>
51  <td align=left><b>Uptime</b></td>
52  <td align=left><b>Downtime</b></td>
53  </tr>
54  EOF
55
56      my ($logpathfiles);
57      if (($SCGI::formlist{type} =~ /day/) or
58          ($SCGI::formlist{type} =~ /mon/))
59      {
60          $logpathfiles=sprintf("%s/%4d%02d*",
61                                  $nstatuslog,
```

```
62                                    $SCGI::formlist{year},
63                                    $SCGI::formlist{mon});
64      }
65      elsif ($SCGI::formlist{type} =~ /year/)
66      {
67          $logpathfiles=sprintf("%s/%04d*",$nstatuslog,$year);
68      }
69
70      my @logfiles = glob($logpathfiles);
71      my (%machine);
72
73      my $selecteddate = sprintf("%4d%02d%02d",
74                                    $SCGI::formlist{year},
75                                    $SCGI::formlist{mon},
76                                    $SCGI::formlist{day});
77
78      for my $file (@logfiles)
79      {
80          open(D,"/usr/local/bin/gunzip -c $file|") or next;
81
82          while(<D>)
83          {
84              chop;
85              next unless(length($_));
86              my ($date,$time,$machine,$status) = split /:/;
87              next unless(defined($date) and defined($time) and
88                          defined($machine) and defined($status));
89              my $yes=0;
90
91              if ($SCGI::formlist{type} =~ "day")
92              {
93                  if ($selecteddate eq $date)
94                  { $yes = 1 }
95                  else
96                  { $yes = 0 }
97              }
98              else
99              { $yes = 1; }
100
101             if ($yes)
102             {
103                 ($status) ? $machine{$machine}{ucount}++
104                     : $machine{$machine}{dcount}++;
```

```
105                    }
106              }
107          close(D);
108      }
109
110      my ($count,$totact,$totdown);
111
112      foreach my $machine (sort keys %machine)
113      {
114          my $actualuptime=($machine{$machine}{ucount}*100)
115              / ($machine{$machine}{ucount}
116                  + (($machine{$machine}{dcount}) ?
117                      ($machine{$machine}{dcount}) : 0));
118
119          my $actualdowntime=100-$actualuptime;
120
121          print("<tr><Td>$machine</td>\n");
122          printf("<td align=right>%3.2f %%</td>\n",
123                  $actualuptime);
124          printf("<td align=right>%3.2f %%</td></tr>\n",
125                  $actualdowntime);
126          $count++;
127          $totact   += $actualuptime;
128          $totdown += $actualdowntime;
129      }
130      printf("<tr><Td><b>Total:</b></td>\n");
131      printf("<td align=right>%3.2f %%</td>\n",
132              ($totact/$count));
133      printf("<td align=right>%3.2f %%</td></tr>\n",
134              ($totdown/$count));
135      print "</table>";
136 }
137
138 print template('footer','www');
```

ANNOTATIONS

The script follows the same layout as the more advanced CGI scripts we have already seen. The script initializes the CGI system using the **SCGI** module from Chapter 8, and it either supplies the form to select the information to be displayed, or it displays the selected information.

```
1    #!/usr/local/bin/perl5 -w
2
3    use strict;
4    use SCGI;
5    use MCConfig;
6
7    print "Content-type: text/html\n\n";
8
9    init_cgi;
10
```

We import the **MCConfig** module, which provides us with the location of the log files. Line 7 prints out the HTTP header so that the user's browser knows what sort of information to expect, and we initialize the CGI variables that hold the values from the form information, if it has been supplied, on line 9.

```
11   my $pagetitle = "Daily Report";
12   my $pageheader = "Daily Report";
13
14   print template('header','www',
15                  'pagetitle' => $pagetitle,
16                  );
17   print template('main','www',
18                  'pageheader' => $pageheader,
19                  );
20
```

Lines 11 to 19 print out the page header, which is consistent regardless of whether we are providing the form or the report, so they are printed outside of the test for form elements.

```
21   my ($mday,$mon,$year) = (localtime(time))[3,4,5];
22   $year += 1900;
23   $mon++;
24
```

We need the date in order to pre-fill the form with values so it is clear what the user has to enter. It also means the user can press the Submit button and obtain an availability report for today without entering today's date.

```
25   if ( $SCGI::formlength < 1 )
26   {
27       print <<EOF;
28   <form method=GET method="/cgi-bin/dr.pl">
29   <b>Report type:</b><select name=type>
30   <option value=day>Day
31   <option value=month>Month
```

```
32   <option value=year>Year
33   </select><br>
34   <b>Date to Review:</b>
35   <input type=text size=2 name=day value=$mday>/
36   <input type=text size=2 name=mon value=$mon>/
37   <input type=text size=4 name=year value=$year><br>
38   <input type="submit" value="send">
39   </form>
40   EOF
41   }
```

If no form elements have been specified, we identify this on line 25 and print out the form on lines 27 to 40. The form has only two elements, the report type, day, month, or year, and the date. The report type defines which fields are used from the date supplied. For example, if the users selects a yearly report, then the day and month will be ignored—we don't need them.

```
42   else
43   {
44       print("<font size=+1><b>",
45               "Report for $SCGI::formlist{day}/",
46               "$SCGI::formlist{mon}/",
47               "$SCGI::formlist{year}<p>\n");
48       print <<EOF;
49   <table border=1>
50   <tr><td><b>Server</b></td>
51   <td align=left><b>Uptime</b></td>
52   <td align=left><b>Downtime</b></td>
53   </tr>
54   EOF
55
```

If there are form fields supplied to the script (presumably from the from provided in the previous section), then we print the report header on lines 44 to 54.

```
56       my ($logpathfiles);
57       if (($SCGI::formlist{type} =~ /day/) or
58           ($SCGI::formlist{type} =~ /mon/))
59       {
60           $logpathfiles=sprintf("%s/%4d%02d*",
61                                   $nstatuslog,
62                                   $SCGI::formlist{year},
63                                   $SCGI::formlist{mon});
64       }
```

The **$logpathfiles** variable, on line 56, holds the specification for a later **glob** function. We need to decipher the list of files that will be processed. Remember that the log files are stored as a six-digit year and month. If the user selects a month or day report, we need to open only one file and process the contents. If the user has selected a year, then we need to open up to 12 files and process the contents of each.

The corresponding file specification for a day or month report is created via the **sprintf** function in lines 60 to 63. The **sprintf** function returns the formatted information as a string, rather than printing the information to a file handle. In the case of a day or month report, we can create a file specification based on the location of the network status log (**$nstatuslog**) and the year and month specified on the HTML form. The use of **sprintf** ensures that if the user has simply entered "1" as the month on the form, it will be correctly used as "01" within the file specification.

```
65      elsif ($SCGI::formlist{type} =~ /year/)
66      {
67          $logpathfiles=sprintf("%s/%04d*",$nstatuslog,$year);
68      }
69
```

If the report type is year, then the file specification can be simply made up of the year.

```
70      my @logfiles = glob($logpathfiles);
71      my (%machine);
72
```

The **@logfiles** array holds the list of valid files from the result of the **glob**, based on the file specification we have just generated. We use the **%machine** hash to store information about the machines and their availability. The key holds the machine name, and the corresponding value holds a count of the number of times the machine was logged as being available.

```
73      my $selecteddate = sprintf("%4d%02d%02d",
74                                  $SCGI::formlist{year},
75                                  $SCGI::formlist{mon},
76                                  $SCGI::formlist{day});
77
```

If we are reporting a specific day, then we need a value to compare to, in order to build up the availability report. If you refer to the previous script, you will remember that the individual records of the availability report are as follows:

```
19981101:2005:Internet Gateway:1
```

Lines 73 to 76 build a date in the same format as the first field of the log file; we'll need this date to compare against the log file.

```
78    for my $file (@logfiles)
79    {
80        open(D,"/usr/local/bin/gunzip -c $file|") or next;
81
```

We start a loop to work through the list of files that contain the information on which we want to report. This could be a single file in the case of a month or day report, or it could be multiple files, up to a maximum of 12, if the user has selected a year report.

Line 80 attempts to open the file, or it skips to the next one if the file cannot be opened. Note that we open the file via gunzip; the **-c** option forces gunzip to decompress the file to standard output without actually decompressing the file. Log files older than the current month are automatically compressed as part of the collection process.

```
82        while(<D>)
83        {
84            chop;
85            next unless(length($_));
86            my ($date,$time,$machine,$status) = split /:/;
87            next unless(defined($date) and defined($time) and
88                        defined($machine) and defined($status));
89            my $yes=0;
90
```

We start a loop to work through the contents of the current log file on line 82. What we need to do here is identify whether the current record from the file needs to be included in the report. We take the new-line character off the end of the record in line 84, and we skip the record unless the length of the record is greater than zero on line 85.

Line 86 extracts the fields from the current record, using **split** to separate the elements by the colon used when the records were created. Just in case there was an error reporting the details, we skip the record if we cannot find valid information in each of the fields.

The **$yes** variable, which we initialize to zero on line 89, decides if the current record should be included in the calculation. If we are producing a month or year report, all lines should be included, but if we are producing a day report, then we need to compare the value of the **$date** variable against the **$selecteddate** variable we created earlier. If they match, the record should be included, but if they don't match we can ignore it. The logic for this is in following lines:

```
91        if ($SCGI::formlist{type} =~ "day")
92        {
```

```
93                  if ($selecteddate eq $date)
94                  { $yes = 1 }
95                  else
96                  { $yes = 0 }
97              }
98          else
99          { $yes = 1; }
100
```

Lines 91 to 99 decide which lines to include; if the report is for a single day (line 91), we must compare the date values (line 93), setting the **$yes** variable to a positive value if they match, or zero if they don't. If we are not producing a report by day, then all lines should be included, which is the purpose of lines 98 and 99.

```
101             if ($yes)
102             {
103                 ($status) ? $machine{$machine}{ucount}++
104                     : $machine{$machine}{dcount}++;
105             }
106         }
107     close(D);
108     }
109
```

On line 101, we test the value of the **$yes** variable. If it's true, it signifies that the current record should be included in the report. Lines 103 and 104 increment either the ucount or dcount keys of the hash within the value of the matching **$machine** key of the **%machine** hash.

To explain this better, the **%machine** hash is made up of keys and values. It is legal, and in fact very practical, to have a hash as the value. This hash also has its own keys and corresponding values. The result is a hash of hashes, which allows us to model complex information in a more natural way. The main key can be thought of as the record, and the subhash key can be thought of as the field within the record. The combination of the two gives us a two-dimensional hash, which is very easy and practical to implement and use, although at first glance it looks more complicated than it is.

The result in our case is a database within a hash variable. The records can be identified by the name of the machine; the two fields, ucount and dcount, specify the number of times that an individual machine has been identified as up and down, respectively.

Once the log file has been processed, we close the current log file on line 107 before moving on to the next log file in the list.

```
110     my ($count,$totact,$totdown);
111
```

Line 110 sets up the variables we use to store the summary information for call machines.

```
112    foreach my $machine (sort keys %machine)
113    {
114        my $actualuptime=($machine{$machine}{ucount}*100)
115            / ($machine{$machine}{ucount}
116            + (($machine{$machine}{dcount}) ?
117                ($machine{$machine}{dcount}) : 0));
118
```

Line 112 starts a loop to work through the sorted list of machines within the hash. Note that we do not have to treat the parent hash specially, even though it is in fact a hash of hashes. This is because keys and values are still treated separately: the values contain references to anonymous hashes, which we can access directly using the notation we have already seen.

Lines 114 to 117 calculate the uptime of an individual machine. The calculation is a fairly simple one. We divide the number of times the machine was recorded as being "up" multiplied by a hundred (line 114) by the total number of up and down counts recorded in all the log files (lines 115 to 117). We have to take account of the fact on lines 116 and 117 that the machine may never have been down, in which case the down count will be undefined.

```
119        my $actualdowntime=100-$actualuptime;
120
```

The downtime of a machine can be calculated by subtracting the actual uptime from 100. (We are dealing with percentages, which makes the calculation much easier!)

```
121        print("<tr><Td>$machine</td>\n");
122        printf("<td align=right>%3.2f %%</td>\n",
123            $actualuptime);
124        printf("<td align=right>%3.2f %%</td></tr>\n",
125            $actualdowntime);
126        $count++;
127        $totact  += $actualuptime;
128        $totdown += $actualdowntime;
129    }
```

Lines 121 to 125 print the uptime and downtime information for the current machine, using **printf** to format the percentages to print with a maximum of two digits past the decimal point. Lines 126 to 128 count the number of machines and total the uptime and downtime so we can report the average uptime and downtime for all of the machines.

```
130      printf("<tr><Td><b>Total:</b></td>\n");
131      printf("<td align=right>%3.2f %%</td>\n",
132              ($totact/$count));
133      printf("<td align=right>%3.2f %%</td></tr>\n",
134              ($totdown/$count));
135      print "</table>";
136  }
137
138  print template('footer','www');
```

Lines 130 to 134 print out the average uptime and downtime information, and line 135 closes the HTML table used to format the data. This is the end of the script, so line 138 prints out the standard footer for the intranet site.

A sample report can be seen in Figure 11-2.

uxstat.pl

Getting Individual Unix Statistics

Our next two scripts obtain statistics about the current machine for use in reporting their status as part of a machine status page, which we'll see later in this script. This script is used on Unix machines (the next script is an NT version), and it obtains the disk space and loading and swap space of the machine, placing the details into a single file. The performance information is then sent by FTP to the collector machine.

Daily Report
Day Report for 01/11/98

Server	Uptime	Downtime
Client FTP Server	100.0 %	0.00 %
Internet Connectivity	100.0 %	0.00 %
Internet Router	100.0 %	0.00 %
MC Server	69.6 %	30.04 %
NT Server	100.0 %	0.00 %
Total:	93.92 %	6.08 %

FIGURE 11-2. The server daily report

There are a few things that we need to take into account in the script. First of all, we have to find reliable ways of obtaining the information we are looking for. This is not as easy as it sounds, since we need to be able to support FTP, which requires, in our case, the excellent **libnet** module from Graham Barr.

Second, we need to make the script as self sufficient as possible. We cannot rely on as many external modules as we have done before; we could be using this script on a machine that doesn't support them, or we may not want to support additional Perl modules. Finally, the collector machine, which needs to be running FTP, may not be available at the time the script needs to send in a report. We need to place the status files in an outgoing directory and have the script send all the status files when it can contact the destination.

Unlike the network status script, this script was designed to record historical information to monitor the performance of individual machines, although the script does provide 'live' status information, as we'll see with the **ms.pl** script later in this chapter. On my own network, I run the script every 15 minutes. The process is quite time-consuming for a simple information gathering exercise, and we don't want to have the machine running the tests so frequently that it distorts the statistics it is trying to gather.

```perl
1   #!/usr/local/bin/perl5 -w
2
3   use strict;
4   use SMTPWrap;
5   use Net::FTP;
6   use MCConfig;
7   require 'hostname.pl';
8
9   my ($min,$hour,$mday,$mon,$year) = (localtime(time))[1,2,3,4,5];
10  $year += 1900;
11  $mon++;
12
13  my $dateref = sprintf("%4d%02d%02d:%02d%02d",
14                        $year,$mon,$mday,$hour,$min);
15
16  my $remlogdir = $colldir;
17  my $machine   = hostname();
18  my $logdir    = '/tmp/statout/';
19  my $logfile   = "$logdir/perf.$machine.$dateref.$$";
20  my $fswarn    = 5000;
21  my $swapwarn  = 5000;
22  my $loadwarn  = 3;
23
24  mkdir($logdir,777);
25
```

```perl
26   unless(open(PERF,">$logfile"))
27   {
28       warn_collector("Monitor failed: Opening $logfile: $!");
29       exit;
30   }
31
32   check_fs();
33   check_swap();
34   check_load();
35
36   unless(close(PERF))
37   {
38       warn_collector("Monitor failed: Closing $logfile: $!");
39       exit;
40   }
41
42   send_perf();
43
44   sub warn_collector
45   {
46       my ($message) = @_;
47       mail_a_message("SM Warn:$message",
48                      "$colluser\@$collector",
49                      "$colluser\@$machine",
50                      $message);
51   }
52
53   sub check_fs
54   {
55       open(FS,"/usr/bin/df -k|") or return;
56       <FS>;
57       while(<FS>)
58       {
59           my ($tot,$used,$avail,$fs) = (split(/\s+/))[1,2,3,5];
60           next if ($tot == 0);
61           warn_collector("$fs\@$machine, $avail")
62               if ($avail <= $fswarn);
63           print PERF "$dateref:df:$fs:$avail:$used\n";
64       }
65       close(FS);
66   }
67
68   sub check_swap
```

```perl
69   {
70       my $swap = `/usr/sbin/swap -s`;
71       $swap =~ s/k//g;
72       my ($used,$avail) = (split(/ /,$swap))[8,10];
73       warn_collector("Swap\@$machine, $avail")
74           if ($avail <= $swapwarn);
75       print PERF "$dateref:sw:$used:$avail\n";
76   }
77
78   sub check_load
79   {
80       my $load = `/usr/bin/uptime`;
81       my ($loada,$loadb,$loadc)
82           = ($load =~ m/.*average:\s+
83                         ([\d.]+)[\s,]+
84                         ([\d.]+)[\s,]+
85                         ([\d.]+)/x);
86       warn_collector("Load\@$machine, $loada")
87           if ($loada >= $loadwarn);
88       print PERF "$dateref:ld:$loada:$loadb:$loadc\n";
89   }
90
91   sub send_perf()
92   {
93       my $ftp = Net::FTP->new($collector);
94       unless($ftp)
95       {
96           warn_collector("Couldn't FTP\n");
97           exit;
98       }
99       $ftp->login($colluser,$collpass);
100      $ftp->cwd($remlogdir);
101      chdir($logdir);
102      my @list = glob("perf.*");
103      for my $file (@list)
104      {
105          if ($ftp->put($file,$file))
106          {
107              unlink $file;
108          }
109      }
110      $ftp->quit;
111  }
```

ANNOTATIONS

The script uses a set of functions that use external programs to obtain the performance information. We have to parse the output of each program in order to identify the information we are looking for. Once the data has been gathered, it's written out, in a standard format, to the file that will eventually be sent to the collection machine. The format for the lines in the performance file is

`date:time:type:typeinfo...`

The date field is formatted as the date in universal format, the time in hours and minutes. The type is the type of information being recorded; for example, sw defines that the typeinfo field contains information about the swap space. The other two types we use in this script are df for disk space and ld for the system loading.

Aside from reporting the information into the file that will be sent to the collector, we also take the opportunity to monitor the different performance information, reporting any possible problems.

The basic operation of the script is to create the log file and discover the performance information for the disk space, swap space, and load average of the machine, writing the details out to the log file. The last stage of the process is to send the file, by FTP, to the collection machine.

```perl
1    #!/usr/local/bin/perl5 -w
2
3    use strict;
4    use SMTPWrap;
5    use Net::FTP;
6    use MCConfig;
7    require 'hostname.pl';
8
9    my ($min,$hour,$mday,$mon,$year) = (localtime(time))[1,2,3,4,5];
10   $year += 1900;
11   $mon++;
12
13   my $dateref = sprintf("%4d%02d%02d:%02d%02d",
14                         $year,$mon,$mday,$hour,$min);
15
```

Lines 4 to 7 include the necessary modules that we are going to use. We need the **SMTPWrap** module to send e-mail messages regarding any failures during the operation of the script; we could have developed a separate function that used an external program like sendmail, but since we require the **libnet** module for FTP transfers we know that the corresponding **Net::SMTP** module will also have been installed. We need the **hostname.pl** script, which provides functions for discovering the name of the host we are running—we need this information for the name of the log file.

We also need the date and time for the log file name and for the log file records. We extract the date and time on line 9; remember on lines 10 and 11 to add the necessary values to the year and month that are returned so that the year includes the century, and the month starts at 1 for January. Lines 13 and 14 then format the date and time field, placing the date in year/month/day format, with separators. As we have seen previously, this can help in sorting and formatting information.

```perl
16    my $remlogdir = $colldir;
17    my $machine   = hostname();
18    my $logdir    = '/tmp/statout/';
19    my $logfile   = "$logdir/perf.$machine.$dateref.$$";
20    my $fswarn    = 5000;
21    my $swapwarn  = 5000;
22    my $loadwarn  = 3;
23
```

Lines 16 to 22 define the local variables, specific to this script, that we need throughout the remainder of the script. Unlike those variables specified by the **MCConfig** module, these variables are used in and customizable for this script only.

The remote collection directory is stored in **$remlogdir**; the value is taken straight from the **MCConfig** specification. Line 17 extracts the name of the machine. Line 18 defines the location of the local log files before they are sent on to the collection machine. The **$logfile** variable stores the name of the log file that will be created. The format of this file must match the format used by the rest of the status monitor system. The format of these files is as follows:

`type.machine.date.id`

The type is the type of log file; this is used by the collector (see "The Collector" sidebar at the end of this script section) to identify what to do with the script. The machine name defines where the log file will be stored—individual directories exist for each of the machines monitored by the status system. The date and ID act as a combination of identifiers for log file names and as a unique sequence number to prevent files from overwriting each other. The **$$** variable is used as the Id; it represents the process ID of the current execution of the Perl script. By using the machine name, date, time, and the process ID, we ensure that other log files are not overwritten when they reach the collection machine.

```perl
24    mkdir($logdir,777);
25
```

We ensure that the log directory that we want to use to store the status in exists by recreating it on line 24.

```perl
26    unless(open(PERF,">$logfile"))
27    {
```

```
28          warn_collector("Monitor failed: Opening $logfile: $!");
29          exit;
30      }
31
```

We attempt to open the log file on line 26, reporting an error via the **warn_collector** function on line 28 if the operation fails. If we cannot open the log file, then there is no point in continuing, so we quit the script on line 29.

```
32      check_fs();
33      check_swap();
34      check_load();
35
```

Lines 32 to 34 call the corresponding functions for checking the file system space, the swap space, and load average of the machine.

```
36      unless(close(PERF))
37      {
38          warn_collector("Monitor failed: Closing $logfile: $!");
39          exit;
40      }
41
```

We close the log file on line 36, again checking to make sure we can close it correctly. Failure to do so causes another warning on line 38. Since a failure to close the file could indicate a failure to write the information out to the log file, we also exit the script before sending the file on to the collector. Note that we don't delete the file, so that the file can be checked by the network administrator and deleted or allowed to be sent the next time the script is run. The error that caused the failure could have been a temporary problem.

```
42      send_perf();
43
```

Line 42 calls the **send_perf** function to transfer the log file to the collection machine for processing.

```
44      sub warn_collector
45      {
46          my ($message) = @_;
47          mail_a_message("SM Warn:$message",
48                         "$colluser\@$collector",
49                         "$colluser\@$machine",
50                         $message);
51      }
52
```

The **warn_collector** function e-mails a warning message to the network administrator at the e-mail address specified in the **MCConfig** module.

```
53   sub check_fs
54   {
55       open(FS,"/usr/bin/df -k|") or return;
56       <FS>;
57       while(<FS>)
58           {
```

We use the **df** program to obtain details about the available file systems and report the amount of space used and available on each. We use Perl's ability to open not a file, but a file handle attached to the execution of the program. The pipe symbol at the end of the filename defines that Perl should open the program specified for reading from; the standard output of the file will be redirected to the file handle and can then be read using familiar commands.

The output of the **df** command with the **-k** option looks like this:

```
$ df -k
Filesystem              kbytes      used     avail  capacity  Mounted on
/dev/dsk/c0t0d0s0       115504     28019     75935      27%   /
/dev/dsk/c0t0d0s4       240516    208755      7711      96%   /usr
/proc                        0         0         0       0%   /proc
fd                           0         0         0       0%   /dev/fd
/dev/dsk/c0t0d0s3        57487      6748     44999      13%   /opt
/dev/dsk/c0t0d0s6       480509    113005    319454      26%   /users
/dev/dsk/c0t0d0s5      1041732    504153    433409      54%   /usr/local
```

We need to extract the **used**, **avail**, and **Mounted on** fields for the log file report. First of all, we need to skip the title line—it contains no useful information. Line 56 skips the first line. You probably recognize the **<FS>** notation from the **while** loop (in fact we use it on line 57). It returns a line from the file, and, when used in the **while** loop, it returns progressive lines from the file until it can no longer read from the file. By using it on its own here, without assigning the return value to anything, we have effectively moved the file pointer to the next line in the file.

```
59           my ($tot,$used,$avail,$fs) = (split(/\s+/))[1,2,3,5];
60           next if ($tot == 0);
61           warn_collector("$fs\@$machine, $avail")
62               if ($avail <= $fswarn);
63           print PERF "$dateref:df:$fs:$avail:$used\n";
```

Line 59 uses **split** with a regular expression of multiple spaces and subscript notation to obtain the total, used, available, and mount point data from the **df** output. If you refer to the sample output, you will see there are file system entries that have a total size of zero. They are the special file systems that manage processes and file descriptors. They don't provide any useful information, and in fact we skip over them on line 60.

Lines 61 and 62 check the available file space against the minimum value specified at the start of the script. Since we have taken the opportunity to extract the information here, we use it to warn the network administrator of any possible problems. We could do this on the collection machine, but that would require postprocessing of the file that is received and that may be some time after the problem first appears. Instead we send an e-mail directly from this script, using the same mechanism that warns of execution problems. The difference is that because this is a warning, we do not quit the script.

Line 63 prints out the performance details to the log file, using the predefined date, time, and type field data.

```
64          }
65      close(FS);
66  }
67
```

Once the **df** command has completed, there is no more information to read from the command, so the loop ends after line 64; we close it on line 65 before finally exiting the function on line 66.

```
68  sub check_swap
69  {
70      my $swap = `/usr/sbin/swap -s`;
71      $swap =~ s/k//g;
72      my ($used,$avail) = (split(/ /,$swap))[8,10];
73      warn_collector("Swap\@$machine, $avail")
74          if ($avail <= $swapwarn);
75      print PERF "$dateref:sw:$used:$avail\n";
76  }
77
```

The **check_swap** function reports the amount of swap space used and available on the machine. The function here is designed for Solaris, which provides the swap program. With the **–s** option, it reports the status of the swap space, including how much has been used and how much is available. The output from the swap command is obtained by using backtick notation—the output from the command is returned and placed into the **$swap** variable. The output of the command looks like this:

```
total: 8376k bytes allocated + 2384k reserved = 10740k used, 4536k available
```

Because we are interested only in the values, we can safely strip the "k" for kilobytes off the end of the values, which we do in line 71. We could use a regular expression match to extract the information, but in fact it's easier to simply split the returned line by spaces and access the resulting fields, and then obtain the total amount of swap space used and available in line 72.

Again we take the opportunity in lines 73 and 74 to warn the network administrator if the amount of swap space is below the value set at the start of the script. Then in line 75 we output the data captured to the log file.

```
78   sub check_load
79   {
80       my $load = `/usr/bin/uptime`;
81       my ($loada,$loadb,$loadc)
82           = ($load =~ m/.*average:\s+
83                         ([\d.]+)[\s,]+
84                         ([\d.]+)[\s,]+
85                         ([\d.]+)/x);
86       warn_collector("Load\@$machine, $loada")
87           if ($loada >= $loadwarn);
88       print PERF "$dateref:ld:$loada:$loadb:$loadc\n";
89   }
90
```

The **uptime** command reports the load average of the machine by showing the average number of jobs executed each second over the last minute, 5 minutes, and 15 minutes. The information is generated automatically by the kernel and is a reliable and well-established method of monitoring the load on a machine's resources. The output from the **uptime** command looks like this:

```
9:24am up 22:34 3 users, load average: 0.12, 0.67, 1.2
```

We extract the load average information via a match regular expression on line 82 to 85. The /x option allows us to put the regular expression on multiple lines. We are looking for the word "average" and then three floating point numbers (defined by [\d.]+), separated by a mixture of spaces and commas.

The results are placed into three variables that we use as the data fields for the log record in line 88. We also take the opportunity in lines 86 and 87 to report a warning to the network administrator if the load average for the last minute exceeds the value specified at the start of the script.

```
91   sub send_perf()
92   {
93       my $ftp = Net::FTP->new($collector);
94       unless($ftp)
95       {
96           warn_collector("Couldn't FTP\n");
97           exit;
98       }
```

The **send_perf** function connects to the collection machine and sends all of the files in an outgoing directory. We need the **Net::FTP** module to do this. Line 93 attempts to contact the collection machine, creating a new FTP object. If we cannot reach the machine, then we report an error to the network administrator in line 96. It's a serious enough error to warrant us exiting from the script on line 97. By the time the function has been called, the performance file will have been created, and because we don't delete the file it will remain in the outgoing directory.

```
99      $ftp->login($colluser,$collpass);
100     $ftp->cwd($remlogdir);
101     chdir($logdir);
102     my @list = glob("perf.*");
```

In line 99 we log in to the FTP server, using the predefined user and password, as obtained from the **MCConfig** module. We then change to the remote incoming directory on line 100, and change the local directory in line 101. I haven't checked these results—we should be in controlled conditions since we manage the entire system. Line 102 obtains the list of files waiting to be sent to the collection machine. Note that the design of the system means that all files from all of the subsystems that are waiting to be sent will also be transferred by this function.

```
103     for my $file (@list)
104     {
105         if ($ftp->put($file,$file))
106         {
107             unlink $file;
108         }
109     }
110     $ftp->quit;
111 }
```

Lines 103 to 109 step through the list of files waiting to be sent, sending each one on line 105. If the transfer was successful, we can delete the file on line 107. If the transfer failed for any reason, then the file will not be deleted and will be available for sending next time this transfer process occurs.

It's difficult to show any specific output from the script, since the information makes little sense outside of the reporting system. We'll take a look at the results when we examine the **ms.pl** script later in this chapter.

The Collector

Once all of the information has been gathered and sent to the incoming directory, we need to process the details. The shell script that gathers the information, studies the name of each file in the incoming directory, and processes the file accordingly. For example, for the machine status information in the **uxstat.pl** script, we append the file to the historical statistics log for the machine, and we also copy a version into a "latest" file. The latter file is used by the **ms.pl** script to identify the latest set of statistics from the machine, saving us from examining the historical log to gain the details we want to report.

Other parts of the status monitor system pass their data in the same way, by supplying a file via FTP to the incoming directory. The collection script parses and reports on those in a similar fashion. I've already set up handlers that process the Web log files each week, update the information into files split by month, and then automatically create the Web log report. Adding another status monitoring system is just a case of creating the necessary script on the host machine and modifying the collector script on the collection machine to handle the information.

The collection script should obviously be run at a reasonable interval in order to process the incoming information. Since the performance scripts are set to run every 15 minutes (at 0, 15, 30, and 45 minutes past the hour), I've also set the collector to process the incoming directory every 15 minutes, but this time at 5, 20, 35, and 50 minutes past the hour.

ntstat.pl

Getting Individual NT Statistics

The **ntstat.pl** script provides similar functionality to the Unix equivalent, extracting performance information from an NT machine, formatting it in the same way for sending to the collection server. The only difference, due in part to a difference between the operating systems, is that we cannot easily obtain the load average information that is available under Unix on NT.

Windows NT and Windows in general provide tools for reporting the available memory and disk space. However, they both have limitations. The mem command reports a huge amount of information about the system, especially when compared to the fact that we only require information on the amount of memory used and the amount available. Although it wouldn't be impossible to parse this information to obtain what we require, it would be exceedingly lengthy and cumbersome: what we want is a quick, easy way to obtain the information, without placing too much load on the NT machine.

The chkdsk command also provides a lot more information than we require. Furthermore, it reports the information for an individual drive, not for all of the drives in the machine like the df equivalent under NT. This requires customization of the script for each machine we install it on, and regular modifications if the drives and configuration change on the machine.

The solution is to use the **Win32::AdminMisc** module from Dave Roth. It provides a set of functions available directly within Perl to obtain the information directly from the machine. This means we can access data without relying on external programs to obtain the information, nor do we have to postprocess the output.

```perl
1    use Win32::AdminMisc;
2    use Win32;
3
4    use strict;
5    my ($min,$hour,$mday,$mon,$year) = (localtime())[1,2,3,4,5];
6    $mon++;
7    $year += 1900;
8    my $fdate = sprintf("%04d%02d%02d",$year,$mon,$mday);
9    my $ftime = sprintf("%02d%02d",$hour,$min);
10   my $Node = Win32::NodeName();
11   $Node =~ tr/ /-/;
12   my $PID  = (Win32::AdminMisc::GetIdInfo())[0];
13   my $logdir = "C:/Temp/Outgoing";
14   my $remlogdir = "/usr/local/etc/statmon/incoming";
15
16   mkdir($logdir,0666) unless ( -d $logdir);
17   my $logfile = "$logdir/perf.$Node.$fdate.$ftime.$PID";
18
19   open(PERF,">$logfile") or die "Couldnt open file: $!";
20
21   my @drives = Win32::AdminMisc::GetDrives(DRIVE_FIXED);
22
23   foreach my $let (@drives)
24   {
25       my ($tot,$free) = Win32::AdminMisc::GetDriveSpace($let);
26       my $reallet = $let;
27       $reallet =~ s/:\\//g;
28       $tot = int($tot/1024);
29       $free = int($free/1024);
30       my $used=$tot-$free;
31       print PERF "$fdate:$ftime:df:$reallet:$free:$used\n";
32   }
33
34   my %Data;
```

```
35
36   if (%Data = Win32::AdminMisc::GetMemoryInfo())
37   {
38       print PERF ("$fdate:$ftime:sw:",
39                   (($Data{PageTotal}-$Data{PageAvail})/1024),
40                   ":",
41                   ($Data{PageAvail}/1024),"\n");
42   }
43
44   close(PERF);
45
46   require Net::FTP;
47
48   my $ftp = Net::FTP->new("collector");
49   die "Couldn't open connection" unless $ftp;
50   $ftp->login("statmon","Status");
51   $ftp->cwd($remlogdir);
52   chdir($logdir);
53   my @list = glob("perf.*");
54   for my $file (@list)
55   {
56       my $realfile = $file;
57       $realfile =~ s/\.\./:/g;
58       if ($ftp->put($file,$realfile))
59       {
60           unlink $file;
61       }
62   }
63
64   $ftp->quit;
```

ANNOTATIONS

Other than the use of internal Perl functions (albeit imported from modules), the only other difference from the previous script is that we do not e-mail the administrator in the case of difficulty. This is a lapse that I have yet to resolve, but I've had a small number of problems with sending e-mail from NT machines. Otherwise the script follows a very similar format to the Unix version.

```
1   use Win32::AdminMisc;
2   use Win32;
3
4   use strict;
```

Aside from incorporating the **Win32::AdminMisc** and **Win32** modules, there are no further requirements for this script. Note also that we do not use the **MCConfig** module—we rely on settings within the script.

```
5    my ($min,$hour,$mday,$mon,$year) = (localtime())[1,2,3,4,5];
6    $mon++;
7    $year += 1900;
8    my $fdate = sprintf("%04d%02d%02d",$year,$mon,$mday);
9    my $ftime = sprintf("%02d%02d",$hour,$min);
10   my $Node = Win32::NodeName();
11   $Node =~ tr/ /-/;
12   my $PID  = (Win32::AdminMisc::GetIdInfo())[0];
13   my $logdir = "C:/Temp/Outgoing";
14   my $remlogdir = "/usr/local/etc/statmon/incoming";
15
```

Lines 5 to 14 initialize the same set of variables as the Unix version. Some things to note, however: The name of the machine is extracted via the **Win32::NodeName** function. Unlike the Unix **hostname** function, which returns the TCP/IP registered name of the machine, this function returns the Windows NT directory name. Because of this, we have to strip the space from the name in line 11—it will only complicate the collection and reporting processes. The process ID is obtained using another function on line 12, rather than using the special **$$** variable.

```
16   mkdir($logdir,0666) unless ( -d $logdir);
17   my $logfile = "$logdir/perf.$Node.$fdate.$ftime.$PID";
18
19   open(PERF,">$logfile") or die "Couldnt open file: $!";
20
```

We ensure the outgoing log file directory exists on line 16, recreating it if it doesn't exist. Line 17 then generates the log file name before we attempt to open it on line 19. Because we don't have the ability to e-mail in case of a problem, we can safely use **die** if the operation fails. It's worth noting that depending on how your system is configured, the information should be reported in the Windows NT event log.

```
21   my @drives = Win32::AdminMisc::GetDrives(DRIVE_FIXED);
22
23   foreach my $let (@drives)
24   {
25       my ($tot,$free) = Win32::AdminMisc::GetDriveSpace($let);
26       my $reallet = $let;
27       $reallet =~ s/:\\//g;
```

Line 21 uses the function from the **Win32::AdminMisc** module to get a list of available drives. The **DRIVE_FIXED** argument specifies that we want a list of fixed drives, not including removable or network mounted drives. This ensures that the script runs correctly and doesn't try to obtain the drive space of the floppy drive or CD-ROM drive that may or may not contain a valid disk. It's also highly likely that we are interested in the contents of removable drives, as they are unlikely to play a significant part in the operation of the NT machine.

Line 23 then sets up the loop to work through the list of drives. Note that I've used **foreach** here for clarity: remember that **for** and **foreach** are identical.

Line 25 gets the total space and the amount of free space, in bytes, of the specified drive. Because the drive specification on an NT machine uses drive letters followed by a colon, we need to strip the colon from the drive letter on lines 26 and 27.

```
28      $tot = int($tot/1024);
29      $free = int($free/1024);
30      my $used=$tot-$free;
31      print PERF "$fdate:$ftime:df:$reallet:$free:$used\n";
32    }
33
```

Line 28 converts the total size of the drive from bytes to kilobytes by dividing the value by 1,024. The use of **int** around the calculation ensures that the resulting value is an integer, not a floating-point value. The performance information should include the amount of space used on the drive and the amount of space free, so we make a calculation on line 30 using the information we know. Then line 31 writes out the performance record to the log file.

```
34    my %Data;
35
36    if (%Data = Win32::AdminMisc::GetMemoryInfo())
37    {
38        print PERF ("$fdate:$ftime:sw:",
39                    (($Data{PageTotal}-$Data{PageAvail})/1024),
40                    ":",
41                    ($Data{PageAvail}/1024),"\n");
42    }
43
```

Line 34 sets up the hash that will be used on line 36 to store the memory information about the current machine. The different value types are defined as keys within the hash, with the sizes stored in the corresponding values. Lines 38 to 41 print out the performance log record using inline calculations to produce the data we require: the amount of memory used and the amount of memory available.

```
44    close(PERF);
45
```

We have finished collecting the information, so it is now safe to close the log file.

```
46  require Net::FTP;
47
48  my $ftp = Net::FTP->new("collector");
49  die "Couldn't open connection" unless $ftp;
50  $ftp->login("statmon","Status");
51  $ftp->cwd($remlogdir);
```

The last stage of the process, as in the Unix script, is to send the log file to the collection machine. Line 48 opens the connection to the collection machine with line 49 reporting an error if the command fails.

Lines 50 and 51 then log into the FTP server and change to the remote collection directory. Note that because we are not using the **MCConfig** module, we can specify the information directly within the functions. This defeats the object somewhat, but it's unlikely to cause too many problems—this is one of the many things that will be resolved in future versions of the system.

```
52  chdir($logdir);
53  my @list = glob("perf.*");
54  for my $file (@list)
55  {
56      my $realfile = $file;
57      $realfile =~ s/\.\./:/g;
58      if ($ftp->put($file,$realfile))
59      {
60          unlink $file;
61      }
62  }
63
64  $ftp->quit;
```

Lines 52 to 64 follow the same format as the Unix **uxstat.pl** script. The only difference is that we transfer just the performance log files (via the file specification to the **glob** function on line 53). We also convert double periods to a colon in line 57 in case the variables in the earlier file specification failed for any reason. I have sometimes experienced problems with this, hence the conversion. As before, we delete the log file only if the file could be sent on line 58.

As in the Unix version, it is difficult to show the result of an execution, but we will look at the results in the next script, **ms.pl**.

ms.pl

Reporting Individual Machine Status

Unlike the previous reporting script, extracting information from the reports supplied by individual machines is incredibly easy because the collector places the latest report for each machine in a set position within the log file directory hierarchy. All we need to do is access each file, reporting the information via an HTML page.

```perl
1    #!/usr/local/bin/perl5 -w
2
3    use strict;
4    use SCGI;
5    use MCConfig;
6
7    print "Content-type: text/html\n\n";
8
9    init_cgi;
10
11   my $pagetitle = "Machine Status";
12   my $pageheader = "Machine Status";
13
14   print template('header','www',
15                  'pagetitle' => $pagetitle,
16                  );
17   print template('main','www',
18                  'pageheader' => $pageheader,
19                  'pagewidth' => 800
20                  );
21
22   if ( $SCGI::formlength < 1 )
23   {
```

```
24      print <<EOF;
25  <form method=GET method="/cgi-bin/ms.cgi">
26  <b>Report type:</b><select name=type>
27  <option value=single>Single Machine
28  <option value=all selected>All Machines
29  </select><br>
30  <b>Machine</b><select name=machine>
31  EOF
32      chdir($MCConfig::netmng_mlogs);
33      my @machines = glob("*");
34      for(my $i=0;$i<($#machines+1);$i++)
35      {
36          print("<option value=$machines[$i]>$machines[$i]\n");
37      }
38      print <<EOF;
39  </select><p>
40  <input type="submit" value="send">
41  </form>
42  EOF
43  }
44  else
45  {
46      print <<EOF;
47  <p>
48  <table cellpadding=0 cellborder=0 cellspacing=0>
49  <tr>
50  <td width=60><b>Filesystem</b></td>
51  <td width=60 align=right><b>Used</b></td>
52  <td width=60 align=right><b>Avail</b></td>
53  <td width=60 align=right><b>Mem Used</b></td>
54  <td width=60 align=right><b>Mem Avail</b></td>
55  <td width=35 align=right><b>15mins</b></td>
56  <td width=35 align=right><b>5mins</b></td>
57  <td width=35 align=right><b>1min</b></td>
58  </tr>
59  EOF
60      my @machines;
61      if ( $SCGI::formlist{type} =~ /single/ )
62      {
63          push(@machines,$SCGI::formlist{machine});
64      }
65      else
66      {
```

```
67          chdir($MCConfig::netmng_mlogs);
68          @machines = glob("*");
69      }
70
71      for my $machine (@machines)
72      {
73          my $lastfile="$MCConfig::netmng_mlogs/" .
74                       "$machine/perf/latest";
75          open(D,"<$lastfile") or next;
76          my $first = 1;
77          while(<D>)
78          {
79              chomp;
80              my ($date,$time,$type,
81                  $opta,$optb,$optc,$optd) = split /:/;
82              $date =~ s:(\d{4})(\d{2})(\d{2}):$3/$2/$1:;
83              $time =~ s/(\d{2})(\d{2})/$1:$2/;
84              if ($first)
85              {
86                  print "<tr><td colspan=9></td></tr>\n";
87                  print("<tr><td colspan=6><font color=red><b>",
88                        lc($machine),
89                        "</b></font></td>",
90                        "<td align=right>$date</td>",
91                        "<td align=right>$time</td>");
92                  $first=0;
93              }
94              if ( $type eq 'df' )
95              {
96                  if ($optb < 5000)
97                  {
98                      print("<tr><td>$opta</td>",
99                            "<td align=right>$optc k</td>",
100                           "<td align=right>",
101                           "<font color=red>",
102                           "$optb k</font></td>\n");
103                 }
104                 else
105                 {
106                     print("<tr><td>$opta</td>",
107                           "<td align=right>$optc k</td>",
108                           "<td align=right>$optb k</td>\n");
109                 }
```

```
110                 }
111             if ( $type =~ "sw" )
112             {
113                 my $used=$opta;
114                 my $avail=$optb;
115                 if ( $avail < 5000 )
116                 {
117                     print("<td>$used align=right k</td>",
118                             "<td align=right><font color=red>",
119                             "$avail k</font></td>\n");
120                 }
121                 else
122                 {
123                     print("<td align=right>$used k</td>",
124                             "<td align=right>$avail k</td>\n");
125                 }
126             }
127
128             if ( $type =~ "ld" )
129             {
130                 print("<td align=right>$opta</td>",
131                         "<td align=right>$optb</td>",
132                         "<td align=right>$optc</td>\n");
133             }
134
135         }
136     close(D);
137     }
138     print("</table>\n");
139 }
140
141 print template('footer','www');
```

ANNOTATIONS

The operation of the script should be easy to follow. We open each of the **latest** files for each of the machines on which we want to report within the log file hierarchy, printing the results. We know the order of the input source: it should be file system, swap space, and loading, and the output format reflects this. However, to save space, when we output the information we set up a table to handle all three elements on a single row. Since we only have one set of information for the load and swap space, we report it on the last line of the file system report. We don't need any complicated programming to do this; we just need to format the HTML table in such a way that it will automatically be reported last.

```
1    #!/usr/local/bin/perl5 -w
2
3    use strict;
4    use SCGI;
5    use MCConfig;
6
7    print "Content-type: text/html\n\n";
8
9    init_cgi;
10
```

We initialize the CGI system and the whole script in the first ten lines.

```
11   my $pagetitle = "Machine Status";
12   my $pageheader = "Machine Status";
13
14   print template('header','www',
15                  'pagetitle' => $pagetitle,
16                  );
17   print template('main','www',
18                  'pageheader' => $pageheader,
19                  'pagewidth' => 800
20                  );
21
```

We print out the header and body of the HTML page that will report the information. Once again, we use the **template** function from the **SCGI** module to ensure that the page generated keeps the same style and format as the rest of the intranet Web site.

```
22   if ( $SCGI::formlength < 1 )
23   {
24       print <<EOF;
25   <form method=GET method="/cgi-bin/ms.cgi">
26   <b>Report type:</b><select name=type>
27   <option value=single>Single Machine
28   <option value=all selected>All Machines
29   </select><br>
30   <b>Machine</b><select name=machine>
31   EOF
```

If no fields were specified on an HTML form, then we print out a selection form. There are two pop-ups: one defines the report type (single machine or all machines), and the other defines the list of available machines. The first pop-up is defined above; the second must be based on the list of machine directories defined in the status hierarchy.

```
32      chdir($MCConfig::netmng_mlogs);
33      my @machines = glob("*");
34      for(my $i=0;$i<($#machines+1);$i++)
35      {
36          print("<option value=$machines[$i]>$machines[$i]\n");
37      }
```

Line 32 changes the directory to that of the log file. The contents of the directory are a list of the individual machines that have some form of log. We are not worried at this time about any specific machine status data, although it's highly likely that the list of machines presented here will be the list of machines with performance information. Line 33 extracts the list of machines, using **glob** to extract the list of directory names. Lines 34 to 37 then print out the selection option for the each machine, building the options on the pop-up list.

```
38      print <<EOF;
39  </select><p>
40  <input type="submit" value="send">
41  </form>
42  EOF
43  }
```

Lines 38 to 41 finish off the form.

```
44  else
45  {
46      print <<EOF;
47  <p>
48  <table cellpadding=0 cellborder=0 cellspacing=0>
49  <tr>
50  <td width=60><b>Filesystem</b></td>
51  <td width=60 align=right><b>Used</b></td>
52  <td width=60 align=right><b>Avail</b></td>
53  <td width=60 align=right><b>Mem Used</b></td>
54  <td width=60 align=right><b>Mem Avail</b></td>
55  <td width=35 align=right><b>15mins</b></td>
56  <td width=35 align=right><b>5mins</b></td>
57  <td width=35 align=right><b>1min</b></td>
58  </tr>
59  EOF
```

If form field information has been supplied, we assume the information relates to the selection of machines that we want to gather performance information for. Lines 46 to 58 print out the table header; remember, we are reporting all the information effectively on one line, so we must print out headers for the file system, swap space, and load average information.

```
60      my @machines;
61      if ( $SCGI::formlist{type} =~ /single/ )
62      {
63          push(@machines,$SCGI::formlist{machine});
64      }
65      else
66      {
67          chdir($MCConfig::netmng_mlogs);
68          @machines = glob("*");
69      }
70
```

Lines 60 to 69 decide which machines we are going to report on. The **@machines** array holds the list. If a single machine has been specified, we the put the machine name, taken from the **machine** field on the form, into the **@machines** array. If the user has selected all machines, then we just put the output of the **glob** command in the machine log directory into the **@machines** array instead.

```
71      for my $machine (@machines)
72      {
73          my $lastfile="$MCConfig::netmng_mlogs/" .
74                      "$machine/perf/latest";
75          open(D,"<$lastfile") or next;
76          my $first = 1;
```

We now need to work through a list of the machine directories, opening the "latest" file in each perf directory for each machine, hence the loop on line 71. The name of the log file is generated on lines 73 and 74. We attempt to open the file on line 75, skipping to the next machine if we cannot open it; it may be that the machine does not record any performance information. The **$first** variable decides when title information for the machine should be printed.

```
77      while(<D>)
78      {
79          chomp;
80          my ($date,$time,$type,
81              $opta,$optb,$optc,$optd) = split /:/;
82          $date =~ s:(\d{4})(\d{2})(\d{2}):$3/$2/$1:;
83          $time =~ s/(\d{2})(\d{2})/$1:$2/;
```

We split the data from the file for the current machine on lines 80 and 81. There will be at most seven fields, starting with the date, time, entry type, and optional additional data.

Lines 82 and 83 format the date and time, respectively, from the stored format to a more friendly English version. We use a regular expression substitution to convert, for example, "19981101" into "01/11/1998." The match converts the groups of 4, 2, 2 digits into a reverse version separated by forward slashes, using the resulting group match for each element. Converting the time is easier since we only really need to insert a colon between the two pairs of digits.

```
84          if ($first)
85          {
86              print "<tr><td colspan=9></td></tr>\n";
87              print("<tr><td colspan=6><font color=red><b>",
88                      lc($machine),
89                      "</b></font></td>",
90                      "<td align=right>$date</td>",
91                      "<td align=right>$time</td>");
92              $first=0;
93          }
```

If this is the first report line for this machine, then we print a title line, including the machine name, and the date and time recorded for the current record; this will give an indication of when the last performance report was filed. Once the title line has been printed out, we set the value of the **$first** variable to zero so subsequent records will not trigger this information to be printed.

```
94          if ( $type eq 'df' )
95          {
96              if ($optb < 5000)
97              {
98                  print("<tr><td>$opta</td>",
99                          "<td align=right>$optc k</td>",
100                         "<td align=right>",
101                         "<font color=red>",
102                         "$optb k</font></td>\n");
103             }
104             else
105             {
106                 print("<tr><td>$opta</td>",
107                         "<td align=right>$optc k</td>",
108                         "<td align=right>$optb k</td>\n");
109             }
110         }
```

If the current record is a file system entry, then we print out the file system mount point, space used, and space available. We account, via the test on line 96, for printing out the available space in red if it falls below 5,000 kilobytes. Otherwise, we print out the information normally. Note, in both cases, that we do not include the </tr> tag to close the current row within the report table so that we can add the swap and load information to the same line if we need to.

```perl
111             if ( $type =~ "sw" )
112             {
113                 my $used=$opta;
114                 my $avail=$optb;
115                 if ( $avail < 5000 )
116                 {
117                     print("<td>$opta align=right k</td>",
118                           "<td align=right><font color=red>",
119                           "$avail k</font></td>\n");
120                 }
121                 else
122                 {
123                     print("<td align=right>$opta k</td>",
124                           "<td align=right>$optb k</td>\n");
125                 }
126             }
127
```

Lines 111 to 127 print out the swap space record from the file, if it has been reached. Because we did end the table row in the HTML table, this information should be printed in the next two columns after the last file system that had been reported. Like the file system report, we highlight the swap space available if it is less than 5,000 kilobytes by printing the value in red.

```perl
128             if ( $type =~ "ld" )
129             {
130                 print("<td align=right>$opta</td>",
131                       "<td align=right>$optb</td>",
132                       "<td align=right>$optc</td>\n");
133             }
134
```

Finally, we print the load average record. This record, too, will appear on the last line of the file system report, in the final three columns of the report.

```
135         }
136         close(D);
137     }
138     print("</table>\n");
139 }
140
141 print template('footer','www');
```

Once we have finished processing the records from one machine, we close the file on line 136 and move on to the next in the list, before printing out the end of the table once all of the machines have been processed. Finally, we print the footer information.

The whole script builds a table that contains information about each machine, with individual lines specifying information about each of the available file systems on a machine. The final file system line also contains the swap space and load average information. We can guarantee that the last line contains the information because we know the order in which the records are added to the file in the first place via one of the **uxstat.pl** or **ntstat.pl** scripts we have already seen.

You can see an example of the output in Figure 11-3.

Machine Status

Filesystem	Used	Avail	Mem Used	Mem Avail	15mins	5mins	1min
NT Server					03/11/1998	21:45	
C	623456 k	3366048 k					
D	1145952 k	83616 k	126912 k	133232 k			
Twinspark					03/11/1998	21:45	
/	29110 k	57705 k					
/usr	191990 k	15737 k					
/opt	512 k	401765 k					
/usr/local	446164 k	709952 k					
/users	569 k	408035 k	120072 k	147572 k	0.75	0.34	0.30

FIGURE 11-3. The machine status report

Summary

As you can see, Perl can make the process of controlling, managing, and monitoring network devices and services much easier. We are still using the same principles and basics that we have seen elsewhere in this book, but now we are applying them to more practical solutions for aiding network administration.

There are many other systems and elements of network administration that can be modeled within the Perl language, and in this chapter I have deliberately attempted to avoid the more obvious choices of users and groups in favor of the problems I have faced as a network administrator.

Using Perl as the basis for the DNS configuration file builder is a logical choice with its combination of text handling features and the networking extensions provided by modules such as **Net::DNS**. Most people also forget that Perl is a capable cross-platform language and that it can be used to plug the gaps in NT's core facilities. The Service manager is just one example of a command-line tool that was crying out to be developed. Here, Perl is a less-than-obvious but still capable choice, and it shows Perl's versatility: Perl is too often pigeonholed as a text processing and CGI solution.

The final set of scripts demonstrate not so much Perl, but how Perl can be used, with planning, to create what appears to be a complex set of tools for monitoring your network. Again, Perl's versatility shines through, although we still use Perl-based CGI scripts to report the information.

Platform Specifics

Unix
Windows 95/NT
MacOS

Although Perl is a standard language, there are some fundamental differences between each operating system and even between system versions that can introduce problems, errors, and incompatibilities that you wouldn't otherwise expect. MacOS is a 100-percent windowed GUI environment: there is no Mac command line as there is with Unix; there isn't even a command-line interface (CLI) like the Windows Command Prompt to work with. Conversely, the basic interface to UNIX is the command line. Even if you use a product like the X Windows System, you are still using a terminal that utilizes a CLI. The same is true under Microsoft Windows versions, although you can still use familiar Windows-based tools for editing and creating your Perl scripts.

This appendix explains some more specific differences between the platforms, covering everything from installation and executing scripts to adding third-party modules, as well as noting differences between the underlying Perl implementations.

If you want some general information on the ports available, you can find some perlport documentation as part of the standard Perl distribution.

PROGRAMMER'S NOTE   *For this book, the bulk of the scripts have been tested under Unix and Windows NT. Where appropriate, I've also included a Mac version or suggested what needs to be changed in the script to make it more Mac compatible.*

Unix

We'll use Unix as our base reference point. It was the original platform for Perl and continues to be the main point of reference for the Perl source, scripts, and most of the documentation and support sites.

INSTALLING AND RUNNING THE PERL APPLICATION

Installation is a little more complex on Unix because for most implementations you will be compiling the actual Perl source code. Once you have downloaded the latest version of the Perl package (from CPAN; see Appendix B), check the documentation for the specific instructions for installing Perl. As a quick guide, you can try the following:

1. Extract the source code from the archive using **tar** and **gunzip**:

   ```
   $ gunzip -c perl5.tar.gz | tar xf -
   ```

2. Change to the newly created directory. It's worth checking the **readme** and **install** files that contain, respectively, general Perl information and specific details on the installation process.

3. Run the configuration script:

```
$ ./configure
```

This command is in fact a GNU-style execution of the real Configure script. The standard Perl Configure script is actually interactive, requiring input from you on a number of questions. The GNU-compatible execution answers the questions automatically for you, though it still shows the process going on behind the scenes.

4. Run **make** to build the application:

```
$ make
```

The application and support files have now been compiled. It's a good idea at this point to run **make test**, which will run a standard selection of tests to ensure that your Perl has compiled properly. If there are any problems, you want to check the build process to see if anything failed. On the mainstream systems, such as Linux and Solaris, it's unlikely that you will notice any test failures.

5. Once the build has completed, install the application, scripts, and modules, again using **make**:

```
$ make install
```

Provided you didn't specify different directories, the usual directory specification will install Perl into the /usr/local/bin and /usr/local/lib/ perl5 directories. You will need to add /usr/local/bin or the installation directory you chose (specified by the $installation_prefix/bin variable in the Makefile) to your $PATH environment variable, if it is not already there.

If you don't want to compile the source yourself, the CPAN archives also now include prebuilt binaries that are ready to install onto your system. You can find the full list of ports that are available at ftp://ftp.funet.fi/pub/languages/perl/CPAN/ports/index.html.

EXECUTING SCRIPTS

There are two ways of executing a Perl script under Unix. You can run the **perl** application, supplying the script's name on the command line, or you can place the following on the first line of the file:

```
#!/usr/local/bin/perl
```

The path given is the path to the **perl** application. You must then change the file mode of the script to be executable.

This latter method is the one I have used throughout this book. Note that because I have a number of different versions of Perl, including the old Perl 4.036, I have specified **perl5** in all of the scripts to ensure that it is the later version of Perl that is being used.

Whenever a script is run, unless errors have been redirected, standard input, output, and errors are sent via the terminal or window, the same as the shell environment.

THIRD-PARTY MODULES

For most modules (particularly those from CPAN), the installation process is fairly straightforward:

1. Download the module, and extract it using **tar** and **gunzip**:

   ```
   $ gunzip -c module.tar.gz | tar xf -
   ```

   This command should create a new directory with the module contents.

2. Change to the module directory.

3. Type the following command:

   ```
   $ perl5 Makefile.PL
   ```

   This command will check that the module contents are complete and that the necessary prerequisite modules are already installed. It will also create a Makefile that will compile (if necessary) and install the module.

   As in the original installation process, a **make test** will verify that the compilation and configuration of the package worked before you install it. Any problems should be reported back to the package's author.

4. To install the module, type

   ```
   $ make install
   ```

   to copy the modules and any required support files into the appropriate directories.

Most CPAN modules (except those specifically for another platform, like the Win32 modules) are developed or supported under Unix. You should not have any compatibility problems. However, if you are using a Unix installation that does not have a C compiler (such as Solaris 2.x), you may have trouble installing certain modules.

LINE TERMINATION

The default line termination character under Unix is **\n**, or ASCII 10 (new line).

VOLUMES, PATH NAMES, AND FILES

There are no volumes under Unix; all directories and files are stored within the same root (/) directory. The file/directory separator is the forward slash (/).

TIME

The time of the epoch is 00:00:00 on 1 January, 1970 UTC, and time values are calculated as the number of seconds since this date and time. The specific of UTC or GMT means that the value is ignorant of the current time zone.

RUNNING EXTERNAL PROGRAMS

You can use any of the methods we have discussed in this book to execute external programs, either directly or through the use of **open** statements. For example, the following line opens the file text.gz via the gunzip application to read uncompressed text from the file:

```
open(D, "gunzip -c text.gz|");
```

You can also run a program directly using the **system** function or by using backticks (`).

NETWORKING

The standard Perl **Socket** module uses TCP/IP, the standard networking protocol under Unix. Both the built-in packages and many of the third-party packages use the standard **Socket** module, so there should not be any major difficulties when using networking scripts within a Unix-based Perl environment.

WEB SERVERS AND CGI

Because I/O is performed by the standard input and output devices, using Perl for CGI scripts is simply a case of installing the script into the CGI directory of your Web server. If you are using Apache as your Web server software, there is a Perl module, **mod_perl** (available on CPAN), that effectively allows you to execute Perl code directly within the Apache server so that you don't need to spawn new Perl processes. For more information on this module, you can visit the Perl Apache Web site, http://perl.apache.org.

MORE INFORMATION

For more information, check the main Perl Web sites (www.perl.com and www.perl.org) and the main Perl distribution. These resources should contain all the information you need to get started.

Windows 95/NT

The Windows 95 and Windows NT versions of Perl are collectively known as Perl for Win32. There are two basic versions, the ActiveState ports and the "Standard" or "Core" ports. The ActiveState ports are now relatively out of date; the most recent supported Perl source is version 5.003_07 (we are currently on version 5.005_05). The base version from ActiveState will work directly on Windows 95 and NT. There are then two extensions: PerlScript and ISAPI. PerlScript will run as an ActiveX scripting engine within Internet Explorer 3 and Microsoft Internet Information Server 3. ISAPI is a dynamically loadable library (DLL) that will execute Perl scripts within the confines of an ISAPI-compliant Web server.

The core binary distributions are more up to date, and are currently based on version 5.004_02. This standard distribution is more like the Perl you will find under Unix and is designed to be a more practical, all-around solution. It is possible to use it with Microsoft's IIS and other Web servers under Windows 95 and NT. If you want to use Standard Perl under 95/NT, this is the best solution, and you should also think about installing Win32 Perl extensions, which provide a standard toolkit for using the features of the 32-bit Windows Perl port.

It's expected that the two versions of Perl available for Windows will eventually merge into a single distribution, eliminating much of the confusion and making Perl under Windows an easier solution for many problems.

INSTALLING AND RUNNING THE PERL APPLICATION

Once you have obtained the required version of the Perl distribution you want, you need to extract it with a decompression tool that supports long filenames. I can recommend WinZip (http://www.winzip.com) and Aladdin's Expander for Windows (http://www.aladdinsys.com). Once the file is extracted, you simply need to run install.bat and answer some easy questions. The result will be an installation in your selected directory of the entire Perl distribution and support modules.

The installation should update your PATH values so that you can type **perl** at the command-line prompt and it will execute correctly. The installation will also associate the .pl extension to the Perl application, so scripts can be double-clicked. If you have IIS installed, then an entry will be made against the script registry for IIS so that you can use Perl for CGI scripting.

EXECUTING SCRIPTS

Once installed correctly, there are two basic ways of executing a Perl script. You can either type

```
C:\> perl cat.pl
```

in a command window, or you can double-click on the script in Windows Explorer. The former method allows you to specify command-line arguments; the latter method requires that you ask the user for any required information.

If you want a more Unix-like method of executing scripts, you can modify the PATHEXT environment variable (in the System control panel) to include .pl as a recognized extension. This modification allows you to call a script just like any other variable on the command line, but with limitations. The following will work:

```
C:\> cat readme.txt
```

but redirection and pipes do not work, so the following lines would do nothing:

```
C:\> cat <readme.txt
C:\> cat readme.txt|more
```

Note that this method works only under Windows NT, not Windows 95. It also does not support the "shebang" method of specifying Perl options, for example:

```
#!/usr/local/bin/perl5 -w
```

PROGRAMMER'S NOTE   *The "shebang" is the #! string at the start of the file. It is used by Unix to identify an alternative program to the shell for executing the script.*

If you want to execute a script with warnings switched on, you must call Perl and the script from the command line. Input and output occurs in a command window (either the current window or a new one if the script was double clicked).

THIRD-PARTY MODULES

How you install a third-party module depends entirely on the module in question. For the Win32 module, it is simply a case of extracting the zip file and then running install.bat. In contrast, for Dave Roth's AdminMisc module, you must install the module and support files manually. Once installed, you can call the modules as usual; there is no special handling required.

WARNING   *When installing the Win32 module and Dave Roth's AdminMisc module, you need to manually remove the AdminMisc module supplied with Win32. Otherwise, you will make calls to the Win32 AdminMisc module that do not exist!*

If the module you are trying to install requires a C compiler, you will also have similar problems. This is not an issue for Win32 specific modules that are supplied as precompiled.

LINE TERMINATION

Text files under Windows are terminated with **\r\n** (a carriage-return and a new-line character), and files are terminated by the SUB (^Z) character. However, within the C libraries that are used to build Perl, the end-of-line characters are converted to a single new-line character, **\n** on input, and a new-line character is converted to carriage-return new-line character on output. This means that Perl scripts using text files are interchangeable between Unix and Windows Perl implementations.

Incidentally, if you are using binary files directly within Perl, you must specify that the file handle is to be treated as binary using the **binmode** function:

```
open(D,"<file.bin");
binmode(D);
```

You need to specify this before you read or write to the file. The change occurs only at the point the function is called.

VOLUMES, PATH NAMES, AND FILES

Volumes, or drives under Widows, are referenced by a drive letter followed by a colon. The boot drive is generally C:, although it is possible to have other drives. This means that if you use colons to separate drive info, you must account for the colon in any file specification. Directories and files are by default separated by the backslash character (\); however, Perl for Windows uses the forward slash (/), as it does under Unix. This means that the code fragment

```
print "Exists\n" if (-f "C:/autoexec.bat");
```

works, but the fragment

```
print "Exists\n" if (-f "C:\autoexec.bat");
```

doesn't.

PROGRAMMER'S NOTE
In the latter example, the lookup will actually fail because the double-quoted string causes Perl to interpret the "\a" as a special character.

It's also worth mentioning that files and directories can be specified irrespective of case. Windows does not distinguish between upper- and lowercase letters within the command prompt.

TIME

The epoch is measured the same as in Unix, from 00:00:00 on 1 January, 1970.

RUNNING EXTERNAL PROGRAMS

Within the core Perl distribution, it is possible to execute external programs in the same manner as you would under Unix. However, if you are using the ISAPI or script versions of the ActiveState version of Perl, it is not a supported option. This is because scripts within these environments are executed within the confines of the host Web server, and executing an external program would probably cause the host application to crash—if the attempt of the operation succeeded at all.

NETWORKING

For most scripts, Unix-style networking will work—the standard **Socket** module is supplied. You can even run a simple TCP/IP server under Windows. However, it is not a good idea to use Windows as a server platform within Perl, because the Win32 implementation does not support **fork()**, so you will only be able to support one connection at a time. The forthcoming threads version of Perl may alleviate this problem, but it's beyond the scope of this book to go into the relative merits of threads against processes.

WEB SERVERS AND CGI

See the general discussion at the start of this section and the "Installing and Running the Perl Application" section for more details.

MORE INFORMATION

The best place to go for more information is the Perl distribution directory on CPAN, http://www.cpan.org/ports/win32. There are ActiveState and core Perl executables there, along with FAQs and links to other sites.

MacOS

The most fundamental difference between MacOS and Windows/Unix is that MacOS does not have any form of command-line environment. This means that MacPerl is both a development environment and the program used to execute the script. This characteristic is no bad thing: the MacPerl environment is very easy to use, and it supports the creation, editing, and execution of Perl, in addition to direct access to the execution process (scripts can be started and stopped from menus and key combinations) and the Perl debugger.

Best of all, POD documents are available and viewable as preformatted online texts. This includes all of the basic Perl information supplied in all versions (that is, the "man" or manual pages), as well as additional general Perl texts and the more specific MacPerl modules and abilities.

Because the MacOS has no CLI, a new range of modules is supplied that support file selection dial boxes and basic text entry forms. You can also produce more complex forms based on lists, check boxes, and radio buttons within Perl, all without having to resort to the Perl Tk interface.

MacPerl was originally ported, and it is continually supported by Matthias Neeracher.

INSTALLING AND RUNNING THE PERL APPLICATION

Perl is available in a number of different guises, depending on what you want to do with it and how extensible and expandable you want the support modules to be. The basic distribution, appl, includes the MacPerl binary, all the Perl and MacPerl libraries and modules, and the documentation. The tool distribution works with MPW (the Macintosh Programmers Workshop/Workbench), allowing you to develop and release Perl programs that are part of a larger overall application, while presenting you with the same interface and development environment you use for C/C++ and Pascal Mac applications. Because MacPerl provides an almost transparent interface to the underlying Mac Toolbox, you can use Perl and C/C++/Pascal programs and code interchangeably. The source, in the src distribution, including all of the toolbox interfaces, is also available.

Installing the application is a case of downloading and decompressing the installer, and then double-clicking on the installer application. This process will install all the modules, the application, and the documentation you need to start programming in Perl. Starting MacPerl is a simple case of double-clicking on the application.

EXECUTING SCRIPTS

Perl scripts are identified using the MacOS Creator and Type codes. The MacPerl environment automatically sets this information when you save the script. In fact, MacPerl specifies three basic formats, which are outlined in Table A-1.

There is a fourth format, CGI Script, that creates a script suitable for working with a Mac Web server application. See "Web Servers and CGI" later on for more information.

File Type	Description
Droplet	A droplet is a mini-application that consists of the original Perl script and a small amount of glue code, which uses AppleEvents to start MacPerl if it is not already running and then executes the script. Using droplets is the recommended method for distributing MacPerl scripts. To save a script as a droplet, go to Save As under the File menu and choose Droplet in the File Type pop-up menu at the bottom of the File dialog box. Files dragged and dropped onto a droplet's icon in the Finder have their names passed to the script as arguments (within @ARGV). If you plan on distributing your scripts to other people, droplets require that the destination users have MacPerl already installed. This might make initial distributions large (about 800K), but later updates should be smaller.
Standalone applications	A standalone application creates a file composed of the Perl application and the script and related modules. This creates a single, double-clickable application that runs and executes your script. This solution lets you provide a single file for a client, if you want to save them the task of installing MacPerl on their machines. However, this file is still an interpreted version: the script is not compiled into an executable; it's just bundled with the Perl interpreter into a single file.
Plain text file	A plain text file can be opened within the MacPerl environment and executed as a Perl script. Make sure that if the script has come from another platform that the script is in MacOS text format. These files will not automatically execute when you double-click on them. They simply open either the built-in editor within MacPerl or the editor you usually use for editing text files (such as SimpleText, BBEdit, or emacs).

TABLE A-1. MacPerl Script Types

When a script is executing, standard input, output, and errors are supported in the MacPerl window. If you want to introduce information on a "command line" (other than files if you are using a droplet), you will need to use the Mac-specific toolbox modules and functions to request the information from the user. For example, the code snippet

```
MacPerl::Answer("Delete File","OK","Cancel");
```

would present a dialog with the message "Delete File" and two buttons. The return value would be 1 if OK were clicked, and 0 if Cancel were clicked. If you want the user to enter a value, use **MacPerl::Ask**:

```
$name = MacPerl::Ask("Enter your name");
```

For more information see the MacPerl documentation.

THIRD-PARTY MODULES

Modules that build on the modules supplied as part of a basic distribution should work without any problems. All of the modules in this book, for example, that do not rely on an external module set work.

Scripts that rely on external modules, such as those from CPAN (especially those that require C source code to be compiled), may cause difficulties, not all of which can be easily overcome. The process for installing a third-party module is as follows:

1. Download and then extract the module. Most modules are supplied as a Gzipped tar file. You can either use the individual tools, MacGzip and suntar, to extract the file, or use Aladdin System's Stuffit Expander with the Expander Extensions. Whichever application set you use, remember to switch linefeed conversion on—this will convert the Unix-style Perl scripts into Macintosh text files, which will be correctly parsed by the MacPerl processor.

2. Read the documentation to find out if the module, or any modules on which it relies, use XS or C source code. If they do, it's best to forget about using the module!

3. Ignore the Makefile.PL file. Although it might run, it will probably report an error like the following:

   ```
   # On MacOS, we need to build under the Perl source directory or
   have the MacPerl SDK installed in the MacPerl folder.
   ```

   Ignore the file: we need to install the Perl modules manually. Even if the Makefile.PL runs successfully, it will generate a Makefile that we can't use on the Mac without the addition of some special tools.

4. Create a new folder (if you don't already have one) to hold your site-specific and contributed modules.

5. Add the new folder to the library folder list in the Preferences of the MacPerl application.

6. Copy across the individual Perl modules to the new directory. If the modules follow a structure, copy across all the directories and subdirectories.

7. Once installed, try running one of the test programs, or write a small script to **use** one of the modules you have installed. Check the MacPerl error window; if you get an error like the following:

```
# Illegal character \012 (carriage return).
File 'Midkemia:MacPerl ƒ:site_perl:Net:DNS:Header.pm'; Line 1
# (Maybe you didn't strip carriage returns after a network transfer?)
```

then the file still has Unix-style linefeeds in it. You can use an application like BBEdit to convert these to Macintosh text. Alternatively, you could write a Perl script to do it.

In my experience, many of the modules on CPAN work okay, including libnet, Net-DNS, and libwww. One that doesn't is the DBD database module that relies on some C source code to interface between Perl and the outside world.

LINE TERMINATION

On the Mac, \n means ASCII 13, not ASCII 10 (under Unix). If you specifically want ASCII 10 you must specify the code, that is, **\012**.

VOLUMES, PATH NAMES, AND FILES

Directories are called folders under the MacOS, and colons, rather than forward or backward slashes separate files and folders. Individual disks, or disk partitions, are called volumes. If you specify a file with

`Folder:File`

then the reference is considered relative—the reference will be relative to the current volume and folder. References of the form

`:Folder:File`

are relative to the current volume only. A reference like

`File`

refers to a file in the current directory. If you want to specify an absolute filename, then just place the name of the volume in the path. For example:

`Volume:Folder:File`

Because we use colons to separate the path elements, we must take care when storing the information in text-delimited databases. Using a colon to separate fields in a database, where one of the fields is a Mac path name, will cause problems.

TIME

If you use the number of seconds since the epoch as a comparative measure, you need to be aware that the time is measured from an epoch of 1904 within MacPerl, not 1970. This shouldn't be a problem under MacOS-only scripts because the comparisons will be using the same base reference, but if you are comparing or exchanging date information based on epoch references with other platforms, you will need to take account of the difference.

RUNNING EXTERNAL PROGRAMS

MacOS does not have (currently) any notion of subprocesses. Therefore, entries like
`open(d, "|command")`
won't work. However, some backtick commands have been hard-coded within
MacPerl to add a certain level of cross-platform support. The entries supported are
shown in Table A-2.

NETWORKING

MacPerl supports the standard Perl 5 **Socket** module, so basic TCP/IP networking
works. I've also got my MacPerl set up with the libnet and lwp modules without any
problems. If you want to use AppleTalk networking, then MacPerl supports using
and selecting certain AppleTalk devices and interfaces via the supplied Mac-specific
toolboxes.

WEB SERVERS AND CGI

Any Mac-based Web server that is MacHTTP and WebStar compliant should be able
to use MacPerl and therefore Perl scripts for CGI operations. The MacPerl
environment allows you to save a standard script as a CGI script. You can then
install the CGI script into the CGI folder on the Web server and reference it as you
would a CGI script on a Unix platform.

The difference between a droplet and a CGI script is that the I/O is redirected to
and from the Web server interface, allowing you to obtain data using GET, PUT, and

Command	Description
`pwd` or `Directory`	Returns the current working directory, followed by a new-line character. Case is significant.
`hostname`	Returns the name of the current machine if MacTCP or Open Transport are running.
`glob xxx`	Expands the glob pattern, returning a list of expanded filenames. Only * and ? are supported. The internal **glob()** function also works.
`stty raw` and `stty -raw`	Switches the console window between raw and sane modes, respectively.
`stty sane` and `stty -sane`	Switches the console window between sane and raw modes, respectively.

TABLE A-2.   MacPerl "Built-in" External Programs

environment variables from the Web server and HTML forms. Printing to standard out sends replies back as HTML to the client Web browser.

MORE INFORMATION

For more information, check out the extensive documentation supplied with the MacPerl application. I really can't praise the quality of this documentation enough. All of the standard Perl documents and manual pages are supplied, in combination with more Mac-specific information. The formatting and ease of use of the documentation is so good that I now use it in preference to manual pages on my Sun workstation!

You can also visit the MacPerl Web site (see Appendix B), which has various links to other excellent MacPerl resources, or simply buy the book (which is also available online).

Resources

From its humble beginnings many years ago, Perl has grown to be one of the cult languages on the Internet. There are many Web sites, books, journals, mailing lists, and newsgroups that supply a seemingly endless stream of information on the topic of Perl and Perl programming.

I've done my best to list a range of resources here that most people will find useful. Many of the entries are personal recommendations—certainly populating your shelf with the book list wouldn't be a bad idea!

However, this appendix is not by any means an attempt to list all the available resources. Perl is too popular, and the Internet is too fluid to make that sort of thoroughness possible.

Print Resources

While it's impossible to list all of the books, journals, and texts that promote Perl as a programming language, there are some standard books and journals that all Perl programmers should probably keep on their bookshelf.

BOOKS

Asbury, S., M. Glover, A. Humphreys, E. Weiss, J. Matthews, S. Sol. 1997. *Perl 5 How-To*. 2d ed. Corte Madera, CA: Waite Group.   By using a question and answer style, this book covers nearly the entire range of Perl's abilities. It solves specific problems and gives step-by-step examples of the solutions and manages to explain even the most complex areas of Perl development.

Brown, V. and C. Nandor. 1998. *MacPerl: Power and Ease*. Sunnyvale, CA: Prime Time Freeware.   This book is a perfect guide to programming Mac-specific Perl scripts, as well as a general guide to Perl programming and making the best of the MacPerl development environment.

Johnson, E. F. 1996. *Cross-Platform Perl*. Foster City, CA: IDG Press.   This book concentrates on creating code that can be easily transported between Unix and NT hosts. Special attention is given to scripts that deal with systems administration and Web sites, although the book covers a wide range of other topics.

Orwant, J. 1997. *Perl 5 Interactive Course: Certified Edition*. Corte Madera, CA: Waite Group.   This book is a thorough guide to Perl 5 programming, taking the reader through a series of different tasks and topics, ranging from building basic scripts to the proper use of variables, functions, and Perl-style regular expressions.

Srinivasan, S. 1997. *Advanced Perl Programming*. Sebastapol, CA: O'Reilly.   This book is an excellent guide to data modeling, networking, and the Tk widget interface. The book also covers the internal workings of Perl, which will help the advanced programmer write more efficient and smaller code, while providing all the information necessary for extending Perl with external C code.

Wall, L., T. Christiansen, R. L. Schwartz. 1996. *Programming Perl.* **2d ed. Sebastapol, CA: O'Reilly.**   Written by the three modern Perl architects, this book is the definitive guide to Perl programming. Most people refer to it as the "camel" book because that is the picture used on the front cover.

JOURNALS

The Perl Journal   A periodical devoted entirely to Perl, *The Perl Journal* covers a wide range of topics, ranging from basic principles for beginners to the advanced topics of Perl internals.

SunExpert Magazine   A magazine targeted at Sun and Unix users, *SunExpert* also covers the use of Perl in a systems administration and Web-serving role.

SunWorld Online (www.sunworldonline.com)   *SunWorld Online* is a monthly Web magazine that covers a number of topics, including using Perl to help manage and monitor Sun workstations.

Web Resources

Although Perl was designed as a simple reporting language, it soon became apparent that it could be used as a suitable language for CGI programming, and there are therefore a vast number of Web sites dedicated to Perl. The main site is The Perl Institute at www.perl.org. It is the home of Perl and is a good place to start your search for more information about Perl.

If you don't find what you are looking for at the sites listed in Table B-1, try visiting Yahoo, www.yahoo.com, or Alta Vista, www.altavista.digital.com.

Site	Description
www.perl.org	The Perl Institute, the official home of Perl, has general information on Perl, links to other sources, ports, and a vast amount of background and support information on the Perl world.

TABLE B-1.   Perl Web Sites

Site	Description
www.perl.com	This is Tom Christiansen's Perl Web site. Tom is one of the major contributors to the modern Perl effort and is a dedicated member of the team developing Perl itself. He is also the author of a number of books on the topic. His site is geared to providing general information and sample scripts and modules.
www.cpan.org	The Comprehensive Perl Archive Network (CPAN) is an online library of scripts, modules, and extensions to Perl. Originally produced with script-specific archives in mind, CPAN now concentrates on supporting and supplying Perl 5 modules. CPAN should be your second port of call (after the CD-ROM) for the modules I've used throughout this book.
www.iis.ee.ethz.ch/~neeri/macintosh/perl.html	The MacPerl Homepage contains links to other sources and information on using Perl on the Mac.
www.ActiveWare.com	ActiveWare has a port of Perl 5 that is usable with Windows NT Web servers (such as Microsoft's Internet Information Server (IIS)). If you want a more general version of Perl for NT, you need the core port available on CPAN.
www.roth.net/perl	This site is maintained by Dave Roth, the author of the Win32::AdminMisc Perl module for Windows NT. You'll also find some general information and other example scripts.
www.virtualschool.edu/mon/Perl/index.html	This site contains a wealth of information on both Mac- and Unix-based Perl scripts and modules.
www.metronet.com/perlinfo/perl5.html	This site is a brilliant independent source for Perl 5 scripts, modules, and examples. It's an excellent starting point for any Perl programmer, beginner or advanced, to further their knowledge.

TABLE B-1.   Perl Web Sites (*continued*)

You may also want to refer to Joseph's Top Ten Tips for Answering Questions Posted to comp.lang.perl.misc, available at http://www.5sigma.com/perl/topten.html, which provides some hints and tips on how best to make use of the question and answer nature of many of these groups. The site style is slightly satirical, but it is still a good reference.

FTP Sites

If you are looking for a specific module, script, or idea, then it's best to visit the CPAN archives (see the preceding list of Web sites), since the CPAN system will automatically take you to a local FTP site. However, if all you want to do is browse around the available files, or download the entire contents, then try some of the sites shown in Table B-2.

PROGRAMMER'S NOTE *ftp.funet.fi is the main CPAN archive site, and it contains an up-to-date list of all the mirror sites. If you access CPAN via the Web, then you can opt to automatically use your nearest CPAN mirror.*

Mailing Lists

Mailing lists fall into two distinct categories: announcements or discussions. If the list is for announcements, you are not allowed to post to the group. These lists tend to be low-volume and are useful for keeping in touch with the direction Perl is taking. If it's a discussion list, then you can post and reply to messages just as you would in a Usenet newsgroup. These lists are higher volume, and the number of messages can become unmanageable very quickly. That said, a discussion list is likely to have experts and users in it who can answer your questions and queries with authority.

GENERAL MAILING LISTS

Perl Institute Announce   This list is for announcements from the Perl Institute on general Perl issues. To subscribe, send an e-mail to majordomo@perl.org with "subscribe tpi-announce" in the body of the message.

Perl5-Porters   If you are porting Perl or Perl modules or want to help in the development of the Perl language in general, then you should be a member of this discussion list. Don't join if you are just interested: this is a high-volume, highly technical

Server Name	Directory
ftp.funet.fi	/pub/languages/perl/CPAN/src/5.0
ftp.netlabs.com	/pub/outgoing/perl5.0
ftp.cis.ufl.edu	/pub/perl/CPAN/src/5.0
ftp.metronet.com	/pub/perl/source
sinsite.doc.ic.ac.uk	/pub/computing/programming/languages /perl/perl.5.0
ftp.cs.ruu.nl	/pub/PERL/perl5.0/src
coombs.anu.edu.au	/pub/perl/CPAN/src/5.0
sungear.mame.mu.oz.au	/pub/perl/src/5.0

TABLE B-2.   Perl FTP Sites

mailing list. To subscribe, send an e-mail to majordomo@perl.org with "subscribe perl5-porters" in the body of the message.

PLATFORM-SPECIFIC LISTS

MacOS   MacOS is a general discussion list of using Perl on the Mac. To subscribe, send an e-mail to mac-perl-request@iis.ee.ethz.ch with a body of "subscribe."

Windows Users   The Perl-Win32-Users mailing list is targeted for Perl installation and programming questions. There are two versions, standard and digest. To subscribe to the *standard* version, send an e-mail to ListManager@ActiveState.com with "SUBSCRIBE Perl-Win32-Users" in the body of the message. To subscribe to the *digest* version, send an e-mail to ListManager@ActiveState.com with "DIGEST Perl-Win32-Users" in the body of the message.

Windows Announce   This mailing list is for announcements of new builds, bugs and security problems, and other information. To subscribe to the *standard* version, send an e-mail to ListManager@ActiveState.com with "SUBSCRIBE Perl-Win32-Announce" in the body of the message. To subscribe to the *digest* version, send an e-mail to ListManager@ActiveState.com with "DIGEST Perl-Win32-Announce" in the body of the message.

Windows Web Programming   This list focuses on using Perl as a CGI programming alternative on Windows NT servers. To subscribe to the *standard* version, send an e-mail to ListManager@ActiveState.com with "SUBSCRIBE Perl-Win32-Web" in the body of the message. To subscribe to the *digest* version, send an e-mail to ListManager@ActiveState.com with "DIGEST Perl-Win32-Web" in the body of the message.

Windows Admin   This lists covers information and discussion on using Perl for administering and managing Windows 95 and NT machines. To subscribe to the *standard* version, send an e-mail to ListManager@ActiveState.com with "SUBSCRIBE Perl-Win32-Admin" in the body of the message. To subscribe to the *digest* version, send an e-mail to ListManager@ActiveState.com with "DIGEST Perl-Win32-Admin" in the body of the message.

Newsgroups

To reach a more general Perl audience, you might want to post a question, query, or announcement to one of the many Perl newsgroups. These are already available on many ISP's Usenet news servers and other ISPs may be happy to add them to their list if you ask nicely. See Table B-3 for a list of Perl-related Newsgroups.

Newsgroup	Description
comp.infosystems.www.authoring.cgi	This group deals with using Perl as a tool for writing CGI programs. This general CGI discussion group is not specifically targeted at Perl users; however, it does provide a lot of useful information on extracting, receiving, and returning information from Web servers and clients.
comp.lang.perl.announce	This group announces news from the Perl world, including new book releases, new version releases, and occasionally major Perl module releases.
comp.lang.perl.misc	This group is a general discussion forum for Perl. It covers everything from queries about how best to tackle a problem to the inside machinations of Perl. Some of the discussion can get quite technical and be more biased to someone interested in Perl's internal workings, but it still represents the best port of call if you are having trouble with a Perl script.
comp.lang.perl.modules	This group was set up to specifically discuss the use and creation of Perl modules. Unlike comp.lang.perl.misc, you should only find problems related to modules in this group. If you are having trouble with something downloaded from CPAN, this is the best place to start asking questions.
comp.lang.perl.moderated	This is a "low noise" newsgroup for serious Perl discussion. Inexperienced Usenet readers should either lurk here or experiment in the comp.lang.perl.misc newsgroup until they are more comfortable with posting and replying to Usenet postings.
comp.lang.perl.tk	Tk is a toolkit that provides a set of functions to support a graphical user interface (GUI) within Perl. It was originally developed to use the TCL (Tool Command Language), but it has been massaged to work with other scripting systems, including Perl. Tk's strength is that, like Perl, it is available for a number of platforms, and therefore building a GUI-style interface within X Windows (under Unix), Microsoft Windows (on the PC), and MacOS, among others, becomes very much easier.

TABLE B-3.   Perl-friendly Newsgroups

Perl
Documentation

Since version 5, the Perl distribution documentation has been supplied in a new text format designed to make it more compatible with the different platforms that now support Perl as a scripting language. Plain Old Documentation, or POD, is a top-level text format that uses tags to format the different text elements that make up a typical document.

Because POD is a very simple, nonimplementation-specific format, it can be easily converted into other, more familiar formats for different platforms. These formats are manual (or "man") pages for Unix and HTML for Windows 95/NT. The MacPerl implementation reads and displays POD documentation directly. Translators are supplied with the Perl distributions (see the section "Formatting for Translated Formats") for making HTML, man, Tex/LaTeX, and even plain text files.

The Perl language also knows about POD documentation, and it will ignore POD information supplied as part of a Perl script or module.

The POD Format

A POD document is made up of three different types of paragraph: verbatim, command, and ordinary text. Each type of paragraph is translated and handled differently, according to the output format of the translator.

In addition to these paragraph types, there are also escape sequences, which allow you to specify an alternative printed format for a word or sentence. This includes things like boldfacing and underlining text, as well as introducing references and links to other parts of the document.

There is no standard format or layout for a POD document, but different translators place certain levels of significance on different elements within the source POD file.

VERBATIM PARAGRAPH

A verbatim paragraph will be reproduced within the final document exactly; you cannot use formatting escapes, and the translator won't make any assumptions about the contents of the paragraph. A verbatim paragraph is identified by indentation in the source text, either with spaces or tabs. Probably the best use for a verbatim paragraph is to reproduce code within the document to ensure that it appears as working code within the final document.

COMMAND PARAGRAPH

A command paragraph specifies that some special element or formatting should be applied to the next section. It is typically used to insert headings, subheadings, and lists into the document. All command paragraphs start with an equal sign, =, and a keyword that specifies the formatting to be applied. The paragraph may include an additional keyword or reference. For example, the paragraph

`=head1 This is a main heading`

would create a level one heading the text of which would be 'This is a main heading.'

The full list of available command paragraphs is in Table C-1.

ORDINARY TEXT PARAGRAPH

Ordinary paragraphs of text are converted by the translation program into justified and filled paragraphs, according to the destination format. It is entirely dependent on the translator and the resulting file how the justification takes place. For example, if the conversion is to HTML, then the browser handles paragraph formatting, so an ordinary text paragraph will simply be copied to the destination file.

Command	Result
=head1 text	Applies first-level heading, using "text" as the description.
=head2 text	Applies second-level heading, using "text" as the description.
=over n	Starts a section for the generation of a list. The value of *n* is used as the indentation value.
=item text	Specifies the title for an item in a list. The value of text will be interpreted differently, according to the translator.
=back	Ends a list/indentation.
=for format	Allows you to specify that the following paragraph be inserted exactly as supplied, according to the specified format. For example: **=for html <font size=+1>Heading</font>** would be inserted into the translated file only by an HTML translator.
=begin format =end format	Acts similarly to =for, except that all the paragraphs between =begin and =end are included by the specified format translator as preformatted text.
=pod	Specifies the start of a POD document. It is best used when the documentation is included as part of a script. The =pod command paragraph tells the compiler to ignore the following text.
=cut	Specifies the end of a =pod section.

TABLE C-1. POD Command Paragraphs

ESCAPE SEQUENCES

Escape sequences are recognized both within ordinary text and command
paragraphs. The escape sequences allow you to specify that a block of text is to be
displayed as italicized, boldfaced, underlined, and so on. An escape sequence
consists of a single letter and a pair of angle brackets that contain the text to be
modified. For example, the POD fragment

```
B<Hello World!>
```

specifies that the string should be boldfaced, producing

Hello World!

A note: the resulting format must support this sort of text formatting!

The full list of escape sequences supported by the POD standard is shown in Table C-2.
The sequences will not always be transferred correctly to the destination format, and
then the sequence is open to interpretation by the resulting file viewing mechanism.

Sequence	Description
I<text>	Italic text
B<text>	Boldfaced text
S<text>	Text with nonbreaking spaces (spaces within text that will not be used to wrap or split lines)
C<code>	Literal code fragment (for example, the C<printf()> function)
L<name>	A link or cross-reference to another section, identified by name. Links are further subdivided as follows:
L<name>	Manual page
L<name/ident>	Item or section within a manual page
L<name/"sec">	Section in other manual page
L<"sec">	Section within the current manual page (quotes are optional, as in L<name>)
L</"sec">	Same as above
L<text | name> L<text | name/ident> L<text | name/"sec"> L<text | "sec"> L<text | /"sec">	Same as above, but destination is identified by *name* but displayed as *text*; the *text* element cannot contain | or >
F<file>	Used for filenames

TABLE C-2.   POD Escape Sequences

Sequence	Description
X<index>	An index entry
Z<>	A zero-width character
E<escape>	A named character (similar to HTML escapes):
E<lt>	A literal <
E<gt>	A literal >
E<n>	Character number (in ASCII)

TABLE C-2.   POD Escape Sequences *(continued)*

Embedding POD Documents in Perl Scripts

You can embed documentation into a Perl script simply by starting the POD section with **=head1** and ending it with **=cut**. The compiler ignores the POD documentation between the two command paragraphs. A POD translator ignores any code outside of the command paragraphs. In this way, you can place both script and documentation within a single file, allowing the compiler and translator to interpret the corresponding sections. For example, the script:

```
=head1 NAME

HelloWorld.pl

=cut

print "Hello World!";

=head1 SYNOPSIS

This programs prints Hello World! on the screen.

=cut
```

produces:

    Hello World!

when parsed with the compiler, and

```
NAME
```

```
HelloWorld.pl

SYNOPSIS

This programs prints Hello World! on the screen.
```

when parsed with a POD viewer.

Formatting for Translated Formats

Different resulting formats have different requirements and restrictions on what can and can't be incorporated within a POD source document. At first glance, this would appear to have an effect on the cross-platform nature of the POD format, but in fact it helps to standardize the base POD documents.

The translated format that has the most stringent rules is the "man" format because the Unix manual format places certain restrictions and requirements on a manual page so that the information can be indexed and displayed in standard format. Within the confines of POD documentation, this restriction aids in the formatting and layout of nearly all the documents that are produced.

The format of a manual page consists of the elements outlined in Table C-3. Element titles are historically shown in uppercase, although this is not a requirement, and each should be the reference with the **=head1** element. Subheadings can be included in **=head2** elements.

Element	Description
NAME	The mandatory comma-separated list of the functions or programs documented by the man page
SYNOPSIS	The outline of the function's or program's purpose
DESCRIPTION	Longer description/discussion of the program's purpose
OPTIONS	The command-line options or function arguments
RETURN VALUE	What the program returns if successful
ERRORS	Any return codes, errors, or exceptions that may be produced
EXAMPLES	Examples of the program's or function's use
ENVIRONMENT	The environment or variables used by and modified by the program

TABLE C-3. Elements of a POD Man Page

Element	Description
FILES	The files used
SEE ALSO	Other entries to refer to
NOTES	Any additional commentary
CAVEATS/WARNINGS	Anything to be aware of during the program's use
DIAGNOSTICS	Errors or messages produced by the program and what they mean
BUGS	Things that do not work as expected
RESTRICTIONS	Items that are built-in design features and limitations
AUTHOR	Who wrote the function or program
HISTORY	The source or origin of the program or function

TABLE C-3.   Elements of a POD Man Page *(continued)*

You can see a sample man page, in POD format, following. It is part of the man page for the pod2html Perl script used to convert POD documentation to HTML documents.

```
=head1 NAME

pod2html - convert .pod files to .html files

=head1 SYNOPSIS

    pod2html --help --htmlroot=<name> --infile=<name> --outfile=<name>
             --podpath=<name>:...:<name> --podroot=<name>
             --libpods=<name>:...:<name> --recurse --norecurse --verbose
             --index --noindex --title=<name>

=head1 DESCRIPTION

Converts files from pod format (see L<perlpod>) to HTML format.

=head1 ARGUMENTS

pod2html takes the following arguments:

=over 4

=item help
```

```
    --help
```

Displays the usage message.

=item htmlroot

```
    --htmlroot=name
```

Sets the base URL for the HTML files. When cross-references are made, the HTML root is prepended to the URL.

=item infile

```
    --infile=name
```

Specify the pod file to convert. Input is taken from STDIN if no infile is specified.

=item outfile

```
    --outfile=name
```

Specify the HTML file to create. Output goes to STDOUT if no outfile is specified.

=item podroot

```
    --podroot=name
```

Specify the base directory for finding library pods.

=item podpath

```
    --podpath=name:...:name
```

Specify which subdirectories of the podroot contain pod files whose HTML converted forms can be linked-to in cross-references.

The result of this POD document is shown in Figure C-1.

NAME

pod2html - convert .pod files to .html files

SYNOPSIS

```
pod2html --help --htmlroot=<name> --infile=<name> --outfile=<name>
         --podpath=<name>:...:<name> --podroot=<name>
         --libpods=<name>:...:<name> --recurse --norecurse --verbose
         --index --noindex --title=<name>
```

DESCRIPTION

Converts files from pod format (see in the *perlpod* manpage) to HTML format.

ARGUMENTS

pod2html takes the following arguments:

help

> --help

> Displays the usage message.

htmlroot

> --htmlroot=name

> Sets the base URL for the HTML files. When cross-references are made, the HTML root is prepended to the URL.

infile

> --infile=name

> Specify the pod file to convert. Input is taken from STDIN if no infile is specified.

outfile

> --outfile=name

> Specify the HTML file to create. Output goes to STDOUT if no outfile is specified.

podroot

> --podroot=name

FIGURE C-1. Sample output of the **pod2html** script via the MacPerl **shuck**

Index